WILLIAM J. McKNIGHT.

1755   1844

A PIONEER HISTORY

OF

JEFFERSON COUNTY, PENNSYLVANIA

and

My First Recollections of
Brookville, Pennsylvania, 1840–1843,
When My Feet Were Bare and
My Cheeks Were Brown

W. J. McKnight, M.D.

HERITAGE BOOKS
2015

HERITAGE BOOKS
AN IMPRINT OF HERITAGE BOOKS, INC.

Books, CDs, and more—Worldwide

For our listing of thousands of titles see our website
at
www.HeritageBooks.com

A Facsimile Reprint
Published 2015 by
HERITAGE BOOKS, INC.
Publishing Division
5810 Ruatan Street
Berwyn Heights, Md. 20740

Copyright © 1898 W. J. McKnight, M.D.

Originally published
Phildelphia:
Printed by J. B. Lippincott Company
1898

— Publisher's Notice —
In reprints such as this, it is often not possible to remove blemishes from the original. We feel the contents of this book warrant its reissue despite these blemishes and hope you will agree and read it with pleasure.

International Standard Book Numbers
Paperbound: 978-0-7884-1216-5
Clothbound: 978-0-7884-6220-7

TO MY

FATHER AND MOTHER

THESE PAGES ARE

AFFECTIONATELY

DEDICATED

PREFACE.

To write a pioneer history of a single county years and years after all the fathers and mothers have gone to that "country from whose bourn no traveller returns" is a task to appall the most courageous. To say it mildly, it is a task requiring a vast amount of labor and research, untiring perseverance, great patience, and discrimination. In undertaking this task I realized its magnitude, and all through the work I have determined that, if labor, patience, and perseverance would overcome error and false traditions and establish the truth, the object of this book would be fully attained. This book is not written for gain, nor to laud or puff either the dead or the living. It is designed to be a plain, truthful narrative of the pioneer men and events of Jefferson County. I have compiled, wherever I could, from the writings of others.

I am indebted to the following historical works,—viz., "Jefferson County Atlas," "Jefferson County History," Day's "Historical Recollections," Egle's "History of Pennsylvania," W. C. Elliott's "History of Reynoldsville," and the county histories of Indiana, Armstrong, Elk, Centre, Lycoming, Venango, Crawford, and Northumberland; also to many individuals. I am greatly indebted to the late Mr. G. B. Goodlander, of Clearfield, for a complete file of the *Brookville Republican* for the year 1837, to Clarence M. Barrett for a file of the *Republican* for 1834, and also to the *Ladies' Home Journal* of Philadelphia, Pennsylvania.

In every instance, as far as possible, credit has been given to the writings of those who have preceded me. But, dear reader,

> "Whoever thinks a faultless work to see,
> Thinks what ne'er was, nor is, nor e'er shall be.
> In every work regard the writer's end,
> Since none can compass more than they intend,
> And if the means be just, the conduct true,
> Applause, in spite of trivial faults, is due."

W. J. McKnight.

Brookville, Pennsylvania.

CONTENTS.

CHAPTER I.
                                                                                                                PAGE
INTRODUCTORY—TIMES, PRIVILEGES, SOCIAL HABITS OF THE PIONEERS, CHRISTIANITY OF THOSE DAYS, ETC. 9

CHAPTER II.
OUR ABORIGINES—THE IROQUOIS, OR SIX NATIONS—INDIAN TOWNS, VILLAGES, GRAVEYARDS, CUSTOMS, DRESS, HUTS, MEDICINES, DOCTORS, BARK-PEELERS, BURIALS, ETC. 12

CHAPTER III.
THE WILDERNESS IN 1755—THE SAVAGE INDIAN—MARIE LE ROY AND BARBARA LEININGER, THE FIRST WHITE PIONEERS TO TREAD THIS WILDERNESS—THE CHINKLACAMOOSE PATH—PUNXSUTAWNEY AND KITTANNING—REV. HECKEWELDER, REV. ZEISBERGER, REV. ETTWEIN, AND ROTHE 32

CHAPTER IV.
THE PURCHASE OF 1784 42

CHAPTER V.
TITLES AND SURVEYS—PIONEER SURVEYS AND SURVEYORS—DISTRICT LINES RUN IN NORTHUMBERLAND, NOW JEFFERSON, COUNTY, PENNSYLVANIA   78

CHAPTER VI.
PIONEER ANIMALS—BEAVER, BUFFALO, ELK, PANTHERS, WOLVES, WILD-CATS, BEARS, AND OTHER ANIMALS—PENS AND TRAPS—BIRDS—WILD BEES . 88

CHAPTER VII.
RUNWAYS, PATHS, TRAILS, DEER RUNS AND CROSSINGS, INDIAN TRAILS—THE WHITE MAN'S PATH—DAVID AND JOHN MEADE—MEADE'S PACK-HORSE TRAIL—PIONEER SETTLEMENT IN THE NORTHWEST—WHITE BOYS CAPTURED AND REARED BY INDIANS—PIONEER EXPLORERS AND SETTLERS 115

CONTENTS.

CHAPTER VIII.

PROVISION FOR OPENING A ROAD—REPORT OF THE COMMISSIONERS TO THE GOVERNOR—STREAMS, ETC. 124

CHAPTER IX.

THE OLD STATE ROAD—EARLY ROADS AND TRAILS—WHY THE STATE ROAD WAS MADE—THE FIRST ATTEMPT TO OPEN THE ROAD—LAWS, ETC., TOUCHING THE SUBJECT—THE SURVEY—THE ROAD COMPLETED—THE ACT OF THE LEGISLATURE WHICH SANCTIONED THE BUILDING OF THE ROAD 137

CHAPTER X.

PIONEER AGRICULTURE—HOW THE FARMERS IN THE OLDEN TIME HAD TO MAKE SHIFT—THE PIONEER HOMES—PIONEER FOOD—PIONEER EVENING FROLICS—TREES, SNAKES, AND REPTILES—SOLDIERS OF 1812—PIONEER LEGAL RELATIONS OF MAN AND WIFE—EARLY AND PIONEER MUSIC—LIST OF TAXABLE INHABITANTS IN 1820—THE TRANSPORTATION OF IRON—THE FIRST SCREW FACTORY—POPULATION OF THE STATE AND OF THE UNITED STATES 150

CHAPTER XI.

THE ERECTION OF THE COUNTY—SITE FOR COUNTY ESTABLISHED, AND DEED FOR PUBLIC LOTS—PIONEER COURT-HOUSE AND JAIL—THE PIONEER ACADEMY 185

CHAPTER XII.

THE COMMON SCHOOL SYSTEM—ITS INCEPTION—INTRODUCTION INTO AMERICA—STATE EFFORT—HISTORY OF EDUCATION IN THE STATE—SCHOOLS OF JEFFERSON COUNTY—PROGRESS OF EDUCATION, ETC. 199

CHAPTER XIII.

PIONEER MISSIONARY WORK—THE FIRST WHITE MAN TO TRAVEL THE SOIL OF JEFFERSON COUNTY—REVS. POST, HECKEWELDER, AND OTHERS . 229

CHAPTER XIV.

PIONEER AND EARLY CHURCHES—PRESBYTERIAN THE PIONEER CHURCH IN THE COUNTY—THE PIONEER PREACHER AND CHURCH 237

CHAPTER XV.

WHITE SLAVERY—ORIGIN—NATURE IN ROME, GREECE, AND EUROPE—AFRICAN SLAVERY IN PENNSYLVANIA—GEORGE BRYAN—PIONEER COLORED SETTLER IN JEFFERSON COUNTY—CENSUS, ETC.—DAYS OF BONDAGE IN THIS COUNTY 266

CONTENTS.

CHAPTER XVI.
PAGE
PIONEER MONEY 296

CHAPTER XVII.
"SCOTCH-IRISH"—ORIGIN OF THE TERM UNDER JAMES I.—LORDS AND LAIRDS—EARLY SETTLERS IN PENNSYLVANIA—THE PIONEER AND EARLY SETTLERS IN JEFFERSON COUNTY 299

CHAPTER XVIII.
FROM 1830 TO 1840 311

CHAPTER XIX.
PIONEER SETTLEMENT OF WESTERN PENNSYLVANIA—PIONEER PENNSYLVANIA INDIAN TRADERS—THE PIONEER ROAD BY WAY OF THE SOUTH BRANCH OF THE POTOMAC AND THE VALLEY OF THE KISKIMINITAS—THE PIONEER ROAD FROM EAST TO WEST, FROM RAYSTOWN, NOW BEDFORD, TO FORT DUQUESNE, NOW PITTSBURG, A MILITARY NECESSITY—GENERAL JOHN FORBES OPENS IT IN THE SUMMER AND FALL OF 1758—COLONEL GEORGE WASHINGTON OPPOSED TO THE NEW ROAD AND IN FAVOR OF THE POTOMAC ROAD—DEATH OF GENERAL JOHN FORBES—PIONEER MAIL-COACHES, MAIL-ROUTES, AND POST-OFFICES 334

CHAPTER XX.
PIONEER ROADS IN PROVISIONAL JEFFERSON COUNTY FROM 1808 TO 1830 . 346

CHAPTER XXI.
PIONEER COURT—PIONEER JUDGES—PRESIDENT AND ASSOCIATES—PIONEER BAR AND EARLY LAWYERS—MINUTES OF PIONEER SESSIONS OF COURT—DECEMBER SESSION, 1830, AND FEBRUARY SESSION, 1831—LIST OF RETAILERS OF FOREIGN MERCHANDISE IN THE COUNTY, FEBRUARY SESSIONS, 1831—EARLY CONSTABLES 364

CHAPTER XXII.
THE PIONEER PHYSICIAN IN THE COUNTY, DR. JOHN W. JENKS, OF PUNXSUTAWNEY—THE PIONEER PHYSICIAN ON THE LITTLE TOBY, DR. NICHOLS—OTHER EARLY PHYSICIANS, DR. EVANS, DR. PRIME, DR. DARLING, DR. BISHOP, DR. A. M. CLARKE, DR. JAMES DOWLING, DR. WILLIAM BENNETT—PIONEER MAJOR OPERATION IN SURGERY IN 1821—EARLY RIDES, FEES, ETC. 391

CHAPTER XXIII.
PIONEER TOWNSHIPS AND BOROUGHS AND PIONEER TAXABLES 396

CONTENTS.

CHAPTER XXIV.

PAGE

PIONEER NEWSPAPER IN THE WEST—PIONEER NEWSPAPER IN THE COUNTY—
TERMS—EARLY MARKET—OTHER PAPERS 407

CHAPTER XXV.

MILITIA AND TOWNSHIPS 414

CHAPTER XXVI.

MY FIRST RECOLLECTIONS OF BROOKVILLE 512

CHAPTER XXVII.

CORNPLANTER—OUR CHIEF—CHIEF OF THE SENECAS, ONE OF THE SIX NATIONS—BRIEF HISTORY—SOME SPEECHES—LIFE AND DEATH—MOSES KNAPP—SAW-MILLS—JOHN JONES 560

CHAPTER XXVIII.

JOSEPH BARNETT—BIOGRAPHICAL SKETCH OF THE PATRIARCH OF JEFFERSON COUNTY 570

APPENDIX 593

A PIONEER HISTORY

OF

JEFFERSON COUNTY, PENNSYLVANIA.

CHAPTER I.

INTRODUCTORY—TIMES, PRIVILEGES, SOCIAL HABITS OF THE PIONEERS, CHRISTIANITY OF THOSE DAYS, ETC.

At this time all the pioneers have passed away, and the facts here given are collected from records and recollections. Every true citizen now and in the future of Jefferson County must ever possess a feeling of deep veneration for the brave men and courageous women who penetrated this wilderness and inaugurated civilization where savages and wild beasts reigned supreme. These heroic men and women migrated to this wilderness and endured all the hardships incidental to that day and life, and through these labors and tribulations they have transmitted to us all the comforts and conveniences of a high civilization. When pioneers pass off a given spot they disappear from that locality forever. This county was redeemed by the Barnetts, Scotts, and others. We will know them or their like no more forever. The graves have closed over all these pioneer men and women, and I have been deprived of the great assistance they could have been to me in writing this history.

In 1800, when Joseph Barnett settled on Mill Creek, then Lycoming County, the United States contained a population of five million three hundred and five thousand nine hundred and twenty-five people. Now, in 1890, we have sixty-two million six hundred and twenty-two thousand two hundred and fifty.

Men at this time wore no beard, whiskers, or moustaches, a full beard being held as fitted only for heathen or Turks.

In 1800 Philadelphia and New York were but overgrown villages, and Chicago was unknown. Books were few and costly, ignorance the rule, and authors famed the world over now were then unborn; now we spend annually one hundred and forty million dollars for schools. Then there was no telegraph, telephone, or submarine cable; now the earth is girdled with telegraph wires, and we can speak face to face through the telephone a thousand miles apart, and millions of messages are sent every year under the waters of the globe. To-day in the United States an average of one to twelve telegraphic messages are sent every minute, day and night, the year through.

In 1800 emigrants to America came in sailing vessels. Each emigrant had to provide his own food, as the vessel supplied only air and water. The trip required a period of from thirty days to three months. Now this trip can be made by the use of Jefferson County coal in less than six days. Now ocean travel is a delight. Then canals for the passage of great ships and transatlantic steamers were unknown.

In 1800 electricity was in its infancy, and travel was by sail, foot, horseback, and by coach. Now we have steamers, street-cars, railroads, bicycles, and horseless carriages. Gas was unheard of for stoves, streets, or lights. Pitch-pine, fat, and tallow candles gave the only light then.

In 1800 human slavery was universal, and irreligion was the order of the day. Nine out of every ten workingmen neither possessed nor ever opened a Bible. Hymn-books were unknown, and musical science had no system. Medicine was an illiterate theory, surgery a crude art, and dentistry unknown. No snap shots were thought of. Photography was not heard of. Now this science has revealed "stars invisible" and microscopic life.

In 1800 there were but few daily papers in the world, no illustrated ones, no humorous ones, and no correspondents. Modern tunnels were unknown, and there was no steam heating. Flint and tinder did duty for matches. Plate-glass was a luxury undreamed of. Envelopes had not been invented, and postage-stamps had not been introduced. Vulcanized rubber and celluloid had not begun to appear in a hundred dainty forms. Stationary wash-tubs, and even wash-boards, were unknown. Carpets, furniture, and household accessories were expensive. Sewing-machines had not yet supplanted the needle. Aniline colors and coal-tar products were things of the future. Stem-winding watches had not appeared; there were no cheap watches of any kind. So it was with hundreds of the necessities of our present life.

"In the social customs of our day, many minds entertain doubts whether we have made improvements upon those of our ancestors. In those days friends and neighbors could meet together and enjoy themselves, and enter into the spirit of social amusement with a hearty goodwill, a geniality of manners, a corresponding depth of soul, both among the old and young, to which modern society is unaccustomed. Our ancestors did not make a special invitation the only pass to their dwellings, and they entertained those who visited them with a hospitality that is not generally practised at the present time. Guests did not assemble then to criticise the decorations, furniture, dress, manners, and surroundings of those by whom they were invited. They were sensible people, with clear heads and warm hearts; they visited each other to promote mutual enjoyment, and believed in genuine earnestness in all things. We may ignore obligations to the pioneer race, and congratulate ourselves that our lot has been cast in a more advanced era of mental and moral culture; we may pride ourselves upon the developments which have been made in science and art, but while viewing our standard of elevation as immeasurably in advance of that of our forefathers, it would be well to emulate their great characteristics for hospitality, honor, and integrity.

"The type of Christianity of that period will not suffer by comparison with that of the present day. If the people of olden times had less for costly apparel and ostentatious display, they had also more for offices of charity and benevolence; if they did not have the splendor and luxuries of wealth, they at least had no infirmaries or paupers, very few lawyers, and but little use for jails. The vain and thoughtless may jeer at their unpretending manners and customs, but in all the elements of true manhood and true womanhood it may be safely averred that they were more than the peers of the generation that now occupy their places. That race has left its impress upon our times,—whatever patriotism the present generation boasts of has descended from them. Rude and illiterate, comparatively, they may have been, but they possessed strong minds in strong bodies, made so by their compulsory self-denials, their privations and toil. It was the mission of many of them to aid and participate in the formation of this great commonwealth, and wisely and well was the mission performed. Had their descendants been more faithful to their noble teachings, harmony would now reign supreme where violence and discord now hold their sway in the land.

"The pioneer times are the greenest spot in the memories of those who lived in them; the privations and hardships they then endured are consecrated things in the recollection of the survivors."

CHAPTER II.*

OUR ABORIGINES—THE IROQUOIS, OR SIX NATIONS—INDIAN TOWNS, VILLAGES, GRAVEYARDS, CUSTOMS, DRESS, HUTS, MEDICINES, DOCTORS, BARK-PEELERS, BURIALS, ETC.

AQUANUSCHIONI, or "united people," is what they called themselves. The French called them the Iroquois; the English, the Six Nations. They formed a confederate nation, and as such were the most celebrated and powerful of all the Indian nations in North America. The confederacy consisted of the Mohawk, the fire-striking people; the Oneidas, the pipe-makers; the Onondagas, the hill-top people; the Cayugas, the people from the lake; the Tuscaroras, unwilling to be with other people; and the Senecas, the mountaineers.

The Iroquois, or Six Nations, were divided into what might be called eight families,—viz., the Wolf, Bear, Beaver, Turtle, Deer, Snipe, Heron, and Hawk. Each of the Six Nations had one of each of these families in their tribe, and all the members of that family, no matter how wide apart or of what other tribe, were considered as brothers and sisters, and were forbidden to marry in their own family. Then a wolf was a brother to all other wolves in each of the nations. This family bond was taught from infancy and enforced by public opinion.

"If at any time there appeared a tendency toward conflict between the different tribes, it was instantly checked by the thought that, if persisted in, the hand of the Turtle must be lifted against his brother Turtle, the tomahawk of the Beaver might be buried in the brain of his kinsman Beaver. And so potent was the feeling that, for at least two hundred years, and until the power of the league was broken by the overwhelming outside force of the whites, there was no serious dissension between the tribes of the Iroquois.

"In peace, all power was confined to 'sachems;' in war, to 'chiefs.' The sachems of each tribe acted as its rulers in the few matters which required the exercise of civil authority. The same rulers also met in

---

* For much in this chapter I am indebted to Rupp's History.

council to direct the affairs of the confederacy. There were fifty in all, of whom the Mohawks had nine, the Oneidas nine, the Onondagas fourteen, the Cayugas ten, and the Senecas eight. These numbers, however, did not give proportionate power in the councils of the League, for all the nations were equal there. There was in each tribe, too, the same number of war-chiefs as sachems, and these had absolute authority in time of war. When a council assembled, each sachem had a war-chief near him to execute his orders. But in a war-party the war-chief commanded and the sachem took his place in the ranks. This was the system in its simplicity.

"The right of heirship, as among many other of the North America tribes of Indians, was in the female line. A man's heirs were his brother,—that is to say, his mother's son and his sister's son,—never his own son, nor his brother's son. The few articles which constituted an Indian's personal property—even his bow and tomahawk—never descended to the son of him who had wielded them. Titles, so far as they were hereditary at all, followed the same law of descent. The child also followed the clan and tribe of the mother. The object was evidently to secure greater certainty that the heir would be of the blood of his deceased kinsman. The result of the application of this rule to the Iroquois system of clans was that if a particular sachemship or chieftaincy was once established in a certain clan of a certain tribe, in that clan and tribe it was expected to remain forever. Exactly how it was filled when it became vacant is a matter of some doubt; but, as near as can be learned, the new official was elected by the warriors of the clan, and was then inaugurated by the council of sachems.

"If, for instance, a sachemship belonging to the Wolf clan of the Seneca tribe became vacant, it could only be filled by some one of the Wolf clan of the Seneca tribe. A clan council was called and, as a general rule, the heir of the deceased was chosen to his place,—to wit, one of his brothers, reckoning only on the mother's side, or one of his sister's sons, or even some more distant male relative in the female line. But there was no positive law, and the warriors might discard all these and elect some one entirely unconnected with the deceased, though, as before stated, he must be of the same clan and tribe. While there was no unchangeable custom compelling the clan council to select one of the heirs of the deceased as his successor, yet the tendency was so strong in that direction that an infant was frequently chosen, a guardian being appointed to perform the functions of the office till the youth should reach the proper age to do so. All offices were held for life, unless the incumbent was solemnly deposed by a council, an event which very seldom occurred. Notwithstanding the modified system of hereditary power in vogue, the constitution of every tribe was essentially republican. Warriors, old men, and women attended the various councils and made their influence felt. Neither in the government of the confederacy nor of the tribes was there any such thing as tyranny over the people, though there was a great deal of tyranny by the league over conquered nations. In fact, there was very little government of any kind, and very little need of any. There was substantially no property interests to guard, all land being in common, and each man's personal property being limited to a bow, a tomahawk, and a few deer-skins. Liquor had not yet lent its disturbing influence, and few quarrels were to be traced to the influence of women, for the American Indian is singularly free from the warmer passions.

"His principal vice is an easily aroused and unlimited hatred; but the tribes were so small and enemies so convenient that there was no difficulty in gratifying this feeling (and attaining to the rank of a warrior) outside of his own nation. The consequence was that although the war-parties of the Iroquois were continually shedding the blood of their foes, there was very little quarrelling at home.

"Their religious creed was limited to a somewhat vague belief in the existence of a Great Spirit and several inferior but very potent evil spirits. They had a few simple ceremonies, consisting largely of dances, one called the 'green-corn dance,' performed at the time indicated by its name, and others at other seasons of the year. From a very early date their most important religious ceremony has been the 'burning of the white dog,' when an unfortunate canine of the requisite color is sacrificed by one of the chiefs. To this day the pagans among them still perform this rite.

"In common with their fellow-savages on this continent, the Iroquois have been termed 'fast friends and bitter enemies.' Events have proved, however, that they were a great deal stronger enemies than friends. Revenge was the ruling passion of their nature, and cruelty was their abiding characteristic. Revenge and cruelty are the worst attributes of human nature, and it is idle to talk of the goodness of men who roasted their captives at the stake. All Indians were faithful to their own tribes, and the Iroquois were faithful to their confederacy; but outside of these limits their friendship could not be counted on, and treachery was always to be apprehended in dealing with them.

"In their family relations they were not harsh to their children and not wantonly so to their wives; but the men were invariably indolent, and all labor was contemptuously abandoned to their weaker sex.

"Polygamy, too, was practised, though in what might be called moderation. Chiefs and eminent warriors usually had two or three wives, rarely more. They could be discarded at will by their husbands, but the latter seldom availed themselves of their privilege.

"Our nation—the Senecas—was the most numerous and comprised the greatest warriors of the Iroquois confederacy. Their great chiefs, Cornplanter and Guyasutha, are prominently connected with the traditions of the head-waters of the Allegheny, Western New York, and Northwestern Pennsylvania. In person the Senecas were slender, middle-sized, handsome, and straight. The squaws were short, not handsome, and clumsy. The skin was a reddish brown, hair straight and jet-black."

There was a village of Indians at Summerville, one at Brookville, and as late as 1815 there were six hundred Indians living between Brookville and New Bethlehem. There was a village at Port Barnett, at Reynoldsville, at Big Run, and a big one at Punxsutawney. The country was

Indian wigwam.

thickly inhabited, especially what is now Warsaw. Their graveyards or burial-places were always some distance from huts or villages. There was one on the Temple farm, in what is now Warsaw; one on Mill Creek, at its junction with the Big Toby Creek, in what was afterwards Ridgway township. They carried their dead sometimes a long way for burial.

"After the death of a Seneca, the corpse was dressed in a new blanket or petticoat, with the face and clothes painted red. The body was then laid on a skin in the middle of the hut. The war and hunting implements of the deceased were then piled up around the body. In the evening after sunset, and in the morning before daylight, the squaws and relations assembled around the corpse to mourn. This was daily repeated until interment. The graves were dug by old squaws, as the young squaws abhorred this kind of labor. Before they had hatchets and other tools, they used to line the inside of the grave with the bark of trees, and when the corpse was let down they placed some pieces of wood across, which were again covered with bark, and then the earth thrown in, to fill up the grave. But afterwards they usually placed three boards, not nailed together, over the grave, in such a manner that the corpse lay between them. A fourth board was placed as a cover, and then the grave was filled up with earth. Now and then a proper coffin was procured.

"At an early period they used to put a tobacco-pouch, knife, tinder-box, tobacco and pipe, bow and arrows, gun, powder and shot, skins, and cloth for clothes, paint, a small bag of Indian corn or dried bilberries, sometimes the kettle, hatchet, and other furniture of the deceased, into the grave, supposing that the departed spirits would have the same wants and occupation in the land of souls. But this custom was nearly wholly abolished among the Delawares and Iroquois about the middle of the last century. At the burial not a man shed a tear; they deemed it a shame for a man to weep. But, on the other hand, the women set up a dreadful howl."

THE ORIGINAL BARK-PEELERS.

An Indian hut was built in this manner. Trees were peeled abounding in sap, usually the linn. When the trees were cut down the bark was peeled with the tomahawk and its handle. They peeled from the top of the tree to the butt. The bark for hut-building was cut into pieces of six or eight feet; these pieces were then dried and flattened by laying heavy stones upon them. The frame of a bark hut was made by driving poles into the ground and the poles were strengthened by cross-beams. This frame was then covered inside and outside with this prepared linnwood bark, fastened with leatherwood bark or hickory withes. The roof ran upon a ridge, and was covered in the same manner as the frame, and an opening was left in it for the smoke to escape, and one on the side of the frame for a door.

HOW THE INDIAN BUILT LOG HUTS IN HIS TOWN OR VILLAGE.

They cut logs fifteen feet long and laid these logs upon each other, at each end they drove posts in the ground and tied these posts together at the top with hickory withes or moose bark. In this way they erected a wall of logs fifteen feet long to the height of four feet. In this same way they raised a wall opposite to this one about twelve feet away. In the centre of each end of this log frame they drove forks into the ground, a strong pole was then laid upon these forks, extending from end to end, and from these log walls they set up poles for rafters to the centre-pole; on these improvised rafters they tied poles for sheeting, and the hut was then covered or shingled with linnwood bark. This bark was peeled from the tree, commencing at the top, with a tomahawk. The bark-strips in this way were sometimes thirty feet long and usually six inches wide. These strips were cut as desired for roofing.

At each end of the hut they set up split lumber, leaving an open space at each end for a door-way, at which a bear-skin hung. A stick leaning against the outside of this skin meant that the door was locked. At the top of the hut, in place of a chimney, they left an open place. The fires were made in the inside of the hut, and the smoke escaped through this open space. For bedding they had linnwood bark covered with bear skins. Open places between logs the squaws stopped with moss gathered from old logs.

There was no door, no windows, and no chimney. Several families occupied a hut, hence they built them long. Other Indian nations erected smaller huts, and the families lived separate. The men wore a blanket and went bare-headed. The women wore a petticoat, fastened about the hips, extending a little below the knees.

Our nation, the Senecas, produced the greatest orators, and more of them than any other. Cornplanter, Red Jacket, and Farmer's Brother were all Senecas. Red Jacket once, in enumerating the woes of the Senecas, exclaimed,—

"We stand on a small island in the bosom of the great waters. We are encircled, we are encompassed. The evil spirit rides on the blast, and the waters are disturbed. They rise, they press upon us, and the waters once settled over us, we disappear forever. Who then lives to mourn us? None. What marks our extinction? Nothing. We are mingled with the common elements."

The following is an extract from an address delivered by Cornplanter to General Washington in Philadelphia, Pennsylvania, in 1790:

"FATHER,—When you kindled your thirteen fires separately the wise men assembled at them told us that you were all brothers, the children of one Great Father, who regarded the red people as his children. They called us brothers, and invited us to his protection. They told us he resided beyond the great waters where the sun first rises, and he was a king whose power no people could resist, and that his goodness was as bright as the sun. What they said went to our hearts. We accepted the invitations and promised to obey him. What the Seneca nation promises they faithfully perform. When you refused obedience to that king he commanded us to assist his beloved men in making you sober. In obeying him we did no more than yourselves had bid us to promise. We were deceived; but your people, teaching us to confide in that king, had helped to deceive us, and we now appeal to your breast. Is all the blame ours?

"You told us you could crush us to nothing, and you demanded from us a great country as the price of that peace which you had offered us, as if our want of strength had destroyed our rights."

"Drunkenness, after the whites were dealing with them, was a common vice. It was not confined, as it is at this day among the whites, principally to the 'strong-minded,' the male sex; but the Indian female, as well as the male, was infatuated alike with the love of strong drink; for neither of them knew bounds to their desire: they drank while they had whiskey or could swallow it down. Drunkenness was a vice, though attended with many serious consequences, nay, murder and death, that was not punishable among them. It was a fashionable vice. Fornication, adultery, stealing, lying, and cheating, principally the offspring of drunkenness, were considered as heinous and scandalous offences, and were punished in various ways.

"The Delawares and Iroquois married early in life; the men usually at eighteen and the women at fourteen; but they never married near relations. If an Indian man wished to marry he sent a present, consisting of blankets, cloth, linen, and occasionally a few belts of wampum, to the nearest relations of the person he had fixed upon. If he that made the present, and the present pleased, the matter was formally proposed to the girl, and if the answer was affirmatively given, the bride was conducted to the bridegroom's dwelling without any further ceremony; but if the other party chose to decline the proposal, they returned the present by way of a friendly negative.

"After the marriage, the present made by the suitor was divided among the friends of the young wife. These returned the civility by a present of Indian corn, beans, kettles, baskets, hatchets, etc., brought in solemn procession into the hut of the new married couple. The latter commonly lodged in a friend's house till they could erect a dwelling of their own.

"As soon as a child was born, it was laid upon a board or straight piece of bark covered with moss and wrapped up in a skin or piece of cloth, and when the mother was engaged in her housework this rude cradle or bed was hung to a peg or branch of a tree. Their children they educated to fit them to get through the world as did their fathers. They instructed them in religion, etc. They believed that Manitou, their God, 'the good spirit,' could be propitiated by sacrifices; hence they observed a great many superstitious and idolatrous ceremonies. At their general and solemn sacrifices the oldest men performed the offices of priests, but in private parties each man brought a sacrifice, and offered it himself as priest. Instead of a temple they fitted up a large dwelling-house for the purpose.

"When they travelled or went on a journey they manifested much carelessness about the weather; yet, in their prayers, they usually begged 'for a clear and pleasant sky.' They generally provided themselves with Indian meal, which they either ate dry, mixed with sugar and water, or boiled into a kind of mush; for they never took bread made of Indian corn for a long journey, because in summer it would spoil in three or four days and be unfit for use. As to meat, that they took as they went.

"If in their travels they had occasion to pass a deep river, on arriving at it they set about it immediately and built a canoe by taking a long piece of bark of proportionate breadth, to which they gave the proper form by fastening it to ribs of light wood, bent so as to suit the occasion. If a large canoe was required, several pieces of bark were carefully sewed together. If the voyage was expected to be long, many Indians carried

Indians moving.

everything they wanted for their night's lodging with them,—namely, some slender poles and rush-mats, or birch bark."

When at home they had their amusements. Their favorite one was dancing. "The common dance was held either in a large house or in an open field around a fire. In dancing they formed a circle, and always had a leader, to whom the whole company attended. The men went before, and the women closed the circle. The latter danced with great decency and as if they were engaged in the most serious business; while thus engaged they never spoke a word to the men, much less joked with them, which would have injured their character.

"Another kind of dance was only attended by men. Each rose in his turn, and danced with great agility and boldness, extolling their own or their forefathers' great deeds in a song, to which all beat time, by a monotonous, rough note, which was given out with great vehemence at the commencement of each bar.

"The war-dance, which was always held either before or after a campaign, was dreadful to behold. None took part in it but the warriors themselves. They appeared armed, as if going to battle. One carried his gun or hatchet, another a long knife, the third a tomahawk, the fourth a large club, or they all appeared armed with tomahawks. These they brandished in the air, to show how they intended to treat their enemies. They affected such an air of anger and fury on this occasion that it made a spectator shudder to behold them. A chief led the dance, and sang the warlike deeds of himself or his ancestors. At the end of every celebrated feat of valor he wielded his tomahawk with all his might against a post fixed in the ground. He was then followed by the rest; each finished his round by a blow against the post. Then they danced all together; and this was the most frightful scene. They affected the most horrible and dreadful gestures; threatened to beat, cut, and stab each other. They were, however, amazingly dexterous in avoiding the threatened danger. To complete the horror of the scene, they howled as dreadfully as if in actual fight, so that they appeared as raving madmen. During the dance they sometimes sounded a kind of fife, made of reed, which had a shrill and disagreeable note. The Iroquois used the war-dance even in times of peace, with a view to celebrate the deeds of their heroic chiefs in a solemn manner.

"The Indians, as well as 'all human flesh,' were heirs of disease. The most common were pleurisy, weakness and pains in the stomach and breast, consumption, diarrhœa, rheumatism, bloody flux, inflammatory fevers, and occasionally the small-pox made dreadful ravages among them. Their general remedy for all disorders, small or great, was a sweat. For this purpose they had in every town an oven, situated at some distance from the dwellings, built of stakes and boards, covered with sods, or were dug in the side of a hill, and heated with some red-hot stones. Into this the patient crept naked, and in a short time was thrown into profuse perspiration. As soon as the patient felt himself too hot he crept out, and immediately plunged himself into a river or some cold water, where he continued about thirty seconds, and then went again into the oven. After having performed this operation three times successively, he smoked his pipe with composure, and in many cases a cure was completely effected.

"In some places they had ovens constructed large enough to receive several persons. Some chose to pour water now and then upon the heated stones, to increase the steam and promote more profuse perspiration. Many Indians in perfect health made it a practice of going into the oven once or twice a week to renew their strength and spirits. Some pretended by this operation to prepare themselves for a business which requires mature deliberation and artifice. If the sweating did not remove the disorder, other means were applied. Many of the Indians believed that medicines had no efficacy unless administered by a professed physician; enough of professed doctors could be found; many of both sexes professed to be doctors.

"Indian doctors never applied medicines without accompanying them with mysterious ceremonies, to make their effect appear supernatural. The ceremonies were various. Many breathed upon the sick; they averred their breath was wholesome. In addition to this, they spurted a certain liquor made of herbs out of their mouth over the patient's whole body, distorting their features and roaring dreadfully. In some instances physicians crept into the oven, where they sweat, howled, roared, and now and then grinned horribly at their patients, who had been laid before the opening, and frequently felt the pulse of the patient. Then pronounced sentence, and foretold either their recovery or death. On one occasion a Moravian missionary was present, who says, 'An Indian physician had put on a large bear skin, so that his arms were covered with the fore legs, his feet with the hind legs, and his head was entirely concealed in the bear's head, with the addition of glass eyes. He came in this attire with a calabash in his hand, accompanied by a great crowd of people, into the patient's hut, singing and dancing, when he grasped a handful of hot ashes, and scattering them into the air, with a horrid noise, approached the patient, and began to play several legerdemain tricks with small bits of wood, by which he pretended to be able to restore him to health.'

"The common people believed that by rattling the calabash the physician had power to make the spirits discover the cause of the disease, and even evade the malice of the evil spirit who occasioned it.

"Their materia medica, or the remedies used in curing diseases, were such as rattlesnake-root, the skins of rattlesnakes dried and pulverized, thorny ash, toothache-tree, tulip-tree, dogwood, wild laurel, sassafras, Canada shrubby elder, poison-ash, wintergreen, liverwort, Virginia poke, jalap, sarsaparilla, Canadian sanicle, scabians or devil's-bit, bloodwort, cuckoo pint, ginseng, and a few others.

"Wars among the Indians were always carried on with the greatest fury, and lasted much longer than they do now among them. The offensive weapons were, before the whites came among them, bows, arrows, and clubs. The latter were made of the hardest kind of wood, from two to three feet long and very heavy, with a large round knob at one end. Their weapon of defence was a shield, made of the tough hide of a buffalo, on the convex side of which they received the arrows and darts of the enemy. But about the middle of the last century this was all laid aside by the Delawares and Iroquois, though they used to a later period bows, arrows, and clubs of war. The clubs they used were pointed with nails and pieces of iron, when used at all. Guns were measurably substituted for all these. The hatchet and long-knife was used, as well as the gun. The army of these nations consisted of all their young men, including boys of fifteen years old. They had their captains and subordinate officers. Their captains would be called among them commanders or generals. The requisite qualifications for this station were prudence, cunning, resolution, bravery, undauntedness, and previous good fortune in some fight or battle.

"'To lift the hatchet,' or to begin a war, was always, as they declared, not till just and important causes prompted them to it. Then they assigned as motives that it was necessary to revenge the injuries done to the nation. Perhaps the honor of being distinguished as great warriors may have been an 'ingredient in the cup.'

"But before they entered upon so hazardous an undertaking they carefully weighed all the proposals made, compared the probable advantages or disadvantages that might accrue. A chief could not begin a war without the consent of his captains, nor could he accept of a war-belt only on the condition of its being considered by the captains.

"The chief was bound to preserve peace to the utmost of his power. But if several captains were unanimous in declaring war, the chief was

then obliged to deliver the care of his people, for a time, into the hands of the captains, and to lay down his office. Yet his influence tended greatly either to prevent or encourage the commencement of war, for the Indians believed that a war could not be successful without the consent of the chief, and the captains, on that account, strove to be in harmony with him. After war was agreed on, and they wished to secure the assistance of a nation in league with them, they notified that nation by sending a piece of tobacco, or by an embassy. By the first, they intended that the captains were to smoke pipes and consider seriously whether they would take part in the war or not. The embassy was intrusted to a captain, who carried a belt of wampum, upon which the object of the embassy was described by certain figures, and a hatchet with a red handle. After the chief had been informed of his commission, it was laid before a council. The hatchet having been laid on the ground, he delivered a long speech, while holding the war-belt in his hand, always closing the address with the request to take up the hatchet, and then delivering the war-belt. If this was complied with, no more was said, and this act was considered as a solemn promise to lend every assistance; but if neither the hatchet was taken up nor the belt accepted, the ambassador drew the just conclusion that the nation preferred to remain neutral, and without any further ceremony returned home.

"The Delawares and Iroquois were very informal in declaring war. They often sent out small parties, seized the first man they met belonging to the nation they had intended to engage, killed and scalped him, then cleaved his head with a hatchet, which they left stick in it, or laid a war-club, painted red, upon the body of the victim. This was a formal challenge. In consequence of which, a captain of an insulted party would take up the weapons of the murderers and hasten into their country, to be revenged upon them. If he returned with a scalp, he thought he had avenged the rights of his own nation.

"Among the Delawares and Iroquois it required but little time to make preparations for war. One of the most necessary preparations was to paint themselves red and black, for they held it that the most horrid appearance of war was the greatest ornament. Some captains fasted and attended to their dreams, with the view to gain intelligence of the issue of the war. The night previous to the march of the army was spent in feasting, at which the chiefs were present, when either a hog or some dogs were killed. Dog's flesh, said they, inspired them with the genuine martial spirit. Even women, in some instances, partook of this feast, and ate dog's flesh greedily. Now and then, when a warrior was induced to make a solemn declaration of his war inclination, he held up a piece of dog's flesh in sight of all present and devoured it, and pronounced these words, 'Thus will I devour my enemies!' After the feast the captain and all his people began the war-dance, and continued till daybreak, till they had become quite hoarse and weary. They generally danced all together, and each in his turn took the head of a hog in his hand. As both their friends and the women generally accompanied them to the first night's encampment, they halted about two or three miles from the town, danced the war-dance once more, and the day following began their march. Before they made an attack they reconnoitred every part of the country. To this end they dug holes in the ground; if practicable, in a hillock, covered with wood, in which they kept a small charcoal fire, from which they discovered the motions of the enemy undiscovered. When they sought a prisoner or a scalp, they ventured, in many instances, even in daytime, to execute their designs. Effectually to accomplish this, they skulked behind a bulky tree, and crept slyly around the trunk, so as not to be observed by the person or persons for whom they lay in ambush. In this way they slew many. But if they had a family or town in view, they always preferred the night, when their enemies were wrapt in profound sleep, and in this way killed, scalped, and made prisoners many of the enemies, set fire to the houses, and retired with all possible haste to the woods or some place of safe retreat. To avoid pursuit, they disguised their footmarks as much as possible. They depended much on stratagem for their success. Even in war they thought it more honorable to distress their enemy more by stratagem than combat. The English, not aware of the artifice of the Indians, lost an army when Braddock was defeated.

PIONEER HISTORY OF JEFFERSON COUNTY, PENNA.

"The Indian's cruelty, when victorious, was without bounds; their thirst for blood was almost unquenchable. They never made peace till compelled by necessity. No sooner were terms of peace proposed than the captains laid down their office and delivered the government of the state into the hands of the chiefs. A captain had no more right to conclude a peace than a chief to begin war. When peace had been offered to a captain he could give no other answer than to mention the proposal to the chief, for as a warrior he could not make peace. If the chief inclined to peace, he used all his influence to effect that end, and all hostility ceased, and, in conclusion, the calumet, or peace-pipe, was smoked and belts of wampum exchanged, and a concluding speech made, with the assurance 'that their friendship should last as long as the sun and moon give light, rise and set; as long as the stars shine in the firmament, and the rivers flow with water.'"

The weapons employed by our Indians two hundred years ago were axes, arrows, and knives of stone. Shells were sometimes used to make knives.

The Indian bow was made as follows: the hickory limb was cut with a stone axe, the wood was then heated on both sides near a fire until it was soft enough to scrape down to the proper size and shape.

A good bow measured forty-six inches in length, three-fourths of an inch thick in the centre, and one and a quarter inches in width, narrowing down to the points to five eighths of inch. The ends were thinner than the middle. Bow-making was tedious work.

"The bow-string was made of the ligaments obtained from the vertebra of the elk. The ligament was split, scraped, and twisted into a cord by rolling the fibres between the palm of the hand and the thigh. One end of the string was knotted to the bow but the other end was looped, in order that the bow could be quickly strung."

Quivers to carry the arrows were made of dressed buckskin, with or without the fur. The squaws did all the tanning.

The arrow-heads were made of flint or other hard stone or bone; they were fastened to the ash or hickory arrows with the sinews of the deer. The arrow was about two feet and a half in length, and a feather was fastened to the butt end to give it a rotary motion in its flight.

Poisoned arrows were made by dipping them into decomposed liver, to which had been added the poison of the rattlesnake. The venom or decomposed animal matter no doubt caused blood-poisoning and death.

Bows and arrows were long used by the red men after the introduction of fire-arms, because the Indian could be more sure of his game without revealing his presence. For a long time after the introduction of fire-arms the Indians were more expert with the bow and arrow than with the rifle.

Their tobacco-pipes were made of stone bowls and ash stems. Canoes

PIONEER HISTORY OF JEFFERSON COUNTY, PENNA.

were made of birch or linnwood bark, and many wigwam utensils of that bark. This bark was peeled in early spring. The bark canoe was the American Indian's invention.

When runners were sent with messages to other tribes the courier took an easy running gait, which he kept up for hours at a time. It was a "dog-trot," an easy, jogging gait. Of course he had no clothes on except a breech-clout and moccasins. He always carried both arms up beside the chest with the fists clinched and held in front of the breast. He eat but little the day before his departure. A courier could make a hundred miles from sunrise to sunset.

When a young squaw was ready to marry she wore something on her head as a notice.

Then kettles were made of clay, or what was called "pot stone."

The stone hatchets were in the shape of a wedge; they were of no use in felling trees. They did this with a fire around the roots of the tree. Their stone pestles were about twelve inches long and five inches thick. They used bird-claws for "fish-hooks." They made their ropes, bridles, nets, etc., out of a wild weed called Indian hemp.

The twine or cords were manufactured by the squaws, who gathered stalks of this hemp, separating them into filaments, and then taking a number of filaments in one hand, rolled them rapidly upon their bare thighs until twisted, locking, from time to time, the ends with fresh fibres. The cord thus made was finished by dressing with a mixture of grease and wax, and drawn over a smooth groove in a stone.

Their hominy-mills can be seen yet about a mile north of Samuel Temple's barn, in Warsaw township.

All the stone implements of our Indians except arrows were ground and polished. How this was done the reader must imagine. Indians had their mechanics and their workshops or "spots" where implements were made. You must remember that the Indian had no iron or steel tools, only bone, stone, and wood to work with. The flint arrows were made from a stone of uniform density. Large chips were flaked or broken from the rock. These chips were again deftly chipped with bone chisels into arrows, and made straight by pressure. A lever was used on the rock to separate chips,—a bone tied to a heavy stick.

From Jones's "Antiquities of the Southern Indians" the writer has gleaned most of the following facts. They had a limited variety of copper implements, which were of rare occurrence, and which were too soft to be of use in working so hard a material as flint or quartzite. Hence it is believed that they fashioned their spear- and arrow-heads with other implements than those of iron or steel. They must have acquired, by their observation and numerous experiments, a thorough and practical knowledge of cleavage,—that is, "the tendency to split in certain directions, which is characteristic of most of the crystallizable minerals." Captain

John Smith, speaking of the Virginia Indians in his sixth voyage, says, "His arrow-head he quickly maketh with a little bone, which he weareth at his bracelet, of a splint of a stone or glasse, in the form of a heart, and these they glue to the ends of the arrows. With the sinews of the deer and the tops of deers' horns boiled to a jelly they make a glue which will not dissolve in cold water." Schoolcraft says, "The skill displayed in this art, as it is exhibited by the tribes of the entire continent, has excited admiration. The material employed is generally some form of horn stone, sometimes passing into flint. No specimens have, however, been observed where the substance is gun-flint. The horn-stone is less hard than common quartz, and can be readily broken by contact with the latter." Catlin, in his "Last Ramble among the Indians," says, "Every tribe has its factory in which these arrow-heads are made, and in these only certain adepts are able or allowed to make them for the use of the tribe. Erratic bowlders of flint are collected and sometimes brought an immense distance, and broken with a sort of sledge-hammer made of a rounded pebble of horn-stone set in a twisted withe, holding the stone and forming a handle. The flint, at the indiscriminate blows of the sledge, is broken into a hundred pieces, and such flakes selected as from the angles of their fracture and thickness will answer as the basis of an arrow-head. The master-workman, seated on the ground, lays one of these flakes on the palm of his hand, holding it firmly down with two or more fingers of the same hand, and with his right hand, between the thumb and two forefingers, places his chisel or punch on the point that is to be broken off, and a co-operator—a striker—in front of him, with a mallet of very hard wood, strikes the chisel or punch on the upper end, flaking the flint off on the under side below each projecting point that is struck. The flint is then turned and chipped in the same manner from the opposite side, and that is chipped until required shape and dimensions are obtained, all the fractures being made on the palm of the hand. In selecting the flake for the arrow-head a nice judgment must be used or the attempt will fail. A flake with two opposite parallel, or nearly parallel, planes of cleavage is found, and of the thickness required for the centre of the arrow-point. The first chipping reaches nearly to the centre of these planes, but without quite breaking it away, and each clipping is shorter and shorter, until the shape and edge of the arrow-head is formed. The yielding elasticity of the palm of the hand enables the chip to come off without breaking the body of the flint, which would be the case if they were broken on a hard substance. These people have no metallic instruments to work with, and the punch which they use, I was told, was a piece of bone, but on examining it, I found it to be of substance much harder, made of the tooth—incisor—of the sperm whale, which cetaceans are often stranded on the coast of the Pacific."

"A considerable number of Indians must have returned and settled

PIONEER HISTORY OF JEFFERSON COUNTY, PENNA.

along the Red Bank as late as 1815-16. James White, of 'Mexico,' informed the writer that three hundred of them, about that time, settled along this stream below Brookville, partly in Armstrong County. Respecting their return to this section, Dr. M. A. Ward wrote to Eben Smith Kelly at Kittanning, from Pittsburg, January 18, 1817,—

" 'I am not at all surprised that the sober, industrious, religious inhabitants of Red Bank should be highly incensed at their late accession of emigrants, not only because by them they will probably be deprived of many fat bucks and delicious turkeys, to which, according to the strict interpretation of all our game laws, they have as good a right, if they have the fortune to find and the address to shoot them, as any "dirty, nasty" Indians whatever, but because the presence and examples of such neighbors must have a very depraving influence upon the morals. Their insinuating influence will be apt to divert the minds of the farmers from the sober pursuits of agriculture and inspire a propensity for the barbarous pleasures of the chase. . . . But what is worse than all, I have heard that they love whiskey to such an inordinate degree as to get sometimes beastly drunk, and even beat their wives and behave unseemly before their families, which certainly must have a most demoralizing tendency on the minds of the rising generation.' "—*History of Armstrong County.*

The Delaware Indians styled themselves "Lenni Lenape," the original or unchanged people. The eastern division of their people was divided into three tribes,—the Unamies, or Turtles of the sea-shore; the Unachlactgos, or Turkeys of the woods; and the Minsi-monceys, or Wolves of the mountains. A few of the Muncy villages of this latter division were scattered as far west as the valley of the Allegheny.

From Penn's arrival in 1682 the Delawares were subject to the Iroquois, or the confederacy of the Six Nations, who were the most warlike savages in America. The Iroquois were usually known among the English people as the *Five* Nations. The nations were divided and known as the Mohawks, the fire-striking people, having been the first to procure fire-arms. The Senecas, mountaineers, occupied Western New York and Northwestern Pennsylvania. They were found in great numbers in the Allegheny and its tributaries. Their great chiefs were Cornplanter and Guyasutha. This tribe was the most numerous, powerful, and warlike of the Iroquois nation, and comprised our Jefferson County Indians.

" But these were Indians pure and uncorrupted. Before many a log fire, at night, old settlers have often recited how clear, distinct, and immutable were their laws and customs; that when fully understood a white man could transact the most important business with as much safety as he can to-day in any commercial centre.

" In this day and age of progress we pride ourselves upon our railroads and telegraph as means of rapid communication, and yet, while it was well known to the early settlers that news and light freight would travel with incomprehensible speed from tribe to tribe, people of the present day fail to understand the complete system by which it was done.

"In many places through the western counties you will find traces of pits, which the early settlers will tell you were dug by white men looking for silver, which, as well as copper, was common among the Indians, and was supposed by first comers to be found in the vicinity; but experience soon proved the copper came, perhaps, from Lake Superior, by this Indian express, as we might term it, and the silver, just as possible, from the far West. Our railroads wind along the valleys, almost regardless of length or circuit, if a gradual rise can only be obtained. To travellers on wheels straight distances between points are much less formidable than is generally supposed. We find traces of the example of the Indian in the first white men. The first settlers of 1799 and 1805 took their bags of grain on their backs, walked fifty miles to the mill in Indiana or Armstrong County, and brought home their flour the same way."

"The following is taken from the 'Early Days of Punxsutawney and Western Pennsylvania,' contributed a few years ago to the *Punxsutawney Plaindealer* by the late John K. Coxson, Esq., who had made considerable research into Indian history, and was an enthusiast on the subject. According to Mr. Coxson, 'More than eighteen hundred years ago the Iroquois held a lodge in Punxsutawney (this town still bears its Indian name, which was their sobriquet for "gnat town"), to which point they could ascend with their canoes, and go still higher up the Mahoning to within a few hours' travel of the summit of the Allegheny Mountains. There were various Indian trails traversing the forests, one of which entered Punxsutawney near where Judge Mitchell now resides.

"'These trails were the thoroughfares or roadways of the Indians, over which they journeyed when on the chase or the "war-path," just as the people of the present age travel over their graded roads. "An erroneous impression obtains among many at the present day that the Indian, in travelling the interminable forests which once covered our towns and fields, roamed at random, like a modern afternoon hunter, by no fixed paths, or that he was guided in his long journeyings solely by the sun and stars, or by the course of the streams and mountains; and true it is that these untutored sons of the woods were considerable astronomers and geographers, and relied much upon these unerring guide-marks of nature. Even in the most starless nights they could determine their course by feeling the bark of the oak-trees, which is always smoothest on the south side and roughest on the north. But still they had their trails, or paths, as distinctly marked as are our county and State roads, and often better located. The white traders adopted them, and often stole their names, to be in turn surrendered to the leader of some Anglo Saxon army, and, finally, obliterated by some costly highway of travel and commerce.

They are now almost wholly effaced or forgotten. Hundreds travel along, or plough over them, unconscious that they are in the footsteps of the red men."* It has not taken long to obliterate all these Indian landmarks from our land; little more than a century ago the Indians roamed over all this western country, and now scarce a vestige of their presence remains. Much has been written and said about their deeds of butchery and cruelty. True, they were cruel, and in many instances fiendish, in their inhuman practices, but they did not meet the first settlers in this spirit. Honest, hospitable, religious in their belief, reverencing their Manitou, or Great Spirit, and willing to do anything to please their white brother,—this is how they met their first white visitors; but when they had seen nearly all their vast domain appropriated by the invaders, when wicked white men had introduced into their midst the "wicked firewater," which is to-day the cause of many an act of fiendishness perpetrated by those who are not untutored savages, then the Indian rebelled, all the savage in his breast was aroused, and he became pitiless and cruel in the extreme.

"'It is true that our broad domains were purchased and secured by treaty, but the odds were always on the side of the whites. The "Colonial Records" give an account of the treaty of 1686, by which a deed for "walking purchase was executed, by which the Indians sold as far as a man could walk in a day. But when the walk was to be made the most active white man was obtained, who ran from daylight until dark, as fast as he was able, without stopping to eat or drink. This much dissatisfied the Indians, who expected to walk leisurely, resting at noon to eat and shoot game, and one old chief expressed his dissatisfaction as follows: 'Lun, lun, lun; no lay down to drink; no stop to shoot squirrel, but lun, lun, lun all day; me no keep up; lun, lun for land.' That deed, it is said, does not now exist, but was confirmed in 1737."

"'When the white man came the Indians were a temperate people, and their chiefs tried hard to prohibit the sale of intoxicating drinks among their tribes; and when one Sylvester Garland, in 1701, introduced rum among them and induced them to drink, at a council held in Philadelphia, Shemekenwhol, chief of the Shawnese, complained to Governor William Penn, and at a council held on the 13th of October, 1701, this man was held in the sum of one hundred pounds never to deal rum to the Indians again; and the bond and sentence was approved by Judge Shippen, of Philadelphia. At the chief's suggestion the council enacted a law prohibiting the trade in rum with the Indians. Still later the ruling chiefs of the Six Nations opposed the use of rum, and Red Jacket, in a speech at Buffalo, wished that whiskey would never be less than "a dollar a quart." He answered the missionary's remarks on drunkenness

---

* Judge Veech.

thus: "Go to the white man with that." A council, held on the Allegheny River, deplored the murder of the Wigden family in Butler County by a Seneca Indian while under the influence of whiskey, approved the sentence of our law, and again passed their prohibitory resolutions, and implored the white man not to give rum to the Indian.'

"Mr. Coxson claims that the council of the Delawares, Muncys, Shawnese, Nanticokes, Tuscorawas, and Mingos, to protest against the sale of their domain by the Six Nations, at Albany, in 1754, was held at Punxsutawney, and cites Joncaire's 'Notes on Indian Warfare,' 'Life of Bezant,' etc. 'It is said they ascended the tributary of La Belle Riviere to the mountain village on the way to Chinklacamoose (Clearfield) to attend the council.' * At that council, though Sheklemas, the Christian king of the Delawares, and other Christian chiefs, tried hard to prevent the war, they were overruled, and the tribes decided to go to war with their French allies against the colony. 'Travellers, as early as 1731, reported to the council of the colony of a town sixty miles from the Susquehanna.' †

"'After the failure of the expedition against Fort Duquesne, the white captives were taken to Kittanning, Logtown, and Pukeesheno (Punxsutawney). The sachem, Pukeesheno (for whom the town was called), was the father of Tecumseh and his twin brother, the Prophet, and was a Shawnese. We make this digression to add another proof that Punxsutawney was named after a Shawnese chief as early as 1750.' ‡

"'I went with Captain Brady on an Indian hunt up the Allegheny River. We found a good many signs of the savages, and I believe we were so much like the savages (when Brady went on a scouting expedition he always dressed in Indian costume) that they could hardly have known us from a band of Shawnese. But they had an introduction to us near the mouth of Red Bank. General Brodhead was on the route behind Captain Brady, who discovered the Indians on a march. He lay concealed among the rocks until the painted chiefs and their braves had got fairly into the narrow pass, when Brady and his men opened a destructive fire. The sylvan warriors retuned the volley with terrific yells that shook the caverns and mountains from base to crest. The fight was short but sanguine. The Indians left the pass and retired, and soon were lost sight of in the deepness of the forest. We returned with three children recaptured, whose parents had been killed at Greensburg. We immediately set out on a path that led us to the mountains, to a lodge the savages had near the head-waters of Mahoning and Red Bank.

"'We crossed the Mahoning about forty miles from Kittanning, and entered a town, which we found deserted. It seemed to be a hamlet, built by the Shawnese. From there we went over high and rugged hills,

---

* Joncaire.   † Bezant.   ‡ History of Western Pennsylvania, p. 302.

through laurel thickets, darkened by tall pine and hemlock groves, for one whole day, and lay quietly down on the bank of a considerable stream (Sandy Lick). About midnight Brady was aroused by the sound of a rifle not far down the creek. We arose and stole quietly along about half a mile, when we heard the voices of Indians but a short distance below us; there another creek unites its waters with the one upon whose banks we had rested. We ascertained that two Indians had killed a deer at a lick. They were trying to strike a light to dress their game. When the flame of pine-knots blazed brightly and revealed the visages of the savages, Brady appeared to be greatly excited, and perhaps the caution that he always took when on a war-path was at that time disregarded. Revenge swallowed and absorbed every faculty of his soul. He recognized the Indian who was foremost, when they chased him, a few months before, so closely that he was forced to leap across a chasm of stone on the slippery rock twenty-three feet; between the jaws of granite there roared a deep torrent twenty feet deep. When Brady saw Conemah he sprang forward and planted his tomahawk in his head. The other Indian, who had his knife in his hand, sprang at Brady. The long, bright steel glistened in his uplifted hand, when the flash of Farley's rifle was the death-light of the brave, who sank to the sands. . . . Brady scalped the Indians in a moment, and drew the deer into the thicket to finish dressing it, but had not completed his undertaking when he heard a noise in the branches of the neighboring trees. He sprang forward, quenched the flame, and in breathless silence listened for the least sound, but nothing was heard save the rustling of the leaves, stirred by the wind. One of the scouts softly crept along the banks of the creek to catch the faintest sound that echoes on the water, when he found a canoe down upon the beach. The scout communicated this to Brady, who resolved to embark on this craft, if it was large enough to carry the company. It was found to be of sufficient size. We all embarked and took the deer along. We had not gone forty rods down the stream when the savages gave a war-whoop, and about a mile off they were answered with a hundred voices. We heard them in pursuit as we went dashing down the frightful and unknown stream. We gained on them. We heard their voices far behind us, until the faint echoes of the hundreds of warriors were lost; but, unexpectedly, we found ourselves passing full fifty canoes drawn up on the beach. Brady landed a short distance below. There was no time to lose. If the pursuers arrived they might overtake the scouts. It was yet night. He took four of his men along, and with great caution unmoored the canoes and sent them adrift. The scouts below secured them, and succeeded in arriving at Brodhead's quarters with the scalps of two Indians and their whole fleet, which disabled them much from carrying on their bloody expeditions.'

"In the legend of Noshaken, the white captive of the Delawares, in

1753, who was kept at a village supposed to have been Punxsutawney, occurs the following: 'The scouts were on the track of the Indians, the time of burning of the captives was extended, and the whole band prepared to depart for Fort Venango with the prisoners. . . . They continued on for twenty miles, and encamped by a beautiful spring, where the sand boiled up from the bottom near where two creeks unite. Here they passed the night, and the next morning again headed for Fort Venango.

"'This spring is believed to have been the "sand spring" at Brookville. Thus both the earlier histories and traditions would lead us to believe that Jefferson County was once the scene of Indian occupation. The early settlers found many vestiges of them, and even at this late day "Indian relics" in the shape of stone tomahawks, flint arrows, darts, etc., are frequently found.

"'But it was long after these scenes, when Joseph Barnett, the first white settler, came into the wilds of what is now Jefferson County. Then nearly all the Indians had gone, some toward the setting sun, others toward Canada. Of all the tribes that once composed the great Indian confederations, only a few Muncies and Senecas of Cornplanter's tribe remained. These Indians, for a number of years after the white men came, extended their hunting excursions into these forests. They were always peaceable and friendly. The first settlers found their small patches of corn, one of which was planted where the fair-grounds are now located, and another in the flat at Port Barnett. Indian corn, or maize, as it was sometimes called, is undoubtedly an American cereal, being first discovered on this continent in 1600, though it is now grown in all civilized lands.'"*—*Kate Scott's History of Jefferson County.*

CHAPTER III.

THE WILDERNESS IN 1755—THE SAVAGE INDIAN—MARIE LE ROY AND BARBARA LEININGER, THE FIRST WHITE PIONEERS TO TREAD THIS WILDERNESS—THE CHINKLACAMOOSE PATH—PUNXSUTAWNEY AND KITTANNING—REV. HECKEWELDER, REV. ZEISBERGER, REV. ETTWEIN, AND ROTHE.

FROM what I can learn, the first white pioneers to tread the soil of Jefferson County, as it now is, were Marie Le Roy and Barbara Leininger. They were Swiss people, and lived with their parents about fifteen miles from where the city of Sunbury now is, in Northumberland County, then

---

* Drs. Sturtevant, Pickering, and other eminent botanists and antiquarians, believed that maize (or Indian corn) is mentioned by the old Icelandic writers, who are thought to have visited the coast of eastern North America as early as 1006.

Lancaster or Berks County. These girls were Indian prisoners, and were being taken to Kittanning, as it is called now, by and over the "Chinklacamoose path" or "Indian trail." This "trail" passed through Punxsutawney, and here the Indians with these captive girls rested *five* days.

I quote from the "Narrative of Marie Le Roy and Barbara Leininger" as follows:

"Early in the morning of the 16th of October, 1755, while Le Roy's hired man went out to fetch the cows, he heard the Indians shooting six times. Soon after eight of them came to the house and killed Marie Le Roy's father with tomahawks. Her brother defended himself desperately for a time, but was at last overpowered. The Indians did not kill him, but took him prisoner, together with Marie Le Roy and a little girl, who was staying with the family. Thereupon they plundered the homestead and set it on fire. Into this fire they laid the body of the murdered father, feet foremost, until it was half consumed. The upper half was left lying on the ground, with the two tomahawks with which they had killed him sticking in his head. Then they kindled another fire, not far from the house. While sitting around it, a neighbor of Le Roy, named Bastian, happened to pass by on horseback. He was immediately shot down and scalped.

"Two of the Indians now went to the house of Barbara Leininger, where they found her father, her brother, and her sister Regina. Her mother had gone to the mill. They demanded rum; but there was none in the house. Then they called for tobacco, which was given them. Having filled and smoked a pipe, they said, 'We are Allegheny Indians, and your enemies. You must all die!' Thereupon they shot her father, tomahawked her brother, who was twenty years of age, took Barbara and her sister Regina prisoners, and conveyed them into the forest for about a mile. There they were soon joined by the other Indians, with Marie Le Roy and the little girl.

"Not long after several of the Indians led the prisoners to the top of a high hill, near the two plantations. Toward evening the rest of the savages returned with six fresh and bloody scalps, which they threw at the feet of the poor captives, saying that they had a good hunt that day.

"The next morning we were taken about two miles farther into the forest, while the most of the Indians again went out to kill and plunder. Toward evening they returned with nine scalps and five prisoners.

"On the third day the whole band came together and divided the spoils. In addition to large quantities of provisions, they had taken fourteen horses and ten prisoners,—namely, one man, one woman, five girls, and three boys. We two girls, as also two of the horses, fell to the share of an Indian named Galasko.

PIONEER HISTORY OF JEFFERSON COUNTY, PENNA.

"We travelled with our new master for two days. He was tolerably kind, and allowed us to ride all the way, while he and the rest of the Indians walked. Of this circumstance Barbara Leininger took advantage, and tried to escape. But she was almost immediately recaptured, and condemned to be burned alive. The savages gave her a French Bible, which they had taken from Le Roy's house, in order that she might prepare for death; and when she told them that she could not understand it, they gave her a German Bible. Thereupon they made a large pile of wood and set it on fire, intending to put her into the midst of it. But a young Indian begged so earnestly for her life that she was pardoned, after having promised not to attempt to escape again, and to stop her crying.

"The next day the whole troop was divided into two bands, the one marching in the direction of the Ohio, the other, in which we were with Galasko, to Jenkiklamuhs,* a Delaware town on the west branch of the Susquehanna. There we stayed ten days, and then proceeded to Puncksotonay,† or Eschentown. Marie Le Roy's brother was forced to remain at Jenkiklamuhs.

"After having rested for five days at Puncksotonay, we took our way to Kittanny. As this was to be the place of our permanent abode, we here received our welcome, according to Indian custom. It consisted of three blows each, on the back. They were, however, administered with great mercy. Indeed, we concluded that we were beaten merely in order to keep up an ancient usage and not with the intention of injuring us. The month of December was the time of our arrival, and we remained at Kittanny until the month of September, 1756.

"The Indians gave us enough to do. We had to tan leather, to make shoes (moccasins), to clear land, to plant corn, to cut down trees and build huts, to wash and cook. The want of provisions, however, caused us the greatest suffering. During all the time that we were at Kittanny we had neither lard nor salt, and sometimes we were forced to live on acorns, roots, grass, and bark. There was nothing in the world to make this new sort of food palatable, excepting hunger itself.

"In the month of September Colonel Armstrong arrived with his men, and attacked Kittanny Town. Both of us happened to be in that part of it which lies on the other (right) side of the river (Allegheny). We were immediately conveyed ten miles farther into the interior, in order that we might have no chance of trying, on this occasion, to escape. The savages threated to kill us. If the English had advanced, this might have happened, for at that time the Indians were greatly in dread of Colonel Armstrong's corps. After the English had withdrawn, we were

---

* Chinklacamoose, on the site of the present town of Clearfield.
† Punxsutawney, in Jefferson County.

again brought back to Kittanny, which town had been burned to the ground.

"There we had the mournful opportunity of witnessing the cruel end of an English woman, who had attempted to flee out of her captivity and to return to the settlements with Colonel Armstrong. Having been recaptured by the savages and brought back to Kittanny, she was put to death in an unheard-of way. First they scalped her, next they laid burning splinters of wood here and there upon her body, and then they cut off her ears and fingers, forcing them into her mouth, so that she had to swallow them. Amidst such torments this woman lived from nine o'clock in the morning until toward sunset, when a French officer took compassion on her and put her out of her misery. An English soldier, on the contrary, named John ——, who escaped from prison at Lancaster and joined the French, had a piece of flesh cut from her body and ate it. When she was dead, the Indians chopped her in two, through the middle, and let her lie until the dogs came and devoured her.

"Three days later an Englishman was brought in, who had likewise attempted to escape with Colonel Armstrong, and burned alive in the same village. His torments, however, continued only about three hours; but his screams were frightful to listen to. It rained that day very hard, so that the Indians could not keep up the fire: hence they began to discharge gunpowder at his body. At last, amidst his worst pains, when the poor man called for a drink of water, they brought him melted lead and poured it down his throat. This draught at once helped him out of the hands of the barbarians, for he died on the instant.

"It is easy to imagine what an impression such fearful instances of cruelty make upon the mind of a poor captive. Does he attempt to escape from the savages, he knows in advance that if retaken he will be roasted alive: hence he must compare two evils,—namely, either to remain among them a prisoner forever or to die a cruel death. Is he fully resolved to endure the latter, then he may run away with a brave heart.

"Soon after these occurrences we were brought to Fort Duquesne, where we remained for about two months. We worked for the French, and our Indian master drew our wages. In this place, thank God, we could again eat bread. Half a pound was given us daily. We might have had bacon, too, but we took none of it, for it was not good. In some respects we were better off than in the Indian towns. We could not, however, abide the French. They tried hard to induce us to forsake the Indians and stay with them, making us various favorable offers. But we believed that it would be better for us to remain among the Indians, inasmuch as they would be more likely to make peace with the English than the French, and inasmuch as there would be more ways open for flight in the forest than in a fort. Consequently we declined the offers of the French and accompanied our Indian master to Sackum,* where we spent the winter, keeping house for the savages, who were continually on the chase. In the spring we were taken to Kaschkaschkung,† an Indian town on the Beaver Creek. There we again had to clear the plantations of the Indian nobles, after the German fashion, to plant corn, and to do other hard work of every kind. We remained at this place for about a year and a half.

"After having, in the past three years, seen no one of our own flesh and blood, except those unhappy beings who, like ourselves, were bearing the yoke of the heaviest slavery, we had the unexpected pleasure of meeting with a German, who was not a captive, but free, and who, as we heard, had been sent into this neighborhood to negotiate a peace between the English and the natives. His name was Frederick Post. We and all the other prisoners heartily wished him success and God's blessing upon his undertaking. We were, however, not allowed to speak with him. The Indians gave us plainly to understand that any attempt to do this would be taken amiss. He himself, by the reserve with which he treated us, let us see that this was not the time to talk over our afflictions. But we were greatly alarmed on his account, for the French told us that if they caught him they would roast him alive for five days, and many Indians declared that it was impossible for him to get safely through, that he was destined for death.

"Last summer the French and Indians were defeated by the English in a battle fought at Loyal-Hannon, or Fort Ligonier. This caused the utmost consternation among the natives. They brought their wives and children from Lockstown,‡ Sackum, Schomingo, Mamalty, Kaschkaschkung, and other places in that neighborhood, to Moschkingo, about one hundred and fifty miles farther west. Before leaving, however, they destroyed their crops and burned everything which they could not carry with them. We had to go along, and stayed at Moschkingo§ the whole winter.

"In February, Barbara Leininger agreed with an Englishman, named David Breckenreach (Breckenridge), to escape, and gave her comrade, Marie Le Roy, notice of their intentions. On account of the severe season of the year and the long journey which lay before them, Marie strongly advised her to relinquish the project, suggesting that it should

---

* Sakunk, outlet of the Big Beaver into the Ohio, a point well known to all Indians; their rendezvous in the French wars, etc. Post, in his Journal, under date of August 20, 1758, records his experience at Sakunk (Reichel). See Post's Journal, Pennsylvania Archives, O. S., vol. iii. p. 527.

† Kaskaskunk, near the junction of the Shenango and Mahoning, in Lawrence County.

‡ Loggstown, on the Ohio, eight miles above Beaver.—*Weiser's Journal.*

§ Muskingum.

be postponed until spring, when the weather would be milder, and promising to accompany her at that time.

"On the last day of February nearly all the Indians left Moschkingo, and proceeded to Pittsburg to sell pelts. Meanwhile, their women travelled ten miles up the country to gather roots, and we accompanied them. Two men went along as a guard. It was our earnest hope that the opportunity for flight, so long desired, had now come. Accordingly, Barbara Leininger pretended to be sick, so that she might be allowed to put up a hut for herself alone. On the 14th of March, Marie Le Roy was sent back to the town, in order to fetch two young dogs which had been left there, and on the same day Barbara Leininger came out of her hut and visited a German woman, ten miles from Moschkingo. This woman's name is Mary——, and she is the wife of a miller from the South Branch.* She had made every preparation to accompany us on our flight; but Barbara found that she had meanwhile become lame, and could not think of going along. She, however, gave Barbara the provisions which she had stored,—namely, two pounds of dried meat, a quart of corn, and four pounds of sugar. Besides, she presented her with pelts for moccasins. Moreover, she advised a young Englishman, Owen Gibson, to flee with us two girls.

"On the 16th of March, in the evening, Gibson reached Barbara Leininger's hut, and at ten o'clock our whole party, consisting of us two girls, Gibson, and David Breckenreach, left Moschkingo. This town lies on a river, in the country of the Dellamottinoes. We had to pass many huts inhabited by the savages, and knew that there were at least sixteen dogs with them. In the merciful providence of God not a single one of these dogs barked. Their barking would at once have betrayed us and frustrated our design.

"It is hard to describe the anxious fears of a poor woman under such circumstances. The extreme probability that the Indians would pursue and recapture us was as two to one compared with the dim hope that, perhaps, we would get through in safety. But, even if we escaped the Indians, how would we ever succeed in passing through the wilderness, unacquainted with a single path or trail, without a guide, and helpless, half naked, broken down by more than three years of hard slavery, hungry and scarcely any food, the season wet and cold, and many rivers and streams to cross? Under such circumstances, to depend upon one's own sagacity would be the worst of follies. If one could not believe that there is a God who helps and saves from death, one had better let running away alone.

"We safely reached the river (Muskingum). Here the first thought in all our minds was, Oh, that we were safely across! And Barbara Lei-

---

* South Branch of the Potomac.

ninger, in particular, recalling ejaculatory prayers from an old hymn, which she had learned in her youth, put them together, to suit our present circumstances, something in the following style:

> "O bring us safely across this river!
> In fear I cry, yea, my soul doth quiver.
> The worst afflictions are now before me,
> Where'er I turn nought but death do I see.
> Alas, what great hardships are yet in store
> In the wilderness wide, beyond that shore!
> It has neither water, nor meat, nor bread,
> But each new morning something new to dread.
> Yet little sorrow would hunger me cost
> If but I could flee from the savage host,
> Which murders and fights and burns far and wide,
> While Satan himself is array'd on its side.
> Should on us fall one of its cruel bands,
> Then help us, Great God, and stretch out Thy hands!
> In Thee will we trust, be Thou ever near,
> Art Thou our Joshua, we need not fear.

"Presently we found a raft, left by the Indians. Thanking God that He had himself prepared a way for us across these first waters, we got on board and pushed off. But we were carried almost a mile down the river before we could reach the other side. There our journey began in good earnest. Full of anxiety and fear, we fairly ran that whole night and all next day, when we lay down to rest without venturing to kindle a fire. Early the next morning Owen Gibson fired at a bear. The animal fell, but when he ran with his tomahawk to kill it, it jumped up and bit him in the feet, leaving three wounds. We all hastened to his assistance. The bear escaped into narrow holes among the rocks, where we could not follow. On the third day, however, Owen Gibson shot a deer. We cut off the hind-quarters and roasted them at night. The next morning he again shot a deer, which furnished us with food for that day. In the evening we got to the Ohio at last, having made a circuit of over one hundred miles in order to reach it.

"About midnight the two Englishmen rose and began to work at a raft, which was finished by morning. We got on board and safely crossed the river. From the signs which the Indians had there put up we saw that we were about one hundred and fifty miles from Fort Duquesne. After a brief consultation we resolved, heedless of path or trail, to travel straight toward the rising of the sun. This we did for seven days. On the seventh we found that we had reached the Little Beaver Creek, and were about fifty miles from Pittsburg.

"And now that we imagined ourselves so near the end of all our troubles and misery, a whole host of mishaps came upon us. Our provisions were at an end, Barbara Leininger fell into the water and was nearly drowned, and, worst misfortune of all! Owen Gibson lost his flint and steel. Hence we had to spend four nights without fire, amidst rain and snow.

"On the last day of March we came to a river, Alloquepy,* about three miles below Pittsburg. Here we made a raft, which, however, proved to be too light to carry us across. It threatened to sink, and Marie le Roy fell off, and narrowly escaped drowning. We had to put back and let one of our men convey one of us across at a time. In this way we reached the Monongahela River, on the other side of Pittsburg, the same evening.

"Upon our calling for help, Colonel Mercer immediately sent out a boat to bring us to the fort. At first, however, the crew created many difficulties about taking us on board. They thought we were Indians, and wanted us to spend the night where we were, saying they would fetch us in the morning. When we had succeeded in convincing them that we were English prisoners, who had escaped from the Indians, and that we were wet and cold and hungry, they brought us over. There was an Indian with the soldiers in the boat. He asked us whether we could speak good Indian. Marie Le Roy said she could speak it. Thereupon he inquired why she had run away. She replied that her Indian mother had been so cross and had scolded her so constantly, that she could not stay with her any longer. This answer did not please him; nevertheless, doing as courtiers do, he said he was very glad we had safely reached the fort.

"It was in the night from the last of March to the first of April that we came to Pittsburg. Most heartily did we thank God in heaven for all the mercy which he showed us, for His gracious support in our weary captivity, for the courage which He gave us to undertake our flight and to surmount all the many hardships it brought us, for letting us find the road which we did not know, and of which He alone could know that on it we would meet neither danger nor enemy, and for finally bringing us to Pittsburg to our countrymen in safety.

"Colonel Mercer helped and aided us in every way which lay in his power. Whatever was on hand and calculated to refresh us was offered in the most friendly manner. The colonel ordered for each of us a new chemise, a petticoat, a pair of stockings, garters, and a knife. After having spent a day at Pittsburg, we went, with a detachment under command of Lieutenant Mile,† to Fort Ligonier. There the lieutenant presented each of us with a blanket. On the 15th we left Fort Ligonier, under protection of Captain Weiser and Lieutenant Atly,‡ for Fort Bedford, where we arrived in the evening of the 16th, and remained a week. Thence, provided with passports by Lieutenant Geiger, we

---

* Chartiers Creek.   † Lieutenant Samuel Miles.
‡ Lieutenant Samuel J. Atlee.

travelled in wagons to Harris' Ferry, and from there, afoot, by way of Lancaster, to Philadelphia. Owen Gibson remained at Fort Bedford and David Breckenreach at Lancaster. We two girls arrived in Philadelphia on Sunday, the 6th of May."

In 1762 the great Moravian missionary, Rev. John Heckewelder, may have, and probably did, spend a day or two in Punxsutawney. In or about the year 1765 a Moravian missionary—viz., Rev. David Zeisberger—established a mission near the present town of Wyalusing, Bradford County, Pennsylvania. He erected forty frame buildings, with shingle roofs and chimneys, in connection with other improvements, and Christianized a large number of the savages. The Muncy Indians were then living in what is now called Forest County, on the Allegheny River. This brave, pious missionary determined to reach these savages also, and, with two Christian Indian guides, he traversed the solitude of the forests and reached his destination on the 16th of October, 1767. He remained with these savages but seven days; they were good listeners to his sermons, but every day he was in danger of being murdered. Of these Indians he wrote,—

"I have never found such heathenism in any other parts of the Indian country. Here Satan has his stronghold. Here he sits on his throne. Here he is worshipped by true savages, and carries on his work in the hearts of the children of darkness." These, readers, were the Indians that roamed over our hills, then either Lancaster or Berks County. In 1768 this brave minister returned and put up a log cabin, twenty-six by sixteen feet, and in 1769 was driven back to what is now called Wyalusing by repeated attempts on his life. He says in his journal, "For ten months I have lived between these two towns of godless and malicious savages, and my preservation is wonderful."

In 1768 the six Indian nations having by treaty sold the land from "under the feet" of the Wyalusing converts, the Rev. Zeisberger was compelled to take measures for the removal of these Christian Indians, with their horses and cattle, to some other field. After many councils and much consideration, he determined to remove the entire body to a mission he had established on the Big Beaver, now Lawrence County, Pennsylvania. Accordingly, "on the 11th of June, 1772, everything being in readiness, the congregation assembled for the last time in their church and took up their march toward the setting sun." They were "divided into two companies, and each of these were subdivided. One of these companies went overland by the Wyalusing path, up the Sugar Run, and down the Loyal Sock, *via* Dushore. This company was in charge of Ettwein, who had the care of the horses and cattle. The other company was in charge of Rothe, and went by canoe down the Susquehannah and up the west branch." The place for the divisions to unite was the Great Island, now Lock Haven, and from there, under the lead of Rev. John Ettwein, to proceed up the west branch of the Susquehanna, and then cross the mountains over the Chinklacamoose path, through what is now Clearfield and Punxsutawney, and from there to proceed, *via* Kittanning, to the Big Beaver, now in Lawrence County, Pennsylvania. Reader, just think of two hundred and fifty people of all ages, with seventy head of oxen and a greater number of horses, traversing these deep forests, over a small path sometimes scarcely discernible, under drenching rains, and through dismal swamps, and

Rattlesnake.

all this exposure continued for days and weeks, with wild beasts to the right and to the left of them, and the path alive with rattlesnakes in front of them, wading streams and overtaken by sickness, and then, dear reader, you will conclude with me that nothing but "praying all night in the wilderness" ever carried them successfully to their destination. This story of Rev. Ettwein is full of interest. I reprint a paragraph or two that applies to what is now Jefferson County,—viz. :

"*1772, Tuesday, July 14th.*—Reached Clearfield Creek, where the Buffaloes formerly cleared large tracts of undergrowth, so as to give them the appearance of cleared fields. Hence the Indians called the creek 'Clearfield.' Here we shot nine deer. On the route we shot one hundred and fifty deer and three bears.

"*Friday, July 17th.*—Advanced only four miles to a creek that comes down from the Northwest." This was and is Anderson Creek, near Curwensville, Pennsylvania.

"*July 18th.*—Moved on . . .

"*Sunday, July 19th.*—As yesterday, but two families kept up with me, because of the rain, we had a quiet Sunday, but enough to do drying our effects. In the evening all joined me, but we could hold no service as the Ponkies were so excessively annoying that the cattle pressed toward and into our camp to escape their persecutors in the smoke of the fire. This vermin is a plague to man and beast by day and night, but in the swamp through which we are now passing, their name is legion. Hence the Indians call it the Ponsetunik, *i.e.* the town of the Ponkies." This swamp was in what we now call Punxsutawney. These people on their route lived on fish, venison, etc.

CHAPTER IV.

THE PURCHASE OF 1784.

THE following article on the purchase made by the Commonwealth from the Indian tribes known as the Six Nations in 1784, of all the lands within the charter boundaries of Pennsylvania in which the Indian title had not been extinguished by previous purchases, was written and compiled by Major R. H. Forster, of the Department of Internal Affairs, for this book:

"At the close of the war of the Revolution, in the year 1783, the ownership of a large area of the territory within the charter boundaries of Pennsylvania was still claimed by the Indians of the several tribes that were commonly known as the Six Nations. The last purchase of lands from the Six Nations by the proprietary government of the province was made at Fort Stanwix in November, 1768, and the limit of this purchase may be described as extending to lines beginning where the northeast branch of the Susquehanna River crosses the northern line of the State, in the present county of Bradford; thence down the river to the mouth of Towanda Creek, and up the same to its head-waters; thence by a range of hills to the head-waters of Pine Creek, and down the same to the west branch of the Susquehanna; thence up the same to Cherry Tree; thence by a straight line, across the present counties of Indiana and Armstrong, to Kittanning,* on the Allegheny River, and thence down the Allegheny and Ohio Rivers to the western boundary line of the province. The Indian claim, therefore, embraced all that part of the State lying to the northwest of the purchase lines of 1768, as they are here described. With the close of the Revolutionary struggle, the authorities of the new Commonwealth, anxiously looking to its future stability and prosperity,

---

* "Canoe Place," so called in the old maps of the State to designate the head of navigation on the west branch of the Susquehanna River, is the point at which the purchase line of 1768 from that river to Kittanning, on the Allegheny River, begins. A survey of that line was made by Robert Galbraith in the year 1786, and a cherry-tree standing on the west bank of the river was marked by him as the beginning of his survey. The same cherry-tree was marked by William P. Brady as the southeast corner of a tract surveyed by him "at Canoe Place," in 1794, on warrant No. 3744, in the name of John Nicholson, Esq. The town of Cherry Tree now covers part of this ground. The old tree disappeared years ago. Its site, however, was regarded as of some historic importance, and under an appropriation of $1500, granted by the Legislature in 1893, a substantial granite monument has been erected to mark the spot where it stood.

soon found themselves confronted with duties and responsibilities different in many respects from those that had engaged their serious attention and earnest effort during the previous seven years of war. They were to enact just and equitable laws for the government of a new State, and to devise such measures as would stimulate its growth in wealth and population and promote the development, settlement, and improvement of its great domain.

"As early as the 12th of March, 1783, the General Assembly had passed an act setting apart certain lands lying north and west of the Ohio and Allegheny Rivers and Conewango Creek to be sold for the purpose of redeeming the depreciation certificates given to the officers and soldiers of the Pennsylvania Line who had served in the war of the Revolution, and also for the purpose of making donations of land to the same officers and soldiers in compliance with a promise made to them by a resolution passed in 1780. It will be observed that when this act was passed the Indian claim of title to the lands mentioned was still in force; but the State authorities, though seemingly slow and deliberate in their actions, were no doubt fully alive to the necessity of securing as speedily as possible the right to all the lands within the State—about five-sixteenths of its area—that remained unpurchased after the treaty at Fort Stanwix in 1768. With that purpose in view, the first movement made by the General Assembly to be found on record was on the 25th day of September, 1783. This action is in the form of a resolution passed on that day by the recommendation of the report of a committee that had been previously appointed ' to digest such plans as they might conceive necessary to facilitate and expedite the laying off and surveying of the lands' set apart by the act of the previous March. The resolution reads,—

"' *Resolved*, unanimously, That the supreme executive council be, and they are hereby authorized and empowered to appoint commissioners to hold a meeting with the Indians claiming the unpurchased territory within the acknowledged limits of the State, for the purpose of purchasing the same, agreeable to ancient usage, and that all the expenses accruing from the said meeting and purchase be defrayed out of the Treasury of the State.'—*Pennsylvania Archives*, vol. x. p. 111.

"It next appears by a minute of the Supreme Executive Council, of February 23, 1784, that Samuel John Atlee, William Maclay, and Francis Johnston were on that day chosen commissioners to treat with the Indians as proposed in the resolution of the General Assembly. The gentlemen named—all of them prominent citizens—were informed on the 29th of the same month of their appointment, but they did not acknowledge the receipt of President Dickinson's letter until the 17th of May following. On that day Messrs. Atlee and Johnston reply in a letter of thanks for the honor conferred upon them, and explain the delay as having been caused by circumstances that required Mr. Maclay and Colonel Atlee to visit their families, the first named still remaining absent. The letter also contains a statement of their views upon various matters pertaining to the mission upon which they are about to enter. They suggest Samuel Weiser, a son of Conrad Weiser, the noted Indian missionary, as a

Conrad Weiser.

proper person to notify the Indians of the desire to treat with them, and, from his familiarity with their language and customs, to act as interpreter. The time and place for holding the treaty are mentioned, but nothing definite suggested, owing to the fact that the Continental Congress had likewise appointed commissioners to meet the Six Nations for the purpose of treating with them in relation to the lands of the Northwest, beyond the limits of Pennsylvania, and it was deemed proper to permit the representatives of Congress to arrange for the meeting.* Fort Stanwix, in the State of New York, was finally agreed upon as the place where the

* Pennsylvania Archives, vol. x. p. 265.

meeting should be held, and thither the commissioners on the part of Pennsylvania were directed to proceed. On the 25th of August, 1784, a committee of the General Assembly, having Indian affairs under consideration, made the following report :

"'That weighty reasons have occurred in favor of the design for holding a conference with the Indians on the part of this State, and if under the present situation of Continental affairs that measure can be conducted on sure ground and without too unlimited an expense, it ought to take place and be rendered as effective as this House can make it, under whose auspices a foundation would thus be laid of essential and durable advantage to the public, by extending population, satisfying our officers and soldiers in regard to their donation lands and depreciation certificates, restoring that ancient, friendly, and profitable intercourse with the Indians, and guarding against all occasions of war with them.'—*Pennsylvania Archives*, vol. x. p. 316.

"To aid the commissioners in their efforts to attain objects so worthy and laudable, the above report was accompanied by a resolution that authorized the Supreme Executive Council to expend $9000 in the purchase of 'such goods, merchandize, and trinkets' as would be acceptable to the Indians, to be given them as part of the consideration in the event of a purchase being made. In pursuance of this resolution the council promptly ordered a warrant to be issued by the treasurer in favor of the commissioners for the sum of £3375 (equivalent in Pennsylvania currency to $9100), to be expended by them in purchasing the necessary articles.*

"After a tedious and fatiguing journey, in which they met with a number of unexpected delays, the commissioners reached Fort Stanwix early in the month of October, where they found some of the tribes already assembled, and with them the commissioners of the Continental Congress. In a letter to President Dickinson, dated October 4, 1784, they announce their arrival, and state that the negotiations had already commenced, and while they would not venture an opinion as to the final issue, they say the disposition of the Indians appeared to be favorable. The negotiations continued until the 23d of the same month, and on that day ended in an agreement by which the Indian title to all the lands within the boundaries of the State that remained after the treaty of 1768 was extinguished. The Indians represented at the conference were the Mohawks, the Oneidas, the Onondagas, the Senecas, the Cayugas, and the Tuscaroras. The consideration fixed for the surrender of their rights was

---

* For a list of the articles designated in the order see Colonial Records, vol. xiv. p. 186. After the negotiations at Fort Stanwix had been concluded the commissioners gave an obligation for an additional thousand dollars in goods, to be delivered at Tioga. For this list see Pennsylvania Archives, vol. x. p. 496.

$5000. The deed is dated October 23, 1784, is signed by all the chiefs of the Six Nations and by the Continental commissioners as witnesses. The boundaries of the territory ceded are thus described : ' Beginning on the south side of the river Ohio, where the western boundary of the State of Pennsylvania crosses the said river, near Shingo's old town, at the mouth of Beaver Creek, and thence by a due north line to the end of the forty-second and the beginning of the forty-third degrees of north latitude, thence by a due east line separating the forty-second and the forty-third degrees of north latitude, to the east side of the east branch of the Susquehanna River, thence by the bounds of the late purchase made at Fort Stanwix, the fifth day of November, Anno Domini one thousand seven hundred and sixty-eight, as follows : Down the said east branch of Susquehanna, on the east side thereof, till it comes opposite to the mouth of a creek called by the Indians Awandac, and across the river, and up the said creek on the south side thereof, all along the range of hills called Burnet's Hills by the English and by the Indians ——, on the north side of them, to the head of a creek which runs into the west branch of Susquehanna, which creek is by the Indians called Tyadaghton, but by the Pennsylvanians Pine Creek, and down the said creek on the south side thereof to the said west branch of Susquehanna, thence crossing the said river, and running up the south side thereof, the several courses thereof to the forks of the same river, which lies nearest to a place on the river Ohio called Kittanning, and from the fork by a straight line to Kittanning aforesaid, and thence down the said river Ohio by the several courses thereof to where said State of Pennsylvania crosses the same river at the place of beginning.' After the commissioners had accomplished in so satisfactory a manner the object for which they had journeyed to Fort Stanwix, it became necessary to appease the Western Indians, the Wyandots and the Delawares, who also claimed rights in the same lands. The same commissioners were therefore sent to Fort McIntosh, on the Ohio River, at the site of the present town of Beaver, where, in January, 1785, they were successful in reaching an agreement with those Indians for the same lands. This deed, signed by the chiefs of both tribes, is dated January 21, 1785, and is in the same words (except as to the consideration money, which is $2000) and recites the same boundaries as the deed signed at Fort Stanwix in the previous month of October.*

"After the purchase of 1768 a disagreement arose between the proprietary government and the Indians as to whether the creek flowing into the west branch of the river Susquehanna, and called in the deed ' Tyadaghton,' was intended for Lycoming Creek or Pine Creek. The In-

---

* The conference of the commissioners at Fort Stanwix and Fort McIntosh with the deeds signed at those places are published in the Appendix to the General Assembly for the session of February to April, 1785.

dians said it was the former, and that the purchase only extended that far, the proprietaries claimed the latter stream to be the extent of the purchase; but, in order to avoid any trouble that might arise from the dis-

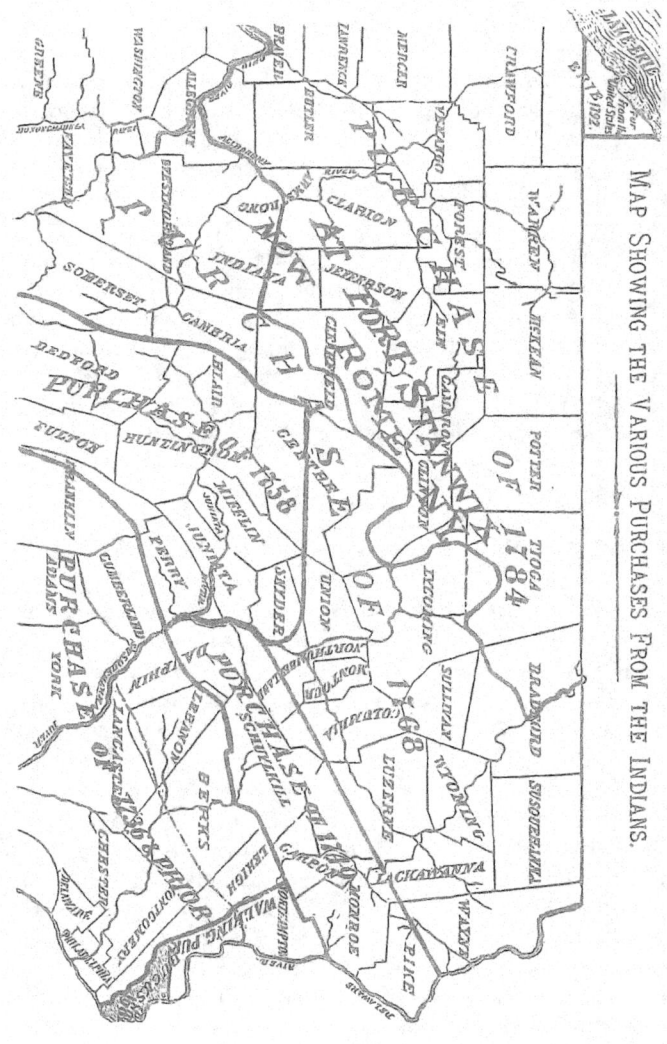

pute, it was wisely determined that no rights should be granted for lands west of Lycoming Creek. This determination, however, did not deter or prevent adventurous pioneers from entering upon and making settlements within the disputed territory, and from their persistency in so doing arose an interesting, not to say serious, condition of affairs, to which reference will again be made. The commissioners at Fort Stanwix were instructed to ascertain definitely from the Indians which of the two streams they meant by 'Tyadaghton.' They then admitted that it was Pine Creek, being the largest emptying into the west branch of the Susquehanna.

"The Indian claim of right to the soil of Pennsylvania, within its charter limits, had thus, in a period of a little more than one hundred years, ceased to exist. A glance at a map of the State will show that within the magnificent domain that comprises the purchase of 1784 are to be found at the present day the counties of Tioga, Potter, McKean, Warren, Crawford, Venango, Forest, Clarion, Elk, Jefferson, Cameron, Butler, Lawrence, and Mercer, and parts of the counties of Bradford, Clinton, Clearfield, Indiana, Armstrong, Allegheny, Beaver, and Erie.* This large and important division of our great Commonwealth, now teeming with population and wealth, the abiding-place of a noble civilization, and containing within its boundaries thousands upon thousands of homes of comfort and many of elegance and luxury, fertile valleys to reward the labor of the husbandman, thriving villages, busy towns, and growing, bustling cities, was, in 1784, largely an uninhabited and untraversed wilderness.

"LANDS EAST OF THE ALLEGHENY RIVER AND CONEWANGO CREEK.

"The General Assembly of the State did not delay in enacting laws which would open to settlers and purchasers that part of the late acquisition that had not been otherwise appropriated. As a matter of fact, in anticipation of the purchase, an act was passed on the 1st day of April, 1784, in which it was provided that as soon as the Indians were 'satisfied for the unpurchased lands,' the supreme executive council should give official information thereof to the surveyor-general, who was then to appoint district surveyors to survey all such lands within the purchase as should 'be found fit for cultivation.' The tracts were to contain not more than 500 nor less than 200 acres each, and were to be numbered on a general draft of each district. When a certain number of lots were surveyed, they were to be sold at public auction, the purchaser having the privilege of paying one moiety at the time of purchase and receiving a credit of two years for the other moiety. The mode of disposing of the lands thus indicated was soon changed by subsequent legislation. By an act passed December 21, 1784, to amend the act of April 1, the provisions of the law for sales by public auction and the giving of credit were repealed. Section 6 of the act provided that the land-office should

---

* See accompanying map, which shows the extent of the purchase.

be open on the 1st day of May, 1785, to receive applications for lands at the rate of £30* for every hundred acres of the same, and that the survey of an application should not contain more than 1000 acres, with the usual allowance of six per centum for highways. This act was intended to apply to all lands within the purchase, except the lands north and west of the Ohio and Allegheny Rivers and Conewango Creek (which, as already mentioned, had been appropriated for the redemption of depreciation certificates and for the donations of land to the soldiers of the Pennsylvania Line) and the disputed territory between Lycoming and Pine Creeks. By Section 7, a warrant issued in pursuance of the act was not descriptive, and was not confined to any particular place, but could be located on any vacant land, not within the excepted districts, that the applicant might select. Sections 8, 9, and 10 of the act provide for the persons who occupied lands between Lycoming and Pine Creek, in violation of the proprietary mandate. The situation of these settlers was peculiar. When the disagreement in regard to the purchase lines of the purchase of 1768 occurred, the proprietaries, always extremely anxious to avoid giving offence to the Indians, decided to withhold the territory between the two streams from sale and settlement until the differences could be properly adjusted by mutual agreement. Though many applications for land west of Lycoming Creek were on file, surveys would not be accepted, and at the same time stringent orders were issued protesting against persons making settlement beyond that stream, and warning those already there to depart. In defiance of warnings, protests, and proclamations, however, many sturdy, self-reliant men persisted in occupying the forbidden ground, where they found themselves beyond the bounds of lawful authority, and could not expect to receive encouragement or protection from the proprietary government. But with the energy and courage common to pioneer settlers they at once began the work of subduing the wilderness and building homes for their families, and from accounts that have come down to us, the little community, if it did not live in luxury, was at least able to earn a subsistence that was not meagre in quantity, whatever may have been its quality. Being without law or government, the members of the community were compelled by the necessities of their situation and surroundings to adopt a system of government of their own, the details of which are not fully known. All, however, were under solemn obligations to support and defend their agreement for mutual support and protection. They called themselves Fair-Play Men, and it is known that annually they elected three of their number to constitute a court, which held stated meetings to dispense justice. To this tribunal all disputes and controversies were referred for settlement, and from its decisions there was no appeal. A stranger

---

* In Pennsylvania currency this was at the rate of 80 cents an acre.

coming among them was obliged to appear before the court and promise under oath to submit to the laws of the community. If he did this, he could remain, take possession of unoccupied land, and receive assistance in building his cabin. If he would not take the obligation, he was quickly notified to absent himself without delay, which he usually did, without awaiting the call of a committee, whose methods of expulsion might be none too gentle. Many of these brave frontiersmen served in the army during the Revolutionary War, and Section 8 of the act recited that by reason of their services as soldiers, they merited the 'pre-emption of their respective plantations.' Sections 9 and 10 of the same act allowed a pre-emption to all settlers and their legal representatives who had settled on the lands between the two streams prior to the year 1780, limiting each claim to 300 acres, providing that the application should be made and the consideration paid on or before November 1, 1785. It will be remembered that the time fixed by the act of December 21, 1784, for the land-office to be opened to receive applications was May 1, 1785. Before that day arrived, however, the Legislature passed another act, which, in many respects, changed the policy previously pursued in disposing of unappropriated lands. This act became a law on the 8th day of April, 1785, and with it came the practice, as provided in the act, of numbering all warrants for land in the last purchase to the east of the Allegheny River and Conewango Creek, a change in practice that has always been regarded as a valuable improvement on the old system. The act is entitled 'An act to provide further regulations, whereby to secure fair and equal proceedings in the land-office, and the surveying of lands.' It was believed that when the office was opened on the day fixed by the law, numerous applications would be made at the same time, and that preference would necessarily be given to some persons to the disadvantage of others, and thereby cause dissatisfaction. In order to prevent any one from profiting by such preference, it was enacted in Section 2 of the act that the priority of all warrants to be granted on applications received during the first ten days after the opening of the office should be determined by a lottery to be drawn under the supervision of the Secretary of the Land-Office. Not more than 1000 acres were to be included in one application, and the warrants were to be numbered 'according to the decision of the lottery.' For conducting the lottery the section contains minute directions. All applications made after the expiration of ten days were to have priority according to the order in which they came into the hands of the Secretary, and were to be numbered accordingly. The other sections of the act relate mainly to the duties of the surveyor-general and the deputy-surveyors to be by him appointed, and the way in which surveys were to be made and returned. It also prescribes the fees to be received by the officers of the land office and the deputy surveyors, and attaches the territory east of the Allegheny

River and Conewango Creek to Northumberland County, a part of which county it remained until Lycoming County was formed in 1795, when it became part of that county. The remaining portion of the purchase was attached to Westmoreland County, and so continued until Allegheny was formed in 1788, when it was included in the boundary of that county. The applications received during the first ten days from the opening of the office were listed and numbered, placed in the lottery-wheel, and drawn therefrom in the manner provided by the second section of the act. They numbered five hundred and sixty-four, and warrants for that number of tracts were issued, and received a number that corresponded with the number drawn from the wheel. These warrants were called 'Northumberland County Lottery Warrants,' and under that designation are yet carried on the warrant registers of the office. They could be, and were, located in such localities within the purchase east of the Allegheny River as the owners might select, except on a reservation of 1000 acres at the forks of Sinnemahoning Creek, for which General James Potter held a pre-emption.

"The surveyor general had authority to appoint deputy-surveyors, and to fix the number, extent, and boundaries of the districts to which they were to be assigned. The territory was divided into eighteen districts, and a deputy-surveyor appointed for each. These districts were numbered consecutively, beginning with No. 1, on the Allegheny River, and running eastward to No. 18, which extended to the north branch of the Susquehanna in the northeast corner of the purchase. This arrangement of the districts continued until after the year 1790, when a change was made by the surveyor-general. The number of districts was then reduced to six, and were numbered westward from district No. 1, beginning at the mouth of Lycoming Creek. In the new arrangement John Adlum was appointed deputy-surveyor for district No. 1, John Broadhead for No. 2, John Canan for No. 3, James Hunter for No. 4, William P. Brady for No. 5, and Enion Williams for No. 6, on the Allegheny River. In 1793, John Adlum, whose surveys were principally along the northern line of the State, was succeeded by William Ellis, and Enion Williams by John Broadhead. After the drawing of the lottery warrants the business of the land-office does not appear to have been very pressing. It would seem that at the price fixed by the act of December, 1784—£30 per hundred, or 80 cents an acre—purchasers were not numerous. The records show that from the time of the drawing and issuing of the lottery warrants in May, 1785, down to the year 1792, not more than 400 warrants were granted for these lands, and among these warrants were many to religious and educational institutions issued under various acts of endowment. There were 32 to Dickinson College,—28 of 300 acres each, and 4 of 400 acres each, making in all 7000 acres; the Episcopal Academy had 33 warrants,—32 of 300 acres each, and 1 of 400 acres, making 10,000 acres; the Lutheran congregation, of Philadelphia, 10 warrants of 500 acres each, making 5000 acres; the Pittsburg Academy, 10 warrants of 500 acres each, making 5000 acres; the Washington Academy, 10 warrants of 500 each, making 5000 acres; the Reading Academy, 7 warrants,—3 of 1000 acres each and 4 of 500 acres each, making 5000 acres; and Franklin College 33 warrants of 300 acres each, and 1 of 100 acres, making 10,000 acres,—making in the aggregate 112 warrants for 52,000 acres of land.

"It had now become apparent to the authorities that the price of land was too high to induce investments of money in them, and that the General Assembly must fix a lower rate to promote sales. Benjamin Franklin, the president of the Supreme Executive Council, under date of February 23, 1787, addressed a letter to that body in which he says, 'We are convinced that it will be of advantage to the State to lower the price of land within the late Indian purchase; only eight warrants have been taken out for lands these six months passed.'* The Legislature accordingly passed an act, October 3, 1788, to reduce the price from the rate of £30 per hundred acres to £20. This rate was to be charged after March 1, 1789, and was a reduction from the old rate of 80 cents an acre to 53⅓ cents an acre. This rate continued until April 3, 1792; but, contrary to expectations, did not have the effect of increasing sales, and, therefore, brought little or no change in the business of the office. By another act, passed April 3, 1792, the price was again reduced. The rate fixed by this act was £5, or \$13.33⅓, for each hundred acres, and at this rate sales almost astonishing in extent were made, and the years 1792–93–94 proved to be noted and important years for disposing of unappropriated lands. The low price at which lands could now be bought, and the alluring prospect of a large increase in their value, undoubtedly induced many large purchasers to enter their applications. The applications received at the land-office were for a large number of tracts, and in the course of the years named more than 5000 warrants of 900 and 1000 acres each, covering almost 5,000,000 acres, were granted for lands north and west of the purchase line of 1768, and east of the Allegheny River. These were all numbered in consecutive order, as required by the act of April, 1785, and were sent to the deputy surveyors of the six districts to be executed. They were issued in the names of a comparatively small number of persons, but the holdings, as a rule, were very large. While it would be tedious to give the names of all the holders of these warrants, generally called 'late purchase warrants,' it may not prove uninteresting to mention a few of those whose purchases were more than usually large, if only to show that a spirit of speculation might have existed in those days, even as it does at the present time. The first to

---

* Colonial Records, vol. xv. p. 167.

be mentioned will be the warrants issued in the names of Wilhelm Willink, Nicholas Van Staphorst, Christian Van Eeghan, Pieter Stadnitski, Hendrick Vollenhoven, and Ruter Jan Schimmelpenninck. These gentlemen were merchants of the city of Amsterdam, Holland. In the land history of Pennsylvania they are known as the 'Holland Land Company,' and through agents they invested a large amount of money in land in the purchase of 1784. The warrant registers show that in the three years, 1792–93–94, they paid for and received 1105 warrants of 900 acres each, aggregating 995,400 acres of land lying east of the Allegheny River. These warrants were divided among the deputy surveyors of the six districts. James Wilson was another large owner of warrants, the number held by him being 510, of 900 acres each, making 451,000 acres. Herman Le Roy and Jan Lincklean, A. Z., also of Amsterdam, 303 warrants of 900 acres each, making 272,700 acres. John Nicholson 300 warrants of 1000 acres each, making 300,000 acres. Thomas M. Willing, 311 warrants of 1000 acres each, making 311,000 acres. George Meade, 306 warrants of 1000 acres each, making 306,000 acres. Robert Gilmore, 200 warrants of 1000 acres each, making 200,000 acres. Samuel Wallis, 100 warrants of 1000 acres each, making 100,000 acres. William Bingham, 125 warrants of 1000 acres each, making 125,000 acres. Robert Morris, 185 warrants, 141 of 1000 acres each, and 44 of 500 acres each, making 163,000 acres. The magnitude of the purchases made by a few individuals is here clearly indicated. There were, however, other large purchasers, such as Robert Blackwell, John Olden, Charles Willing, Philip Nicklin and Robert Griffith, James Strawbridge, Jeremiah Parker, and others whose names we are obliged to omit. The surveys generally were carefully and correctly made, and, considering the extent of territory covered by them, and the large interests involved, no great amount of litigation from conflicting locations afterwards grew out of defective or careless work by the surveyor, as was too often the case with surveys made in other sections of the State. In 1817 the price of the lands was again changed to 26⅔ cents an acre, to correspond with the price in the older purchases. At the same time warrants were made descriptive, and have since been carried in the warrant registers by counties. The surveys made on the numbered warrants did not appropriate all the land within the limits to which they were restricted, and since then many warrants have been granted in all the counties erected from the territory that in 1785 was made to form a part of the county of Northumberland.

"LANDS NORTH AND EAST OF THE OHIO AND ALLEGHENY RIVERS AND CONEWANGO CREEK.

"After the surveys of the tracts to be sold for the redemption of depreciation certificates and the donation lots to be given to the soldiers of the Pennsylvania Line had been made, there remained in this part of the purchase a large surplus of lands to be otherwise appropriated. The Legislature, on the 3d of April, 1792, passed an act for the sale of these lands, entitled 'An act for the sale of vacant lands within this Commonwealth.' This act differs from all previous laws for disposing of the public lands, by providing that they should only be offered for sale to such persons as would 'cultivate, improve, and settle the same, or cause the same to be cultivated, improved, and settled.' The price fixed was £7 10s. in Pennsylvania currency, for every hundred acres, or in other words, 20 cents an acre, and the warrants were limited to 400 acres each. The surveyor-general was authorized to divide the territory offered for sale into proper and convenient districts and appoint deputy-surveyors, who were to give the customary bond for the faithful performance of their duties. They were to execute warrants according to their priority, but 'not to survey any tract actually settled and improved prior to the date of the entry of such warrant with the deputy, except to the owner of such settlement and improvement.' The territory was divided into eleven districts, and a deputy-surveyor appointed for each; Thomas Reese for district No. 1, William Powers for No. 2, Benjamin Stokely for No. 3, Thomas Stokely for No. 4, John Moore for No. 5, Samuel Nicholson for No. 6, John McCool for No. 7, Stephen Gapen for No. 8, Jonathan and Daniel Leet for Nos. 9 and 10, John Hoge for No. 11.

"By Section 8 of the act, on application being made to the deputy-surveyor of the proper district by any person who had made an actual settlement and improvement, that officer, on being paid the legal fees, was required to survey the lines of the tract, not exceeding 400 acres, to which such person may have become entitled by virtue of his settlement. Many such surveys were returned to the land-office and constituted pre-emptions to persons for whom they were made. Some of the tracts thus returned still remain unpaid, as a glance at the land lien docket of the land-office will show. By Section 9, no warrant or survey made in pursuance of the act was to vest title to the lands unless the guarantee had, 'prior to the date of such warrant made, or caused to be made, or should within the space of two years next after the date of the same, make, or cause to be made, an actual settlement thereon, by clearing, fencing, and cultivating at least two acres for every hundred acres contained in one survey, erecting thereon a messuage for the habitation of man, and residing or causing a family to reside thereon, for the space of five years next following his first settling of the same, if he or she shall so long live.' In default of such actual settlement and residence the right was forfeited, and new warrants, reciting the original warrants and the lack of compliance with the requirements of the act, could be granted to other actual settlers. It was provided, however, 'that if any actual settler or any grantee in any such original or succeeding warrant, shall by force of arms of the enemies of the United States, be prevented from making such actual settlement, or be driven therefrom and shall persist in his endeavors to make such actual settlement as aforesaid, then, in either case, he and his heirs shall be entitled to have and to hold the said lands in the same manner as if the actual settlement had been made and continued.' Under the provisions of this act many surveys, as already stated, were returned for actual settlers, and many warrants were taken out immediately after its passage. The warrants were for 400 acres each, and immense numbers of them in fictitious names, in which great families of Inks, Pims, etc., appear, were taken out by a few individuals. For instance, the Holland Land Company, previously mentioned, again appears in the territory west of the Allegheny. That company alone took out 1162 warrants representing 464,800 acres of land, and making the entire purchases of the company from the State amount to more than 1,500,000 acres. John Nicholson was another purchaser who held a large number of these warrants. To the 'Pennsylvania Population Company' he assigned 100,000 acres lying principally in the present County of Erie, and proposed to assign 250,000 acres lying along Beaver Creek and the western line of the State to another of his land schemes called the 'North American Land Company.' The warrants all contained the actual settlement clause, but not any of the large owners of warrants made the slightest pretence of complying with it. Owing to the disturbed condition of the western border at the time it was impossible to do so. A state of war existed with the western Indians. The United States forces had met with serious reverses in the defeat of Harmer and St. Clare in 1791, and it was not until after Wayne's treaty, in December, 1795, gave peace and safety to the borders that settlers with their families could enter upon those lands free from the fear and danger of Indian incursions.

"But with the settling of the Indian disorders and the return of peace, there soon came other troubles, with expensive and vexatious litigation, to annoy and harass settlers and warrantees by the uncertainty that was cast upon their titles. This uncertainty grew out of differences of opinion in relation to the construction the two years' clause of the law requiring actual settlement, after the termination of the Indian hostilities that had prevented such settlement from being made, should receive. The opposite views held by those interested in titles are clearly stated in Sergeant's 'Land Laws,' page 98: 'On one side it was contended that the conditions of actual settlement and residence, required by the act, was dispensed with, on account of the prevention for two years after the date of the warrant[*] by Indian hostilities; and that the warrant holder was not bound to do anything further, but was entitled to a patent. On the other side it was insisted that the right under the warrant was forfeited, at the expiration

---

[*] Nearly all of these warrants were granted in 1792–93.

of two years, without a settlement, and that actual settlers might then enter on such tracts and hold them by making a settlement. On this and other constructions, numbers of persons entered on the lands of warrantees and claimed to hold under the act, as settlers, after a forfeiture.' The authorities of the State at the time—1796 to 1800—held to the first opinion, and by the advice of Attorney-General Ingersoll, the Board of Property devised what was called a 'prevention certificate,' which set forth the fact of the inability of the warrantee or settler to make the required settlement. This certificate was to be signed by two justices, and on its presentation, properly signed, the land officers freely granted a patent for the land described. Under prevention certificates of this kind many patents were granted. The Holland Land Company received more than one thousand, and John Field, William Crammond, and James Gibson, in trust for the use of the Pennsylvania Population Company, more than eight hundred. These patents all contained a recital of the prevention certificate, as follows: 'And also in consideration of it having been made to appear to the Board of Property that the said (name of warrantee) was by force of arms of the enemies of the United States prevented from making settlement as is required by the ninth section (act of April 3, 1792), and the assignees of the said (warrantee) had persisted in their endeavors to make such settlement,' etc. With a change of administration in October, 1799, there followed a change of policy. The new authorities did not regard the policy and proceedings of the former Board of Property binding, and the further issuing of patents on prevention certificates was refused. In the mean time, the contentions between the owners of warrants and settlers were carried into the courts, where a like difference of opinion in regard to the rights of the contending parties under the act of 1792 soon manifested itself, the judges disagreeing as widely in their construction of the ninth section as the parties in interest. It was only after years of exciting and troublesome litigation, and the enactment of a number of laws by the Legislature of the State to facilitate an adjustment of the contentions, that titles became settled and owners felt secure in their possessions. It may be said that while the judges of the courts often differed in their opinions on the points at issue, the litigation ended generally in favor of the holders of the warrants. The Holland Land Company, being composed of foreigners, could appeal to the courts of the United States. In one case carried to the Supreme Court, the company was actually absolved from making the settlement prescribed by the ninth section. Chief Justice Marshall, holding that a warrant for a tract of land under the Act of 1792 'to a person who, by force of arms of the enemies of the United States, was prevented from settling and improving the said land, and from residing thereon from the date of the warrant until the 1st of January, 1796, but who, during the said period, persisted in his endeavors to make such settlement and residence, vests in such grantee a fee-simple in said land.'* That the uncertainty in regard to land titles during these years did much to retard the growth and prosperity of this northwestern section of the State cannot be doubted; but, under the influence of better conditions, brought about by the adjustment of land rights and the allaying of local strife, it afterwards made marvellous strides forward in the march of progress and improvement.

"The dispositions made of the unsold depreciation and the undrawn donation lots in this part of the purchase were fully treated of in former papers, and, therefore, need no further notice. It may not, however, be amiss to say a word in relation to the purchase of the Erie triangle, an acquisition that was of vast importance to Pennsylvania by reason of the outlet of Lake Erie. The triangle was claimed by the States of New York and Massachusetts, but was ceded by both States, in the years 1781 and 1785, to the United States. The Pennsylvania authorities, anticipating its possession, had, through a treaty made at Fort McIntosh by General St. Clair, Colonel Harmer, and others, secured a deed from the Indians by which their claim of title was extinguished. This deed, signed by the chiefs of the Six Nations, is dated January 9, 1789, and the consideration paid was $2000. It was then, by a deed dated March 3, 1792, ceded by the United States to Pennsylvania. This deed is signed by George Washington, President, and Thomas Jefferson, Secretary of State. In 1790, Andrew Ellicott made a survey of the triangle and found it to contain 202,287 acres, and the purchase-money paid to the United States, at the rate of 75 cents an acre, amounted to $151,640.25. This purchase having been completed before the passage of the act of April 3, 1792, the lands within it, except the reservations, were sold under the provisions of that act. Before the completion of the purchase, John Nicholson had made application for the entire tract, and probably held a larger number of warrants for lands within its boundaries than any other individual.

"THE RESERVATIONS NORTH AND WEST OF THE OHIO AND ALLEGHENY RIVERS AND CONEWANGO CREEK.

"In the act of March 12, 1783, setting apart the depreciation lands, two reservations for the use of the State were made,—one of 'three thousand acres, in an oblong of not less than one mile in depth from the Allegheny and Ohio Rivers, and extending up and down the said rivers, from opposite Fort Pitt, so far as may be necessary to include the same;' and the other 'three thousand acres on the Ohio, and on both sides of Beaver Creek, including Fort Mackintosh.' There was also reserved on Lake Erie for the use of the State the peninsula of Presque Isle, a tract extending eight miles along the shores of the lake and three miles

---

* Smith's Laws, vol. ii. p. 228.

in breadth, and another tract of 2000 acres on the lake at the mouth of Harbor Creek; and also tracts at the mouth of French Creek, at Fort Le Bœuf, and at the mouth of Conewango Creek. For the purpose of raising an additional sum by the sale of town lots to be used in paying the debts of the State, the President of the Supreme Executive Council was authorized by an act passed the 11th day of September, 1787, to cause a town to be laid out on the reservation opposite Fort Pitt. The tract, except 312 acres within its boundaries, was accordingly surveyed into town and out lots and sold at public auction. The regular lots of the town, as laid down in the survey, were in dimensions 60 by 240 feet, while the out lots contained from five to ten acres. The part containing 312 acres, not included in the plan of the town, was patented to James O'Hara on the 5th day of May, 1789. This town has grown into the large and flourishing city of Allegheny. By another act, passed September 28, 1791, the governor was given power to authorize the surveyor-general to cause a part of the reservation at the mouth of Beaver Creek to be laid out in town lots, 'on or near the ground where the old French town stood,' in such manner as commissioners, to be appointed by the governor, should direct. By this act 200 acres were to be surveyed into town lots, and 1000 acres, adjoining on the upper side, into out lots to contain not less than five acres, nor more than ten acres. Daniel Leet, a deputy-surveyor, who had previously surveyed district No. 2, of the depreciation lands and one of the donation districts, was employed to lay out these town and out lots, and his survey of the town and out lots was confirmed by an act passed in March, 1793. The same act directed the governor to proceed to make sale of the lots and grant conveyances for them, in the manner prescribed by the act authorizing the laying out of the town. The town was called Beavertown, and when the county of Beaver was erected in 1800 was made the county seat. The act erecting the county appropriated 500 acres of the reservation for the use of such school or academy as might thereafter be established in the town. The town then called Beaver was incorporated into a borough in 1802, and the boroughs of Rochester and Bridgewater, on opposite sides of the creek, also occupy parts of this reservation.

"The towns of Erie, Franklin, Waterford, and Warren were established by an act passed on the 18th day of April, 1795. Of the large reservation on Lake Erie, at Presque Isle, the governor was authorized to appoint two commissioners to survey 1600 acres for town lots and 3400, adjoining thereto, for out lots, with such streets, alleys, lanes, and reservations for public uses as the commissioners should direct. The town lots were to contain not more than one-third of an acre,* the out lots not

---

* The regular town lots of Erie as laid down in the map of the town are 82 feet 6 inches front and 165 feet in depth.

more than five acres, the reservations for public uses not to exceed twenty acres, and the town was to be called Erie. After the survey of the town, made by General William Irvine and Andrew Ellicott, was filed in the office of the secretary of the Commonwealth, the governor was directed to sell at public auction one-third of the town lots and one-third of the out lots to the highest bidders, and grant patents to the purchasers upon the condition that within two years they respectively should 'build a house, at least sixteen feet square, and contain at least one brick or stone chimney,' on each lot purchased, the patent not to be issued until after the expiration of two years, and then only on proof that the condition of the sale had been complied with. In addition to the surveys of the town and out lots, the act provided that three lots—one of 60 acres on the southern side of the harbor, another of 30 on the peninsula, and a third of 100 acres also on the peninsula—should be surveyed for the 'use of the United States in erecting and maintaining forts, magazines, and dock-yards thereon.' Of the tract at the mouth of French Creek, 300 acres for town lots and 700 acres for out lots were to be surveyed for the town of Franklin ; and of the tract at the mouth of Conewango Creek, 300 acres for town lots and 700 acres for out lots were to be surveyed for the town of Warren. At the time the act providing for the laying out of these towns became a law a settlement had been made at Fort Le Bœuf. Andrew Ellicott had surveyed and laid out a town, and his draft of the town was accepted and confirmed by the Legislature. It was provided, however, that in addition to the town lots of Ellicott's survey, 500 acres should be surveyed for out lots, and that the town should be called Waterford. The size of the town and out lots for Franklin and Warren, the out lots for Waterford, and the provisions for streets, lanes, alleys, and reservations for public use,—the reservations reduced to ten acres,—were the same as for the town of Erie, as were also the regulations for the sale of the lots. At Waterford a number of settlers who had built houses were given a right of pre emption to the lots on which they settled. A subsequent act passed April 11, 1799, provided that surveys should be made of the reserved tracts adjoining Erie, Franklin, Warren, and Waterford, not laid out in town or out lots, into lots not to exceed 150 acres in each, to be sold by commissioners, one of whom was to reside in each town. The tracts were to be graded in quality, and no sale was to be made at less than four dollars an acre for land of the first quality ; three dollars for the second quality, and two dollars for the third quality, and purchasers, before title could vest in them, were required within three years from the date of their purchases to make an actual settlement on the land ' by clearing, fencing, and cultivating at least two acres for every fifty contained in one survey, and erect on each lot or tract a messuage for the habitation of man and reside thereon for the space of five years following their first settlement of the same.' The same act required 500 acres in each of the reserved tracts to be surveyed for the use of schools or academies, and provision was made for the appraisement of the residue of the town and out lots, and for their sale by the commissioner residing in the town. It was also provided in this act that the reserved lot in the town of Erie, at the mouth of Cascade Creek, was to be sold at public sale, on consideration of settlement and improvement, provided it brought $50 an acre. By an act passed February 19, 1800, the clause of the act that required settlement and improvement of lots was repealed. The other reservation of 2000 acres in the Erie triangle, at the mouth of Harbor Creek, was donated by an act of the Legislature to General William Irvine to indemnify him for the loss of Montour's Island (now called Neville Island), in the Ohio River below the city of Pittsburg. General Irvine held the island under a Pennsylvania patent, but was divested of his title by a judgment of the Supreme Court of the United States in an ejectment suit brought against him by a party who claimed ownership under a Virginia right, which, under the agreement between Pennsylvania and Virginia for settling the southwestern boundary dispute, was held by the court to be good."

INDIAN TREATIES AT FORTS STANWIX AND McINTOSH.

" Proceedings of the treaties held at Forts Stanwix and McIntosh, between the commissioners of the Commonwealth of Pennsylvania and the deputies of the *Six Nations* and the *Wyandott* and *Delaware Indians*, claiming the unpurchased territory within the acknowledged limits of the said Commonwealth:

"FORT STANWIX, October 4, 1784.

" The commissioners of Indian affairs from the State of Pennsylvania, pursuant to their letter of the 3d instant, met in conference with the commissioners on part of the Continent.

" PRESENT.

The Hon. OLIVER WOLCOTT, RICHARD BUTLER, and ARTHUR LEE, ESQS., } *Commissioners on part of the United States.*

The Hon. SAMUEL F. ATLEE, WILLIAM McCLAY, and FRANCIS JOHNSTON, ESQS., } *Commissioners on part of the State of Pennsylvania.*

" It was requested by the State commissioners that the commissioners for the United States should introduce and announce them in their official character to the Indians, and to inform them that they, by consent of Congress, had some business of importance to transact with them, relating to the affairs of said State, to be brought forward at a proper period.

"Which requisition, after being discussed, was unanimously agreed to.

"FORT STANWIX, October 17, 1784.

"At the request of the commissioners from the United States, the commissioners from the State of Pennsylvania met them this day in conference on the same subject as above. Present as before.

"Whereupon it was agreed, That upon the close of the council to be held this day with the Indians in the council-house of Fort Stanwix, the commissioners on part of said State should be introduced and announced in due form to the Indian chiefs or sachems in full council.

"The same day, in council held between the commissioners on part of the United States and the representatives of the Six Indian Nations, present also the commissioners for the State of Pennsylvania, General Wolcott arose and addressed the Indians as follows,—viz. :

"'SACHEMS AND WARRIORS,—We now announce to you Colonel Atlee, Mr. McClay, and Colonel Johnston, three honorable gentlemen from the State of Pennsylvania, who have come, by the consent of Congress, as commissioners, to transact some affairs with you, on the part of their State, after the conclusion of the present treaty, should it be concluded in a manner satisfactory to the United States.'

"After which Colonel Atlee, in behalf of the Indian commissioners for the State of Pennsylvania, delivered the following speech,—viz. :

"'SACHEMS AND WARRIORS,—You have been now told by the honorable commissioners from Congress that we attend as commissioners from your old friends of Pennsylvania to transact business with you on the part of that State. At a proper season we will produce to you our commission, and lay before you the business committed to our charge, and we doubt not but you will take it under immediate consideration and return a favorable answer.'

"(FOUR STRINGS.)

"IN CONFERENCE, FORT STANWIX, October 22, 1784.

"PRESENT:

The HON. SAMUEL F. ATLEE,
FRANCIS JOHNSTON, and
WILLIAM MCCLAY, ESQS.
GRIFFITH EVANS, *Secretary.*
The REV. SAMUEL KIRKLAND } *Interpreters.*
and MR. JAMES DEAN,

And the deputies of the Six Indian Nations.

"The commissioners, through Colonel Atlee, opened their business by addressing them as follows,—viz.:

PIONEER HISTORY OF JEFFERSON COUNTY, PENNA.

"'BROTHERS OF THE SIX NATIONS,—It is probable that the business between you and the Continental commissioners will be settled this day in council. Previous to which we are desirous of meeting you this morning with a view of laying before you the particular objects of our mission, and which we have attended here so long to negotiate with you on the part of the State of Pennsylvania. It is not our wish to settle any matters finally until the conclusion of the Continental treaty. The design of our present interview is to prepare your minds for the introduction of our business at a proper season, to discuss with freedom and seriously deliberate upon the subjects necessary to be taken into consideration, that we may fully and perfectly understand each other.

"We now inform you that we are commissioned, and sent from your old friends in Pennsylvania to purchase from you, according to ancient custom, the unpurchased lands within the acknowledged limits of the said State. This has been the invariable usage of our forefathers, and we, desirous of pursuing their good example, wish that our young men, who have become very numerous and require more lands, should settle and improve the same in quietness and peace ; for this desirable purpose we have brought with us a valuable cargo of goods, suited to your various wants and necessities, as a compensation for your right to these lands. But these lands being more remote and consequently less valuable than those our fathers have heretofore purchased, you ought not, therefore, to expect so great a consideration for them.'

"(The commissioners then produced a map of the State, pointing out to them the unpurchased land now intended to be purchased.)

"'We here produce to you all the deeds of purchase made by our forefathers from their first coming into this country, which, if you require, shall be read and explained to you for your information and satisfaction, by which you will learn the extreme regard the people of Pennsylvania have ever shown the Six Confederated Nations.'

"To which Captain O'Bale,* a chief of the Seneca Nation, replied in behalf of the Six Nations :

"'BROTHERS OF PENNSYLVANIA,—We now call your attention to our reply to what you have said. We greatly rejoice in meeting our brothers of Pennsylvania once more in peace and friendship. Your language has been friendly and agreeable to us, as that of your forefathers always was. You have informed us of the business you are commissioned from the State of Pennsylvania to transact with us. We have seen the deeds given by our fathers to yours and understand you well. We will take up the matter, keep it in mind, and deliberate upon it till the close of the Continental business.'

---

* Captain O'Bale was more generally known as the great chief "Cornplanter," who lived on the Allegheny River, in what is now Warren County. He received two thousand acres of land from the State.

"The commissioners then thanked them, and proceeded as follows,—viz.:

"'We come in the most peaceable and friendly manner, and do not wish to irritate your minds with a recapitulation of former grievances, but to make the road between us smooth and even. We are to inform you that one of our brothers present (pointing to Mr. McClay) is appointed by the government of Pennsylvania to run the boundary line between you and us next spring, when we will expect some of you to accompany him, in order to prevent all disputes in future touching the same.

"'Having it in charge from the State, we must not omit to be informed by you the Indian name of Burnet's Hills, mentioned in our deed of 1768. And also which of the two streams, Lycoming or Pine Creek (both of which empty into the west branch of Susquehanna) is known among you by the name of TIADAGHTON.' ('To which they answered:) As to Burnet's Hills, they call them the Long Mountains, and knew them by no other name, and that TIADAGHTON was Pine Creek or the uppermost and largest of the two, but of this they would consider and return a more positive answer.

"The conference was then closed.

"October 23, 1784, IN CONFERENCE.
"PRESENT as before.

"The commissioners again produced the map of the State, pointing out the purchased and unpurchased lands within the same, particularly describing and explaining to them the forty-second degree or line of latitude (being the northern boundary of the State), and also mentioned the place where it was supposed it would pass. All which Captain Aaron Hill, a Mohock chief, who spoke English very well, perfectly understood and explained in a satisfactory manner to the other chiefs.

"Captain O'Bale then spoke, and informed the commissioners 'that it is not the wish of the Six Nations at present to part with so much of their hunting-grounds,' and pointed out a line on the map which he hoped would be agreeable to them.

"This being far short of the boundary of the State, was, therefore, deemed by the commissioners totally inadmissible.

"The commissioners then spoke to them as follows:

"'BROTHERS,—Though the lands that we are about to purchase are already ceded by the line of cession described in the Articles of Peace between the United States and Great Britain, yet we mean not to take advantage of you, but are desirous of paying you a valuable consideration for them, after the manner of our ancestors, your brothers of Pennsylvania. This consideration we have with us, and consists of an excellent assortment of goods, amounting in value to four thousand dollars, and which you will find to be of the first quality, which will certainly convince you that many advantages will flow to you from a trade and correspondence with your brothers of Pennsylvania.

"'We now desire you would make up your minds on these important matters, that our business may be in such forwardness on the conclusion of the Continental treaty as to be ready to receive a public and final sanction, on the completion of which we will deliver you a belt.

"'We wish once more to impress our brothers with an idea that our intention is to pursue the same method of obtaining lands from you that our forefathers did, with whose conduct we conceive you must be perfectly satisfied, as they never wronged you, but have fulfilled all their engagements and paid you faithfully for all the lands they have from time to time purchased of you.

"'Least any doubts should arise respecting the quality of the goods, if such chiefs as are desirous of seeing them will attend at the stores, the several packages shall be opened and shown to them.

"'It has been intimated by some of you that you are desirous of having a privilege of hunting on these lands. To this we have no objections, more especially as the Continental commissioners have granted you the same indulgence. This, in our opinions, will tend to our mutual advantage.

"'Brothers, to-morrow being Sunday, on which we can transact no public business, being a great way from our respective families and winter approaching fast upon us, we must, therefore, again request you to come to a conclusion on these matters, and let us know your minds as soon as possible.'

"The commissioners then withdrew, the chiefs still remaining in consultation. After some time the Indians requested their attendance. They returned accordingly, when the chiefs present spoke by Captain O'Bale as follows:

"'BROTHERS OF PENNSYLVANIA,—You have communicated to us your business, you have pointed out the lands you are directed to purchase of us, and we understand you. You have likewise shown your authority, of which we are satisfied. And as we wish to keep the way between us smooth and even, and to brighten the chain of friendship and make it lasting, we have agreed that the lands you have described be granted to you in the same manner as you have requested. But as lands afford a lasting and rising profit, and as the Pennsylvanians have always been generous, we hope you will give us something next year as a farther consideration.'

"The commissioners, after consulting together, replied,—

"'We thank you for meeting us here, and are glad to find you so well disposed to peace and friendship. We expected we had brought you sufficient presents for the lands we are commissioned to purchase, but have nevertheless agreed to give you goods to the amount of one thousand dollars more, which we will deliver to you or to any persons you may appoint to receive them at Tioga, the 1st day of next October. This cargo of goods shall be assorted in the best manner to serve you, for the performance of which we will obligate ourselves, if you think it necessary.'

"Then the chiefs, by Captain O'Bale, spoke as follows,—viz.:

"'We most cheerfully agree to this. We will make an obligation for the purpose of securing to us the privilege of hunting on the lands, and also for delivery of the goods, which will perfectly satisfy us. We wish that our brothers of Pennsylvania would send us a faithful gun- and blacksmith to reside at or near Tioga, who would be of great advantage to us when we come down in hunting-parties; and also that the government of Pennsylvania would establish trading-houses at the same place, that we may be conveniently and honestly supplied with such articles as we stand in need of.'

"The commissioners answered, 'We will make true report of these requests to the State, and make no doubt they will be complied with.'

"Two of the principal chiefs,—Captain Aaron Hill, of the Mohawks, and Captain O'Bale, of the Senecas,—desirous of having each a rifle of the manufacture of Pennsylvania, being informed they were very good, requested the commissioners to give them two of the best quality, to be delivered to them on the 1st day of April next, at the new store at Newtown, near Tioga, which the commissioners complied with and gave their obligation for that purpose.

"The conference ended.

"*The same day In Council.*

"PRESENT:

The Hon. Oliver Wolcott, Richard Butler, and Arthur Lee, Esqs.,	Commissioners on part of United States.
The Hon. Samuel F. Atlee, William McClay, and Francis Johnston, Esqs.,	Commissioners on part of the State of Pennsylvania.
The Rev. Samuel Kirkland and Mr. James Dean,	Interpreters.

And a full representation of the Six Indian Nations.

"At the close of the Continental business, General Wolcott addressed the Indians as follows:

"'SACHEMS AND WARRIORS,—We informed you some time past that these gentlemen commissioners from the State of Pennsylvania had some public business to transact with you on the part of the said State. If they are ready to bring it forward, now will be a proper time.'

"Upon which Colonel Atlee, in behalf of the Pennsylvania commissioners, delivered the following speech, prepared for the purpose:

"'BROTHERS OF THE SIX NATIONS,—After a long separation of nine years, during which period the great Congress have been at war with and conquered their enemies from the other side of the great water, we, the commissioners from your old friends of Pennsylvania, with the consent of the United States in Congress assembled, are well pleased to meet you this day; and from our hearts rejoice with you that peace and friendship are once more established by these honorable gentlemen, the commissioners of Congress.'

"(SIX STRINGS.)

"'BROTHERS,—Listen with great attention to what we are going to say to you. We come in the name and from the government of Pennsylvania, of which you have already been informed; our commission we here produce, which we will read to you publicly.'

"(The commission was read.)

"'BROTHERS,—From the first coming of our fathers to this country, about one hundred years ago, to the time of the last treaty and purchase in 1768 at this place, which many of you now present must well remember, your brothers of Pennsylvania, as they wanted lands for their young men to settle on, applied for and purchased from the natives from time to time such quantities within the bounds of their charter as they judged sufficient.

"'The several deeds for the different purchases we here produce, as authentic proofs of the justice of our conduct towards our brethren the Six Nations, and others claiming and possessing the country,—testimonies which cannot lie.'

"(Produced the deeds.)

"'This last deed, brothers, with the map annexed, are descriptive of the purchase made sixteen years ago at this place; one of the boundary lines calls for a creek by the name of Tyadoghton; we wish our brothers the Six Nations to explain to us clearly which you call the Tyadoghton, as there are two creeks issuing from the Burnet's Hills, Pine and Lycoming.

"'Brothers, you will observe by our commission just now read to you that our present business is to satisfy you, as was our ancient custom, for the lands lying within the acknowledged limits of Pennsylvania, for which you have not heretofore received any compensation.

"'This compensation has been mutually agreed to by you and us in conference this morning. It was also agreed that, in addition to the goods we have now on this ground for your use, we should give our obligation for the amount of one thousand dollars in such goods as will best suit yourselves to be delivered at or near Tioga, on the Susquehanna, on the first day of October next. It now remains for us mutually to carry into execution our respective agreements, and that in the most solemn and public manner, as it is our fixed determination that they shall be inviolate for ever.

"'Brothers, before we conclude we desire you to appoint some suitable persons among yourselves to receive and distribute the goods with impartiality and justice, and that you will also nominate a fit person to attend running the boundary between you and us, when due notice shall be given thereof.'

"(A LARGE BELT.)

"To which they replied by Captain Aaron Hill,—

"'BROTHERS FROM PENNSYLVANIA,—We have heard what you have said, and are well pleased with the same. The consideration we have fully agreed on, which we are to receive for the lands, and agreeable to your request have appointed Captain Aaron Hill, Onequiandahonjo, and Honeghariko, of the Mohawk tribe; Kayenthogkke, Thaghneghtanhari, and Teyagonendageghte, of the Seneca; Obendirighton and Thoneeyade, of the Cayuga; Sagoyahalongo and Otoghfelonegh, Ojestalale, Oneyanha, Gaghsawweda, and Odaghfeghte, of the Oneida; and Onefaghweughte and Tharondawagon, of the Tuscarora, as suitable persons to receive the goods from you.

"'With regard to the creek called Tyadoghton, mentioned in your deed of 1768, we have already answered you, and again repeat it, it is the same you call Pine Creek, being the largest emptying into the west branch of the Susquehannah.

"'Agreeable to your wish we have appointed Thaghneghtanhari to attend your surveyor in running the line between you and us.'

"'We do certify that the foregoing speech was this day made by Captain Aaron Hill, on behalf of the Six Nations, to the Pennsylvania commissioners.

"'Witness our hands this twenty-third day of October, Anno Domini one thousand seven hundred and eighty-four.

(Signed) "'SAMUEL KIRKLAND, *Missionary*.
JAMES DEAN, *Interpreter*.'

"The deed was then produced and publicly read, when the chiefs of the respective nations sealed and delivered the same, saying, 'We deliver this as our grant and deed, and give up the land therein mentioned, according to the description thereof, to their brothers, the Pennsylvanians, for their use forever.' After the same being witnessed, the commissioners sealed and delivered the two obligations mentioned above, one for the delivery of the goods and the other for securing to them the privilege of hunting on the lands now purchased.

PIONEER HISTORY OF JEFFERSON COUNTY, PENNA.

" The council arose.
" The foregoing is a true state of the proceedings of the Indian treaty at Fort Stanwix.

"GRIFFITH EVANS, *Secretary*.
"October 23, 1784."

"The six Indian Nations, to the Commonwealth of Pennsylvania, DEED for lands purchased October 23, 1784.

" To ALL PEOPLE to whom these presents shall come, WE Anigwendahonji and Teweghnitogon, Sachems or Chiefs of the Indian nation called the Mohocks. Kanonghgwenya, Atyatonenghtha, and Tatahonghteayon, Sachems or Chiefs of the Indian nation called the Oneidas. Obendarighton and Keatarondyon, Sachems or Chiefs of the Indian nation called the Onondagoes. Oraghgwanentagon, Sachem of the Indian nation called the Cayogaes. Tayagoneatageghti, Tehonweeaghreyagi, Thaghnaghtanhari, Sachems or Chiefs of the Indian nation called the Senecas. And Ononghsawanghti and Tharondawagon, Sachems or Chiefs of the Indian nation called the Tuscaroras, being met together in a general council of the Six Nations convened at Fort Stanwix, by the Honorable Oliver Wolcott, Richard Butler and Arthur Lee, Esquires, commissioners of Indian affairs, duly appointed by the honorable the Congress of the United States, for the northern and middle districts, SEND GREETING. KNOW YE that WE the said Sachems or Chiefs, for and in consideration of the sum of five thousand dollars, to us in hand paid, before ensealing and delivery of these presents, by the honorable Samuel John Atlee, Esquire, and William M'Clay, and Francis Johnson, Esquires, commissioners for and in behalf of the commonwealth of Pennsylvania, the receipt whereof WE do hereby acknowledge HAVE granted bargained, sold, released and confirmed, and by these presents, for us and the said Six Nations, and their confederates and dependent tribes, all of whom we represent, and by whom we are thereunto authorized and impowered, Do grant, bargain, sell, release and confirm unto the said Commonwealth, all that part of the said Commonwealth not yet purchased of the Indians within the acknowledged limits of the same, BEGINNING on the south side of the river Ohio, where the western boundary of the state of Pennsylvania crosses the said river, near Shingo's old Town, at the mouth of Beaver creek, and thence by a due north line to the end of the forty second and beginning of the forty-third degrees of north latitude, thence by a due east line seperating the forty second and forty third degrees of north latitude, to the east side of the east branch of the river Susquehanna, thence by the bounds of the late purchase made at Fort Stanwix, the fifth day of November, anno domini, one thousand seven hundred and sixty eight, as follows : ' Down the said east branch of Susquehanna, on the east side thereof, till it comes opposite to the mouth of a creek called by the Indians, Awandac, and across the river, and up the said creek on the south side thereof, and along the range of hills, called Burnett's Hills by the English, and by the Indians, . . . on the north side of them to the head of a creek which runs into the west branch of Susquehannah, which creek is by the Indians called Tyadaghton, but by the Pennsylvanians Pine Creek, and down the said creek on the south side thereof, to the said west branch of Susquehanna, then crossing the said river, and running up the same on the south side thereof, the several courses thereof, to the fork of the same river, which lies nearest to a place on the river Ohio called Kittaning, and from the fork by a straight line to Kittaning aforesaid, and then down the said river Ohio by the several courses thereof, to where the western bounds of the said state of Pennsylvania crosses the same river,' at the place of BEGINNING. Together with all lakes, rivers, creeks, rivulets, springs, waters, soils, lands, fields, woods, underwoods, mountains, hills, valleys, savannahs, fens, swamps, isles, inlets, mines, minerals, quarries, rights, liberties, privileges, advantages, hereditaments, and appurtenances whatsoever, to the said tract of land and country belonging or in any wise appertaining, and all the right, title, interest, claim and demand whatsoever, of us the said sachems or chiefs, and of the said Six Nations, and their confederates and dependent tribes, and every of them, TO HAVE AND TO HOLD the said tract of land and country, with the appurtenances thereunto belonging, unto the said commonwealth to the only proper use and behoof of the said commonwealth, FOR EVER, so that we, the said sachems or chiefs, nor any of us, nor the said Six Nations, nor their confederates and dependent tribes, nor any of them, nor any of our or their heirs, children or descendents, shall claim, demand or chalenge, any right, title, interest, or property, of, in, or to the said tract of land or country, but from the same shall be forever barred and excluded ; and the same tract of land and country, shall forever hereafter be peaceably and quietly possessed by the said commonwealth, and all persons, who shall settle thereon, under the authority of the same, without the let, hindrance, molestation, interruption, or denial of us the said sachems or chiefs, or the said Six Nations, or their confederates, and dependent tribes, or any of them, or of our or their heirs, children, or descendents. IN WITNESS Whereof, We the said sachems or chiefs, for ourselves and the rest of the Six Nations, and their confederates and dependent tribes, have hereunto set our hands and seals. Dated at Fort Stanwix aforesaid, this twenty third day of October, in the year of our Lord, one thousand seven hundred and eighty four.

"ORAGHGWANENTAGON, his X mark, L. S.
TAYAGONEATAGEGHTI, his X mark, L. S.
TEHONWEEAGHREYAGI, his X mark, L. S.
THAGHNAGTANHARI, his X mark, L. S.

"ONONGHSAWANGHTI, his X mark, L. S.
THARONDAWAGON, his X mark, L. S.
ANIGWENDAHONJI, his X mark, L. S.
TEWEGHNITOGON, his X mark, L. S.
KANONGHGWENYA, his X mark, L. S.
ATYATONENGHTHA, his X mark, L. S.
TATAHONGHTEAYON, his X mark, L. S.
OBENDARIGHTON, his X mark, L. S.
KEATARONDYON, his X mark, L. S.

"Sealed and delivered in the presence of us,

"OLIVER WOLCOTT,
ARTHUR LEE,   } United States Commissioners.
RICHARD BUTLER,
AARON HILL,
SAMUEL KIRKLAND, *Missionary*.
"JAMES DEAN, *Interpreter*.
ALEXANDER CAMPBELL, *Sec. Com. U. S.*
SAMUEL MONTGOMERY, *Ag. & St. K. C. C.*
G. EVANS, *Sec. Penns. Ind. Commis.*

"STATE OF PENNSYLVANIA, *S.S.*

"BE IT REMEMBERED, That on the seventeenth day of February, in the year of our Lord one thousand seven hundred and eighty five, and in the ninth year of the independence of the United States of America, came the honourable Arthur Lee, Esquire, LL.D. one of the commissioners of the United States of America for holding treaties with the Indian nations, and Griffith Evans, Esquire, Secretary to the commissioners of the said State of Pennsylvania, for treating and purchasing, &c. of said Indians, before the honourable Thomas McKean Esq., doctor of Laws, chief justice of the supreme court of the said state of Pennsylvania, and made oath on the holy Evangelists of Almighty God, that they were present and did see the thirteen Indian sachems or chiefs, in the above deed named as grantors, make the signatures or marks to their respective names adjoining, and seal and deliver the above conveyance, as and for their act and deed, that they severally subscribed their names as witnesses thereof, and also seen the other seven witnesses subscribe their names as witnesses to the same, and that the names Arthur Lee and G. Evans above subscribed, are of their respective hand writing.

"IN TESTIMONY, Whereof I have hereunto put my hand and seal the day and year above said.

"THOS M'KEAN, L. S."

FORT McINTOSH.

After having successfully completed their mission to Fort Stanwix, the Pennsylvania commissioners, accompanied by those representing the

United States, immediately proceeded to Fort McIntosh, on the Ohio River, now the site of the present town of Beaver, to treat with the Wyandott and Delaware Indians, who claimed rights in the same lands ceded to the State by the treaty at Fort Stanwix. The following are the proceedings:

"FORT MCINTOSH, January, 1785.

"*In Council, January 9, 1785.*

"PRESENT.

The HON. GEORGE ROGERS CLARKE, RICHARD BUTLER, and ARTHUR LEE, ESQS., } *Commissioners on part of the United States.*

THE HON. SAMUEL F. ATLEE and FRANCIS JOHNSTON, ESQS., } *Commissioners on part of the State of Pennsylvania.*

GRIFFITH EVANS, *Secretary.*
JOHN MONTOUR, *Interpreter.*

And the chiefs, etc., of the Wyandott, Delaware, Chippewa, and Ottawa Indian Nations.

"The commissioners on part of the United States, in consequence of the State commissioners' letter of yesterday, addressed the Indians as follows:

"'SACHEMS AND WARRIORS,—These gentlemen, Colonel Atlee and Colonel Johnston, are commissioners from the State of Pennsylvania, who have attended here by consent of Congress to transact some public business with you on the part of said State, which they will be ready to introduce after the present treaty is concluded.'

"NOTE.—It appearing to the commissioners that the Wyandott and Delaware nations were the only claimants of the unpurchased lands in Pennsylvania among the western Indians, consequently the present negotiations on part of the State are confined to them.

"*In Conference, January 14, 1785.*

"PRESENT.

The HON. SAMUEL F. ATLEE and FRANCIS JOHNSTON, ESQS., } *Commissioners.*

GRIFFITH EVANS, *Secretary.*

JOHN MONTOUR and JOSEPH NICHOLSON, } *Interpreters.*

And the chiefs of the Wyandott and Delaware Indian nations.

"The commissioners addressed them in the following words by Colonel Atlee:

"'BROTHERS,—We have been long separated by the wars that have subsisted between us, which are now terminated and over. We are very glad to meet you here, and have great occasion to rejoice that we have an opportunity of brightening the chain of friendship between us, and we hope soon to take you by the hand in a happy and lasting peace,—when established by the commissioners from Congress.

"'We have called you together this morning with a view of explaining to you the nature of the business we have to negotiate with you.

"'Brothers, we are commissioned and sent from your old friends of Pennsylvania to purchase of the natives all the unpurchased lands within the territory of Pennsylvania. For this purpose we met your brothers and uncles, the Six Nations, last October at Fort Stanwix, and, according to our ancient custom, purchased the said lands of them, and this is the deed they gave us to confirm the same.'

"(Then produced the deed executed by the Six Nations last October, and also a map of the country explaining the same to them.)

"'Your brothers and uncles suggested to us that they had a right to act for you also in disposing of this land; but hearing you claimed, and knowing that you hunted on, part of this ground, we conceived we had better meet you ourselves on the subject, that we might also see each other and remove all obstructions out of the way between us. We have, therefore, reserved a proportion of the presents, and have brought them with us to give you as a compensation for your right to this country.

"'The amount of what we have reserved is two thousand dollars, consisting of an excellent assortment of goods of the first quality, calculated in the best manner to supply your wants, which is a greater proportion than what we have given to your uncles the Six Nations, and is certainly a very generous consideration.

"'You are now fully informed of our business with you. We earnestly desire that you may think seriously of it, for what we are about to do must be as permanent as the sun. We wish you to go and consult together upon our words, and let us know your minds as soon as convenient.

"'Brothers, we inform you that it is not our wish to settle our business finally with you previous to the conclusion of the Continental treaty, but only that we may fully understand each other and have our minds prepared, that when the commissioners on the part of the United States shall have completed their business we may have ours ready to bring on.'

"To which they replied by Captain Pipe, of the Delawares,—viz.:

"'BROTHERS,—We rejoice from our hearts to see our brothers from Pennsylvania, and are very glad that we are likely once more to live in peace and friendship with you. Your speech is very pleasing to us. You have told us the business you have meet us here upon, and we think we fully understand you. We will council together and let you know our minds some time soon.

"'Brothers, we are glad to hear of your having met with our uncles, the Six Nations, at Fort Stanwix, and that they have given up their lands to you, agreeable to the deed you just showed us.'

"*In Conference. Present as before.*

"Captain Pipe spoke in behalf of the Wyandott and Delaware nations as follows:

"'BROTHERS OF PENNSYLVANIA,—We met last night and counselled together upon the speech you delivered to us yesterday. We thank you for saving some of your presents for us, for in this, brothers, you were very right, for our fathers always told us, and we tell our children, that from Vinango to Little Beaver Creek, and out to the lake was our hunting-ground. But we have now all agreed to let our brothers, the Pennsylvanians, have it, excepting a few tracts, which we would wish to reserve, that we might make a present of a piece of ground to you and your young men for meeting us here at this inclement season, and that we may have it in our power to fulfil our promise to some of our friends, which we made long ago.'

"To which the commissioners replied,—

"'BROTHERS,—We thank you for your kind offer, but we cannot, consistent with our instructions from the State, agree to any reservations. Our purchase must be for our whole claim. At the same time, we have no doubt, but that if any individuals have just claims to any part of these lands, that upon application being made to the government of Pennsylvania, they will be properly attended to.'

"The chiefs, after consulting together for some time, answered,—

"'Well, then, we have agreed that this country shall be yours, and that our brothers of Pennsylvania shall have it forever.'

"The commissioners then thanked them, and said,—

"'We shall expect a deed from you for these lands, and we request you will nominate the persons who are to sign it, that it may be ready for execution at the proper season, when we will meet you in public council; and also that you would appoint fit persons to receive the goods from us, when we shall be ready to deliver them out.'

"They replied that Montour, the interpreter, should wait on the commissioners the next day and give them the names of those persons.

"Conference ended.

"January 16, 1785.

"Montour, agreeable to the appointment of yesterday, attended the commissioners, and returned the names of the following persons, who were to sign the deed,—viz., Deungquat, or the Half King, Tauwarah, or the Sweat House, and Abraham Kuhn, of the Wyandotts; and Kee-skanohen, or the Pipe, Peechemelind, or the Present, Wialindeoghin, or the Council Door, Hyngapushes, or the Big Cat, Tatabaughsey, or the Twisting Vine, and Whingohatong, or the Volunteer, of the Delawares. And Abraham Kuhn, Wialindeoghin, and Wingenum, to receive the goods.

"*In Council, January 21, 1785.*

"PRESENT.

The Hon. GEORGE ROGERS CLARKE, RICHARD BUTLER, and ARTHUR LEE, ESQS., } *Commissioners on part of the United States.*

ALEXANDER CAMPBELL, *Secretary*.

The Hon. SAMUEL F. ATLEE and FRANCIS JOHNSON, ESQS., } *Commissioners on part of the State of Pennsylvania.*

GRIFFITH EVANS, *Secretary*.

JOSEPH NICHOLSON and JOHN MONTOUR, *Interpreters*.

And the deputies of the Wyandott, Delaware, Chippewa, and Ottawa and Muncy Indian nations.

"Upon the completion of the Continental treaty, the Pennsylvania commissioners delivered the following speech by Colonel Atlee:

"'BROTHERS OF THE WYANDOTT AND DELAWARE NATIONS,—Listen with attention to what your brothers of Pennsylvania are going to say. You have been informed by the Continental commissioners at their first meeting that we come from the government of Pennsylvania as commissioners duly authorized to transact public business with you, as will appear by our commission under the seal of the State, which we will read to you.'

"(Read the commission.)

"'Pursuant to this commission, we met your brothers and uncles, the Six Nations, at Fort Stanwix in October last, and after a solemn peace was established with them by the honorable commissioners of the United States, we, in conformity to ancient custom, purchased their right to all the lands within the acknowledged limits of Pennsylvania not already purchased of them, for which we gave a valuable consideration in goods of the first quality.

"'That this may be known to all, we here produce their deed executed to us in the most public manner, and witnessed by the honorable commissioners of Congress, Captain Aaron Hill, a chief of the Mohawk tribe, and several others.

"'Now, brothers, as you have been called together to this place by the honorable the commissioners of the United States, we, by consent of Congress, are happy to meet you, and rejoice that peace and friendship are once more established among us. In testimony of our sincerity we present you with these strings.'

"(FIVE STRINGS.)

"'BROTHERS,—Knowing that for some time past you have hunted upon and claimed a portion of the lands within Pennsylvania, and being actuated by the strict principles of peace and justice towards you in the same degree that you have seen we have manifested to your brothers and uncles, the Six Nations, and to prevent future trouble between your people and ours, we have determined, according to the known usage of Pennsylvania, to give you the consideration agreed upon between us, for this purpose we have brought with us a quantity of the best goods such as will minister to your relief and comfort. These goods shall be delivered out to proper persons appointed by each nation to receive them; and that no misunderstanding may arise in future, a map of the land we wish to have confirmed to the Commonwealth shall be afixed to the deed to be executed by you, that your children and ours, may hereafter have recourse to the same.'

"(A BELT.)

"To which they, by the Half King, chief of the Wyandotts, replied,—

"'BROTHERS OF PENNSYLVANIA,—Give attention to what we shall say to you. Your words have pleased us very much, and we all thank you for your kindness towards us; our grandfathers have always said that your conduct towards them was just the same you discover to us now. Pennsylvania has never deceived or wronged us out of anything, and we all thank you not only from our lips, but also from our hearts for your honesty.'

"(THREE STRINGS.)

"The commissioners then produced the deed* that was prepared, and informed them it was ready for them to execute, when the persons who had been appointed for the purpose walked forward and sealed and delivered the same, in the most solemn manner, in the presence of many witnesses, as their quit-claim and deed for the land therein described, for the use of Pennsylvania forever.

"The council fire was raked up.

"The foregoing is a true state of the proceedings of the Indian treaty held at Fort McIntosh.

"GRIFFITH EVANS, *Secretary.*

"January 23, 1785."

---

* The deed executed at Fort McIntosh, excepting the consideration money mentioned, which was two thousand dollars instead of five thousand dollars, is in the same

PIONEER HISTORY OF JEFFERSON COUNTY, PENNA.

GOODS TO BE DELIVERED TO THE INDIANS AT FORT STANWIX.

"*The Supreme Executive Council met.*

"PHILADELPHIA, August 28, 1784, Saturday.

"PRESENT.

His Excellency JOHN DICKINSON, ESQUIRE, *President.*
The Honorable JAMES IRVINE, SAMUEL JOHN ATLEE,
JOHN McDOWELL, BERNARD DOUGHERTY,
and STEPHEN BALLIOTT, JOHN BOYD, } *Esqrs.*

"Council having considered the resolution of the General Assembly of the twenty fifth instant, it was

"*Ordered,* That the Commissioners be requested to procure immediately the undermentioned articles, but if the sum of three thousand and three hundred and seventy five pounds will not be sufficient to purchase the whole, that then they be desired to reduce the quantity or number of such of the articles as they shall think fit.

---

words, and for the same lands with the same boundaries as the deed previously signed by the Sachems and Chiefs of the Six Nations at Fort Stanwix. It is dated at Fort McIntosh, the 21st day of January, 1785, and signed by the Sachems and Chiefs of the two tribes as follows:

    WIALINDEOGHIN, or the COUNCIL DOOR, X his mark, L. S.
    HYNGAPUSHES, or the BIG CAT, X his mark, L. S.
    TATABAUGHSEY, or the TWISTING VINE, X his mark, L. S.
    WHINGOHATONG, or the VOLUNTEER, X his mark, L. S.
    DEUNGQUAT, or the HALF KING, X his mark, L. S.
    TAUWARAH, or the SWEAT HOUSE, X his mark, L. S.
    ABRAHAM KUHN, X his mark, L. S.
    KEESKANOHEN, or the PIPE, X his mark, L. S.
    PEECHEMELIND, or the PRESENT, X his mark, L. S.
                                                [Sealed.]

Sealed and delivered in presence of
    G. R. CLARK,
    RICHARD BUTLER, } *Commissioners of the United States,*
    ARTHUR LEE,
    JOS. HARMER, Lieutenant-Colonel Com.,
    ALEXD. LOWREY,
    JOHN BOGGS,
    WM. BUTLER,
    ALEX. CAMPBELL, *Secretary Commissioners United States,*
    W. BRADFORD,
    DANIEL ELLIOT,
    JOHN MONTOUR, *Interpreter,*
    G. EVANS, *Secretary Pennsylvania Commissioners,*
    EDW. BUTLER.

PIONEER HISTORY OF JEFFERSON COUNTY, PENNA.

20½ casks of gun powder.
1 ton of bar lead.
2 groce of thimbles.
2 do jews harps.
50 dozen white ruffled shirts.
5 do laced hats.
50 do knives.
10 do hatchets.
10 do pipe tomahawks.
12 do looking glasses.
2 M awl blades.
5 M needles.
1 C. Vermillion.
50 rifles.
60 M wampum—30 white, 30 black.
12 dozen silver arm bands.
12 do wrist bands.
20 dozen pipes, Moravian.
20 do callicoe shirts.
1 hogshead of tobacco.
500 lb of brass kettles in nests, complete.
100 lb of small white beads.
2 gross of morrice bells.
5 dozen of pieces of yellow, green and purple ribbon.
5 pieces of embossed flannel.
60 dozen broaches.
2 do gorgets.
12 do nosebobs.
12 do hair pipes.
12 do rings.
6 pieces scarlet broad cloth.
100 lb of brass wire.
20 dozen silk handkerchiefs.
2 do pieces of callicoe
4 dozen of saddles and bridles.
1,000 flints, or 1 keg.
1 gross sheers.
1 do scissars.
1 do horn combs.
1 do ivory do.
50 lb of thread sorted.
12 gross scarlet and star gartering.
12 do green and yellow bedlace.
3 hogsheads of rum.
30 p's best London stroud.
30 do French match coats.
10 do blankets.
20 do half thicks, purple and white nap.

"*Ordered*, That a warrant be issued to the Treasurer for the sum of three thousand three hundred and seventy five pounds specie, in favor of the Commissioners appointed to negotiate a purchase from the Indians claiming the unpurchased territory within the limits of this State, to be applied to the purchase of the article above enumerated, in pursuance of the resolution of the General Assembly of the twenty fifth inst."—*Colonial Records*, vol. xiv. p. 186.

COMMISSIONERS ON INDIAN TREATY, 1785.

"SIR,—In pursuance of the Order of Council of 30th July last, I have made out a List of the Goods necessary to be furnished the Indians in October next w^h I do myself the honor to inclose.

"I am your Excellency's
"most Obedient Serv't,
"F. JOHNSTON.

"Directed,
"To His Excellency JOHN DICKINSON, ESQR.

PIONEER HISTORY OF JEFFERSON COUNTY, PENNA.

"A list of the goods to be furnished the six nations of Indians on the First day of October next.

8 pieces Blue Stroud.	2 Dozen Ivory ditto.
20 pairs 3 point Match Coats.	25 lb Vermillion.
60 pairs 2½ point ditto.	50 Gallons Barbadoes rum.
25 yards Scarlet Flannel.	56 lb Gun powder.
1 Piece Scarlet Broad Cloth.	400 lb Barr Lead.
100 White Ruffled Shirts.	300 lb Tobacco.
50 Callico ditto.	1 Kegg pipes.
18 French Castors.	3 Pieces Gartering.
6 Dozen coarse Combs.	

"Aug't 10, 1785.'

—*Pennsylvania Archives*, vol. x. p. 496.

CHAPTER V.

TITLES AND SURVEYS—PIONEER SURVEYS AND SURVEYORS—DISTRICT LINES RUN IN NORTHUMBERLAND, NOW JEFFERSON, COUNTY, PENNSYLVANIA.

"IN 1670 Admiral Sir William Penn, an officer in the English navy, died. The government owed this officer sixteen hundred pounds, and William Penn, Jr., fell heir to this claim. King Charles II. liquidated this debt by granting to William Penn, Jr., 'a tract of land in America, lying north of Maryland and west of the Delaware River, extending as far west as plantable.' King Charles signed this deed March 4, 1661. William Penn, Jr., was then proprietor, with power to form a government. Penn named the grant Pennsylvania, in honor of his father. In 1682 Penn published his form of government and laws. After making several treaties and visiting the Indians in the interior as far as Conestoga, Penn sailed for England, June 12, 1684, and remained away till December 1, 1699. On his return he labored to introduce reforms in the provincial government, but failed. He negotiated a new treaty of peace with the Susquehanna Indians and also with the Five Nations. In the spring of 1701 he made a second journey into the interior, going as far as the Susquehanna and Swatara. Business complications having arisen, Penn sailed for England in the fall, and arrived there the middle of December, 1701. Owing to straitened financial circumstances, he entered into an agreement with Queen Anne, in 1712, to cede to her the province of Pennsylvania and the Lower Counties for the sum of twelve thousand pounds sterling; but before the legal papers were completed he was stricken with paralysis, and died July 30, 1718, aged seventy-four. While Penn accomplished much, he also suffered much. He was persecuted for his religion, imprisoned for debt, and tried for treason. After his death it was found that, owing to the complication of his affairs and the peculiar construction of his will, a suit in chancery to establish his legal heirship was necessary. Several years elapsed before the question was decided, when the Proprietaryship of the province descended to John, Richard, and Thomas Penn. John died in 1746 and Richard in 1771, when John, Richard's son, and Thomas became sole Proprietaries. But the Revolution and the Declaration of Independence soon caused a radical change in the provincial government."—*Meginnis.*

During the Revolution the Penn family were Tories, adherents of England, and on the 27th of November, 1779, the Legislature of Pennsylvania confiscated all their property except certain manors, etc., of which surveys and returns had been made prior to the 4th of July, 1776. The Penns were granted as a compensation for these confiscations one hundred and thirty thousand pounds sterling. This ended the rule of the Penns in America. The treaty of peace between England and what is now the United States was ratified by Congress in January, 1784. All foreign domination or rule in the colonies then ceased, but internal troubles with the savages still continued in this State in the north and northwest.

"The Indians were jealous of their rights, and restive under any real or fancied encroachments that might be made upon them, and it required the exercise of great care, caution, and prudence on the part of the authorities to avert trouble on the northern and western boundaries of the State; and this they did not always succeed in doing, as many adventurous spirits, pushing far out into the unsettled wilderness, discovered to their sorrow. Fortunately, however, by the treaty of October, 1784, with the Six Nations at Fort Stanwix, and that of January, 1785, with the Wyandots and Delawares at Fort McIntosh, the Indian title was extinguished to all the remaining territory within the then acknowledged limits of the State which had been previously purchased. The boundaries of that great northwestern section of the State covered by this purchase may be briefly described as follows: Beginning on the east branch of the Susquehanna River where it crosses the northern boundary of the State in Bradford County; thence down the east branch to the mouth of Towanda Creek; thence up Towanda Creek to its headwaters; thence by a straight line west to the head waters of Pine Creek; thence down Pine Creek to the west branch of the Susquehanna; thence up the west branch to Cherry Tree in Clearfield County; thence by a straight line to Kittanning, on the Allegheny River, in Armstrong County; thence down the Allegheny River to the Ohio River; thence down the Ohio River to where it crosses the western boundary to Lake Erie; and thence east along the northern boundary of the State to the beginning. And within this territory at the present day we find the counties of

PIONEER HISTORY OF JEFFERSON COUNTY, PENNA.

Tioga, Potter, McKean, Warren, Crawford, Venango, Forest, Clarion, Elk, Jefferson, Cameron, Butler, Lawrence, and Mercer, and parts of the counties of Bradford, Clinton, Clearfield, Indiana, Armstrong, Allegheny, Beaver, and Erie."—*Annual Report of Internal Affairs.*

The Indians received for this territory ten thousand dollars in cash. Our wilderness was then in Northumberland County. "All land within the late (1784) purchase from the Indians, not heretofore assigned to any other particular county, shall be taken and deemed to be within the limits of Northumberland County and Westmoreland County. And that from Kittanning up the Allegheny to the mouth of Conewango Creek, and from thence up said creek to the northern line of this State, shall be the line between Northumberland County."—*Smith's Laws,* vol. ii. p. 325.

"Under the Proprietary government which ended 27th November, 1779, land was disposed to whom, on what terms, in such quantities, and such locations as the proprietor or his agents saw proper. The unoccupied lands were never put in the market, nor their sale regulated by law. Every effort made by the Assembly to secure uniformity in the sale and price of land was resisted by the proprietor as an infringement upon his manorial rights. After the Commonwealth became vested with the proprietary interests, a law was passed April 9, 1781, for establishing the land-office, for the purpose of enabling those persons to whom grants had been made to perfect their titles. July 1, 1784, an act was passed opening the land-office for the sale of vacant lands in the purchase of 1768. The price was fixed at £10 per 100 acres, or 33⅓ cents per acre, in addition to the warrant survey and patent fees, and the quantity in each warrant limited to 400 acres and the 6 per cent. allowance. The purchase of 1784 having been completed and confirmed by the treaty at Fort McIntosh, January, 1785, the land-office was opened for the sale of lands in the new purchase December 21, 1785, at which the price was fixed at £30 per 100 acres, and warrants were allowed to contain 1000 acres, with 10 per cent. overplus, besides the usual allowance." This is the reason why so many old warrants contained 1100 acres, with 6 per cent., or 60 more acres. "Nevertheless, the price of the land was placed so high that but few speculators ventured to invest in the hilly and heavily timbered lands of Northern Pennsylvania. Under the pressure of certain land-jobbers, who were holding important offices (?) in the Commonwealth, like John Nicholson, Robert Morris, and William Bingham, an act was passed April 3, 1792, in which the price of vacant lands was reduced to 50 shillings per 100 acres, or 6⅔ cents per acre. Speculation ran wild. Applications for warrants poured into the office by tens of thousands. The law, while it appeared to favor persons of small means, and prevent the wealthy from acquiring large portions of the public domain, was so drawn that by means of fictitious applications and poll deeds—

that is, mere assignments of the application without the formalities of acknowledgment—any party could possess himself of an unlimited quantity of the unappropriated lands. Within a year or two nearly all the lands in the county (then Northumberland) had been applied for, Nicholson, Morris, Bingham, James D. Le Roy, Henry Drinker, John Vaughan, Pickering, and Hodgdon being the principal holders."— *Craft's History of Bradford County*, pp. 40, 41.

"When, in the pursuance of this policy which had been adopted by William Penn, by treaties with and by purchases of the Indians, they finally became divested of their original title to all the lands in Pennsylvania; then, under what was called 'The Late Purchase,' which covered all of this section of country and included it in Northumberland County, in the year 1785 certain warrants, called 'Lottery Warrants,' were issued by governmental authority to persons who would pay twenty pounds per hundred acres, authorizing them to enter upon the lands and make selections where they pleased. This was done to some extent, and on those warrants surveys were made; but, as there was no road by which emigrants could come into the country, no settlements could be made in any place except where the sturdy pioneer could push his canoe, ignoring, or overcoming all the privations and difficulties incident to a pioneer life in such a wilderness."

With a desire to give a complete history of the pioneer surveys of the county, I addressed a letter to Hon. I. B. Brown, Deputy Secretary of Internal Affairs, asking for all the information known by the State. I herewith submit his reply,—viz.:

"DEPARTMENT OF INTERNAL AFFAIRS,
"HARRISBURG, PA., March 7, 1895."

"MR. W. J. McKNIGHT, Brookville, Pa.

"DEAR SIR,—In answer to your letter of the 5th instant, we beg to say that prior to the opening of the land office in May, 1785, for the sale of lands within the purchase of 1784, that part of the purchase lying east of the Allegheny River and Conewango Creek was divided into eighteen districts, and a deputy surveyor appointed for each. These districts were numbered consecutively, beginning with No. 1, on the Allegheny River, and running eastward. The southern line of district No. 1 began on the old purchase line of 1768 at Kittanning, and following that line in successive order were districts Nos. 2, 3, 4, 5, and 6, the latter terminating at the marked cherry-tree on the bank of the west branch of the Susquehanna River at Canoe Place. From that point the district line between the sixth and seventh districts, as then constituted, is supposed to be the line that divides the present counties of Indiana and Jefferson from the county of Clearfield as far north as Sandy Lick Creek.

"An old draft and report, found among the records of this department, show that Robert Galbraith, one of the early surveyors of Bedford County, ran the purchase line of 1768 from the cherry-tree to Kittanning for the purpose of marking it and ascertaining also the extent of the several survey districts north of the line and between the two points. This draft and accompanying report are without date, but the survey was presumably made during the summer of 1786. A reference to the appointment of Mr. Galbraith by the surveyor-general to perform this work, and the confirmation of the appointment by the Supreme Executive Council on the 8th of April, 1786, appear in the 'Colonial Records,' vol. xv. pp. 3 and 4. In the same volume, p. 85, is found the record of an order in favor of Galbraith for forty-five pounds, twelve shillings, to be in full for his services in running and marking the line and 'laying off' the districts of the deputy-surveyors. He says in his report, 'I began at the marked cherry-tree and measured along the purchase line seven miles and forty perches for James Potter's district, thence fifty-four perches to the line run by James Johnston for the east line of his district; from the post marked for James Potter's district seven miles and forty perches to a post marked for James Johnston's district, thence fifty-two perches to the line run by James Hamilton for the east line of his district; from Johnston's post seven miles and forty perches to the post marked for James Hamilton's district, thence fifty-two perches to the line run by George Wood, Jr., for the east line of his district; from the post marked for Hamilton's district six miles and one hundred and fifty-two perches to the line run by Thomas B. McClean for the east line of his district, thence two hundred and eight perches to the post marked for George Wood, Jr.'s, district, thence six miles and one hundred and fifty perches to the line run by John Buchanan for the east line of his district, thence two hundred and ten perches to the post marked for Thomas Brown McClean's district, thence two miles and one hundred and twenty perches to the Allegheny River for John Buchanan's district.'

"With the exception of the first, these districts each extended seven miles and forty perches along the purchase line, with the division lines between them running north to the line of New York. Undoubtedly the fourth, fifth, and sixth districts, of which James Hamilton, James Johnston, and General James Potter were respectively the deputy-surveyors, must have embraced, if not all, at least much the larger part of the territory that subsequently became the county of Jefferson, while the earliest surveys were made within that territory during the summer of 1785 by the surveyors named. It is possible, however, that part of the third district, of which George Wood, Jr., was the deputy-surveyor, may have been within these limits, and if so, surveys were no doubt also made by him. These first surveys were principally made and returned on the first warrants granted within the purchase, commonly known as the lottery warrants, and many of them in the name of Timothy Pickering and Company were located on lands that are now within Jefferson County.

"General James Potter died in the year 1789, and was succeeded by his son, James Potter, who was appointed in 1790. One of the reasons given for the appointment of James Potter, second, was that he had filled the position of an assistant to his father, and had done so much of the actual work in the field, and was therefore so thoroughly conversant with the lines of surveys already run, that he would avoid the interferences another person might fall into, thus preventing future trouble arising from conflicting locations. It does not appear, however, that the second James Potter ever did any work in the district, as the deputies' lists of surveys on file in the land-office show no returns from him.

"Soon after the year 1790 a change was made by the surveyor-general in the arrangement of the districts within the purchase of 1784, by which the number was reduced to six, counting west from the mouth of Lycoming Creek to the Allegheny River. In this arrangement the two western districts, Nos. 5 and 6, were assigned respectively to William P. Brady and Enion Williams. Williams was succeeded in 1794 by John Broadhead. Brady's district is described as 'beginning at a cherry-tree of late General Potter's district, and from thence extending by district No. 4 due north to the northern boundary of Pennsylvania, thence by the same west fourteen miles, thence south to the line of purchase of 1768, late the southern boundary of James Johnston's and General Potter's districts, and by the same to the place of beginning.'

"The sixth district comprised all the territory west of Brady's district to the Allegheny River and Conewango Creek. All of the present county of Jefferson must have been within these districts. The surveys made and returned by Brady, Williams, and Broadhead, for the Holland Company, John Nicholson, Robert Morris, and other large purchasers of lands, are so numerous as to practically cover all the lands left unsurveyed by their predecessors within that particular section of the State. A small part of the county, in the vicinity of Brockwayville, was in Richard Shearer's district, No. 7, east of General Potter's line, and a number of lottery warrants was surveyed by Shearer in that locality in 1785. That part of the county subsequently fell within district No. 4, of which James Hunter was the surveyor, who also returned a few surveys.

"In what manner these pioneer surveyors in the wilderness were equipped, and what the outfit for their arduous and difficult labors may have been, we do not know and have no means of ascertaining. Doubtless they had many severe trials and endured many hardships in preparing the way for future settlements and advancing civilization, for which they receive little credit or remembrance at this day. Possibly their only equipment was the ordinary surveyor's compass and the old link chain of those days, but they nevertheless accomplished much work that remains valuable down to the present time. For their labor they were paid by fees fixed by law. The law of that day also provided a per diem wage of three shillings for chain-carriers, to be paid by the purchaser of the land.

"Very truly yours,
"ISAAC B. BROWN,
"*Secretary.*"

You will see from the above that in 1785, Richard Shearer, with his chain-carriers and his axe-men, traversed what is now Brockwayville and the forest east of it; that James Potter, with his chain-carriers and axe-men, traversed the forests near Temples, now Warsaw; that James Johnston, with his chain-carriers and axe-men, traversed the forest where Brookville now is, and that James Hamilton, with his chain-carriers and axe-men, traversed the forest near or where Corsica now is. Each of these lines ran directly north to the New York line. Where these lines ran was then all in Northumberland County. In 1794, James Hunter, with his chain-carriers and axe-men, was in what is now Brockwayville region, William P. Brady, with his chain-carriers and axe-men, was in what is now the Temple region, and Enion Williams and John Broadhead, with chain-carriers and axe-men, were between where Brookville now is and the Clarion region. This wilderness was then in Pine Creek township, Northumberland County.

Elijah M. Graham was born in Dauphin County, Pennsylvania, October 19, 1772. His father's name was John Graham, who served five years in the Continental army.

Elijah M. Graham was one of the original explorers of what is now Jefferson County, Pennsylvania. He explored this region in 1794 under Deputy-Surveyor John Broadhead. In that year Broadhead surveyed the district line which now forms the western boundary of Brookville borough. Broadhead and his party of nine men were in this wilderness surveying from May until the middle of October, 1794. The party consisted of Department-Surveyor Broadhead, two chain-carriers (Elijah M. Graham and Elisha Graham, brothers), two axe-men (unknown), one cook (unknown), one driver with two horses (unknown), and two other men (unknown), one of whom was a hunter. These parties crossed streams on log floats, encamped in log huts, and carried their outfit and their provisions on pack-horses from what is now Franklin, Pennsylvania, and from some point then in Westmoreland County, Pennsylvania. Graham was six months on this survey without seeing a paleface other than those that comprised the party.

In 1797, Elijah M. Graham located on French Creek, now Crawford County, Pennsylvania, where he resided with his father until 1804, when he returned to this wilderness and worked on Joseph Barnett's mill for three years, when and where he married Miss Sarah Ann Barnett and located on the State Road near and afterwards in what is now Eldred township. He was the first court crier, and served in various township offices.

In 1804 there were but seven or eight families here,—viz., the Barnetts, Longs, Joneses, Vasbinders, and Dixons, and one colored family.

Mr. Graham reared a family of ten children, only three or four of whom, including J. B., are now living. Elijah M. Graham died in 1854, aged eighty-two years.

John Graham, Elijah M. Graham's father, moved to Jefferson County from Crawford County about 1812, locating about three miles northeast of Brookville, where he died in 1813, and this Revolutionary soldier was buried in the first graveyard, now in East Brookville, the land owned and occupied by W. C. Evans.

"By an act of the Legislature, passed April 1, 1794, the sale of these lands was authorized. The second section of this law provides that all lands west of the Allegheny Mountains shall not be more than three pounds ten shillings for every one hundred acres.

"Section four provides that the quantity of land granted to one person shall not exceed four hundred acres. Section six provides for the survey and laying out of these lands by the surveyor-general or his deputies into tracts of not more than five hundred acres and not less than two hundred acres, to be sold at public auction at such times as the 'Supreme Executive Council may direct.'

"When all claims had been paid, 'in specie or money of the State,' for patenting, surveying, etc., a title was granted to the purchaser. In case he was not ready or able to make full payment at the time of purchase, by paying all the fees appertaining thereto, he was allowed two years to complete the payment by paying lawful interest, and when the last payment was made a completed title was given.

"By the act of April 8, 1785, the lands were sold by lottery, in portions not to exceed one thousand acres to each applicant. Tickets, commencing with number one, were put in a wheel, and the warrants, which were called 'Lottery Warrants,' issued on the said applications, were severally numbered according to the decision of the said lottery, and bore date from the day on which the drawing was finished.

"Section seven of this act allowed persons holding these warrants to locate them upon any piece or portion of unappropriated lands. The land upon each warrant to be embraced in one tract, if possible.

"On the 3d of April, 1792, the Legislature passed an act for the sale of these lands, which, in some respects, differed from the laws of 1784 and 1785. It offers land only to such persons as shall settle on them, and designates the kind and duration of settlement.

"By section two of this act all lands lying north and west of the Ohio and Allegheny Rivers and Conewango Creek, except such portions as had been or should be appropriated to public or charitable uses, were offered to such as would 'cultivate, improve, and settle upon them, or cause it to be done, for the price of seven pounds ten shillings for every hundred acres, with an allowance of six per centum for roads and highways, to be located, surveyed, and secured to such purchasers, in the manner hereinafter mentioned.'

"Section three provided for the surveying and granting of warrants by the surveyor-general for any quantity of land within the said limits, to not exceed four hundred acres, to any person who settled upon and improved said land.

"The act provided for the surveying and division of these lands. The warrants were, if possible, to contain all in one entire tract, and the form of the tract was to be as near, as circumstances would admit, to an oblong, whose length should not be greater than twice the breadth thereof. No warrants were to be issued in pursuance of this act until the purchase-money should have been paid to the receiver-general of the land-office.

"The surveyor-general was obliged to make clear and fair entries of all warrants in a book to be provided for the purpose, and any applicant should be furnished with a certified copy of any warrant upon the payment of one-quarter of a dollar.

"In this law the rights of the citizen were so well fenced about and so equitably defined that risk and hazard came only at his own. But controversies having arisen concerning this law between the judges of the State courts and those of the United States, which the Legislature, for a long time, tried in vain to settle, impeded for a time the settlement of the district. These controversies were not settled until 1805, by a decision of Chief Justice Marshall, of the Supreme Court of the United States.

"At the close of the Revolutionary War several wealthy Hollanders,—Wilhelm Willink, Jan Linklaen, and others,—to whom the United States was indebted for money loaned in carrying on the war, preferring to invest the money in this country, purchased of Robert Morris, the great financier of the country at that time, an immense tract of land in the State of New York, and at the same time took up by warrant (under the law above cited) large tracts in the State of Pennsylvania, east of the Allegheny River. Judge Yeates, on one occasion, said, 'The Holland Land Company has paid to the State the consideration money of eleven hundred and sixty-two warrants and the surveying fees on one thousand and forty eight tracts of land (generally four hundred acres each), besides making very considerable expenditures by their exertions, honorable to themselves and useful to the community, in order to effect settlements. Computing the sums advanced, the lost tracts, by prior improvements and interferences, and the quantity of one hundred acres granted to each individual for making an actual settlement on their lands, it is said that,

PIONEER HISTORY OF JEFFERSON COUNTY, PENNA.

averaging the whole, between two hundred and thirty and two hundred and forty dollars have been expended by the company on each tract.'

"An act was passed by the Legislature, March 31, 1823, authorizing Wilhelm Willink, and others of Holland to 'sell and convey any lands belonging to them in the Commonwealth.'

"Large tracts of lands in Jefferson County were owned by the Holland Company, and Charles C. Gaskill, of Punxsutawney, was the agent of the company for their sale. He was appointed by John J. Vandercamp, the general agent. He finally sold out to Alexander Caldwell, and Lee, and Gilpin. Mr. Gaskill conveyed much of these lands to actual settlers in this county. Mr. Gaskill was very lenient to settlers. A day was generally set for those parties who had payments to make to meet the owners or their agents, from whom they had purchased lands, at a certain place; but money was scarce, and it was hard for the early settlers to meet their obligations, small as was the price paid in those days. In order to stir his delinquent debtors up to a sense of their indebtedness Mr. Gaskill inserted the following notice in a paper published at Kittanning:

"'NOTICE.—Having been very indulgent towards those persons indebted for "HOLLAND LAND" in Indiana, Jefferson, and Armstrong Counties for some time past, I am now under the necessity of informing them that it will be necessary for them to exert themselves and make as considerable payments, and as soon as possible, on their respective bonds, etc.

"'CHARLES C. GASKILL.

"'PUNXSUTAWNEY, November 20, 1819.'"

—*Kate Scott's History of Jefferson County.*

"Legally, there never was any such thing as the Holland Land Company, or the Holland Company, as they were usually called.

"The company, consisting of Wilhelm Willink and eleven associates, merchants and capitalists of the city of Amsterdam, placed funds in the hands of friends who were citizens of America to purchase several tracts of land in the United States, which, being aliens, the Hollanders could not hold in their names at that time; and in pursuance of the trust created, there were purchased, both in New York and Pennsylvania, immense tracts of land, all managed by the same general agent at Philadelphia.

"The names of the several persons interested in these purchases, and who composed the Holland Land Company, so called, were as follows: Wilhelm Willink, Nicholas Van Staphorst, Pieter Van Eeghen, Hendrick Vollenhoven, and Ruter Jan Schimmelpenninck. Two years later the five proprietors transferred a tract of about one million acres, so that the title vested in the original five, and also in Wilhelm Willink, Jr., Jan Willink, Jr., Jan Gabriel Van Staphorst, Roelif Van Staphorst, Jr., Cornelius Vollenhoven, and Hendrick Seye."

Charles C. Gaskill came to Punxsutawney about 1820 from Philadelphia, Pennsylvania. He resided there until 1849, during which time he visited regularly the courts of this and adjoining counties, making sales and receiving payments for land. In this year he disposed of all the Holland land to Reynolds, Smith, Gilpin & Co., when he returned to Philadelphia, Pennsylvania. Mr. Gaskill was a kind, courteous Quaker gentleman. He died at Cooper's Point, New Jersey, in 1872.

CHAPTER VI.

PIONEER ANIMALS—BEAVER, BUFFALO, ELK, PANTHERS, WOLVES, WILD-CATS, BEARS, AND OTHER ANIMALS—PENS AND TRAPS—BIRDS—WILD BEES.

THE mountainous character of this county and the dense forests that covered almost its whole area made the region a favorite haunt of wild beasts. "Many of them have disappeared, and it is difficult to believe that animals now extinct on the continent at large were once numerous within the boundaries of this county."

The beaver, the buffalo, the elk, and the deer were probably the most numerous of the animals. "Beaver will not live near man, and at an

Beaver.

early period after the settlement of this State these animals withdrew into the secluded regions and ultimately entirely disappeared." The last of them known in this State made their homes in the great "Flag Swamp," or Beaver Meadow, of what was then Jefferson County. This swamp was in Jenks township, and is now situated in Jenks township, Forest County. The beavers were still in this swamp in the thirties. Late in the thirties a trapper named George W. Pelton would occasionally bring a "beaver pelt" from this swamp on Salmon Creek to Brookville and "barter" it for merchandise. Centuries ago herds of wild buffaloes fed in our valleys and on our hills. Yes, more, the "buffalo, or American bison, roamed in great droves over the meadows and uplands from the Susquehanna to Lake Erie."

HOW THE BEAVER BUILT HIS DAM.

If the place chosen was stagnant water or a swamp, he at once commenced building on the bank with low entrances from the water, but if the stream was a running one, a large company of beavers would co-operate in order to keep the water at its level. Then they would go up the stream, gnaw down trees from two feet in diameter down, trim them, float them down to the "site," lay them crosswise, and fill in with mud and stone, which they carried between their forepaws and chin. When the water was high enough in a dam to prevent freezing to the bottom of it in winter, they separated into families and built their houses against the bank or dam. The entrance to the house was beneath the water, and the roof of the house was well covered with mud to protect against wolves. Beavers laid up food for winter by sinking bark and logs in the dam near their house, and in summer fed on grass, roots, etc. Every stream in the county, big or little, had beaver meadows, but they were mostly located on the smaller streams.

The American elk was widely distributed in this great forest in 1794. The habitat of this noble game was the forest extending across the northern part of the State. These animals were quite numerous in Jefferson County in the thirties.

In 1834, Mike, William, and John Long and Andrew Vasbinder captured a full-grown, live elk. Their dogs chased the animal onto a high rock, and while there the hunters lassoed it. The elk only lived three weeks in captivity. The last elk in the State was killed in our forests. A noted hunter thus describes a battle between wolves and a drove of elk: "I heard a rush of feet from the opposite direction, and the next moment a band of elks swept into sight. Magnificent fellows they were, eight males and three does, with a couple of calves. They had evidently been stampeded by something, and swept past me without seeing me, but stopped short on catching sight of the wolves. The does turned back and started to gallop away in the direction from which they came, but one of the bucks gave a cry, and they stopped short and huddled together with the fawns between them, while the bucks surrounded them. Each buck lowered his horns and awaited the attack. The wolves, seeing the cordon of bristling bone, paused, disconcerted for a moment; then the foremost, a gaunt old wolf, gave a howl and threw himself upon the lowered antlers. He was flung fully ten feet with a broken back, but his fate did not deter the others. They threw themselves upon the elks only to be pierced by the prongs. It was not until fully twenty had in this way been maimed and killed that they seemed to realize the hopelessness of the thing."

The largest carnivorous beast was the panther. After the advent of white men into this wilderness panthers were not common. In the early days, however, there were enough of them in the forests to keep the settler or the hunter ever on his guard. They haunted the wildest glens and made their presence known by occasional raids on the flocks and herds. It is probable that here in our northwestern counties there are still a few of these savage beasts.

The puma, popularly called by our pioneers panther, was and is a large animal with a cat head. The average length of a panther from nose to tip of tail is about six to twelve feet, the tail being over two feet long, and the tip of which is black. The color of the puma is tawny, dun,

Panther.

or reddish along the back and side, and sometimes grayish-white underneath or over the abdomen and chest, with a little black patch behind each ear. The panther is a powerful animal, as well as dangerous, but when captured as a cub can be easily domesticated. These animals are occasionally to be found in this wilderness. The pioneers shot them and captured many in panther- and bear-traps. The pelts sold for from one to two dollars.

The Longs, Vasbinders, and other noted hunters in our county killed many a panther. A law was enacted in 1806 giving a bounty of eight dollars for the "head" of each grown wolf or panther killed, and the "pelts" bringing a good price for fur, stimulated these hunters greatly to do their best in trapping, hunting, and watching the dens of these dangerous animals. The bounty on the head of a wolf pup was three dollars. The bounty on the head of a panther whelp was four dollars. The county commissioners would cut the ears off these heads and give an order on the county treasurer for the bounty money. A panther's pelt sold for about four dollars. On one occasion a son of Bill Long, Jackson by name, boldly entered a panther's den and shot the animal by the light of his glowing eyes. Jackson Long's history would fill this volume. In 1833, Jacob and Peter Vasbinder found a panther's den on Boone's Mountain. They killed one, the dogs killed two, and these hunters caught a cub, which they kept a year and then sold it to a showman. In 1819 the Legislature enacted a law giving twelve dollars for a full-grown panther's head and five dollars for the head of a cub.

"One hundred years ago wolves were common in Northern and Western Pennsylvania. In the middle of the last century large packs of

Wolf.

them roamed over a great portion of the State. To the farmer they were an unmitigated nuisance, preying on his sheep, and even waylaying belated travellers in the forest. After the State was pretty well settled these beasts disappeared very suddenly. Many people have wondered as to the cause of their quick extinction. Rev. Joseph Doddridge in his ' Notes' ascribes it to hydrophobia, and he relates several instances where settlers who were bitten by wolves perished miserably from that terrible disease."

I have listened in my bed to the dismal howl of the wolf, and for the benefit of those who never heard a wolf's musical *soirée* I will state here that one wolf leads off in a long tenor, and then the whole pack joins in the chorus.

Wolves were so numerous that, in the memory of persons still living in Brookville, it was unsafe or dangerous to permit a girl of ten or twelve years to go a mile in the country unaccompanied. In those days the Longs have shot as many as five and six without moving in their tracks, and with a single-barrelled, muzzle-loading rifle, too. The sure aim and steady and courageous hearts of noted hunters made it barely possible for the early settlers to live in these woods, and even then they had to exercise "eternal vigilance." In 1835, Bill Long, John and Jack Kahle captured eight wolves in a "den" near the present town of Sigel. Wolf-pelts sold for three dollars. Wild-cats were numerous; occasionally a cat is killed in the county yet, even within the borough limits.

One of the modes of Mike Long and other pioneer hunters on the Clarion River was to ride a horse with a cow-bell on through the woods over the deer-paths. The deer were used to cow-bells and would allow the horse to come in full view. When the deer were looking at the horse, the hunter usually shot one or two.

Buffalo.

Every pioneer had one or more cow-bells; they were made of copper and iron. They were not cast, but were cut, hammered, and riveted into shape, and were of different sizes.

The black bear was always common in Pennsylvania, and especially was this so in our wild portion of the State. The early settlers in our county killed every year in the aggregate hundreds of these bears. Bear-skins were worth from three to five dollars a-piece. Reuben Hickox, of Perry township, as late as 1822, killed over fifty bears in three months. Captain Hunt, a Muncy Indian, living in what is now Brookville, killed sixty-eight in one winter. In 1831, Mrs. McGhee, living in what is now

Washington township, heard her pigs squealing, and exclaimed, "The bears are at the hogs!" A hired man, Phillip McCafferty, and herself each picked up an axe and drove the bears away. One pig had been killed. Every fall and winter bears are still killed in our forests.

Peter Vasbinder when a boy shot a big bear through the window of his father's house, and this, too, by moonlight. This bear had a scap of bees in his arms, and was walking away with them. The flesh of the bear was prized by the pioneer. He was fond of bear meat. Bears weighing four or five hundred pounds rendered a large amount of oil, which the pioneer housewife used in cooking.

Trapping and pens were resorted to by the pioneer hunters to catch the panther, the bear, the wolf, and other game.

The bear-pen was built in a triangular shape of heavy logs. It was in shape and build to work just like a wooden box rabbit-trap. The bear steel-trap weighed about twenty-five pounds. It had double springs and spikes sharpened in the jaws. A chain was also attached. This was used as a panther-trap, too. "The bear was always hard to trap. The cautious brute would never put his paw into visible danger, even when allured by the most tempting bait. If the animal was caught, it had to be accomplished by means of the most cunning stratagem. One successful method of catching this cautious beast was to conceal a strong trap in the ground covered with leaves or earth, and suspend a quarter of a sheep or deer from a tree above the hidden steel. The bait being just beyond the reach of the bear, would cause the animal to stand on his hind feet and try to get the meat. While thus rampant, the unsuspecting brute would sometimes step into the trap and throw the spring. The trap was not fastened to a stake or tree, but attached to a long chain, furnished with two or three grab-hooks, which would catch to brush and logs, and thus prevent the game from getting away."

An old settler informs me that in the fall of the year bears became very fat from the daily feasts they had on beechnuts and chestnuts, and the occasional raids they made on the old straw beehives and ripe cornfields. In pioneer times the bear committed considerable destruction to the corn. He would seat himself on his haunches in a corner of the field next the woods, and then, collecting a sheaf of the cornstalks at a time, would there and then enjoy a sumptuous repast.

Wolves usually hunt in the night, so they, too, were trapped and penned. The wolf-pen was built of small round logs about eight or ten feet high and narrowed at the top. Into this pen the hunter threw his bait, and the wolf could easily jump in, but he was unable to jump out. The wolf-trap was on the principle of the rat-trap, only larger, the jaws being a foot or two long.

Trappers rated the fox the hardest animal to trap, the wolf next, and the otter third. To catch a fox they often made a bed of chaff and got him to lie in it or fool around it, the trap being set under the chaff. Or a trap was set at a place where several foxes seemed to stop for a certain purpose. Or a fox could be caught sometimes by putting a bait a

Fox.

little way out in the water, and then putting a pad of moss between the bait and the shore, with the trap hid under the moss. The fox, not liking to wet his feet, would step on the moss and be caught.

THE AMERICAN ELK—DEER AND DEER COMBATS—HUNTERS, PROFESSIONAL AND NON-PROFESSIONAL—STALKING AND BELLING DEER—OTHER ANIMALS, ETC.

The American elk is the largest of all the deer kind. Bill Long and other noted hunters killed elk in these woods seven feet high. The early hunters found their range to be from Elk Licks on Spring Creek, that empties into the Clarion River at what is now called "Hallton," up to and around Beech Bottom. In winter these heavy footed-animals always "yarded" themselves on the "Beech Bottom" for protection from their enemies,—the light footed wolves. The elk's trot was heavy, clumsy, and swinging, and would break through an ordinary crust on the snow, but in the summer-time he would throw his great antlers back on his shoulders and trot through the thickets at a Nancy Hanks gait, even over fallen timber five feet high. One of his reasons for locating on the Clarion River was that he was personally a great bather and enjoyed spending his summers on the banks and the sultry days in bathing in that river. Bill Long presented a pair of enormous elk-horns, in 1838, to John Smith, of Brookville, who used them as a sign for the Jefferson Inn.

"The common Virginia white-tailed deer, once exceedingly numerous in our county, is still to be found in limited numbers. This deer when loping or running elevates its tail, showing the long white hair of the lower surface. If the animal is struck by a bullet the tail is almost invariably tucked close to the hams, concealing the white.

Elk.

"The American deer, common deer, or just deer, is peculiar to Pennsylvania. It differs from the three well-known European species,—the red deer, the fallow deer, and the pretty little roe. Of these three, the red deer is the only one which can stand comparison with the American.

"The bucks have antlers peculiar in many cases, double sharp, erect spikes or tines. The doe lacks these antlers. The antlers on the bucks are shed and removed annually. Soon after the old antlers fall, swellings, like tumors covered with plush, appear; these increase in size and assume the shape of the antlers with astonishing rapidity, until the new antlers have attained their full size, when they present the appearance of an ordinary pair of antlers covered with fine velvet. The covering, or 'velvet,' is filled with blood-vessels, which supply material for the new growth. The furrows in the complete antler show the course of the circulation during its formation, and no sooner is the building process completed than the 'velvet' begins to wither and dry up. Now the buck realizes that he is fully armed and equipped for the fierce joustings which must decide the possession of the does of his favorite range, and he busies himself in testing his new weapons and in putting a proper polish upon

every inch of them. He bangs and rattles his horn daggers against convenient trees and thrusts and swings them into dense, strong shrubs, and if observed during this honing-up process he frequently seems a disreputable-looking beast, with long streamers of blood-stained 'velvet' hanging to what will shortly be finely polished antlers with points as sharp as knives. When the last rub has been given and every beam and tine is furbished thoroughly, our bravo goes a-wooing with the best of them. He trails the coy does through lone covers and along favorite runways unceasingly; he is fiery and impetuous and full of fight, and asks no fairer chance than to meet a rival as big and short-tempered as himself. He meets one before long, for every grown buck is on the warpath, and when the pair fall foul of each other there is frequently a long and desperate combat, in which one gladiator must be thoroughly whipped or killed. All deer fight savagely, and occasionally two battling rivals find a miserable doom by managing to get their antlers securely interlocked, when both must perish. Two dead bucks thus locked head to head have been found lying as they fell in an open glade, where the scarred surface of the ground and the crushed and riven shrubs about told an eloquent tale of a wild tourney long sustained, and of miserable failing efforts of the wearied conqueror to free himself of his dead foe.''
—*Outing*. The Vasbinders, Longs, and all the early hunters found just such skulls in these woods.

Artificial deer-licks were numerous, and made in this way: A hunter would take a coffee-sack and put in it about half a bushel of common salt, and then suspend the sack high on the branch of a tree. When the rain descended the salt water would drip from the sack to the ground, making the earth saline and damp, and to this spot the deer would come, paw and lick the earth. The hunter usually made his blind in this way: A piece of board had two augur-holes bored in each end, and with ropes through these holes was fastened to a limb on a tree. On this board the hunter seated himself to await his game. Deer usually visit licks from about 2 A.M. until daylight. As a rule, deer feed in the morning and evening and ramble around all night seeking a thicket for rest and seclusion in the daytime.

"For ways that were dark and for tricks that were vain" the old pioneer was always in it. When real hungry for a venison steak he would often use a tame deer as a decoy, in this way: Fawns were captured when small, tamed, reared, and permitted to run at large with the cattle. A life insurance was "written" on this tame deer by means of a bell or a piece of red flannel fastened around the neck. Tame deer could be trained to follow masters, and when taken to the woods usually fed around and attracted to their society wild deer, which could then be shot by the secreted hunter. At the discharge of a gun the tame deer invariably ran up to her master. Some of these does were kept for five or six years.

Deer generally have two fawns at a time, in May, and sometimes three. The horns of a deer drop off about New-Year's.

Love of home is highly developed in the deer. You cannot chase him away from it. He will circle round and round, and every evening come to where he was born. He lives in about eight or ten miles square of his birthplace. In the wilds of swamps and mountains and laurel-brakes he has his "roads," beaten paths, and "crossings," like the civilized and cross roads of man. When hounded by dogs he invariably strikes for a creek or river, and it is his practice to take one of these "travelled paths," which he never leaves nor forgets, no matter how circuitous the path may be. Certain crossings on these paths where the deer will pass are called in sporting parlance "stands." These "stands" never change, unless through the clearing of timber or by settlement the old landmarks are destroyed.

"The deer loves for a habitation to wander over hills, through thick swamps or open woods, and all around is silence save what noise is made by the chirping birds and wild creatures like himself. He loves to feed a little on the lowlands and then browse on the high ground. It takes him a long time to make a meal, and no matter how much of good food there may be in any particular place, he will not remain there to thoroughly satisfy his appetite. He must roam about and eat over a great deal of territory. When he has browsed and fed till he is content, he loves to pose behind a clump of bushes and watch and listen. At such times he stands with head up as stanch as a setter on point, and if one watches him closely not a movement of his muscles will be detected. He sweeps the country before him with his keen eyes, and his sharp ears will be disturbed by the breaking of a twig anywhere within gunshot.

"When the day is still the deer is confident he can outwit the enemy who tries to creep up on him with shot-gun or rifle. But when the wind blows, he fears to trust himself in those places where he may easily be approached by man, so he hides in the thickets and remains very quiet until night. To kill a deer on a still day, when he is not difficult to find, the hunter must match the deer in cunning and must possess a marked degree of patience. The deer, conscious of his own craftiness, wanders slowly through the woods; but he does not go far before he stops, and like a statue he stands, and can only be made out by the hunter with a knowledge of his ways and a trained eye.

"The deer listens for a footfall. Should the hunter be anywhere within the range of his ear and step on a twig, the deer is off with a bound. He does not stop until he has reached what he regards as a safe locality in which to look and listen again. A man moving cautiously behind a clump of bushes anywhere within the sweep of his vision will start him off on the run, for he is seldom willing to take even a small chance against man. Should the coast be clear, the deer will break his pose, browse and wander about again, and finally make his bed under the top of a fallen tree or in some little thicket.

"To capture the deer by the still-hunting method, the hunter must know his ways and outwit him at his own game. First of all, the still-hunter wears soft shoes, and when he puts his foot on the ground he is careful not to set it on a twig which will snap and frighten any deer that may be in the vicinity. The still-hunter proceeds at once to put into practice the very system which the deer has taught him. He strikes a pose. He listens and looks. A deer standing like a statue two hundred yards away is not likely to be detected by an inexperienced hunter, but the expert is not deceived. He has learned to look closely into the detail of the picture before him, and he will note the difference between a set of antlers and a bush.

"The brown sides of a deer are very indistinct when they have for a background a clump of brown bushes. But the expert still-hunter sits quietly on a log and peers into the distance steadily, examining all details before him. Occasionally his fancy will help him to make a deer's haunch out of a hump on a tree, or he will fancy he sees an antler mixed with the small branches of a bush, but his trained eye finally removes all doubt. But he is in no hurry. He is like the deer, patient, keen of sight, and quick of hearing. He knows that if there are any deer on their feet in his vicinity he will get his eyes on them if he takes the time, or if he waits long enough he is likely to see them on the move. At all events he must see the deer first. Then he must get near enough to him to bring him down with his rifle."—*Outing.*

Deer will not run in a straight line. They keep their road, and it is this habit they have of crossing hills, paths, woods, and streams, almost invariably within a few yards of the same spot, that causes their destruction by the hounding and belling methods of farmers, lumbermen, and other non-professionals. Deer-licks were numerous all over this county. A "deer-lick" is a place where salt exists near the surface of the earth. The deer find these spots and work them during the night, generally in the early morning. One of the methods of our early settlers was to sit all night on or near a tree, "within easy range of a spring or a 'salt-lick,' and potting the unsuspecting deer which may happen to come to the lick in search of salt or water. This requires no more skill than an ability to tell from which quarter the breeze is blowing and to post one's self accordingly, and the power to hit a deer when the gun is fired from a dead rest."

"Belling deer" was somewhat common. I have tried my hand at it. The mode was this: Three men were located at proper distances apart along a trail or runway near a crossing. The poorest marksman was placed so as to have the first shot, and the two good ones held in reserve for any accidental attack of "buck fever" to the persons on the first and second stands. An experienced woodsman was then sent into a laurel thicket, carrying with him a cow-bell; and when this woodsman found and started a deer, he followed it, ringing the bell. The sound of this bell was notice to those on the "stand" of the approach of a deer. When the animal came on the jump within shooting distance of the first stand, the hunter there posted would bleat like a sheep; the deer would then come to a stand-still, when the hunter could take good aim at it; the others had to shoot at the animal running. The buck or doe rarely escaped this gauntlet.

"The deer was always a coveted prize among hunters. No finer dish than venison ever graced the table of king or peasant. No more beautiful trophy has ever adorned the halls of the royal sportsman or the humble cabin of the lowly hunter on the wild frontier than the antlers of the fallen buck. The sight of this noble animal in his native state thrills with admiration alike the heart of the proudest aristocrat and the rudest backwoodsman. In the days when guns were rare and ammunition very costly, hunters set stakes for deer, where the animal had been in the habit of jumping into or out of fields. A piece of hard timber, two or three inches thick and about four feet long, was sharpened into a spear shape, and then driven firmly into the ground at the place where the deer were accustomed to leap over the log fence. The stake was slanted towards the fence, so as to strike the animal in the breast as it leaped into or out of the fields. Several of these deadly wooden spears were often set at the same crossing, so as to increase the peril of the game. If the deer were seen in the field, a scare would cause them to jump over the fence with less caution, and thus often a buck would impale himself on one of the fatal stakes, when but for the sight of the hunter the animal might have escaped unhurt. Thousands of deer were killed or crippled in this way generations ago."—*Outing.*

A deer-skin sold in those days for seventy-five to ninety cents. Of the original wild animals still remaining in our county, there are the fox, raccoon, porcupine, musk-rat, martin, otter, mink, skunk, opossum, woodchuck, rabbit, squirrel, mole, and mouse. Fifty years ago the woods were full of porcupines. On the defensive is the only way he ever fights. When the enemy approaches he rolls up into a little wad, sharp quills out, and he is not worried about how many are in the besieging party. One prick of his quills will satisfy any assailant. When he sings his blood-curdling song, it is interpreted as a sign of rain.

The wholesale price of furs in 1804 were: Otter, one dollar and a half to four dollars; bear, one to three dollars and a half; beaver, one to two dollars and a half; martin, fifty cents to one dollar and a half; red fox, one dollar to one dollar and ten cents; mink, twenty to forty cents; muskrat, twenty-five to thirty cents; raccoon, twenty to fifty cents; deer-pelts, seventy-five cents to one dollar.

The pioneer hunter carried his furs and pelts to the Pittsburg market in canoes, where he sold them to what were called Indian traders from the East. In later years traders visited the cabins of our hunters in the county, and bartered for and bought the furs and pelts from the hunters or from our merchants.

Porcupine.

Old William Vasbinder, a noted hunter and trapper in this wilderness, and pioneer in what is now Warsaw township, was quite successful in trapping wolves one season on Hunt's Run, about the year 1819 or 1820; but for some unknown reason his success suddenly stopped, and he could not catch a single wolf. He then suspected the Indians of robbing his traps. So one morning bright and early he visited his traps and found no wolf, but did find an Indian track. He followed the Indian trail and lost it. On looking around he heard a voice from above, and looking up he saw an Indian sitting in the fork of a tree, and the Indian said, "Now, you old rascal, you go home, Old Bill, or Indian shoot." With the Indian's flint-lock pointed at him, Vasbinder immediately became quite hungry and started home for an early breakfast.

Bill Long often sold to pedlers fifty deer-pelts at a single sale. He had hunting shanties in all sections and quarters of this wilderness.

In 1840 the late John Du Bois, founder of Du Bois City, desired to locate some lands near Boone's Mountain. So he took Bill Long with him, and the two took up a residence in a shanty of Long's near the head-waters of Rattlesnake Run, in what is now Snyder township. After four or five days' rusticating, the provisions gave out, and Du Bois got hungry. Long told him there was nothing to eat here and for him to leave for Bundy's. On his way from the shanty to Bundy's Mr. Du Bois killed five deer.

George Smith, a Washington township early hunter, who is still living in the wilds of Elk County, has killed in this wilderness fourteen panthers, five hundred bears, thirty elks, three thousand deer, five hundred catamounts, five hundred wolves, and six hundred wild-cats. He has killed seven deer in a day and as many as five bears in a day. All these animals were killed in what was originally Jefferson County. Mr. Smith has followed hunting as a profession for sixty years.

NATURAL LIFE OF SOME OF OUR WILD AND DOMESTIC ANIMALS.

	Years.		Years.
Elk	50	Hog	20
Beaver	50	Wolf	15
Panther	25	Cat	15
Catamount	25	Fox	15
Buffalo	20	Dog	10
Cow	20	Sheep	10
Horse	20	Squirrel	7
Bear	20	Rabbit	7
Deer	20		

BIRDS.

"If a bird's nest chance to be before thee in the way in any tree, or on the ground, whether they be young ones, or eggs, and the dam sitting upon the young, or upon the eggs, thou shalt not take the dam with the young: but thou shalt in anywise let the dam go, and take the young to thee; that it may be well with thee, and that thou mayest prolong thy days."
—*Deut.* xxii. 6, 7.

With the exception of the wild turkey and raven, which are now about extinct, we have almost the same variety of birds here that lived and sung in this wilderness when the Barnetts settled on Mill Creek. Some of these original birds are quite scarce. We have one new bird,—viz., the English sparrow.

Wild turkey.

Before enumerating our birds it might be proper to give a few sketches of some of the principal ones.

THE RAVEN.

A very handsome bird, numerous here in pioneer time, now extinct. He belonged to the crow family. He had a wonderful intellect. He could learn to talk correctly, and was a very apt scholar. He lived to an extreme old age, probably one hundred years. He was blue-black, like the common crow. He made his home in the solitude of the forest, preferring the wildest and most hilly sections. In such regions, owing to his intellect and strength, his supremacy was never questioned, unless by the eagle. In the fall of the year he would feast on the saddles of venison the hunters would hang on a tree, and the Longs adopted this method to save their meat: Take a small piece of muslin, wet it, and rub it all over with gunpowder; sharpen a stick and pin this cloth to the venison. The raven and crow would smell this powder and keep away from the venison.

THE "BALD" EAGLE OUR NATIONAL EMBLEM.

The name "Bald" which is given to this species is not applied because the head is bare, but because the feathers of the neck and head of adults are pure white. In Jefferson County, as well as throughout the United States, we had but two species of eagles, the bald and the golden. The "Black," "Gray," and "Washington" eagles are but the young of the bald eagle. Three years, it is stated, are required before this species assumes the adult plumage. The bald eagle is still found in Pennsylvania at all seasons of the year. I have seen some that measured eight feet from tip to tip of wing.

"The nest, a bulky affair, built usually on a large tree, mostly near the water, is about four or five feet in diameter. It is made up chiefly of large sticks, lined inside with grass, leaves, etc. The eggs, commonly two, rarely three, are white, and they measure about three by two and a half inches. A favorite article of food with this bird is fish, which he obtains mainly by strategy and rapine. Occasionally, however, according to different observers, the bald eagle will do his own fishing. Geese and brant form their favorite food, and the address displayed in their capture is very remarkable. The poor victim has apparently not the slightest chance for escape. The eagle's flight, ordinarily slow and somewhat heavy, becomes, in the excitement of pursuit, exceedingly swift and graceful, and the fugitive is quickly overtaken. When close upon its quarry the eagle suddenly sweeps beneath it, and turning back downward, thrusts its powerful talons up into its breast. A brant or duck is carried off bodily to the nearest marsh or sand-bar. But a Canada goose is too heavy to be thus easily disposed of; the two great birds fall together to the water beneath, while the eagle literally tows his prize along the surface until the shore is reached. In this way one has been known to drag a large goose for nearly half a mile.

"The bald eagle occasionally devours young pigs, lambs, and fawns. Domestic fowls, wild turkeys, hares, etc., are also destroyed by this species. I have knowledge of at least two of these birds which have killed poultry (tame ducks and turkeys) along the Susquehanna River. Sometimes, like the golden eagle, this species will attack raccoons and skunks. I once found two or three spines of a porcupine in the body of an immature bald eagle. The golden eagle occurs in this State as a winter visitor. The only species with which it is sometimes compared is the bald eagle in immature dress. The two birds, however, can be distinguished at a glance, if you remember that the golden eagle has the tarsus (shin) densely feathered to the toes, while, on the other hand, the bald eagle has a bare shin. The golden eagle breeds in high mountainous regions and the Arctic countries.

"Golden eagles are rather rare in this region, hence their depredations to poultry, game, and live-stock occasion comparatively little loss. Domestic fowls, ducks, and turkeys especially, are often devoured; different species of water-birds, grouse, and wild turkeys suffer chiefly among the game birds. Fawns are sometimes attacked and killed; occasionally it destroys young pigs, and frequently many lambs are carried off by this powerful bird. Rabbits are preyed upon to a considerable extent."

Of our birds, the eagle is the largest, swiftest in flight, and keenest-eyed, the humming-bird the smallest, the coot the slowest, and the owl the dullest.

The spring birds, such as the bluebird, the robin, the sparrow, and the martin, were early to come and late to leave.

I reproduce from Olive Thorne Miller's Lectures the following,—viz. :

"There are matrimonial quarrels also among birds. As a rule, the female is queen of the nest, but once I saw a male sparrow assert his power. He was awfully angry, and tried to oust his spouse from a hole in a maple-tree in which they had made their home. He did drive her out at last, and absolutely divorced her, for he was back before long with a bride whom, with some trouble and a good many antics, he coaxed to accept the nest.

"The female bird is the queen of the home, and usually selects the place for the nest, the male bird sometimes lending a beak in building it, but most of the time singing his sweet song to encourage his mate.

"That the female is queen is shown by a little story related of a sparrow. She was hatching her eggs, and was relieved now and then by her mate while she went off for exercise and food. One day the male bird was late and the female called loudly for him. He came at last, and she gave him an unmerciful drubbing, which he took without a murmur. Thoroughly ashamed of himself, he sat down meekly on the eggs.

"The robin is the most familiar of our birds. Running over the lawns, with head down, it suddenly grabs a worm, which it shakes as a cat does a mouse. Having swallowed it, the robin looks up with infinite pride. They are great insect-destroyers, though they insist on having the earliest spring peas and the first mulberries, raspberries, and grapes. The robin is the great enemy of the bird observer, giving warning of his approach to every bird in the neighboring thickets. They are brave, and will help any bird in distress. A sparrow-hawk had seized an English sparrow, one of the robin's worst enemies, but the robin attacked the hawk so viciously that it released the sparrow. In another instance a cat had captured a young robin, but was so fearlessly attacked by an older bird that she parted with her tender meal and sought shelter under the barn.

"The robins make charming but most mischievous pets. I heard of a case where a child helped bring up a brood of these birds. When they were fledged they would follow her about the yard like a flock of chickens.

"The wood-thrush or wood-robin is of a shy and retiring nature, frequenting thick woods and tangled undergrowth, and at daybreak and sundown this bird carols forth its thankfulness for a day begun and a day ended. The nest is made in some low tree, with little or no mud in its composition, and contains from four to six eggs. The veery, or tawny thrush, is a wonderful songster, but a most retiring bird.

"The American cuckoo, unlike her English cousin, builds her own nest, and is a most devoted parent. These birds, with white breast, are numerous here in the summer, and the male bird's courting is most grotesque. After each note he makes a profound bow to the mate, and then opens his mouth as wide as possible, as if about to emit a loud cry, but only the feeblest of 'coos' can be heard.

"The blue-jay, though one of our best-known birds, is greatly misunderstood. It is said he is always quarrelling and fighting, whereas really he is only full of frolic and mischief and is a most affectionate bird, and instead of tyrannizing over other birds is most kind to them. These birds have shared a room with a dozen others much smaller than themselves and were never known to molest them. They will defend their young against all comers, and James Russell Lowell tells a story of discovering three young birds who were held to their nest by a string, in which they had got entangled. He determined to cut them loose. The old birds flew at him at first, but on learning what his object was, sat quietly within reach of him, watching the operation, and when the birds were released noisily thanked him.

"A story is told of the frolicsomeness of this bird. One was seated on a fence-rail, and two kittens, having espied him, essayed to stalk him. They got up near him ; then he began playing leap-frog over those two kittens until they returned full of offended dignity to the house. The bird tried to coax them out to a game several times afterwards, but the kittens had had enough of it.

"The kingbird is said to fight and drive away every bird that comes near it, but this is a libel. He attends to his own business almost wholly, and though not particularly social, is no more belligerent in the bird world than most birds are when they have nests to protect. He is a character, and interesting to watch.

"The shrike, or butcher-bird, has imputed to him the worst character of any of our birds. He is not only accused of killing birds, but of impaling them afterwards on thorns. That he does kill birds is undoubted, but only when other food is scarce, for he much prefers field-mice, grasshoppers, and other noxious insects. That he impales his prey is certain, and the reason for this is, I think, that he has such small, delicate feet that they are not strong enough to hold down a mouse or insect while he tears it to pieces.

"Blackbirds are gregarious, forming blackbird cities in the tops of trees. He and the fishhawk have a strange friendship for one another, often three or four pairs building their nests in the straggling outskirts of the hawk's large nest, and they unite in protecting one another.

"The red-winged blackbirds are the most independent of birds, as far as the two sexes are concerned. The dull brown-streaked females come up in flocks some time after the males have arrived, and as soon as the breeding season is over they separate again, the males keeping to the marshes, while the females seek shelter in the uplands, but always near water. They nest in marshy places, and insist on plenty of water.

"The cowbird is undoubtedly the most unpopular of this class of birds, simply from the fact that no nest is built, the egg always being placed in the nest of some vireo, warbler, or sparrow, and the rearing of one of these birds means the loss of at least two song-birds, for they always smother the rightful owners. The popular idea that the foster-parents are unaware of this strange egg is doubtful. I believe it to be another instance of the great good nature of the birds to the young of any sort. The cowbirds nearly kill with overwork whatever birds they have been foisted on.

"The bobolink, who later in the year becomes the reed- or rice-bird, is a handsome bird in his plumage of black and white and buff. The female is a quieter-colored bird. While breeding they are voracious insect-eaters, but when they get down to the rice marshes it is almost impossible to drive them away. A hawk seems to be the only thing they are afraid of.

"The Baltimore oriole is one of the most beautiful and best-known birds. Its long, pendant, woven nest is known to every one, and it is wonderful how the bird, with only its beak, can build such a splendid structure. They have been known to use wire in the structure of their nests.

"The meadow-lark, one of the largest of this family, is a wonderful singer, sitting on a fence-rail, carolling forth its quivering silvery song. All these birds, except the oriole, walk while hunting for food, and do not hop as most other birds do.

"The crow does not belong to the blackbird family, but owing to his uniform I will speak about him. Much has been said against him, but the truth is that he is a most useful bird in killing mice, snakes, lizards, and frogs, and is a splendid scavenger. He has been persecuted for so many generations that perhaps he is the most knowing and wary of birds. He will always flee from a man with a gun, though paying little attention to the ordinary pedestrian. These birds are gregarious in their habits, and make their large, untidy nests at the tops of trees.

"They have regular roosting-places, and, curious to say, it is not first come first served. As each flock reaches the sleeping-grove they sit around on the ground, and it is only when the last wanderer returns that they all rise simultaneously and scramble for nests. Crows as pets are intensely funny.

"In July, when nesting is over, there are no more frolicsome birds than the highholes, or woodpeckers. They are like boys out of school, and actually seem to play games with each other, one that looks very much like 'tag' being a favorite.

Woodpeckers.

"The young of these birds never cease in their clamor for food, and even when they have left their hole-nest they are fed by the parent birds.

"The feeding process is a strange one. The old one half loses its long bill down the throat of the youngster, and from its crop gives up a sufficient supply of half-digested food for a full meal.

"The courtship of these birds is exquisitely quaint, and a correspondent has given an account of a game, or dance, in which they began with a waltz of an odd sort and went through various evolutions, ending with crossing their beaks, and standing so for a moment before they drew back and did the whole thing over.

"The downy woodpecker is particularly fond of apple-trees, and though popularly supposed to be an enemy of the orchard, is in reality one of its greatest friends. They tunnel for the worms, and it has been conclusively proved that trees drilled with their holes have long outlived in usefulness the trees unvisited by these birds.

"The clown of the family is the red-headed woodpecker, which, as well as the others shown, is a Pennsylvanian, and a most original and quaint character. He has been studied for many years in Ohio and many of his tricks described by Mr. Keyser, of that State. He lays up food for the winter, and in places where he has been accustomed to depend on the sweet beechnut for provisions he refuses to stay when the nut crop fails, but at once betakes himself to a more inviting region.

"The sapsucker, or yellow-breasted woodpecker, was shown with his mate and a young one, and his characteristics defended against the charge of sap sucking, which has been made against him. Sufficient evidence from several scientific ornithologists was produced to show that the bird is insectivorous in a great degree, and the small amount of sap he may drink is well paid for by the insects he consumes.

"The junco, or snowbird, is often found in flocks, except in the nesting season. Their favorite nesting-place is in the roots of trees that have been blown over. That birds are considerate of one another is certain. I know of a case where a family had fed a flock of juncos during a long spell of cold weather. They got so tame that they would come up to the stoop to be fed; but it was noticed that one bird always remained on the fence and the other ones fed it. On examination, it was found that the bird had an injured wing, and in case of sudden danger would not have been able to leave with the flock in the rush, so it was left in a place of safety and fed.

"The snow-bunting is to be seen in our part of the world only in blizzard times, or when there are snow-scurries around."—*Miller*.

OF HAWKS.

The red-shouldered hawk, called by farmers and hunters the hen-hawk, nests in trees in April or May. The eggs are two to four, white and blotched, with shades of brown. The nest is built of sticks, bark, etc.

The goshawk was a regular breeder in our woods and mountains. He is a fierce and powerful bird. The hawk feeds upon wild turkeys, pheasants, ducks, chickens, robins, rabbits, and squirrels. The cooper-hawk, known as the long-tailed chicken-hawk, is an audacious poultry thief, capturing full-grown chickens. This hawk also feeds upon pigeons, pheasants, turkeys, and squirrels. This bird nests about May in thick woods; the nest containing four or five eggs. In about twelve weeks the young are able to care for themselves. The sharp-shinned hawk bears a close resemblance to the cooper, but feeds by choice upon young chickens and pullets, young turkeys, young rabbits, and squirrels. If a pair of these birds should nest near a cabin where chickens were being raised, in a very few days they would steal every one.

When I was a boy large nestings of wild pigeons in what was then Jenks, Tionesta, and Ridgway townships occurred every spring. These big roosts were occupied annually early in April each year. Millions of pigeons occupied these roosts, and they were usually four or five miles long and one or two miles wide. In this territory every tree would be occupied, some with fifty nests. These pigeons swept over Brookville on their migration to these roosts, and would be for days passing, making the day dark at times. The croakings of the pigeons in these roosts could be heard for miles.

Wild pigeon.

The coopers and the bloody goshawk, the great-horned and barred owls, like other night wanderers, such as the wild bear, panther, wolf, wild cat, lynx, fox, the mink, and agile weasel, all haunted these roosts and feasted upon these pigeons. The weasel would climb the tree for the pigeons' eggs and the young, or to capture the old birds when at rest. The fox, lynx, and mink depended on catching the squabs that fell from the nests.

Like the buffaloes of this region, the wild pigeon is doomed. These once common birds are only to be seen occasionally. Isolated and scattered pairs still find a breeding-place in our wilds, but the immense breeding colonies that once visited our county will never be seen again. The extermination of the passenger pigeon has gone on so rapidly that in another decade the birds may become a rarity. The only thing that will save the birds from this fate is the fact that they no longer resort to the more thickly populated States as breeding-places, but fly far into the woods along our northern border. Thirty years ago wild pigeons were found in New York State, and in Elk, Forest, Warren, McKean, Pike, and Cameron Counties, Pennsylvania, but now they only figure as migrants, with a few pair breeding in the beech-woods.

To give an idea of the immensity of these pigeon-roosts, I quote from the *Elk Advocate* as late as May, 1851:

"The American Express Company carried in one day, over the New York and Erie Railroad, over seven tons of pigeons to the New York market, and all of these were from the west of Corning. This company alone have carried over this road from the counties of Chemung, Steuben, and Allegheny fifty-six tons of pigeons."

The wild pigeon lays usually one or two eggs, and both birds do their share of the incubating. The females occupy the nest from 2 P.M. until the next morning, and the males from 9 or 10 A.M. until 2 P.M. The males usually feed twice each day, while the females feed only during the forenoon. The old pigeons never feed near the nesting-places, always allowing the beechmast, buds, etc., there for use in feeding their young when they come forth. The birds go many miles to feed,—often a hundred or more.

Our birds migrate every fall to Tennessee, the Carolinas, and as far south as Florida. Want of winter food is and was the cause of that migration, for those that remained surely picked up a poor living. Migrating birds return year after year to the same locality. In migrating northward in the spring, the males usually precede the females several days, but on leaving their summer scenes of love and joy for the south, the sexes act in unison.

Of the other pioneer birds, there was the orchard-oriole, pine-grosbeak, rose-breasted grosbeak, swallow, barn-swallow, ruff-winged swallow, bank swallow, black and white warbler, chesnut-sided warbler, barn-owl, American long-eared owl, short-eared owl, screech-owl, great-horned owl, yellow-billed cuckoo, black-billed cuckoo, kingbird, crested flycatcher, phœbe-bird, wood-pewee, least flycatcher, ruffed grouse (pheasant, or partridge), quail, also known as the bob-white, marsh-hawk, sparrow-hawk, pigeon-hawk, fish-hawk, red-tailed hawk, American ruff-legged hawk, horned grebe, loon, hooded merganser, wood-duck, buff-headed duck, red-headed duck, American bittern, least bittern, blue heron, green heron, black-crowned night-heron, Virginia rail, Carolina rail, American coot, American woodcock, Wilson's snipe, least sandpiper, killdeer

Grouse, or pheasant.

plover, belted kingfisher, turtle-dove, turkey-buzzard, whippoorwill, nighthawk, ruby-throated humming-bird, blue-jay, bobolink, or reed-bird, or rice-bird, purple grackle, cowbird (cow-bunting), red-winged blackbird, American grosbeak, red-poll, American goldfinch, or yellow-bird, towhee-bunting, cardinal- or redbird, indigo bunting, scarlet tanager, cedar- or cherry-bird, butcher-bird, or great northern scarlet tanager, red-eyed vireo, American redstart, cootbird, brown thrush, bluebird, house-wren, wood-wren, white-breasted nuthatch, chickadee, golden-crowned knight.

Humming-birds.

NATURAL LIFE OF SOME OF OUR BIRDS.

	Years.		Years.
Raven	100	Pheasant	15
Eagle	100	Partridge	15
Crow	100	Blackbird	10
Goose	50	Common fowl	10
Sparrowhawk	40	Robin	10
Crane	24	Thrush	10
Peacock	24	Wren	5
Lark	16		

WILD BEES—BEE-HUNTING, BEE-TREES, BEE-FOOD, ETC.

In pioneer times these woods were alive with bee-trees, and even yet that condition prevails in the forest part of this region, as the following article on bees, from the pen of E. C. Niver, clearly describes:

"Although the natural range of bee-pasturage in this section is practically unlimited, singular to relate, apiculture is not pursued to any great extent. With all the apparently favorable conditions, the occupation is too uncertain and precarious to hazard much capital or time on it. At the best, apiculture is an arduous occupation, and in the most thickly populated farming communities it requires constant vigilance to keep track of runaway swarms. But in this rugged mountain country, with its thousands of acres of hemlock slashings and hard-wood ridges, it is virtually impossible to keep an extensive apiary within bounds. The rich pasturage of the forests and mountain barrens affords too great a temptation, and although the honey-bee has been the purveyor of sweets for the ancients as far back as history reaches, she has never yet become thoroughly domesticated. At swarming time the nomadic instinct asserts itself. Nature lures and beckons, and the first opportunity is embraced to regain her fastness and subsist upon her bounty. Never a season goes by but what some swarms escape to the woods. These take up their habitation in hollow trees or some other favorable retreat, and in time throw off other swarms. Thus it is that our mountains and forests contain an untold wealth of sweetness, but little of which is ever utilized by man.

"Here is the opportunity of the bee-hunter. In the backwoods counties of Western Pennsylvania bee-hunting is as popular a sport with some as deer-hunting or trout-fishing. It does not have nearly so many devotees, perhaps, as these latter sports, for the reason that a greater degree of woodcraft, skill, and patience is required to become a proficient bee-hunter. Any backwoodsman can search out and stand guard at a deer runway, watch a lick, or follow a trail; and his skill with a rifle, in the use of which he is familiar from his early boyhood, insures him an equal chance in the pursuit of game. It does not require any nice display of woodcraft to tramp over the mountains to the head of the trout stream, with a tin spice-box full of worms, cut an ash sapling, equip it with the hook and line, and fish the stream down to its mouth. But to search out a small insect as it sips the nectar from the blossoms, trace it to its home, and successfully despoil it of its hoarded stores, requires a degree of skill and patience that comparatively few care to attain. Yet in every community of this section are some old fellows who do not consider

Straw bee scap.

life complete without a crockful of strained honey in the cellar when winter sets in. Then, as they sit with their legs under the kitchen-table while their wives bake smoking-hot buckwheat cakes, the pungent flavor of decayed wood which the honey imparts to their palates brings back the glory of the chase. Whenever a man takes to bee-hunting he is an enthusiastic devotee, and with him all other sport is relegated to the background.

"There are many methods employed in hunting the wild honey-bee. The first essential is a knowledge of bees and their habits. This can only be acquired by experience and intelligent observation. The man who can successfully 'line' bees can also successfully 'keep' them in a domestic state, but a successful apiarist is not necessarily a good bee-hunter.

"September and October are the best months for securing wild honey, as the bees have then in the main completed their stores. At that season they can also be most readily lined, for the scarcity of sweets makes them more susceptible to artificial bait. But the professional bee-hunter does not, as a rule, wait until fall to do all his lining. He wants to know what is in prospect, and by the time the honey-bee suspends operations for the winter the hunter has perhaps a dozen bee-trees located which he has been watching all summer in order to judge as near as possible as to the amount of stored honey they contain. If the hunter wants to save the bees he cuts the tree in June and hives the inmates in the same manner as when they swarm in a domestic state. Many swarms are thus obtained, and the hunter scorns to expend any money for a swarm of bees which he can get for the taking. As a matter of course, when the honey is taken in the fall the bees, being despoiled of their subsistence, inevitably perish.

"'I'll gather the honey-comb bright as gold,
And chase the elk to his secret fold.'

"The first warm days of April, when the snows have melted from the south side of the hills, and the spring runs are clear of ice, find the bee-hunter on the alert. There is nothing yet for the bees to feed upon, but a few of the advance-guard are emerging from their long winter's hibernations in search of pollen and water, and they instinctively seek the water's edge where the warm rays of the sun beat down. Where the stream has receded from the bank, leaving a miniature muddy beach, there the bees congregate, dabbling in the mud, sipping water and carrying it away. The first material sought for by the bees is pollen, and the earliest pasturage for securing this is the pussy-willow and skunk-cabbage, which grow in the swamps. After these comes the soft maple, which also affords a large supply of pollen. Sugar-maple is among the first wild growth which furnishes any honey. Then comes the wild cherry, the locust, and the red raspberries and blackberries. Of course, the first blossoms and the cultivated plants play an important part, but the profusion of wild flowers which are honey-bearing would probably supply as much honey to the acre as the cultivated sections.

"The wild honeysuckle, which covers thousands of acres of the mountain ranges with a scarlet flame in May, is a particular favorite with bees, as is also the tulip-tree, which is quite abundant in this section. Basswood honey has a national reputation, and before the paper-wood cutters despoiled the ridges and forests the basswood-tree furnished an almost unlimited feeding-ground. This tree blooms for a period of two or three weeks, and a single swarm has been known to collect ten pounds of honey in a day when this flower was in blossom. Devil's-club furnishes another strong feed for bees, as well as the despised sumach. Last, but not least, is the golden-rod, which in this latitude lasts from August until killed by the autumn frosts. While these are the chief wild-honey producing trees and plants, they are but a fractional part of the honey resources of the country.

"Having discovered the feeding-ground and haunts of the wild honey-bee, the hunter proceeds to capture a bee and trace it to its habitation. This is done by 'lining,'—that is, following the bee's flight to its home. The bee always flies in a direct line to its place of abode, and this wonderful instinct gives rise to the expression, 'a bee-line.'

"To assist in the chase the hunter provides himself with a 'bee-box,' which is any small box possessing a lid, with some honey inside for bait. Arrived at any favorable feeding-ground, the hunter eagerly scans the blossoms until he finds a bee at work. This he scoops into his box and closes the lid. If he can capture two or more bees at once, so much the better. After buzzing angrily for a few moments in the darkened box the bee scents the honey inside and immediately quiets down and begins to work. Then the box is set down and the lid opened. When the bee gets all the honey she can carry she mounts upward with a rapid spiral motion until she gets her bearings, and then she is off like a shot in a direct line to her habitation. Presently she is back again, and this time when she departs her bearings are located and she goes direct. After several trips more bees appear, and when they get to working the bait and the line of their flight is noted, the box is closed when the bees are inside and moved forward along the direction in which they have been coming and going. The hunter carefully marks his trail and opens the box again. The bees are apparently unconscious that they have been moved, and work as before. This manœuvre is repeated until the spot where the swarm is located is near at hand, and then comes the most trying part of the quest to discover the exact location of the hive. Sometimes it is in the hollow of a dead tree away to the top; sometimes it is near the bottom. Again, it may be in a hollow branch of a living tree of gigantic proportions, closely hidden in the foliage, or it may be in an old stump or log. To search it out requires the exercise of much patience, as well as a quick eye and an acute ear.

"To determine the distance of the improvised hive after a line has been established from the bee-box the hunter resorts to 'cross-lining.' This is done by moving the box when the bees are at work in it some distance to one side. The bees as usual fly direct to their home, the second line of flight converging with the first, forming the apex of a triangle, the distance between the first and second locations of the box being the base and the two lines of flight the sides. Where the lines meet the habitation is to be found.

"Different kinds of bait are frequently used in order to induce the bees to work the box. In the flowering season a little anise or other pungent oil is rubbed on the box to attract the bees and keep them from being turned aside by the wealth of blossoms along their flight. It is a mistake to mix the oil with the bait, as it spoils the honey the bees make and poisons the whole swarm. Sometimes in the early spring corn-cobs soaked in stagnant brine proves an attractive bait, while late in the fall beeswax burned on a heated stone will bring the belated straggler to the bee-box.

"Cutting a bee-tree is the adventuresome part of the sport. An angry swarm is a formidable enemy. Then, too, the treasure for which the hunter is in search is about to be revealed, and the possibilities bring a thrill of anticipation and excitement. So far as the danger goes the experienced hunter is prepared for that, and protects his head and face by a bag of mosquito-netting drawn over a broad-brimmed hat. With gloves on his hands he is tolerably protected, but sometimes a heavy swarm breaks through the netting, and instances are on record where bee-hunters have been so severely stung in despoiling wild swarms as to endanger their lives. In felling a tree great care must be exercised in order that the tree may not break up and destroy the honey. Sometimes trees are felled after night, as bees do not swarm about in the darkness, and the danger of getting stung is not so great.

"The amount of honey secured depends upon the age of the swarm. Frequently much time and labor have been expended in lining and cutting a tree which yielded nothing, while again the returns have been large. There are instances in this community where a single tree yielded over two hundred pounds of good honey. Not long since a hunter cut a tree in which a hollow space about eighteen inches in diameter was filled with fine honey for a length of fifteen feet. Often a tree is cut which has been worked so long that part of the honey is spoiled with age. Often the comb is broken and the honey mingled with the decayed wood of the tree. The bee-hunter, however, carefully gathers up the honey, wood and all, in a tin pail, and strains it, and the pungent flavor of the wood does not in the least detract from the quality in his estimation.

"Bee-hunting as a sport could be pursued in nearly every section of Western Pennsylvania, particularly in the lumbering and tannery districts. In these sections thousands of acres are annually stripped of timber, extending many miles back from the settled districts. Fire runs through these old slashings every year or so, and a dense growth of blackberry and raspberry briers spring up. These, with the innumerable varieties of wild flowers, afford a rich and vast pasturage for the honey-bee which has thrown off the restraints of civilization. Swarm upon swarm is propagated, the surplus product of which is never utilized. With a little encouragement bee-hunting might become as popular a form of sport with the dweller of the town as with the skilled woodsman."

CHAPTER VII.

RUNWAYS, PATHS, TRAILS, DEER RUNS AND CROSSINGS, INDIAN TRAILS—THE WHITE MAN'S PATH—DAVID AND JOHN MEADE—MEADE'S PACK-HORSE TRAIL—PIONEER SETTLEMENT IN THE NORTHWEST—WHITE BOYS CAPTURED AND REARED BY INDIANS—PIONEER EXPLORERS AND SETTLERS.

PREVIOUS to the white man's advent here this wilderness had public highways, but they were for the wild deer and savage Indians. These thoroughfares were called "deer paths" and "Indian trails." These paths were usually well beaten and crossed each other as civilized roads now do. The first trail discovered and traversed by the white man was the Indian Chinklacamoose path, which extended from what is now Clearfield town to what is now Kittanning. This Indian trail passed through what is now Punxsutawney, and over this path and through this Indian town Allegheny Indians carried their white prisoners from the eastern part of the State to what was then called Kittany, on the Allegheny River. From a most careful and thorough search to ascertain when the first path or trail of the white man was made through or in what is now our county, I find it to be in the year 1787. In this year of grace two hardy and courageous men, David and John Meade, were living in what is now Sunbury, Pennsylvania, where John was keeping an inn or tavern. These two brothers having read General George Washington's report to Governor Dinwiddie, of Virginia, of the rich lands and valleys that were unoccupied in what is now called Venango and Crawford Counties, Pennsylvania, determined to explore that region for themselves. To reach this uninhabited section they were compelled to open a path from east to west, through what is now called Jefferson County, then Northumberland County, and which path is now called in history "Meade's Trail." This trail passed through what are now West Reynoldsville, Port Barnett, and Brookville.

Fired with the zeal and energy of youth, David and John Meade blazed their way through this wilderness, over or through streams and across hills until they reached a broad valley upon whose bosom now reposes the city of Meadville. Being pleased with the valleys and hills, these two brothers returned to Sunbury over their trail in the spring of 1788, only to invite and bring with them in the same year, over the same trail, to the rich valleys they had found, the following-named friends and neighbors:

Thomas Martin, John Watson, James F. Randolph, Thomas Grant, Cornelius Van Horn, and Christopher Snyder.

These men, with their goods packed on four horses, passed through where Brookville now is in 1788, and settled in and around what is now Meadville, then Allegheny County. Meade's trail commenced at the mouth of Anderson's Creek, near Curwinsville, Clearfield County, Pennsylvania, and over this trail until 1802 all transportation had to be carried into or through this wilderness on pack-saddles by pack-horses. A pack-horse load was from two to three hundred pounds. In 1802–3 the first wagon-road, or the old Milesburg and Waterford State Road, was opened for travel. The Meade settlers in Crawford County in 1788 comprised the pioneer permanent settlement in Northwestern Pennsylvania.

Soon after David Meade and his neighbors reached their new home the great chief of the Six Nations, accompanied by a number of his tribe, made these pioneers a social visit. This chief was Cornplanter, and he was then chief over our Indians who belonged to this confederation. In one of these friendly visits Meade discovered that five white men who had been captured when boys were reared by the Indians and were then living under Cornplanter; that these boys had all attained manhood and three of them had married Indian women. The five white men were Lashley Malone, of Bald Eagle Valley, Pennsylvania, Peter Krause, of Monongahela, Elijah Matthews, of Ohio, Nicholas Rosencrants and Nicholas Tanewood, of Mohawk Valley, New York State.

In 1789, Darius Meade, father of David and John, Robert F. Randolph, and Frederick Baum passed over this "trail" on their way to what is now Meadville. Many of the pioneers who travelled over this trail to the northwest were captured and murdered by the Indians in the raids of 1791–92 and 1793. In 1791, Darius Meade was captured by two Indians while ploughing in a field. His captors were Captain Bull, a Delaware chief, and Conewyando, a Seneca chief. Meade in an effort to escape got possession of Bull's knife and killed Bull with it, and after a fierce struggle with Conewyando was killed, but Conewyando died in a few days from the wounds Meade gave him. Two of our soldiers buried Meade and Bull side by side where they fell.

"Indian trails were 'bee lines,' over hill and dale, from point to point. Here and there were open spots on the summits, where runners signalled their coming by fires when on urgent business, and were promptly met at stated places by fresh men."

Of the pioneer settlers who came over this trail and settled in what is now Jefferson and Clarion Counties, Judge Peter Clover, of Clarion County, in 1877, wrote as follows:

"As stated in the outset, I will give a brief account of the pioneer settlement of Jefferson County. In 1800, Joseph Barnett and Samuel Scott settled forty miles west of Curwinsville, Clearfield County. They were men of great energy and industry, and soon made valuable improvements. They built a saw-mill, which was a great help to the people, providing them with boards, etc. They settled among the Indians of the Seneca tribe, who were, however, civil. Joseph Barnett was a very eccentric, high-minded man, and took a leading part in all the business transactions of the day ; a man long to be remembered by those who knew him. Shortly after their mill was made, perhaps as early as 1802, Henry Fir, a German, and a number of other families settled on the west of Mill Creek,—Jacob Mason, L. Long, John Dickson, Freedom Stiles, and a very large negro by the name of Fudge Vancamp, whose wool was as white as the wool of a sheep and whose face was as black as charcoal, and yet he was married to a white woman (?).

"In about 1802, John Scott came to the county and settled on the farm where Corsica now stands, and about 1805, Peter Jones, John Roll, Sr., the Vasbinder families, and Elijah Graham, and, in 1806, John Matson and some others, settled near where Brookville now stands. In the southern part of the county, near Mahoning, John Bell settled at an early day. He was a man of iron will and great perseverance, afraid of neither man nor beast, and was a mighty hunter. Moses Knapp was also an early settler. 'Port Barnett,' as the settlement of Barnett and Scott was called, was the only stopping-place from Curwinsville for all those who came in 1801–2 through or for the wilderness over the 'trail.' We imagine that these buildings would have a very welcome look to those footsore and weary travellers,—an oasis in the desert, as it were.

"In the year 1801, with a courage nothing could daunt, ten men left their old homes and all the comforts of the more thickly settled and older portions of the eastern part of the State for the unsettled wilderness of the more western part, leaving behind them the many associations which render the old home so dear, and going forth, strong in might and firm in the faith of the God of their fathers, to plant homes and erect new altars, around which to rear their young families. Brave hearts beat in the bosoms of those men and women who made so many and great sacrifices in order to develop the resources of a portion of country almost unknown at that time. When we look abroad to-day and see what rapid strides have been made in the march of civilization, we say all honor to our forefathers who did so great a part of the work. It would be difficult for those of the present day to imagine how families could move upon horseback through an almost unbroken wilderness, with no road save an 'Indian trail,' the women and children mounted upon horses, the cooking utensils, farming implements, such as hoes, axes, ploughs, and shovels, together with bedding and provision, placed on what were called pack-saddles, while following upon foot were the men with guns upon their shoulders, ready to take down any small game that might cross their path, which would go towards making up their next meal. After a long and toilsome journey these pioneers halted on their course in what was then called Armstrong County (now Clarion County), and they immediately began the clearing of their lands, which they had purchased from General James Potter, of the far-famed 'Potter Fort,' in Penn's Valley, in Centre County, familiar to every one who has ever read of the terrible depredations committed by the Indians in that part of the country at an early period of its history.

"The names of the men were as follows: William Young, Sr., Philip Clover, Sr., John Love, James Potter, John Roll, Sr., James McFadden,

Bear.

John C. Corbett, Samuel Wilson, Sr., William Smith, and Philip Clover, Jr. Samuel Wilson returned to Centre County to spend the winter, but death removed him. In the following spring of 1802 his widow and her five sons returned,—namely, Robert, John, William, Samuel, and David. Those who did not take their families along in 1801, built their cabins, cleared some land, put in some wheat, raised potatoes and turnips, put them in their cabins and covered them with earth for safe-keeping for the next summer's use, and when they got all their work done, in the fall they returned to their families in Centre and Mifflin Counties, in the spring of 1802. Those, with some others, who also came at an early date, James Laughlin and Frederick Miles, built a saw-mill in 1804, at or near the mouth of Pine Creek, and they were the first to run timber to Pittsburg from what is now Clarion County.

"The food and raiment of the first settlers made a near approach to that of John the Baptist in the wilderness. Instead of locusts they had wild turkey, deer, and bear meat, and their raiment consisted of homespun woollen, linen, or tow cloth, the wool and flax being all prepared for weaving by hand, there being no carding-machines in the county for many years after its first settlement; then women carded by hand. When woollen cloth was wanted for men's wear, the process of fulling was as follows: The required quantity of flannel was laid upon the bare floor, and a quantity of soap and water thrown over it; then a number of men seated upon stools would take hold of a rope tied in a circle and begin to kick the flannel with their bare feet. When it was supposed to be fulled sufficiently, the men were released from their task, which was a tiresome one, yet a mirth provoking one, too, for, if it were possible, one or so must come from his seat, to be landed in the midst of the heap of flannel and soapsuds, much to the merriment of the more fortunate ones. Flax was prepared by drying over a fire, then breaking, scutching, and hackling before being ready to spin. The linen and tow cloth supplied the place of muslin and calico of the present day. That which was for dress goods was made striped, either by color or blue through the white, which was considered a nice summer suit, when made into what was called a short gown and petticoat, which matched very well with the calfskin slippers of that day. The nearest store was at Kittanning, thirty-five miles distant, and calico was fifty cents per yard, and the road but a pathway through the woods.

"In those days men appeared at church in linen shirts with collars four inches wide turned down over the shoulders, linen vest; no coat in summer. Some wore cowhide shoes, others moccasins of buckskin, others again with their feet bare. In winter, men wore deerskin pantaloons and a long loose robe called a hunting-shirt, bound round the body with a leathern girdle, and some a flannel warmus, which was a short kind of a coat, the women wearing flannel almost exclusively in the winter.

"During the first two years after the first settlement the people had to pack their flour upon horseback from Centre, Westmoreland, and Indiana Counties; also their iron and salt, which was at ten dollars per barrel; iron fifteen cents per pound. Coffee and tea were but little used, tea being four dollars per pound, coffee seventy-five cents. Those articles were considered great luxuries, both from the high price at which they came, and the difficulties attending their transportation through the woods, following the Indian trail. As to vegetables and animal food, there was no scarcity, as every one had gardens and the forest abounded with wild game, and then there were some expert huntsmen that kept the settlement supplied with meat. Those who were not a sure shot themselves would go and work for the hunter while he would go out and supply his less fortunate neighbor. Many, however, got along badly, some having nothing but potatoes and salt for substantials. I knew one hunter who killed one hundred and fifty deer and twenty bears in the first two years of the settlement, besides any amount of small game. When people began to need barns and larger houses, one would start out and invite the whole country for miles around, often going ten or twelve miles, and then it often took two or three days to raise a log barn, using horses to help to get up the logs."

THE PIONEER EXPLORERS, ANDREW BARNETT AND SAMUEL SCOTT—THE PIONEER SETTLERS, JOSEPH HUTCHISON AND WIFE—THE PATRIARCH OF THE COUNTY, JOSEPH BARNETT—OTHER EARLY SETTLERS.

In regard to the first settlement and early history of the county I have made diligent research, and find, what is not unusual, some conflicting accounts and statements. These I have endeavored to compile, arrange, and harmonize to the best of my ability.

From the best information I am enabled to gather and obtain, Andrew Barnett and Samuel Scott were sent in 1795 by Joseph Barnett, who was then living in either Northumberland, Lycoming, or Dauphin County, Pennsylvania, to explore the famous region then about French Creek, now Crawford County, Pennsylvania. But when these two "explorers" reached Mill Creek, now Port Barnett, they were forcibly impressed with the great natural advantages of the place for a saw-mill. They stopped over two or three days to examine the creek. They explored as far down as to where Summerville now is, and, after this careful inspection, concluded that this spot, where "the lofty pine leaned gloomily over every hill-side," was just the ideal home for a lumberman.

They went no farther west, but returned east, and informed Joseph Barnett of the "Eureka" they had found. In the spring of 1797, Joseph and Andrew Barnett, Samuel Scott, and Moses Knapp came from their home at the mouth of Pine Creek, then in Lycoming County, to the ideal mill-site of Andrew, and so well pleased were they all that they commenced the erection of the pioneer cabin and mill in the wilderness, in what was then Pine Creek township, Lycoming County. The cabin and mill were on the present site of Humphrey's mill and grounds at Port Barnett. The Indians assisted, about nine in number, to raise these buildings, and not a stroke of work would these savages do until they had eaten up all the provisions Mr. Barnett had. This took three days. Then the rascals exclaimed, "Me eat, me sleep; now me strong, now me work." In the fall of the same year Joseph Barnett returned to his family, leaving his brother Andrew and Scott to finish some work. In a short time thereafter Andrew Barnett became ill and died, and was buried on the north bank of the creek, at the junction of Sandy Lick and Mill Creek, Scott and two Indians being the only attendants at the funeral. Joseph Barnett was, therefore, soon followed by Scott, who was his brother-in-law, bringing the melancholy tidings of this event, which for a time cast a gloom over the future prospects of these sturdy pioneers.

In 1798, however, Joseph Barnett, Scott, Knapp, and a married man by the name of Joseph Hutchison, came out with them and renewed their work. Hutchison brought his wife, household goods, also two cows and a calf, and commenced housekeeping, and lived here two years before Joseph Barnett brought his family, who were then living in Dauphin County. Hutchison is clearly the pioneer settler in what is now Jefferson County. He was a sawyer. In that year the mill was finished by Knapp and Scott, and in 1799 there was some lumber sawed. In the fall of 1800, Joseph Barnett brought his wife and family to the home prepared for them in the wilderness. Barnett brought with him two cows and seven horses, five loaded with goods as pack-horses and two as riding or family horses. His route of travel into this wilderness was over Meade's trail.

The first boards were run in 1801 to what is now Pittsburg. About four thousand feet were put in a raft, or what would be a two-platform piece. Moses Knapp was the pioneer pilot.

In a paper contributed to the *Jefferson County Graphic* by Mrs. Sarah Graham, a daughter of Joseph Barnett, this portion of the county is there described as "the home of the Indian, the panther, the bear, and deer; and wolves were as plenty as dogs in Brookville."

Farther on this interesting account continues: "The first white child born in the county was J. P. Barnett. The next person that came here was Peter Jones. He settled on the farm now owned by John McCullough, and the next was a Mr. Roll, who settled on the farm now owned by John S. Barr. Then came Fudge Vancamp (negro), who built his cabin on the farm now owned by John Clark; and then Adam Vasbinder, who settled on the farm at the present time owned by Samuel Bullers. William Vasbinder pitched his tent on the Kirkman homestead. Ludwick Long put up his wigwam on the place now owned by Mr. McConnell. Here Long erected a distillery, and the great dragon first opened his mouth and cast out his flood of water in the wilderness. John Dixon came next. He was our first school-master. The school-house was built on the McConnell farm; built of round logs, and oiled paper for glass. Everything had to be carried from the settlements on horseback; glass was too easily broken to try to bring so far. The second school-house was built on the south side of the pike, at the forks of the Ridgway road.

Here the first graveyard was laid out, and the first person buried in it was a child of Samuel Scott.

"An old Muncy Indian, called Captain Hunt, was a frequent visitor at Port Barnett, and had his camp for several years on the Red Bank, within the limits of the southwestern part of what is now the town of Brookville. It is related of him that a cave near what is now the confluence of Sandy Lick and North Fork was occupied by him for several years as a hiding-place. He was a fugitive from his tribe for having killed a fellow Indian, and was frequently pursued by members of his race to avenge the crime. On these occasions he always managed to escape to his cave, approaching it by running in the water of the stream to avoid being followed by his track, and in this way he safely secreted himself and successfully evaded his pursuers.

"In this same connection, a story is told of the capture of a child in Westmoreland County by the Muncy Indians, who carried him to their tribe and adopted him. By the law of this tribe, when one of their number was a fugitive from them for killing another, he was not permitted to return until the place of the murdered Indian was supplied by the capture of another male from the whites or some other tribe. It is, therefore, alleged and generally supposed that the little boy from Westmoreland County, who had been sent by his mother on an errand to his father in the field, was observed by these Indians, seized and carried off to their camp, and that after this old Captain Hunt was at liberty to return to his tribe. It is also related of the boy, that when he grew to be a man he was permitted to visit his parents and friends, but declined to remain among them, and returned to his Indian home.

"Old Captain Hunt was a noted and successful hunter, obtaining his living in this way, and John Jones was often his companion on hunting excursions. One year he is said to have killed seventy-eight bears, and having the Indian appetite for whiskey, the skins of these were nearly all expended by him in procuring this beverage.

"These dense forests were the abode of wild animals and game in greater numbers than most any other part of the country. Panthers, bears, and wolves roamed the woods undisturbed, the deer travelled about in droves, and flocks of wild turkeys were numerous."

I may not be able to give the names of all the early settlers and the date of their arrival, but John, William, and Jacob Vasbinder reached here about the year 1802 or 1803, John Matson, Sr., about 1806, and the Lucases soon after.

In 1803 the name Keystone was first applied to the State. This was in a printed political address to the people. Pennsylvania was the central State of the original thirteen.

John and Archibald Bell settled in the southern part of the county about 1809 or 1810, and that locality was then an unbroken wilderness for miles around. Archie Hadden came and settled a mile southeast of him about 1812, and in 1815 Hugh McKee settled half a mile east of Perrysville. Jacob Hoover came in 1814 and settled at the present site of Clayville. John Postlethwait, Sr., came in 1818 from Westmoreland County, and located with his family a mile and a half northwest of Perrysville. A family by the name of Young settled about two miles west of this place about the same time. People began to settle in the vicinity of Punxsutawney about the year 1816, the first being Abram Weaver, and

Deer and fawn.

Rev. David Barclay, Dr. John W. Jenks, and Nathaniel Tindle, with their families, and Elijah Heath arrived there about 1817 or 1818. Charles C. Gaskill, Isaac P. Carmalt, John B. Henderson and John Hess came some time later. About 1818, David, John, and Henry Milliron settled on Little Sandy, and Henry Nolf located on the same stream, where Langville now stands, and erected a saw-mill. In 1820, Lawrence Nolf came to Pine Run, two miles south of Ringgold, but made no improvement, and afterwards sold to John Miller, who opened up a farm. Hon. James Winslow and others were also among the first settlers in the neighborhood of Punxsutawney. James McClelland and Michael Lantz came into the southwestern part of the county, within the limits of what is now Porter township, previous to the year 1820. William Stewart and Benjamin McBride made a settlement in the Round Bottom, west of Whitesville, in 1821, and in the same year James Stewart came and located three miles northwest of Perrysville. The year 1822 brought a number of families to the county, among whom were the following : David Postlethwait, who purchased Stewart and McBride's right of settlement in the Round Bottom, and settled with his brother John on Pine Run, who had preceded him there; John McHenry, James Bell, and some others, who moved into the Round Bottom, near Whitesville, and a Mr. Baker, who settled across the creek east of Whitesville ; Jesse Armstrong and Adam Long, the former locating near where Clayville now is, and the latter at a place near Punxsutawney ; John Fuller, who settled near Reynoldsville ; and Samuel Newcome, who settled on Pine Run, about a mile above the Postlethwaits. In 1823, John McIntosh and Henry Keys settled in Beech Woods, now Washington township, and the year 1824 brought Alexander Osborn. John McGee, Matthew and William McDonald, Andrew Smith, John Wilson, William Cooper, and William McCullough were also among the first settlers in the northeastern part of the county. Other names of early settlers will be found in that part of this history devoted to the different towns and townships.

CHAPTER VIII.

PROVISION FOR OPENING A ROAD—REPORT OF THE COMMISSIONERS TO THE GOVERNOR—STREAMS, ETC.

"AN ACT TO PROVIDE FOR OPENING A ROAD FROM NEAR THE BALD EAGLE'S NEST, IN MIFFLIN COUNTY, TO LE BŒUF, IN THE COUNTY OF ALLEGHENY.

"WHEREAS, A road has, under the direction of the Legislature, been in part laid out from Reading and Presque Isle ; AND WHEREAS, It is considered that opening and improving said road would be greatly conducive to the interests of the community by opening a communication with the northwest part of the State, and would much facilitate an intercourse with Lake Erie ;

"SECTION 1. *Therefore be it enacted by the Senate and House of Representatives of the Commonwealth of Pennsylvania in General Assembly met, and it is hereby enacted by the authority of the same,* That the governor be empowered to contract for the opening and improving of the road between the Bald Eagle's Nest and the Allegheny River to Le Bœuf.

"SECTION 2. *And be it further enacted by the authority aforesaid,* That when it shall appear to the persons who may contract for the opening of

Pioneer transportation, travel, and team.

said road that deviations from such parts of the road as laid out are essentially necessary, he or they shall be authorized to make such deviations, provided that such deviations do not depart materially from the survey already made.

"SECTION 3. *And be it further enacted by the authority aforesaid*, That in order to carry this into effect the governor is empowered to draw his warrant on the State Treasurer for five thousand dollars, to be paid out of the sale of reserved lands and lots in the towns of Erie, Franklin, Warren, and Waterford."

Passed April 10, 1799. Recorded in Law Book No. 6, p. 443.

The Bald Eagle's Nest referred to above was Milesburg. The nest was not that of a bird, but that of an Indian warrior of that name, who built his wigwam there between two large white oaks. The western terminus of the road, then called Le Bœuf, is now known as Waterford, Erie County, Pennsylvania. On the completion of the turnpike most of this road was abandoned in this county. It is still in use from Brookville, about seven or eight miles of it, to the Olean road north of Corsica. It passed through where Brookville now is, near or on what is now Coal Alley. It was a great thoroughfare for the pioneers going to the West and Northwest.

"DEPARTMENT OF INTERNAL AFFAIRS,
"HARRISBURG, PA., May 18, 1895."

"MR W. J. MCKNIGHT, Brookville, Pa.

"DEAR SIR,—In answer to your letter of the 1st instant, we send you this contract and the accompanying papers, which are among the records of the department. As requested, we send you a copy of the report of the commissioners who made the survey of the road.

"Very truly yours,
"ISAAC B. BROWN,
"*Deputy Secretary.*"

REPORT OF THE COMMISSIONERS TO THE GOVERNOR.

"WHEREAS, In and by an Act of the General Assembly entitled 'An Act for laying out and opening sundry Roads within this Commonwealth and for other purposes,' it is among other things provided and declared, that your Excellency shall be empowered and required to appoint three persons as Commissioners, 'to view the ground and estimate the expense of opening and making a good Waggon Road from the Bald Eagle's Nest, or the end of Nittany Mountain, to the Town of Erie at Presqueisle, and to cause the said Road to be Surveyed and staked out, by the most practicable Route, and also cause a draft of the survey to be made out in Profile, and to report to the Legislature the several parts of the expense that will be incurred in each County through which the said Road will pass: *Provided*, That the Commissioners thus appointed shall not stake out any part of the said Road when it may be carried on Roads heretofore laid out and opened, agreeably to the Provisions of former laws of this State.'

"AND WHEREAS, In pursuance of the power and authority given and granted in and by the said recited Act of Assembly, William Irvine, Andrew Ellicott, and George Wilson, Esquires, were by Letters Patent under your Excellency's hand, and the great Seal of the State, bearing date the thirteenth day of April, in the year of our Lord one thousand seven hundred and ninety-six, appointed Commissioners for the purposes aforesaid; but the said Andrew Ellicott, Esq., hath since resigned the said appointment, and his resignation hath been duly accepted.

"AND WHEREAS, In pursuance of the power and authority given and granted in and by the said recited Act of Assembly, Joseph Ellicott was, by Letters Patent, under your Excellency's Hand and the great Seal of the State, bearing date the nineteenth day of August, in the year of our Lord one thousand seven hundred and ninety-six, appointed a Commissioner in the lieu and stead of the said Andrew Ellicott, Esq., who had resigned as aforesaid, and in conjunction with the said William Irvine and George Wilson, Esquires, the two other Commissioners for the purpose of viewing and laying out the said Road in manner as stated in and by the above recited Act of Assembly.

"Now THEREFORE, The said George Wilson and Joseph Ellicott, two of the Commissioners appointed as aforesaid for the purposes aforesaid, beg leave to report:

"I. That the said William Irvine, George Wilson, and Joseph Ellicott, the Commissioners appointed as aforesaid, in conformity to your Excellency's Instructions in pursuance of the above recited Act of Assembly, with all convenient dispatch, in the execution of the trust reposed in them, proceeded to examine the situation of the Country at the Bald Eagle's Nest and to the end of Nittany Mountain, and having viewed the respective *scites*, they unanimously agreed to take their departure from the Bald Eagle's Nest. As soon as this decision took place the said William Irvine left the other Commissioners and returned home.

"II. That the said George Wilson and Joseph Ellicott then proceeded to view, survey, and stake out by a route, in their opinion, deemed the most practicable, a Road from the Bald Eagle's Nest towards the town of Erie at Presque-isle, and that they have ascertained the various courses and distances, the topographical situation, &c., of the said Road for the length of one hundred and sixteen miles, as represented in and by the Draft in profile hereunto annexed.

"III. That in consequence of the failure of Horses, the scarcity of Provisions, the advanced season of the year, and various other obstacles which retarded the prosecution of the business, they were compelled to relinquish the object of their mission, and have left above thirty-six miles of the Road unfinished.

"IV. That they have used their utmost diligence and attention to direct the course of the said Road over firm and level ground; but that frequently became totally impracticable, and where the ascent and descent of hills and mountains became unavoidable they made use of an altitude level, and have so adjusted its course that in its greatest elevation or depression it never exceeds an angle of six degrees with the horizon : Hence it may easily be inferred that considerable deviations from a straight line have necessarily occurred.

"V. That the land in that part of Mifflin County through which the Road passes is generally of an indifferent quality. For a part of this distance the Road passes over the declivities of the Allegheny Mountain and the Mushanon Hills. The country, however, for several miles between the summit of the Allegheny Mountain and the Mushanon hills, and also that part of Huntingdon County which the Road intersects, is generally level and free from stones, well timbered with Hickory, White and Black Oak, Dogwood, Ash, Chestnut, Poplar, White Pine, &c., and upon the whole well calculated for settlements. The soil of that part of Lycoming County which is intersected by the Road is generally of a luxuriant quality, abounding in many places with Stone coal, well timbered with various species of wood, and adapted to the production of all kinds of grain, &c., peculiar to the climate.

"VI. Your Commissioners with pleasure remark that from the Susquehanna River at Anderson's Creek to the first navigable stream of Sandy Lick Creek (a branch of Allegheny River) the portage along the said road is but twenty-two Miles. The road crosses Sandy Lick Creek about fifty miles from its junction with the Allegheny River, and from the Susquehanna to the North-Western branch of Sandy Lick Creek the portage is thirty-three miles. The North-Western branch discharges its waters into Sandy Lick Creek, about sixty perches below the place where it is intersected by the Road at the junction of the North-Western branch. The Sandy Lick Creek is as large as the Susquehanna River at Anderson's Creek, and the distance of the said Creek from the Allegheny River is about thirty-five miles. The Portage from the Susquehanna at Anderson's to Toby's Creek is forty-nine miles. Toby's Creek is twenty-two perches wide, and its distance from the intersection of the Road to the Allegheny River is about forty miles. It is navigable for boats, rafts, &c., from the intersection of the Road to the Allegheny River and about fifty or sixty miles above the place of intersection. The portage from the Susquehanna to the Allegheny River at Sussunadohtaw is seventy-two miles, and for the greater part of the distance of these portages the Road passes through a rich and fertile country.

"VII. That your Commissioners have formed their estimate of expenses upon the supposition that the said Road, as far as it has been surveyed, will be opened thirty feet in width ; sixteen feet in the middle to

PIONEER HISTORY OF JEFFERSON COUNTY, PENNA.

be cut and cleared as nearly level with the surface of the earth as practicable, but where digging and levelling on the sides of Hills and Mountains shall become necessary that a passage will be dug twelve feet wide, and that Bridges and causeways will be erected and formed over all miry places to enable Waggons to pass.

"A general estimate of expenditures requisite in opening, clearing, digging, levelling, erecting Bridges and forming causeways over the said Road.

"The expenses in opening the Road through the County of Mifflin, commencing at the Bald Eagle's Nest and ending at the Big Mushanon Creek, nineteen miles & sixteen perches.

"For opening, cleaning, digging, levelling, forming causeways on the said Road and erecting a Bridge over the Little Mushanon in the said County. } Dolls. 3316.74.

"The expenses in opening the Road through the County of Huntingdon, commencing at the Big Mushanon Creek and ending at the West branch of the Susquehanna River, twenty-one miles one hundred and fifty-seven perches.

"For opening, clearing, digging, levelling, forming causeways on the said Road and erecting a Bridge over Alder Run in said County. } 2643.37.

"The expenses in opening the Road through the County of Lycoming, commencing at the West branch of Susquehanna and ending at the Allegheny River, seventy-two miles & 193 perches.

"For opening, clearing, digging, levelling, and forming Causeways on the said Road. } 7215.20.

"VIII. That the said Road in its whole length passes through one entire and uninterrupted Wilderness, and the expenses already incurred in the execution of the business have considerably exceeded the legal appropriation intended for its completion.

"GEO. WILSON.
JOSEPH ELLICOTT."

DELAWARE INDIAN AND PIONEER NAMES FOR RIVERS AND CREEKS; ALSO ACTS OF LEGISLATURE DECLARING THESE STREAMS PUBLIC HIGHWAYS.

"Where skimmed the Indian bark,
And the song of the boatman re-echoed through the forest."

Topi-hanne—Toby Creek; 1749, Rivière au Fiel—Gall River.
Ma-onink—Mahoning.
Tangawunsch-hanne—North Fork.
Legamwi mahonne—Sandy Lick, or Red Bank; 1749, Rivière au Vermillon.

Legamwi-hanne—Sandy Creek.

The reason why Toby Creek was subsequently called Clarion River was because there were no less than three or four Toby Creeks in Pennsylvania. There was one in Monroe County, one in Luzerne, and one in Venango, which is now Clarion. Now, Tobyhanna, or Toby Creek, is corrupted from Topi-hanne, signifying alder stream; that is, a stream whose banks were fringed with alders. I find also that the Clarion River was called by the Delawares Gawunsch-hanne; that is, brier stream, a stream whose banks are overgrown with briers. There seems to be an incongruity, but the probabilities are that farther down in what is now Clarion County the stream was overgrown with alder-bushes. Mahoning is a corruption of Ma-onink, and signifies where there is a lick, or at the lick; sometimes a stream flowing there or near a lick. This name is a very common one for rivers and places in the Delaware country, along which or where the surface of the ground was covered with saline deposits, provisionally called "licks," from the fact that deer, elk, buffalo, and other animals frequented these places and licked the salted earth.

Mahonitty signifies a small lick, and Ma-oning a stream flowing from or near a lick.

By the act of Assembly, March 21, 1808, this creek was declared to be a public highway for the passage of rafts, boats, and other vessels from its confluence with the Allegheny River to the mouth of Canoe Creek, in Indiana County. That act authorized the inhabitants along its banks, and others desirous of using it for navigation, to remove all natural and artificial obstructions in it, except dams for mills and other water-works, and to erect slopes at the mill and other dams, which must be so constructed as not to injure the works of such dams. Any person owning or possessing lands along this stream has the liberty to construct dams across it, subject, however, to the restrictions and provisions of the general act authorizing the riparian owners to erect dams for mills on navigable streams. William Travis and Joseph Marshall were appointed to superintend the expenditure of eight hundred dollars for the improvement of this stream, authorized by the act of March 24, 1817, to whom an order for their services for two hundred and one dollars was issued by the commissioners of this county December 23, 1818.

The Act of Legislature, No. 129, declaring part of Big Mahoning Creek a public highway, approved April 13, 1833, reads as follows:

"SECTION 2. From and after the passage of this act, that part of Big Mahoning Creek, in Jefferson County, from the mouth of Canoe Creek, in said county, is hereby declared a public highway for the passage of rafts, boats, and other craft; and it shall and may be lawful for persons desirous of using the navigation of said creek between the points aforesaid to remove all natural and artificial obstructions from the bed or channel of said creek, except dams for mills and other water works, and also to erect such slopes at the mill or other dams on said creek as may be necessary for the passage of rafts, boats, and other vessels. *Provided,* such slopes be so constructed as not to injure the works of such dams. *And provided also,* that any person or persons owning or possessing lands on said creek shall have liberty to construct any dam or dams across the same, agreeably and subject to all the restrictions and provisions of an act of the General Assembly of this Commonwealth, passed the twenty-third day of March, one thousand eight hundred and three, entitled 'An Act to authorize any person or persons owning lands adjoining navigable streams of water declared public highways to erect dams on such streams for mill and other water-works.'"

Tangawunsch-hanne, North Fork, meant in the Indian tongue Little Brier Stream, or stream whose banks are overgrown with green brier.

The following act of the Legislature declared it a public highway.

An act, No. 64, declaring the North Fork of Sandy Lick Creek, in the county of Jefferson, from the mouth thereof to Ridgway, in said county, a public highway:

"SECTION 1. *Be it enacted, etc.,* That the North Fork of Sandy Lick Creek, in the county of Jefferson, from the mouth thereof to Ridgway, in said county, be, and the same is hereby declared a public highway; and it shall and may be lawful for any person or persons desirous of improving or using the navigation of said stream to remove thereout all obstructions, except dams for mills and other water-works already built, on which dam any such person or persons as aforesaid shall have full power to make slopes, such as are hereinafter described, and to keep the same in repair for the passage of boats, rafts, and other craft. *Provided,* that such slopes be so constructed as not to injure such dams.

"Approved—the thirteenth day of March, A.D. one thousand eight hundred and thirty-three.

"GEORGE WOLF,
"*Governor.*"

"Legamwi-mahonne means a sandy lick creek; that is, Sandy Lick, which was the name of this stream as late as 1792, from its source to its mouth, according to Reading Howell's map of that year. It bore that name even later. By the act of Assembly, March 21, 1798, 'Sandy Lick or Red Bank Creek' was declared to be a public stream or highway 'from the mouth up to the second or great fork.' The writer has not been able to ascertain just when, why, or at whose suggestion its original name was changed to Red Bank, by which it has been known by the oldest inhabitants now living in the region through which it flows. Perhaps the change may have been suggested by the red color of the soil of its banks many miles up from its mouth."—*History of Armstrong County, Pennsylvania.*

PIONEER HISTORY OF JEFFERSON COUNTY, PENNA.

THE ORIGIN OF THE NAME OF RED BANK CREEK.

In 1749 the governor-general of Canada sent an expedition under Celeron de Bienville down what is now known as the Allegheny and Ohio Rivers, to take possession of the country in the name of the king of France. The command embraced two hundred and fifteen French and Canadian soldiers and fifty-five Indians. Father Bonnecamp, a chaplain of this expedition, drew a map of the route, locating the tribes of Indians, and giving the Indian names of the tributaries of these rivers and also the name of the Indian villages. This manuscript map was deposited and is still in the archives of the Department de la Marine in Paris, and is styled "Map of a Voyage made on the Beautiful River in New Flanders, 1749, by Rev. Father Bonnecamp, Jesuit Mathematician." The map is very correct, considering all the circumstances. It has been reproduced on a smaller scale by George Dallas Albert and published in "The Frontier Forts of Pennsylvania," in vol. ii., with an explanation of the map, French names, and their corresponding American designations. In this map I find Rivière au Vermillon emptying into the Allegheny River, corresponding to the exact location of what is now called Red Bank Creek, and unfortunately translated by Mr. Albert as Mahoning Creek. On the Allegheny River going downward I find Rivière aux Bœuf, Beef, or Buffalo River, now called French Creek; then Rivière au Fiel,—Gall River or Clarion River; third, Rivière au Vermillon or Red Bank Creek; fourth, a stream not named, which must have been Mahoning; and then Attique, a village, or what is now Kittanning. Mr. Albert should have named the undesignated stream Mahoning and the Vermilion River Red Bank.

In 1798 this stream was designated by legal statute as Sandy Lick or Red Bank Creek, but later by common acceptance the name Sandy Lick was applied to that portion above where the North Fork unites, and Red Bank from Brookville to the mouth.

"The first lot of lumber which Barnett and Scott sent down the Red Bank was a small platform of timber, with poles instead of oars as the propelling power. There was a flood in this stream in 1806 which reached eight or ten feet up the trees on the flats.

"One thousand dollars was appropriated by the act of Assembly 'making appropriations for certain internal improvements,' approved March 24, 1817, for the purpose of improving this creek, and Levi Gibson and Samuel C. Orr were appointed commissioners to superintend the application of the money. By the act of April 4, 1826, 'Sandy Lick, or Red Bank Creek,' was declared a public highway only for the passage of boats, rafts, etc., descending it. That act also made it lawful for all persons owning lands adjoining this stream to erect mill-dams across it, and other water-works along it, to keep them in good repair, and draw off enough water to operate them on their own land, but required them 'to make a slope from the top, descending fifteen feet for every foot the dam is high, and not less than forty feet in breadth,' so as to afford a good navigation, and not to infringe the rights and privileges of any owner of private property.

"The first flat-boat that descended this stream was piloted by Samuel Knapp, in full Indian costume. In 1832 or 1833 two boats loaded with sawed lumber owned by Uriah Matson, which found a good market in Cincinnati, with the proceeds of which Matson purchased the goods with which he opened his store at Brookville."—*History of Armstrong County.*

An act declaring the rivers Ohio and Allegheny, and certain branches thereof, public highways:

"SECTION 1. *Be it enacted, etc.*, That from and after the passing of this act, the river Ohio, from the western boundary of the State up to the mouth of the Monongahela, Big Beaver Creek, from the mouth of the first fork in the seventh district of donation land, Allegheny River, from the mouth to the northern boundary of the State, French Creek to the town of Le Bœuf, and Conewango Creek, from the mouth thereof to the State line, Cussawago Creek, from the mouth of the main forks, Little Coniate Creek, from the mouth up to the inlet of the Little Coniate Lake, Toby's Creek, from the mouth up to the second fork (now Clarion River, and Johnsonburg was the second fork), Oil Creek, from the mouth up to the main fork, Broken Straw Creek, from the mouth up to the second fork, Sandy Lick, or Red Bank Creek, from the mouth up to the second great fork, be, and the same are hereby declared to be public streams and highways for the passage of boats and rafts; and it shall and may be lawful for the inhabitants or others desirous of using the navigation of the said river and branches thereof to remove all natural obstructions in the said river and branches aforesaid." Passed 21st March, 1798. Recorded in Law Book No. VI. page 245.

The first fork was at Brookville's site, the second great fork was at Port Barnett.

An act, No. 189, declaring Little Toby's Creek, Black Lick Creek, Little Oil Creek, and Clark's Creek public highways:

"SECTION 1. *Be it enacted, etc.*, That from and after the passage of this act Little Toby's Creek, in the counties of Clearfield and Jefferson, from the mouth of John Shaffer's mill run, on the main branch of Toby's Creek, and from the forks of Brandy Camp (or Kersey Creek) to the Clarion River,

*   *   *   *   *   *   *   *   *

be, and the same are hereby declared public highways for the passage of rafts, boats, and other craft, and it shall and may be lawful for, etc. (The same provisions follow here as in No. 129.)

"Approved—the fourteenth day of April, A.D. one thousand eight hundred and twenty-eight.

"J. ANDW. SHULTZ,
"*Governor.*"

The Little Sandy Creek makes a long circuit through about what is now the centre of the county. Numerous runs approach it from the east and north. The principal streamlets are Big Run, Elk Run, and Pine Run. This region of the county is hilly and the ravines are deep, and at some points wide ranges of bottom flats. When the pioneer settled here the stream was the southwestern portion of the county. The tablelands along this stream range in height from twelve hundred to eighteen hundred feet above the sea.

"THAT FLOOD."

"The flood is here. During the past week all has been bustle and hurry. Our lumbermen have had an excellent time to start their lumber to market, and now the great body of the lumber manufactured on the Clarion and its tributaries during the past year is floating down-stream. The waters have been very accommodating for a few days past,—neither too high nor too low. Pilots are in their glory. Each one was the first to discover that stray 'snag' which had hid itself beneath the foaming waters in some critical spot, and although some of them happened to run pretty close to it, yet all knew it was there, and would have missed it, if they could; and some of them did miss it by dint of 'cracking her up behind' with all their power.

"The rafting season on these waters is a season of life and activity, bustle and confusion, wet limbs and red wamuses. It gives to our town an important and business-like appearance. The landing of steamers and other craft in a great commercial mart may be some, but the landing of rafts in 'Dick's Pond' and 'the Eddy' is considerable more. The skill, nerve, and muscle here exhibited—to say nothing of an occasional big word that accidentally falls from some excited pilot or proprietor—can find its equal nowhere only on some lumbering stream during a rafting freshet. There is something fascinating about this rafting business, notwithstanding its incessant hard labor. As they proceed downward, floating majestically over the virgin bosom of the mighty waters, the scene changes with them, the fare changes, the atmosphere changes, the waters change. Here the hungry raftmen recruit their drooping energies with 'the best the country can afford,' and such as are so disposed (and we are happy to say there are but few of this class) can wet their whistles with pure, unadulterated 'rot gut,' with which 'our bar' is always bountifully supplied. On their course they soon find beef and potatoes and hot cakes more scarce, but are cheered up by a change from this fare to 'a great many molasses,' lots of flitch, and mouldy bread that has been kept over from the last rafting for their especial benefit, with common corn whiskey. But anything for a change. No matter if you do flop out of the frying-pan into the fire. Peradventure, our hardy fellow citizens, with rough exterior, but large, generous souls glowing within them, arrive at towns below, where they are greeted with 'Olean hoosiers' from every long nine, with a smutty-faced urchin attached to it, they meet. But no matter. They have 'better clothes' at home and more

Banking logs.

rhino in their pockets than any score of these foppish nobodies. They command respect wherever they land, whether it be in a skiff at some little settlement to get a small stock of provisions, or in the populous cities where they find a market. Their frank, open countenances, their independent swagger, and their muscular appearance is enough to secure them from molestation. They see all the curiosities of the city, visit the theatre, take a peep into the 'punch-room,' just to see what is there. They get a view of all the fashionable resorts of the city. But we are not going to speak of *all* the places they frequent! They do not care for expenses. They go down the river for fun, not for profit, and as they did not have much going down,—tugging away at an oar, in rain-, hail-, and snow-storms,—they are bent on making up for lost time. Finally, after they have become sick and tired of smoke and confusion, they turn their steps homeward, and in due time they arrive at their mountain home, and are ready to go to work—when they get rested."—*Elk Advocate*.

In 1844 the waters of what is now called the Clarion were as clear as crystal, pure as life, and gurgled into the river from mountain springs. No tannery or other refuse was to be found in it. In 1749 the French named the stream Gall River. It was declared a public highway, as

Driving logs.

Toby's Creek, by an act of the Legislature, March 21, 1798, up to the second great fork.

In early times this river was known as Stump Creek, and sometimes as Toby's Creek, and it is said that it got these two names after two Indian hunters, who were in the habit (in the winter) of going up this river in canoes to hunt and trap. They would return each spring with their furs and meat to their villages down the Allegheny and Ohio Rivers.

It was called Toby's Creek as early as 1758. Unable myself to find any authority for a change to Clarion, I wrote to the Secretary of Internal Affairs, and received the following reply,—viz. :

PIONEER HISTORY OF JEFFERSON COUNTY, PENNA.

"June 3, 1897.

"Hon. W. J. McKnight, Brookville, Pa.

"Dear Sir,—In answer to your letter of recent date, we beg to say that we are unable to find any act of Assembly changing the name of Toby's Creek to Clarion River. In an act to authorize the erection of a dam, passed in 1822, this stream is designated as 'Toby's Creek, otherwise called Clarion River.'

"Very truly yours,
"James W. Latta,
"Secretary."

CHAPTER IX.

THE OLD STATE ROAD—EARLY ROADS AND TRAILS—WHY THE STATE ROAD WAS MADE—THE FIRST ATTEMPT TO OPEN THE ROAD—LAWS, ETC., TOUCHING THE SUBJECT—THE SURVEY—THE ROAD COMPLETED—THE ACT OF THE LEGISLATURE WHICH SANCTIONED THE BUILDING OF THE ROAD.

In 1791 and 1793 a State road through this wilderness to what is now called Waterford was incepted, agitated, and legalized; but, owing to the Indian troubles of 1791, '92, '93, and '94, all efforts had to be stopped and all legal proceedings annulled and repealed. The Indian troubles were settled in 1794 by war and purchases, and then legal steps were again taken to open up this great northwest in 1795 and 1796. The reader will please bear in mind that Le Bœuf is now Waterford, Pennsylvania, Presque Isle is now Erie City, Pennsylvania, and Bald Eagle's Nest is now Milesburg, Centre County, Pennsylvania.

EARLY ROADS AND TRAILS.

In 1784–85 the old State Road from the east was opened through to Fort Pitt in the west over what had been previously a path, or what was called Forbes's Trail. This trail passed through Bedford, Westmoreland, and other counties. In those days the State surveyed and laid out county seats and sold the lots. The lots were generally sold at auction. All government stores, as well as groceries and goods of every description, were for a long time carried from the east to the west on pack-horses over trails. One man would sometimes drive a hundred horses.

Guards from the militia were a necessity for their trains. Guards were also a necessity for the road surveyors and road-makers. A body of about fifty militia was the usual number, and sometimes these soldiers would do some work as well as guard the road-makers. Transportation was also carried over Meade's trail, which passed through West Reynoldsville, in the same way. In 1787 the only road from Fort Pitt to Le Bœuf (now Waterford) was a trail or path through what is now Butler County and up the Allegheny River. The turnpike over or across the old Forbes's trail was finished to Pittsburg in 1819.

In 1794 the great problem was a thoroughfare from the east to the northwest. The defence of the western portion of the State from Indians required the State and the national authorities to be constantly on the alert. On the 28th of February, 1794, the Legislature passed an act for "raising soldiers for the defence of the western frontiers." Also at this time a combined effort of the nation and State was made to lay out a town at Presque Isle (now Erie) on Lake Erie.

WHY THE STATE ROAD WAS MADE.

In order to protect these frontiers from the British and Indians a road through this wilderness seemed an absolute necessity, hence an act was passed through the Legislature previous to or in 1794, authorizing the surveying and making of a State road from Reading to Presque Isle (Erie City). Colonel William Irvine and Andrew Ellicott were the commissioners. These men were also commissioners to lay out the town of Erie (Presque Isle). The official instructions to the commissioners and Captain Denny were as follows:

"PHILADELPHIA, March 1, 1794.

"GENTLEMEN,—In providing for the general defence of the frontiers, the Legislature has authorized me to form a detachment of troops, for carrying into effect the act directing a town to be laid out at or near Presque Isle; and as the subject of the commission to survey and lay out a road from Reading to Presque Isle may be promoted by the same measure, I have instructed Captain Denny, the commanding officer of the detachment, to grant to you as commissioners all the aid and protection that is compatible with a due attention to the particular charge which is confided to him. Under these circumstances, I trust you will find it convenient to proceed immediately in the execution of your work.

"I am, gentlemen,
"Your most obedient servant,
"THOMAS MIFFLIN.

"To WILLIAM IRVINE and ANDREW ELLICOTT, Commissioners for laying out a road from Reading to Presque Isle."

"PHILADELPHIA, March 1, 1794.

"The Legislature having made provision for surveying and opening two roads,—one from Reading and the other from French Creek to Presque Isle,—it is obvious that the establishment of the town is intimately connected with those objects; and, therefore, you shall deem it your duty to grant all the aid and protection to the respective commissioners and contractors employed in surveying and opening those roads that is compatible with due attention to the particular charge confided in you.

"Your most obedient servant,
"THOMAS MIFFLIN.

"To EBENEZER DENNY, ESQ., Captain of the Allegheny Company, &c."

FIRST ATTEMPT TO OPEN THE ROAD.

Captain Ebenezer Denny, with a detachment of soldiers, was ordered by the government to accompany these men. On the arrival of Denny and the soldiers at what is now Franklin, Venango County, he discovered that the Indians were cross and ugly, and General Wilkins, in talking to Mr. Dallas, said, "The English are fixed in their opposition to the opening of the road to Presque Isle, and are determined to prevent it by the English and Indians." Orders were then given to Captain Denny to go no farther than Le Bœuf (now Waterford), and occupy two small blockhouses, which had been erected for Commissioners Irvine and Ellicott.

This was the first attempt to open up a road through the wilderness of what is now Jefferson County. Governor Mifflin applied to the President for a thousand militia soldiers to enforce this work; but the President counselled peace. Work was suspended at Presque Isle, and it was not until in April, 1795, that all difficulties were removed and Colonel William Irvine and Andrew Ellicott resumed work. At this time Irvine commanded the troops and Ellicott had charge of the surveyors.

LAWS, ETC., TOUCHING THE SUBJECT.

The following letter to the author from Hon. Isaac B. Brown, Secretary Pennsylvania Department of Internal Affairs, of Harrisburg, gives some valuable information concerning the road.

"HARRISBURG, April 29, 1895.
"MR. W. J. MCKNIGHT, Brookville, Pa.

"DEAR SIR,—In answer to your letter of the 13th instant, we beg to say that you will find 'An Act to provide for opening a road from near the Bald Eagle's Nest, in Mifflin County, to Le Bœuf, in the county of Allegheny,' passed April 10, 1790, published in full in Bioren's 'Laws of Pennsylvania,' vol. vi. p. 24. The reference in the preamble of this act to a road 'in part laid out from Reading to Presque Isle,' is probably to an act passed April 11, 1793, appropriating certain sums of money for laying out a large number of roads within the State. The following appropriation is made in the first section: 'For viewing and laying out a road from Reading to Presque Isle, one thousand three hundred and thirty-three dollars.' This act appears in Bioren's 'Laws,' vol. iv. p. 277 *et seq.* It is possible, however, that the reference was intended to apply to a road from the Bald Eagle's Nest to the Allegheny River, which was surveyed and laid out under an act passed April 4, 1796, entitled 'An Act for laying out and opening sundry roads within this Commonwealth, and for other purposes.' This act will be found in full in Bioren's 'Laws,' vol. v. p. 187. By this act the governor was authorized and empowered to appoint 'three skilful persons to view the ground, and estimate the expense of opening and making a good wagon road from the Bald Eagle's Nest, or the end of the Nittany Mountain, to the town of Erie at Presque Isle.'

"Under this last act the governor, on the 13th day of April, 1796, appointed William Irvine, Andrew Ellicott, and George Wilson commissioners to make the survey. Andrew Ellicott declined the appointment, and Joseph Ellicott was appointed in his place. These men met to examine the situation of the country at the Bald Eagle's Nest and at the end of Nittany Mountain, and determined to start at the Bald Eagle's Nest, now Milesburg, Centre County. It appears, however, that William Irvine returned home, and George Wilson and Joseph Ellicott proceeded to make the survey. Their draft and report are among the records of this department, and show their work from the Bald Eagle's Nest to the Allegheny River, a distance of one hundred and sixteen miles by their measurement. After reaching the Allegheny River, they say that 'in consequence of the failure of horses, the scarcity of provisions, the advanced season of the year, and various other obstacles which retarded the prosecution of the business, they were compelled to relinquish the object of their mission, and have left above thirty-six miles of the road unfinished.'

"Very truly yours,
"ISAAC B. BROWN,
"*Secretary.*"

THE SURVEY.

The point on the Allegheny River where these surveyors stopped in the fall of 1796 was on the land where Eli Holeman settled in 1800. It is three miles below Tionesta borough, Forest County, Pennsylvania. For the sixteen years of travel and traffic of emigrants and others over this old State Road each and all had to force or cross this ferry. The old State Road never passed through where Clarion now is, or through Franklin or Meadville. It passed through the wilderness away north of these towns, but connected with other State roads running through them. All of the county histories which have been written prior to this one confound this road with the turnpike, which was not built or opened for traffic until November, 1820. At Brookville the turnpike survey in 1818 took a separate and distinct southerly course from the old State Road, and passed through Franklin, Meadville, and so forth.

THE ROAD COMPLETED.

The road was officially taken from the contractors and a quietus entered as to the contract April 2, 1804. The course of the road through what is now Winslow township was through Rathmel, down Sandy Lick to the south side, crossing the creek between Sandy Valley and near where West Reynoldsville now is, where it deflected to the right over the hill, through the farm now occupied by Robert Waite. This State road was the great public thoroughfare for emigrants from the east to the northwest for a period of sixteen years, until the turnpike was finished in 1820. A portion of about seven miles is still in use from Brookville to the Clarion County line, parallel, but north of that part of the turnpike which extends from Brookville to Corsica.

SANCTIONED BY THE LEGISLATURE.

The following is the act which authorized the building of the State Road, of which this article is a history:

"AN ACT FOR LAYING OUT AND OPENING SUNDRY ROADS WITHIN THIS COMMONWEALTH, AND FOR OTHER PURPOSES.

"WHEREAS, From the increasing population of the northern and northwestern parts of this State, it becomes expedient at this time to provide for the laying out and opening the necessary roads, for the accommodation of the same; therefore,

"SECTION 1. *Be it enacted by the Senate and House of Representatives of the Commonwealth of Pennsylvania in General Assembly met, and it is hereby enacted by the authority of the same,* That the governor be, and he is hereby, authorized and empowered to appoint three skilful persons to view the ground and estimate the expense of opening and making a good wagon road from the town of Northampton, in the county of Northampton, to the mouth of Tioga, in the county of Luzerne, and from thence, by the most practicable route, to the northern line of this State; and three skilful persons to view the ground and estimate the expense of opening and making a good wagon road from the Bald Eagle's Nest, or the end of the Nittany Mountain, to the town of Erie, at Presque Isle; and to cause the said roads to be surveyed and staked out by the most practicable routes; and also to cause drafts of the roads to be made in profile, and report to the Legislature the proportional parts of the expense that will be incurred in each county through which the said road will pass; provided that the commissioners thus appointed shall not stake out any part of the said roads when they may be carried on roads heretofore laid out and opened agreeably to the provisions of former laws of this State.

"SECTION 2. *And be it further enacted by the authority aforesaid,* That the governor be, and he is hereby, empowered to contract, either with individuals, or with companies, for opening a road from Pittsburg, by the way of Fort Franklin, to Le Bœuf, and to draw his warrant on the State Treasurer for a sum not exceeding two thousand dollars, to defray the expense of laying out the roads to Tioga and Erie; a sum not exceeding four thousand dollars, to defray the expense of opening the road from Pittsburg, by Fort Franklin, to Le Bœuff. *Provided always*, That all contracts to be made by virtue of this act shall be registered by the governor, according to the directions of the eighth section of the act, entitled 'An Act to provide for the opening and improving sundry navigable waters and roads within the Commonwealth,' passed the thirteenth day of April, one thousand seven hundred and ninety-one.*

"SECTION 3. *And be it further enacted by the authority aforesaid*, That the governor be, and he is hereby, empowered to draw his warrant in favor of Joseph Horsefield for any sum not exceeding five hundred dollars, to be applied towards removing the fallen timber and other obstructions in the road leading from Jacob Heller's tavern, in Northampton County, to Wilkesbarre, in Luzerne County. Passed 4th April, 1796."

"DEPARTMENT OF INTERNAL AFFAIRS,
"HARRISBURG, PA., June 7, 1895.

"HON. W. J. MCKNIGHT, Brookville, Pa.

"DEAR SIR,—Herewith you will find copies of the contract and the reports of John Fleming relating to the road from Bald Eagle's Nest to Le Bœuff.

"Very truly yours,
"JAMES W. LATTA,
"*Secretary.*"

"ARTICLES OF AGREEMENT made and entered into this third day of July, in the year of our Lord one thousand seven hundred and ninety-nine, between Thomas Mifflin, Governor of the Commonwealth of Pennsylvania, of the one part, and Samuel Miles and Roger Alden, of the City of Philadelphia, Esquires, of the other part.

"WHEREAS, In and by an Act of the General Assembly, entitled 'An Act to provide for opening a Road from near the Bald Eagle's Nest, in Mifflin county, to Le Bœuff, in the county of Allegheny,' passed the tenth day of April, in the year one thousand seven hundred and ninety-nine, the Governor is empowered to contract for opening and improving the said road in the manner and on the terms in the said act prescribed: AND WHEREAS, The said Samuel Miles and Roger Alden have made proposals for entering into the said contract upon principles which appear to the Governor most likely to accomplish the good purposes by the Legis-

---

* For the act referred to in this section, see vol. iv. chap. 1558.

lature intended: NOW THESE ARTICLES WITNESS, That the said Samuel Miles and Roger Alden, jointly and severally for themselves, their Heirs, Executors, and Administrators, covenant, promise, and agree to and with the said Thomas Mifflin and his successors, Governors of the Commonwealth of Pennsylvania, in consideration of the Covenant on behalf of the said Commonwealth hereinafter made, That they, the said Samuel Miles and Roger Alden, their Heirs, Executors, and Administrators, shall and will, well and faithfully, and with all convenient diligence, open, extend, and improve the said Road in manner following,—that is to say: That the Road shall be opened generally of such width as to enable and admit two waggons to pass each other, except only in such place or places as from great natural difficulty of Mountains, Hills, Rocks, and Morasses shall render such an undertaking impracticable or unreasonably laborious and expensive, considering the public consideration therefor given. But in all such place or places there shall be a good passage of at least ten feet wide, with proper and convenient passing places in view: And that the said Contractors will advance by anticipation (if necessary) the sums of money requisite to open the said Road in the manner aforesaid. And the said Thomas Mifflin, in consideration of the Covenants and undertaking of the said Contractors, and by virtue of the power in the said Act of Assembly to him given, covenants, promises, and agrees to and with the said Samuel Miles and Roger Alden, their Executors, Administrators, and Assigns, that they shall have and receive the sum of Five Thousand Dollars, to be paid out of the first money arising from the sale of the reserved Lands & Lots at the Towns of Erie, Franklin, Warren, and Waterford: And for which sum of Five Thousand Dollars, the said Thomas Mifflin covenants, promises, and agrees to draw his Warrant or Warrants on the State Treasurer in favor of the said Contractors. In Witness whereof the parties have hereunto set their respective hands & seals the day and year first above written.

                    (Signed)   "SAMUEL MILES, [seal]
                                        ROGER ALDEN, [seal]
                                        THOS. MIFFLIN. [seal]

"Sealed and Delivered
   in the presence of
      A. W. FOSTER,
      JNO. MILES."

To the above contract appear the names of George Fox, James Phillips, and Tench Coxe as sureties for its "true, faithful, perfect, and diligent performance," and also the following endorsement on the back of the same:

"The Governor, being satisfied, from three several reports of John Fleming, Esquire, (the two first dated on the 16th of December, 1801,

& the 10th of January, 1803, respectively; & the last without date, but delivered into the Secretary's Office in the month of January last,) that Samuel Miles & Roger Alden, Esquires, have completed their contract for opening a road from near the Bald Eagle's Nest to Le Bœuff, by opening & improving the same agreeably to the terms of said contract, as far as could reasonably be expected from the situation and nature of the country through which said road passes, & the public consideration given therefore, this day directed a quietus to be entered upon the contract.

       (Signed)   "T. M. THOMPSON, *Sec.*
" April the 2nd, 1804."

"To HIS EXCELLENCY THOMAS MCKEAN, ESQUIRE, *Governor of the State of Pennsylvania :*

" SIR,—In pursuance of your Excellency's letter appointing me a Commissioner to view and report on that part of the State Road from Milesburg to Le Bœuff, which was undertaken to be opened by Col. Samuel Miles, I proceeded to Milesburg and viewed the said Road as shewn to me by Mr. Richard Miles, and beg leave to submit the following Report :

" Beginning at Milesburg the road crosses Bald Eagle creek, over which is a sufficient wooden Bridge, thence up the said creek on the north side of it for five miles; the road passable for waggons. Within these five miles, on the west side of Wallis's run, there is some wet ground a little swampy.

" Leaving the Bald Eagle creek and thence to the foot of the Allegheny mountain, five miles, the Road is good excepting some trees that have fallen across it since it was opened.

Across the mountain is three miles. The ascent is one mile, of which 240 perches are dug, in some places, nine feet wide. Towards the top it is too steep for carriages. The descent of the mountain is about two miles and gradual.

" About one mile from the foot of the mountain is a small run difficult to pass.

" Here I must beg leave to remark, as applicable to this as well as to other small runs that may be mentioned in this Report, that many very small streams in the country over which this road passes run in narrow channels, the bottoms of which lie from one to three feet below the surface of the earth. A footman can step over many of them, where, from the nature of the soil at the bottom, a horse is in great danger of being mired.

" After crossing the last-mentioned run there is a hill of which in ascent there are thirty perches, and in descent twelve perches not passable for waggons for want of digging. Near this are two small runs, both difficult to pass.

"To Phillipsburg from thence, a distance of more than eight miles, the Road is good, excepting some very swampy ground on the east of what is called the five mile run, and some miry ground at Coldstream, one mile from Phillipsburg. Some more work is necessary on the hill west of the five mile run. The whole distance from Milesburg to Phillipsburg is twenty-six miles.

"Passing Phillipsburg one mile is Moshannon creek. It is not bridged nor is it fordable at the place where the Road crosses it at any season. There is some timber prepared at the place for a bridge. It is about six perches wide with steep banks. There is a Fording about half a mile below. Three miles further the road is good excepting a few wet places. Within two miles further there are two runs, the banks of which are dug, and the road is good.

"Thence to Clearfield creek, four miles, some digging done in two places, and on the hill descending to Clearfield forty perches are well dug; the road is good.

"Thence to the Susquehanna river, five miles, the road good. The breadth of the river is twelve perches.

"Thence to Anderson's creek, nearly three miles, some digging done on Hogback hill. The road in general good.

"Thence to a branch of Anderson's creek, about eight miles, several places dug and some bridges made: the road is tolerably good. More digging and bridging wanted.

"Thence to the waters of Stump creek, about three miles, several bridges made and digging done in some places; the road good.

"Thence five miles, crossing two ridges on each of which there is digging done, and several runs, two of which are bridged. In the latter part of these five miles are two runs necessary to be bridged. With this exception the road is tolerably good.

"Thence to a branch of Sandy Lick creek, about six miles, in several places the road is dug and some bridges made. The road tolerably good.

"Thence about three miles; several steep banks, deep runs and wet places; road not passable.

"Thence to the end of Col. Miles' opening is four miles. The road good.

"From Milesburg until the road crosses the Susquehanna the road is opened from sixteen to twenty feet wide, and from thence to the end it is opened from twelve to sixteen feet wide. The whole length of the road opened as aforesaid by Col. Miles is seventy-four miles and eighty-six perches.

(Signed)　　　"JNO. FLEMING.

"December 16th, 1801."

Only the commonest goods were hauled into this county from Philadelphia over the old State Road. The freightage from Philadelphia to

Port Barnett was about six dollars per one hundred pounds, and it took four weeks to come from Philadelphia. In 1800 wheat brought one dollar and a half a bushel, wheat flour four and five dollars per one hundred pounds, corn one dollar per bushel, oats seventy-five cents, potatoes sixty-five cents. Tobacco was sold by the yard at four cents per yard, common sugar thirty-three cents, and loaf (white sugar) fifty cents per pound. A hunter's rifle cost twenty-five dollars, a yoke of oxen eighty dollars, boots from one to three dollars, a pair of moccasins about three or four shillings.

S. B. Rowe, in his "Pioneer History of Clearfield County," says, "The State, in order to connect the western frontier with the eastern settlements, had laid out several roads, among others one leading from Milesburg to Erie. This road was opened in the year 1803. It crossed the Susquehanna River near the residence of Benjamin Jordan.

"The Milesburg and Le Bœuff road became subsequently an important and leading thoroughfare. It was a road of the worst kind, laid out with very little skill, and made with a great deal of dishonesty. It had but one bridge—at Moshannon—between Bellefonte and Anderson's Creek, and to avoid digging the hill-side, Anderson's Creek was crossed three times in less than two miles. Large quantities of merchandise passed over it, principally upon pack-horses, companies of which, exceeding a score in number, might often be seen traversing it. Until the place of this road was supplied by an artificial road, located on or near its bed, it was the principal road leading to Erie and the great West. About the time the State Road was supplanted by the turnpike the now almost forgotten Conestoga wagon, with its heavy horses, walking leisurely along, their tread measured by the jingling of bells, afforded cheaper and better mode of transportation for goods. A trip to Philadelphia to purchase goods or to 'see the sights' of that village was then quite an undertaking, and called for weeks of preparation."

"To HIS EXCELLENCY THOMAS MCKEAN, ESQUIRE, *Governor of the Commonwealth of Pennsylvania:*

"Agreeably to your Instructions received through the Secretary of the Commonwealth, I proceeded to review that part of the road leading from Milesburg to Le Bœuff, opened by Major Roger Alden, and beg leave to submit the following report:

"Beginning at the west end of Col. Samuel Miles' opening,

"2 miles, a hill with some digging; the road good.

"1½ miles to the crossing of the north branch of Sandy Lick creek. The road good.

"9 m farther. The road good.

"4 m of rough road. There is in this distance four streams of water crossing it, with bad hills on each side of each of them. They are generally all dug that carriages may pass.

"4 m farther to Toby's creek: some digging done on the descent of the hill going down to the creek—the road tolerably good.

"2 m farther to the hill descending to Little Toby's creek. The road good. When I reported before, this descent to the creek was impassable with waggons; since that time the road has been changed, and laid on better ground, and the road dug. The road good. West of the creek the road is somewhat difficult for carriages.

"4 m. The road passable for carriages.

"1 m. A hill descending to Licking creek, bad, as is also the hill on the west side of the creek. There is some digging done here. These hills comprehend a distance exceeding a mile.

"10 m. Road good, lying on chestnut ridges. In this distance there is little difference in the road.

"4 m to the Allegheny river, lying over pine ridges, some of them steep. The hill to the river near a mile long. Since my last report some bridging and digging has been done. Passable for carriages.

"6 m from the crossing of the Allegheny river to Pithole creek. The road crosses several ridges, one of which is dug.

"2 m of good road.

"2 m of very swampy ground, principally bridged and causewayed. Passable with carriages.

"3 m to the crossing of the south-east branch of Oil creek There are several bridges made in this distance. There is a good one across the creek. The road good.

"7 m to the crossing of the N. W. branch of Oil creek. There are several bridges made in this distance. Since my last report the fording of the creek is changed for the better.

"1 m. West of the creek for near a mile the road is altered, making the ascent of the hills that I noticed easier. They are still difficult for carriages.

"7 m to where this road intersects the public road from Pittsburg to Le Bœuff by the way of Franklin. In this distance the road in general is good. A number of bridges are made on it.

"3 m to the crossing of Muddy creek—several bridges made. The road something wet.

"12 m to the crossing of French creek—a number of bridges made.

"3 m to Le Bœuff—a number of bridges made, and the road good. From the intersection of the Franklin road to Le Bœuff the soil is generally wet.

"I would generally observe that a considerable quantity of timber is fallen across the road, and the sprouts in such quantities grown up in many places, since the road was opened, as to render travelling difficult.

There has not been any cutting done since I reported, unless where the road is changed in the two places before mentioned.

"I am Sir,
"Your Excellency's very humble servant,
"JOHN FLEMING."

"AN ACT MAKING APPROPRIATION FOR CERTAIN INTERNAL IMPROVEMENTS.

"SECTION 14. *And be it further enacted by the authority aforesaid,* That the sum of four hundred and fifty dollars be, and the same is hereby appropriated to be paid to John Litle and James Weston, for improving the following roads in the county of Erie: to wit, two hundred and twenty-five dollars for the State Road from Milesburgh to Waterford, etc.

"SECTION 17. That the sum of five hundred dollars be, and the same is hereby appropriated to be paid to the commissioners of Venango County for improving the following roads: viz., . . . and two hundred and fifty dollars for the State Road from Waterford to Milesburgh, where it passes through the county of Venango, and crosses the Allegheny River at the ferry of Eli Holeman.

"SECTION 20. That the sum of seven hundred dollars be, and the same is hereby appropriated to be paid to the commissioners of Indiana County for improving the State Road from Milesburgh to Waterford, where it passes through the county of Jefferson, between the counties of Clearfield and Armstrong; and that the further sum of seven hundred dollars be, and the same is hereby appropriated to be paid to the commissioners of Armstrong County; three hundred dollars thereof for improving that part of the Milesburgh and Waterford road which passes through the County of Armstrong, etc.

"SECTION 22. That the sum of seven hundred dollars be, and the same is hereby appropriated to be paid to the commissioners of Centre County for improving the roads in Clearfield County, as follows: viz., . . . four hundred dollars for the road from Milesburgh to Waterford between the west branch of the Susquehanna River and the line between the counties of Clearfield and Jefferson, and one hundred dollars for the said road from Clearfield Creek to the line of Centre County.

"SECTION 29. That it shall be the duty of the county commissioners, and trustees, and the commissioners appointed by this act, to whom the sums hereby appropriated are to be paid respectively, to advertise that proposals will be received at a certain time and place, to be by them fixed, for making the improvements in this act specified, and shall contract with such person or persons as will in their judgment secure the most advantageous expenditure of the several sums herein appropriated; and they shall furnish to the auditors of their several counties a detailed statement of the manner in which the said monies shall have been expended; and the county commissioners, and trustees, and commissioners appointed by this act, as soon as their accounts shall have been settled and adjusted, shall transmit a certified copy of the detailed statement aforesaid to the auditor-general, together with the vouchers, which accounts shall be settled by the accountant department in the usual manner.

"SECTION 30. *And be it further enacted by the authority aforesaid,* That at any time after the first day of August next, the State treasurer be, and he is hereby authorized and directed to pay to the county commissioners, and trustees, and commissioners appointed by this act, on their producing satisfactory evidence that the several contracts have been made, and the necessary securities for the faithful application of the monies taken, and the work actually commenced, the several sums hereby appropriated out of any monies in the treasury not otherwise appropriated.

"Approved—the second day of April, one thousand eight hundred and eleven.

"SIMON SNYDER."

The road was opened and finished to Holeman's Ferry, on the Allegheny River, in 1804. This point is now in Forest County. There was no provision made to complete the road from there to Waterford by the Legislature until 1810. At that time Clarion County was not organized, and the part of the State Road that now lies in Clarion County was then in Venango County. As near as can be learned, the following contracts were let for work on the road in the year 1811 :

"Wm. Hays contracted to dig a part of said road on the north side of 'Three Mile Run at 40 cts. per perch.'

"Isaac Connelly contracted to dig a part of said road on the north side of 'Hemlock Creek at 50 cts. per perch.'

"William Hays contracted to dig and open a part of said road on the south side of 'Hemlock Creek at 40 cts. a perch.'

"Samuel and Alexander McHatten agree to open and bridge a part of the said road near Hicks cabin at eight dollars.

"Charles Holman contracted to open and dig a part of said road for 66 cts. per perch for digging, and a reasonable prize for any part which may be opened.

"Samuel and Alexander McHatten contracted to dig and open a part of said road at 57 cts. a perch on the north side of Little Toby's Creek.

"Alexander McElhaney contracted to bridge a part of said road, supposed to be 26 rods, at 99 cts. per perch, and to open and repair at a reasonable price.

"Samuel and Alex McHatten agree to dig and open a part of said road on Toby's Creek Hill at twenty-four and a half cents per perch."

In Brookville the State Road came up the hill between Mrs. Showalter's and the Lutheran church, turned to the right and over what is now an alley between Dr. McKnight and Robert Darrah.

CHAPTER X.

PIONEER AGRICULTURE—HOW THE FARMERS IN THE OLDEN TIME HAD TO MAKE SHIFT—THE PIONEER HOMES—PIONEER FOOD—PIONEER EVENING FROLICS—TREES, SNAKES, AND REPTILES—SOLDIERS OF 1812—PIONEER LEGAL RELATIONS OF MAN AND WIFE—EARLY AND PIONEER MUSIC—LIST OF TAXABLE INHABITANTS IN 1820—THE TRANSPORTATION OF IRON—THE FIRST SCREW FACTORY—POPULATION OF THE STATE AND OF THE UNITED STATES.

FOR convenience in description I may here state that the soil of Jefferson County was covered in sections with two different growths of timber,—viz., sections of oak and other hard-wood timber, with underbrush and saplings. Some of these sections were called the barrens. The other sections were covered with a dense and heavy growth of pine, hemlock, poplar, cucumber, bass, ash, sugar, and beech, with saplings, down timber, and underbrush in great profusion. The mode of clearing in these different sections was not the same. In the first-mentioned or sparsely covered section the preliminary work was grubbing. The saplings and underbrush had to be grubbed up and out with a mattock and piled in brush-piles. One man could usually grub an acre in four days, or you could let this at a job for two dollars per acre and board. The standing timber then was usually girdled or deadened, and allowed to fall down in the crops from year to year, to be chopped and rolled in heaps every spring. In the dense or heavy growth timber the preliminary work was underbrushing, cutting the saplings close to the ground, piling the brush or not, as the necessity of the case seemed to require. The second step was the cutting of all down timber into lengths of ten or fifteen feet. After this came the cutting of all standing timber, which, too, had to be brushed and cut into twelve- or fifteen-foot lengths. This latter work was always a winter's job for the farmer, and the buds on these falling trees made excellent browsing feed for his cattle. In the spring-time, after the brush had become thoroughly dry, and in a dry time, a good burn of the brush, if possible, was obtained. The next part of the process was logging, usually after harvest. This required the labor of five men and a team of oxen,—one driver for the oxen and two men at each end of the log-heap. Neighbors would "morrow" with each other, and on such occasions each neighbor usually brought his own handspike. This was a round pole, usually made of beech-, dog-, or ironwood, without any iron on or in it, about six feet long, and sharpened at the large end. Logs were rolled on the pile over skids. Sometimes the cattle were made to draw or roll the logs on the heap. These piles were then burned, and the soil was ready for the drag or the triangular harrow. I have looked like a negro many a time while working at this logging. Then money was scarce, labor plenty and cheap, and amusements few, hence grubbing, chopping, and logging "frolics" were frequent and popular. For each frolic one or more two-gallon jugs of whiskey were indispensable. A jolly good time was had, as well as a good dinner and supper, and every one in the neighborhood expected an invitation.

As there was a fence law then, the ground had to be fenced, according to this law, "horse-high, bull-strong, and hog-tight." The effort made by the pioneer to obey this law was in four ways,—viz.: First, by slashing trees and placing brush upon the trees; second, by using the logs from the clearing for the purpose of a fence; third, by a post- and rail-fence, built straight, and the end of each rail sharpened and fastened in a mortised post; fourth, by the common rail- or worm-fence. These rails were made of ash, hickory, chesnut, linn, and pine. The usual price for making rails per hundred was fifty cents with board. I have made them by contract at that price myself.

> "I seem to see the low rail-fence,
>   That worming onward mile on mile,
> Was redolent with pungent scents
>   Of sassafras and camomile.
> Within a fence-rail tall and bare,
> The saucy bluebird nested there;
> 'Twas there the largest berries grew,
> As every barefoot urchin knew!
> And swiftly, shyly creeping through
>   The tangled vine and the bramble dense,
> The mingled sunshine and the dew,
>   The Bob-White perched atop the fence;
> And, flinging toil and care away,
> He piped and lilted all the day."

In 1799, when Joseph Hutchison lived here, wheat sold in this section of the State for two dollars and fifty cents per bushel, flour for eighteen dollars per barrel, corn two dollars, oats one dollar and fifty cents, and potatoes one dollar and fifty cents per bushel.

The early axes were called pole-axes. They were rude, clumsy, and heavy, with a single bit. About 1815 an improved Yankee single-bit axe was introduced, but it, too, was heavy and clumsy. In about 1825 the present double-bitted axe came to be occasionally used.

I have never seen the wooden plough, but I have seen them with the iron shoe point and coulter. These were still in use in the late twenties. I have driven an ox-team to the drag or triangular harrow. This was the principal implement used in seeding ground, both before and after the introduction of the shovel-plough in 1843.

PIONEER HISTORY OF JEFFERSON COUNTY, PENNA.

"The greatest improvement ever made on ploughs, in this or any other country, was made by Charles Newbold, of Burlington, New Jersey, and patented in 1797. The mould-board, share, landside, and point were all cast together in one solid piece. The plough was all cast iron except the beam and handles. The importance of this invention was so great that it attracted the attention of plough-makers and scientific men all over the country. Thomas Jefferson (afterwards President of the United States) wrote a treatise on ploughs, with a particular reference to the Newbold plough. He described the requisite form of the mould-board, according to scientific principles, and calculated the proper form and curvature of the mould-board to lessen the friction and lighten the draught.

"The Newbold plough would have been nearly perfect had it not been for one serious defect. When the point, for instance, was worn out, which would soon be accomplished, the plough was ruined and had to be thrown aside. This defect, however, was happily remedied by Jethro Wood, who was the first to cast the plough in sections, so that the parts most exposed to wear could be replaced from the same pattern, by which means the cast-iron plough became a complete success. His plough was patented in 1819, twenty-two years after Newbold's patent. It is a wonder that so long a time should have elapsed before any one thought of this improvement. These two men did more for the farmers in relation to ploughs than any others before their time or since."

In harvest-time the grain was first reaped with a sickle; then came the cradle. In my boyhood all the lying grain thrown down by storms was still reaped with a sickle. I carry the evidence of this on my fingers. Grain was usually thrashed by a flail, though some tramped it out with horses. By the flail ten bushels of wheat or twenty bushels of oats was a good day's work. Men who travelled around thrashing on shares with the flail charged every tenth bushel, including board. The tramping was done by horses and by farmers who had good or extra barn floors. The sheaves were laid in a circle, a man stood in the middle of the circle to turn up and over the straw as needed, and then, with a boy to ride one horse and lead another, the "tramping" in this circuit commenced. This was hard work for the boy; it made him tired and sore *where* he sat down. To prevent dizziness, the travel on the circuit was frequently reversed. One man, a boy, and two horses could tramp out in this way in a day about fifteen bushels of wheat or thirty-five bushels of oats. Grain was cleaned by means of two hand-riddles, one coarse and one fine. These riddles had no iron or steel about them, the bottom of each being made of wooden splints woven in. The riddles were two and one-half feet in diameter and the rings about four inches wide. Three men were required to clean the grain,—one to shake the riddle, while two others, one at each end of a tow sheet, doubled, swayed the sheet to and fro in front of the man shaking the riddle. These three men in this way could clean about ten or fifteen bushels of wheat in a day. This process was practised in the twenties. Windmills came into use about 1825. For many years there were extremely few wagons and but poor roads on which to use them. The early vehicles were the prongs of a tree, a sled made of saplings, called a "pung," and ox-carts. In fact, about all the work was done with oxen, and in driving his cattle the old settler would halloo with all his might and swear profusely. This profanity and hallooing was thought to be necessary. The pioneer sled was made with heavy single runners, the "bob"-sled being a later innovation.

"HAYING IN THE OLDEN TIME.

"Haying in the old days was a much more formidable yearly undertaking than it is to modern farmers. Before the era of labor-saving haying implements farmers began the work of haying early in the day and season, and toiled hard until both were far spent. Human muscle was strained to exert a force equal to the then unused horse-power. On large farms many 'hands' were required. Haying was an event of importance in the farmer's year. It made great demands upon his time, strength, and pocket-book. His best helpers were engaged long in advance, sometimes a whole season. Ability to handle a scythe well entitled a man to respect while haying lasted. Experts took as much pains with a scythe as with a razor. Boys of to-day have never seen such a sight as a dozen stalwart men mowing a dozen-acre field.

"On the first day of haying, almost before the sun was up, the men would be at the field ready to begin. The question to be settled at the very outset was as to which man should cut the 'double.' This was the first swath to be cut down and back through the centre of the field.

"The boys brought up the rear in the line of mowers. Their scythes were hung well 'in,' to cut a narrow swath. They were told to stand up straight when mowing, point in, keep the heel of the scythe down, and point out evenly, so as not to leave 'hog-troughs' on the meadow when the hay was raked up. Impatient of these admonitions, they thought they could mow pretty well, and looked ambitiously forward to a time when they might cut the 'double.'"

DRESS OF MEN.

Moccasin shoes, buckskin breeches, blue broadcloth coats and brass buttons, fawn-skin vests, roundabouts, and woollen warmuses, leather or woollen gallowses, coon- or seal-skin caps in winter with chip or oat-straw hats for summer. Every neighborhood had then usually one itinerant shoemaker and tailor, who periodically visited cabins and made up shoes or clothes as required. All material had to be furnished, and these itinerant mechanics worked for fifty cents a day and board. Corduroy pants and corduroy overalls were common.

The warmuses, breeches, and hunting-shirts of the men, the linsey petticoats, dresses, and bed-gowns of the women, were all hung in some corner of the cabin on wooden pegs. To some extent this was a display of pioneer wealth.

DRESS OF WOMEN.

Home made woollen cloth, tow, linen, linsey-woolsey, etc. I have seen "barefoot girls with cheek of tan" walk three or four miles to church, when, on nearing the church, they would step into the woods to put on a pair of shoes they carried with them. I could name some of these who are living to-day. A woman who could buy eight or ten yards of calico for a dress at a dollar a yard put on queenly airs. Every married woman of any refinement then wore day-caps and night-caps. The bonnets were beaver, gimp, leghorn, and sun-bonnets. For shoes, women usually went barefoot in the summer, and in the winter covered their feet with moccasins, calf-skin shoes, buffalo overshoes, and shoe-packs.

Linen and tow cloth were made from flax. The seed was sown in the early spring and ripened about August. It was harvested by "pulling." This was generally done by a "pulling frolic" of young people pulling it out by the root. It was then tied in little sheaves and permitted to dry, hauled in, and thrashed for the seed. Then the straw was watered and rotted by laying it on the ground out of doors. Then the straw was again dried and "broken in the flax-break," after which it was again tied up in little bundles and then scutched with a wooden knife. This scutching was a frolic job too, and a dirty one. Then it was hackled. This hackling process separated the linen part from the tow. The rest of the process consisted of spinning, weaving, and dyeing. Linen cloth sold for about twenty-four cents a yard, tow cloth for about twenty cents a yard.

In the State Constitutional Convention of 1837 to amend the constitution I find the occupation of the members elected to that body to be as follows,—viz.: Farmers, 51; iron-masters, 3; manufacturer, 1; mechanics, 2; house-carpenters, 2; brick-maker, 1; paper-maker, 1; printers, 2; potter, 1; judge, 1; attorneys, 41; doctors, 12; editor, 1; merchants, 9; surveyors, 4; clerks, 4; total membership, 136. From this it will be seen that farmers received proper recognition in the earlier elections.

THE PIONEER HOMES OF JEFFERSON COUNTY, PENNSYLVANIA.

> "This is the land our fathers loved,
> The homestead which they toiled to win.
> This is the ground whereon they moved,
> And here are the graves they slumber in."

The home of the pioneer in Jefferson County was a log cabin, one story high, chinked and daubed, having a fireplace in one end, with a chimney built of sticks and mud, and in one corner always stood a big wooden poker to turn back-logs or punch the fire. These cabins were usually small, but some were perhaps twenty by thirty feet, with a hole cut in two logs for a single window,—oiled paper being used for glass.

Pioneer cabin.

For Brussels carpet they had puncheon floors, and a clapboard roof held down by weight poles to protect them from the storm. Wooden pegs were driven in the logs for the wardrobe, the rifle, and the powder-horn. Wooden benches and stools were a luxury upon which to rest or sit while feasting on mush and milk, buckwheat cakes, hog and hominy.

Hospitality in this log cabin was simple, hearty, and unbounded. Whiskey was pure, cheap, and plenty, and was lavished bountifully on each and all social occasions. Every settler had his jug or barrel. It was the drink of drinks at all merry-makings, grubbings, loggings, choppings, house-warmings, and weddings. A drink of whiskey was always proffered to the visitor or traveller who chanced to call or spend a night in these log cabins.

Puncheon boards or planks were made from a log of straight grain and clear of knots, and of the proper length, which was split into parts

Cabin barn.

and the face of each part smoothed with a broadaxe. The split parts had to be all started at the same time, with wedges at the end of the log, each wedge being struck alternately with a maul until all the parts were separated.

The furniture for the table of the pioneer log cabins consisted of pewter dishes, plates, and spoons, or wooden bowls, plates, and noggins. If noggins were scarce, gourds and hard-shelled squashes answered for drinking-cups.

The iron pots, knives and forks, along with the salt and iron, were brought to the wilderness on pack-horses over Meade's trail or over the Milesburg and Le Bœuf State road.

Some of these log cabins near Brookville were still occupied in the forties. I have been in many of them in my childhood. In proof of the smallness of the early cabin I reproduce the testimony on oath of Thomas Lucas, Esq., in the following celebrated ejectment case,—viz.:

"EJECTMENT.

"In the Court of Common Pleas of Jefferson County. Ejectment for sixteen hundred acres of land in Pine Creek township. Elijah Heath vs. Joshua Knap, et al.

"16th September, 1841, a jury was called *per minets*. The plaintiff after having opened his case in support of the issue, gave in evidence as follows:

"Thomas Lucas.—Masons have in the surveys about twelve acres of land, a cabin house, and stable thereon. They live near the line of the town tract, the town tract takes in the apple-trees; think they claim on some improvement. Some of this improvement I think is thirty-five years old,—this was the Mason claim. The first improvement was made in 1802; I call it the Pickering survey, only an interference. Jacob Mason has been living off and on since 1802,—two small cabin houses on the interference, one fifteen or sixteen feet square, the other very small, twelve or fifteen feet,—a log stable."

At this time and before it many of these cabins were lighted by means of a half window,—viz., one window-sash, containing from four to six panes of seven by nine glass. Up to and even at this date (1841) the usual light at night in these cabins was the old iron lamp, something like the miner wears in his hat, or else a dish containing refuse grease, with a rag in it. Each smoked and gave a dismal light, yet women cooked, spun, and sewed and men read the few books they had as best they could. The aroma from this refuse grease was simply horrible. The cabin was daily swept with a split broom made of hickory. The hinges and latches of these cabins were made of wood. The latch on the door was raised from without by means of a buckskin string. At night, as a means of safety, the string was "pulled in," and this locked the door. As a further mark of refinement each cabin was generally guarded by from two to six worthless dogs.

Of pests in and around the old cabin, the house-fly, the bed-bug, and the louse were the most common on the inside; the gnat, the wood-tick, and the horse-fly on the outside. It was a constant fight for life with man, cattle, and horses against the gnat, the tick, and the horse-fly, and if it had not been for the protection of what were called "gnat-fires," life could not have been sustained, or at least it would have been unendurable. The only thing to dispel these outside pests was to clear land

PIONEER HISTORY OF JEFFERSON COUNTY, PENNA.

and let in the sunshine. As an all-around pest in the cabin and out, day and night, there was the flea.

PIONEER FOOD—WHAT THE PIONEER COULD HAVE, OR DID HAVE, TO EAT.

Buckwheat cakes, mush, and souens, corn-mush and milk, rye-mush and bread, hominy, potatoes, turnips, wild onions or wramps, wild meats, wild birds, fish, and wild fruits.

In the early cooking everything was boiled and baked; this was healthy. There was no "rare fad," with its injurious results. The common dishes served were wheat- and rye bread, wheat- and rye-mush, corn-pone, cakes, and mush, sweet and buttermilk boiled and thickened, doughnuts, and baked pot-pies. Soda was made by burning corn-cobs.

Buckwheat souens was a great pioneer dish. It was made in this wise: Mix your buckwheat flour and water in the morning; add to this enough yeast to make the batter light; then let it stand until evening, or until the batter is real sour. Now stir this batter into boiling water and boil until it is thoroughly cooked, like corn-mush. Eat hot or cold with milk or cream.

MEATS.

Hogs, bears, elks, deer, rabbits, squirrels, and woodchucks.

The saddles or hams of the deer were salted by the pioneer, then smoked and dried. This was a great luxury, and could be kept all the year through.

The late Dr. Clarke wrote, "Wild game, such as elks, deer, bears, turkeys, and partridges, were numerous, and for many years constituted an important part of the animal food of the early settlers in this wilderness. Wolves and panthers came in for a share of this game, until they, too, became game for the hunters by the public and legal offer of bounties to be paid for their scalps, or rather for their ears, for a perfect pair of ears was required to secure the bounty. All these have become nearly extinct. The sturdy elk no longer roves over the hills or sips 'salty sweetness' from the licks. The peculiar voice of the stately strutting wild turkey is heard no more. The howl of the wolf and the panther's cry no longer alarm the traveller as he winds his way over the hills or through the valleys, and the flocks are now permitted to rest in peace. Even the wild deer is now seldom seen, and a nice venison steak rarely gives its delicious aroma among the shining plate of modern well-set tables."

FISH.

Pike, bass, catfish, suckers, sunfish, horn-chubs, mountain trout, and eels.

The old settler shot, seined, hooked with a line, and gigged his fish. Gigging was done at night by means of a light made from burning fagots of pitch-pine. It usually required three to do this gigging, whether "wading" or in a canoe,—one to carry the light ahead, one to gig, and one to care for the fish.

BIRDS.

Pheasants were plentiful, and enlivened the forests with their drumming. The waters and woods were full of wild ducks, geese, pigeons, and turkeys.

The most remarkable bird in America was the wild turkey. It is the original turkey, and is the stock from which the tame turkeys sprung. In the wild state it was to be found in the wooded lands east of the Rocky Mountains. In pioneer times it was called gobbler or Bubly Jock by the whites, and Oo-coo-coo by the Indians. Our pioneer hunters could mimic or imitate the gobbling of a turkey, and this deceptive ruse was greatly practised to excite the curiosity and bring the bird within shooting distance. The last wild turkey in our county was killed in the seventies near the town of False Creek.

To obtain a turkey roast when needed, the pioneer sometimes built in the woods a pen of round logs and covered it with brush. Whole flocks of turkeys were sometimes caught in these pens, built in this wise:

"First, a narrow ditch, about six feet long and two feet deep, was dug. Over this trench the pen was built, leaving a few feet of the channel outside of the enclosure. The end of the part of the trench enclosed was usually about the middle of the pen. Over the ditch, near the wall of the pen, boards were laid. The pen was made tight enough to hold a turkey and covered with poles. Then corn was scattered about on the inside, and the ditch outside baited with the same grain. Sometimes straw was also scattered about in the pen. Then the trap was ready for its victims. The turkeys came to the pen, began to pick up the corn, and followed the trench within. When they had eaten enough, the birds tried to get out by walking around the pen, looking up all the time. They would cross the ditch on the boards, and never think of going to the opening in the ground at the centre of the pen. When the hunter found his game he had only to crawl into the pen through the trench and kill the birds."

In the fall turkeys became very fat, and gobblers were sometimes captured for Christmas in this way weighing over twenty pounds.

FRUITS.

Apples, crab-apples, wild, red, and yellow plums, blackberries, huckleberries, elderberries, wild strawberries, choke-cherries, and wild gooseberries.

SWEETS.

Domestic and wild honey, maple-sugar, maple-molasses, and corn-cob molasses. Bee-trees were numerous, and would frequently yield from eight to twelve gallons of excellent honey. These trees had to be cut in the night by the light of pitch-pine fagots.

DRINK.

Metheglin, a drink made from honey; whiskey, small beer, rye coffee, buttermilk, and fern, sassafras, sage, and mint teas.

To fully illustrate the pioneer days I quote from the "History of Crawford County, Pennsylvania,"—viz. :

"The habits of the pioneers were of a simplicity and purity in conformance to their surroundings and belongings. The men were engaged in the herculean labor, day after day, of enlarging the little patch of sunshine about their homes, cutting away the forest, burning off the brush and *débris*, preparing the soil, planting, tending, harvesting, caring for the few animals which they brought with them or soon procured, and in hunting. While they were engaged in the heavy labor of the field and forest, or following the deer, or seeking other game, their helpmeets were busied with their household duties, providing for the day and for the winter coming on, cooking, making clothes, spinning, and weaving. They were fitted by nature and experience to be the consorts of the brave men who first came into the western wilderness. They were heroic in their endurance of hardship and privation and loneliness.

"Their industry was well directed and unceasing. Woman's work then, like man's, was performed under disadvantages, which have been removed in later years. She had not only the common household duties to perform, but many others. She not only made the clothing, but the fabric for it. That old, old occupation of spinning and of weaving, with which woman's name has been associated in all history, and of which the modern world knows nothing, except through the stories of those who are great-grandmothers now,—that old occupation of spinning and weaving which seems surrounded with a glamour of romance as we look back to it through tradition and poetry, and which always conjures up thoughts of the graces and virtues of the dames and damsels of a generation that is gone,—that old, old occupation of spinning and of weaving was the chief industry of the pioneer woman. Every cabin sounded with the softly whirring wheel and the rhythmic thud of the loom. The woman of pioneer times was like the woman described by Solomon : 'She seeketh wool and flax, and worketh willingly with her hands; she layeth her hands to the spindle, and her hands hold the distaff.'

"Almost every article of clothing, all of the cloth in use in the old log cabins, was the product of the patient woman-weaver's toil. She spun the flax and wove the cloth for shirts, pantaloons, frocks, sheets, and blankets. The linen and the wool, the 'linsey-woolsey' woven by the housewife, formed all of the material for the clothing of both men and women, except such articles as were made of skins. The men commonly wore the hunting-shirt, a kind of loose frock reaching half-way down the figure, open before, and so wide as to lap over a foot or more upon the chest. This generally had a cape, which was often fringed with a ravelled piece of cloth of a different color from that which composed the garment. The bosom of the hunting-shirt answered as a pouch, in which could be carried the various articles that the hunter or woodsman would need. It was always worn belted, and made out of coarse linen, or linsey, or of dressed deer-skin, according to the fancy of the wearer. Breeches were made of heavy cloth or of deer-skin, and were often worn with leggings of the same material or of some kind of leather, while the feet were most usually encased in moccasins, which were easily and quickly made, though they needed frequent mending. The deer-skin breeches or drawers were very comfortable when dry, but when they became wet were very cold to the limbs, and the next time they were put on were almost as stiff as if made of wood. Hats or caps were made of the various native furs. The women were clothed in linsey petticoats, coarse shoes and stockings, and wore buckskin gloves or mittens when any protection was required for the hands. All of the wearing apparel, like that of the men, was made with a view to being serviceable and comfortable, and all was of home manufacture. Other articles and finer ones were sometimes worn, but they had been brought from former homes, and were usually relics handed down from parents to children. Jewelry was not common, but occasionally some ornament was displayed. In the cabins of the more cultivated pioneers were usually a few books, and the long winter evenings were spent in poring over these well-thumbed volumes by the light of the great log-fire, in knitting, mending, curing furs, or some similar occupation.

"As the settlement increased, the sense of loneliness and isolation was dispelled, the asperities of life were softened and its amenities multiplied; social gatherings became more numerous and more enjoyable. The log-rollings, harvestings, and husking-bees for the men, and apple-butter-making and the quilting-parties for the women, furnished frequent occasions for social intercourse. The early settlers took much pleasure and pride in rifle-shooting, and as they were accustomed to the use of the gun as a means often of obtaining a subsistence, and relied upon it as a weapon of defence, they exhibited considerable skill.

"Foot-racing, wrestling, and jumping matches were common. The jumping matches consisted of the 'single jump,' backward jump, high jump, three jumps, and the running hop, step, and jump.

"A wedding was the event of most importance in the sparsely settled new country. The young people had every inducement to marry, and generally did so as soon as able to provide for themselves. When a marriage was to be celebrated, all the neighborhood turned out. It was customary to have the ceremony performed before dinner, and in order to be in time, the groom and his attendants usually started from his father's house in the morning for that of the bride. All went on horseback, riding in single file along the narrow trail. Arriving at the cabin of the bride's parents, the ceremony would be performed, and after that dinner served. This would be a substantial backwoods feast, of beef, pork, fowls, and bear- or deer-meat, with such vegetables as could be procured. The greatest hilarity prevailed during the meal. After it was over, the dancing began, and was usually kept up till the next morning, though the newly made husband and wife were, as a general thing, put to bed in the most approved fashion and with considerable formality in the middle of the evening's hilarity. The tall young men, when they went on the floor to dance, had to take their places with care between the logs that supported the loft-floor, or they were in danger of bumping their heads. The figures of the dances were three- and four-hand reels, or square sets and jigs. The commencement was always a square four, which was followed by 'jigging it off,' or what is sometimes called a 'cut out jig.' The 'settlement' of a young couple was thought to be thoroughly and generously made when the neighbors assembled and raised a cabin for them."

PIONEER EVENING FROLICS, SOCIAL PARTIES, PLAYS, AND AMUSEMENTS—HOW THE PIONEER AND EARLY SETTLERS MADE THEIR LOG CABINS MERRY WITH SIMPLE, PRIMITIVE ENJOYMENTS.

In the pioneer days newspapers were few, dear, printed on coarse paper, and small. Books were scarce, only occasional preaching, no public lectures, and but few public meetings, excepting the annual Fourth of July celebration, when all the patriots assembled to hear the Declaration of Independence read. The pioneer and his family had to have fun. The common saying of that day was that "all work and no play makes Jack a dull boy." As a rule, outside of the villages, everybody lived in log cabins, and were bound together by mutual dependence and acts of neighborly kindness. At every cabin the latch-string was always out. The young ladies of the "upper ten" learned music, but it was the humming of to "knit and spin;" their piano was a loom, their sunshade a broom, and their novel a Bible. A young gentleman or lady was then as proud of his or her new suit, woven by a sister or a mother on her own loom, as proud could be, and these new suits or "best clothes" were always worn to evening frolics. Social parties among the young were called "kissing parties," because in all the plays, either as a penalty or as part of the play, all the girls who joined in the amusement had to be kissed by some one of the boys. The girls, of course, objected to the kissing, but then they were gentle, pretty, and witty, and the sweetest and best girls the world ever knew. This was true, for I attended these parties myself. To the boys and girls of that period—

> "The earth was like a garden then,
> And life seemed like a show,
> For the air was rife with fragrance,
> The sky was all rainbow,
> And the heart was warm and joyous;
> Each lad had native grace,
> Sly Cupid planted blushes then
> On every virgin's face."

The plays were nearly all musical and vocal, and the boys lived and played them in the "pleasures of hope," while usually there sat in the corner of the cabin fireplace a granddad or a grandma smoking a stone or clay pipe, lighted with a live coal from the wood-fire, living and smoking in the "pleasures of memory."

The plays were conducted somewhat in this way :

A popular play was for all the persons present to join hands and form a ring, with a dude of that time, in shirt of check and bear-greased hair, in the centre. Then they circled round and round the centre person, singing,—

> "King William was King James's son,
> And of that royal race he sprung;
> He wore a star upon his breast,
> To show that he was royal best.
> Go choose your east, go choose your west,
> Go choose the one that you like best;
> If he's not here to take your part,
> Go choose another with all your heart."

The gentleman in the centre then chose a lady from the circle, and she stepped into the ring with him. Then the circling was resumed, and all sang to the parties inside,—

> "Down on this carpet you must kneel,
> Just as the grass grows in the field;
> Salute your bride with kisses sweet,
> And then rise up upon your feet."

The play went on in this manner until all the girls present were kissed.

Another popular play was to form a ring. A young lady would step into the circle, and all parties would join hands and sing,—

> "There's a lily in the garden
> For you, young man;
> There's a lily in the garden,
> Go pluck it if you can," etc.

The lady then selects a boy from the circle, who walks into the ring with her. He then kisses her and she goes out, when the rest all sing,—

> "There he stands, that great big booby,
> Who he is I do not know;
> Who will take him for his beauty?
> Let her answer, yes or no."

This play goes on in this way until all the girls have been kissed. Another favorite play was:

> "Oats, peas, beans, and barley grows;
> None so well as the farmer knows
> How oats, peas, beans, and barley grows;
> Thus the farmer sows his seed,
> Thus he stands to take his ease;
> He stamps his foot and claps his hands,
> And turns around to view his lands," etc.

Another great favorite was:

> "Oh, sister Phœbe, how merry were we
> The night we sat under the juniper-tree,
> The juniper-tree, I, oh.
> Take this hat on your head, keep your head warm,
> And take a sweet kiss, it will do you no harm,
> But a great deal of good, I know," etc.

Another was:

> "If I had as many lives
> As Solomon had wives,
> I'd be as old as Adam;
> So rise to your feet
> And kiss the first you meet,
> Your humble servant, madam."

Another was:

> "It's raining, it's hailing, it's cold, stormy weather;
> In comes the farmer drinking of his cider.
> He's going a-reaping, he wants a binder,
> I've lost my true love, where shall I find her."

A live play was called "hurly-burly." "Two went round and gave each one, secretly, something to do. This girl was to pull a young man's hair; another to tweak an ear or nose, or trip some one, etc. When all had been told what to do, the master of ceremonies cried out, 'Hurly-burly.' Every one sprang up and hastened to do as instructed. This created a mixed scene of a ludicrous character, and was most properly named 'hurly-burly.'"

TREES, SNAKES, AND REPTILES.

Our forests were originally covered by a heavy growth of timber-trees of various kinds. Pine and hemlock predominated. Chestnut and oak grew in some localities. Birch, sugar-maple, ash, and hickory occupied a wide range. Birch- and cherry-trees were numerous, and linnwood-, cucumber-, and poplar-trees grew on many of the hill-sides, butternut, sycamore, black ash, and elm on the low grounds.

In all, about one hundred varieties of trees grew here. These forests have become the prey of the woodman's axe. There has been no voice raised effectively to restrain the destruction, wanton as it has been, of the best specimens of the pine which the eye of man ever saw. The growth of hundreds of years felled to the ground, scarified, hauled to the streams, tumbled in, and floated away to the south and east and west for the paltry pittance of ten cents a foot! Oh, that there could have been some power to restrain the grasping, wasteful, avaricious cupidity of man, of some voice of thunder crying, "Woodman, woodman, spare that tree! That old familiar forest-tree, whose glory and renown has spread over land and sea, and woodmen hacked it down!"

But they are gone, all gone from the mountain's brow. The hands, also, that commenced the destruction are now mouldering into dust, thus exemplifying the law of nature, that growth is rapidly followed by decay, indicating a common destiny and bringing a uniform result. And such are we; it is our lot thus to die and be forgotten.

Reptiles and snakes were very numerous. The early pioneer had to contend against the non-poisonous and poisonous snakes. The non-poisonous were the spotted adder, blacksnake, the green-, the garter-, the water-, and the house-snake. The blacksnake sometimes attained a length of six and eight feet. But dens of vicious rattlesnakes existed in every locality in the county. In the vicinity of Brookville there was one at Puckerty, several on the north fork, one at Iowa Mills, and legions of rattlers on Mill Creek. The dens had to be visited by bold, hardy men annually every spring to kill and destroy these reptiles as they emerged in the sun from their dens. Hundreds had to be destroyed at each den every spring. This was necessary as a means of safety for both man and beast. Of copperheads, there were but a few dens in the county, and these in the extreme south and southwest,—viz., in Perry township, in Beaver township, on Beaver Run; and two or three dens in Porter township, on the head-waters of Pine Run,—viz., Nye's Branch and Lost Hill. Occasionally one was found in Brookville.

The copperhead is hazel-brown on the back and pinkish on the belly. On each side there are from fifteen to twenty-six chestnut blotches or bands, that somewhat resemble an inverted Y. His head is brighter and almost copper-colored on top, and everywhere over his back are found very fine dark points. The sides of his head are cream-colored. The dividing line between the cream of the side and the copper of the top passes through the upper edge of the head, in front of the eye, and involves three-fourths of the orbit. The line is very distinct.

He is commonly found wherever the rattler is, but he does not live quite so far north. He has a variety of names,—upland moccasin, chunkhead, deaf-adder, and pilot-snake among the rest. It is agreed that he is a much more vicious brute than the rattlesnake. He is more easily irritated and is quicker in his movements. It is said that he will even follow up a victim for a second blow. On the other hand, his bite is very much less dangerous for a variety of reasons. In the first place, he is no more than three feet long, and his fangs are considerably shorter than those of a rattler of the same size, while his strength is less, and the blow, therefore, less effective. So he cannot inflict as deep a wound nor inject so much venom. The chances of his getting the venom directly into a large vein are proportionately less.

Rattlesnakes, copperheads, and other large snakes do most of their travelling in the night. "Snakes, it appears, are extremely fastidious, every species being limited to one or two articles of diet, and preferring to starve rather than eat anything else apparently quite as toothsome and suitable. Individual snakes, too, show strange prejudices in the matter of diet, so that it is necessary in every case to find out what the snake's peculiarities are before feeding him."

Rattlesnakes eat berries for food, hence they avoid ash and sugar, and live on barren, rocky, or on huckleberry land. They like to bathe, drink, and live in the sunshine. This, too, makes them avoid ridgy, heavily timbered land.

The bigger the reptile, of course, the more poison it has. Furthermore, it is to be remembered that of all American serpents the rattlesnake is the most dangerous, the copperhead less so, and the water-moccasin least. It is a fact that the poisonous snakes are proof against their own venom. That this is true has been demonstrated repeatedly by inoculating such serpents with the poisonous secretion from their salivary glands. It is believed that there exists in the blood of the venomous snake some agent similar to the poison itself, and that the presence of this toxic principle is accountable for the immunity exhibited.

One safety from the snakes to the pioneer and his family was the great number of razor-back hogs. These animals were great snake-hunters, being very fond of them.

RATTLESNAKES FIRST KILL THEIR PREY, THEN SWALLOW IT WHOLE.

The rattlesnake is not found anywhere but in America. It belongs to the viper family. There are twelve species and thirteen varieties. They vary in size and color, one variety being red. A rattle is formed at each renewal of the skin, and as the skin may be renewed more than once a year, rattles do not indicate the exact age. They live to a ripe old age, and have sometimes as many as thirty rattles. Some writers call our variety the "banded snake." In the natural state the rattler sheds his skin but once a year, but in confinement he can be forced to shed the skin two or three times annually by giving him warm baths and keeping him in a warm place. Rattlers are unable to climb trees, are fond of

Dr. Ferd. Hoffman and rattlesnakes.

music, and do not chase a retreating animal that has escaped their "strike."

The rattlesnake of Jefferson County, Pennsylvania, is the *Crotalus horridus*, or North American species, and is the black variety, somewhat spotted. Our snake attains the length of five feet, but usually only four and one-half feet, and they inhabit the barren, rocky portions of our county, formerly in immense numbers, but of late years they are not so plentiful.

Dr. Ferd. Hoffman, of our town, celebrated as a snake-charmer, brought a rattlesnake into our store one day, in a little box covered with wire screen. The snake was small, being only thirty inches long and having seven rattles. Desiring to see the reptile eat, and knowing that they will not eat anything but what they kill themselves, we conceived the idea of furnishing his kingship a repast. Mr. Robert Scofield went out and captured a large field-mouse (not mole) and brought it in, and, in the presence of myself, Scofield, Albert Gooder, 'Squire McLaughlin and brother, and Frank Arthurs, dropped it into the box under the screen. The box was fourteen inches long and seven inches wide. The snake, being lively, immediately struck the mouse back of the head. The mouse gave a little squeak of terror and ran fourteen inches, then staggered fourteen inches, the length of the box, then was apparently seized with spinal paralysis, for it had to draw its hind limbs with its front feet to a corner of the box. It then raised up and fell dead on its back. After striking the mouse, the snake paid no attention to anything until the mouse dropped over dead, then his snakeship wakened up and apparently smelled (examined) the mouse all over. Satisfied it was healthy and good food, the snake caught the mouse by the nose and pulled it out of the corner. After this was done, the snake commenced the process of swallowing in this manner,—viz.: He opened his jaws and took the head of the mouse in one swallow, pulling alternately by the hooks in the upper and lower jaw, thus forcing the mouse downward, taking an occasional rest, swallowing and resting six times in the process. He rattled vigorously three times during this procedure. It is said they rattle only when in fear or in danger. This rattling of his must have been a notice to us that he was dining, and to stand back.

I am informed by my friend Dr. Hoffman, of Brookville, Pennsylvania, that the rattlesnake is possessed of both a high intelligence and a memory; that he can be domesticated, and in that state become quite affectionate and fond of his master, and that snakes thus domesticated will vie and dispute with each other in manifestations of affection to and for their master. He also informs me that rattlesnakes are unlike in disposition,—some are cross and ugly, while others are docile and pleasant.

He also informs me that the rattlesnake can be trained to perform tricks, as he has thus trained them himself and made them proficient in numerous acrobatic tricks, such as suspending a number by the head of one on his thumb, the forming of a suspension chain or bridge, and permitting them to kiss him, and many other tricks too numerous to relate.

To my personal knowledge, he has educated or trained the rattlers in numbers to perform in the manner indicated here, and without removing, in a single instance, any poisonous tooth or sac. These trained rattlers will fight any stranger the moment he presents himself; but if the master or their acquaintance presents himself, the rattlers will at once recognize him, and to him be kind, docile, and affectionate.

The snapping-turtle, the mud-turtle, and the diamond-backed terrapin existed in great numbers in the swamps and around the streams, and formed a part of the Indian's food. The tree-toad, the common toad, common frog, lizard, and water-lizard lived here before the pioneers took possession of the land.

The tools of the pioneer were the axe, six-inch auger, the drawing-knife, the shaving-knife, a broadaxe, and a cross-cut saw. These were "all used in the erecting of his shelters." The dexterity of the pioneer in the "slight" and use of the axe was remarkable and marvellous. He used it in clearing land, building cabins, making fences, chopping firewood, cutting paths and roads, bridges and corduroy. In fact, in all work and hunting, in travelling by land, in canoeing and rafting on the water, the axe was ever the friend and companion of the pioneer.

The civilized man in his first beginning was farmer, carpenter, mason, merchant, and manufacturer—complete, though primitive, in the individual. But he was a farmer first and foremost, and used the other avocations merely as incidentals to the first and chief employment. Less than half a century has elapsed since the spinning-wheel and the loom were common and necessary in the home.

SOLDIERS OF 1812 WHO PASSED THROUGH PINE CREEK TOWNSHIP TO FIGHT GREAT BRITAIN—AN INTERESTING ACCOUNT OF THE PENNSYLVANIA MILITIA WHICH MARCHED OVER THE OLD STATE ROAD THROUGH BROOKVILLE AND WITHIN TWO MILES OF WHERE REYNOLDSVILLE NOW STANDS, WHILE ON ITS WAY TO ERIE.

George Washington never passed through any portion of Jefferson County with soldiers; neither did Colonel Bird, who was stationed at Fort Augusta in 1756; neither was there a "road brushed out for the purpose of transferring troops to Erie." In 1814, early in the spring, a detachment of soldiers, under command of Major William McClelland, travelled through our county, over the old State Road (Bald Eagle's Nest and Le Bœuf road) to Erie. They encamped at Soldiers' Run, in what is now Winslow township, rested at Port Barnett for four days, and encamped over night at the "four-mile" spring, on what is now the Afton farm. Elijah M. Graham was impressed with his two "pack-horses" into their service, and was taken as far as French Creek, now in Venango County.

Joseph B. Graham gave me these facts in regard to McClelland. These soldiers were Pennsylvania volunteers and drafted men, and were from Franklin County. Major McClelland, with his officers and men, passed through where Brookville now is, over the old Milesburg and Waterford Road. Three detachments of troops left Franklin County during the years 1812-14 at three different times,—one by way of Pittsburg, one by way of Baltimore, and the last one through this wilderness. All of these troops in these three detachments were under the supervision of the brigade inspector, Major McClelland.

N. B. BOILEAU TO WILLIAM MCCLELLAND.

"HARRISBURG, February 1, 1814.

"To WILLIAM MCCLELLAND, ESQ., *Inspector Second Brigade, Seventh Division*.

"SIR,—By last evening's mail the Governor received a letter from the Secretary of War, requiring a detachment of one thousand militia to march to the defence of Erie. He has it in contemplation to order them from the counties of Cumberland, York, Adams, and Franklin. The Governor directs me to give you this intimation in order that you may make arrangements to execute as promptly as possible the orders which which will be sent to you in a few days.

"Very respectfully, sir,
"Your obedient servant,
"N. B. BOILEAU."

NOTE.—Similar letters were written to George Welsh, James Lamberton, and Archibald S. Jordan.

GOVERNOR SIMON SNYDER TO N. B. BOILEAU.

"GENERAL ORDERS.

"HARRISBURG, February 7, 1814.

"To N. B. BOILEAU, *Aide-de-Camp*.

"In compliance with a requisition by the President of the United States, I do order into the service of the Union one thousand men, rank and file, of the Pennsylvania militia, and a competent number of officers, to be composed of the quotas of the First and Second Brigades of the Seventh Division, and of the Second Brigade of the Fifth Division, designated for the service of the United States, under general orders of the 12th of May, 1812, to rendezvous at Erie on the 5th day of March, then, or as soon thereafter as possible, to be organized into one regiment, and to be agreeably to law.

"SIMON SNYDER,
"*Governor of the Commonwealth of Pennsylvania*."

N. B. BOILEAU TO WILLIAM MCCLELLAND.

"HARRISBURG, February 24, 1815.

"To WILLIAM MCCLELLAND, ESQ., *Inspector of Second Brigade, Seventh Division.*

"SIR,—In answer to yours of the 21st ult., to the Governor, I am directed to state that in case your first draft does not furnish a quota sufficient when added to those from Mr. Lamberton's and Welsh's brigades to make one thousand men, rank and file, then you put under the direction of Major Lamberton the number you may have ready to march, and proceed to make another draft to make up the deficiency of your quota, and march them on to the general place of rendezvous as expeditiously as practicable. You will make an arrangement with Mr. Lamberton as to the point where your detachment will join his. A sufficient number of tents, together with those at Carlisle, to accommodate the whole detachment, are now on the road from Philadelphia, and will be at Carlisle on Saturday next.

"By order of the Governor.

"N. B. BOILEAU."

I quote from an early history of Franklin County, Pennsylvania:

"In the early part of the year 1814, the general government having made a call upon the State of Pennsylvania for more troops, Governor Simon Snyder, about the beginning of February of that year, ordered a draft for one thousand men from the counties of York, Adams, Franklin, and Cumberland, Cumberland County to raise five hundred men and the other counties the balance. The quota of Franklin County was ordered to assemble at Loudon on the 1st of March, 1814. What was its exact number I have not been able to ascertain.

"At that time Captain Samuel Dunn, of Path Valley, had a small volunteer company under his command, numbering about forty men. These, I am informed, volunteered to go as part of the quota of the county, and were accepted. Drafts were then made to furnish the balance of the quota, and one full company of drafted men, under the command of Captain Samuel Gordon, of Waynesburg, and one partial company, under command of Captain Jacob Stake, of Lurgan township, were organized, and assembled at Loudon in pursuance of the orders of the Governor. There the command of the detachment was assumed by Major William McClelland, brigade inspector of the county, who conducted it to Erie. It moved from Loudon on the 4th of March, and was twenty-eight days in reaching Erie. According to Major McClelland's report on file in the auditor-general's office at Harrisburg, it was composed of one major, three captains, five lieutenants, two ensigns, and two hundred and twenty-one privates.

PIONEER HISTORY OF JEFFERSON COUNTY, PENNA.

"Captain Jacob Stake lived along the foot of the mountain, between Roxbury and Strasburg. He went as captain of a company of drafted men as far as Erie, at which place his company was merged into those of Captains Dunn and Gordon, as the commissions of those officers antedated his commission and there were not men enough in their companies to fill them up to the required complement."

Upon the arrival of these troops at Erie, and after their organization into companies, they were put into the Fifth Regiment of the Pennsylvania troops, commanded by Colonel James Fenton, of that regiment. James Wood, of Greencastle, was major, and Thomas Poe, of Antrim township, adjutant, the whole army being under the command of Major-General Jacob Brown.

Adjutant Poe is reputed to have been a gallant officer, one to whom fear was unknown. On one occasion he quelled a mutiny among the men in camp, unaided by any other person. The mutineers afterwards declared that they saw death in his eyes when he gave them the command to "return to quarters." He fell mortally wounded at the battle of Chippewa, July 5, 1814, and died shortly afterwards.

These soldiers did valiant service against the British. They fought in the desperate battles of Chippewa and Lundy's Lane, on July 5 and 25 of the year 1814.

War has cost the United States nearly $10,000,000,000 and over 680,000 lives, to say nothing of 30,000 lives lost in colonial wars before the Revolution. Here are the details:

	Cost.	Lives.
Revolution	$135,193,703	30,000
War of 1812	107,159,003	2,000
Mexican war	74,000,000	2,000
Civil war	8,500,000,000	600,000
Indian wars	1,000,000,000	49,000

The two Napoleons cost France in war nearly $3,500,000,000. For the Napoleonic wars France paid $1,275,000,000. Over 5,000,000 men were killed in these wars.

AN OUTLINE OF THE PIONEER LEGAL RELATIONS OF MAN AND WIFE.

Up to and later than 1843, Pennsylvania was under the common law system of England. Under this law the wife had no legal separate existence. The husband had the right to whip her, and only in the event of her committing crimes had she a separate existence from her husband. But if the crime was committed in her husband's presence, she was then presumed not guilty. Her condition was legally little, if any, better than a slave.

Under the common law, husband and wife were considered as *one person*, and on this principle all their civil duties and relations rested.

The wife could not sue in her own name, but only through her husband. If she suffered wrong in her person or property, she could, with her husband's aid and assistance, prosecute, but the husband had to be the plaintiff. For crimes without any presumed coercion of her husband, the wife could be prosecuted and punished, and for these misdemeanors the punishments were severe. The wife could make no contract with her husband. The husband and she could make a contract through the agency of trustees for the wife, the wife, though, being still under the protection of her husband.

All contracts made between husband and wife before marriage were void after the ceremony. The husband could in no wise convey lands or realty to his wife, only and except through a trustee. A husband at death could bequeath real estate to his wife.

Marriage gave the husband all right and title to his wife's property, whether real or personal, but he then became liable for all her debts and contracts, even those that were made before marriage, and after marriage he was so liable, except for "superfluities and extravagances."

If the wife died before the husband and left no children, the husband and his heirs inherited her real estate. But if there were children, the husband remained in possession of her land during the lifetime of the wife, and at his death the land went to the wife's heirs.

All debts due to the wife became after marriage the property of the husband, who became invested with power to sue on bond, note, or any other obligation, to his own and exclusive use. The powers of discharge and assignment and change of securities were, of course, involved in the leading principle. If the husband died before the recovery of the money, or any change in the securities, the wife became entitled to these debts, etc., in her own right. All personal property of the wife, such as money, goods, movables, and stocks, became absolutely the property of the husband upon marriage, and at his death went to his heirs.

Property could be given to a wife by deed of marriage settlement.

Property could be settled on the wife after marriage by the husband, provided he was solvent at the time and the transfer not made with a view to defraud.

The wife could not sell her land, but any real estate settled upon her to a trustee she could bequeath.

The husband and wife could not be witnesses against each other in civil or criminal cases where the testimony could in the least favor or criminate either. One exception only existed to this rule, and that was this, "the personal safety or the life of the wife gave her permission to testify for her protection." For further information, see my "Recollections."

PIONEER HISTORY OF JEFFERSON COUNTY, PENNA.

A PIONEER SONG THAT WAS SUNG IN EVERY FAMILY.

"OLD GRIMES.

"Old Grimes is dead, that good old man,
    We ne'er shall see him more;
He used to wear a long black coat
    All buttoned down before.

"His heart was open as the day,
    His feelings all were true;
His hair was some inclined to gray,
    He wore it in a queue.

"When'er he heard the voice of pain
    His breast with pity burned;
The large round head upon his cane
    From ivory was turned.

"Kind words he ever had for all;
    He knew no base design;
His eyes were dark and rather small,
    His nose was aquiline.

"He lived in peace with all mankind,
    In friendship he was true;
His coat had pocket-holes behind,
    His pantaloons were blue.

"Unharmed, the sin which earth pollutes
    He passed securely o'er,
And never wore a pair of boots
    For thirty years or more.

"But good Old Grimes is now at rest,
    Nor fears misfortune's frown;
He wore a double-breasted vest,
    The stripes ran up and down.

"He modest merit sought to find,
    And pay it its desert:
He had no malice in his mind,
    No ruffles on his shirt.

"His neighbors he did not abuse,
    Was sociable and gay;
He wore large buckles on his shoes,
    And changed them every day.

"His knowledge hid from public gaze
    He did not bring to view,
Nor make a noise town-meeting days,
    As many people do.

> "His worldly goods he never threw
> In trust to fortune's chances,
> But lived (as all his brothers do)
> In easy circumstances.
>
> "Thus undisturbed by anxious cares
> His peaceful moments ran;
> And everybody said he was
> A fine old gentleman."
>
> —ALBERT G. GREENE.

EARLY AND PIONEER MUSIC—PIONEER MUSIC-SCHOOLS AND PIONEER SINGING-MASTERS IN JEFFERSON COUNTY.

I. D. Hughes, of Punxsutawney, informs me that the first music-book he bought was Wyeth's "Repository of Sacred Music," second edition. I have seen this book myself, but a later edition (the fifth), published in 1820. Mr. Hughes says that Joseph Thompson, of Dowlingville, was the pioneer "singing-master" in Jefferson County, and that he sang from Wakefield's "Harp," second edition. He used a tuning-fork to sound the pitches, and accompanied his vocal instruction with violin music.

George James was an early "master," and used the same book as Thompson. These two taught in the early thirties. I. D. Hughes taught in 1840 and used the "Missouri Harmony." This was a collection of psalm and hymn tunes and anthems, and was published by Morgan & Co., Cincinnati, Ohio. The first tune in this old "Harmony," or "buckwheat" note-book, was "Primrose":

> "Salvation, oh, the joyful sound,
> 'Tis pleasure to our ears,
> A sovereign balm for every wound,
> A cordial for our fears."

On the second page was "Old Hundred," and on the same page "Canaan":

> "On Jordan's stormy banks I stand,
> And cast a wishful eye
> To Canaan's fair and happy land,
> Where my possessions lie."

The dear old pioneers who used to delight in these sweet melodies have nearly all crossed this Jordan, and are now doubtless singing "Harwell":

> "Hark! ten thousand harps and voices
> Sound the note of praise above;
> Jesus reigns, and heaven rejoices;
> Jesus reigns, the God of love."

Rev. George M. Slaysman, of Punxsutawney, was the pioneer teacher of round notes—the *do ra me's*—in the county. Judge William P. Jenks was also an early instructor in these notes.

PIONEER HISTORY OF JEFFERSON COUNTY, PENNA.

We talk about progress, rapid transit, and electricity, but modern music-teachers have failed to improve on the melody of those old pioneer tunes, "that seemed like echoes from a heavenly choir; echoes that seemed to have increased power every time the pearly gates opened to admit some sainted father or mother."

"God sent these singers upon earth
With songs of sadness and of mirth,
That they might touch the hearts of men
And bring them back to Heaven again."

A PIONEER SONG FOR THE SUGAR-TROUGH CRADLE.
DR. WATTS'S CRADLE HYMN.

"Hush, my babe, lie still and slumber,
    Holy angels guard thy bed;
Heavenly blessings, without number,
    Gently falling on thy head.

"Sleep, my babe, thy food and raiment,
    House and home thy friends provide,
All without thy care or payment,
    All thy wants are well supplied.

"How much better thou'rt attended
    Than the Son of God could be,
When from heaven He descended
    And became a child like thee.

"Soft and easy is thy cradle,
    Coarse and hard thy Saviour lay,
When His birthplace was a stable,
    And his softest bed was hay.

"Blessed babe! what glorious features,
    Spotless, fair, divinely bright!
Must He dwell with brutal creatures?
    How could angels bear the sight?

"Was there nothing but a manger
    Wicked sinners could afford
To receive the heavenly stranger?
    Did they thus affront the Lord?

"Soft, my child, I did not chide thee,
    Though my song may sound too hard:
'Tis thy mother sits beside thee,
    And her arms shall be thy guard.

"Yet, to read the shameful story,
    How the Jews abused their King;
How they served the Lord of Glory,
    Makes me angry while I sing.

"See the kinder shepherds round Him,
    Telling wonders from the sky;
There they sought Him, there they found Him,
    With his virgin mother by.

"See the lovely babe a dressing,
    Lovely infant! how He smiled!
When He wept, His mother's blessing
    Soothed and hushed the holy child.

"Lo! He slumbers in a manger
    Where the horned oxen fed!
Peace, my darling, here's no danger,
    Here's no ox about thy bed.

"'Twas to save thee, child, from dying,
    Save my dear from burning flame,
Bitter groans, and endless crying,
    That thy blest Redeemer came.

"May'st thou live to know and fear Him,
    Trust and love Him all thy days!
Then go dwell forever near Him,
    See His face and sing His praise.

"I could give thee thousand kisses
    Hoping what I most desire;
Not a mother's fondest wishes
    Can to greater joys aspire."

COMPLETE LIST OF TAXABLE INHABITANTS IN JEFFERSON COUNTY, PENNSYLVANIA, IN A.D. 1820.

PINE CREEK TOWNSHIP.

Robert Andrews, William Andrews, single man, Joseph Barnett, saw- and grist-mill, John Barnett, single man, Andrew Barnett, single man, Thomas Barnett, grist-mill, Summers Baldwin, single man, half a saw-mill, Israel Bartlett, David Butler, single man, Peter Bartle, Harmen Bosley, single man, J. Bowen, Joseph Clements, Paul Campbell, Joseph Carr, Euphrastus Carrier, single man, Samuel Corbett, single man, John Dixon, Robert Dixon, single man, John Z. Early, two saw-mills, J. Stephens, half a saw-mill, Henry Feye, Sr., Henry Feye, Jr., single man, George Feye, single man, Aaron Fuller, Solomon Fuller, saw-mill and grist-mill, John Fuller, saw-mill, Elijah Graham, Andrew Grinder, Alexander Hatter, single man, John Hise, Christopher Himes, William Himes, single man, Frederick Hetrick, John Jones, single man, Robert Knox, Henry Kailor, Moses Knapp, Lewis Long, John Lucas, John Lattimer, single man, Thomas Lucas, Henry Latt, John Matson, half a saw-mill, Jacob Mason, Abraham Milliron, Philip Milliron, William Morrison, Joseph McCullough, Samuel McGill, William Milliron, John

PIONEER HISTORY OF JEFFERSON COUNTY, PENNA.

Mason, single man, John McCartney, single man, John McClelland, single man, Adam Newenhouse, John Nolf, Jr., John Nolf, Sr., saw-mill, Peter B. Ostrander, half a saw-mill, Alexander Powers, Jacob Pierce, single man, John Reed, Hulet Smith, James Shields, Samuel Shaffer, Henry Sharp, Walter Templeton, Adam Vasbinder, Sr., Jacob Vasbinder, William Vasbinder, Henry Vasbinder, John Vasbinder, Andrew Vasbinder, Jr., single man, Fudge Van Camp, colored, Richard Van Camp, single man, colored, Sarah Van Camp, colored, Enos Van Camp, colored, Hugh Williamson, John Welsh, saw-mill, Charles Sutherland, colored.

PERRY TOWNSHIP.

Jesse Armstrong, James Brady, Jr., John Bell, Esq., James Bell, single man, Joseph Bell, single man, John Bell, single man, Asa Crossman, Sr., Asa Crossman, Jr., Joseph Crossman, Elisha Dike, Benjamin Dike, Nathaniel Foster, Charles C. Gaskill, David Hamilton, James Hamilton, Archibald Hadden, Jacob Hoover, saw-mill, Elijah Heath, John Hoover, James Hutchinson, James Irven, Dr. John W. Jenks, Stephen Lewis, Isaac Lewis, Michael Lantz, Jacob Lantz, single man, Adam Long, James McClelland, Elizabeth McHenry, John McDonald, David Milliron, John Milliron, Hugh McKee, James McKee, John Newcome, John Postlethwait, David Postlethwait, single man, John Pifer, Thomas Pagne, Peter Reed, Samuel Stokes, William Smith, James Stewart, John Stewart, Jacob Smith, William Thompson, James Wachob, John Young.

MAPLE-SUGAR INDUSTRY.

One of the pioneer industries in this wilderness was maple-sugar-making. The sugar season commenced either in the last of February or the first of March. In any event, at this time the manufacturer always visited his camp to see or set things in order. The camp was a small cabin made of logs, covered usually with clapboards, and open at one end. The fireplace or crane and hooks were made in this way: Before the opening in the cabin four wooden forks were deeply set in the ground, and on these forks was suspended a strong pole. On this pole was hung the hook of a limb, with a pin in the lower end to hang the kettle on. An average camp had about three hundred trees, and it required six kettles, averaging about twenty-two gallons each, to boil the water from that many trees. The trees were tapped in various ways,—viz.: First, with a three-quarter-inch auger, one or two inches deep. In this hole was put a round spile about eighteen inches long, made of sumach or whittled pine, two spiles to a tree. The later way was by cutting a hollow notch in the tree and putting the spile below with a gouge. This spile was made of pine or some soft wood. When a boy I lived about five years with Joseph and James McCurdy, in what is now Washington township, and the latter method of opening trees was practised by them. Indeed, all I say here about this industry I learned from and while with them. At the camp there were always from one to three storage-troughs made of cucumber or poplar, and each trough held from ten barrels upward. Three hundred trees required a storage of thirty barrels and steady boiling with six kettles. The small troughs under the trees were

Stirring off maple-sugar.

made of pine and cucumber and held from three to six gallons. We hauled the water to the storage-troughs with one horse and a kind of "pung," the barrel being kept in its place by plank just far enough apart to hold it tight. In the fireplace there was a large back log and one a little smaller in front. The fire was kept up late and early with smaller wood split in lengths of about three feet. We boiled the water into a thick syrup, then strained it through a woollen cloth while hot into the syrup-barrel. When it had settled, and before putting it on to "sugar off," we strained it the second time. During this sugaring we skimmed the scum off with a tin skimmer and clarified the syrup in the kettle with eggs well beaten in sweet milk. This "sugaring off" was always done in cloudy or cold days, when the trees wouldn't run "sap." One barrel of sugar-water from a sugar-tree, in the beginning of the season, would make from five to seven pounds of sugar. The sugar was always made during the first of the season. The molasses was always made at the last of the season, or else it would turn to sugar in a very few days. The sugar was made in cakes, or "stirred off" in a granulated condition, and sold in the market for from six and a quarter to twelve and a half cents a pound. In "sugaring off," the syrup had to be frequently sampled by dropping some of it in a tin of cold water, and if the molasses formed a "thread" that was brittle like glass, it was fit to stir. I was good at sampling, and always anxious to try the syrup, as James McCurdy, who is still living, can substantiate. In truth, I was never very hungry during sugar-making, as I had a continual feast during this season of hot syrup, treacle, and sugar.

Skill and attention were both necessary in "sugaring off," for if the syrup was taken off too soon the sugar was wet and tough, and if left on too long, the sugar was burnt and bitter. Time has evolved this industry from our county. In the census chapter of 1840 you will find how many pounds of maple-sugar were manufactured in each township and the sum total in pounds for the county.

"While maple-sugar-making has passed in Jefferson County, it still is quite an important industry in many parts of the country. According to the statistics gathered in the census of 1890, Vermont leads in the production of maple-sugar, at least in the number of large producers. There were 23,533 producers who manufactured each 500 pounds or over of sugar, according to that census. Of these, Vermont reported 10,099; New York, 7884; New Hampshire, 1725; Michigan, 1135; Pennsylvania, 1101; Ohio, 930; Massachusetts, 415; Maryland, 78; Maine, 39; West Virginia, 26; Indiana, 24; Iowa and Minnesota, 23 each; Illinois, 8; Connecticut and Missouri, 5 each; Wisconsin and Virginia, 4 each; Tennessee and North Carolina, 2 each; and Kentucky, 1.

"It is the hard-maple tree that makes the sugar. Windham County, Vermont, Somerset County, Pennsylvania, and Delaware County, New York, are the three greatest maple-sugar producing counties in the Union, the first leading the list with an annual yield of about 3,000,000 pounds, the second producing 2,500,000 pounds, and the third 2,000,000 pounds. The largest single sugar-bush is in Windham County; it contains 7000 sap-bearing trees."

Joseph and James McCurdy were pioneer settlers. Joseph has been dead many years, and I can cheerfully say that he was an honest and true Christian.

THE TRANSPORTATION OF IRON THROUGH JEFFERSON COUNTY.

Centre County, Pennsylvania, was richly supplied by nature with the finest quality of iron ore and all the other requisites for its manufacture into iron. The pioneer in the iron business in what is now Centre County was Colonel John Patton, of the Revolutionary war. Immediately after peace was declared he removed to this region and erected

PIONEER HISTORY OF JEFFERSON COUNTY, PENNA.

"Centre Furnace." He died in 1804. The iron in early days, before 1800, was called "Juniata Iron," and the market was to be found on the Atlantic seaboard.

The development of this rich iron field, thus early commenced, gradually developed under the old charcoal system, until in 1826, when, from an increased demand from the Western market, there was in active operation in that county thirteen furnaces making annually eleven thousand six hundred tons of pig-metal and three thousand one hundred tons of bar-iron,—with such a production of iron new markets had to be sought out. The completion of the Susquehanna and Waterford Turnpike through this wilderness suggested the feasibility to the Greggs, Curtins, and others of transporting pig-metal, blooms, and iron to the waters of Red Bank by horse power, a distance of about eighty-eight miles, and from here by water to Pittsburg, Cincinnati, Ohio, and Louisville, Kentucky.

As near as I can ascertain, about the year 1828 a contract was entered into by iron men of Centre County with Henry Riley, of Armstrong County, Pennsylvania, to deliver blooms and pig-iron to Pittsburg and the Western market at a stated price per ton. The transportation on land to Port Barnett was principally carried on during the winter months by farmers in subcontracts. Port Barnett was so named because it was a shipping-point. Henry Feye hauled with an ox-team, and Joseph McGiffin, of this county, hauled with a horse-team. The late Uriah Matson and Peter B. Ostrander took subcontracts from Riley for delivering at Port Barnett. They hauled with oxen and sleds and carried their own board and ox-feed with them. The round trip took them about ten days. Matson and Ostrander received about ten dollars per ton for their work. Peter B. Ostrander was a veteran of the war of 1812. Other Port Barnett teamsters were Samuel Jones and David Butler. Fudge Van Camp, our colored patriarch and brother, hauled this pig-metal as well as fiddled in the old inns and taverns. Riley's teamsters were Captain F. Downs, Christ Shick, and others. These men were all well supplied with old rye and used it freely. They hauled with wooden sleds, having wooden soles. The iron was principally hauled from Phillipsburg. A number of Armstrong farmers (now Clarion) took subcontracts from Riley,—viz., the Joneses, Crookses, Hindmans, and Shieldses. The "silver craze" prevailed then, for Riley paid his contract workers all in silver.

From Port Barnett the pioneer transportation to Pittsburg was on rafts. The rafts were made of dry or dead pine timber, in this wise: The sticks were notched on each side and a hole was bored through each; then the sticks were placed side by side in the water to form a platform, and poles were driven through these flat platforms and wedged on each side. These dry pine logs forming the platform were marketed in Pittsburg for wood. Samuel T. Corbett, uncle of W. W. Corbett, was the pioneer to pilot one of these rafts to market. Henry Feye conceived the idea that barges would afford better transportation facilities for the iron, and he built one, loaded it, and had the misfortune to stove it on what is now called, on that account, "Iron Bar Ripple." This ripple is about one and one-half miles from the mouth of Red Bank. William Jack, of Brookville, built boats on the North Fork, at the head of what is now Heidrick, Matson & Co.'s dam. The late James K. Hoffman and John Dixon worked on these boats and helped run them to market. The barge business continued, and Major William Rodgers, of Brookville, and Thomas Chapman, of Westmoreland County, Pennsylvania, received the contract in 1832 for the transportation of three hundred tons. This contract was for but two years, and was for bar-iron to be delivered at Louisville, Kentucky. Their shipping-point was the mouth of the North Fork. Joseph McGiffin, William Kennedy, and William Kelso, of this county, hauled for this firm. Chapman and Rodgers shipped entirely by barges or flat-boats about eighty feet long. After the iron was unloaded an eighty-foot boat brought them eighty dollars.

This mode of transportation ceased in 1834, but iron and nails were still brought here for our local market for many years thereafter.

THE FIRST SCREW FACTORY.

"It is an especially noteworthy fact, known to comparatively few persons, that the first screw-mill in the United States was erected in 1821 by Mr. Phillips in the little mountain village of Phillipsburg, hundreds of miles distant from any of the great marts of the country. The necessary buildings were put up near the Moshannon Creek, in a suburb of the town that is now called Point Lookout. The capacity of the factory was fifteen hundred gross per week, but the largest quantity produced during the time it was in operation was one thousand gross per week, the material for which was prepared from the blooms by rolling and wire-drawing machinery operated by steam- and water-power. The nearest and best market was at Pittsburg, through Port Barnett, and the products of the forge- and screw-mill had to be hauled at no inconsiderable expense to the waters of the Allegheny River in wagons, and thence transported in arks to their destination."

The old Chinklacamoose trail passed through and over the high table-lands in the county of Centre, passing through or near Milesburg, Phillipsburg, and Snow Shoe. Snow Shoe took its name from the following circumstances : About or previous to the year 1775, "a party of white hunters went out on the old Chinklacamoose trail and were overtaken on these high table-lands of the Allegheny Mountains, near the forks of Moshannon Creek, by a heavy snow-storm. Their provisions becoming exhausted they had to make snow-shoes and walk in them to the Bald

Eagle settlement. It required about two days to travel in these snow-shoes a distance of thirty miles." This old Indian path passed through the Indian town of Chinklacamoose,—old town, or what is now called Clearfield. "This was the central point of the great Chinklacamoose path." "Post lodged at this village on his way to the Ohio country in the night of August 2, 1758. 'We arrived,' he writes in his journal, 'this night at Shinglimuce, where we saw the posts painted red and stuck in the ground, to which the Indians tie their prisoners. It is a disagreeable and melancholy sight to see the means they use to punish flesh and blood.'"

At this point Indian trails connecting the great eastern and western waters crossed the mountains in various directions. There was a trail towards Fort Venango (through Brookville), another towards Kittanning (through Punxsutawney), and one towards the source of the Sinnemahoning (through Brockwayville). Punxsutawney was another central point for Indian paths, and this Chinklacamoose trail is famous, made so by the fact that the "white prisoners" were carried over it to Kithan-ne, in Munsi Indian, and Gicht-han-ne, in Delaware, meaning Kittanning, or a town near or on the main stream,—viz., the Allegheny River.

I copy from the Armstrong history a few of the early cruelties practised on the prisoners carried over this trail.

"At a council, held in Philadelphia, Tuesday, September 6, 1756, the statement of John Coxe, a son of the widow Coxe, was made, the substance of which is: He, his brother Richard, and John Craig were taken in the beginning of February of that year by nine Delaware Indians from a plantation two miles from McDowell's mill, which was between the east and west branches of the Conococheague Creek, about twenty miles west of the present site of Shippensburg, in what is now Franklin County, and brought to Kittanning 'on the Ohio.' On his way hither he met Shingas with a party of thirty men, and afterwards, with Captain Jacobs and fifteen men, whose design was to destroy the settlements in Conogchege. When he arrived at Kittanning he saw here about one hundred fighting men of the Delaware tribe, with their families, and about fifty English prisoners, consisting of men, women, and children. During his stay here Shingas's and Jacobs's parties returned, the one with nine scalps and five prisoners. Another company of eighteen came from Diahogo with seventeen scalps on a pole, which they took to Fort Duquesne to obtain their reward. The warriors held a council, which, with their war-dances, continued a week, when Captain Jacobs left with forty-eight men, intending, as Coxe was told, to fall upon the inhabitants of Paxton. He heard the Indians frequently say that they intended to kill all the white folks except a few, with whom they would afterwards make peace.

"They made an example of Paul Broadley, whom, with their usual cruelty, they beat for half an hour with clubs and tomahawks, and then, having fastened him to a post, cropped his ears close to his head and chopped off his fingers, calling all the prisoners to witness the horrible scene.

"Among other English prisoners brought to Kittanning were George Woods, father-in-law of the eminent lawyer, James Ross (deceased), and the wife and daughter of John Grey, who were captured at Bigham's Fort, in the Tuscarora Valley, in 1756. Mr. Grey came out here with Armstrong's expedition, hoping to hear from his family. These three prisoners were sent from Kittanning to Fort Duquesne and subsequently to Canada.

"Fort Granville, which was situated on the Juniata, one mile above Lewistown, was besieged by the Indians July 30, 1756. The force then in it consisted of twenty-four men under the command of Lieutenant Armstrong, who was killed during the siege. The Indians having offered quarter to those in the fort, a man by the name of John Turner opened the gate to them. He and the others, including three women and several children, were taken prisoners. By order of the French commander the fort was burned by Captain Jacobs. When the Indians and prisoners reached Kittanning, Turner was tied to a black post, the Indians danced around him, made a great fire, and his body was run through with red-hot gun-barrels. Having tormented him for three hours, the Indians scalped him alive, and finally held up a boy, who gave him the finishing stroke with a hatchet.

"Such were a few of the terrible enactments of which Kittanning was the scene in the eighteenth century."

POPULATION OF THE STATE OF PENNSYLVANIA AND OF THE UNITED STATES FROM 1790 TO 1840 INCLUSIVE.

1790.

Whites.	Free Colored.	Negro Slaves.	Total in Pennsylvania.
424,099	6,537	3,737	434,373

Population in the United States, 3,929,827.

1800.

| 586,098 | 14,561 | 1,706 | 602,365 |

Population in the United States, 5,305,941.

1810.

| 786,704 | 22,492 | 795 | 810,091 |

Population in the United States, 7,239,814.

1820.

| 1,017,094 | 32,153 | 211 | 1,049,458 |

Population in the United States, 9,638,191.

PIONEER HISTORY OF JEFFERSON COUNTY, PENNA.

1830.

Whites.	Free Colored.	Negro Slaves.	Total in Pennsylvania.
1,309,900	37,930	403	1,348,233

Population in the United States, 12,866,020.

1840.

1,676,115	47,854	64	1,724,033

Population in the United States, 17,069,453.

RATIO FOR A MEMBER OF CONGRESS.

1790—33,000	Number in Pennsylvania,	13	Total membership,	105
1800—33,000	" " "	18	" "	141
1810—35,000	" " "	23	" "	181
1820—40,000	" " "	26	" "	213
1830—47,000	" " "	28	" "	240
1840—70,680	" " "	24	" "	223

Salary of a Congressman, eight dollars a day.

CHAPTER XI.

THE ERECTION OF THE COUNTY—SITE FOR COUNTY ESTABLISHED, AND DEED FOR PUBLIC LOTS—PIONEER COURT-HOUSE AND JAIL—THE PIONEER ACADEMY.

ERECTION OF JEFFERSON COUNTY.

WHEN William Penn came to what is now the State of Pennsylvania and organized what has become our present Commonwealth, he erected three counties, which were Bucks, Philadelphia, and Chester. Chester County extended over the western portion of the State at that time. In reality, it had jurisdiction over only the inhabitable portion, but its boundary lines extended west of what is now Jefferson County.

On May 10, 1729, Lancaster County was erected from Chester. On January 27, 1750, Cumberland County was erected from Lancaster. On March 9, 1771, Bedford County was erected from Cumberland. March 27, 1772, Northumberland County was erected, and for thirteen years our wilderness was in this county. On April 13, 1795, Lycoming County was erected from Northumberland, and on March 26, 1804, Jefferson County was erected from Lycoming County. Thus you will see that this wilderness was embraced in six other counties before it was erected into a separate county. The name of the county was given in honor of Thomas Jefferson, who was then President of the United States. The original area of Jefferson County contained 1203 square miles, but it now has only about 413,440 acres; highest altitude, from 1200 to 1880 feet above sea-level; length of county, 46 miles; breadth, 26 miles.

"Jefferson County is now in the fourth tier of counties east of the Ohio line, and in the third tier south of the New York line, and is bounded by Forest and Elk on the north, Clearfield on the east, Indiana on the south, and Armstrong and Clarion on the west. Its south line now runs due west twenty-three and one-third miles from the Clearfield-Indiana corner;

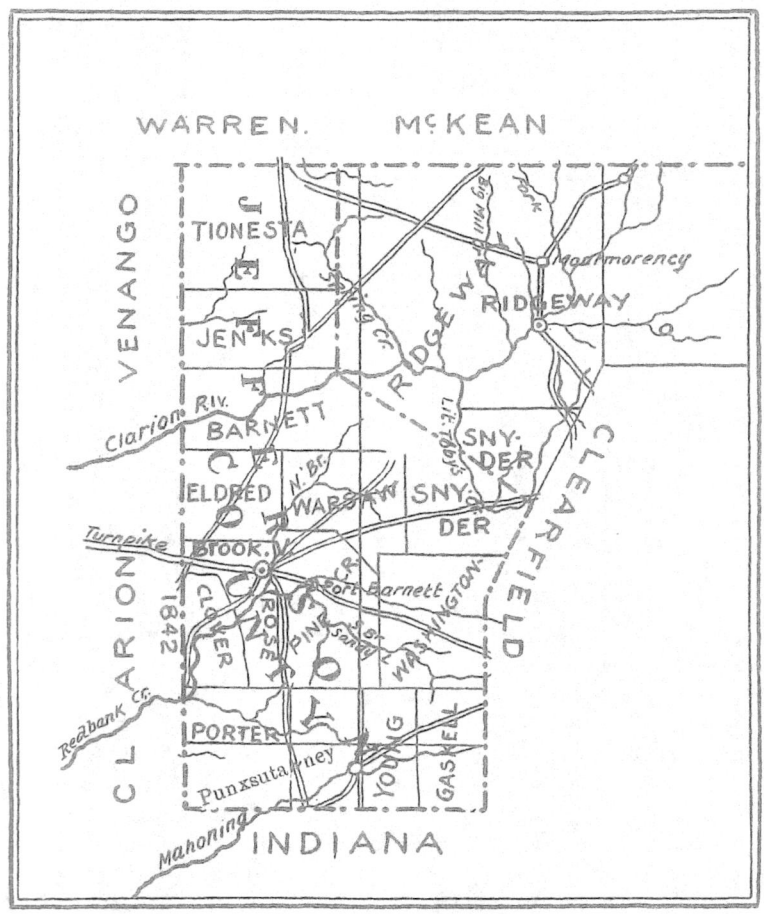

Map of Jefferson County, 1842.

its west line thence due north twenty-eight and one-quarter miles to the Clarion River; its north line, first up the Clarion River to Elk County, thence due south one-half mile, thence southeast thirteen and three-quarter miles, to Clearfield County; its east line runs first southwest ten miles, thence due south fifteen and one-third miles, to the starting-place at the Clearfield-Indiana corner.

PIONEER HISTORY OF JEFFERSON COUNTY, PENNA.

GEOGRAPHY.

"The original boundary lines enclosed an area of more than one thousand square miles, embracing much of what is now Forest and Elk, beyond the Clarion River. At what time the present boundaries were erected is not certain; but much shifting took place, especially along the northern border, until comparatively recent years.

"The pioneer people were mainly of Scotch-Irish descent, with a considerable intermixture of the German element, industrious, prudent, and thrifty.

TOPOGRAPHY.

"The surface of Jefferson County is uniformly broken and hilly; everywhere occupied by the same set of rock strata, lying nearly horizontal, and excavated into valleys and ravines in the same style. Although one valley cannot be said to be the exact counterpart of another, nor the streams be considered of equal size and importance, yet the type of the topography is the same wherever we look at it, and any one part of the county, therefore, is, in this respect, a picture of the whole.

"Standing upon one of the many elevated points of the region, the observer may see beneath him a broad valley, from three hundred to five hundred feet deep, and as irregular in its trend and course as its slopes are variable in their fall. Here precipitous walls face the stream on both sides; there a sharp descent upon the one side is faced by a long gentle slope upon the other, according as the dips are arranged; at another place the valley widens under the influence of a synclinal, and both its slopes are gradual. Numerous ravines, some short, some long, some deep, others shallow, debouch into the valley from both sides. Uplands undulating, but of a pretty uniform height, stretch away in both directions. No mountain ridges are anywhere visible on the horizon. As far as the eye can see there spreads an elevated table-land, broken by vales, valleys, and ravines.

"The height above tide of the upland summits ranges from twelve hundred to eighteen hundred and eighty feet. They are lowest at the southern end of the county, and highest at the northern end, in obedience to a topographical law prevailing throughout Western Pennsylvania: that the surface elevations gradually increase in the direction of the rising anticlinal axes,—*i.e.*, towards the northeast.

"To this law there is one notable exception in Jefferson County; the southeast corner borders on the high table-land of the Chestnut Ridge anticlinal, whose summits frequently attain an elevation of two thousand feet; and some few points in Gaskill township rise nearly to that height; but these points are related more closely to the topography of Indiana and Clearfield Counties than to that of Jefferson, which is in fact a mere continuation of that prevailing throughout Clarion, Armstrong, and western Indiana Counties.

PIONEER HISTORY OF JEFFERSON COUNTY, PENNA.

ELEVATION.

	Feet
Hillman	above sea-level, 1880
Perrysville	" " 1170
Winslow	" " 1636
Horatio	" " 1211
Falls Creek	above tide, 1405
Evergreen	" " 1398
Magee's (Sandy Valley P. O.)	" " 1387
Panther Run	" " 1386
Reynoldsville	" " 1377
Prior Run	" " 1366
Prindible	" " 1360
McAnnulty's Run	" " 1359
Camp Run	" " 1341
Fuller's	" " 1327
Wolf Run	" " 1319
Iowa Mills	" " 1299
Bell's Mills	" " 1268
Brookville Tunnel, east end	" " 1242
Brookville Station	" " 1235
Coder's Run	" " 1223
Puckerty Point	" " 1214
Rattlesnake Run	" " 1207
Baxter	" " 1206
Troy	" " 1186
Heathville	" " 1161
Patton's	" " 1131

ELEVATION ABOVE TIDE FROM FALLS CREEK TO RIDGEWAY.

Near Falls Creek Station	above tide, 1406
Surface of ground, McMinn's Summit	" " 1625
(McMinn's Summit is the Boon Mountain divide.)	
Brockwayville	" " 1466
Ordinary low water in Little Toby	" " 1441
On the main Ridgway Road	" " 1451
Mouth of Little Toby Creek	" " 1321
(This is the ordinary water-level.)	
Big Run	" " 1287
Sykesville	" " 1350
Punxsutawney	" " 1225

DRAINAGE.

"The drainage of Jefferson County is all westward towards the Ohio River, through (1) the Clarion River at the north end of the county, (2) Red Bank Creek in the centre, and (3) Mahoning Creek on the south. Each of these streams has its own complex system of tributaries, each with its own system of small branches and branchlets; and thus the surface of the whole county is broken into hills.

PIONEER HISTORY OF JEFFERSON COUNTY, PENNA.

"Although the Clarion and Mahoning are larger streams, yet they flow on the borders of the county, and are less important to it than the Red Bank.

"Red Bank Creek is the principal stream, as a glance at the map will at once show. Its water basin is unsymmetrical on the two sides, a much larger part of its drainage coming in from the north than from the south. Excepting indeed from the Little Sandy branch its basin on the south side would be confined pretty much to the hills which overlook the creek; whereas towards the north its far-reaching arms extend to what is now the Elk County line.

"Red Bank Creek in the original maps and drafts of Jefferson County bore the name of Sandy Lick, which name is still retained for its main branch, coming from Clearfield County, along which the Bennett's Branch Railroad is laid. The creek assumes the name of Red Bank at Brookville, where Sandy Lick unites with the North Fork, and both branches carry enough water during floods to float rafts and logs.

"Mill Creek, a branch of the Sandy Lick, is also a rafting stream.

"Little Sandy, before alluded to as occupying the southwestern part of the county, is a rafting stream.

"The volume of water, however, in all the streams, large and small, is extremely irregular, varying as it does from stages of high flood when the larger streams are destructive torrents, to stages of almost complete exhaustion during periods of severe drought. This extreme of variability is largely the consequence of the porous and loose condition of the surface rocks, which thus copiously yield water so long as they hold it. In 1879, an exceptional year, after a succession of prolonged droughts, there was a dearth of water in all parts of the county; the larger streams had barely enough in them to turn a mill; and considerable difficulty was experienced, especially in the upland country, to obtain water for the cattle. As a rule, the county is abundantly watered for agricultural purposes, and for domestic supply in towns and villages.

"The Red Bank-Mahoning divide in the southeast corner of the county crosses from Clearfield at a point nearly due east of Reynoldsville. Thence it follows an irregular southwest line, around the heads of Elk Run, and around the heads of Little Sandy. Paradise settlement stands at the top of it; so does Shamoka, Oliveburg, and Frostburg. Porter Post-Office at the southwest end of the county marks the top of the divide in that region.

"The Red Bank-Clarion divide on the north enters Jefferson south of Lane's Grove, where one branch of Rattlesnake Run takes its rise. After passing Brockwayville the water-shed is forced almost to the edge of Little Toby valley, as will be seen on examination of the county map. Along the last-named stream it passes in Elk County, where curving about the heads of the North Fork (Red Bank system), it returns again to Jefferson, whence closely skirting the Clarion River, it runs southwest of Sigel.

There it turns sharply about and next sweeps around the head of Big Mill Creek, extending thence south to within a few miles of the Red Bank valley. It therefore describes a semicircle in northern Jefferson, stretching from one side of the county to the other."

FOREST-TREES.

"The southern portion of Jefferson County was mostly covered with white oak, black oak, rock oak, chestnut, sugar, beech, and hickory.

"The rock areas of northern Jefferson were covered with pine and hemlock, with scarcely a trace of white oak. There is still a considerable quantity of marketable hemlock left.

"White oak, chestnut, sugar, beech, and hickory were the principal kinds of wood on the cleared lands.

"White oak was found mostly on the high uplands.

"W. C. Elliott says, 'There were four kinds of maple, four of ash, five of hickory, eight of oak, three of birch, four of willow, four of poplar, four of pine, and from one to three of each of the other varieties. The following are the names of all of them; some of the trees are not correctly named, but the names given are the only English names by which they go. Their Latin names are all correct and would be given, but would not be understood. Sweet-bay, cucumber, elkwood, long-leaved cucumber, white basswood, toothache-tree, wafer-ash, spindle-tree, Indian-cherry, feted buckeye, sweet buckeye, striped maple, sugar-maple, white maple, red maple, ash-leaved maple, staghorn sumach, dwarf sumach, poison elder, locust, coffee-nut, honey-locust, judas-tree, wild plum, hog-plum, red cherry, black cherry, American crab-apple, crab-apple, cockspur, thorn, scarlet haw, blackthorn, Washington thorn, service-tree, witch-hazel, sweet-gum, dogwood, boxwood, sour-gum, sheep-berry, stag-bush, sorrel-tree, spoonwood, rosebay, southern buckthorn, white ash, red ash, green ash, black ash, fringe-tree, catalpa, sassafras, red elm, white elm, rock elm, hackberry, red mulberry, sycamore, butternut, walnut, bitter-nut, pignut, kingnut, shagbark, white hickory, swamp white oak, chestnut oak, yellow oak, red oak, shingle oak, chinquapin, chestnut, iron-wood, leverwood, beech, gray birch, red birch, black birch, black alder, speckled alder, black willow, sand-bar willow, almond-willow, glaucous willow, aspen, two varieties of soft poplar, two varieties of cottonwood, two varieties of necklace-poplar, liriodendron (incorrectly called poplar), white cedar, red cedar, white pine, hemlock, balsam, fir, hickory, pine, pitch-pine or yellow pine, red pine, Virginia date, and forest olive. In addition to the above were numerous wild berries, vines, etc.'

GEOLOGICAL STRUCTURE.

"The rocks of Jefferson County are folded in a regular succession of parallel anticlinal ridges and synclinal basins, stretching from southwest to northeast. The folds are not all equidistant from each other. Those west of Perrysville anticlinical are nearly so.

"The anticlinical arches are low, and the synclinal basins are shallow; and while they are not equal in height and depth, when compared with one another, the difference is small, although of considerable importance in its effect upon mining interests. Some idea of how gently the rocks incline from the horizontal may be got from the fact that the whole thickness of strata outcropping at the surface in any basin does not exceed five hundred feet, although the basin is in some cases six miles wide.

"The axes of the rolls and troughs being parallel, the line of strike is necessarily uniform in all parts of the county; about N. 40° E. (S. 40° W.).

"The normal dip, therefore, is either to the N. 50° W. or S. 50° E. But the real dip is somewhat different, owing to the plainly marked rise of the whole region (with its anticlinals and synclinals) towards the northeast."—*Geological Report of Jefferson County, Pennsylvania.*

"AN ACT TO ERECT PARTS OF LYCOMING, HUNTINGDON, AND SOMERSET COUNTIES INTO SEPARATE COUNTY DISTRICTS.

"SECTION 1. *Be it enacted, etc., and it is hereby enacted by the authority of the same,* That part of the county of Lycoming, included within the following lines, to wit: Beginning at the northeast corner of Venango County, and thence east thirty miles (part along the line of Warren County), and thence by a due south line fifteen miles, thence a southwesterly course to Sandy Lick Creek, where Hunter's district line crosses said creek; thence south along Hunter's district line to a point twelve miles north of the canoe-place, on the west branch of Susquehanna; thence a due west line until it intersects the eastern boundary of Armstrong County; thence north along the line of Armstrong and Venango Counties, to the place of beginning, be, and the same is hereby erected into a separate county, to be henceforth called Jefferson County; and the place of holding the courts of justice shall be fixed by the Legislature at any place at a distance not greater than seven miles from the centre of the said county, which may be most beneficial and convenient for the said county.

"SECTION 7. *And be it further enacted by the authority aforesaid,* That the Governor shall, as soon as convenient, appoint three Commissioners to run and mark the boundary lines of the counties of Jefferson, Clearfield, and Cambria, and shall appoint three other Commissioners to run and mark the boundary lines of the counties of McKean, Potter, and Tioga, according to the true intent and meaning of this act; and the said Commissioners, or any two of them, shall have power to run the aforesaid lines, and shall have, for their services, the sum of two dollars for every mile so run and marked, to be paid out of the treasury of this Commonwealth.

"SECTION 8. *And be it further enacted by the authority aforesaid*, That as soon as it shall appear by an enumeration of the taxable inhabitants within the counties of Jefferson, McKean, Clearfield, Potter, Tioga, and Cambria, that any of the said counties, according to the ratio which shall then be established for apportioning the representation among the several counties of this Commonwealth, shall be entitled to a separate representation, provision shall be made by law apportioning the said representation, and enabling such county to be represented separately, and to hold the courts of justice at such place in the said county as is or may hereafter be fixed for holding the same by the Legislature, and to choose their county officers in like manner as in the other counties of this Commonwealth.

"SECTION 9. *And be it further enacted by the authority aforesaid*, That the Governor be, and he is hereby authorized and required to appoint three suitable persons for trustees in each of the said counties, who shall receive proposals in writing from any person or persons, or any bodies corporate or politic, for the grant or conveyance of any lands within the said counties respectively, and within the limits prescribed by this act for fixing the place of holding courts of justice in said counties respectively, or the transfer of any other property, or payment of money for the use of said counties, and transmit to the Legislature from time to time a copy of the proposals so received under their hands; and when the place of holding courts of justice in the said counties respectively shall be fixed by the Legislature, to take assurances in the law for the lands and other valuable property, or money contained in any such proposals, which shall or may be accepted of.

"SECTION 13. *And be it further enacted by the authority aforesaid*, That for the present convenience of the inhabitants of the county of Jefferson, and until an enumeration of the taxable inhabitants of said county shall be made, and it shall be otherwise directed by law, the said county of Jefferson shall be, and the same is hereby annexed to the county of Westmoreland; and the jurisdiction of the several courts of the county of Westmoreland, and the authority of the judges thereof, shall extend over and shall operate and be effectual within the said county of Jefferson.

"SECTION 15. *And be it further enacted by the authority aforesaid*, That the electors within the counties erected by this act shall continue to elect at the same places and with the same counties as heretofore.

"Approved—the twenty-fifth day of March, in the year of our Lord one thousand and eight hundred and four.
"THOMAS McKEAN,
"*Governor of the Commonwealth of Pennsylvania.*"

"An Act approving the Appointment of Commissioners to fix upon a Proper Site for the Seat of Justice in Jefferson County.

"Section 1. *Be it enacted, etc., and it is hereby enacted by the authority of the same,* That John Mitchell, of the county of Centre, Alexander McCalmont, of the county of Venango, and Robert Orr, Junior, of Armstrong County, be and they are hereby appointed Commissioners, who, or a majority of whom, shall meet at the house of Andrew Barnett, in the county of Jefferson, on the first Monday in September next, and from thence proceed to view and determine the most eligible and proper situation for the seat of justice for the said county of Jefferson, and make report into the office of the Secretary of the Commonwealth on or before the first Monday of December next; and each of said Commissioners shall receive three dollars per day for every day they shall be necessarily employed in the duty aforesaid, to be paid by warrants drawn by the Commissioners of Jefferson County on the treasurer of said county: *Provided,* That in case of death, resignation, or inability of any one or more of the Commissioners to serve, the Governor shall be authorized and required to appoint such suitable person or persons to fill such vacancy or vacancies.

"Section 2. *And be it further enacted by the authority aforesaid,* That the Commissioners of Jefferson County shall have power, and it shall be their duty to take assurances, by deed, bond, or otherwise, of any land, lots, money, or other property which hath or may be offered for the use and benefit of the said county, either for the purpose of erecting public buildings, or for the support of an academy or other public use.

"Approved—the eighth day of April, A.D. one thousand eight hundred and twenty-nine.

"J. Andw. Shulze."

In accordance with the provisions of this act these men met at the house of Joseph Barnett on the first Monday of September, 1829, and located the site on the Waterford and Susquehanna turnpike, at the confluence of the Sandy Lick and North Fork, where they form the Red Bank, and named the place Brookville.

The boundaries of the town as then laid out were as follows: Butler Alley, running east and west, north of the second (or old graveyard), thence east, taking in the mills and dam of Robert P. Barr, now Heidrick, Matson & Co. On the west was an alley, now east of the Presbyterian church, down that alley to Water Street, taking in or including "Hunt's Point," thence along Water Street to Pickering Street, and across Red Bank, near the bridge, and out Pickering Street to lot No. 25, and thence to the Sandy Lick.

'An Act to authorize the Provisional County of Jefferson, to elect County Commissioners, and for Other Purposes.

"Section 1. (The citizens to elect three County Commissioners and three Auditors on the second Tuesday of October next :)

"*Provided,* that the largest in vote of the said County Commissioners, and also the lowest in vote of the said County Auditors, shall only serve one year, the next lowest two years, whose places respectively shall be supplied according to the laws of this Commonwealth. *Provided always,* That all and singular the costs and expenses in laying out and opening roads, all costs chargeable to the county of Jefferson, arising from criminal prosecutions instituted against persons within said county, and all other costs and expenses incidental to said county, and which of right should be paid by the same, on account of the jurisdiction of the several Courts of Indiana County, and the authority of the judges thereof extending over the said county of Jefferson, shall be paid by the said county of Jefferson, on warrants drawn by the Commissioners of Indiana County, and countersigned by the Commissioners of the county of Jefferson.

"Section 2. *And be it further enacted by the authority aforesaid,* That it shall and may be lawful for the said Commissioners of the county of Jefferson, or their successors, to call on the Commissioners of the county of Indiana for the purpose of examining, liquidating, and receiving such balances as shall be found due to the said county of Jefferson, and if, on such examination, it be found that a balance is due from the county of Jefferson to the county of Indiana, then it shall be the duty of the Commissioners of Indiana County to call on the Commissioners of Jefferson County and receive said balance.

"Section 3. *And be it further enacted by the authority aforesaid,* That the said County Commissioners and Auditors so elected shall hold their office and transact the public business as Commissioners and Auditors of said county at such place as shall be fixed upon by a majority of the Commissioners first elected in said county of Jefferson, until the seat of justice is ascertained, and thereafter at the seat of justice.

"Section 4. *And be it further enacted by the authority aforesaid,* That so much of any act or acts of the General Assembly of this Commonwealth as is altered or supplied by this act be, and the same is, hereby repealed.

"Passed 21st January, 1824."

* * * * * * * * *

PIONEER COMMISSIONERS, TREASURERS, AUDITORS, COLLECTORS, AND ASSESSORS—SATURDAY AFTERNOON A TIME TO PREPARE FOR SUNDAY.

In pursuance of this act of Assembly, approved January 21, 1824, granting to the provisional county of Jefferson the privilege of electing

PIONEER HISTORY OF JEFFERSON COUNTY, PENNA.

its own commissioners, auditors, etc., an election was held the 12th day of October, 1824. Andrew Barnett was duly elected commissioner of Jefferson County for three years, John Lucas was duly elected for two years, and John W. Jenks was elected for one year, the election of these three being certified to by Alexander Taylor, prothonotary of Indiana and Jefferson Counties. Andrew Barnett and John Lucas took the oath of office before Joseph McCullough, of Pine Creek township, Friday, October 29, and John W. Jenks before John Bell, Esq., of Perry township, on the 3d day of November, 1824.

November 12, 1824, Barnett, Lucas, and Jenks met at the home of Joseph Barnett, in Pine Creek township, and organized as a board. Ira White was appointed clerk for one year at one dollar a day for the "time employed in the office." A room was rented in Barnett's Inn for an office "at the rate of one dollar a week for the time occupied," "and a closet in said room to be in the use of the county continually."

On the 16th day of February, 1825, John Matson, Sr., was appointed county treasurer.

The pioneer county auditors were elected in 1825,—viz., Thomas Robinson, James Corbett, and Alonzo Baldwin. They were sworn in before Joseph McCullough, Esq., January 2, 1826.

The pioneer assessors and collectors under the commissioners for Jefferson County were, in 1825: Pine Creek—assessor, James Shields; collector, John Barnett; Perry—assessor, Elijah Heath; collector, Isaac McKinley.

The pioneer contract to supply the public buildings with wood and coal for fuel was in November, 1831, for one year, by Joseph Clements, for thirty-seven dollars and fifty cents. As the county buildings had only ten-plate stoves, wood, three feet in length, and no coal, was supplied under this contract.

Previous to and as late as 1850 it was the rule for mill-men, woodsmen, and laboring men generally to stop work every Saturday at noon. The idea was to better prepare for the observance of the Sabbath. As far as my observation reminds me, I can assure you that spiritualizing was practised freely on these Saturday afternoons.

COPY OF DEED DELIVERING GROUND FOR THE PUBLIC PURPOSES.

"JOHN PICKERING *et al.*   Deed dated July 31st, 1830.
           to   Recorded in Deed Book No. 1, at
COMMISSIONERS OF JEFFERSON Co.   page 133.

"AND WHEREAS, The said John Pickering, with the approbation and consent of a majority of the said Company, being the parties of the second part hereto, which consent is signified by their becoming parties to this indenture, for and in consideration of the seat of justice for Jefferson

County being established upon the said tract of land, did agree (*inter alia*) to grant and convey unto the said parties of the third part, and their successors in office, ground for the public buildings, and also for churches and a public burying-ground, as also ten inlots in the town to be laid out upon said tract of land.

"AND WHEREAS, The General Assembly of the Commonwealth of Pennsylvania, by an act passed on the second day of April, A.D. one thousand eight hundred and thirty, did establish the seat of justice for said county of Jefferson at the town of Brookville, to be laid out upon said tract of land, and thereby authorize and empower the said parties of the third part to receive (*inter alia*) from the party of the first part a deed in fee simple for the purposes above mentioned.

"*Now this Indenture Witnesseth*, That the said John Pickering, as well as for and in consideration of the sum of one dollar, lawful money of the United States to him in hand paid by the said Thomas McKee, Thomas Lucas, and Elijah Heath, Commissioners of Jefferson County, at and before the ensealing and delivery hereof, the receipt whereof is hereby acknowledged, hath granted, bargained, and sold, aliened, enfeofed, released, and confirmed, and by these presents doth grant, bargain, and sell, alien, enfeof, release, and confirm unto the said Thomas McKee, Thomas Lucas, and Elijah Heath, Commissioners of Jefferson County, and their successors in office, all that square or piece of ground in the said town of Brookville, situated, lying between, and bounded by Pickering Street, Market Street, Chestnut Alley, and Court Alley, and marked in the general plan of said town, Public Square, and also the outlots known and numbered in the general plan of the same by the numbers twelve (12) and thirteen (13). And also all those ten inlots of ground known and numbered in the general plan of said town by the numbers thirty-four (34), thirty-five (35), thirty-six (36), thirty-seven (37), thirty-eight (38), sixty-four (64), sixty-five (65), sixty-six (66), sixty-seven (67), and sixty-eight (68), together with the privileges and appurtenances thereunto belonging or in any wise appertaining. To have and to hold the same to the said Thomas McKee, Thomas Lucas, and Elijah Heath, Commissioners of Jefferson County, and their successors in office, to the only proper use and behoof of the said Thomas McKee, Thomas Lucas, and Elijah Heath, Commissioners of Jefferson County, and their successors in office, forever. In trust, nevertheless, and to and for the uses and purposes hereinafter declared,—that is to say, that the said square shall be and remain for the use of the Public Buildings. That outlot Number twelve (12) shall be and remain for the purpose of erecting churches or houses of public worship thereon for any denomination that sees proper to build thereon. That outlot Number thirteen (13) shall be and remain a public burying-ground. That as to the said ten inlots before mentioned and described, the said parties of the third part and their successors in office shall sell and dispose of the same and pay the proceeds thereof into the Treasury of said county, to be applied towards the erection of the public buildings in the Town of Brookville.

"In witness whereof the said parties have hereunto set their hands and seals the day and year first above written.

"JNO. PICKERING, *Trustee*. [L. S.]
JNO. PICKERING, *Executor*. [L. S.]
OCTAVIUS PICKERING, *Executor*. [L. S.]

"THOMAS A. DEXTER,
SAMUEL HUNT,

"Witnesses to the signature of John Pickering and Octavius Pickering.

"NICH'S FISH. [L. S.]
LEONARD KIP. [L. S.]
MARIA I. KIP. [L. S.]

"DAVID CLYDE, *Clerk*.
WM. H. MAXWELL, *Counsellor and Commissioner, New York*.

"Witnesses to the signatures of Nich's Fish: WM. JOHNSON, LEONARD KIP, LEONARD KIP, as attorney, and MARIA I. KIP, his wife.

"LEONARD KIP. [L. S.]
"*Attorney for all the heirs of Duncan Ingraham.*
"REDWOOD FISHER, *Executor*. [L. S.]

"Witnesses to the signature of Redwood Fisher: ANDREW GEYER and J. C. WIKOFF.

"JABOY M. FISHER, *Executor*. [L. S.]

"Witnesses to the signature of Jaboy M. Fisher: ANDREW GEYER and RALPH SMITH.

"ANN WIKOFF. [L. S.]

"Witnesses to the signature of Ann Wikoff: ANDREW GEYER and J. C. WIKOFF."

The pioneer court-house was contracted for in 1830 and finished in 1833. The county records show this "Article of Agreement, made the 14th day of December, 1830, between Thomas Lucas and Robert Andrews, Commissioners of Jefferson County, of the first part, and John Lucas, of Jefferson County, and Robert Barr, of the county of Indiana, of the second part. The party of the second part agrees to build court-house, two offices, one fire-proof, within two years from the 1st day of January next. The Commissioners, on their part, agree to pay contractors the sum of three thousand dollars, in manner as follows : two thousand dollars as the work progresses, and one thousand dollars in full on the 1st day of January, 1833, to be paid out of the funds arising from the sale of lots in said town of Brookville, if there shall be sufficient; if not, to be made up out of the county funds.

(Signed)   "THOMAS LUCAS,
ROBERT ANDREWS,
"Commissioners.
"JOHN LUCAS,
ROBERT BARR,
"Contractors.

"Witnesses:
"WILLIAM M. KENNEDY,
JAMES HALL."

Our first jail was a stone structure, built of common stone, in 1831. It was two stories high, was situated on the northeast corner of the public square lot, near Joseph Darr's residence, and fronting on Pickering Street. Daniel Elgin was the contractor. The building was divided into eight rooms, two down-stairs and two up-stairs for jail proper, and two down-stairs and two up-stairs for the sheriff's residence and office. The sheriff occupied the north part. It cost eighteen hundred and twenty-four dollars and twenty-three cents.

The pioneer academy in Jefferson County was authorized by an act of the Legislature, approved April 13, 1838. This act authorized the treasurer of the Commonwealth to subscribe two thousand dollars, to be expended in building an academy building in Brookville, Pennsylvania. The trustees appointed by said act were John J. Y. Thompson, C. A. Alexander, Thomas Hastings, Levi G. Clover, John Pierce, and Richard Arthurs. In 1841 the Legislature authorized the commissioners of Jefferson County to subscribe five hundred dollars, and five hundred dollars being raised by subscription of citizens, this made a fund of three thousand dollars to erect the building.

The site selected was the lot on the corner of Jefferson and Barnett Streets, and the lot was kindly donated for this purpose by John Pickering. The lot was in a state of nature then, being covered with pine-trees. The contractors were Robert P. Barr, Thomas M. Barr, and Robert Larrimer. The building was of brick, and was completed in 1843. Professor J. M. Coleman was the first to teach classics and high mathematics in this institution.

CHAPTER XII.

THE COMMON SCHOOL SYSTEM—ITS INCEPTION—INTRODUCTION INTO AMERICA—STATE EFFORT—HISTORY OF EDUCATION IN THE STATE—SCHOOLS OF JEFFERSON COUNTY—PROGRESS OF EDUCATION, ETC.

As an introduction to this chapter, I cannot do better than reproduce an extract from a speech delivered by myself before a convention of Jefferson County school directors,—viz. :

"GENTLEMEN OF THE CONVENTION,—I thank you for this honor. I highly appreciate it. As the representatives of thirty-two school districts, two hundred and forty schools, and twelve thousand pupils, we have met this day to consider modes and methods by which we can best advance the cause of education. This is wise and patriotic. Perhaps it might be well as an introduction to our work to review a little history as to the origin and present status of our common schools. Martin Luther, a German, was the first to advocate the public school system. This he did in 1524, ably, vigorously, and boldly. He asserted that the 'government, as the natural guardian of all the young, has the right to compel the people to support schools.' He further said, 'Now, nothing is more necessary than the training of those who are to come after us and bear rule.' The education of the young of all classes in free schools was one of the objects nearest Luther's heart. Scotland is the only other country of Europe that took an early interest in public school education. In 1560, John Knox urged the necessity of schools for the poor. These grand humane impulses of John Knox and other Scotch fathers have spread abroad, 'wide as the waters be,' only to germinate, bud, and bloom into the grandest social, theological, and political conditions ever attained by man. But it remained for the Puritan fathers of New England (America) to completely develop the common school system of our time. In New England education early made great progress. Under the eaves of their church the Puritans always built a school-house. As early as 1635, Boston had a school for 'the teaching of all children with us.' In 1647, Massachusetts made the support of schools compulsory and education universal and free by the enactment of the following law,—viz. : 'It is therefore ordered that every township in this jurisdiction, after the Lord hath increased them to the number of fifty householders, shall then forthwith appoint one within the town to teach all such children as shall resort to him to write and read, whose wages shall be paid either by the parents or masters of such children, or by the inhabitants in general by way of

supply, as the major part of those who order the prudentials of the town shall appoint, provided those that send their children be not oppressed by paying much more than they can have them taught for in other towns.'
In Connecticut, in 1665, every town that did not keep a school for three months in the year was liable to a fine. On April 1, A.D. 1834, one hundred and eighty-seven years later than the enactment of the common school law of Massachusetts, the law creating the common school system of Pennsylvania was approved by George Wolf, governor. Our second State superintendent of public instruction was appointed under this law. His name was Thomas H. Burrowes.

"The foundation of our common school system was built by the convention to form a State constitution in 1790. The article as incorporated in that document reads as follows:

"'SECTION 1. The Legislature shall, as soon as conveniently may be, provide by law for the establishment of schools throughout the State, in such a manner that the poor may be taught gratis.

"'SECTION 2. The arts and sciences shall be promoted in one or more seminaries of learning.'

"This educational article was also incorporated into the constitution of 1838. But little effort was made under the first constitution by legislative bodies to establish schools under the first section. Their only aim seemed to be to aid the churches and neighborhood schools to carry on the work they had been doing for a hundred years. The pioneer effort by the Legislature seems to have been in 1794, when, on December 8, 1794, a committee was appointed by the House to report a proper mode of carrying into effect that part of the governor's message in regard to schools. The committee reported as follows:

"'*Resolved*, That schools may be established throughout the State, in such a manner that the poor may be taught gratis.

"'*Resolved*, That one-fifth part of the expense necessary to support the masters of said schools be paid out of the general funds of the State.

"'*Resolved*, That the remaining four-fifths of the said expense be paid in each county, respectively, by means of a county tax.

"'*Resolved*, That the said schools be put under the direction of trustees in each county, subject to such limitations and regulations, as to the distribution of their funds, the appointment of masters, and their general arrangements, as shall be provided by law.

"'*Resolved*, That the schools thus established shall be free schools, and that at least spelling, reading, writing, and arithmetic shall be taught therein.

"'*Resolved*, That ten thousand dollars a year be appropriated out of the funds of this Commonwealth to encourage the establishment of academies, in which grammar, the elements of mathematics, geography, and history shall be taught.

"'*Resolved*, That the said sum be apportioned amongst the city and several counties of the State in proportion to their respective population.

"'*Resolved*, That whenever a sum sufficient, with the addition of the sums proposed to be given by the public, to support an academy for the purpose aforesaid shall have been subscribed, or contributed, the additional sum of one hundred dollars a year shall be given out of the public treasury in aid of such academy.

"'*Resolved*, That when the number of academies in any county shall be so great that the sum to which such county is entitled becomes insufficient to afford one hundred dollars to each, it shall be divided by the trustees aforesaid among the whole of such academies, in proportion to the number of masters employed and scholars taught, and the length of time in each during which each academy is so kept and supported.

"'*Resolved*, That whenever a sum is subscribed and contributed sufficient, if added to the income of any of the inferior schools, to procure the instruction contemplated to be given in the academies, such school shall become an academy and receive the additional bounty of one hundred dollars as aforesaid, subject to a reduction in the manner aforesaid.'

"A bill was prepared in accordance with these resolutions and passed both branches, but was lost in conference committee. This was forty years before the enactment of 1834."

THE PIONEER ACT.

On the 1st day of March, 1802, Governor McKean approved the pioneer law of this State making a provision for the education of the poor, the title being "An Act to provide for the Education of Poor Children gratis."

"WHEREAS, By the first section of the seventh article of the Constitution of this Commonwealth it is directed 'That the Legislature shall as soon as conveniently may be provide by law for the establishment of schools throughout the State, in such manner as that the poor may be taught gratis;' therefore,

"SECTION 1. *Be it enacted, etc.*, That from and after the passing of this act the Guardians and Overseers of the Poor of the City of Philadelphia, the District of Southwark, and Townships and Boroughs within this Commonwealth, shall ascertain the names of all those children whose parents or guardians they shall judge to be unable to pay for their schooling, to give notice in writing to such parent or guardian that provision is made by law for the education of their children or the children under their care, and that they have a full and free right to subscribe at the usual rates and send them to any school in their neighborhood, giving notice thereof as soon as may be to the Guardians or Overseers of the term for which they have subscribed, the number of scholars and the rate of tuition; and in those Townships where there are no Guardians or

Overseers of the Poor, the Supervisors of the Highways shall perform the duties herein required to be done by the Guardians or Overseers of the Poor.

"SECTION 2. *And be it further enacted by the authority aforesaid*, That every Guardian or Overseer of the Poor, or Supervisor of the Highways, as the case may be, in any township or place where any such child or children shall be sent to school as aforesaid, shall enter in a book the name or names, age, and length of time such child or children shall have been so sent to school, together with the amount of schooling, schoolbooks, and stationery, and shall levy and collect in the same way and manner and under the same regulations as poor taxes or road taxes are levied and collected a sufficient sum of money from their respective townships, boroughs, wards, or districts to discharge such expenses, together with the sum of five per cent. for their trouble.

"SECTION 3. *And be it further enacted by the authority aforesaid*, That the Guardians or Overseers of the Poor for the time being, or Supervisors of the Highways, as the case may be, shall use all diligence and prudence in carrying this act into effect, and shall settle their accounts in the same way and manner as by the existing laws of the State, the Guardians, Overseers of the Poor, and Supervisors of the Poor, and Supervisors of the Highways are authorized and required to settle their accounts.

"SECTION 4. *And be it further enacted by the authority aforesaid*, That this act shall continue in force for the term of three years, and from thence to the end of the next sitting of the General Assembly and no longer."

It was found that the act of 1802 was unsatisfactory, and, in the hope of betterment, this act of 1804 was passed:

"AN ACT TO PROVIDE FOR THE MORE EFFECTUAL EDUCATION OF THE CHILDREN OF THE POOR GRATIS.

"WHEREAS, The law passed the first day of March, Anno Domini one thousand and eight hundred and two, entitled 'An Act to provide for the Education of Poor Children gratis,' has not been found by experience to answer the constitutional purposes intended by it; therefore,

"SECTION 1. *Be it enacted, etc.*, That from and after the passing of this act it shall be enjoined as a duty on all school-masters and school-mistresses teaching reading and writing in the English or German languages and arithmetic to receive into their schools and teach as aforesaid all such poor children as shall be recommended to them by the Overseers of the Poor, or where there are no Overseers of the Poor, by a Justice of the Peace and two respectable freeholders of the city, district, or township where such school is kept.

"SECTION 2. *And be it further enacted by the authority aforesaid*, That upon the performance of any such service by any school-master or school-mistress as aforesaid, the Overseers of the Poor or Justices of the

Peace and freeholders who have recommended as aforesaid, shall certify to the Commissioners of the proper county or city the names of such poor children, the time they have been respectively taught, and the usual rate of schooling paid for other children at the same school, who shall examine such certificate, and, finding it correct, shall draw an order in favor of such school-master or school-mistress for the amount on the treasurer of the proper county or city, to be paid out of the county stock.

"SECTION 3. *And be it further enacted by the authority aforesaid,* That this act shall continue in force for three years, and from thence to the end of the next session of the General Assembly and no longer, and the act entitled 'An Act to provide for the Education of Poor Children gratis,' shall be and hereby is repealed."

That this act also was considered an incomplete fulfilment of the constitution appears from the message of the governor the next year after its passage.

Agitation and discussion over the law resulted in the act of 1809, better drawn, with the same title and aim.

THE LAW OF 1809.

"AN ACT TO PROVIDE FOR THE EDUCATION OF THE POOR GRATIS.

"SECTION 1. *Be it enacted by the Senate and House of Representatives of the Commonwealth of Pennsylvania in General Assembly met, and it is hereby enacted by the authority of the same,* That it shall be the duty of the Commissioners of the several counties within this Commonwealth, at the time of issuing their precepts to the assessors, annually to direct and require the assessor of each and every township, ward, and district to receive from the parents the names of all the children between the ages of five and twelve years who reside therein, and whose parents are unable to pay for their schooling; and the Commissioners when they hold appeals shall hear all persons who may apply for alterations or additions of names in the said list, and make all such alterations as to them shall appear just and reasonable, and agreeably to the true intent and meaning of this act; and after adjustment they shall transmit a correct copy thereof to the respective assessor, requiring him to inform the parents of the children therein contained that they are at liberty to send them to the most convenient school free of expense; and the said assessor, for any neglect of the above duty, shall forfeit and pay the sum of five dollars, to be sued for by any person, and recovered as debts of that amount are now recoverable, and to be paid into the county treasury, for county purposes: *Provided always,* That the names of no children whose education is otherwise provided for shall be received by the assessors of any township or district.

"SECTION 2. *And be it further enacted by the authority aforesaid*, That the said assessor shall send a list of the names of the children aforesaid to the teachers of schools within his township, ward, or district, whose duty it shall be to teach all such children as may come to their schools in the same manner as other children are taught, and each teacher shall keep a day-book, in which he shall enter the number of days each child entitled to the provisions of this act shall be taught, and he shall also enter in said book the amount of all stationery furnished for the use of said child, from which book he shall make out his account against the county, on oath or affirmation, agreeably to the usual rates of charging for tuition in the said school, subject to the examination and revision of the trustees of the school where there are any; but where there are no trustees, to three reputable subscribers to the school; which account, after being so examined or revised, he shall present to the County Commissioners, who, if they approve thereof, shall draw their order on the county treasurer for the amount, which he is hereby authorized and directed to pay of any moneys in the treasury.

"Approved—the fourth day of April, one thousand eight hundred and nine.

"SIMON SNYDER."

Each of these acts compelled parents to publish to the world their poverty and to send their children to school as paupers.

The method of organizing schools and hiring masters under these laws was as follows: A school-meeting was called by a notice posted in the district. The inhabitants then met and elected in their own way three of their number to act as a committee or as trustees with power to hire a master or mistress, and this committee executed a supervision over the school. A rate bill was always made out by the master and handed to the committee, who collected the moneys and paid it to the master.

The pioneer and early modes of school discipline were the cat-o'-nine-tails and the rod, carrying the offender on the back of a pupil and then flogging him, setting the boys with the girls and the girls with the boys, fastening a split stick to the ear or the nose, laying the scholar over the knee and applying the ferule to the part on which he sat. These punishments lasted for years after the common schools came into use. For the benefit of young teachers I will give the mode of correction. The masters invariably kept what was called toms, or, more vulgarly, cat-o'-nine-tails, all luck being in odd numbers. This instrument of torture was an oaken stick about twelve inches long to which was attached a piece of raw-hide cut in strips, twisted while wet, and then dried. It was freely used for correction, and those who were thus corrected did not soon forget it, and not a few carried the marks during life. Another and no less cruel instrument was a green cow-hide. Comment upon the above is useless, as the words cruelty and barbarity will suggest themselves to the minds of all who read it. For our text-books we had Dilworth's and the "United States Speller," and our readers were the good old Bible and Testament. The "Western Calculator" was all the arithmetic that was in use, and the one who got through the "rule of three" was called tolerably good in figures, and the lucky wight who got through the book was considered a graduate in mathematics. Grammar

Governor Joseph Ritner.

and geography were not taught in common schools, being considered higher branches.

Not one of the governors of the State during the time the law of 1809 was in force believed it met the requirements of the constitution, hence in 1824 an act was passed repealing it and another one substituted. The new act was violently opposed, never went into effect, was repealed in 1826, and the act of 1809 was re-enacted. The policy enforced in our State for fifty years after the Revolutionary War was the endowment of academies and the free instruction of poor children in church and neighborhood schools.

Governor Wolf, in 1833-34, made education the leading topic of his message. Among other things he said,—

"'To provide by law 'for the establishment of schools throughout the State, and in such a manner that the poor may be taught gratis,' is one of the public measures to which I feel it to be my duty now to call your attention, and most solemnly to press upon your consideration. Our apathy and indifference in reference to this subject becomes the more conspicuous when we reflect that whilst we are expending millions for the physical condition of the State, we have not hitherto appropriated a single dollar that is available for the intellectual improvement of its youth, which, in a moral and political point of view, is of tenfold more consequence, either as respects the moral influence of the State or its political power and safety.

Governor George Wolf.

"According to the returns of the last census, we have in Pennsylvania five hundred and eighty-one thousand one hundred and eighty children under the age of fifteen years, and one hundred and forty-nine thousand and eighty-nine between the ages of fifteen and twenty years, forming an aggregate of seven hundred and thirty thousand two hundred and sixty-nine juvenile persons of both sexes under the age of twenty years, most of them requiring more or less instruction. And yet with all this numerous youthful population growing up around us, who, in a few years, are to be our rulers and our law-givers, the defenders of our country and the pillars of the State, and upon whose education will depend in great measure the preservation of our liberties and the safety of the republic, we have neither schools established for their instruction nor provision made by law for establishing them as enjoined by the constitution."

PIONEER HISTORY OF JEFFERSON COUNTY, PENNA.

In 1827, William Audenreid, then a senator from Schuylkill County, introduced a bill into the Senate, the title of which was, "To provide a Fund in support of a General System of Education in Pennsylvania." This bill passed the Senate that session, but was defeated in the House, but being urged and pressed every season it became a law April 2, 1831. This law entitled Senator Audenreid to be called the author of our school system. The law reads as follows:

"SECTION 1. That there shall be and there hereby is established a fund, to be denominated a Common School Fund, and the Secretary of the Commonwealth, the Auditor-General, and the Secretary of the Land-Office shall be Commissioners thereof, who, or a majority of them, in addition to the duties they now perform, shall receive and manage such moneys and other things as shall pertain to such fund, in the most advantageous manner, and shall receive and hold to the use of said fund all such gifts, grants, and donations as may be made; and that said Commissioners shall keep a correct record of their proceedings, which, together with all papers and documents relative to said fund, shall be kept and preserved in the office of the Auditor-General.

"SECTION 2. That from and after the passage of this act, all moneys due and owing this Commonwealth by the holders of all unpatented lands; also all moneys secured to the Commonwealth by mortgages or liens on land for the purchase-money of the same; also all moneys paid to the State Treasurer on any application hereafter entered, or any warrant hereafter granted for land, as also fees received in the land-office, as well as all moneys received in pursuance of the provisions of the fourth section of an act entitled 'An Act to increase the County Rates and Levies for the Use of the Commonwealth,' approved the twenty-fifth day of March, 1831, be and the same are hereby transferred and assigned to the Common School Fund; and that at the expiration of twelve months after the passage of this act, and regularly at the expiration of every twelve months thereafter, the State Treasurer shall report to the said Commissioners the amount of money thus received by him during the twelve months last preceding, together with a certificate of the amount thereof, and that the same is held by the Commonwealth for the use of the Common School Fund, at an interest of five per cent.

"SECTION 3. That the interest of the moneys belonging to said fund shall be added to the principal as it becomes due, and the whole amount thereof shall be held by the Commonwealth, and remain subject to the provisions of an act entitled 'An Act relative to the Pennsylvania Canal and Railroad,' approved the twenty-second of April, 1829, until the interest thereof shall amount to the sum of one hundred thousand dollars annually, after which the interest shall be annually distributed and applied to the support of common schools throughout this Commonwealth, in such a manner as shall hereafter be provided by law."

THE PIONEER SCHOOLS—SCHOOL-MASTERS AND SCHOOL-HOUSES.

"The pioneer school-house in the southern part of the county was built of logs, in the fall of 1820, near John Bell's, a little more than a mile northeast of where Perrysville stands. It was built after the fashion of the first school-house in the county, with paper instead of window-

Pioneer school-house.

glass, boards pinned to the wall for desks, floors and seats made of puncheons, and fireplace along one end. John Postlethwait, Sr., John Bell, Archibald Hadden, Hugh McKee, and James Stewart were the principal citizens engaged in organizing and starting the school. John B. Henderson, of Indiana County, taught the school in this part of the county, in that pioneer house, the first winter after it was built. The Testament, Bible, Catechism, and the 'United States Spelling-Book' were used as text-books in the school. Ira White, a Yankee from the State of New York, succeeded Mr. Henderson as master. Some time afterwards a school was taught by Crawford Gibson, in a house near the county line. Some parties claim that Gibson taught before Henderson, about a mile south of Perrysville. Somewhat later a school was taught by John Knox, in a log house across the creek, southeast of Perrysville. They paid him with grain, in part at least. James C. Neal, Sr., then a young man, hauled a load of grain with a yoke of oxen, to pay Mr. Knox for teaching, from Perrysville to some place near Troy, a distance of about twenty miles, through the woods.

"The pioneer school held in Punxsutawney was opened by Andrew Bowman, about 1823, in a house then owned by John B. Henderson. Dr. Jenks, Charles Barclay, Judge Heath, Rev. David Barclay, Mr. Black, and others took an active part in starting the school. They hired a master by the year. The tuition for the small pupils was twelve dollars each, and for the large ones fifty dollars a year. The first school-house was

PIONEER HISTORY OF JEFFERSON COUNTY, PENNA.

built in Punxsutawney by the above-named gentlemen about 1827, where the Baptist church stands. Hugh Kenworthy was the first man who was well educated that was employed as a master there. The next master was Dr. Robert Cunningham. After him came Thomas Cunningham, since Judge Cunningham.

"The pioneer master in Rose township was Robert Knox. When he taught the house was not floored and the pupils sat on the sleepers. The venerable Joseph Magifen, still living, taught a six months' term in 1827. Tuition, fifty cents a month per scholar and to board with the scholars.

"A school was taught in the vicinity of Brockwayville in 1828,—then Ridgway township,—for which the master was to receive twelve dollars per month in maple-sugar.

"Alexander Cochran taught the pioneer school in what is now Washington township, in 1831, in a school-house near the Beechwoods graveyard. Messrs Cooper, Keys, McIntosh, and the Smiths were instrumental in organizing the school.

"Brookville's pioneer school was taught by Alexander McKnight, father of Dr. McKnight, in a small brick school-house in 1832–33.

"A pioneer school was commenced within the present limits of Union township about 1834 or 1835. James Barr taught first, in the summer. There were about twenty pupils, and the tuition was fifty cents a month for each pupil. Samuel Davison, Robert McFarland, John W. Monks, John Hughes, and Robert Tweedy were prominent in organizing the school.

"In every locality in the county in which the population was dense enough to support a school one seems to have been organized previous to the common school system."—*Blose.*

The creation of the common schools in Pennsylvania was not the work of any one man or set of men, nor was it imported from any other State. It was the outgrowth of freedom. In a book like mine I cannot enumerate all the glorious workers in the fight. The Pennsylvania Society for the Promotion of Public Schools, organized in Philadelphia in 1827, was a great factor in the work. Senator Audenreid, Dr. Anderson, and Senator Smith, of Delaware County; N. B. Fetterman, of Bedford; Samuel Breck, a senator from Philadelphia; and Thaddeus Stevens, all deserve to be forever remembered for their able and untiring labor in this direction.

The pioneer school in the United States for the education of teachers was the model school of Philadelphia, established and opened in 1838. The finest and most costly educational structures in the world are the Girard College buildings in Philadelphia.

In the session of 1834, Samuel Breck, a senator from Philadelphia, was made chairman of a joint committee on education. The members of this committee on the part of the Senate were Samuel Breck, Charles B.

Penrose, William Jackson, Almon H. Read, and William Boyd; of the House, Samuel Anderson, William Patterson, James Thompson, James Clarke, John Wiegand, Thomas H. Crawford, and Wilmer Worthington. This committee secured all possible information on the subject from all sources. The author of the bill as passed was Samuel Breck. It was but little discussed and met with but little opposition in the Legislature.

THE LAW OF 1834 AND ITS WORKINGS IN JEFFERSON COUNTY.

"WHEREAS, It is enjoined by the constitution, as a solemn duty which cannot be neglected without a disregard of the moral and political safety of the people; and

"WHEREAS, The fund for the common school purposes, under the act of the 2d of April, 1831, will, on the 4th of April next, amount to the sum of $546,563.72, and will soon reach the sum of $2,000,000, when it will produce at five per cent. an increase of $100,000, which, by said act, is to be paid for the support of common schools; and

"WHEREAS, Provisions should be made by law for the distribution of the benefits of this fund to the people of the respective counties of the Commonwealth; therefore,

"SECTION 1. *Be it enacted by the Senate and House of Representatives of the Commonwealth of Pennsylvania in General Assembly met, and it is hereby enacted by the authority of the same*, That the city and county of Philadelphia, and every other county in this Commonwealth, shall each form a school division, and that every ward, township, and borough, within the several school divisions, shall each form a school district.

"SECTION 2. It shall be the duty of the sheriff of each county, thirty days previous to the third Friday in September of the current year, 1834, to give notice, by proclamation, to the citizens of each school district to hold elections in their respective townships, wards, and boroughs at the places where they hold their elections for supervisors, town councils, and constables, to choose six citizens, of each school district, to serve as school directors of said districts respectively; which elections shall, on the said day, be conducted and held in the same manner as elections for supervisors and constables are by law held and conducted; and on the day of the next annual election of supervisors in the respective townships, and of constables in the respective cities of the Commonwealth, a new election for directors shall take place in the said townships, boroughs, and cities, at which election, and annually thereafter at that time, and in manner and form aforesaid, two directors shall be chosen, who shall serve for three years; the sheriff giving thirty days' notice previous to such election."

OF MANUAL SCHOOLS.

"SECTION 10. WHEREAS, Manual labor may be advantageously connected with intellectual moral instruction in some or all of the schools, it shall be the duty of the school directors to decide whether such connection in their respective districts shall take place or not; and if decided affirmatively, they shall have power to purchase materials and employ artisans for the instruction of the pupils in the useful branches of the mechanic arts, and where practicable, in agricultural pursuits: *Provided, nevertheless,* That no such connection shall take place in any common school, unless four out of the six directors shall agree thereto."

Many of the sections were found to contain requirements that were crude, hence they were repealed in 1836 and perfected. These referred to the building of school-houses, employing masters, locating houses, etc. No pay was allowed a director other than as a delegate to the county convention.

PROCLAMATION—COMMON SCHOOLS.

"WHEREAS, The act of Assembly approved 1st April, 1834, and entitled 'An Act to establish a General System of Education by Common Schools,' provides 'that the city and county of Philadelphia, and every other county in this Commonwealth, shall each form a school division, and that every ward, township, and borough within the several school divisions shall each form a school district: *Provided,* That any borough which is or may be connected with a township in the assessments of county rates and levies shall, with the same township, so long as it remains so connected, form a district, and each of said districts shall contain a competent number of common schools for the education of every child within the limits thereof, who shall apply either in person, or by his or her parents, guardian, or next friend, for admission and instruction.'

"AND WHEREAS, The said act further directs, 'that it shall be the duty of the sheriff of each county to give notice by proclamation to the citizens of each school district to hold elections in their respective townships, wards, and boroughs, on the third Friday of September next, at the places where they hold their elections for supervisors, town council, and constables are by law held and conducted.'

"*Now, therefore,* I, William Clark, High Sheriff of the county of Jefferson, in pursuance of the duty enjoined on me by the above recited act, do issue this, my proclamation, giving notice to the citizens of said county, qualified as aforesaid, that an election will be held on the third Friday of September next, to choose six citizens residing therein, to serve as school directors of said districts respectively.

"The electors of the borough of Brookville are to meet at the Court-House in said borough.

"The electors of Rose township are to meet at John Lucas'.

"The electors of the township of Pine Creek are to meet at Joseph Barnett's.

"The electors of Barnett township are to meet at the house of William Armstrong.

PIONEER HISTORY OF JEFFERSON COUNTY, PENNA.

"The electors of Perry township are to meet at the house of Christopher Heterick.

"The electors of Young township are to meet in Punxsutawney.

"The electors of Ridgeway township are to meet at the house of James Gallagher.

"Given under my hand at Brookville, this fifth day of August, one thousand eight hundred and thirty-four, and of the independence of the United States the fifty-eighth.

"WILLIAM CLARK,
"Sheriff.

"SHERIFF'S OFFICE, August 5, 1834."

PIONEER SCHOOL DIRECTORS IN THE COUNTY.

Those elected under this proclamation and the law of 1834 were:

Rose township and Brookville borough—Alexander McKnight, James Green, James Linn, Robert Andrews, Irwin Robinson, Darius Carrier.

Barnett township—Cyrus Blood, William Armstrong, Edwin Forsythe, Trumble Hunt, Alexander Murray, John Hunt.

Pine Creek township—David Butler, John Lattimer, Andrew Barnett, William Cooper, Samuel Jones.

Young township—John W. Jenks, William Campbell, Jos. Winslow.

Perry township—John Philliber, William Postlethwait, Martin Shoff, Esq., William Marshall, Andrew Gibson, David Lewis.

Ridgeway township—L. Wilmarth, James Gallagher, J. L. Gillis.

As soon as these proclamations were made by the sheriff the liveliest discussion took place for and against the system. The majority of the citizens in most of the counties were against it. It was not so, however, in Jefferson, six of the districts adopting it. Nearly half of the nine hundred and eighty-seven districts in the State rejected it. Families quarrelled over and about it. In some districts a free-school man was ostracized. Life-long enmities were engendered. Several religious denominations placed themselves against this law,—Catholics, Episcopalians, Mennonites, Friends, and Lutherans. These were not opposed to education, but they believed in religious instruction and secular education, and that the two should go hand in hand, as their fathers had it. The Germans opposed it on account of a change in language. But the ignorant, the penurious, and the narrow-minded fought against it most bitterly, on account of supposed increased taxation. James Findlay was the pioneer superintendent of common schools.

The school question entered into the nomination and election of members for the session of 1834–35, and perhaps a majority of those elected were anti-school. But Governor Wolf and friends of the common school were undismayed, bold, and able, and braved the tempest of that session. Competent judges who witnessed that struggle in the

Legislature agree that had it not been for Thaddeus Stevens, a young member from Adams County, the law of 1834 would have been repealed, or only saved by a veto from the governor. This session ended the last bitter and great fight in the State and Legislature for common schools.

Thaddeus Stevens.

The ablest and most determined leaders of the anti-school were William Hopkins, of Washington County, and Henry W. Conrad, of Schuylkill.

Children as late as 1842 were admitted to the schools at the age of four years.

APPOINTMENT OF SCHOOL INSPECTORS UNDER THE LAW OF 1834.

"SECTION 12. The several courts of quarter sessions of this Commonwealth shall annually, at their first session, after the election of school directors, within their respective counties or divisions, appoint two competent citizens of each school district to be inspectors of the public school therein, established by this act, who shall be exempt during the performance of the duties of their said office from militia duty, and from serving in any township or borough office.

"SECTION 13. It shall be the duty of the school inspectors to visit every three months, and as much oftener as they may think proper, to inquire into the moral character, learning, and ability of the several teachers employed therein; they shall have power to examine any persons wishing to be employed as a teacher, and of good moral character, shall give him or her a certificate to that effect, naming therein the branches which he or she is found qualified to teach, certificates shall be valid for one year from the date thereof, and no longer; and no person who shall not have obtained such certificate shall receive from the county treasury, or the treasury of the Commonwealth, any compensation for his services.

"SECTION 14. The inspectors of any school division may meet at such times and places as they may deem expedient, and adopt such rules for the examination of teachers and schools, and prescribe such form or certificates, as they may deem necessary to produce uniformity in such examinations and certificates throughout the school division, and they may, if they deem it expedient, appoint days for the public examination of teachers to be examined in public, and said inspectors, or any one of them, may visit all district schools in their school division and examine the same.

"SECTION 15. Whenever the inspectors meet together, as they are empowered by the preceding section, they shall organize themselves for the proper transaction of business, and each inspector shall be governed by the rules then adopted in his examinations and observe such forms in his certificates as shall be prescribed by the majority of the inspectors of the school division thus assembled, and no certificate of qualification shall be given by the inspectors, or any of them, to any teacher unless he or she shall be found qualified to teach reading, writing, and arithmetic.

"SECTION 16. The school inspectors shall minutely examine into the state and condition of the schools, both as respects the progress of the scholars in learning and the good order of the schools, and make an annual report to the superintendent of the public schools on or before the first Monday in November of the situation of the schools in their respective districts, founded on their own observation and the report of the respective school directors; to include the characters of the teachers; the number of scholars admitted during the year in the several schools under their inspection; the branches of study taught in each school; the number of days in the year during which each school shall have been kept open; the cost of the school-house for either building, renting, or repairing, and all other costs that may have been incurred in maintaining the several schools in their respective districts, and also shall cause the same to be published in the school division, at the expense of the respective city or county."

PIONEER STATE AID.

"The first money received from the State for school purposes, by this county, was by an order drawn August 5, 1836, on the State Treasurer, Joseph Lawrence, Esq., to the Treasurer of Jefferson County, by Thomas H. Burrowes, Superintendent of Common Schools, under an act entitled 'An Act to establish a General System of Education by Common Schools,' passed on the 1st of April, 1834, and a supplement thereto passed April 15, 1835, for one hundred and four dollars and ninety-four cents, for the year 1835. Also, on the same date, one hundred and four dollars and ninety-four cents, for the year 1836.

Thomas H. Burrowes.

"The following table will show the townships receiving the State aid, the officers of their school boards, the number of the warrants, and the amounts received:

	No. of Warrant.	State Aid.
Barnett township—W. P. Armstrong, President; Cyrus Blood, Treasurer and Secretary	76	$49.20
Eldred township—Thomas Hall, President; Wm. M. Hindman, Treasurer; John W. Monks, Secretary	37	23.95
Perry township—Thomas Williams, President; Isaac Lewis, Treasurer; John Philliber, Secretary	209	35.31
Pine Creek township—Wm. Cooper, President; Samuel Jones, Treasurer; A. Barnett, Secretary	103	66.68
Ridgeway township—J. Gallagher, President; L. Wilmarth, Treasurer and Secretary	40	25.89
Rose township—Wm. Kelso, President; B. McCreight, Treasurer; C. A. Alexander, Secretary	252	163.14
Snyder township—A. Brockway, President; A. Ross, Treasurer; Wm. Shaw, Secretary	41	26.54
Young township—Wm. Campbell, President; J. W. Jenks, Treasurer; J. Winslow, Secretary	146	94.52
		$485.23

PIONEER HISTORY OF JEFFERSON COUNTY, PENNA.

"It would seem from the above table that it includes the appropriation of 1837 also."

ORGANIZATION UNDER THE COMMON SCHOOL SYSTEM IN JEFFERSON COUNTY.

"From the best information to be had, it appears that in 1837 Cyrus Crouch taught the first school in Brookville under the common school system. He taught two terms, and was followed by Jesse Smith, Craighead, and Hannibal.

"As early as the fall of 1835 a man by the name of Timblin made application for the school in Punxsutawney. He was examined by the Board of Directors, and was the first master under the new school system. The members of the Board were C. C. Gaskill, James Winslow, and James Torrence. Mr. Gaskill attended to the examination of the masters. It was held in an old log house in which Mr. Torrence lived. The house known as the old farm-house of Dr. Jenks was the first house built in Punxsutawney. The master was examined in reading, writing, and arithmetic. The 'United States Speller,' the 'English Reader,' and the 'Western Calculator' were the text-books used in the school. At that time Young township included Bell, McCalmont, Gaskill, Henderson, and parts of Winslow and Oliver.

"There was a great deal of hostility to the school system at first in Punxsutawney. Four schools were organized, under the common school system, in the fall of 1835 in Pine Creek township,—one near where Nathaniel Butler lives, another near the Bowers school, then called the Frederick school, another near Richardsville, and the other in the school-house near the Beechwoods graveyard. The directors were John Lattimer, William Cooper, and Andrew Barnett. A school-master of the time says that David Butler, John Lattimer, and Andrew Barnett examined the masters at Andrew Barnett's house. Mr. Thomas Kirkman taught first under the school system at the Butler school-house. Mrs. Mary McKnight taught the summer term in this house in 1840. Mr. Kirkman taught thirty days for a month, receiving fourteen dollars a month and boarding himself. They used the 'English Reader' and the 'United States Spelling-Book.' The schools began some time in November, and continued three months. Thomas Reynolds taught the Waite school in Beechwoods first under the school system. He received twelve dollars a month and 'boarded round' with the scholars. They had a ten-plate stove in the school-house, and their fuel consisted entirely of chestnut and hemlock bark, which the large pupils helped the master to pull from dead trees in the vicinity. There were about twenty-eight pupils attending the school, with an average daily attendance of eighteen. Judge Andrew Barnett, John Lattimer, and William Cooper were the principal citizens who took part in having the schools started. John Wilson was probably the first master at Richardsville. They had about fifteen pupils there."

PAUL DARLING, A PIONEER SCHOOL-MASTER.

Dr. George Darling located in Brookville in 1834 and was the father of Paul. When still young, about thirteen years old, Paul was obliged

Paul Darling.

to help himself. In the year 1836 Paul taught a school in Pine Creek township. His certificate read as follows:

"We, the undersigned School Directors of Pine Creek township, do hereby certify that we have examined Paul Darling, and have found him qualified to teach Reading, Writing, and Arithmetic and the principal rules of Grammar and Geography.

(Signed)   "JAMES MOORE,
ARCHD. McMURRAY,
JOHN LONG,
GEO. S. MATTHEWS."

From a long and intimate acquaintance with Paul Darling, I can truthfully say that he was a type of the truest men of his time; he was modest, yet determined, honest in deeds as well as in words, industrious and intelligent, frugal and liberal, kind-hearted, friendly and charitable, social and poetic, yet prudent and just. As a financier he was eminently successful, as his large estate of over five hundred thousand dollars fully attested.

"In 1836 a school-house was built above Mr. Prescott's, at Prescottville, called the Fuller school-house. Mr. Thomas Reynolds taught the first school in it. During the summer of the same year a contract for building a hewed log school-house near Mr. Dickey's, in Henderson township, was given to Mr. Caufman, and a school was commenced the following winter, under a Mr. Heisy as master. From the best information to be had, a school appears to have been organized in the Bowers settlement some time before that. About 1836 a school was organized under the school system in Perry township, and taught in one of the old log dwelling-houses in the vicinity of Perrysville. No one remembers who the master was.

"In the winter of 1835 or 1837 a school was kept in an old house near Frederick Stears', by a Mr. Travis. That was the first school in that locality under the school system. A Mrs. Travis taught a summer school in the same place. It was then in Perry, but was included in Porter township when it was organized. About the year 1839 a frame school-house was built just above Perrysville. T. S. Smith, Sr., furnished the nails and spikes, and some other citizens furnished other material and built the house. The same year a hewed log school-house was built near George Blose, Sr.'s. Wm. Postlethwait, George Blose, Sr., Youngs, and some others were prominent in having the school organized.

"The first common school was commenced in what is now Eldred township in the beginning of the winter of 1837. The house was built the same fall, near where the Hall school-house now stands. It was a hewed log house, and was built by the citizens. John Lucas taught the first school in it. There were about forty scholars. About 1837 or 1838 a round log school-house, called the Milliron school, was built a short distance northwest of where Ringgold now is. Samuel Hice was the first master there. He received not more than ten dollars a month. They used 'Cobb's Spellers' as text-books. Henry Freas, John Hice, Ben-

PIONEER HISTORY OF JEFFERSON COUNTY, PENNA.

jamin Campbell, and others were the principal citizens in having the school organized. A school-house was built in Rose township, near Mr. Spyker's, in 1836. They previously rented a house on what is now the Pleasantville road, near John J. Miller's. The first school in Union township under the school system was taught by Jesse or Theophilus Smith, about 1838, in a log school-house, with a wooden chimney along one end. The house was about two miles from Corsica, near Dallas Monks'. The pupils studied their lessons out loud. The teacher was paid sixteen or eighteen dollars a month, and boarded himself. Some of the citizens who took part in starting the school were John Fitzsimmons, the Barrs, Hindmans, Mr. Kennedy, and Mr. Monks. John Kahle taught the first school in Kahletown, Eldred township, about 1837 or 1838, in one end of his father's house. That was the first school in that part of the county. Clover township was organized into a separate school district in 1842. The first board of directors was organized May 24, 1842. Rev. C. Fogle was President, John Shields, Secretary, and D. Carrier, Treasurer. The wages of male teachers were from eighteen to twenty-five dollars a month, and of female teachers from twelve to fifteen dollars a month, and board themselves and make their own fires."—*Blose.*

PIONEER SCHOOL INSPECTORS.

Pioneer school inspectors appointed by the court December 8, 1834, under the act of 1834:

Rose township—Dr. George Darling, Rev. John Shoap.
Young township—Charles C. Gaskill, Charles R. Barclay.
Perry township—David Lewis, Parlen White.
Pine Creek township—Andrew Barnett, John Lattimer.
Ridgeway township—Lyman Wilmarth, Reuben A. Aylesworth.
Barnett township—Cyrus Blood, William Armstrong.

EXTRACT FROM COMMON SCHOOL LAW OF 1834.

"SECTION 3. It shall be the duty of the said school directors, within ten days after the period of their election, annually to meet in their respective school districts, when such board shall choose, out of their own body, a president and secretary, and a delegate to join the delegate meeting provided for in the following section; they shall appoint a treasurer for the district where no township or borough treasurer shall be otherwise appointed; and it shall be the duty of each board, on the day of their first assembling as aforesaid, to divide themselves into three classes, the first of which shall serve until the next election, the second until the second election, and the third until the third election following, so that one-third of each board may be chosen annually; and if any vacancy shall occur, by death or otherwise, it shall be the duty of the body in which such vacancy may occur to fill the same until the next election.

"SECTION 4. On the first Tuesday of November, in the year one thousand eight hundred and thirty-four, and the first Monday in May in each year thereafter, there shall be held, at the county court-house in each division, a joint meeting of the county commissioners and one delegate from each board of school directors within said county or school division, in which it shall be decided whether or not a tax for the expenditure of each district be levied; and if a tax be authorized by a majority of the joint meeting, it shall be apportioned among the several districts as county levies are now by law apportioned. Each delegate to the joint meeting shall be entitled to receive one dollar per day for each day's attendance spent by him in travelling to and from and attending said meeting, to be paid out of the county treasury."

PIONEER SCHOOL CONVENTION UNDER THE COMMON SCHOOL LAW OF 1834.

From *The Jeffersonian*, Brookville, Pennsylvania, Thursday, November 6, 1834:

"The delegates appointed by the several boards of school directors in the respective districts of Jefferson County, together with the commissioners of said county, met agreeably to law at the court-house, in the borough of Brookville, on Tuesday, the 4th of November, inst. (being the first Tuesday of the month). The following delegates were in attendance:

"County Commissioners—Levi G. Clover, James Corbett.

"Rose—Robert Andrews.

"Barnett—Cyrus Blood.

"Pine Creek—Andrew Barnett.

"Young—John Hoover.

"Perry—John Philliber.

"Ridgeway—James L. Gillis.

"The above delegates met the 4th of November and adjourned until the 5th in consequence of the absence of some delegates.

"They met the 5th of November in pursuance to previous adjournment, and proceeded to business.

"On motion, the convention was organized by calling Robert Andrews to the chair and appointing John Beck secretary.

"On motion of Mr. Andrew Barnett, and seconded, it was unanimously resolved that an appropriation for common schools be made.

"'*Resolved*, That a tax be levied and raised of double the amount of the appropriation made by the Commonwealth for common schools.'

"The following shows the proportionable share due each township out of the money appropriated by the Commonwealth,—viz.: Barnett township, $6.13; Ridgeway township, $7.06; Perry township, $21.86; Pine Creek township, $13.20; Rose township, $37.60; Young township, $19.20; total, $105.05.

"The tax to be raised off the people, for the pupose of carrying into effect the 'free school' system, is estimated at double the amount appropriated by the Commonwealth.

"'SECTION 17. The Secretary of the Commonwealth shall be superintendent of all the public schools established by virtue of this act.'"

COMMON SCHOOL NOTICE.

"For the purpose of settling controversies, of collecting and imparting information connected with the Common School System, so as to produce harmony and vigor in every department of its operations, the Superintendent will be at the county towns mentioned in the following lists on the days therein designated at 10 o'clock A.M.

"Directors, Teachers, and all others who may have business to transact with the Superintendent, under the 4th paragraph of 10th section of the school law, will meet him at their proper county towns on the days respectively named. As the chain of appointments now made will not admit of more than one day's delay at each place, early and punctual attendance is earnestly requested.

Town.	County.	Date.
* * *	* * *	* * *
Brookville.	Jefferson.	Saturday, Sept. 2.
* * *	* * *	* * *

"THOS. H. BURROWES,
"*Superintendent Common Schools.*

"SECRETARY'S OFFICE, HARRISBURG, July 18, 1837."

"SECTION 19. Seventy-five thousand dollars are hereby appropriated out of the school fund for the year one thousand eight hundred and thirty-five, which amount shall be annually thereafter appropriated and paid as hereinafter directed until the year when the school fund shall yield an interest of one hundred thousand dollars annually, when that sum shall be distributed in each year amongst the school divisions created by the adoption of this act in manner following: The superintendent of common schools shall give notice in at least one public newspaper in every division in this Commonwealth for the space of three weeks of the sum to which such division may be entitled, having reference in such distribution to the number of taxable inhabitants in said division, and these funds shall again be distributed to the different districts according to the provisions of this act, and as soon as practicable thereafter the said superintendent shall cause the distributive share of each school division entitled thereto to be paid to the county treasurer, which share shall be appointed amongst the respective districts of the several divisions according to the said principle of distribution prescribed for the superintendent; and the same rule shall be observed in the distribution of the proceeds of the tax imposed upon the county for the same purpose by the delegate meeting hereinbefore provided for."

The law of 1831 of Senator Audenreid is the foundation-stone, and that of 1834 and the act of 1837 completed our common school system, erroneously called "the free school system."

I cannot do better than to reproduce here a little speech of mine in response to the toast "Our Free Schools":

"The free school is our nation's hope. It is education that forms the common mind, and the continuance of our free institutions requires an educated common mind. To thoroughly educate the common people our schools should be free and equal. No special privileges or conditions should be permitted in them, either for the rich or the poor. We pride ourselves on our common schools, and well we may; but the schools are not equal, and only partially free. Before they can become either we must emancipate them from favoritism and unequal burdens. The conditions are unequal because the rich can buy all needful books to make the schools thorough and efficient for them, but the widow, the day laborer, and the mechanic cannot. True, we have free houses, free desks, free fuel, free black-boards, free maps, and free teachers, everything free except the most important, the one thing needful,—books. It is our duty, then, to perfect the school system by furnishing free books, free paper, free pens, free ink, free slates, free pencils, and free sponges. For it must be plain to all that with this heavy burden yet remaining on the shoulders of poor parents and pupils the word free schools is a misnomer and a mockery. Give us, then, by legislation equal privileges in the schools, and free text-books for all.

> "Hasten the day, just Heaven,
> Accomplish Thy design,
> And let the blessings of the school Thou hast given us
> On all men and women shine,
> Until free schools be everywhere and equally enjoyed,
> And human power be for human good employed."

For much of the local information in this chapter, and which I quote, I am indebted to the writings of Professor G. Ament Blose.

PIONEER LICENSES IN JEFFERSON COUNTY FROM 1812 TO 1830.*

Name.	Place.	Date.
Joseph Barnett	Bald Eagle road	December 16, 1812.
John Matson	Bellefonte road	Issued.
Joseph Barnett	Residence	March 6, 1819.

* Copied from the records of Indiana County by J. N. Banks, Esq.

PIONEER HISTORY OF JEFFERSON COUNTY, PENNA.

Name.	Place.	Date.
Joseph Barnett	Residence	September 27, 1820.
Henry Feye	Sandy Lick settlement	December 15, 1812.
Joseph Barnett	Residence on State Road	December 12, 1814.
Isaac Packer	Where Northern pike crosses Sandy Lick Creek	December 12, 1823.
Joseph Barnett	Continued	December 24, 1821.
Joseph Barnett	"	March 23, 1823.
Elijah Heath	Punxsutawney	December 25, 1822.
Elizabeth Winslow	"	March 24, 1829.
Joseph Long	"	" "
William Vasbinder	Rose township	March 23, 1829.
Joseph Potter	On Turnpike road	" "
John W. McAnulty	Bellefonte road	March 25, 1825.
Joseph Barnett		Dated Sept. 27, 1824.
Elijah Heath	Punxsutawney	March 22, 1824.
Alexander Powers	Pine Creek township	December 26, 1824.
Isaac Packer	" " "	March 30, 1824.
John Barnett	House formerly owned by Joseph Barnett	Granted.
Joseph Barnett	Port Barnett	September 22, 1822.
Andrew Vasbinder	Pine Creek township	June 25, 1827.
Joseph Barnett	Port Barnett	March 27, 1827.
Isaac Packer	At his residence	" "
Elijah Heath	Punxsutawney	Marked granted.
Alexander Powers	Pine Creek township	June 27, 1827.

PIONEER CONSTABLES IN JEFFERSON COUNTY FROM 1811 TO 1830.

Name.	Place.	Date of Election.
Freedom Styles	Pine Creek	March 15, 1811.
Freedom Styles	"	March 20, 1812.
Joseph Barnett	"	March 18, 1814.
Freedom Styles	"	March 17, 1815.
Elijah Graham	"	March 15, 1816.
Elijah Graham	"	March 15, 1817.
Freedom Styles	"	March 20, 1818.
David Hamilton	Perry	" "
Jesse Armstrong	"	March 19, 1819.
Jacob Mason	Pine Creek	" "
Jacob Hoover	Perry	March 17, 1820.
John Dixon	Pine Creek	March 18, 1820.
Moses Knapp	"	March 16, 1821.
James Wachob	Perry	" "
David McDonald	"	March 15, 1822.
Silas Sally	Pine Creek	" "
Elijah Heath	Perry	March 14, 1823.
James Diven	Pine Creek	" "
Isaac McHenry	Perry	March 19, 1824.
Stephen Reed	Pine Creek	" "
Thomas Robison	"	March 18, 1825.
Charles R. Barclay	Perry	" "

223

PIONEER HISTORY OF JEFFERSON COUNTY, PENNA.

Name.	Place.	Date of Election.
Thomas Robison	Pine Creek	March 17, 1826.
Thomas McKee	Perry	" "
James Park	Pine Creek	March 16, 1827.
Joseph Lowry	Young	" "
Nehemiah Bryant	Ridgeway	" "
William McAndrish	Perry	" "
James Wachob	"	March 20, 1829.
Peter Ostrander	Pine Creek	" "
William Love	Rose	" "
Clark Eggleston	Ridgeway	" "
William Bowers	Young	March 19, 1830.
William Smith	Perry	" "
James McCollough	Pine Creek	" "
James M. Brockway	Ridgeway	" "
Herbert Smith	Rose	" "
William Bowers	Young	" "

EARLY CONSTABLES IN JEFFERSON COUNTY FROM 1831 TO 1843.

Name.	Place.	Date of Election.
John George	Rose	1831.
Stephen Tibbets	Ridgeway	"
John B. Williams	Young	"
Joseph Cochran	Perry	"
Adam George	Rose. Tie vote. Adam George acted as constable, no doubt by appointment of court.	1832.
John George		
James Wachob	Perry. Tie vote. James Wachob evidently appointed by the court.	"
Alvah Payne		
John George	Pine Creek	"
Henry Walburn	Ridgeway	"
Wiliam Clark	Rose	1833.
John Dixon, Sr.	Pine Creek	"
Caleb Dill	Ridgeway	"
John Maize	Barnett	"
John Drum	Young	"
William M. Cochran	Perry	"
John Smith	Rose	1834.
George Newcomb	Perry	"
William Clawson	Young	"
Jacob Dobbins	Ridgeway	"
Edwin Forsythe	Barnett	"
James K. Hoffman	Pine Creek	"
John Christy	Rose	1835.
Joseph Sharp	Brookville	"
George Newcomb	Perry	"
Nathan Phipps	Barnett	"
Thomas W. Barber	Ridgeway	"
John Wilson	Pine Creek	"
William Clawson	Young	"

PIONEER HISTORY OF JEFFERSON COUNTY, PENNA.

Name.	Place.	Date of Election.
Miram Gibbs	Snyder	1835.
Joseph Sharp	Brookville	1836.
Joseph Chitister	Rose	"
Joseph Cochran	Young	"
Andrew Alcorn	Perry	"
Thomas W. Barber	Ridgeway	"
Miram Gibbs	Snyder	"
John Wilson	Pine Creek	"
Elijah M. Graham	Eldred	"
James Aharrah	Barnett	"
John McLaughlin	Brookville	1837.
William Kelso	Rose	"
Henry Smith	Young	"
Henry Philliber	Perry	"
John McGhee	Washington	"
Edward Adams	Pine Creek	"
Elijah M. Graham	Eldred	"
Henry Shaffer	Snyder	"
George Dickinson	Ridgeway	"
James Aharrah	Barnett	"
John McLaughlin	Brookville	1838.
William Kelso	Rose	"
William Robinson	Young	"
James R. Postlethwait	Perry	"
John McGhee	Washington	"
Henry Shaffer	Snyder	"
Thomas Dixon	Pine Creek	"
T. B. Maize	Barnett	"
Cyrus Blood	Jenks	"
John Gallagher	Brookville	1839.
Samuel Newcomb	Rose	"
David Barnett	Young	"
Robert E. Kennedy	Perry	"
Robert McIntosh	Washington	"
George S. Matthews	Pine Creek	"
Galbraith Wilson	Snyder	"
Christ. McNeil	Eldred	"
Matthew L. Ross	Ridgeway	"
James Aharrah	Barnett	"
George R. James	Rose	1840.
William Long	Young	"
Andrew Gibson	Perry	"
John Hice	Porter	"
George Matthews	Pine Creek	"
David Riggs	Washington	"
Christ. McNeil	Eldred	"
Peter Rickard, Jr	Snyder	"
Robert Huling	Barnett	"
David Thayer	Ridgeway	"
John Dougherty	Brookville	"

PIONEER HISTORY OF JEFFERSON COUNTY, PENNA.

Name.	Place.	Date of Election.
George R. James	Rose	1841.
James St. Clair	Young	"
Michael Palmer	Perry	"
John Hice	Porter	"
Michael Elliott	Washington	"
Nicholas McQuiston	Pine Creek	"
James Wilkins	Snyder	"
Joseph Winslow	Gaskill	"
Charles Gillis	Ridgeway	"
James Steele	Eldred	"
James Aharrah	Barnett	"
William Rodgers	Brookville	"
William McGarey	Rose	1842.
David L. Moore	Clover	"
Absalom De Haven	Young	"
Michael Palmer	Perry	"
James Dickey	Paradise	"
John McAninch	Porter	"
Michael Elliott	Washington	"
Peter Rickard	Snyder	"
Nicholas McQuiston	Pine Creek	"
David Thayer	Ridgeway	"
John D. Kahle	Eldred	"
Robert Wallace	Barnett	"
Oran Bennett	Jenks	"
John Brownlee	Brookville	"
Isaac Hughes	Rose	1843.
William E. Gillespie	Young	"
Nicholas McQuiston	Pine Creek	"
De Witt C. White	Snyder	"
David C. Riggs	Warsaw	"
John McAninch	Porter	"
Samuel Kyle	Washington	"
Charles Jacox	Clover	"
David Thayer	Ridgeway	"
John Reynolds	Barnett	"
Job M. Carley	Eldred	"
John Coffman	Gaskill	"
James H. Ames	Jenks	"
M. Palmer	Perry	"
William Rodgers	Brookville	"

"PIONEER CENSUS OF LYCOMING AND JEFFERSON COUNTIES.

	Total.	Negro Slaves.	
"Lycoming County, Pennsylvania, in 1800	5414	39	
	Whites.	Colored.	Slaves.
'Jefferson County, Pennsylvania, in 1810	161	1	..
" " " in 1820	561	10	..
" " " in 1830	2003	21	1
" " " in 1840	7196	57	..

PIONEER HISTORY OF JEFFERSON COUNTY, PENNA.

"Taxable list of Jefferson County, Pennsylvania, from 1807 up to and including 1842: 1807, 23; 1814, 35; 1821, 161; 1828, 256; 1835, 904; 1842, 1788.

"Receipts and expenditures of Jefferson County from January 2, 1816, to January 1, 1817, both days inclusive:

"John Taylor, Esq., Treasurer.

"Dr.

"To cash of Joseph Barnett, Collector of Pine Creek township for 1813, in full	$17.43¾
Received on unseated lands	2475.61¼
" land sold	101.92
	$2594.97
List of outstanding debts due from the collectors for 1815	$7.70½
On unseated lands before 1816, for which the lands have been sold to the Commissioners	2140.27
County tax, 1816	790.92
	$2938.89½

"Cr.

"By cash paid on sundry road orders	$1626.76
" " on election orders	34.00
" " on wolf orders	157.37½
" " to road viewers	18.00
" " on contingent expenses	102.00
Paid to Indiana County the proportionate part of the general expenses	298.56
Treasurer's fees of sixty-five tracts of land sold to Commissioners	182.92
Treasurer's fees on $1933.13½ at 2 per cent.	38.66
Balance in treasury	136.69½
	$2594.97

"Garwin Sutton,
Thomas Sharp,
Thomas Laughlin,
"*Commissioners.*

"Attest:
"Daniel Stanard,
"*Clerk.*"
—*Indiana American*, February 10, 1817.

INCIDENTS.

On October 23, 1819, was the "dark day." Between nine and ten o'clock in the morning the darkness was so great that the pioneer had to light his old lamp or blaze his pitch-pine knot.

In January, 1828, there was a great flood in Jefferson County, and also a great one on February 10, 1832.

1816, or the year without a summer. Frost occurred in every month in 1816. Ice formed half an inch thick in May. Snow fell to the depth of three inches in June. Ice was formed to the thickness of a common window-glass on the 5th day of July. Indian corn was so frozen that the greater part was cut in August and dried for fodder, and the pioneers supplied from the corn of 1815 for the seeding of the spring of 1817.

In 1809, Fulton patented the steamboat.

The pioneer steam-vessels that made regular trips across the Atlantic Ocean were the "Sirius" and "Great Western" in the year 1830.

The pioneer use of gas for practical illumination was in 1802.

The pioneer mill to make finished cloth from raw cotton was erected in Waltham, Massachusetts, in 1813.

In 1807 wooden clocks were made by machinery.

The anthracite coal business was established about 1820.

In 1836 matches were patented.

"The first practical friction matches were made in 1827 by an English apothecary named Walker, who coated splints of card-board with sulphur and tipped them with a mixture of sulphate of antimony, chlorate of potash, and gum. A box of eighty-four matches sold for one cent, a piece of glass-paper being furnished with it for obtaining ignition. In 1830 a London man named Jones devised a species of match which was a little roll of paper soaked in chlorate of potash and sugar, with a thin glass globule filled with sulphuric acid attached to one end. The globule being broken, the acid acted upon the potash and sugar, producing fire. Phosphorus matches were first introduced on a commercial scale in 1833, and after that improvements were rapid.

"The modern lucifer match combines in one instrument arrangements for creating a spark, catching it on tinder, and starting a blaze,—steps requiring separate operations in primitive contrivances. It was in 1836 that the first United States patent for friction matches was issued. Splints for them were made by sawing or splitting blocks of wood into slivers slightly attached at the base. These were known as 'slab' or 'block' matches, and they are in use in parts of this country to-day."

The pioneer strike in America was that of the journeymen bootmakers of Philadelphia in 1796. The men struck, or "turned out," as they phrased it, for an increase of wages. After two weeks' suspension of trade their demands were granted, and this success gained them greater strength and popularity, so that when they "turned out in 1798, and again in 1799, for further increases, they were still successful and escaped indictment.

Vulcanized rubber was patented in 1838.

In 1840, Daguerre first made his pictures.

The express business was started about 1840.

The pioneer telegram was sent in 1845.

The pioneer steamer to cross the Atlantic was built in New York in

PIONEER HISTORY OF JEFFERSON COUNTY, PENNA.

1818 by Francis Picket. The vessel was called the "Savannah." In the trip she carried seventy-five tons of coal and twenty-five cords of wood. She left Savannah, Georgia, in May, 1819, and arrived at Liverpool in June, 1819. She used steam eighteen of the twenty-six days.

James Piles was the pioneer blacksmith, in 1808, in Jefferson County. Joseph McCullough was the second blacksmith, in 1819. Before "stocks" were invented oxen had to be thrown and tied and the shoes nailed on while down. McCullough did this.

In 1811 a furious tornado swept across this county.

In 1828, March 9, an earthquake shock was felt in Jefferson County.

The earliest recorded tornado in the United States was in 1794. It passed north of Brookville, in what is now Heath and other townships, and extended to Northford, Connecticut.

PIONEER THANKSGIVING DAYS.

The first recorded Thanksgiving was the Hebrew feast of the Tabernacles.

The New England Thanksgiving dates from 1633, when the Massachusetts Bay colony set apart a day for thanksgiving.

The first national Thanksgiving proclamations were by Congress during the Revolutionary War.

The first great American Thanksgiving day was in 1734, for the declaration of peace. There was one more national Thanksgiving in 1789, and no other till 1862, when President Lincoln issued a national proclamation for a day of thanksgiving.

The pioneer Thanksgiving day in Jefferson County, Pennsylvania, was on the last Thursday of November, 1819, by proclamation of Governor Findlay.

CHAPTER XIII.

PIONEER MISSIONARY WORK—THE FIRST WHITE MAN TO TRAVEL THE SOIL OF JEFFERSON COUNTY—REVS. POST, HECKEWELDER, AND OTHERS.

THE pioneer minister to travel through what is now Jefferson County was a Moravian missionary or a preacher of the United Brethren Church, the Rev. Christian Frederic Post. He travelled from Philadelphia to the Ohio (Allegheny) River in 1758 on a mission from the government of Pennsylvania to the Delaware, Shawanese, and Mingo Indians. These Indians were then in alliance with the French, and Rev. Post's mission was to prevail on them to withdraw from that alliance. Post passed through what is now Jefferson County, from Clearfield, over Boone's Mountain, crossed Little Tobec (Little Toby), and then over Big Tobec (Big Toby) Creek.

From Post's journal I quote the following extract:

"*August 2nd*—We came across several places where two poles, painted red, were stuck in the ground by the Indians, to which they tye the prisoners, when they stop at night, in their return from their incursions. We arrived this night at Shinglimuce, where was another of the same posts. It is a disagreeable and melancholy sight, to see the means they make use of, according to their savage way, to distress others.

"*3rd*—We came to a part of a river called Tobeco, over the mountains, a very bad road.

"*4th*—We lost one of our horses, and with much difficulty found him, but were detained a whole day on that account [at what is now Brockwayville]. I had much conversation with Pisquetumen [an Indian chief that travelled with him]; of which I think to inform myself further when I get to my journey's end.

"*5th*—We set out early this day, and made a good long stretch, crossing the big river Tobeco, and lodged between two mountains. I had the misfortune to lose my pocket book with three pounds five shillings, and sundry other things. What writings it contained were illegible to any body but myself.

"*6th*—We passed all the mountains, and the big river, Weshawaucks, and crossed a fine meadow two miles in length, where we slept that night, having nothing to eat.

"*7th*—We came in sight of fort Venango, belonging to the French, situate between two mountains, in a fork of the Ohio [Allegheny] river. I prayed the Lord to blind them, as he did the enemies of Lot and Elisha, that I might pass unknown. When we arrived, the fort being on the other side of the river, we hallooed, and desired them to fetch us over: which they were afraid to do; but showed us a place where we might ford. We slept that night within half gun shot of the fort."

*   *   *   *   *   *   *   *   *

"Christian Frederic Post accompanied by several friendly Indians, set out from Bethlehem on the 19th of July, for Fort Augusta (Sunbury). There he took the path along the right bank of the West Branch, leading over the Chillisquaque, over Muncy, Loyalsock, and Pine Creeks, crossed the Susquehanna at the Great Island, and then struck one of the main Indian thoroughfares to the West. On the 3rd of July he forded Beech Creek, on whose left bank he came to the forks of the road. One branch led southwest along the Bald Eagle, past the Nest to Frankstown, and thence to the Ohio country; the other due west to Chinklacamoose. Post took the latter. It led over the Moshannon, which he crossed on the 1st of August. Next day he arrived at the village of Chinklacamoose in the 'Clear Fields.' Hence the travellers struck a trail to the northwest, crossed Toby's Creek (Clarion River), and on the 7th of August reached Fort Venango, built by the French in 1753, in the forks of the Allegheny. 'I prayed the Lord,' writes Post, 'to blind the French, as he did the enemies of Lot and Elisha, that I might pass unknown.'

"Leaving Venango, Post and his companions turned their horses' heads to the southwest, struck the Conequenessing on the 12th of August, crossed the Big Beaver, and next day arrived at Kaskadkie, the terminus of their journey and the head-quarters of 'the Beavers' and 'Shingas,' war-chiefs of the western Delawares." Post was, therefore, the first Moravian west of the Alleghenies. He closes his interesting journal with these words:

"Thirty-two days that I lay in the woods, the heavens were my covering, and the dew fell so hard sometimes that it pricked close to the skin. During this time nothing lay so heavily on my heart as the man who went along with me [Shamokin Daniel], for he thwarted me in everything I said or did; not that he did it against me, but against the country on whose business I was sent. When he was with the French he would speak against the English, and when he was with the English he would speak against the French. The Indians observed that he was unreliable, and desired me not to bring him any more to transact business between them and the prisoners. But praise and glory be to the lamb that was slain, who brought me through a country of dreadful jealousy and mistrust, where the Prince of this world holds rule and government over the children of disobedience. It was my Lord who preserved me amid all difficulties and dangers, and his Holy Spirit directed me. I had no one to commune with, but Him; and it was he who brought me from under a thick, heavy and dark cloud into the open air, for which I adore, and praise and worship him. I know and confess that He, the Lord my God, the same who forgave my sins and washed my heart in his most precious blood, grasped me in his almighty hand and held me safe,—and hence I live no longer for myself, but for Him, whose holy will to do is my chiefest pleasure."

"Christian Frederic Post, the most adventurous of Moravian missionaries employed among the North American Indians, was born at Conitz, Polish Prussia, in 1710. He immigrated to this country in June, 1742. Between 1743 and 1749 he was a missionary to the Moravian Indians in New York and Connecticut. He first married Rachel, a Wampanoag, and after her death, Agnes, a Delaware. Having become a widower a second time, he, in 1751, returned to Europe: hence he sailed for Labrador in 1752, engaging in an unsuccessful attempt to bring the gospel to the Esquimaux. Having returned to Bethlehem in 1754, he was sent to Wyoming, where he preached to the Indians until in November of 1755. In the summer of 1758, Post undertook an embassy in behalf of government to the Delawares and Shawanese of the Ohio country, which resulted in the evacuation of Fort Duquesne by the French and the restoration of peace. In September of 1761 he engaged in an independent mission to the Indians of that distant region, and built him a hut on the Tuscarawas, near Bolivar, in Stark County, Ohio. John Heckewelder joined him in the spring of 1762. But the Pontiac war drove the missionaries back to the settlements, and the project was abandoned. Impelled by his ruling passion, Post now sought a new field of activity in the southern part of the continent, and in January of 1764 sailed from Charleston, *via* Jamaica, for the Mosquito coast. Here he preached to the natives for upward of two years. He visited Bethlehem in July of 1767, returned to Mosquito, and was in Bethlehem, for the last time, in 1784. At this date he was residing with his third wife, who was an Episcopalian, in Germantown. Here he deceased April 29, 1785. On the 5th of May his remains were interred in the Lower Graveyard of that place, Rev. William White, of Christ Church, conducting the funeral service. A marble slab, bearing an appropriate obituary record, was placed, some thirty years ago, upon the veteran missionary's grave."—*Transactions of the Moravian Historical Society*, vol. i.

The second minister to cry aloud in this wilderness was the Rev. John Heckewelder in 1762. He came from Bethlehem over the Chinklacamoose trail to Punxsutawney. He was a Moravian missionary, and travelled some thirty thousand miles in Indian missionary work between the years 1762 and 1814.

The third preacher to penetrate this wilderness was a Moravian minister, the Rev. David Zeisberger, and he passed through or near Brockwayville over the northwest trail to what was then the Ohio, now the Allegheny (in what is now Forest County) River.

I quote as follows from "Day's Collections":

"In the year 1767 an unarmed man of short stature, remarkably plain in his dress, and humble and peaceable in his demeanor, emerged from the thick forest upon the Allegheny River, in the neighborhood of the Seneca towns. This was the Moravian missionary, Rev. David Zeisberger, who, led by Anthony and John Papanhunk, Indian guides and assistants in his pious labors, had penetrated the dense wilderness of Northern Pennsylvania, from Wyalusing, on the Susquehanna, to preach the gospel to the Indians in this region. His intended station was at Goshgoshunk, which appears to have been on the left bank of the Allegheny, not far from the mouth of Tionesta. Possibly Goshgoshunk was the same as the Indian name Cush-cush.

"The Seneca chief, believing Brother Zeisberger to be a spy, received him roughly at first; but, softened by his mild demeanor, or perhaps by the holy truths which he declared to the chief, he at length bade him welcome, and permitted him to go to Goshgoshunk. He warned him, however, not to trust the people there, for they had not their equals in wickedness and thirst for blood. This was but another incentive to him who came to preach 'not to the righteous, but to sinners.' However, on his arrival he was well received, and shared the hospitality of a relative of one of his guides. 'Goshgoshunk, a town of the Delawares, consisted of three villages on the banks of the Ohio [Allegheny]. The whole town seemed to rejoice at the novelty of this visit. The missionary found, however, that the Seneca chief had told him truly. He was shocked at their heathenish and diabolical rites, and especially by their abuse of the holy name of God. An Indian preacher, called Wangomen, strenuously resisted the new doctrines of the missionaries, especially that of the incarnation of the Deity, and instigated the jealousy of his people; but the truth, preached in its simplicity and power, by the missionaries, overcame him, and he yielded his opposition so far as to join the other Indians in an invitation to the missionaries to settle among them. The old blind chief, Allemewi, was awakened, and afterwards baptized, with the Christian name of Solomon. The missionary went home to report his progress to his friends in Bethlehem. The following year Zeisberger returned, accompanied by Brother Gottlob Senseman and several Moravian Indian families from the Susquehanna, to establish a regular mission at Goshgoshunk. They built a block-house, planted corn, and, gathering round their block-house several huts of believing Indians, they formed a small hamlet, a little separated from the other towns. 'To this a great number resorted, and there the brethren ceased not, by day and night, to teach and preach Jesus, and God in Christ, reconciling the world unto himself.' These meetings were fully attended, 'and it was curious to see so many of the audience with their faces painted black and vermilion and heads decorated with clusters of feathers and fox-tails.' A violent opposition, however, succeeded, occasioned by the malicious lies of the magicians and old women,—' the corn was blasted, the deer and game began to retire from the woods, no chestnuts nor bilberries would grow any more, merely because the missonaries preached a strange doctrine, and the Indians were changing their way of life.' Added to this, the grand council at Onondaga and Zeneschio (Ischua) looked with extreme jealousy upon this new encroachment of white men upon their territories and discountenanced the establishment. In consequence of these things the missionaries left Goshgoshunk, and retired fifteen miles farther up the river, to a place called Lawanakanuck, on the opposite bank, probably near Hickorytown. Here they again started a new settlement, built at first a hunting-den, and afterwards a chapel and a dwelling-house, 'and a bell, which they received from Bethlehem, was hung in a convenient place.'

"About the year 1765 the Moravian missionary David Zeisberger established the mission of Friedenschnetten, near the present town of Wyalusing, in Bradford County. This town, the name of which signifies 'tents of peace,' contained 'thirteen Indian huts, and upward of forty frame houses, shingled, and provided with chimneys and windows.' There was another mission about thirty miles above Friedenschnetten,—

'Tschechsehequanink,' or, as it was translated, 'where a great awakening had taken place.' This latter mission was under the charge of Brother Roth.

"These missions prospered greatly, and much good was done among the Indians, until 1768, when the Six Nations, by the treaty made that year, 'sold the land from under their feet,' and the missionaries encountered so much trouble from both the Indians and whites, that in 1772 the brethren decided to abandon these missions and remove to the new field which had been planted by the indefatigable Zeisberger on the banks of the Ohio. They therefore started from Wyalusing on the 12th day of June, 1772, in number two hundred and forty-one souls, mostly Indians, of all ages, with their cattle and horses. Their destination was Friedenstadt,* near the present site of Beaver, Pennsylvania. They were under the guidance of Brothers Roth and Ettewein, and their course was from the North Branch across the Allegheny Mountains, by way of Bald Eagle, to the Ohio River. Brother Roth conducted those who went by water and Brother Ettewein those who travelled by land. In 1886 the *Moravian*, published at Bethlehem, gave the journal of Rev. John Ettewein, and we give the extracts from it of the progress of the party through the territory now comprised by southern Jefferson County, with the explanatory foot-notes in the *Moravian*, translated by Mr. Jordan:

"'*1772*.

"'*Tuesday, July 14*.—Reached Clearfield Creek, where the buffalos formerly cleared large tracts of undergrowth, so as to give the appearance of cleared fields. Hence, the Indians called the creek 'Clearfield.' Here at night and next morning, to the great joy of the hungry, nine deer were shot. Whoever shoots a deer has for his private portion, the skin and inside; the meat he must bring into camp and deliver to the distributors. John and Cornelius acted in this capacity in our division. It proved advantageous for us not to keep so closely together, as we had at first designed; for if the number of families in a camp be large, one or two deer, when cut up, afford but a scanty meal to each individual. So it happened that scarce a day passed without there being a distribution of venison in the advance, the centre and the rear camp. (On the route there were one hundred and fifty deer and but three bears shot.) In this way our Heavenly Father provided for us; and I often prayed for our hunters, and returned thanks for their success.

"'*Thursday, July 16*.— . . . I journeyed on, with a few of the brethren, two miles in a falling rain, to the site of Chinklacamoose, where we found

---

* "The Annals of Friedenschnetten, on the Susquehanna, with John Ettewein's Journal of the Removal of the Mission to Friedenstadt, 1765 and 1772, by John W. Jordan."

but three huts, and a few patches of Indian corn. The name signifies 'No one tarries here willingly.' It may, perhaps, be traced to the circumstance that some thirty years ago an Indian resided here as a hermit, upon a rock, who was wont to appear to the Indian hunters, in frightful shapes. Some of these, too, he killed, others he robbed of their skins; and this he did for many years. We moved on four miles, and were obliged to wade the West Branch three times, which is here like the Lehigh at Bethlehem, between the island and the mountain, rapid and full of ripples.

"'*Friday, July 17.*—Advanced only four miles to a creek that comes down from the northwest.* Had a narrow and stony spot for our camp.

"'*Saturday, July 18.*—Moved on without awaiting Roth and his division, who on account of the rain had remained in camp. To-day Shebosch lost a colt from the bite of a rattlesnake. Here we left the West Branch three miles to the Northwest, up the creek, crossing it five times. Here, too, the path went precipitately up the mountain, and four or five miles up and up to the summit—to a spring the head-waters of the Ohio.† Here I lifted up my heart in prayer as I looked westward, that the Son of Grace might rise over the heathen nations that dwell beyond the distant horizon.

"'*Sunday, July 19.*—As yesterday, but two families kept with me, because of the rain, we had a quiet Sunday, but enough to do drying our effects. In the evening all joined me, but we could hold no service as the Ponkis were so excessively annoying that the cattle pressed towards and into our camp, to escape their persecutors in the smoke of the fires. This vermin is a plague to man and beast, both by day and night. But in the swamp through which we are now passing, their name is legion. Hence the Indians call it the Ponksutenink, *i.e.*, the town of the Ponkis.‡ The word is equivalent to living dust and ashes, the vermin being so small as not to be seen, and their bite being hot as sparks of fire, or hot ashes. The brethren here related an Indian myth, to wit: That the aforecited Indian hermit and sorcerer, after having been for so many years a terror to all Indians, had been killed by one who had burned his bones, but the ashes he blew into the swamp, and they became living things, and hence the Ponkis.

"'*Monday, July 20.*—After discoursing on the daily word—' The Lord

---

* "Anderson's Creek, in Clearfield County, which they struck at a point near the present Curwensville."

† "Probably the source of the North Branch of the Mahoning, which rises in Brady township, Clearfield County, and empties into the Allegheny, in Armstrong County, ten miles above Kittanning."

‡ "Kept down the valley of the Mahoning, into Jefferson County. Punxsutawney is a village in Young township, Jefferson County. The swamp lies in Gaskill and Young townships."

our God be with us, may he not forsake us'—we traveled on through the swamp, and after five miles crossed the path that leads from Frankstown* to Goshgoshunk, and two miles from that point encamped at a run. At 5 P.M., came Brethren Peter, Boaz, and Michael, with fourteen unbaptized Indians, from Lagundontenink, to meet us with four horses, and five bushels of Indian corn, also Nathaniel's wife from Sheninga † with a letter from Brother Jungman. I thought had I but milk or meat, I would add rice, and prepare a supper for the new-comers. But two of them went to hunt, and in half an hour Michael brought in a deer to my fire. My eyes moistened with tears. Sister Esther hunted up the large camp kettle, and all had their fill of rice and venison, and were much pleased. That night and the following morning there were four deer shot by the company.

" ' *Tuesday, July 21.*—The rear division came up, and the destitute, viz., such as had lived solely upon meat and milk, were supplied each with one pint of Indian corn. We proceeded six miles to the first creek. In the evening a number of the brethren came to my fire, and we sat together right cheerful until midnight. Once when asleep I was awakened by the singing of the brethren who had gathered around the fire of the friends from Lagundontenink. It refreshed my inmost soul.

" ' *Wednesday, July 22.*—We journeyed on four miles, to the first fork ‡ where a small creek comes down from the mouth.

" ' *Thursday, July 23.*—Also four miles to the second fork, to the creek, coming in from the south-east.§ As a number of us met here in good time we had a meeting. Corneliu's brother-in-law stated that he was desirous of being the Lord's; therefore he had left his friends so as to live with the brethren, and to hear of the Saviour.

" ' *Friday, July 24.*—The path soon left the creek, over valleys and heights to a spring. Now we were out of the swamp, and free from the plague of the Ponkis. Also found huckleberries, which were very grateful. Our to-day's station was five miles, and about so far we advanced on.

" ' *Saturday, July 25.*—On which day we encamped at a Salt Lick, and kept Sunday some three miles from the large creek, which has so many curves, like a horseshoe, so that if one goes per canoe, when the water is high, four days are consumed in reaching the Ohio, whereas, by land, the point can be reached in one day.|| Our youngsters went to the creek

---

* "Near Hollidaysburg. See Scull's map of 1759 for this path."
† "Sheninga is a township in Lawrence County, just above Friedenstadt."
‡ "A branch of the Mahoning."
§ "*Query.*—The creek that comes in and up below Punxsutawney."
|| "The Mahoning, formed by the junction of the East and South Branch, which meets at Nicholsburg, in Indiana County. This route to the Allegheny was the same path taken by Post in 1758, when returning from his second visit to the Ohio Indians in that year, and between Chinklacamoose and the Allegheny, over the same path

to fish, and others to hunt; and at sunset they came in with two deer, and four strings of fish.'"

"John Roth was born in Brandenburg, February 3, 1726, of Catholic parents, and was brought up a locksmith. In 1748 he united with the Moravians and emigrated to America, arriving at Bethlehem in June of 1756. He deceased at York, Pennsylvania, July 22, 1791.

"John Ettewein was born 29th of June, 1721, in Freudenstadt, Würtemberg. He united with the Moravians in 1740, and came to Bethlehem in April of 1754. Here he was set apart for service in the schools of his adopted church, when, in 1758, a new field of labor was assigned him at the Brethren's settlements in Western North Carolina (Forsyth and adjacent counties). During his residence in Wachovia he itinerated among the spiritually destitute Germans of South Carolina (1762), and visited the Salzburgers and Swiss of Ebenezer (in Georgia) in 1765. The following year he was recalled to Bethlehem. This place was the scene of his greatest activity, as here, under God, he led the Moravian Church in safety through the stormy times of the Revolution. He was ordained a bishop in 1784. In 1789 he sailed for Europe, and attended a general synod convened at Herrnhut. John Ettewein was one of the remarkable men of the Brethren's Church in North America. He deceased at Bethlehem, 2d of January, 1802."

CHAPTER XIV.

PIONEER AND EARLY CHURCHES—PRESBYTERIAN THE PIONEER CHURCH IN THE COUNTY—THE PIONEER PREACHER AND CHURCH.

THE pioneer Presbyterian preaching in Pennsylvania was in Philadelphia in 1698. In 1704 they erected a frame church on Market Street and called it "Buttonwood."

I quote from Rev. Fields as to the organization of the pioneer Presbyterian Church of Jefferson County:

"Its first name was Bethel, and continued to be for many years. The records of the church are not to be found farther back than September 20, 1851. Records were in existence as far back as 1832, but where they are or who has them cannot now be ascertained. The church had its beginning in Port Barnett. Preaching seems to have been in the settlement in June, 1809. At that time a communion service was held in the house of Peter Jones, near where John McCullough now lives. Robert

---

travelled by Barbara Leininger in 1755, when Chinklacamoose and Punxsutawney were villages."

McGarraugh administered the supper. He was then pastor of Licking and New Rehoboth, now in Clarion County. He had come to the Clarion region as a licentiate of the Presbytery of Redstone in the fall of 1803. Whether he visited Port Barnett settlement at that time cannot now be ascertained. At all events, when he returned from Fayette County with his family, June, 1804, and was ordained pastor of Licking and New Rehoboth churches, November 12, 1807, he seems to have taken the Port Barnett settlement under his care. When he 'held the communion,' June, 1809, certain persons were received into the church in such a way that he baptized their children. This much is plain from the memory and Bible record of Mrs. Sarah Graham, daughter of Joseph Barnett.''

A word here with regard to that good and God-fearing man. He was highly educated and able in prayer, yet, like Moses, slow of speech, often taking two and three hours to deliver a sermon. He preached without notes, and with great earnestness pleaded with his hearers to forsake their sins and the errors of their ways and turn to the Lord. So earnest would he become at times that the great tears would roll from his eyes to the floor. It was often said that he preached more eloquently by his tears than by the power of his voice. He lived poor and died poor, and preached in the clothes in which he worked.

"How long Robert McGarraugh continued to preach in the house of Peter Jones remains uncertain. After some years religious services were held in the house of Samuel Jones, five miles west of Brookville. The church was fully organized in a school-house, near the present site of the United Presbyterian Jefferson Church on the Andrews farm. That seems to have been in 1824. The Allegheny Presbytery reported to the Synod of Pittsburg twenty-three churches in 1823. In 1824 the Presbytery reported twenty-five churches, and among them Bethel and Zelienople, so that the record of the Synod establishes conclusively the fact that in that year (1824) Bethel for the first time was recognized as a separate congregation. The next record is in the minutes of the Allegheny Presbytery, April, 1825. It there appears as vacant, and, shortly afterwards, as connected with Red Bank, both having sixty-eight members.

"Bethel Church, as organized in the Jefferson school-house, was removed, in the fall of 1824, to a farm on the road from Brookville to Clarion. The farm was owned by Joseph Hughes (the father of Isaac D. Hughes, of Brookville), and was distant from Brookville three miles. There they built a church, and dedicated it *The Bethel* of Jefferson County. The church was built of logs, small and closely notched together. It stood to the right of the road as one goes towards Clarion, near the pike, and on a line between it and the 'Old Graveyard.' The latter is still in existence, but all traces of the old meeting-house are gone. The floor was genuine mother-earth, and the seats slabs or boards on logs. A board on two posts constituted the 'pulpit-stand,' and a seat was made out of a slab or a block of wood. The first stated preacher in that log church was Rev. William Kennedy. His name appears as a stated supply October 13, 1825; also April, 1827. Bethel was then connected with Red Bank. He ceased to be a member of the Allegheny Presbytery after April, 1827. He was dismissed to Salem Presbytery, Indiana Synod. He became a member of Clarion Presbytery January 17, 1843, and died November 2, 1846, aged sixty-seven years and four months. The last years of his life were devoted to the congregations of Mount Tabor and Mill Creek.

"The next record concerning Bethel is that the Rev. Cyrus Riggs was appointed to supply at Bethel on the second Sabbath of July, 1827. Bethel and Red Bank were marked vacant April, 1828. Mr. Riggs was appointed April, 1829, to supply one Sabbath at discretion. Rev. John Core and Rev. John Munson were selected to 'administer the Lord's Supper at Bethel on the fifth Sabbath of August, 1829.' Bethel and Red Bank were still vacant April, 1831. 'Rev. Cyrus Riggs and Rev. John Core were appointed to administer the Lord's Supper on the third Sabbath of August, 1831.' Mr. Core afterwards preached that same year at discretion.

"The first jail building in Brookville was of stone, two stories in height. It was built before the first court-house, and for that reason became the first place of preaching, in the second story. Bethel Church seems to have renewed its youth in the summer of 1831. No further trace of preaching in 'the old log church' is found after that date. In the summer of 1832 the first court-house was erected, and religious services were then held in it. Bethel does not appear in the minutes of April, 1832. In 1833, Mr. Riggs was appointed to supply Bethel on the fifth Sabbath of June, and Messrs. McGarraugh and Riggs to administer the Lord's Supper the fourth Sabbath of August. On the 1st of July, 1833, the following persons were dismissed to form the organization of Pisgah,—viz.: Samuel Davidson and wife, Samuel Lucas and wife, Philip Corbett and wife, John Wilson and wife, William Corbett and wife, John Hindman and wife, John M. Flemming and wife, David Lamb and wife, Christwell Whitehill and wife, and William Douglass. They were organized the next day by Mr. Riggs, in the house of Philip Corbett, a short distance west of Corsica, where his son, Robert Corbett, now resides.

"The next record of Presbytery is August 24, 1834: 'The congregations of Bethel, Pisgah, and Beechwoods requested by their commissioners that Mr. John Shoap, a licentiate of Allegheny Presbytery, be appointed to preach steadily in those congregations until the spring meeting of Presbytery.' The request was granted, and Mr. Shoap accepted the call, October 8, 1834, from the churches of Bethel and Pisgah. The conditions of the call were, 'Each half-time and two hundred dollars by each.' 'To be paid,' as one lady remarked, 'in pork and maple-sugar.' Mr. Shoap was never ordained, never installed. He died March 13, 1835, of con-

The Presbyterian Church of Brookville. Erected in 1869.

sumption. His body was interred in the 'Old Graveyard' in Brookville, and perhaps but one person can identify his grave. Rev. Gara Bishop, M.D., came to Brookville June 23, 1835. He supplied in that year

Beechwoods more frequently than either Bethel or Pisgah. April 3, 1838, Bethel requested the one-half of the labors of the Rev. Gara Bishop as a stated supply. One-fourth of his labors were given to Beechwoods. He remained until the spring of 1840. Rev. David Polk, a cousin of President James K. Polk, was then invited to give one-half of his labors to Bethel. On the 22d of October Clarion Presbytery was formed from Allegheny, and Bethel's history henceforward was a part of the records of Clarion. Rev. Bishop died in Brookville, October 17, 1852, and was buried in the 'Old Graveyard.' In 1841 a small frame church (contract price being eleven hundred dollars) was erected on the site of the present edifice, and was dedicated in August, 1842. Rev. Polk remained until December 24, 1845."—*Fields*.

Bethel Church was changed to "The Bethel Congregation of the Brookville Presbyterian Church" by articles and charter of incorporation May 13, 1842. The trustees named in the articles were James Corbett, Samuel Craig, and Andrew Barnett. On May 13, 1842, the court decided that the persons associated in the articles should "become a corporation and a body politic," and that the charter be entered in the office for recording deeds in the said county of Jefferson. In accordance with this decree the articles were recorded in Deed Book No. 3, pages 521, 522.

On August 18, 1843, at a meeting held for that purpose, Jameson Hendricks, W. A. Sloan, and Thomas M. Barr were duly elected elders.

The pioneer regular preacher for Bethel was the Rev. William Kennedy,—viz., from October, 1825, to April, 1827, one-half of his time. The membership then was sixty-eight. When Bethel removed to Brookville in 1830, all west of the old log church moved west, thus forming two churches out of one. On July 2, 1833, the members of the western division were organized into Pisgah Church (the third organization) by a committee from the Allegheny Presbytery, Rev. Cyrus Riggs, chairman, and on that date the organization was completed in Philip Corbett's barn, one mile west of where Corsica now stands. In this society there were twenty-five members,—twelve men and their wives and one widower. The elders elected at that time were William Corbett, William Douglass, Samuel Lucas, Samuel Davison, James Hindman, and John M. Flemming. Two meetings preliminary to the organization were held at the house of Robert Barr, Sr., one mile east of where Corsica now stands,—viz., February 22, 1833, and April 13, 1833. On February 22 it was resolved that the congregational name be Pisgah, and that the edifice for worship be erected on the hill south of McAnulty's, close to the Olean road. A committee was appointed to purchase the land, and a committee was appointed to present the petition of the church people to Presbytery for an organization. At the April meeting the committee reported the purchase of ten acres of ground on the west side of the Olean road for the sum of fifteen dollars and a deed of trust received. It was also resolved that Philip Corbett's barn, in Clarion County, be the place for worship that summer. The pioneer house of worship was built on that hill in 1841, at a cost of one thousand dollars.

Pisgah was first regularly supplied by Rev. John Shoap in connection with Bethel (Brookville) in 1834 and 1835. Rev. Shoap was a married man, and lived in Brookville, where Judge John Mills now resides. Rev. Gara Bishop was put in for one-third time, from May, 1835, to May, 1836. During the next four years only supplies. The first installed minister was Rev. David Polk, one-half time, from 1840 to 1845.

THE BEECHWOODS PRESBYTERIAN CHURCH.

Rev. W. H. Filson, in his history of this church, says, "The Presbyterian Church of Beechwoods was organized December 2, 1832, and is, therefore, nine years younger than the settlement. In 1826, Rev. Cyrus Riggs visited the settlement, and the same year a Sunday-school was started, and at its close a sermon was read. Andrew Smith was the first reader. Rev. Riggs frequently visited these people between 1826 and 1832. The following is a copy of the minutes as found on the sessional records:

"'On the first day of December, 1832, the Rev. Cyrus Riggs, accompanied by three elders of Bethel (Brookville) Church, arrived in Beechwoods, and having preached on Sabbath, the second, after sermon gave public notice that they would proceed at the house of Matthew Keys, on Monday, the third of December, to organize a church, and hold an election for elders in this congregation. At the time appointed the following persons, having presented certificates or given other satisfaction of their standing and right to membership in the church, did publicly agree and covenant to and with each other that they would walk together as a church of Christ, according to the order and discipline of the Presbyterian Church in the United States of America; and, further, that they would love, watch over each other, and not suffer sin on any brother, but would faithfully, and in the spirit of the gospel only, exhort and admonish one another, wherever they saw or knew of any one overtaken, or in danger of being overtaken, with evil, and that they would endeavor to provoke each other to love and good works. An election was then held for ruling elders, and Robert McIntosh, William McConnell, and Robert Morrison were duly elected.' Then following is a list of members: William McConnell, Robert McIntosh, William Cooper, Martha Cooper, David Dennison, Martha Dennison, Susan Keys. The first communion was held in the hewed log house of William Cooper, and was conducted by Rev. Robert McGarraugh, of Clarion County. The only person received into membership at that time was James Smith, the father of Elder William Smith.

"Rev. Riggs was born in Morris County, New Jersey, October 15,

PIONEER HISTORY OF JEFFERSON COUNTY, PENNA.

1774. While yet a boy his father emigrated to Washington County, Pennsylvania. Rev. Riggs studied theology under Dr. McMillen. He graduated from Jefferson College in 1803, and was licensed to preach October 7, 1805. He was married to Miss Mary Ross, of New Jersey, July 25, 1797. He died in Illinois in 1849.

"In 1835, Rev. Gara Bishop, M.D., pastor at Brookville, began to preach for them, and continued to do so for eleven years. During his ministry Joseph McCurdy, John Hunter, and John Millen were elected elders and thirty-three members added to the church. During all this time the congregation had worshipped in the log school-house on the farm of James Wait."

THE PERRY CHURCH IN PERRY TOWNSHIP.

"The Presbyterian Church of Perry stands tenth in order of age in Clarion Presbytery. The older churches were organized as follows: New Rehoboth and Licking, 1802; Concord, 1807; Rockland, 1822; Richland, 1823; Brookville, 1824; Beechwoods, 1832; Pisgah, at Corsica, 1833; Bethesda, at Rimersburg, 1836.

"This church of Perry, so called from the name of the township, was organized September 4, 1836, by Revs. John Reed and E. D. Barret, a committee appointed by the Presbytery of Blairsville. It was composed of the following twenty-four members: William Stunkard, Stephen Lewis, and Samuel Kelly, elders, and their wives, Ruth Stunkard, Ann Lewis, and Elizabeth Kelly, James and Sarah Chambers, John and Mary Frampton, Thomas and Eleanor Gourley, Elizabeth and Margaret Kelly, David and Elizabeth Lewis, William and Rebecca Marshall, Joseph and Jane Manners, Margaret McKinstry, and Elizabeth McKee. All of these were received by letter, and Robert Gaston and Sarah Wachob on examination.

"The original members brought their letters from churches in Indiana and Armstrong Counties. The Gourley family came from Sinking Valley, though John Gourley, a brother of Thomas, was elected an elder in this church in 1841 while residing at Covode, and George Gourley (the first) came here from Smicksburg.

"John Perry was precentor. Isaac Lewis, and after him David Harl, lined out the hymns. The precentor and outliner stood in an elevated box, and the pulpit was high over the heads of the people, as is still the case in some instances in modern times.

"PASTORS.

"This church has had six pastors. For four years after its organization its pulpit was filled by supplies, during which time thirty-two members were received by letter and nineteen on examination, or fifty-one in all.

PIONEER HISTORY OF JEFFERSON COUNTY, PENNA.

"The first pastor was Rev. John Carothers, who was ordained and installed June 4, 1840, by the Presbytery of Blairsville as pastor of the churches of Gilgal and Perry.

"During this pastorate additions to the eldership were received at three different times. May 8, 1841, Joseph Manners and John Gourley were ordained and installed, and James Chambers installed. May 13, 1842, John Sprankle; May 6, 1848, Wm. M. Johnston, Wm. Newcomb, and Isaac McHenry."

THE CUMBERLAND PRESBYTERIAN CHURCH.

This denomination has five congregations within the limits of Jefferson County. The first society was organized in a log school-house, in the borough of Punxsutawney, February 1, 1836, and is called the Jefferson Congregation. At the time of the organization there were seventeen communicants and two elders,—Alex. Jordan and Dr. John W. Jenks. Their first pastor was Rev. Charles R. Barclay.

Writing under date of March 5, 1895, J. B. Morris, Sr., of Punxsutawney, Pennsylvania, says,—

"This organization continued to worship in the same house until about the year 1834. In the fall of 1833 they began the erection of a brick church on what is now known as the Public Square.

"History tells us that the first organization of the Cumberland Presbyterian Church was in the old log school-house above mentioned. This is an error in history, for reasons which can be explained. The first organization of the Cumberland Presbyterian Church was formed in the home of Dr. John W. Jenks, now the City Hotel, in the room now used as a dining-hall, during the afternoon of February 1, 1836, with the following-named members, as recorded in the minutes of the meeting taken from the session-book: John Hutchinson, Isabella Hutchinson, Obed Morris, Mary Morris, Alexander Jordan, Flora Jordan, John White, Kesiah White, Richard Kendall, William Shields, Eleanor Shields, John W. Jenks, Mary D. Jenks, Elizabeth Barclay, Mary Barclay, Rev. David Barclay, and Rachel Williams. At the meeting above mentioned Obed Morris was called to preside, with Charles R. Barclay as clerk. Resolutions were adopted as follows: 'Dissolving our connection with the Presbytery of Blairsville, we seek to unite ourselves with the Pennsylvania Presbytery of the Cumberland Presbyterian Church; also that Charles R. Barclay is hereby appointed commissioner of this congregation to meet the Pennsylvania Presbytery of the Cumberland Presbyterian Church at its next meeting,' which convened at Carmichael's, Greene County, Pennsylvania, April 7, 1836. The moderator and clerk were to sign the resolutions, attested by the two elders, John W. Jenks and Alexander Jordan. Upon presentation of the resolutions to the Pennsylvania Presbytery by the commissioner, the request of the congregation was granted, and so recorded in the minutes of the Presbytery. At this meeting of Presbytery, Charles R. Barclay was examined as a candidate for the ministry, was ordained, and on his return preached his first sermon in April, 1836, in the old brick church, and was pastor of the congregation until the fall of 1841. During about six months of this pastorate, while the pastor was absent, his son-in-law, Samuel McCollum, occupied the pulpit. The pastor was also frequently assisted by such men as John Morgan, Milton Bird, and A. M. Bryan, from all of whom the writer remembers hearing noble gospel sermons.

"A regular Presbyterian Church had been formed in Punxsutawney in 1826, and in about 1833 they built a brick church in the Public Square, but the feeble organization was not permanent.

"A brief sketch of the old brick church erected on the Public Square might not be out of place. The bricks were prepared and delivered on the ground by John Hunt, familiarly known as 'Old Pappy' Hunt, in the summer of 1833, at two dollars and fifty cents per thousand, and late in the fall of the same year, perhaps October or November, they were laid. The carpenter-work was managed by John Drum, father of Mrs. Evans and Mrs. Winslow, and perhaps there are now none living who worked on the building, except Mr. Ephraim Bair and Mr. Daniel Rishel. The house was not finished for years afterwards, although used for religious and school purposes.

"Early ruling elders of the Punxsutawney congregation in the order of their ordination : John W. Jenks, Alexander Jordan, James E. Cooper, Thomas McKee, Edward Means, John McHenry, Sr., John Couch, Charles R. White, C. R. B. Morris, John Hutchinson."

UNITED PRESBYTERIAN CHURCH.

This church is one of the youngest of the Presbyterian bodies in America, but the history of its antecedents extends back more than a century. Its original antecedents were the Associate and Reformed Presbyterian bodies. The former body was composed of Presbyterians who seceded from the General Assembly of Scotland in 1733 and formed themselves into what was known as the "Associate Presbytery," or, as the masses knew them, "the Seceders." The first minister of that denomination to arrive in America was Rev. Alexander Gellatly, who settled at Octoraro, Pennsylvania, in 1753, where he labored for eight years. Many members of the body had preceded him to this country, settling along the seaboard, and some of them going as far south as the Carolinas. The church was largely increased by immigration from year to year, and the Presbytery of Pennsylvania was organized in 1758.

The first minister of the Reformed Presbyterian or Covenanter Church to arrive in America was Rev. John Cuthbertson, who came in 1752.

Soon after he was joined by two other ministers from the Reformed Presbyterian Church of Ireland.

A Presbytery was formed in 1774, and the church, as a body, obtained a foothold in the New World. The subject of union between these bodies was agitated before either was many years old, the leading ministers believing that such an alliance would add to the efficiency of both. During the Revolutionary War several meetings of ministers of the two denominations were held, at which the matter was thoroughly discussed. In 1782 three Presbyteries met in Philadelphia, and a union was consummated. The new organization took the name of the "Associate Reformed Synod of North America." A few of the ministers of both bodies refused to enter into the alliance, and the original bodies maintained a separate existence.

The Associate Reformed Church flourished. It spread rapidly to the westward, and was largely and steadily increased by immigration. In 1793 it had a firm hold on the territory now known as Western Pennsylvania. In that year the original Presbytery of Pennsylvania was divided into two,—the First and Second Associate Reformed Presbyteries of Pennsylvania. The Second, by order of the Synod, took the name of the Monongahela. It was composed of four ministers,—Revs. John Jamison, Henderson, Warwick, and Rankin, with their elders. This was the first Presbytery organized in connection with any of the Reformed Churches west of the Allegheny Mountains. Its boundary lines were the Allegheny Mountains on the east and the Pacific Ocean on the west.

The prosperity of the new body in Western Pennsylvania was remarkable. Soon it became necessary to form new Presbyteries in the territory originally covered by the Presbytery of the Monongahela, and the church commanded the attention of the entire country.

A union of the Associate with the Associate Reformed Churches of North America had been for a long time considered desirable by the leading ministers of both denominations, and it was accomplished in 1858. The consummation took place in Old City Hall, Pittsburg, and was the occasion of general rejoicing among the ministers and members of both bodies. It was in this city of ecclesiastical reunions that the United Presbyterian Church as a distinct Presbyterian body was born.

The Rev. John Jamison mentioned as one of the original four in the Second or Monongahela Presbytery was my maternal great-grandfather.* He was born at Ellerslie, Renfrewshire, Scotland. His mother was a Wallace, of Sir William's clan. He read theology with John Brown, of Haddington. He migrated to America, landing in Philadelphia, Pennsylvania, in November, 1782. He came from the Associated Burgher Synod of Scotland. He moved from Philadelphia, Pennsylvania, to

---

* Dr. McKnight.

Cumberland County, Pennsylvania, where he purchased a grist-mill and six hundred acres of land, including what is known as Big Springs. He was for some years pastor of a Shippensburg church. Mentally, he was able and educated; physically, he was six feet two inches high, possessing wonderful energy and powerful endurance. In the year 1790 he crossed the mountains with his wife and three children, locating near Blairsville, Pennsylvania, being the first minister to locate in Indiana County, Pennsylvania. In 1791 he was installed pastor of Brush Creek, Hannahstown, and Conemaugh Churches. In 1793 his time was given to New Alexandria and Conemaugh. Rev. Jamison travelled as a supply for his church from New York to Georgia, organizing churches. In May, 1795, he was charged with misconstruing the action of Synod in reference to the use of Watts's hymns, days of fasting, the use of tokens, etc., in connection with the Lord's Supper, being opposed to innovations. He was hyper-Calvinistic in his views. These charges were sustained in Philadelphia at the trial, and he was suspended. Nothing daunted, he wrote a book, defending his views and the old-time customs of his church. Also he continued to preach as an Independent till the day of his death. The country being new, he preached from settlement to settlement, in the cabins, barns, and in tents in the woods. For roads he had forest-paths, bridges there were none, and, in devotion to duty, he braved alike the beasts of the forests, the summer's heat, and the winter's cold.

Rev. John Jamison married Nancy Gibb in Scotland. He died in 1821, aged seventy-six years. He is buried in the United Presbyterian Church graveyard at Crete, Indiana County, Pennsylvania. Nancy, his wife, died in 1841, aged ninety-one years.

"The pioneer church organized in Jefferson County was the Jefferson, now United Presbyterian, Congregation.

"About the year 1820 a number of families of like faith settled in Jefferson County. These had most of them been settled in Huntingdon County, in this State, for a few years (some more, some less), but were originally from the same neighborhood in the north of Ireland. Drawn together by a common faith, as they had all been educated in the secession church, and stimulated by the laudable enterprise of securing homes for themselves and for their families, they struck for this country, then an almost unbroken wilderness, covered mostly with pine forests.

"The place selected for their settlement is north of the Red Bank and southwest of what is now Brookville, the county seat. At that time justice for them was administered in Indiana, some forty-five miles south. This arrangement for the administration of justice continued for some ten years after their location here.

"From the circumstance adverted to,—of these people being emigrants from Ireland,—the neighborhood was long known as the Irish Settlement.

PIONEER HISTORY OF JEFFERSON COUNTY, PENNA.

"The names of the founders were John Kelso and Isabella, his wife; John Kennedy and Ann, his wife; James Shields and Elizabeth, his wife; William Morrison and Nancy, his wife; Samuel McGill and Margaret, his wife; James McGiffin and Sarah, his wife; Matthew Dickey and Elizabeth, his wife; James Ferguson and Margaret Bratton, his wife; Robert Andrews and Jane Lucas, his wife; Alexander Smith and Annie Knapp, his wife; Christopher Barr and Sarah Lucas, his wife; also, by subsequent marriage, Elizabeth McGiffin, widow of Joseph Thompson; Clement McGarey and Mary, his wife; Hugh Millen and Esther, his wife; Joseph Millen and Polly Brown, his wife. These last three settled south of Red Bank, and constituted the nucleus of what became Beaver Run Congregation.

"Then there were Moses Knapp and Susanna, his wife; none of that name are now members of the United Presbyterian Church here.

"There were also a William Ferguson and family south of Red Bank; none of that family are now in the county or members of this church.

"ORGANIZATION.

"As nearly as I can ascertain, the first dispensation of the Lord's Supper in this congregation was in the autumn of 1828. The ministers officiating were Revs. Joseph Scroggs and Thomas Ferrier. James Fulton, an elder from Piney Congregation, which seems to have been organized some time previous, was present at this communion. He and James McGiffin were the officiating elders on that occasion. About that time John Kelso was elected and ordained to the eldership. These two, Kelso and McGiffin, were the only elders, as would appear, until after their first pastoral settlement.

"Matthew Dickey and his family moved into these bounds in 1832, and the first recorded minutes of Jefferson Session which has come into my hands is dated August 31, 1833, and is said to be in the handwriting of Mr. Dickey. The Session as then constituted consisted of Rev. James McCarrell, moderator; James McGiffin, John Kelso, Matthew Dickey, and John Shields.

"The next minute of Session is dated July 14, 1838. At this meeting the name of Solomon Chambers appears as a member of the court. It is probable he was elected at the same time with the others mentioned in the pastorate of Brother McCarrell.

"The next recorded minute is dated July 3, 1842, and is in a different handwriting, without any name subscribed. Changes had taken place, which are not noticed in these records. Rev. McCarrell had left (when or for what cause does not appear), and Rev. John McAuley appears, who at that time examined three applicants for admission,—viz., John Thompson, Joseph Millen, and John Millen. These three men are elders in the church,—one in Brookville, the others in Beaver Run. At the same time

PIONEER HISTORY OF JEFFERSON COUNTY, PENNA.

eight children were baptized,—William T. Love, Mary A. Ferguson, Elizabeth Campbell, Martha Chambers, Margaret Lucas, Chambers Millen, Joseph K. Gibson, and Hugh McGill.

"The next date in the minute-book, May 16, 1843, states that Rev. John Hindman, upon the occasion of the moderation of a call, moderated the Session, and baptized two children,—John Kelso Moore and Rebecca McGiffin. Rev. John McAuley disappears as unceremoniously as did his predecessor, and we are left to infer that the call moderated at this time by Brother Hindman was for Mr. John Tod, as the next minute, dated October 15, 1843, represents the same Rev. Tod administering an admonition as the organ of a constituted court.

"PASTORS AND PASTORAL CHANGES.

"No one with whom I have conversed in this vicinity is able to inform me who first ministered in preaching the gospel to these people of Jefferson. When last I met our aged father, Rev. David Blair, in 1872, he informed me that he, first of all his ministerial brethren, visited and preached to this people. Then, as a result, he supplied them to some extent, as he and they were long in the same Presbytery, and, in the absence of evidence to the contrary, I am disposed to admit his claim. One circumstance, however, renders it doubtful. When the first of these people came here, Rev. John Dickey was ministering as the settled pastor of Piney, Cherry Run, and Rich Hill; this last is where he spent most of his ministerial service and ended his life. But Piney is so near, and the relations were so intimate, it seems improbable that they should enjoy a regular dispensation of gospel ordinances and Jefferson not even have any supply.

"The names of Thomas McClintock, Daniel McLean, Joseph Scroggs, David Blair, Thomas Ferrier, and some others have been mentioned to me as having preached here at an early day, some before the congregation organized and some afterwards.

"The first communion was held in 1828, as has been before mentioned, and it would seem that measures were taken soon afterwards to call a pastor. It is not possible from any data within my reach to determine the date of the settlement of the first pastor. There is no doubt but that the man was Rev. James McCarrell and that his settlement was about 1830.

"In the minute-book of this Session there are only two recorded minutes under his pastorate,—the first, August 31, 1833, and the second, May 24, 1834.

"I remember having seen Mr. McCarrell once when a probationer, about the year 1829. This was shortly before his settlement here.

"Of Mr. McCarrell's capabilities as a minister of the Word, or of his success as a pastor, I can form no judgment. His place of residence was

Strattanville, so far out of the bounds of Jefferson Congregation that few of these people had opportunity of becoming acquainted with him. He was a man of blameless life, exemplary in his deportment, and attentive, as much as his domestic cares would permit, to all pastoral duties.

"The next date in the minute-book of Session reveals the presence of Rev. John Hindman and John McAuley. It seems to be the occasion of Mr. McAuley's first communion here after his settlement. Mrs. McAuley, whose maiden name was Reed, and raised in the vicinity of South Hanover, in Southern Indiana,—raised in the Presbyterian Church,—presented a certificate, and it is recorded that on this certificate and her 'acceding to the principles of our church' she was received. It would seem that the pastorate of Brother McAuley in Jefferson lasted about four years. He must have left in 1842, as the next settlement was in the following year.

"Rev. John Tod was installed pastor of Jefferson, Beaver Run, and Piney on the 15th of August, 1843. His time was divided,—one-half to Jefferson, one-third to Beaver, and one-sixth to Piney. This congregation was organized in the Associate Church, under the care of the Presbytery of Allegheny.

"The United Presbyterian Congregation of Brookville was organized in the Associate Reformed Church, and continued in that connection till the union of the Associate and Associate Reformed Church was consummated in the city of Pittsburg, May, 1858.

"Jefferson is perhaps the most recently settled of the counties in Western Pennsylvania. The first of those who settled here and felt an interest in our cause came about the year 1830, some earlier, some later, but no movement was made to have preaching here till 1836.

"Isaac Temple, who was one of the first elders, went to Presbytery, and solicited preaching for the place where he lived. Of course he was encouraged, hence a subscription was taken for service to be rendered during the year 1837.

"The first name on the list is that of David McCormick. I think he was one of the elders of the congregation, but whether he was ordained here or in the place of his former residence we have at present no means of knowing. Then follows Thomas McCormick, Job McCreight, Job and W. Rogers, Levi G. Clover, Benjamin McCreight, William Clark, C. A. Alexander, A. Vasbinder, Daniel Coder, Joseph Kerr, James M. Craig, Isaac Temple, Andrew Moor, John McClelland, William McCullough, David Dennison, William McDonald, Alexander Hutchinson, Andrew McCormick, Charles Boner, Andrew Hunter.

"This comes into my hands as the roll of honor. The first men who gave their names, and with their names their money, built up and sustained the Secession or Reformed Presbyterian cause in this county. Some of these were not then, nor ever became, members of the church which they chose to patronize. Some of them had perhaps little sympathy with

PIONEER HISTORY OF JEFFERSON COUNTY, PENNA.

Christianity at all; but I find them here signing their names and giving their support to a cause to which I have given the labor of my life. I honor them. Most of the names on that paper represent men of worth and weight of character, known in the neighborhood in which they reside as such, and over all Jefferson County as it then was. It will be seen that the parties subscribing to this paper were widely scattered,—from Brookville to the vicinity of Rockdale and Brockwayville. The amount of this first subscription is fifty-four dollars. The compensation agreed upon among the psalm-singing churches was six dollars per Sabbath. This same paper upon which is the subscription contains also the disbursement of the money. In this connection we find, first of all, the name of Joseph Osburn. With this brother I had no acquaintance. He belonged to the Associate Reformed branch of the United Presbyterian Church, and died several years before the union, while yet a young man.

"The next name is that of Jonathan Fulton, of whom the same thing may be said. He died young. He is represented as gifted in a very high degree, both as a reasoner and a pulpit orator. Many of you well remember him. His ministrations here did much to give respectability to our cause. Joseph H. Pressly also ministered here at an early day and with much acceptance. This brother, who has now gone to his rest, represented to me, when in the act of moving to this place, that it was the place of all others he ever visited, the one where he wished to live. But a Providence shapes our ends differently from our anticipations, and even wishes and efforts to the contrary. This brother performed all his life-work in the city of Erie, and there he ended his life.

"I find also among those who rendered acceptable service the names of M. H. Wilson,—this brother labored in Jacksonville, Indiana County, Pennsylvania,—A. G. Wallace, Samuel Brown, William Jamison, and others. These services covered a space of about twenty years, and were the means of keeping the people together and keeping up their sympathy with the cause. The pioneer church edifice was on Church Street, and was built about 1845.

"BEECHWOODS CONGREGATION.

"David Dennison was a member of the Beechwoods Congregation, and died some time during the winter of 1875.

"As far as I have the means of judging, it appears that Rev. Joseph Osburn was the first Associate Reformed minister who visited this section of country, I suppose in 1837. After him the name of N. C. Weed occurs as dispensing the Lord's Supper for the first time in this wilderness in 1842.

"Shortly after this Rev. Alexander McCahen rendered service here as a stated supply for the space of four years.

"The number of communing members at the first sacrament was

thirteen. This communion was held in the barn of Elder Isaac Temple. David McCormick was also an elder officiating at the first communion, but whether either of these fathers, long since departed, was ordained here or had been in the exercise of that office previous to their coming here does not appear from any record. Warsaw was the residence of the brethren, and the congregation up to this time went by that name. The place of worship was about eight miles to the northeast of Brookville." *—*Miss Scott's History of Jefferson County*.

This church has always been a consistent opponent of human slavery. The Scotch-Irish element, of which the church is largely composed, is usually stalwart on the side of all reforms and all right.

This denomination holds a few distinctive principles, by which it is distinguished from the larger Presbyterian bodies. It holds to the exclusive use of an inspired psalmody; in theory it is opposed to the affiliation of its members with secret orders, and it practises a restricted communion.

PIONEER METHODISM—CIRCUIT RIDERS—CHURCH AND MEMBERS IN JEFFERSON COUNTY.

On the 7th of March, 1736, John Wesley preached the pioneer Methodist sermon in America, in Savannah, Georgia. Other early Methodist service in the United States was conducted in New York City by a Mr. Embury, urged and assisted by Barbara Heck. Barbara Heck emigrated from Ireland to New York in 1765. From her zeal, activity, and pious work as a Christian she is called the mother of American Methodism. Methodism was introduced into Pennsylvania in 1767 by Captain Thomas Webb, a soldier in the British army. Webb was a preacher, and is called the apostle of American Methodism. In 1767 he visited Philadelphia, preached, and formed a class of seven persons. The first Annual Conferences of the Methodist Church held in America were in Philadelphia,— viz.: in the years 1773, 1774, and 1775. After this year all Conferences were held in Baltimore, Maryland, until the organization of the church in the New World.

The pioneer Methodist preaching in Pennsylvania was in Philadelphia, in a sail-loft near Second and Dock Streets. St. John's Church was established in 1769. Methodism was to be found in Philadelphia in 1772, York in 1781, Wilkesbarre in 1778, Williamsport in 1791, and in Pittsburg in 1801.

The pioneer Sunday-school in the world was opened at Glencastle, in England, in 1781, by Robert Raikes. The idea was suggested to him by a young woman, who afterwards became Sophia Bradburn. This lady assisted him in the opening of the first school. The pioneer Sunday-schools were started in the New World in 1790 by an official ordinance

---

* Dr. Vincent.

of the Methodist Conference establishing Sunday-schools to instruct poor children, white and black : " Let persons be appointed by the bishops, elders, deacons, or preachers to teach (gratis) all that will attend and have a capacity to learn, from six o'clock in the morning till ten, and from two o'clock in the afternoon until six, when it does not interfere with public worship."

The Methodist Church was really the first temperance organization in America. The general rules of the society prohibited the use of liquor as a beverage. Other modern temperance organizations are supposed to have their beginning about 1811. But little was done after this period outside of the churches for about twenty-five years.

Rev. William Watters was the pioneer American itinerant Methodist preacher. He was born in Baltimore County, Maryland, October 16, 1751.

Until 1824 Western Pennsylvania, or "all west of the Susquehanna River, except the extreme northern part, was in the Baltimore Conference." In 1824 the Pittsburg Conference was organized, and our wilderness came under its jurisdiction. In 1833 the first Methodist paper under the authority of the church was started. It was in Pittsburg, Pennsylvania, and the paper is now called *The Pittsburg Christian Advocate*. In 1836 the Erie Conference was formed, and Jefferson County was placed within its jurisdiction.

Methodism in Jefferson County has been, first, in the Baltimore Conference ; second, in the Pittsburg Conference ; and third, is now in the Erie Conference.

The Methodists were slow in making an inroad in Jefferson County. The ground had been occupied by other denominations, and a hostile and bitter prejudice existed against the new "sect."

The pioneer Methodist minister in the county was the Rev. Elijah Coleman. He was a local.

The pioneer Methodist Church in the county was organized by him in Punxsutawney in 1821, ten members in all. This circuit was a part of the Baltimore Conference then, and contained forty-two appointments. It took the preacher six weeks to travel over it. In 1830 Punxsutawney was in the Pittsburg Conference. In 1836 this church was taken into the Erie Conference.

The pioneer church edifice in the county was erected there in 1833. Services previous to that time were held in Jacob Hoover's grist-mill.

The pioneer circuit in the county was the Mahoning district, which was created in 1812 by the Baltimore Conference, but no appointments were made in our county until 1822.

The pioneer circuit riders in this district were as follows,—viz. : Revs. Ezra Booth, William Westlake, 1822 ; Revs. Dennis Goddard, Elijah H. Field, 1823 ; Revs. Ira Eddy, B. O. Plimpton, 1824 ; Rev. I. H. Tackett, 1825 ; Rev. James Babcock, 1826–27 ; Rev. Nathaniel Callender, 1828 ;

Revs. John Johnson, John C. Ayers, 1829; Revs. Fleck and Day, 1830; Rev. Summerville, 1832; Rev. Bump, 1833; Rev. Kinnear, 1834; Rev. Butt, 1835; Rev. S. Heard, 1837; Rev. J. P. Benn, 1838—associate, Rev. R. Peck; Revs. Shinebaugh and Peck, 1839; Revs. Mershon and George Reeser, 1840; Revs. John Graham and George Reeser, 1841; Revs. H. W. Monks and I. Scofield, 1842; Revs. D. H. Jack and H. W. Monks, 1843.

Summerville, or Troy, was an early field of Methodism. Darius and Nathan Carrier were zealous Methodists, and frequently opened their homes for service as early as 1825–26. The first church was organized there in 1830 by Rev. Ayers.

Missionary Methodist preachers travelled through this wilderness in those times, preaching anywhere and everywhere they could. This itinerancy makes it hard to systemize the church history.

The Brookville Church seems to have been the head-quarters for the northern part of the county, and the first class was organized in 1828 in an old log barn at the head of Litch's dam, on the east side of the North Fork. The members of this class were five,—Cyrus Butler and wife, David Butler and wife, and John Dixon, Jr. A Sunday-school was started, with Cyrus Butler as superintendent. Services were held in private houses, the old jail, and in the court-house, as the congregation was too weak to build a house even as late as 1845.

The pioneer church was organized in Brookville under Rev. Johnson in 1829. In 1829 and 1830 all services were held in the house of David Butler, on the east side of the North Fork Creek, at the upper end of Litch's dam.

The pioneer and early members (1829) were David Butler and wife, Cyrus Butler and wife, John Long and wife, William McKee, William Steel, and John Dixon, Jr. The last is the only one now living.

The pioneer circuit riders in the north side of the county were: Rev. John Johnson, 1829; Rev. Jonathan Ayers, 1830; Rev. Job Watson, 1831; Revs. Abner Jackson and A. C. Barnes, 1832; Rev. Abner Jackson, 1833, who had twenty-nine preaching-places and a circuit of two hundred and fifty miles (it was the Brookville and Ridgeway mission); Rev. A. Kellar, 1834; Revs. John Sava and Charles C. Best, 1835; Revs. J. A. Hallock and J. R. Locke, 1836; Rev. Stephen Heard, 1837; Rev. L. Whipple, 1838; Rev. H. S. Hitchcock, 1839; Rev. D. Prichard, 1840. In 1841, supplies and Revs. G. F. Reeser and John Graham; in 1842, Revs. Isaac Scofield and William Monks; in 1843, Revs. William Monks and D. H. Jack; in 1844, Revs. S. Churchill and J. K. Coxson; in 1845, Revs. R. M. Bear and Thomas Benn.

These ministers always travelled on horseback. The horse was usually "bobbed," and you could see that he had a most excellent skeleton. These itinerants all wore leggings, and carried on the saddle a large pair of saddle-bags, which contained a clean shirt, a Bible, and a hymn-book. The sermon was on a cylinder in the head of the preacher, and was ready to be graphophoned at any point or time.

The pioneer presiding elders were: Rev. Wilder P. Mack, 1828–31; Rev. Joseph S. Barris, 1832; Rev. Zerah P. Caston, 1833–34; Rev. Joshua Monroe, 1835; Rev. Joseph S. Barris, 1836; Rev. William Carroll, 1837–40; Rev. John Bain, 1841–42; Rev. John Robinson, 1843.

Methodist Episcopal Church, Brookville, Pennsylvania. Erected in 1886.

Pioneer Presiding Elder, Brookville Mission District: "Rev. William Carroll, presiding elder on the Brookville Mission District, was a stout, energetic man, of medium preaching talents, and was selected for this field of labor because it required bone and muscle, as well as faith and zeal, to accomplish its duties. That entire region of country was new, wild, rough, and mountainous, with many rapid bridgeless streams to cross. The settlements were far from each other, and the people poor but generous. Never since the days of Young and Finley did any presiding elder encounter such difficulties. Calvinism in its primitive characteristics had been planted there, and its advocates contested the ground with great tenacity and zeal. But to this field of toil and sacrifice the new presiding elder and his little band of youthful heroes hastened away and sowed the good seed with tears, and reaped a rich harvest of souls. That sterile soil has since become very fruitful."—*Gregg's History of Methodism.*

Ridgeway Mission was created in 1834. Pioneer circuit riders: Rev. G. D. Kinnear; 1835, Rev. Alured Plimpton.

As a rule, these pioneer Methodists were good singers, and when and wherever they held a service in this wilderness they usually made our hills and valleys vocal with the glorious and beautiful hymns of John and Charles Wesley.

The pioneer female to pray in public or in the general prayer-meetings in Brookville was "Mother Fogle," Rev. Christopher Fogle's first wife.

The pay of the pioneer Methodist ministers and preachers, and for their wives and children, was as follows:

"*1800.*—' 1. The annual salary of the travelling preachers shall be eighty dollars and their travelling expenses.

" ' 2. The annual allowance of the wives of travelling preachers shall be eighty dollars.

" ' 3. Each child of a travelling preacher shall be allowed sixteen dollars annually to the age of seven years, and twenty-four dollars annually from the age of seven to fourteen years; nevertheless, this rule shall not apply to the children of preachers whose families are provided for by other means in their circuits respectively.

" ' 4. The salary of the superannuated, worn-out, and supernumerary preachers shall be eighty dollars annually.

" ' 5. The annual allowance of the wives of superannuated, worn-out, and supernumerary preachers shall be eighty dollars.

" ' 6. The annual allowance of the widows of travelling, superannuated, worn-out, and supernumerary preachers shall be eighty dollars.

" ' 7. The orphans of travelling, superannuated, worn-out, and supernumerary preachers shall be allowed by the Annual Conference, if possible, by such means as they can devise, sixteen dollars annually.'

"*1804.*—The following inserted in clause 3, before 'nevertheless': 'and those preachers whose wives are dead shall be allowed for each child annually a sum sufficient to pay the board of such child or children during the above term of years.'

PIONEER HISTORY OF JEFFERSON COUNTY, PENNA.

"The following added at the close of the section:

"'8. Local preachers shall be allowed a salary in certain cases as mentioned.'

"*1816.*—'The allowance of all preachers and their wives raised to one hundred dollars.'

"*1824.*—Under clause 2 (allowance to wives) it is added, 'But this provision shall not apply to the wives of those preachers who were single when they were received for trial, and marry under four years, until the expiration of said four years.'

"*1828.*—The seventh clause (relating to orphans) was altered so as to read as follows:

"'7. The orphans of travelling, supernumerary, superannuated, and worn-out preachers shall be allowed by the Annual Conferences the same sums respectively which are allowed to the children of living preachers. And on the death of a preacher, leaving a child or children without so much of worldly goods as should be necessary to his or her or their support, the Annual Conference of which he was a member shall raise, in such manner as may be deemed best, a yearly sum for the subsistence and education of such orphan child or children, until he, she, or they shall have arrived at fourteen years of age, the amount of which yearly sum shall be fixed by the committee of the Conference at each session in advance.'

"*1832.*—The following new clause was inserted:

"'8. The more effectually to raise the amount necessary to meet the above-mentioned allowance, let there be made weekly class collections in all our societies where it is practicable; and also for the support of missions and missionary schools under our care.'

"*1836.*—The regulation respecting those who marry 'under four years' was struck out, and bishops mentioned by name as standing on the same footing as other travelling preachers. Clauses 1, 2, 4, and 5 thrown into two, as follows:

"'1. The annual allowance of the married travelling, supernumerary, and superannuated preachers and the bishops shall be two hundred dollars and their travelling expenses.

"'2. The annual allowance of the unmarried travelling, supernumerary, and superannuated preachers and the bishops shall be one hundred dollars and their travelling expenses.'

"The pioneer members were prohibited from wearing 'needless ornaments, such as rings, earrings, lace, necklace, and ruffles.'"—*Strickland's History of Discipline.*

PIONEER AND EARLY CAMP-MEETINGS.

The pioneer camp-meeting in the United States was held, between 1800 and 1801, at Cane Ridge, in Kentucky. It was under the auspices of several different denominational ministers. The meeting was kept up day and night. It was supposed that there were in attendance during the meetings from twelve to twenty thousand people. Stands were erected through the woods, from which one, two, three, and four preachers would be addressing the thousands at the same time. It was at this place and from this time our camp-meetings took their rise.

Evans, the Shaker historian, who is strong in the gift of faith, tells us that "the subjects of this work were greatly exercised in dreams, visions, revelations, and the spirit of the prophecy. In these gifts of the Spirit they saw and testified that the great day of God was at hand, that Christ was about to set up his kingdom on earth, and that this very work would terminate in the full manifestation of the latter day of glory."

From another authority, endowed perhaps with less fervor but with more of common sense, we get a description of these "exercises," which has a familiar ring that seems to bring it very near home. "The people remained on the ground day and night, listening to the most exciting sermons, and engaging in a mode of worship which consisted in alternate crying, laughing, singing, and shouting, accompanied with gesticulations of a most extraordinary character. Often there would be an unusual outcry, some bursting forth into loud ejaculations of thanksgiving, others exhorting their careless friends to 'turn to the Lord,' some struck with terror and hastening to escape, others trembling, weeping, and swooning away, till every appearance of life was gone and the extremities of the body assumed the coldness of a corpse. At one meeting not less than a thousand persons fell to the ground, apparently without sense or motion. It was common to see them shed tears plentifully about an hour before they fell. They were then seized with a general tremor, and sometimes they uttered one or two piercing shrieks in the moment of falling. This latter phenomenon was common to both sexes, to all ages, and to all sorts of characters.

"After a time these crazy performances in the sacred name of religion became so much a matter of course that they were regularly classified in categories as the rolls, the jerks, the barks, etc. The rolling exercise was effected by doubling themselves up, then rolling from one side to the other like a hoop, or in extending the body horizontally and rolling over and over in the filth like so many swine. The jerk consisted in violent spasms and twistings of every part of the body. Sometimes the head was twisted round so that the face was turned to the back, and the countenance so much distorted that not one of its features was to be recognized. When attacked by the jerks they sometimes hopped like frogs, and the face and limbs underwent the most hideous contortions. The bark consisted in throwing themselves on all-fours, growling, showing their teeth, and barking like dogs. Sometimes a number of people crouching down in front of the minister continued to bark as long as he preached. These last were supposed to be more especially endowed with the gifts of prophecy, dreams, rhapsodies, and visions of angels."

Exactly when the pioneer camp-meeting was held in Jefferson County is unknown to me. Darius Carrier advertised one in the *Jeffersonian* as early as 1836, to be held near Summerville. The first one I remember was near Brookville, on the North Fork, on land now owned by F. Swartzlander. Others were held near Roseville, and in Perry township and kindred points. The rowdy element attended these services, and there was usually a good deal of disturbance from whiskey and fights, which, of course, greatly annoyed the good people. The first "Dutch camp-meeting" was held in what is now Ringgold township. In fact, these German meetings were only abandoned a few years ago. I reproduce a " Dutch camp-meeting hymn" :

"CAMP-MEETING HYMN.

" Satan and I we can't agree,
Halleo, halleolujah!
For I hate him and he hates me,
Halleo, halleolujah!

"I do believe without a doubt,
Halleo, halleolujah!
The Christian has a right to shout,
Halleo, halleolujah!

" We'll whip the devil round the stump,
Halleo, halleolujah!
And hit him a kick at every jump,
Halleo, halleolujah!"

The mode of conducting our wood meetings was patterned after the original in Kentucky. The manner of worship and conversions were the same, and while a great deal of harsh criticism has been made against this mode of religious worship, there is one thing that must be admitted, —many bad, wicked persons were changed into good religious people. Pitch-pine fagots were burned at night to light the grounds.

BAPTIST CHURCH.

The pioneer Baptist preaching in Pennsylvania was at Cold Spring, Bucks County, in 1684, by Rev. Thomas Dungan. This church died in 1702.

In 1818, Rev. Jonathan Nichols settled on Brandy Camp, in the Little Toby Valley. He was a regularly ordained Baptist minister and an educated physician. His labors extended all over this county. He was the pioneer Baptist. His was "the voice of one crying in the wilderness, Prepare ye the way of the Lord, make his paths straight." Rev. Jonathan Nichols migrated to this region from Connecticut. He died in 1846, aged seventy-one years. His wife Hannah died in 1859, aged eighty-two years. As a physician his labors were extended, and his ministry was well received by the scattered people of all beliefs. For a while he adhered to the close communion, but owing to the different beliefs adhered to by his hearers, he after a few years invited all Christian people who attended his services to the "Lord's table." His daughter told me his heart would not let him do otherwise. One who knew him well wrote of him: "He was a generous, kind-hearted gentleman, genial and urbane in his manners, with a helping hand ready to assist the needy, and had kind words to comfort the sorrowing." Winter's snow never deterred him from pastoral work or visits to the sick. After Nichols came Rev. Samuel Miles, of Clearfield County. The first regular Baptist church was organized in what is now Washington township, in June, 1834, with thirteen members, in Henry Keys' barn, by Rev. Brown. Henry Keys and James McConnell were elected deacons. The members of this pioneer church were James McConnell, Henry Keys and wife, Miss Betty Keys, Mrs. Eliza Haney, Mary Ann McConnell, Mrs. Catharine Keys, Margaret McConnell, Mrs. Nancy McGhee, Mrs. McClelland, Miss Hall, and Robert McIntosh and wife. The pioneer church in the county was erected on the Keys farm in 1841–42. It was a frame. James McConnell was the carpenter. The immersions took place in Mill Creek, now Allen's Mills. Before organizing their own church the men and women of the McIntosh, Keys, and McConnell families would start early on Sunday morning and walk to Zion Church, in Clarion County, thirty miles, and return the same day.

BROOKVILLE BAPTIST CHURCH MISSION.

The pioneer minister to do mission labor was Rev. Samuel Miles. He appeared on this field in 1833.

The pioneer Baptist communicant to locate in Brookville was James Craig, in 1834.

The pioneer convert in the borough was Miss Jane Craig. She was "immersed" near the covered bridge by Rev. Samuel Miles in 1838.

The second minister to perform mission work was Rev. Thomas E. Thomas, called Father Thomas. He came here from 1839 to 1843. The third minister to pioneer as a missionary in Brookville was the Rev. Thomas Wilson. He preached in Brookville in 1844. He pioneered in the county as early as 1840.

The early Baptists in this mission were Thomas Humphrey and wife, John Bullers and wife, Michael Troy and wife, William Humphrey and wife, Mrs. John Baum, William Russell and wife, Samuel C. Espy and wife, and others.

The pioneer and early "immersion" points were at the covered bridge at the junction of Sandy Lick and North Fork Creeks,—at or in the tail-race and in the sluice,—the mill-dam of R. P. Barr.

PIONEER HISTORY OF JEFFERSON COUNTY, PENNA.

The Punxsutawney Church was organized October 30, 1840, by Rev. Thomas E. Thomas and Benoni Allen, with the following members by letter,—viz.:

Brookville Baptist Church.   Erected in 1883.

Isaac London, Hiram London, Lemuel Carey, Sr., Hannah Carey, John R. Reed, Margaret Reed, James Armstrong, Mary Armstrong,

Esther McMillan, Eliza Cochrane, Sarah Gilhausen, and Elizabeth McCracken. Revs. Thomas and Allen continued to preach, each one-fourth of his time, until April 1, 1841. William Campbell was elected clerk. The pioneer immersions were Stephen London and James McConaughey,—viz., on November 1, 1840. On the 2d the following were immersed,—viz.: William Davis, William Campbell, Ephraim Bair, Jacob Bair, Samuel Gilhausen, John Hunt, and Prudence Stewart. On the 3d day of this month the following were immersed: James H. Bell, Ann Bell, William Torance, Lemuel Carey, Jr., Mary Davis, Jane Hunt, Elizabeth McDermott, and Jane Major. The Rev. Thomas continued with this church until October, 1841, when he was succeeded by the Rev. Thomas Wilson.

THE WASHINGTON TOWNSHIP BAPTIST CHURCH.
THE BEECHWOODS CHURCH.

"The society was organized in 1835, under the direction of Rev. Stoughton. The first members were Henry Keys and wife, Eliza Keys, Joseph Keys, James McConnell and two sisters, Mrs. Osborne, and several others whose names are forgotten. The first elders were Henry Keys and James McConnell. The first stated pastor was Rev. Samuel Miles, of Milesburg, Centre County, Pennsylvania. The first Baptist in the county was Eliza Keys, a sister of Henry and daughter of Joseph Keys. She was a woman of unusual energy, and whose qualities of mind and heart were eminently designed for the duties of a missionary, as she was in *deed* if not in name. From 1824 to the organization of the church in the county they went to Clarion County, and worshipped in the old 'Zion' Church and in the houses of Messrs. Lewis, Frampton, and Williams, and latterly in a little frame church near Corbett's Mills. The distance travelled by the members of the congregation was from twenty-eight to forty miles, and many of the good people traversed the country on foot, and nothing but sickness prevented them from a regular attendance on divine services. Rev. Thomas E. Thomas, whose services are mentioned in brief in a sketch of the Punxsutawney Baptist Church, was one of the leading preachers in the Clarion region, and by his efforts built up the cause in Western Pennsylvania. In 1825 the only Baptist churches in Western Pennsylvania were Pittsburg, one; Huntington, one; Milesburg, one; and Freeport, one. In 1826 a Baptist church was erected near Corbett's Mills, Clarion County, and thither the people of that faith were accustomed to congregate till the erection of a little church in Beechwoods, the date being 1837. This in time was succeeded by the present edifice."

THE CATHOLIC CHURCH.

The pioneer Catholic service in Pennsylvania was in Philadelphia in 1708. The pioneer priest was either Polycarp Wicksted or James Haddock. The pioneer church erected was St. Joseph's, in Philadelphia, in 1730.

The pioneer Catholic to locate in the county was perhaps John

Catholic Church, Brookville, Pennsylvania.   Erected in 1875.

Dougherty, of Brookville. He came in 1831. The pioneer priest to visit Brookville was the Rev. John O'Neill, of Freeport, Pennsylvania. He visited here in 1832, and performed the pioneer baptism,—viz., of

PIONEER HISTORY OF JEFFERSON COUNTY, PENNA.

Miss Kate, the daughter of John Dougherty. There was no resident priest here until 1847. The pioneer Catholics in the county were attended by priests from Armstrong and Westmoreland Counties. Pioneer services were held in the houses of John Dougherty, John Gallagher, Jacob Hoffman, and others.

THE MORMON CHURCH IN JEFFERSON COUNTY.

About 1815 there lived in Wayne County, New York, a young man by the name of Joseph Smith. In the twenties he proclaimed himself a prophet from God. In 1827 he published to the world that an angel had placed in his hands some golden plates, with a pair of spectacles, too, through which he alone could decipher the writing on the plates. His revelation from God consisted of a book styled the Book of Mormon. The book is a silly, childish kind of a romance. I possessed a copy for many years and tried at different times to read it through, but never had the grace or gift of continuance. This book pretends to give a history of Nephi, a Hebrew, who, six hundred years before the advent of Christ, was miraculously carried from Palestine in vessels to this American continent. When Nephi landed on this continent there were no inhabitants, and the American Indians are declared by the book to be the descendants of Nephi. The Mormons taught that there were many Gods in in heaven, and that each God had many wives and children,—viz.: Smith would be a god; his superior would be Jesus; above Jesus would be Adam, above Adam would be Jehovah, and above all would be Elohim. In 1830, Smith had about thirty believers, and organized his church at Manchester, New York. In 1831, under the lead of an angel, this band moved to Kirtland, Ohio. In 1838 they migrated to Missouri. From here they moved to Illinois, and built the city of Nauvoo. In the early forties Smith received a "revelation" establishing polygamy in the church. This caused internal dissensions, Smith was arrested, placed in jail, and finally shot by a mob. Brigham Young was then elected prophet, and the church migrated in a body beyond the Rocky Mountains to what is now the State of Utah.

PIONEER MORMON MISSIONARY.

"Mormonism! On Saturday evening last our borough was visited by a youth of apparently not more than twenty-two years of age, a graduate of the disciple Jo Smith, S. Rigdon, and others of the Mormon creed, fresh from the 'Holy Land.' He remained here over Sabbath, during which time he kept himself principally secluded from company till evening, when he appeared in the court-house, and attempted to instruct the citizens of this place in the 'sublime mysteries' of Mormonism (?), but his 'new-fangled doctrine' didn't take.

PIONEER HISTORY OF JEFFERSON COUNTY, PENNA.

"In the prosecution of his mission he labored to prove that events of transcendent importance were about being ushered in; that the millennium was dawning on our astonished visions; that a revelation had been made on plates of gold to the said Jo Smith by the hands of an angel, and last, though not least, that a revelation of the hidden mysteries were important, etc.

"He taxed his most deceptive genius—a science in which he appears to be well versed—to rivet the attention of the congregation, by telling them that he had 'strange things yet to tell them,' and finally brought his exhibition to a close. We have not learned that he discipled any here, but believe that the decision and intelligence of the people of Jefferson County is a sure and certain guarantee against such delusions ever gaining their credence. He was permitted to depart in peace."—*Brookville Republican*, Thursday, October 12, 1837.

Our brother, the editor, was not exactly correct in his estimate of the *intelligence* of the people of Jefferson County, for quite a little congregation of Mormons was formed in the extreme eastern end of Snyder township, this county, and the western portion of Fox township, Clearfield County. The principal members were some of the Cobbs, Heaths, Bundys, Hoyts, and others. Religious meetings were held in each other's houses for some time. A number of these members migrated to the "Holy Land."

LUTHERAN CHURCH.

The pioneer Lutheran congregation in the United States was at New Hanover, Montgomery County, Pennsylvania, with Justus Faulkner, pastor, in 1703.

The pioneer Lutheran minister to visit this county was the Rev. George Young, of Armstrong County, Pennsylvania. Rev. Young organized the pioneer church in the county in 1835, and erected a log building for that purpose, to which was attached a cemetery. The pioneer services were held in the barn of Abraham Hoch, one mile south of Sprankle's Mill, and now Oliver township. Communion was commemorated in this barn. The pioneer log church building was erected in 1838, about half a mile from Mr. Hoch's, on the farm now occupied by Boaz D. Blose. This log church was used for ten years, when it was abandoned for school purposes, and a large frame house of worship was then erected on the ridge two miles from Sprankle's Mill. This congregation was and is still known as St. John's, General Council.

The second Lutheran church organized was in 1838, and a log building erected. This church was also called St. John's, and belonged to the General Synod branch of the denomination. Joel Spyker and Peter Thrush took an active part in the organization. This church was on what is now Andrew Ohl's farm, and was about three and one-half miles south of Brookville. The pioneer members at this communion were Thomas Holt, Peter Thrush and wife, Samuel Johns and wife, Mattie Chesly, Charles Merriman and wife, Armenia Grove, Hannah Himes, Mary Johnson, Jacob Wolfgang and wife, Mary Spyker, and Joseph Kaylor.

The pioneer preaching in Brookville was by the Rev. Young. He preached in the homes of members and in the second story of the old stone jail. Rev. John Rengan, of Indiana, Pennsylvania, preached in the jail in 1844. No organization was effected. Rev. John Nuner came after Rengan, but in what year and for how long is unknown.

The pioneer Lutherans in Brookville were John and Catherine Eason, Daniel Coder and wife, Hannah McKinley, Mary A. Yoemans, Jacob Burkett and wife, Jacob Steck and wife, John Boucher and wife, Maria Von Schroeder. Pioneer elder, Daniel Coder. Pioneer deacon, John Boucher.

Lutheran services were also held at Paradise, Grubes, Reynoldsville, Emerickville, Punxsutawney, and Ringgold, but no dates of service or records of organization can be found. I acknowledge valuable aid in this compilation to Mrs. Virginia Blood.

CHAPTER XV.

WHITE SLAVERY—ORIGIN—NATURE IN ROME, GREECE, AND EUROPE—AFRICAN SLAVERY IN PENNSYLVANIA—GEORGE BRYAN—PIONEER COLORED SETTLER IN JEFFERSON COUNTY—CENSUS, ETC.—DAYS OF BONDAGE IN THIS COUNTY.

WHITE slavery is older than history. Its origin is supposed to be from kidnapping, piracy, and in captives taken in war. Christians enslaved all barbarians and barbarians enslaved Christians. Early history tells us that Rome and Greece were great markets for all kinds of slaves, slave-traders, slave-owners, etc. The white slaves of Europe were mostly obtained in Russia and Poland in times of peace. All fathers could sell children. The poor could be sold for debt. The poor could sell themselves. But slavery did not exist in the poor and ignorant alone. The most learned in science, art, and mechanism were bought and sold at prices ranging in our money from one hundred to three hundred dollars. Once sold, whether kidnapped or not, there was no redress, except as to the will of the master. At one time in the history of Rome white slaves sold for sixty-two and a half cents apiece in our money. The state, the church, and individuals all owned slaves. Every wicked device that might and power could practise was used to enslave men and women without regard to nationality or color. And when enslaved, no matter how well educated, the slaves possessed no right in law and were not deemed persons in law, and had no right in and to their children. Slavery as it existed among the Jews was a milder form than that which

Branding slaves.

existed in any other nation. The ancients regarded black slaves as luxuries, because there was but little traffic in them until about the year 1441, and it is at that date that the modern African slave-trade was commenced by the Portuguese. The pioneer English African slave-trader was Sir John Hawkins. Great companies were formed in London to carry on African traffic, of which Charles II. and James II. were members. It was money and the large profits in slavery, whether white or black, that gave it such a hold on church and state. The English were the most cruel African slave-traders. Genuine white slavery never existed in what is now the United States. In the year A.D. 1620 the pioneer African slaves were landed at Hampton Roads in Virginia, and nineteen slaves were sold. In 1790 there were six hundred and ninety-seven thousand six hundred and eighty-one African slaves in the Middle States.

Slavery was introduced in Pennsylvania in 1681, and was in full force until the act quoted below for its gradual abolition was enacted in 1780, by which, as you will see, adult slaves were liberated on July 4, 1827, and the children born before that date were to become free as they reached their majority. This made the last slave in the State become a free person about 1860.

In 1790 Pennsylvania had slaves					3737
In 1800	"	"	"		1706
In 1810	"	"	"		795
In 1820	"	"	"		211
In 1830	"	"	"		403
In 1840	"	"	"		64
In 1860	"	"	"	(in Lancaster County)	1

On December 4, 1833, sixty persons met in Philadelphia, Pennsylvania, and organized the American Anti-Slavery Society.

NEGRO SLAVERY.

"He found his fellow guilty—of a skin not colored like his own; for such a cause dooms him as his lawful prey."

Negro slaves were held in each of the thirteen original States.

In March, 1780, Pennsylvania enacted her gradual abolition law. Massachusetts, by constitutional enactment in 1780, abolished slavery. Rhode Island and Connecticut were made free States in 1784, New Jersey in 1804, New York in 1817, and New Hampshire about 1808 or 1810. The remaining States of the thirteen—viz., Maryland, Delaware, Virginia, North and South Carolina, and Georgia—each retained their human chattels until the close of the Civil War. In one hundred years, from 1676 until 1776, it is estimated that three million people were imported and sold as slaves in the United States.

As late as 1860 there was still one slave in Pennsylvania; his name was Lawson Lee Taylor, and he belonged to James Clark, of Donegal township, Lancaster County.

PIONEER HISTORY OF JEFFERSON COUNTY, PENNA.

The first man who died in the Revolution was a colored man, and Peter Salem, a negro, decided the battle of Bunker Hill; clinging to the Stars and Stripes, he cried, "I'll bring back the colors or answer to God the reason why!" His example fired the hearts of the soldiers to greater valor, and the great battle was won by our men.

"It was on the soil of Pennsylvania in 1682 that the English penalty of death on over two hundred crimes was negatived by statute law, and the penalty of death retained on only one crime,—viz., wilful murder. It was in the province of Pennsylvania that the law of primogeniture was abolished. It was on the soil of Pennsylvania that the first mint to coin money in the United States was established. It was on the soil of Pennsylvania in 1829, and between Honesdale and Carbondale, that the pioneer railroad train, propelled by a locomotive, was run in the New World. It was on the soil of Pennsylvania that the first Continental Congress met. It was on the soil of Pennsylvania that the great *Magna Charta* of our liberties was written, signed, sealed, and delivered to the world. It was on the soil of Pennsylvania that the fathers declared 'that all men are born free and equal, and are alike entitled to life, liberty, and the pursuit of happiness.' It was on the soil of Pennsylvania that the grand old Republican party was organized, and the declarations of our fathers reaffirmed and proclaimed anew to the world. It was on the soil of Pennsylvania that Congress created our national emblem, the Stars and Stripes; and it was upon the soil of Pennsylvania that fair women made that flag in accordance with the resolution of Congress. It was upon the soil of Pennsylvania that our flag was first unfurled to the breeze, and from that day to this that grand old flag has never been disgraced nor defeated. It was upon the Delaware River of Pennsylvania that the first steamer was launched. It was in Philadelphia that the first national bank opened its vaults to commerce. It was upon the soil of Pennsylvania that Colonel Drake first drilled into the bowels of the earth and obtained the oil that now makes the 'bright light' of every fireside 'from Greenland's icy mountains to India's coral strand.' It was on the soil of Pennsylvania that the first Christian Bible Society in the New World was organized. It was on the soil of Pennsylvania that the first school for the education and maintenance of soldiers' orphans was erected. It was on the soil of Pennsylvania that the first medical college for the New World was established.

"And now, Mr. President, I say to you that it was permitted to Pennsylvania intelligence, to Pennsylvania charity, to Pennsylvania people, to erect on Pennsylvania soil, with Pennsylvania money, the first insane institution, aided and encouraged by a State, in the history of the world."

The above is an extract from a speech made by me when Senator in the Senate of Pennsylvania in 1881. I reproduce it here only to reassert it and crown it with the fact that Pennsylvania was the first of the united colonies to acknowledge before God and the nations of the earth, by legal enactment, the Fatherhood of God and the brotherhood of man. Pennsylvania was the first State or nation in the New World to enact a law for the abolition of human slavery. This act of justice was passed, too, when the struggle for independence was still undetermined. The British were pressing us on the east, and the savages on the west were torturing and killing the patriot fathers and mothers of the Revolution.

George Bryan originated, prepared, offered, and carried this measure successfully through the Legislature. I quote from his remarks on this measure: "Honored will that State be in the annals of mankind which shall first abolish this violation of the rights of mankind; and the memories of those will be held in grateful and everlasting remembrance who shall pass the law to restore and establish the rights of human nature in Pennsylvania." George Bryan did this. He was born in Dublin, Ireland, in 1732, died in Philadelphia, Pennsylvania, in 1791. To exhibit the advanced sentiment of George Bryan, I republish his touching and beautiful preamble to his law, and a section or two of the law which will explain its work.

"AN ACT FOR THE GRADUAL ABOLITION OF SLAVERY.

"When we contemplate our abhorrence of that condition to which the arms and tyranny of Great Britain were exerted to reduce us, when we look back on the variety of dangers to which we have been exposed, and how miraculously our wants in many instances have been supplied, and our deliverances wrought, when even hope and human fortitude have become unequal to the conflict, we are unavoidably led to a serious and grateful sense of the manifold blessings which we have undeservedly received from the hand of that Being from whom every good and perfect gift cometh. Impressed with these ideas, we conceive that it is our duty, and we rejoice that it is in our power, to extend a portion of that freedom to others which hath been extended to us, and release from that state of thraldom to which we ourselves were tyrannically doomed, and from which we have now every prospect of being delivered. It is not for us to inquire why, in the creation of mankind, the inhabitants of the several parts of the earth were distinguished by a difference in feature or complexion. It is sufficient to know that all are the work of an Almighty hand. We find, in the distribution of the human species, that the most fertile as well as the most barren parts of the earth are inhabited by men of complexions different from ours, and from each other; from whence we may reasonably, as well as religiously, infer that He who placed them in their various situations hath extended equally His care and protection to all, and that it becometh not us to counteract His mercies. We esteem it a peculiar blessing granted to us that we are enabled this day to add one more step to universal civilization, by removing, as much as possible, the sorrows of those who have lived in undeserved bondage, and from which, by the assumed authority of the kings of Great Britain, no effectual legal relief could be obtained. Weaned, by a long course of experience, from those narrow prejudices and partialities we had imbibed, we find our hearts enlarged with kindness and benevolence towards men of all conditions and nations; and we conceive ourselves at this particular period extraordinarily called upon, by the blessings which we have received, to manifest the sincerity of our profession and to give a substantial proof of our gratitude.

"II. And whereas the condition of those persons, who have heretofore been denominated Negro and Mulatto slaves, has been attended with circumstances which not only deprived them of the common blessings that they were by nature entitled to, but has cast them into the deepest afflictions, by an unnatural separation and sale of husband and wife from each other and from their children, an injury the greatness of which can only be conceived by supposing that we were in the same unhappy case. In justice, therefore, to persons so unhappily circumstanced, and who, having no prospect before them whereon they may rest their sorrows and their hopes, have no reasonable inducement to render their service to society, which they otherwise might, and also in grateful commemoration of our own happy deliverance from that state of unconditional submission to which we were doomed by the tyranny of Britain.

"III. *Be it enacted, and it is hereby enacted,* That all persons, as well Negroes and Mulattoes as others, who shall be born within this State from and after the passage of this act, shall not be deemed and considered as servants for life, or slaves; and that all servitude for life, or slavery of children, in consequence of the slavery of their mothers, in the case of all children born within this State from and after the passing of this act as aforesaid, shall be, and hereby is, utterly taken away, extinguished, and forever abolished.

"IV. *Provided always, and be it further enacted,* That every Negro and Mulatto child born within this State after the passing of this act as aforesaid (who would, in case this act had not been made, have been born a servant for years, or life, or a slave) shall be deemed to be, and shall be, by virtue of this act, the servant of such person, or his or her assigns, who would in such case have been entitled to the service of such child, until such child shall attain unto the age of twenty-eight years, in the manner and on the conditions whereon servants bound by indenture for four years are or may be retained and holden; and shall be liable to like correction and punishment, and entitled to like relief, in case he or she be evilly treated by his or her master or mistress, and to like freedom, dues, and other privileges, as servants bound by indenture for four years are or may be entitled, unless the person to whom the service of such child shall belong, shall abandon his or her claim to the same; in which case the overseers of the poor of the city, township, or district, respectively, where such child shall be so abandoned, shall by indenture bind out every child so abandoned as an apprentice, for a time not exceeding the age herein before limited for the service of such children." Passed March 1, 1780.

PIONEER COLORED SETTLER.

The pioneer colored settler in this wilderness was Fudge Van Camp. He was jet-black, fine-featured, and thin-lipped. Fudge Van Camp was born a slave, but purchased his freedom after he grew to manhood. He came to Port Barnett from Easton, Northumberland County, Pennsylvania, in the winter of 1801, and travelled this distance on foot. The last thirty-three miles were travelled without food, in a heavy snow-storm and in a two-foot fall of snow. Van Camp was a large and powerful man, but gave out and had to work his way for the last mile or two on his hands and knees to Port Barnett. He arrived there at midnight exhausted and almost frozen. He came over what was then called the Military or Milesburg and Le Bœuf State road. Being pleased with the country, he returned to Easton only to migrate here with his four children, bringing his effects on two horses, and settled on what is now the John Clark farm. He brought apple-seeds with him and planted them on this farm, this being the first effort to raise fruit in this wilderness. Some of the trees are still living. Fudge Van Camp married a white woman. She died in Easton. His family consisted of two sons and two daughters,—viz., Richard and Enos, Susan and Sarah. Susan married Charles Sutherland, and Sarah married William Douglass. Douglass was a hunter. Richard married Ruth Stiles, a white woman, and left the county.

Fudge Van Camp was the only colored person living in the county as late as 1810. He was a fiddler and a great fighter, and was the orchestra for all the early frolics.

In 1824 I find James Parks is assessed in Pine Creek township (but lived then where Christ's brewery is now) with one negro man, "Sam," valuation fifty dollars. "Sam" was a miller. In 1826 he is assessed at one hundred dollars. Transferred to Rose township in 1829 and assessed at one hundred dollars. In 1830 Parks's log-mill is assessed at fifty dollars and "Sam" at one hundred dollars. Now "Sam" disappears. According to the census of 1830, the county contained twenty-two colored people,—one of these a slave. This slave was James Parks's man Sam. Master and slave lived in Brookville. I find one negro slave in Brookville in 1833. William Jack is assessed among other property with "one boy of color," valuation forty dollars. Jack lived at that time in the Darr residence, north of the court-house. This slave boy fled to Canada and secured his liberty. In 1836, Jesse Smith, a Presbyterian minister living one mile north of where Corsica now is, on the Olean road, and then in Rose township, is assessed with one mulatto, valuation fifty dollars. It appears from this that slavery existed in Jefferson County from 1824 until 1836,—twelve years.

Thank God this cruel slavery, which existed once in Jefferson County, is forever wiped out in these United States! There is now no master's call, no driver's lash, no auction-block on which to sell, and no blood-hounds to hunt men and women fugitives not from justice, but fugitives for justice. Thank God for John Brown, and may "his soul go marching on!"

Van Camp's real name was Enos Fudge. His owner's name was Van Camp. Fudge was hired by his master to the patriot army of the Revolution to drive team, and by playing the violin to the soldiers and in other ways he accumulated five hundred dollars, which he presented to his master, who in consideration of this gave him his freedom. Two white men, Stephen Roll and August Shultz, came with Van Camp into this wilderness. Van Camp died about the year 1835, and is buried in the old graveyard in Brookville.

THE "UNDERGROUND RAILROAD" IN JEFFERSON COUNTY.

> "My ear is pained,
> My soul is sick with every day's report
> Of wrong and outrage with which this earth is filled."

The origin of the system to aid runaway slaves in these United States was in Columbia, Lancaster County, Pennsylvania. In 1787, Samuel Wright laid out that town, and he set apart the northeastern portion for colored people, and to many of whom he presented lots. Under these circumstances this section was settled rapidly by colored people. Hundreds of manumitted slaves from Maryland and Virginia migrated there and built homes. This soon created a little city of colored people, and in due time formed a good hiding-place for escaped slaves. The term "underground railroad" originated there, and in this way: At Columbia the runaway slave would be so thoroughly and completely lost to the pursuer, that the slave hunter, in perfect astonishment, would frequently exclaim, "There must be an underground railroad somewhere." Of course, there was no railroad. There was only at this place an organized system by white abolitionists to assist, clothe, feed, and conduct fugitive slaves to Canada. This system consisted in changing the clothing, secreting and hiding the fugitive in daytime, and then carrying or directing him how to travel in the night-time to the next abolition station, where he would be cared for. These stations existed from the Maryland line clear through to Canada. In those days the North was as a whole for slavery, and to be an abolitionist was to be reviled and persecuted, even by churches of nearly all denominations. Abolition meetings were broken up by mobs, the speakers rotten-egged and murdered; indeed, but few preachers would read from their pulpit a notice for an anti-slavery meeting. Space will not permit me to depict the degraded state

Charles Brown handcuffed and shackled in Brookville jail, 1834.

"The shackles never again shall bind this arm, which now is free."

"My world is dead,
A new world rises, and new manners reign."

of public morals at that time, or the low ebb of true Christianity in that day, excepting, of course, that exhibited by a small handful of abolitionists in the land. I can only say, that to clothe, feed, secrete, and to convey in the darkness of night, poor, wretched, hunted human beings fleeing for liberty, to suffer social ostracism, and to run the risk of the heavy penalties prescribed by unholy laws for so doing, required the highest type of Christian men and women,—men and women of sagacity, coolness, firmness, courage, and benevolence; rocks of adamant, to whom the down-trodden could flock for relief and refuge. A great aid to the ignorant fugitive was that every slave knew the "north star," and, further, that if he followed it he would eventually reach the land of freedom. This knowledge enabled thousands to reach Canada. All slave-holders despised this "star."

To William Wright, of Columbia, Pennsylvania, is due the credit of putting into practice the first "underground railroad" for the freedom of slaves. There was no State organization effected until about 1838,

PIONEER HISTORY OF JEFFERSON COUNTY, PENNA.

when, in Philadelphia, Robert Purvis was made president and Jacob C. White secretary. Then the system grew, and before the war of the Rebellion our whole State became interlaced with roads. We had a route, too, in this wilderness. It was not as prominent as the routes in the more populated portions of the State. I am sorry that I am unable to write a complete history of the pure, lofty, generous men and women in our county who worked this road. They were Quakers and Methodists, and the only ones that I can now recall were Elijah Heath and wife, Arad Pearsall and wife, James Steadman and wife, and the Rev. Christopher Fogle and his first and second wife, of Brookville (Rev. Fogle was an agent and conductor in Troy), Isaac P. Carmalt and his wife, of near Clayville, James A. Minish, of Punxsutawney, and William Coon and his wife, in Clarington, now Forest County. Others, no doubt, were connected, but the history is lost. Our route started from Baltimore, Maryland, and extended, *via* Bellefonte, Grampian Hills, Punxsutawney, Brookville, Clarington, and Warren, to Lake Erie and Canada. A branch road came from Indiana, Pennsylvania, to Clayville. At Indiana, Pennsylvania, Dr. Mitchell, James Moorhead, James Hamilton, William Banks, and a few others were agents in the cause.

In an estimate based on forty years, there escaped annually from the slave States fifteen hundred slaves; but still the slave population doubled in these States every twenty years. Fugitives travelled north usually in twos, but in two or three instances they went over this wilderness route in a small army, as an early paper of Brookville says, editorially, "Twenty-five fugitive slaves passed through Brookville Monday morning on their way to Canada." Again: "On Monday morning, October 14, 1850, forty armed fugitive slaves passed through Brookville to Canada."

Smedley's "Underground Railroad" says, "Heroes have had their deeds of bravery upon battle-fields emblazoned in history, and their countrymen have delighted to do them honor; statesmen have been renowned, and their names have been engraved upon the enduring tablets of fame; philanthropists have had their acts of benevolence and charity proclaimed to an appreciating world; ministers, pure and sincere in their gospel labors, have had their teachings collected in religious books that generations might profit by the reading; but these moral heroes, out of the fulness of their hearts, with neither expectations of reward nor hope of remembrance, have, within the privacy of their own homes, at an hour when the outside world was locked in slumber, clothed, fed, and in the darkness of night, whether in calm or in storms, assisted poor degraded, hunted human beings on their way to liberty.

* * * * * * * * *

"When, too, newspapers refused to publish antislavery speeches, but poured forth such denunciations as, 'The people will hereafter consider abolitionists as out of the pale of legal and conventional protection which society affords its honest and well-meaning members,' that 'they will be treated as robbers and pirates, and as the enemies of mankind ;' when Northern merchants extensively engaged in Southern trade told abolitionists that, as their pecuniary interests were largely connected with those of the South, they could not afford to allow them to succeed in their efforts to overthrow slavery, that millions upon millions of dollars were due them from Southern merchants, the payment of which would be jeopardized, and that they would put them down by fair means if they could, by foul means if they must, we must concede that it required the manhood of a man and the unflinching fortitude of a woman, upheld by a full and firm Christian faith, to be an abolitionist in those days, and especially an ' underground railroad' agent."

SLAVE TRAFFIC AND TRADE.

"And he that stealeth a man, and selleth him, or if he be found in his hand, he shall surely be put to death."—*Exod.* xxi. 16.

In the United States Constitutional Convention of 1787 the Carolinas, Georgia, and New York wanted the slave-trade continued and more slave *property*. To the credit of all the other colonies, they wanted the foreign slave traffic stopped. After much wrangling and discussion a compromise was effected by which no enactment was to restrain the slave-trade before the year 1808. By this compromise the slave-trade was to continue twenty-one years. On March 2, 1807, Congress passed an act to prohibit the importation of any more slaves after the close of that year. But the profits from slave trading were enormous, and the foreign traffic continued in spite of all law. It was found that if one ship out of every three was captured, the profits still would be large. Out of every ten negroes stolen in Africa, seven died before they reached this *market*. A negro cost in Africa twenty dollars in gunpowder, old clothes, etc., and readily brought five hundred dollars in the United States. Everything connected with the trade was brutal. The daily ration of a captive on a vessel was a pint of water and a half-pint of rice. Sick negroes were simply thrown overboard. This traffic "for revolting, heartless atrocity would make the devil wonder." The profits were so large that no slave-trader was ever convicted in this country until 1861, when Nathaniel Gordon, of the slaver "Erie," was convicted in New York City and executed. It was estimated that from thirty to sixty thousand slaves were carried to the Southern States every year by New York vessels alone. A wicked practice was carried on between the slave and free States in this way. A complete description of a free colored man or woman would be sent from a free State to parties living in a slave State. This description would then be published in hand-bills, etc., as that of a runaway slave.

These bills would be widely circulated. In a short time the person so described would be arrested, kidnapped in the night, overpowered, manacled, carried away, and sold. He had no legal right, no friends, and was only a "nigger." Free colored men on the borders of Pennsylvania have left home to visit a neighbor and been kidnapped in broad daylight, and never heard of after. A negro man or woman would sell for from one to two thousand dollars, and this was more profitable than horse-stealing or highway robbery, and attended with but little danger. A report in this or any other neighborhood that kidnappers were around struck terror to the heart of every free colored man or woman. Negroes in Brookville have left their shanty homes to sleep in the stables of friends when such rumors were afloat.

Before giving any official records in this history, I must pause to present the fact that one Butler B. Amos, an all-around thief, then in this county, was, in 1834, in our jail, sentenced to "hard labor" under the law.

Early convicts were sentenced to hard labor in the county jail, and had to make split-brooms from hickory-wood, as will be seen from this agreement between the commissioners and jailer:

"Received, Brookville, Sept. 29th, 1834, of the commissioners of Jefferson county, thirty-seven broomsticks, which I am to have made into brooms by Butler B. Amos, lately convicted in the Court of Quarter Sessions of said county for larceny and sentenced to hard labour in the gaol of said county for six months, and I am also to dispose of said brooms when made as the said commissioners may direct, and account to them for the proceeds thereof as the law directs. Received also one shaving horse, one hand saw, one drawing knife and one jack knife to enable him to work the above brooms, which I am to return to the said commissioners at the expiration of said term of servitude of the said Butler B. Amos, with reasonable wear and tear.

"ARAD PEARSALL, *Gaoler.*"

Amos had been arrested for theft, as per the following advertisement in the *Jeffersonian* of the annexed date:

"Commonwealth *vs.* Butler B. Amos. Defendant committed to September term, 1834. Charge of Larceny. And whereas the act of General Assembly requires that notice be given, I therefore hereby give notice that the following is an inventory of articles found in the possession of the said Butler B. Amos and supposed to have been stolen, viz.: 1 canal shovel, 1 grubbing hoe, 2 hand saws, 2 bake kettles, 1 curry comb, 2 wolf traps, 1 iron bound bucket, 1 frow, 3 log chains, 1 piece of log chain, 2 drawing chains, 1 piece of drawing chain, 1 set of breast chains, 1 hand ax, &c. The above mentioned articles are now in possession of the subscriber, where those interested can see and examine for themselves.

"ALX. M'KNIGHT, *J. P.*

"BROOKVILLE, August 25th, 1834."

A few years after this sentence was complied with Amos left Brookville on a flat-boat for Kentucky, where he was dirked in a row and killed. Although Amos was a thief, he had a warm "heart" in him, as will be seen farther on.

The earliest official record I can find of our underground road is in the *Jeffersonian* of September 15, 1834, which contained these advertisements,—viz.:

"$150 REWARD.

"ESCAPED from the jail of Jefferson county, Pennsylvania, last night—a black man, called *Charles Brown*, a slave to the infant heirs of *Richard Baylor*, deceased, late of Jefferson county Virginia; he is about 5 feet 7 inches high, and 24 years of age, of a dark complexion—pleasant look, with his upper teeth a little open before. I was removing him to the State of Virginia, by virtue of a certificate from Judges' *Shippen, Irvin & M'Kee*, of the Court of Common Pleas of the county of Venango, as my warrant, to return him to the place from which he fled. I will give a reward of $150 to any person who will deliver him to the Jailor of Jefferson county Virginia, and if that sum should appear to be inadequate to the expense and trouble, it shall be suitably increased.

"JOHN YATES,
" *Guardian of the said heirs.*

"Sept. 15, 1834."

"$150 REWARD!!

"ESCAPED from the Jail of Jefferson county; Pennsylvania last night, a black man, nam'd WILLIAM PARKER alias ROBINSON a slave, belonging to the undersigned: aged about 26 years, and about 5 feet 6 inches high; broad shoulders; full round face, rather a grave countenance, and thick lips, particularly his upper lip, stammers a little, and rather slow in speech.—I was removing him to the State of Virginia, by virtue of a cirtificate, from Judges *Shippen and Irvin*, of the Court of Common Pleas, of Venango county; as my warrant to return him to the place, from which he fled. I will give a reward of $150, to any person, who will deliver him to the Jailor of Jefferson county Virginia; and if that sum should appear to be inadequate to the expense and trouble, it shall be suitably increased.

"STEPHEN DELGARN.

"September 15, 1834."

Arad Pearsall was then our jailer, and he was a Methodist and an abolitionist.

PIONEER HISTORY OF JEFFERSON COUNTY, PENNA.

Our pioneer jail, as I remember it, was constructed from stone spawls, with wooden doors and big iron locks. For safety, the prisoners were usually shackled and handcuffed, and they were fed on " bread and water." When recaptured, escaped slaves were lodged in county jails and shackled for safety. These slaves had been so lodged, while their captors slept on beds " as soft as downy pillows are." Charles Brown and William Parker reached Canada. Heath and Steadman furnished augers and files to the thief Amos, who filed the shackles loose from these human beings, and with the augers he bored the locks off the doors. Pearsall, Heath, and Steadman did the rest. Some person or persons in Brookville were mean enough to inform, by letter or otherwise, Delgarn and Yates that Judge Heath, Arad Pearsall, and James Steadman had liberated and run off their slaves, whereupon legal steps were taken by these men to recover damages for the loss of property in the United States Court at Pittsburg, the minutes of which I here reproduce :

"CLERK'S OFFICE, UNITED STATES CIRCUIT COURT,
"WESTERN DISTRICT OF PENNSYLVANIA,
"PITTSBURG, October 9, 1897.

"W. J. MCKNIGHT, Brookville, Pa.

"DEAR SIR,—Judge Buffington has referred your letter to me, and I enclose a pencil memoranda of the proceedings in the two suits against Heath and others.

"This is about as full as we can give it, except the testimony in so far as it appears in depositions filed. Most of the evidence was oral, the names of the witnesses appearing in subpœnas on file.

"Yours truly,
"H. D. GAMBLE,
"*Clerk United States Circuit Court.*"

"At No. 4 of October Term, 1835, in the District Court of the United States for the Western District of Pennsylvania, suit in trespass, brought July 10, 1835, by Thomas G. Baylor and Anna Maria Baylor, minors, by John Yates, Esq., their guardian, all citizens of Virginia, against Elijah Heath, James M. Steadman, and Arad Pearsall.

"At No. 5, October Term, 1835, suit in trespass by Stephen Delgarn, a citizen of Virginia, against same defendants as in No. 4, brought at same time. Burke and Metcalf, Esqs., were attorneys for the plaintiffs in each case, and Alexander M. Foster for the defendants.

"Suit, as No. 4, was tried on May 3, 4, and 5, 1836, and on May 6, 1836, verdict rendered for plaintiff for six hundred dollars.

"Suit No. 5 was tried May 6 and 7, 1836, and verdict rendered May 7, 1836, for eight hundred and forty dollars. November 24, 1836, judgments and costs collected upon execution and paid to plaintiffs' attorneys.

"In suit No. 4 the allegations as set forth in the declarations filed are: That plaintiffs, citizens of Virginia, were the owners of 'a certain negro man' named Charles Brown, otherwise 'Charles,' of great value,—to wit, of the value of one thousand dollars,—to which said negro they were lawfully entitled as a servant or slave, and to his labor and service as such, according to the laws of the State of Virginia. That on or about the 1st day of August, 1834, the said negro man absconded, and went away from and out of the custody of said plaintiffs, and afterwards went and came into the Western District of Pennsylvania; and the said plaintiffs, by their guardian, did, on or about the 13th day of September, 1834, pursue the said servant or slave into the said Western District of Pennsylvania, and finding the said servant or slave in said district, and there and then claimed him as a fugitive from labor, and caused him to be arrested and brought before the judges of the Court of Common Pleas of Venango County, in said Western District of Pennsylvania; and it appearing upon sufficient evidence before them produced in due and legal form, that the said negro man did, under the laws of Virginia, owe service and labor unto said plaintiffs, and that the said negro man had fled from the service of his said master in Virginia into Venango County, Pennsylvania, aforesaid; and the said plaintiffs, by their guardian, did, on the said 18th day of September, 1834, obtain from the said judges of the Court of Common Pleas of Venango County aforesaid a warrant for the removal of the said negro man to Virginia aforesaid; and the said guardian was returning and taking with him, under and by virtue of the said warrant, said servant or slave to the said plaintiffs' residence in Virginia; and while so returning—to wit, on or about the day and year last aforesaid—the said guardian at Jefferson County, in the Western District of Pennsylvania aforesaid, did, with the assent and by the permission of the person or persons having charge of the public jail or prison in and for said County of Jefferson, place the said servant or slave in said jail or prison for safe-keeping, until he, the said guardian, could reasonably proceed on his journey with the said aforesaid servant or slave to Virginia aforesaid. Yet the said defendants, well knowing the said negro man to be the servant or slave of the plaintiffs and to be their lawful property, and that they, the said plaintiffs, by their guardian aforesaid, were entitled to have the possession and custody of him, and to have and enjoy the profit and advantage of his labor and services; but contriving and unlawfully intending to injure the said plaintiffs, and to deprive them of all benefits, profits, and advantages of and which would accrue to these said plaintiffs from said services, then and there, on or about the day and year aforesaid at Jefferson County aforesaid, did secretly and in the night-time unlawfully, wrongfully, and *unjustly* release, take, and assist in releasing and taking, or procure to be released or taken, the said negro man, then being as aforesaid the servant or slave of the said plaintiffs, from and out of the said prison or jail, where said servant or slave was placed for safe-keeping by said guardian as aforesaid; whereby said servant or slave escaped, ran off, and was and is wholly lost to said plaintiffs, and said plaintiffs deprived of all the profits, benefits, and advantages which might and otherwise would have arisen and accrued to said plaintiffs from the said services of said servant or slave.

"The allegations and declarations in No. 5 were materially the same as in No. 4."

Isaac P. Carmalt was co-operating with Heath and others at this time. Heath was a Methodist, and so was Pearsall. Heath moved away about 1846, and Pearsall died in Brookville about 1857.

Isaac P. Carmalt was a Quaker, a relative of William Penn, and was born in Philadelphia, Pennsylvania, in 1794. He learned the carpenter trade. In 1818 he left his native city with two horses and a dearborn wagon, and in three weeks he crossed the Allegheny Mountains and located in Indiana County, Pennsylvania. In 1821 he moved to Punxsutawney. In 1822 he bought a farm near Clayville. In 1823 he married Miss Hannah A. Gaskill, a Quakeress, in Philadelphia, Pennsylvania. But little can be given of his great work in this direction owing to his death. His daughter, Mrs. Lowry, writes me as follows:

"The last slave that came to our house was after the insurrection at Harper's Ferry. He claimed to have been in the insurrection. He came with a colored man who lived near Grampian Hills, whose name was George Hartshorn. This one was a mulatto, and claimed to be the son of Judge Crittenden, who, I think, held some important office at Washington,—Senator or Congressman. The slave was very nervous when he came, and asked for a raw onion, which, he said, was good to quiet the nerves. He was also quite suspicious of Joe Walkup, who was working at our house at the time. He called him out and gave him his revolver, and told him he would rather he would blow his brains out than to inform on him, for if he was taken he would certainly be hung. He left during the night for Brookville. Most of the fugitives came through Centre and Clearfield Counties. One of the underground railroad stations was in Centre County, near Bellefonte, kept by a friend by the name of Iddings, who sent them to the next station, which was Grampian Hills, from thence to our house, and from here to Brookville. I remember well one Sabbath when I was coming home from church; Lib Wilson was coming part way with me. We noticed a colored man ahead of us. I paid but little attention, but she said, 'I know that is a slave.' I knew Wilson's pro slavery sentiments, and replied very carelessly that 'there was a colored family living near Grampian Hills. I supposed he was going to our house, as we had been there a short time before, wanting to trade horses for oxen to haul timber with.' But as soon as she left me I quickened my pace and tried to overtake him. I was afraid he might go through Clayville, where I knew there was a perfect nest of pro-slavery men, who had made their threats of what they would do if father assisted any more slaves to gain their freedom. Among them were the Gillespies, who boasted of being overseers or slave-drivers while they were in the South. He kept ahead of me and stopped at James Minish's, and I thought it was all over with him, as they and the Gillespies were connected, and most likely were of the same sentiment in regard to slavery. But imagine my surprise when I came up, Mr. Minish handed me a slip of paper with the name of 'Carmalt' on it, and remarked that I was one of the Carmalt girls. (I suppose it was the name of a station.) But he hurried the fugitive on, and I directed him to go up over the hill through the woods. I then hurried home for father to go and meet him. But when I got home, father was not there, so I put on my sun-bonnet and went but a short distance, when I met him. There were several persons in the house, so I slipped him in the back way. He seemed to be in great misery and could not eat anything, but asked for something to bathe his foot in. Then he gave a short account of his escape from slavery three years previous. After escaping he stopped with a man near Harrisburg, at what he called Yellow Breeches Creek, and worked for him, during which time he married and had a little home of his own. One day when ploughing in the field he discovered his old master from whom he had escaped and two other men coming towards him. He dropped everything and ran to his benefactor's house, and told him whom he had seen. His benefactor then pulled off his coat and boots and directed him to put them on, as he was in his bare feet, having left his own coat and boots in the field. Being closely pursued, he ran to the barn, and the men followed him. He was then compelled to jump from a high window, and, striking a sharp stone, he received a severe cut in one heel, not having had time to put on the boots given him by his benefactor. When he came to our house he was suffering terribly, not having had an opportunity to get the wound dressed. His benefactor had charged him not to tarry on the road. But father, seeing the seriousness of his wound, persuaded him to go to bed until midnight. But the poor fellow could not sleep, but moaned with pain. We gave him his breakfast, and then father had him get on a horse, while he walked, and it was just breaking day when they arrived at Brookville. A gentleman by the name of Christopher Fogle was waiting to receive them. We heard afterwards that the poor slave succeeded in reaching Canada, but returned for his wife, and was captured and taken back to slavery.

"There is just one more incident that I will mention, which occurred at an earlier date. One morning I went to the door and saw four large colored men hurrying to the barn. I told father, and he went out and brought them in. Our breakfast was just ready. We had them sit down and eat as fast as they could, taking the precaution to lock the door, for several persons came along while they were eating. Father noticed that one of the slaves looked dull and stupid, and inquired if he was sick. One of the others replied that he was only a little donsey. When they were through eating, father hurried them to the woods and hid them somewhere near the old school-house then on the farm. When father went to take their dinner to them, the one said he was still a little donsey, and then showed father his back. His shirt was sticking to his back. He had been terribly whipped, and they had rubbed salt in the gashes. They then gave a short history of their escape. They said they had a good master and mistress, but their master had died and the estate was sold. The master's two sons then sold them, and they were to be taken to the rice-swamps to toil their lives away. They were determined to make their escape, but the one who had been so terribly whipped was captured and taken back. Their old mistress planned and assisted him to make his escape by dressing him as a coachman, and with her assistance found his way to Washington, where he met his companions and friends. From Washington they were guided by the north star, travelling only by night.

"I think but few fugitives came by the way of Indiana, though I remember of hearing father tell of one or two that he brought with him when he first came from Indiana who had escaped by way of Philadelphia. I think most came through Baltimore, where a Quaker friend by the name of Needles assisted the runaways through this branch of the underground railroad. From Baltimore they came through the Quaker settlements in Centre and Clearfield Counties. Father was the only one who conveyed them from our house near Clayville to Brookville. This he generally did by going himself or by sending some reliable person with them. Father concealed a man from Baltimore, a German, who used to smuggle slaves through. He had a furniture wagon, in which he concealed them, but was discovered and put in jail at York, Pennsylvania, but he escaped to Iddings, near Bellefonte, thence to Grampian Hills, and from there to father's, where he worked five years. He then left, and moved to Ohio. He became afraid to stay, for there were a few who had an inkling of his history and knew there was a reward of three thousand dollars for his arrest. One day in going to his work he met the sheriff from Baltimore, who knew him well, and told him to keep out of his sight, that there was a big reward offered for him. When he was first arrested he had a colored girl concealed in a bureau which he was hauling on his wagon."

Christopher Fogle was born in Baden, Germany, in 1800. His father came with his family to Philadelphia, Pennsylvania, in 1817, and Christopher learned the tanning trade in Germantown. On June 26, 1826, he was married in Dauphin County, Pennsylvania. About this time he joined the Methodist Church. In 1835 he migrated to Heathville, Jefferson

County, Pennsylvania, and built a tannery. In 1843 he moved to Troy and had a tannery. This he afterwards sold out to Hulett Smith, when he moved to Brookville and purchased from Elijah Heath and A. Colwell what was called the David Henry tannery. Rev. Fogle was in the underground railroad business in Heathville, and Mrs. Jane Fogle, his second wife, who still survives him, informs me that he continued in that business until the war for the Union, and she assisted him. The points in and around Brookville where the Rev. Fogle lived and secreted fugitives were, first, the old tannery; second, the K. L. Blood farm; third, the little yellow house where Benscotter's residence now is; and, fourth, the old house formerly owned by John J. Thompson, opposite the United Presbyterian Church. Officers frequently were close after these fugitives, and sometimes were in Brookville, while the agents had the colored people hid in the woods. The next station on this road to Canada was at the house of William Coon, in Clarington, Pennsylvania. Coon would ferry the slaves over the Clarion, feed, refresh, and start them through the wilderness for Warren, Pennsylvania, and when Canada was finally reached, the poor fugitive could sing with a broken heart at times, thinking of his wife, children, and parents yet in bonds,—

> "No more master's call for me,
> No more, no more.
> No more driver's lash for me,
> No more, no more.
> No more auction-block for me,
> No more, no more.
> No more bloodhounds hunt for me,
> No more, no more.
> I'm free, I'm free at last; at last,
> Thank God, I'm free!"

INDENTURED APPRENTICES, WHITE SLAVERY, AND REDEMPTIONERS.

Colored people were not the only class held in servitude by Pennsylvanians. Another form of slavery was carried on by speculators called Newlanders. These traders in "white people" were protected by custom and legal statutes. They ran vessels regularly to European seaports, and induced people to emigrate to Pennsylvania. By delay and expensive formalities these emigrants were systematically robbed during the trip of any money they might have, and upon their arrival at Philadelphia would be in a strange country, without money or friends to pay their passage or to lift their goods from the villanous captains and owners of these vessels which brought them to the wharves of Philadelphia. Imagine the destitute condition of these emigrants. Under the law of imprisonment for debt the captain or merchant either sold these people or imprisoned them.

PIONEER HISTORY OF JEFFERSON COUNTY, PENNA.

The Newlanders were the first German emigrants to Pennsylvania. Actuated by sinister motives, the Newlander would return to Germany, and rely on his personal appearance and flattering tongue to mislead and induce all classes, from the minister down to the lowest strata of humanity, to migrate to the New World. The Newlanders would receive from the owner or captain of a vessel a stipulated sum per passenger. By arts and representations the Newlander ingratiated himself into the confidence of the emigrant, securing possession of his property, and before taking passage the emigrant had to subscribe to a written contract in English, which enabled the Newlander the more fully to pluck his victim, for when the vessel arrived at Philadelphia the list of passengers and their agreements were placed in the hands of merchants. The Newlander managed it so that the emigrant would be in his debt, and then the poor foreigners had to be sold for debt. The merchants advertised the cargo ; the place of sale on the ship. The purchasers had to enter the ship, make the contract, take their purchase to the merchant and pay the price, and then legally bind the transaction before a magistrate. Unmarried people and young people, of course, were more readily sold, and brought better prices. Aged and decrepit persons were poor sale ; but if they had healthy children, these children were sold at good prices for the combined debt, and to different masters and in different States, perhaps never to see each other in this world. The parents then were turned loose to beg. The time of sale was from two to seven years for about fifty dollars of our money. The poor people on board the ship were prisoners, and could neither go ashore themselves or send their baggage until they paid what they did not owe. These captains made more money out of the deaths of their passengers than they did from the living, as this gave them a chance to rob chests and sell children. This was a cruel, murdering trade. Every cruel device was resorted to in order to gain gold through the misfortune of these poor people. One John Stedman, in 1753, bought a license in Holland that no captain or merchant could load any passengers unless he had two thousand. He treated these deluded people so cruelly on shipboard that two thousand in less than one year were thrown overboard. This was monopoly.

As will be seen in this chapter, under the head of advertisements, many of the leading merchants in Philadelphia were engaged in this nefarious business. In answer to the daily advertisements of "Redemptioners for Sale," citizens from all parts of Pennsylvania and adjoining States visited Philadelphia and bought these poor white people, the same as sheep and oxen. Many of the best families and people in this State are descendants of these "white slaves." We have some such descendants in Jefferson County. I could name them.

Under this debasing system of indentured apprentices, the legal existence of African slavery, and the legalized sale of white emigrants in our

State, is it any wonder that among the people intemperance, illiteracy, lottery schemes for churches, gambling, and profanity was the rule, or that to the poor, the weak, and the wretched the prisons were the only homes or hospitals for them, and that the "driver's lash" fell alike on the back of the old and young, black or white, minister, school-master, or layman?

> "I pity the mother, careworn and weary,
> As she thinks of her children about to be sold;
> You may picture the bounds of the rock-girdled ocean,
> But the grief of that mother can never be told."

ACT OF 1700.

"An Act for the Better Regulation of Servants in this Province and Territories.

"For the just encouragement of servants in the discharge of their duty, and the prevention of their deserting their masters' or owners' service, *Be it enacted*, That no servant, bound to serve his or her time in this province, or counties annexed, shall be sold or disposed of to any person residing in any other province or government, without the consent of the said servant, and two Justices of the Peace of the county wherein he lives or is sold, under the penalty of ten pounds; to be forfeited by the seller.

"II. *And be it further enacted*, That no servant shall be assigned over to another person by any in this province or territories, but in the presence of one Justice of the Peace of the county, under the penalty of ten pounds; which penalty, with all others in this act expressed, shall be levied by distress and sale of goods of the party offending.

"III. *And be it enacted*, That every servant that shall faithfully serve four years, or more, shall, at the expiration of their servitude, have a discharge, and shall be duly clothed with two complete suits of apparel, whereof one shall be new, and shall also be furnished with one new axe, one grubbing-hoe, and one weeding-hoe, at the charge of their master or mistress.

"IV. And for prevention of servants quitting their masters' service, *Be it enacted*, That if any servant shall absent him or herself from the service of their master or owner for the space of one day or more, without leave first obtained for the same, every such servant shall, for every such day's absence, be obliged to serve five days, after the expiration of his or her time, and shall further make such satisfaction to his or her master or owner, for the damages and charges sustained by such absence, as the respective County Court shall see meet, who shall order as well the time to be served, as other recompense for damages sustained.

"V. And whosoever shall apprehend or take up any runaway servant, and shall bring him or her to the Sheriff of the county, such person shall, for every such servant, if taken up within ten miles of the servant's abode, receive ten shillings, and if ten miles or upwards, twenty shillings reward, of the said Sheriff, who is hereby required to pay the same, and forthwith to send notice to the master or owner, of whom he shall receive five shillings, prison fees, upon delivery of the said servant, together with all other disbursements and reasonable charges for and upon the same.

"VI. And to prevent the clandestine employing of other men's servants, *Be it enacted*, That whosoever shall conceal any servant of this province or territories, or entertain him or her twenty-four hours, without his or her master's or owner's knowledge and consent, and shall not within the said time give an account thereof to some Justice of the Peace of the county, every such person shall forfeit twenty shillings for every day's concealment. And in case the said Justice shall not, within twenty-four hours after complaint made to him, issue his warrant, directed to the next constable, for apprehending and seizing the said servant, and commit him or her to the custody of the Sheriff of the county, such Justice shall, for every such offence, forfeit five pounds. And the Sheriff shall by the first opportunity, after he has received the said servant, send notice thereof to his or her master or owner; and the said Sheriff, neglecting or omitting in any case to give notice to the master or owner of their servant being in his custody as aforesaid, shall forfeit five shillings for every day's neglect after an opportunity has offered, to be proved against him before the next County Court, and to be there adjudged.

"VII. And for the more effectual discouragement of servants imbezzling their masters' or owners' goods, *Be it enacted*, That whosoever shall clandestinely deal or traffic with any servant, white or black, for any kind of goods or merchandise, without leave or order from his or her master or owner, plainly signified or appearing, shall forfeit treble the value of such goods to the owner; and the servant if a white, shall make satisfaction to his or her master or owner by servitude, after the expiration of his or her time, to double the value of the said goods; And if the servant be a black, he or she shall be severely whipped, in the most public place of the township where the offence was committed."

ACT OF 1705.

"SECTION 2. *Provided*, That no person shall be kept in prison for debt or fines, longer than the second day of the next session after his or her commitment, unless the plaintiff shall make it appear that the person imprisoned hath some estate that he will not produce, in which case the court shall examine all persons suspected to be privy to the concealing of such estate; and if no estate sufficient shall be found, the debtor shall make satisfaction by servitude to the judgment of the court where such action is tried (not exceeding seven years if a single person, and under the age of fifty and three years, or five years if a married man, and under the age of forty and six years) if the plaintiff require it; but if the plaintiff refuse such manner of satisfaction, according to the judgment of the court as aforesaid, then and in such case the prisoner shall be discharged in open court.

"SECTION 3. *Provided*, That nothing in this act contained shall be construed to subject any master of ship or other vessel, trading into this province from other parts, to make satisfaction for debt by servitude as above said."

Up to 1842 this law of Pennsylvania authorized the imprisonment of men for debt. The act of July 12 of that year abolished such imprisonment. Quite a number of men were committed to the old jail in Brookville because of their inability to pay their debts. Sometimes their friends paid the debt for them, and sometimes they came out under the insolvent debtor's law. Below I give an exact copy of an execution issued by 'Squire Corbett, a justice of the peace in Brookville:

"JEFFERSON COUNTY, *ss*.

"The Commonwealth of Pennsylvania to James Cochran, constable of borough, greeting: *Whereas* judgment against Stephen Tibbits for the sum of 5 dollars and 27 cents and the costs was had the 6th day of Jany, '39, before me, at the suit of Heath, Dunham & Co.: These are therefore in the name of the commonwealth, to command you to levy distress on the goods and chattels of the said Stephen Tibbits, and make sale thereof according to law to the amount of said debt and costs, and what may accrue thereon, and make return to me in twenty days from the date thereof; and for want of goods and chattels whereon to levy, you are commanded to convey the body of said Stephen Tibbits to the jail of the said county, the jailer whereof is hereby commanded to receive the same, in safe custody to keep until the said debt and costs are paid, or otherwise discharged by due course of law. Given under my hand and seal the 15 day of May, 1841.
"JAMES CORBETT."

This execution was numbered 811. The debt was $5.27; interest, 60 cents; justice's costs, 25 cents; execution and return, 20½ cents; total, $6.32½. The whole sum was paid May 26, 1841.

By the act passed April 8, 1785, entitled "An Act for establishing the office of a register of all German passengers who shall arrive at the port of Philadelphia, and of all indentures by which any of them shall be bound servants for their freight, and of the assigments of such servants in the city of Philadelphia," it was provided that the register should understand and speak both German and English languages, and that he could have "all the powers and authorities of a justice of the peace, as far as the same shall be required for the support and efficiency of his office, and the laws respecting the importation of German passengers and binding them out servants." All indentures and assignments to be made and acknowledged before the register or his deputy, and he to register all indentures or assignments, as servants' indentures or assignments.

Under the act for regulating the importation of German and other passengers, passed February 7, 1818, the captain was compelled to give a bill of lading of merchandise to passengers, under a penalty of one hundred dollars. Passengers to be discharged on payment of freight. When passengers were sold for servitude, the indenture to be acknowledged before the mayor of the city of Philadelphia; "but no master, captain, owner, or consignee of any ship or vessel shall separate any husband and wife, who came passengers in any such ship or vessel, by disposing of them to different masters or mistresses, unless by mutual consent of such husband and wife; nor shall any passenger, without his or her consent, be disposed of to any person residing out of this Commonwealth, under the penalty of one hundred dollars." The goods of each passenger to be a pledge for freight.

AN ACT FOR THE RELIEF OF REDEMPTIONERS.

"SECTION 1. *Be it enacted by the Senate and House of Representatives of the Commonwealth of Pennsylvania, in General Assembly met, and it is hereby enacted by the authority of the same,* That the several provisions of an act of Assembly of this Commonwealth, passed the twenty-ninth day of September, one thousand seven hundred and seventy, entitled 'An Act for the regulation of apprentices within this province,' and of an act passed the eleventh day of April, one thousand seven hundred and ninety-nine, entitled a supplement to the act, entitled 'An Act for the regulation of apprentices,' be and the same are hereby extended to all Redemptioners bound to service for a term of years." Passed 9th February, 1820.

ACT OF SEPTEMBER 29, 1770.

"SECTION 1. All and every person or persons that shall be bound by indenture, to serve an apprentice in any art, mystery, labour, or occupation, with the assent of his or her parent, guardian or next friend, or with the assent of the overseers of the poor, and approbation of any two Justices, although such persons, or any of them, shall be within the age of twenty-one years at the time of making their several indentures, shall be bound to serve the time in their respective indentures contained, so as such time or term of years of such apprentice, if female, do expire at or before the age of eighteen years, and if a male, at or before the age of twenty-one years, as fully to all intents and purposes as if the same apprentices were of full age at the time of making the said indentures.

"SECTION 2. If any master or mistress shall misuse, abuse, or evilly treat, or shall not discharge his or her duty towards his or her apprentice, according to the covenants in the indentures between them made, or if the said apprentice shall abscond or absent him or herself from his or her master's or mistress's service without leave, or shall not do and discharge his or her duty to his or her master or mistress, according to his or her covenants aforesaid, the said master or mistress, or apprentice, being aggrieved in the premises, shall or may apply to any one Justice of the Peace, of any county or city, where the said master or mistress shall reside, who, after giving due notice to such master or mistress, or apprentice, if he or she shall neglect or refuse to appear, shall thereupon issue his warrant for bringing him or her, the said master, mistress, or apprentice, before him, and take such order and direction, between the said master or mistress and apprentice, as the equity and justice of the case shall require : And if the said Justice shall not be able to settle and accommodate the difference and dispute between the said master or mistress and apprentice, through a want of conformity in the master or mistress, then the said Justice shall take a recognizance of the said master or mistress, and bind him or her over, to appear and answer the complaint of his or her apprentice, at the next county court of Quarter Sessions, to be held for the said county or city, and take such order with respect to such apprentice as to him shall seem just; and if through want of conformity in the said apprentice he shall, if the master or mistress or apprentice request it, take recognizance of him or her with one sufficient surety, for his or her appearance at the said sessions, and to answer the complaint of his or her master or mistress, or commit such apprentice for want of such surety, to the common gaol or work-house of the said county or city respectively; and upon such appearance of the parties and hearing of their respective proofs and allegations, the said court shall, and they are hereby authorized and empowered, if they see cause, to discharge the said apprentice of and from his or her apprenticeship, and of and from all and every the articles, covenants, and agreements in his or her said indenture contained ; but if default shall be found in the said apprentice, then the said court is hereby authorized and empowered to cause, if they see sufficient occasion, such punishment by imprisonment of the body, and confinement at hard labour, to be inflicted on him or her, as to them, in their discretion, they shall think his or her offence or offences shall deserve."

ACT OF APRIL 11, 1799.

"SECTION 1. If any apprentice shall absent himself or herself from the service of his or her master or mistress, before the time of his or her apprenticeship shall be expired, without leave first obtained, every such apprentice, at any time after he or she arrives at the age of twenty-one years, shall be liable to, and the master or mistress, their heirs, executors, or administrators, are hereby enabled to sustain all such actions, and other remedies against him or her, as if the said apprentice had been of full age at the time of executing his or her indenture of apprenticeship.

"SECTION 2. When any master or mistress shall die before the term of apprenticeship shall be expired, the executors or administrators of such master or mistress, provided the term of the indenture extended to executors and administrators, shall and may have a right to assign over the remainder of the term of such apprenticeship to such suitable person of the same trade or calling mentioned in the indenture, as shall be approved of by the court of Quarter Sessions of the county where the master or mistress lived, and the assignee to have the same right to the service of such apprentice as the master or mistress had at the time of his or her death ; and also when any master or mistress shall assign over his or her apprentice to any person of the same trade or calling mentioned in the indenture, the said assignment shall be legal, provided the terms of the indenture extended to assigns, and provided the apprentice, or his or her parents, guardian or guardians, shall give his, her, or their consent to such assignment before some Justice of the Peace of the county where the master or mistress shall live.''

These advertisements are selected from a large number of a similar kind that are found in Relf's *Philadelphia Gazette and Daily Advertiser* for the years 1804–5 :

"GERMAN REDEMPTIONERS.

"To be disposed of, the time of a number of German Redemptioners, consisting of Clerks, Shoemakers, Taylors, Cloth makers, Weavers, Stocking weavers, Blacksmiths, Watch makers, Miniature painters &c. on board the Ship Cato, Capt. Barden, from the river Jade, lying off Vine Street, apply to the captain on board Cato.

"SMITH RIDGWAY & CO.

"No. 50 n. front street.

"Nov. 3rd (1804)."

"TO BE DISPOSED OF.

"The Time of a German Servant Girl, who has eight years to serve. She is strong and hearty, understands English, and can be well recommended. Enquire at No. 15 South Third Street.

" January 9th 1805."

"GERMAN REDEMPTIONERS.

"A number of German Redemptioners of different ages and professions, to be disposed of on board ship Venus from Amsterdam. For terms apply on board, opposite Callowhill street.

"Sept. 9th 1805."

"SWISS AND GERMAN PASSENGERS.

" *The Time*

"Of the following passengers mostly farmers and a few mechanics, viz: 17 men, 11 women, 13 boys and 14 girls now to be seen at the

Spread Eagle Tavern, Callowhill street near the water, to be disposed of by their agents Winkleblick & Bund, at the Red Lion Tavern, Market Street, between 6 and 7 street, South from 9 in the morning till 6 o'clock in the evening. The payment to be made at the counting house of Mr. L. Huson, No. 19 South Wharves."

"GERMAN REDEMPTIONERS.

" On board the ship Indostan laying in the stream above Vine street, consisting of carpenters, bakers, butchers, gardeners, blacksmiths, sugar refiners, glass makers, taylors, servants &c. &c. whose times are to be disposed of, by

"ISAAC HAZELHURST & SONS.
"April 16th 1804."

"20 DOLLARS REWARD.

" RAN AWAY on Saturday last from the subscriber, a German indentured servant man, named Tobias Schwenck, a weaver by trade, about 25 years of age, about 5 feet 6 inches high. When he speaks he has a fashion of swinging his arms in a very passionate manner, pale face, slender made, light straight hair, speaks a little English; took with him a tight body blue coat made in the German fashion, a blue surtout coat, two pair of Russia sheeting trousers, and a pair of blue velvet pantaloons, and a number of other clothing, a pair of new full boots broad round toed.

" Whoever secures the above run-away in any gaol, or delivers him to the subscriber, shall receive the above reward and reasonable charges paid by

"HENRY DOTTERER,
"Sign of the Buck, Second street, Philadelphia.
"Oct. 1804."

"2 DOLLARS REWARD.

"Ran away, an indentured Dutch servant girl, (the property of Richard Baily, near the 7 mile stone, Germantown) about 8 years of age, light complection, named Maria, was dressed in a striped lindsey short gown and petticoat, blue worsted stockings, and speaks but little of her native language. All persons are cautioned against detaining or harboring the said girl. In addition to the above reward, any reasonable expense will be allowed.

" Dec. 18th 1804."

"10 DOLLARS REWARD.

" Ran away from the subscriber living in the village of New-Holland, Lancaster County, on the evening of the 7th last, a German indentured servant Girl, named Anna Maria Wagner, she came from Germany last fall in the brig Newton, Capt. Reilly. She is about 19 or 20 years old, of a low stature, she hath short and sandy hair, freckled face, her arms, hands, and feet, very small. Had on when she went away, a blue and white striped petticoat of German manufacture, and a blue jacket, which is remarkable, being lined after the German manner with whalebone. It is said that she hath a sister living in the neighborhood of Kutz town, Berks county, bound to Mr. Lesher. Whoever will secure and deliver her in any gaol, and give notice to the subscriber thereof, so that he may get her again, shall have the above reward, and reasonable charges paid. All persons are hereby forewarned not to harbour her at their peril.

"JONATHAN ROLAND.

"NEW-HOLLAND, Jan. 3rd 1805."

"In law, this system was known as an apprenticeship, or service entered into by a free person, voluntary, by contract for a term of years on wages advanced before the service was entered. The servants, by performing the service, were redeeming themselves, and therefore called 'Redemptioners.' In practice, however, with a certain class of people, and in instances hereinafter related, this system was as revoltingly brutal and degenerating as the negro slavery abolished in our own time in its worst aspects.

"It was conceived and had its beginning in the harmless and in some respects benevolent idea to help a poor person in Europe who wished to emigrate to America and had not the money to pay for his passage across the ocean, by giving him credit for his passage-money, on condition that he should work for it after his arrival here, by hiring as a servant for a term of years to a person who would advance him his wages by paying his passage-money to the owner or master of the vessel.

"There are instances on record when school-teachers, and even ministers of the gospel, were in this manner bought by congregations to render their services in their respective offices. Laws were passed for the protection of the masters and of the servants. Whilst this is the bright side of the Redemptioners' life, it had also a very dark side. The Redemptioners on their arrival here were not allowed to choose their masters nor kind of service most suitable to them. They were often separated from their family, the wife from the husband, and children from their parents; were disposed of for the term of years, often at public sale, to masters living far apart, and always to the greatest advantage of the shipper. I have read many reports of the barbarous treatment they received, how they were literally worked to death, receiving insufficient food, scanty clothing, and poor lodging. Cruel punishments were inflicted on them for slight offences when they were at the mercy of a hard and brutal master. Their fellow black slave was often treated better, for he was a slave for life, and it was in the interest of the master to treat him well to preserve him, whilst the poor Redemptioner was a slave for a number of years only, and all his vital force was worked out of him during the years of his service.

"No public records were kept of the contracts entered into abroad by the Redemptioners, nor of the time of the expiration of their service. The Redemptioners were not furnished with duplicates of their contracts. They were sometimes, and could be, mortgaged, hired out for a shorter period, sold, and transferred like chattel by their masters. The Redemptioners belonging to the poor and most of them to the ignorant class, it is apparent that under these conditions they were at a great disadvantage against a rapacious master, who kept them in servitude after the expiration of their true contract time, claiming their services for a longer period.

"For many years the Redemptioners in Maryland had come principally from England and Ireland. The abuses of the system having become known in England, rigorous laws and measures were adopted in England for their better protection, and letters and articles appeared in the newspapers warning the poor people from entering into these contracts. The first and early immigration of Germans came into Maryland from Pennsylvania. From Lancaster County it extended into Baltimore, Harford, Frederick, and the western counties of our State. As wages advanced, the trade of shipping Redemptioners to the colony became highly lucrative. Large profits were made in a successful voyage with a full cargo of human beings, who, on their arrival here, were sold to the highest bidder for a term of years.

"The Dutch, who, in 1620, had sent the first cargo of negro slaves to this country, and had amassed great wealth in the pursuit of the negro slave-trade from distant Africa, discovered that it was less troublesome and equally remunerative to engage in a sort of a white slave-trade, by shipping Redemptioners from their own country, Germany, Switzerland, and adjoining countries, to the American colonies. The shipping merchants of Holland would send regular agents, or drummers, as we now would call them, who received one-half of a doubloon for every Redemptioner shipped by them into these colonies. These agents generally appeared in gaudy dress, with flourish of trumpets, and in glowing language depicted the wealth and happiness of the people of this country, whereof all could partake if they only would come here; that they did not need any money for their passage, as all they had to do was to sign a contract that on their arrival here they would pay for the same out of their first earnings. In this manner these agents would travel from village to village, deluding the poorest and most ignorant to follow them to the New Eldorado.

"Whenever such an agent had collected a sufficient number, he would take them personally to the shipping harbor in Holland. It was a gay crowd which travelled in this manner in wagons across the country. The horses and wagons were decorated with gay ribbons, and joyous songs were heard from the emigrants, who believed they were leaving toil and poverty to go to the fabulously rich America to enjoy the ease and plenty of this world's goods. This spirit was artificially kept up by the liberality of the agent until they were safely aboard the ship. From thence such a life of suffering, privation, and hardship commenced, that it seems incredible that the Christian nations of Europe and America should have permitted such a trade to flourish up to nearly the end of the first quarter of the present century. I myself know several very old persons yet living in Baltimore who came to this country in this manner. The contracts which these Redemptioners had to sign in Holland, and which few of them then understood, contained the proviso that if any passenger died on the voyage, the surviving members of the family, or the surviving Redemptioner passengers, would make good his loss. Thereby a wife who had lost her husband during the sea-voyage, or her children, on her arrival here would be sold for five years for her own voyage and additional five more years for the passage-money of her dead husband or dead children, although they may have died in the very beginning of the voyage. If there were no members of the family surviving, the time of the dead was added to the time of service of the surviving fellow-passengers. The effects and property of the dead were confiscated and kept by the captain. By this the shipping merchant and the captain of the vessel would gain by the death of a part of the passengers, for the dead did not require any more food and provision. It seems that many acted on this principle. The ships were often so overcrowded that a part of the passengers had to sleep on deck. Christoph Saur, in his petition to the governor of Pennsylvania in 1775, asserts that at times there were not more than twelve inches room for each passenger (I presume he means sleeping room below deck), and but half sufficient bread and water. Casper Wister, of Philadelphia, in 1752, writes, 'Last year a ship was twenty-four weeks at sea, and of the one hundred and fifty passengers on board thereof more than one hundred died of hunger and privation, and the survivors were imprisoned and compelled to pay the entire passage-money for themselves and the deceased.' In this year ten ships arrived in Philadelphia with five thousand passengers. One ship was seventeen weeks at sea, and about sixty passengers thereof died. Christoph Saur, in 1758, estimates that two thousand of the passengers on the fifteen ships which arrived that year died during the voyage. Heinrich Keppele, the first president of the German Society of Pennsylvania, writes in his diary that of the three hundred and twelve passengers on board of the ship wherein he crossed the ocean, two hundred and fifty died during the voyage. In February, 1775, Christoph Saur relates in his newspaper, 'Another ship has arrived. Of the four hundred passengers, not more than fifty are reported alive. They received their bread every two weeks. Some ate their portion in four, five, and six days, which should have lasted fifteen days. If they received no cooked victuals in eight days, their bread gave out the sooner, and as they had to wait until the fifteen days were over, they starved, unless they had money with which to buy of the mate flour at three pence sterling a pound, and a bottle of wine for seven kopstick thalers.' Then he relates how a man and his wife, who had ate their bread within eight days, crawled to the captain and begged him to throw them overboard, to relieve them of their misery, as they could not survive till bread-day. The captain refused to do it, and the mate in mockery gave them a bag filled with sand and coals. The man and his wife died of hunger before the bread-day arrived. But, notwithstanding, the survivors had to pay for the bread which the dead ought to have had. Pennsylvania, in 1765, at the instigation of the German Society, passed rigorous laws for the protection of the Redemptioners, but Maryland remained inactive until more than fifty years later."—*Hennighausen.*

In Pennsylvania this traffic in white people continued until about 1820–25, when public sentiment compelled it to be discontinued.

CHAPTER XVI.

PIONEER MONEY.

"THE subject of a national mint for the United States was first introduced by Robert Morris, the patriot and financier of the Revolution. As head of the finance department, Mr. Morris was instructed by Congress to prepare a report on the foreign coins then in circulation in the United States. On the 15th of January, 1782, he laid before Congress an exposition of the whole subject. Accompanying this report was a plan for American coinage. But it was mainly through his efforts, in connection with Thomas Jefferson and Alexander Hamilton, that a mint was established in the early history of the Union of the States. On the 15th of April, 1790, Congress instructed the Secretary of the Treasury, Alexander Hamilton, to prepare and report a proper plan for the establishment of a national mint, and Mr. Hamilton presented his report at the next session. An act was framed establishing the mint, which finally passed both houses and received President Washington's approval April 2, 1792.

"A lot of ground was purchased on Seventh Street near Arch, and appropriations were made for erecting the requisite buildings. An old still-house, which stood on the lot, had first to be removed. In an account-book of that time we find an entry on the 31st of July, 1792, of the sale of some old materials of the still-house for seven shillings and sixpence, which 'Mr. Rittenhouse directed *should be laid out for punch* in laying the foundation-stone.'

"The first building erected in the United States for public use under the authority of the federal government was a structure for the United States Mint. This was a plain brick edifice, on the east side of Seventh Street near Arch, Philadelphia, Pennsylvania, the corner-stone of which was laid by David Rittenhouse, director of the mint, on July 31, 1792. In the following October operations of coining commenced. It was occupied for about forty years. On the 19th of May, 1829, an act was passed by Congress locating the United States Mint on its present site.

"The first coinage of the United States was silver half-dimes, in October, 1792, of which Washington makes mention in his address to Congress, on November 6, 1792, as follows: 'There has been a small beginning in the coinage of half-dimes, the want of small coins in circulation calling the first attention to them.' The first metal purchased for coinage was six pounds of old copper at one shilling and three pence per pound, which was coined and delivered to the treasurer in 1793. The first deposit of silver bullion was made on July 18, 1794, by the Bank of Maryland. It consisted of 'coins of France,' amounting to eighty thousand seven hundred and fifteen dollars and seventy-three and a half cents. The first returns of silver coins to the treasurer was made on October, 15, 1794. The first deposit of gold bullion for coinage was made by Moses Brown, merchant, of Boston, on February 12, 1795; it was of gold ingots, worth two thousand two hundred and seventy-six dollars and seventy-two cents, which was paid for in silver coins.

"The first return of gold coinage was on July 31, 1795, and consisted of seven hundred and forty-four half-eagles. The first delivery of eagles was on September 22, same year, and consisted of four hundred pieces.

"Previous to the coinage of silver dollars at the Philadelphia Mint, in 1794, the following amusing incidents occurred in Congress while the emblems and devices proposed for the reverse field of that coin were being discussed.

"A member of the House from the South bitterly opposed the choice of the eagle, on the ground of its being the 'king of birds,' and hence neither proper nor suitable to represent a nation whose institutions and interests were wholly inimical to monarchical forms of government. Judge Thatcher playfully, in reply, suggested that perhaps a goose might suit the gentleman, as it was a rather humble and republican bird, and would also be serviceable in other respects, as the goslings would answer to place upon the dimes. This answer created considerable merriment, and the irate Southerner, conceiving the humorous rejoinder as an insult, sent a challenge to the judge, who promptly declined it. The bearer, rather astonished, asked, 'Will you be branded as a coward?' 'Certainly, if he pleases,' replied Thatcher; ' I always was one, and he knew it, or he would never have risked a challenge.' The affair occasioned much mirth, and, in due time, former existing cordial relations were restored between the parties, the irritable Southerner concluding there was nothing to be gained in fighting with one who fired nothing but jokes.

" Previous to the passage of the law by the federal government for regulating the coins of the United States, much perplexity arose from the use of no less than four different currencies or rates, at which one species of coin was recoined, in the different parts of the Union. Thus, in New Hampshire, Massachusetts, Maine, Rhode Island, Connecticut, Vermont, Virginia, and Kentucky the dollar was recoined at six shillings; in New York and North Carolina at eight shillings; in New Jersey, Pennsylvania, and Maryland at seven shillings and six pence; in Georgia and South Carolina at four shillings and eight pence. The subject had engaged the attention of the Congress of the old confederation, and the present system of the coins is formed upon the principles laid down in their resolution of 1786, by which the denominations of money of account were required to be dollars (the dollar to be the unit), dimes or tenths, cents or hundredths, and mills or thousandths of a dollar. Nothing can be more simple or convenient than this decimal subdivision. The terms are proper because they express the proportions which they are intended to designate. The dollar was wisely chosen, as it corresponded with the Spanish coin, with which we had been long familiar."—*G. G. Evans's History of the United States Mint.*

TABLE OF THE DENOMINATIONS OF UNITED STATES MONEY.

Standard Weight as established by Law.

		Dwt.	Gr.
	$\tfrac{1}{2}$ cent	3	12
10 mills make	1 cent	7	00
	$\tfrac{1}{2}$ dime	0	$20\tfrac{8}{10}$
10 cents make	1 dime	1	$17\tfrac{6}{18}$
	$\tfrac{1}{4}$ dollar	4	8
	$\tfrac{1}{2}$ dollar	8	16
10 dimes make	1 dollar	17	8
	$\tfrac{1}{4}$ eagle	2	$16\tfrac{5}{10}$
	$\tfrac{1}{2}$ eagle	5	9
10 dollars make	1 eagle	10	18

The mills were imaginary and never coined. The old cents were made of copper, round, and about one inch in diameter and one-sixth of an inch in thickness.

PIONEER BANKS.

The pioneer act of the Legislature of Pennsylvania regulating banks was passed March 21, 1813, but Governor Snyder vetoed the bill. On the 21st of March, 1814, this bill was "log-rolled" through the Legislature and became a law over Governor Snyder's veto. Previous to that time banks were organized under articles of association.

CURRENCY.

"The best currency of those times was New York bank-notes, and the poorest those of the Western banks. Pennsylvania bank-notes had only a small circulation in the county, and held a place in popular estimation intermediate between the above. There was a discount on all these, ranging from one to twenty per cent. It was for the interest of the private bankers to circulate the notes on which there was the largest discount, and as a consequence the county was flooded with the bills of banks the locations of which were hardly known. Every business man had to keep a 'Bank-Note Detector,' revised and published monthly or weekly, on hand, and was not sure then that the notes he accepted would not be pronounced worthless by the next mail. There was hardly a week without a bank failure, and nearly every man had bills of broken banks in his possession. To add to the perplexities of the situation, there were innumerable counterfeits which could with difficulty be distinguished from the genuine. Granting that the bank was good, and that the discount was properly figured, there was no assurance that the bill was what it purported to be. All this was a terrible annoyance and loss to the people, but it was a regular bonanza to the 'shaving-shops.' Even of the uncertain bank-notes there was not enough to do the business of the community. Most of the buying and selling was done on long credit, and occasionally a manufacturing firm, to ease itself along and relieve the necessities of the public, would issue a mongrel coin, which went by the name of 'pewterinctum.' "

CHAPTER XVII.

"SCOTCH-IRISH"—ORIGIN OF THE TERM UNDER JAMES I.—LORDS AND LAIRDS—EARLY SETTLERS IN PENNSYLVANIA—THE PIONEER AND EARLY SETTLERS IN JEFFERSON COUNTY.

SCOTCH-IRISH.

THE term "Scotch-Irish" is so frequently used, particularly in Pennsylvania, and is so little understood, even by those who claim such relationship, that I consider it appropriate in this place to explain its derivation. In the time of James I. of England the Irish earls of Tyrone and Tyrconnell conspired against his government, fled from Ireland, were proclaimed outlaws, and their estates, consisting of about five hundred thousand acres of land, were seized by the crown. The king divided these lands into small tracts, and gave tracts to persons from his own country (Scotland), on the sole condition that each individual securing a tract of land should cross over into Ireland within four years and reside upon the land permanently. A second insurrection soon after gave occasion for another large forfeiture, and nearly six counties in the province of Ulster were confiscated and taken possession of by the officers of the crown. King James was a zealous sectarian, and his primary object was to root out the native Irish, who were all Catholics, hostile to his government, and almost continually plotting against it, and to populate Ireland with those from his own country, Scotland, whom he knew would be loyal to him.

The distance from Scotland to County Antrim, in Ireland, was but twenty miles. The lands offered by James free of cost were among the best and most productive in the Emerald Isle, though they had been made barren by the strifes of the times and the indolence of a degraded peasantry. Having the power of the government to encourage and protect them, the inducements offered to the industrious Scotch could not be resisted. Thousands went over. Many of them, though not lords, were lairds, or those who held lands direct from the crown, and all were men of enterprise and energy, and above the average in intelligence. They went to work to restore the land to fruitfulness, and to show the superiority of their habits and belief compared with those of the natives among whom they settled. They soon made to blossom as a rose the counties of Antrim, Armagh, Caven, Donegal, Down, Fermanagh, Londonderry, Monaghan, and Tyrone,—all names familiar to Jefferson County and Pennsylvania settlers.

These were the first Protestants to settle in Ireland, and they at once secured the ascendency in the counties in which they settled, and their descendants have maintained that ascendency to the present time against the efforts of the Church of England on the one hand and the Roman Catholic Church on the other. These Scots refused to intermarry with the Irish who surrounded them. The Scotch were Saxon in blood and Presbyterian in religion, while the Irish were Celtic in blood and Roman Catholic in religion. These were elements that would not coalesce; hence the races are as distinct in Ireland to-day, after a lapse of more than two hundred and fifty years, as when the Scotch first crossed over. The term Scotch-Irish is purely American. It is not used in Ireland; in the United States it is given to the Protestant emigrants from the north of Ireland, simply because they were descendants of the Scots who had in former times taken up their residence in Ireland.

But few Scotch-Irish emigrants found their way to the Province of Pennsylvania prior to 1719. Those that came in that year came from the north of Ireland. Subsequently the descendants of the Scots in Ire-

PIONEER HISTORY OF JEFFERSON COUNTY, PENNA.

land were bitterly persecuted by the English government; hence thousands of them migrated to and settled in Pennsylvania. In 1729 thousands of Scotch-Irish arrived in Philadelphia from Ireland, as well as some English, Welsh, and Scotch people, many of whom were sold in servitude for a term of from three to seven years, for about forty dollars each, to pay passage-money or for their goods. For a further description of this form of slavery, see Chapter XV., German Redemptioners.

In September, 1736, one thousand Scotch-Irish families sailed from Belfast because of an inability to renew their land leases upon satisfactory terms, and the most of these people settled in the eastern and middle counties of Pennsylvania. By a change of residence they hoped to find an unrestrained field for the exercise of industry and skill, and for the enjoyment of religious opinions. They brought with them a hatred of oppression and a love of freedom that served much to give that independent tone to the sentiments of the people of the province which prevailed in their controversies with the English government years before these Scots entertained a thought of American political independence.

The Scotch-Irish who settled in the Cumberland Valley of Pennsylvania brought its fair lands under cultivation. They fought the savages and stood as a wall of fire against savage forays eastward. It is said that between 1771 and 1773 over twenty-five thousand of these Scotch-Irish were driven from Ireland by the rapacity of Irish lairds or landlords, and located either in that rich valley or west of the Allegheny Mountains in Pennsylvania. This was just before the Revolutionary War, and while the angry controversies that preceded it were taking place between the colonists and the English government. Hence these Pennsylvanians were in just the right frame of mind to make them espouse to a man the side of the patriots. A Tory was unheard of among them. They were found as military leaders in all times of danger, and were among the most prominent law-makers through and after the seven years' struggle for freedom and human rights. The Scotch-Irish in the United States have furnished Presidents, United States Senators, Congressmen, judges, and many others in civil as well as in all stations of life.

The pioneers of Westmoreland, Indiana, and Jefferson Counties were made up principally of these Scotch-Irish or their descendants.* I am indebted to the "History of Franklin County, Pennsylvania," 1876, for the data and facts contained in this article.

PIONEER RECORD OF CIVIL LIST.

Roster of State Officers in 1804, at Organization.—Thomas McKean, Governor; Thomas McKean Thompson, Secretary of the Commonwealth;

---

* The Barnetts and others were of this origin. Washington township was settled almost exclusively by them.

PIONEER HISTORY OF JEFFERSON COUNTY, PENNA.

George Duffield, Auditor-General; Andrew Ellicott, Secretary of Land-Office; Timothy Matlack, Master of Rolls; John McKissick, Receiver-General; Samuel Bryan, Controller-General; Clement Biddle, Escheator-General; Samuel Cochran, Surveyor-General; Isaac Weaver, State Treasurer; Joseph B. McKean, Attorney-General; Richard Hampton, Adjutant-General; Simon Snyder, Speaker of the House of Representatives; Robert Whitehill, Speaker of the Senate; Edward Shippen, Chief Justice of Supreme Court. Pennsylvania then had eighteen Congressmen. Her United States Senators were George Logan and Samuel Maclay.

In 1838 the amended constitution as adopted limited the rights of any one man to serve in the office of governor to six years out of nine. Under the first constitution of 1790 the limit of service in this office was nine years out of twelve.

Up to 1840 the judges were all appointed by the governor with the advice and consent of the Senate. Supreme Court judges were appointed for fifteen years, district judges of the Court of Common Pleas were appointed for ten years, and the associate judges were appointed for five years.

OFFICIALS OF WESTMORELAND AND JEFFERSON COUNTIES.

President judge, 1805, Alexander Addison; 1806, John Young.

OFFICIALS OF INDIANA AND JEFFERSON COUNTIES.

Jefferson was attached to Indiana from 1806 until 1830. Hon. John Young, of Greensburg, was president judge from 1806 until 1830.

Associate Judges appointed and elected.—James Smith, Charles Campbell, 1806; Joshua Lewis, 1818; John Taylor, 1828; Andrew Browning, 1829; Samuel Morehead, 1830.

Prothonotary, Clerk, and Register and Recorder.—James McLain, 1806-18; John Taylor, 1818-21.

Prothonotary, Clerk, etc.—James McCahan, 1821-24; Alexander Taylor, 1824-28; William Banks, 1828-30.

Register and Recorder.—James Speer, 1821-24; Alexander Taylor, 1824-28; William Banks, 1828-30.

Sheriff.—Thos. McCartney, 1806-9; Thos. Sutton, 1809-12; Robert Robinson, 1812-15; Thos. Sutton, 1815-18; James Elliott, 1818-21; Henry Kinter, 1821-24; Clements McGara, 1824-27; and James Gordon, 1827-30.

Treasurer.—James McKnight, 1811-12; Thos. Sutton, 1813; John Taylor, 1815-16; William Lucas, 1817-18; William Douglass, 1820-21; Alexander Taylor, 1822-23; William Trimble, 1824-26; William Lucas, 1827-29; and Blaney Adair, 1830.

Commissioners.—William Clark, 1806-7; James Johnson, 1806;

PIONEER HISTORY OF JEFFERSON COUNTY, PENNA.

Alexander McLain, 1806; Wm. Clark, 1808; Alexander McLain, 1808; Wm. Clark, 1809; Rev. John Jamison, 1809; James McKnight, 1810; Rev. John Jamison, 1810; Robt. Robinson, 1810-11; Joshua Lewis, 1811-12; Rev. John Jamison, 1811; Robt. Robinson, 1812; Joseph Moorhead, 1812; Francis Boals, 1813-14; Joshua Lewis, 1813; Joseph Moorhead, 1813-14; Francis Boals, 1814-15; Alexander McLain, 1814-16; Garvin Sutton, 1815-17; Thomas Sharp, 1816-18; John Smith, 1817-19; Thomas Laughlin, 1818-19; Joseph Henderson, 1819-21; Wm. Clark, 1820; John Smith, 1820; Clements McGara, 1821-22; Stewart Davis, 1822-24; Wm. Clark, 1822; Clements McGara, 1823; Alexander Pattison, 1823-24; James Gordon, 1824-25.

Clerk to Commissioners.—James Riddle, 1806; James McKnight, 1807; Daniel Stannard and James M. Biddle, 1808; Daniel Stannard, 1809-10; James McKnight, 1811; James M. Kelley, 1812-13; John Wilson and James Coulter, 1814; John Wilson and John Taylor, 1815; Garvin Sutton and John Taylor, 1816; Daniel Stannard and Stewart Davis, 1817; Stewart Davis, 1818-20; Robert Young, 1822-23; Ephraim Carpenter, 1824.

In 1824 Jefferson County elected three commissioners independent of Indiana.

The pioneer elections in Jefferson County for President and governor were as follows:

For President.—1832, Andrew Jackson, 175; William Wirt, 105. 1836, Martin Van Buren, 244; William H. Harrison, 231. 1840, Martin Van Buren, 592; William H. Harrison, 476. 1844, James K. Polk, 731; Henry Clay, 591.

For Governor.—1832, Geo. Wolf, 250; Joseph Ritner, 173. 1835, Geo. Wolf, 356; Joseph Ritner, 246; Muhlenberg, 3. 1838. David R. Porter, 591; Joseph Ritner, 421. 1841, David R. Porter, 678; John Banks, 447. 1844, Francis R. Shunk, 727; Joseph Markle, 617.

Pioneer Congressional Districts and Early Members.—Pioneer district, Indiana, Westmoreland, and Jefferson: 1816-17, David Marchand; 1820-24, Rev. Plummer; 1826-28-30, Richard Coulter. Early districts, Armstrong, Butler, Clearfield, and Jefferson: 1832-34, Samuel S. Harrison; 1836-38, William Beatty; 1840, William Jack, first Congressman from Jefferson County. Clearfield, McKean, Warren, Potter, Erie, Venango, and Jefferson: 1833, Chas. M. Reed.

Pioneer Senatorial Districts and Senators.—Pioneer district, Indiana, Westmoreland, and Jefferson: 1815, John Reed; 1819, Henry Allshouse. Early districts, Indiana, Cambria, Armstrong, Venango, Warren, and Jefferson: 1822, Robert Orr, Jr.; 1825, Ebon S. Kelley. Jefferson, Indiana, Armstrong, Venango, and Warren: 1829, Joseph Fox; 1830, William D. Barclay; 1831, Philip Mechling; 1834, Meek Kelley. Jefferson, Venango, Warren, McKean, and Tioga: 1838, Samuel Hays.

Elk, Jefferson, McKean, Potter, Warren, and Clarion: 1842, William P. Wilcox. Twenty-eight years and Jefferson no Senator.

Pioneer Legislative Districts and Members.—Pioneer district, Jefferson, Indiana, and Armstrong: 1816, Joshua Lewis, James M. Kelley; 1817, James M. Kelley, Samuel Houston; 1818, Samuel Houston, Robert Orr, Jr.; 1819, Robert Orr, Jr.; 1820, Robert Orr, Jr., Robert Mitchell; 1821, Robert Mitchell, James Taylor; 1822–23, John Taylor, Joseph Rankin; 1824, Joseph Rankin, William Lawson; 1825, William Lawson, Thomas Johnson; 1826, David Lawson, Joseph Rankin; 1827, Robert Mitchell, Joseph Rankin; 1828, Joseph Rankin, David Lawson. Early districts, Indiana and Jefferson, with one member: 1829, Robert Mitchell; 1830–31, William Houston; 1832, James M. Stewart; 1833–34, William Banks; 1835, James Taylor; thirty years connected with Indiana and Jefferson never conceded a member by Indiana. Jefferson, Warren, and McKean, with one member: 1836–37, C. B. Curtis; 1838–39, William P. Wilcox; 1840, James L. Gillis, first member from Jefferson; 1841, Lewis B. Dunham, of Jefferson; 1842, Joseph Y. James. In 1843 another district was formed, and James Dowling, of Jefferson, was elected in 1844.

"At the election held in 1835 votes were cast on the question of a convention to amend the constitution of the State, which resulted in Jefferson as follows: for a convention, 424; against a convention, 59.

"In 1836 the votes cast for delegate to the convention were as follows: Thomas Hastings, 303; O. Hamlin, 284; Benjamin Bartholomew, 127; and —— Powell, 10.

"In 1838 the vote on the amendment to the constitution stood as follows: for amendment, 593; against amendment, 356.

"At the general election in 1839 the first prothonotary was chosen. Levi G. Clover received therefor 544 votes, and William Campbell 358 votes.

"The first county treasurer chosen by the people was at the election in the year 1841. Samuel Craig received 357 votes; Thomas Hastings, 300; David Henry, 230; and Samuel Carey, 219.

"The act of Assembly, passed April 8, 1830, having bestowed full powers, rights, and privileges upon the citizens of Jefferson, and investing complete authority in the county, as an organized body politic, the first general election for State and county officers was held on the second Tuesday of October of that year. The number of townships was then five,—viz.: Pine Creek, Ridgeway, Perry, Rose, and Young. The officers voted for and the number of votes received by each candidate are as follows:

"*Congress.*—Richard Coulter, 162; James Pollock, 121.

"*Senate.*—Philip Mechling, 143; Joseph M. Fox, 41; William D. Barclay, 103.

PIONEER HISTORY OF JEFFERSON COUNTY, PENNA.

"*Assembly.*—William Houston, 176 ; Meek Kelley, 108.

Sheriff.—Thomas McKee, 130; Frederick Heterick, 129; William Bowers, 93.

"*Coroner.*—John Lucas, 230; John Barnett, 2; Joseph Long, 51; John Hess, 1.

"*Commissioner.*—Robert Andrews, 90; Jacob Hoover, 83; John Lattimer, 36 ; William Kennedy, 6 ; Isaac Lewis, 59 ; John McClelland, 13.

"*Auditor.*—John Hess, 138 ; John Welsh, 102 ; John Easor, 20 ; John Bell, 2 ; Peter Sutton, 1."—*Atlas.*

The county was erected in 1804, but there was no election of any kind held until Friday, March 20, 1807. Pine Creek township was established in 1806, and the election district made at Joseph Barnett's. In 1819, Perry was created. This made two election districts, one at Barnett's and one at Bell's. Little Sandy was the dividing line. Previous to 1826 all the settlers on the north of this line had to vote at Port Barnett, and all south at John Bell's. All legal business had to be transacted at Indiana until 1830. No voters in the county before 1814 could vote at a general election. Yet even after 1814 there was no record of our vote, for Jefferson votes were counted in with Indiana.

PIONEER ANNOUNCEMENTS FOR OFFICE PREVIOUS TO NOMINATING CONVENTIONS.

"To the free and independent electors of Jefferson County, who are opposed to petty aristocracies and serving friends out of the public treasury, I offer myself as a candidate for the office of COUNTY AUDITOR, and pledge myself, if elected, to pay some regard to the oath of office, and oppose the settling of any account paid out of the county treasury that is not strictly legal.

"ELIJAH HEATH."

—*Brookville Republican,* August 24, 1837.

"TO THE FREE AND INDEPENDENT ELECTORS OF JEFFERSON COUNTY.

"To all who are opposed to petty aristocracies, to serving friends and pensioners out of the public treasury, and, in short, to all who are opposed to petty monopolies, petty larceny, and to those who sacrifice honor, truth, and honesty at the shrine of Mammon, or in any manner worship the golden calf at the hazard of the damnation of their souls, I, on the suggestion, and at the earnest solicitation of many friends, offer myself, at the ensuing election, as a candidate for the office of COUNTY AUDITOR, and I hereby stand pledged, if elected, to pay full and complete regard to the oath of office and to oppose settlement of any account not in good faith strictly honest.

"C. A. ALEXANDER."

—*Brookville Republican,* August 31, 1837.

PIONEER HISTORY OF JEFFERSON COUNTY, PENNA.

PIONEER ATTEMPT TO ESTABLISH NOMINATING CONVENTIONS FOR COUNTY OFFICERS IN JEFFERSON COUNTY.

Previous and up to the year 1837 everybody who wished announced and ran for office in the county without a caucus nomination, but in that year the pioneer effort was made to organize a party system of nominating candidates,—viz. :

"PUBLIC MEETING.

" In pursuance of a notice in the *Brookville Republican* the Democratic citizens of Jefferson County assembled at the court-house in the borough of Brookville, on Saturday, the 26th of August, instant, to take into consideration the propriety of electing delegates to meet similar delegates at Montmorency from the counties of Warren and McKean, to put in nomination a suitable person to be supported at the next general election to represent the district composed of the counties of Warren, McKean, and Jefferson.

"On motion, Richard Arthurs, Esq., was appointed President, William Rodgers, Esq., and Daniel Coder, Vice-Presidents, and Jesse G. Clark, Secretary.

" The object of the meeting being briefly and ably stated by John J. Y. Thompson, Esq., the following resolutions were adopted,—viz. :

" *Resolved*, That Uriah Matson and Thomas Hastings, Esqrs., be appointed delegates of the Democratic party to meet similar delegates from Warren and McKean Counties, at Montmorency, on the 30th day of August, inst., to put in nomination a suitable person to be supported at the general election to represent this district in the next Legislature.

" *Resolved*, That a notice be published in the *Brookville Republican,* requesting the several townships in the county to send delegates to meet at the court-house on the Wednesday evening of the next September court, to put in nomination suitable persons to fill the various offices in said county, to be supported at the next annual election.

" *Resolved*, That the proceedings of this meeting be signed by the officers and published in the *Brookville Republican.*

"R. ARTHURS,
President.
WILLIAM RODGERS,
DANIEL CODER,
Vice-Presidents.
JESSE G. CLARK,
Secretary."

PIONEER NOMINATING CONVENTION—ORGANIZATION OF THE SYSTEM OF CONVENTION NOMINATIONS IN THE COUNTY.

"TOWNSHIP MEETINGS.

"The citizens of the several townships throughout this county are requested to hold meetings in their several townships, and appoint delegates to meet in convention, in the court-house, on Wednesday evening, the 13th of September next (court week), for the purpose of putting in nomination suitable persons to be supported by the Democratic Anti-Bank, Anti-Shinplaster party for the several county officers.

"DEMOCRATS."
—*Brookville Democrat-Republican*, August 31, 1837.

PIONEER ELECTION OF DELEGATES—DEMOCRATIC GENERAL COUNTY MEETING.

"Pursuant to a resolution of the convention which assembled in Warren on the 6th of September last, for the purpose of nominating a candidate to represent the legislative district composed of the counties of Jefferson, Warren, and McKean in the General Assembly, it is enjoined on the several counties in the assembly district to appoint two delegates from each county to meet in convention on future occasions to bring up a candidate for this district, and that they assemble for said purpose at the house of Gould Richardson, in Montmorency, Jefferson County, on the last Wednesday in August next.

"Agreeable to the foregoing resolve the Democratic citizens of Jefferson will meet at the court-house, in the borough of Brookville, on Saturday, the 26th instant, at five o'clock, to appoint two delegates to confer with the delegates from other counties in said convention.

"MANY DEMOCRATS."
—*Brookville Republican*, August 10, 1837.

PIONEER JUSTICES OF THE PEACE.

It appears by the records in the office of the Secretary of the Commonwealth at Harrisburg, Pennsylvania, that the pioneer justices of the peace for Jefferson County were appointed in the year 1809,—viz.: Thomas Lucas, on the 16th of January, A.D. 1809, and John Scott on the 17th of March, A.D. 1809.

In the books at Harrisburg, Pennsylvania, containing the appointments of justices of the peace from the year 1809 until the year 1840, when the office became elective, the following record of justices of the peace of Jefferson County, Pennsylvania, appears:

FIRST DISTRICT.

Composed of the townships of Perry and Young and that part of Pine Creek lying south of the State Road leading from Milesburg to Erie, bounded by the county line and said road:

John Bell, appointed March 8, 1818.

Thomas Lucas, appointed January 16, 1809.

Charles C. Gaskill, appointed August 15, 1822. Resigned March 12, 1824.

Andrew H. Bowman, appointed February 28, 1826. Resigned.
Elijah Heath, appointed May 16, 1828.
John Hess, Sr., appointed August 20, 1830. Resigned March 7, 1831.
John Winslow, appointed May 20, 1831.
William Stunkard, appointed October 22, 1831.
James Bell, appointed November 13, 1832.
John Robinson, appointed May 27, 1833.
Alexander McKnight, appointed October 25, 1833.
Martin Shoaf, appointed October 31, 1833.
James M. Steedman, appointed January 1, 1834.
William Ferguson, appointed May 27, 1835.
John Robinson, appointed in 1836.
James Corbett, appointed June, 1837, for District No. 1, composed of the townships of Perry, Young, and that part of Pine Creek lying south of the State Road leading from Milesburg to Erie, bounded by the county line and said road, including the borough of Brookville.

SECOND DISTRICT.

To include the remainder of said county lying north of the State Road leading from Milesburg to Erie, bounded by the county line and said State Road, including Ridgeway township:

Joseph McCullough, appointed December 1, 1823.
John Stratton, appointed March, 31, 1837.
Reuben A. Aylesworth, appointed February 18, 1832, and resides in Ridgeway township. Resigned March 15, 1836.
John Wilson, appointed January 8, 1835.
Stephen Tibbetts, appointed February 14, 1835.

EARLY JUSTICES OF THE PEACE—PIONEER ELECTION, 1840.
Young Township.—William Davis, Lemuel Carey.
Porter Township —John Robinson.
Paradise Township.—
Pine Creek Township.—John J. Y. Thompson, Nathaniel Butler.
Washington Township.—Andrew Smith, William Reynolds.
Eldred Township.—William McNeil, David Lamb.
Snyder Township.—Milton Johnston, Asaph M. Clarke.
Barnett Township.—Oran Butterfield, John A. Maize.
Ridgeway Township.—James Gallagher, Lyman Wilmarth.
Tionesta Township.—John G. Williamson.
Jenks Township.—Cyrus Blood.

1842.

Rose Township.—William Kelso.
Clover Township.—Darius Carrier.
Porter Township.—Martin H. Shannon.

PIONEER HISTORY OF JEFFERSON COUNTY, PENNA.

Snyder Township.—Isaac Ingalls.
Pine Creek Township.—Samuel Howe.
Jenks Township.—Russell Buffum.

JEFFERSON COUNTY ROSTER.

The various offices in Jefferson County have been filled by the following persons, either by election or appointment, since 1824. The commissioners, treasurer, and auditors, being the first officers of the provisional county, we commence with them. The figures at the commencement of the line denote the year they were elected or appointed.

Year.	Commissioners.	Treasurers.	Auditors.
1824	And. Barnett / John Lucas / J. W. Jenks		
1825	D. Postlethwait	John Matson	A. Baldwin. / James Corbett. / T. Robinson.
1826	F. Heterick		J. Brockway.
1827	Thos. McKee	Christopher Barr	Jonathan Coon.
1828	Thos. Lucas		John Christy.
1829	Elijah Heath	Andrew Barnett	J. McCullough.
1830	R. Andrews		John Hess.
1831	J. Henderson	J. B. Evans	Wm. Kelso.
1832	C. R. Barclay		D. Postlethwait.
1833	L. G. Clover	Wm. A. Sloan	John Welsh.
1834	Jas. Corbett	J. M. Stedman	Wm. Ferguson.
1835	Jas. Winslow	Jas. L. Gillis	J. J. Y. Thompson.
1836	J. Philliber	A. McKnight	H. Robinson.
1837	John Pierce		C. Alexander.
1838	Daniel Coder	Daniel Smith	Jesse Smith.
1839	Irwin Robinson	Wm. Rodgers	M. Johnston.
1840	B. McCreight	J. G. Clark	James Gray.
1841	Joel Spyker	Nathaniel Butler	James Perry.
1842	J. Gallagher	Samuel Craig	W. Reynolds.
1843	John Drum	J. Henderson	John Pifer.
1844	Enoch Hall		A. McKinstry.

The first election for treasurer took place in 1841, when Samuel Craig was elected. Previous to that time they were appointed by the commissioners for one year, and were eligible to reappointment.

Jonathan Coon died in the spring of 1838, and Samuel Newcomb was elected in his place at the general election to fill the unexpired term as auditor.

Charles R. Barclay, commissioner, resigned in the spring of 1834. John Lattimer was appointed until the election, and then James Winslow was elected to fill the vacancy one year.

Treasurer McKnight died June 20, 1837, and on the 22d of the same month Daniel Smith was appointed to fill the vacancy.

PIONEER HISTORY OF JEFFERSON COUNTY, PENNA.

Prothonotaries were appointed by the governor until 1839, the amended constitution making them elective for three years. James Corbett, appointed in 1830; Thomas Hastings in 1832; Thomas Lucas in 1835; Levi G. Clover, appointed in 1839, and elected in the fall of the same year; John McCrea, elected in 1842.

Sheriffs.—1830, Thomas McKee; 1833, William Jack, appointed in June, in room of McKee, dead; in the fall of the same year William Clark was elected; in 1836, Joseph Henderson elected; 1839, John Smith; 1842, Thompson Barr.

Coroners.—1830, John Lucas; 1833, J. Christy; 1836, Joseph Sharp; 1838, John Earheart; 1839, John Lucas; 1842, Henry Frease. The office of coroner has been considered of such small importance that but few persons lift their commissions.

President Judges.—1830, Thomas Burnside appointed; resigned in 1835, and Nathaniel B. Eldred appointed; Eldred resigned in 1839, and Alexander McCalmont appointed, whose term expired in 1849.

Associate Judges.—In 1830, John W. Jenks and Elijah Heath were appointed; Heath resigned in 1835, and William Jack was appointed; Jack resigned in 1837, and Andrew Barnett was appointed. In 1841 James Winslow was appointed in room of John W. Jenks, whose term of office expired under the amended constitution. In February, 1843, Andrew Barnett's time expired, and James L. Gillis was appointed, but in consequence of the erection of Elk County, Gillis resigned in November of the same year, and Levi G. Clover was appointed.

COMMISSIONERS' CLERKS.

1824-26, Ira White; 1828, James Diven; 1829, William Morrison; 1830-31, William M. Kennedy; 1832, Benjamin Bartholomew; 1833, Jesse Smith; 1834-35, John Beck; 1836, John Wilson; 1838-39, Jesse G. Clark; 1840-41, William Rodgers; 1842-43, Hugh Brady.

PIONEER APPEALS.
"NOTICE.

"The taxable inhabitants of Jefferson County will take notice that the commissioners will hold the appeals for said county as follows,—viz.:

"On Tuesday, the 17th day of February next, at James Caldwell's in Punxsutawny for Young township.

"On Wednesday, the 18th February next, at Sprankle's Mill for Perry township.

"On Thursday, the 19th day of February next, at Andrew Barnett's for Pine Creek township.

"On Friday, the 20th day of February next, at the commissioners' office in Brookville for Rose township.

"On Tuesday, the 24th day of February next, at James Gallagher's for Ridgeway township.

"On Tuesday, the 24th day of February next, at William Armstrong's for Barnett township.

"By order of the commissioners.
"JOHN BECK, *Clerk.*
"COMMISSIONERS' OFFICE, BROOKVILLE, Feb. 12, 1835."

CHAPTER XVIII.

FROM 1830 TO 1840.

I COPY from a book published in Philadelphia, Pennsylvania, in 1832, the following:

"Jefferson County was provisionally erected by an act of 26th March, 1804, and is bounded north by McKean and Warren, east by McKean and Clearfield, south by Indiana, and west by Armstrong and Venango Counties. Greatest length 46 miles, mean breadth 26; area, 1200 square miles. Central lat. 41° 15' N., long. 2° W. from W. C.

"Like the rest of Northwestern Pennsylvania, the county is hilly, and iron and coal are in abundance; the latter is in every part of the county. The soil in the valleys is in many places highly fertile, but the great body of the county cannot be rated above second quality. It is abundantly watered, having on the south Mahoning Creek; on the west Little Sandy Lick Creek and Big Sandy Lick Creek, whose branches stretch across the county. Clarion River, or Toby's Creek, with its many and large ramifications, intersects the northern half of the county in every direction.

"The State Road from Kittanning to Hamilton, in the State of New York, runs diagonally across the county from southwest to northeast, and the turnpike road from Phillipsburg to Franklin traverses it from southeast to northwest, passing through the town of Brookville; and a company has lately been incorporated for making a turnpike road from Ridgeway, through Warren County, to the State line in New York, in the direction of Jamestown.

"There are three small villages in the county, including the seat of justice,—viz.: Brookville, Punxsutawney, and Ridgeway. At the first, which was commenced in August, 1830, there are about 40 dwellings, 4 taverns, and 4 stores; at Punxsutawney 10 or 15 dwellings, 2 taverns, and 1 store; and at Ridgeway some half-dozen dwellings, etc. Port Barnett, Centre, Cooper, and Jefferson are marked on the map as towns. There is a tavern at the first. The others are mere names.

"There are two or three grist-mills only, but more than four times as many saw-mills, and the export of the county is lumber solely, unless venison hams be included. Two million of feet of white pine boards, etc., were cut in 1830 and rafted down the Big Mahoning, Red Bank, or Sandy Lick Creek, and Clarion River, to the Allegheny River, and thence to Pittsburg and other towns on the Ohio.

"The population is composed of Germans, some English, and some settlers from New York, and consisted, by the census of 1830, of 2025. That there is room for great increase is obvious, when we observe that this population might be comfortably supported on 2000 acres, whilst 766,000 acres are unsettled. There are several sects of Christians in these wilds, chiefly Presbyterians, Seceders, and Methodists. But there is not a church in the county.*

"Venango, Warren, Armstrong, Indiana, and Jefferson form the twenty-fourth senatorial district of the State, sending one member to the Senate. Indiana and Jefferson, united, send one member to the House of Representatives. Jefferson belongs to the fourth judicial district, and to the western district of the Supreme Court, and, connected with Westmoreland and Indiana, constitutes the seventeenth Congressional district.

"This county paid into the State treasury in 1831 for—

"Tax on writs, $35; for tavern licenses, $33.44; for duties on dealers in foreign merchandise, $31.69; total, $100.13. Value of taxable property in 1829, real estate, $509,801; of personal estate, $14,777; rate of levy, 7½ mills on the dollar.

"Unimproved lands are offered for sale in this county at from 150 to 200 cents per acre."

"STATISTICAL TABLE OF JEFFERSON COUNTY, 1832.

Townships.	Greatest		Area in Acres.	Population.		Taxables.
	Length.	Breadth.		1820.	1830.	
Perry	11	9	49,280	205	2025 in	86
Pine Creek	15	12	85,760	356	the whole	49
Rose	39	12	289,520	. . .	county.	115
Ridgeway	23	17	262,040	. . .	. . . .	26
Young	9	9	51,840	. . .	. . . .	70

"The population has not been classed by townships in 1830.

"JEFFERSON COUNTY, 1832.

Post-Offices.	Names of Postmasters.	Miles from Washington.	Miles from Harrisburg.
Brockwayville	Alonzo Brockway	226	154
Brookville	Jared B. Evans	238	165
Montmorency	James L. Gillis	242	171
Punxsutawney	John W. Jenks	216	160
Ridgeway	Reuben A. Aylesworth	236	165."

—*Gordon's Gazetteer*, 1832.

---

* There was one abandoned log church building in the county near Roseville,— viz.: Rehoboth.—McKNIGHT.

PIONEER HISTORY OF JEFFERSON COUNTY, PENNA.

OFFICIAL ELECTION RETURNS FOR JEFFERSON COUNTY, 1837.

	Borough.	Rose.	Pine Creek.	Young.	Perry	Snyder.	Eldred.	Ridgeway.	Barnett.
ASSEMBLY.									
Carleton B. Curtis .	22	27	13	2	4	8	15	15	26
William Clawson .	52	64	47	115	84	9	9	. .	. .
COMMISSIONER.									
John Pierce . . .	32	28	28	12	9	7	12	1	6
Christopher Barr .	20	34	18	4	28	1	6	. .	1
David Henry . . .	13	. .	5	48	7	1	3	. .	14
William Kelso . .	6	50	1	. .	16	. .	2	14	2
John Smith . . .	2	4	53	12	12	1	. .	. .	3
Robert K. Scott . . .		6	5	1	. .	2	. .	. .	1
James P. Stewart .	7	. .	1	. .	22	3	. .	. .	1
AUDITOR.									
Daniel Coder . .	24	33	6	10	16	9	5	5	5
C. A. Alexander .	43	6	42	93	69	6	14	. .	6
Elijah Heath . . .	13	18	14	15	2	8	1	2	9
Joseph Magiffin .	6	43	1	. .	7	. .	5	. .	11

1837—APPOINTED BY THE COMMISSIONERS.

"Alexander McKnight, Esq., to be treasurer of Jefferson County for the current year of 1837 from the 1st instant.

"(NOTE.—We are gratified to be able to announce the reappointment of Esquire McKnight. He has filled the office with honor to himself and credit to the county.)"—*Brookville Republican*, January 12, 1837.

"DIED.

"In this borough, on Thursday last, of pulmonary consumption, ALEXANDER MCKNIGHT, Esquire, treasurer of Jefferson County, aged twenty-seven years and six days, leaving a disconsolate widow and three helpless children to deplore his untimely exit.

"In the death of Esquire McKnight it may truly be said that this county and community at large have sustained an irreparable loss. His deportment through life was frank, open, and circumspect. Honesty was one of his most ennobling characteristics. Esteemed by those with whom he had intercourse in life, his decease was equally lamented. In a word, he was a faithful officer, the honest man, and the good citizen. Peace to his memory.—*Brookville Democrat-Republican*, June 22, 1837.

Pioneer book- and medicine-store advertised in the *Brookville Republican*, August 31, 1837:

"'BOOKS AND MEDICINES'
"just received and for sale at this office."

*   *   *   *   *   *   *   *   *

PIONEER HISTORY OF JEFFERSON COUNTY, PENNA.
A RAILROAD COLLISION OF 1837.
"FATAL RAILROAD ACCIDENT.

"STEAMBOAT 'COLUMBUS,'
"August 12, 1837.

"The most serious accident has occurred in Eastern Virginia since my recollection happened on the Portsmouth and Roanoke Railroad, one and a half miles from Suffolk, yesterday, between nine and ten o'clock. A company, consisting of about one hundred and fifty ladies and gentlemen, from the counties of the Isle of Wight, Nansemond, and Southampton, came down on the railroad on Thursday, the 10th inst., with the view of visiting Portsmouth, Norfolk, Fortress Monroe, and returning the next day. On their return, at the time and place above mentioned, they met a locomotive and train of burden-cars, and, horrible to relate, the two ran together while going at the rate of ten or twelve miles an hour."
—*Brookville Republican,* August 31, 1837.

NOTICE.
"LIST OF RETAILERS.

"In pursuance of an act of Assembly, approved the 7th day of April, 1830, requiring the county treasurer to publish a list of the retailers of foreign merchandise, designating those who have and those who have not paid for license on or before the 1st day of June, I publish the following list, certified by the associate judges and commissioners on the 14th day of February, 1837:

Retailers.	Class.	Paid.
William Campbell	7	Not.
Charles R. Barclay	8	"
James McKennon & Co.	7	"
James Robinson	8	"
Evans & Clover	6	"
Jared B. Evans	7	"
Heath, Dunham & Co.	6	"
Enos Gillis	8	"
Hughes & Dickenson	8	"

"All retailing foreign merchandise in Jefferson County and not enumerated in the above list are requested, under penalty of law, to take out license.

"The eighth section of the above act requires the treasurer to bring suits in June against all delinquent retailers of foreign merchandise.

"It is hoped that those interested will prevent legal action by calling in due time for the license. Those who neglect may rest assured the requisitions of the law will be strictly complied with. All persons having

PIONEER HISTORY OF JEFFERSON COUNTY, PENNA.

obtained liberty to keep public houses are requested to call and take their license. Those who neglect will be returned to court as the law directs.

"A. McKnight,
"*Treasurer.*

"Treasurer's Office, Brookville, May 15, 1837."

Table of taxable inhabitants of Jefferson County, together with the seated and unseated township taxes, for the year 1837:

Township.	Inhabitants.	Seated Tax.	Unseated Tax.
Ridgeway	40	$42.32	$38.27
Barnett	76	74.34	74.34
Eldred	37	39.14	36.43
Perry	209	221.12	205.80
Pine Creek	103	108.97	101.38
Rose	252	264.50	248.14
Snyder	41	43.38	40.37
Young	146	154.46	143.47

Table of township assessors for the year 1837:

Rose township	Samuel Lucas.
Perry township	Thomas Gourley.
Ridgeway township	Lyman Wilmarth.
Eldred township	John Wilson.
Tionesta township	David Mead.
Barnett township	James Aharrah.
Jenks township	Cyrus Blood.
Pine Creek township	Joseph Carr.
Washington township	Henry Keys.
Snyder township	Joseph McAfee.
Young township	John Grube.

"ONE CENT REWARD.

"Ran away from the subscriber on the 5th inst. an indentured apprentice to the tailoring business, named Michael Stine, of German descent. His clothing consisted of a straw hat, flannel roundabout, black cloth pantaloons, and coarse shoes. Any person returning said runaway shall receive the above reward, but neither thanks nor charges.

"Benjamin McCreight.

"Brookville, March 7, 1837."

PAMPHLET LAWS.

"Persons wishing to subscribe for the pamphlet laws of the present session will do well to apply soon.

"A. McKnight,
"*Treasurer.*

"Treasurer's Office, Brookville, December 22, 1836."

The laws were bound in "board" and sold at fifty cents, and were then published in English and German editions.

"JACKSON DEMOCRATIC REPUBLICAN CELEBRATION.

"Pursuant to previous arrangements, the citizens commemorated the 4th day of July by appointing

"Colonel Wm. Jack, president of the day.
"Hon. E. Heath, vice-president.
"C. G. M. Prime, orator.
"L. B. Dunham, reader of the Declaration of Independence.
"J. J. Y. Thompson, reader of toasts.
"Colonel John Smith, marshal of the day.

"REGULAR TOASTS.

"1. The day we celebrate.

"2. President and Vice-President of the United States.

"3. General George Washington. His virtue and patriotism will long remain in the minds of the American people. May laurels thicken around his grave.

"4. The heroes of the Revolution, who fought our battles and in the dark days of our adversity wrought out our political salvation; men whose disinterested achievements are not transcended in all the annals of chivalry, and who for us confronted horrors not surpassed in all the history of the martyrs. They are entitled to the gratitude and liberality of American people.

"5. Governor Wolf, our venerable chief magistrate, a consistent Democrat and faithful servant of the people, his administration insures him the suffrages and gratitude of his constituents.

"6. General Lafayette, the benefactor of the old and the liberator of the new world. His generous virtue and patriotic principles, more powerful than the armed hosts of nations, swayed empires and controlled the destinies of the earth. Alas! death has summoned his choice spirit home to that celestial bower, where he sits in the highest niche in that bright constellation of patriots. His memory is indelibly engraven on the hearts of all freemen. The hero, philanthropist, and champion of liberty.

"7. The Constitution of the United States. The highest evidence of learning, genius, profound wisdom, and devout patriotism; our nation's most redoubtable fortress defends the invasions of aspiring demagogues or intriguing political jugglers. The first who dare attack it, may he perish beneath its ramparts.

"8. The United States Bank. Old Nick's kingdom. Satan and his angels are roving to and fro, from the east to the west, seeking whom they may devour; but, fortunate for America's people, the meridian is fast approximating, when Satan shall be bound and his kingdom washed away.

"9. United States Senate. An ambitious and turbulent cabal; they present to the people of the United States a perfect picture of what man is when deprived of the divine faculty of reason.

"10. Agriculture and commerce. The bone and sinew of our republic; our stronghold in war, our wealth in peace; twin stars that will light us into prosperity and glory.

"11. Arts and manufactures. To encourage and foster them is placing a *dome* over our national fabric, and finishing the stately edifice with the touch of a masterly hand.

"12. Thomas Jefferson, the illustrious author of the Declaration of Independence, the able supporter and advocate of the Federal Constitution, the champion of civil and religious liberty.

"13. The American fair. Last in our toasts, first in our hearts, and last to be forgotten.

> "'The fair, how fairer can they be?
> From all corruptions and faults are free.
> Their hearts all beat for sacred liberty,
> For union to a man, and so are we.'

"VOLUNTEER TOASTS.

"By the president of the day, Colonel Wm. Jack. Samuel McKean. Unworthy the situation he holds, the next Legislature will request his retiring to his original obscurity.

"By the vice-president of the day, Hon. Elijah Heath. The judiciary of Pennsylvania. May they always keep themselves untrammelled from politics.

"By the orator of the day, C. G. M. Prime. Andrew Jackson. Like Moses, he has rescued us by the rod of his miracles; but unlike Aaron, with that *rod* he smote the *Golden Calf.*

"By C. J. Dunham. Anti-Masons. Although the noisy advocates of '*law and order*,' they are usually the first to outrage the one and mar the harmony of the other.

"By John Dougherty. The hero of New Orleans. The undaunted chieftain, ever ready to drop the gauntlet to the foes of freedom. The liberal sons of Neptune in Charleston have rigged him with a constitutional shillalah from the timber of old *Ironsides.* May it defend the *deposits* from the grasp of King Biddle, as it did liberty from the chains of King George.

"By J. J. Y. Thompson. Hon. Samuel McKean. The fawning sycophant of *Clay, Webster and Co.*, against whom no prudence can guard, no courage defend. The insidious smile upon his cheek should warn his constituents of the canker in his heart.

"By Robert Larrimore. Anti-Masonry. A rotten ladder for down-hill politicians to climb to power.

"By Jesse Clark. General Lafayette. He sat by the cradle of our independence, and never in a long and eventful life was he for a moment unfaithful to the principles of our independence, to the maintenance of which his youth and manhood were devoted. Americans will hold him in grateful remembrance while the earth bears a plant or the sea rolls a wave.

"By Richard Arthurs. May Congress lay by their political weapons of rebellion and unite in protecting the Union.

"By John Gallagher. The President of the United States. In spite of nullifiers and *blue lights*, he will ride out the storm in safety, the vestal fire of liberty, whose light illuminates the path of the patriot to the temple of freedom, may its genial rays not be shed in vain o'er the green fields of America.

"By L. B. Dunham. Henry Clay, the great grand high priest of envy, malice, and all uncharitableness. His efforts to sacrifice our beloved President at the altar of his horrid deity, the *United States Bank*, will only sink him deeper in the bog.

"By John B. Butler. Martin Van Buren. May the laurels he has won so nobly in defending the principles of Andrew Jackson and hurling political *Anti-Masonry* to the regions of darkness eventually elevate him to the Presidential chair.

"By Colonel John Smith. John Quincy Adams. A great politcal sinner.

"By Wm. Clark, Esq. Martin Van Buren. The next candidate for the Presidential chair. All opposition to him will be in vain. His enemies will vanish away like snow in the grasp of a heated hand.

"By John Earheart. To the afflicted. Down-hill politicians are hereby informed that there is yet room for them in the *Anti-Masonic ranks*.

"By John Beck. Hon. William Wilkins, our talented Senator in Congress. His able and zealous support of our venerable President and the acts of his administration, particularly in reference to the *British bank*, merits and will receive the approbation of all true Pennsylvanians.

"By George R. Barrett. The Democratic party of Jefferson County. God speed its progress!

"By C. Blood. The citizens of Brookville. May peace, prosperity, and independence ever attend them for their disinterested attention and hospitality to strangers.

"By C. J. Dunham. The orator of the day. Mighty in the cause of truth.

"By Daniel Smith. The fair sex.

> "'Auld nature smiles, his lovely dears
> Her noblest work she classes, O.
> Her 'prentice han' she tried on man,
> And then she made the lasses, O.'

"By L. B. Dunham. The fair sex. The patent work of God's invention.

"By Richard Arthurs. He that tramples upon the rights and speaks disdainful of the fair sex, may all good society treat him with unlimited contempt.

"By a guest. Political blacklegs: Senator Clay, two bullets and a bragger. *Hard case!* Senator Forsyth, two bullets and a bragger, and the eldest hand. Do you give it up? Tune, Sweep-Stakes.

"By a guest. The liberty pole. May we see it rising in strength as long as Democracy shall dwell in the breasts of man, and those who would attempt to put it down be treated as tyrants trampling upon the liberties of their country.

"By the company. The officers of the day. The dignity with which they presided and the faithful discharge of their duty is calculated to raise them in the estimation of their fellow-citizens.

"By the company. Our worthy host and hostess: for our excellent entertainment receive our warmest thanks."

"FOURTH OF JULY.

"JACKSON CELEBRATION.

"The citizens of Brookville and vicinity friendly to a National and State administration celebrated the fifty-eighth anniversary of American independence in a manner creditable to themselves and to the party to which they have the honor to belong. The evening immediately preceding the Fourth of July preparations were made to raise a liberty pole, which had been previously drawn to the place for that purpose (a hickory-tree about one hundred feet in length). Our opponents boasted through the streets that our force was too weak, and that we would not find ten Jackson men in our town to aid in planting our POLE. But when we made an attempt to rally our force, we soon found forty stern Democrats surrounding the tree, and some of them willingly yielded their services to guard it until morning, for fear of an attack by the enemy.

"Our cannon was prepared; but some person, having no other way of giving vent to a confined genius or displaying their cunning, stole it from the place where it had been left. We wish it to be understood that we do not, neither do we believe it to be the opinion of one of the party, that any of the respectable citizens would be guilty of so mean and contemptible an act; none would condescend to such insignificance. We believe the act to be done by some wag, hawbuck, or scullion possessing more impudence than brains, willing to be called the ready tool of every sycophant who would put themselves on a level with him.

"The morning of the Fourth every preparation was made, and at one o'clock a large and respectable company of ladies and gentlemen assembled at the court-house at the ringing of the bell, where the Declaration of Independence was read by L. B. Dunham, Esq., and an excellent address delivered by C. G. M. Prime, Esq., well adapted to the occasion.

"After which the company repaired in perfect order to the Franklin House, and partook of an excellent dinner, and we are much pleased to state that the ladies to a considerable number—we know not exactly how many—honored us with their presence, and, to the great gratification of the guests and credit of our village, participated in the festival, joined us in a glass of wine, etc., after which they were accompanied to their respective homes. We must say to the credit of our village that we doubt indeed whether we have a precedent in any of the country towns in the western part of Pennsylvania. The ladies were dressed rich and elegant,—in the line of procession from the court-house as well as at the dinner-table, presented a most magnificent appearance. We wish our readers to remember, when we speak of the manner in which the birthday of American Independence was celebrated by the citizens of Brookville, that four years ago the place where this town now stands was an entire wilderness; where stately edifices are now erected four years ago was the abode of beasts of the forest; the ground where the liberty pole now stands was then probably occupied by a howling wolf or panther. Little did any who then viewed the site where our flourishing village is situated expect four years hence to see the tall pines and scrubby oaks removed, and in their stead stately dwellings reared; little did they expect at this time to see a court-house not surpassed in the western country where then the prospective eye could only view a doleful-looking forest. However, we will not at this time leave the subject which we have commenced to portray, the grandeur of our village and its rapid progress.

"After the ladies had retired the cloth was removed, and the table covered with the choicest and best selection of liquors; the company reassembled and drank their toasts with loud cheers. Every member of the celebration displayed great zeal in defending the administration of General Andrew Jackson. After the toasts which had been committed to paper were passed, a proposition was made that each member should give a sentiment extemporaneously, which was complied with by several gentlemen present, some of which we will cite: 'Hon. John McLean, of Ohio, the Devil on two sticks;' second, 'General Andrew Jackson: may the sons of America appreciate his worth, and never suffer the independence which he aided in achieving to be trampled by the foes of American freedom.' Received with cheers and shouts of applause. The company were blessed while together with the prevalence of an unanimity of sentiment and identity of feeling; they joined, as we predicted, like a band of brothers cemented together by the fond endearing ties of Jacksonism, and celebrated the day without a single occurrence calculated to disturb their peace or mar their harmony. They separated in the evening in perfect order."—*The Jeffersonian*, Brookville, Pennsylvania, Thursday, July 10, 1834. George R. Barrett, editor. Mr. Barrett afterwards became the distinguished Judge Barrett.

A CALL FOR AND A REPORT OF THE DOINGS, AND AN EDITORIAL NOTICE OF AN OLD-TIME POLITICAL FOURTH OF JULY CELEBRATION.

"JACKSON DEMOCRATIC REPUBLICAN MEETING.

"A large and respectable meeting of the Democratic Republican citizens of Brookville and vicinity, friendly to the national and State administration, convened at the house of William Clark, Esq., on Monday, the 23d inst., for the purpose of making arrangements preparatory to celebrating the approaching anniversary of our National independence.

"On motion, Colonel William Jack was called to the chair, and J. J. Y. Thompson appointed secretary.

"Whereupon the following persons were chosen a committee of arrangements: C. G. M. Prime, J. J. Y. Thompson, A. McKnight, J. Beck, and William Rodgers, Esqrs. On motion,

"*Resolved*, That C. G. M. Prime, C. J. Dunham, G. R. Barrett, be a committee to draft regular toasts suitable to the occasion."

"FOURTH OF JULY.

"We, the undersigned, a committee appointed to make arrangements for celebrating the anniversary of American independence, beg leave to inform their constituents and the public that in pursuance of the duties incumbent upon them they have made necessary arrangements for the entertainments of that day. A dinner will be prepared at the Franklin House by Mr. Clark, and an appropriate address delivered in the court-house at the hour of twelve o'clock.

"WILLIAM RODGERS,
C. G. M. PRIME,
J. J. Y. THOMPSON,
J. BECK,
ALEXANDER MCKNIGHT.

"BROOKVILLE, June 25, 1834."
—*The Jeffersonian.*

IMPROVEMENT MEETING—RESIGNATION OF JUDGE BURNSIDE.

"At a meeting of the citizens of Jefferson County, on Thursday afternoon of court week, the following proceedings were adopted :

"On motion, James Clover was called to the chair, and R. A. Aylesworth appointed secretary.

"On motion,

"*Resolved*, That the following persons compose a committee to draft resolutions expressive of the sense of the meeting, to be reported at an adjourned meeting to be held in the court-house this evening at early candle-light,—viz.: William Jack, Thomas Hastings, G. R. Barrett, A. McKnight, and R. A. Aylesworth.

"*Resolved*, That James M. Stedman, James Clover, and John Gallagher be a committee to wait on the Hon. Thomas Burnside and General William R. Smith, and solicit them to address the meeting this evening.

"*Resolved*, That the meeting adjourn to meet this evening at early candle-light.

"ADJOURNED MEETING.

"At an adjourned meeting of the citizens of Jefferson County, held at the court-house on Thursday evening of the February court, the following proceedings were had :

"On motion, the Hon. Elijah Heath was called to the chair.

"Thomas Lucas and James H. Bell, Esqs., vice-presidents.

"James M. Steedman and John Beck, Esqrs., secretaries.

"When Judge Burnside opened the meeting by reading the part of the bill relative to extending the Pennsylvania Canal to the mouth of French Creek, by means of canal or railway, and, to the gratification of all present, delivered a very elaborate and appropriate address.

"He was succeeded by General William R. Smith, who addressed the meeting with great earnestness in a brief but pithy address, after which the committee reported the following resolutions :

"*Resolved*, That we view with deep interest the importance of extending the West Branch Canal, or slack-water navigation, to the mouth of Anderson's Creek, in Clearfield County, and from thence a water navigation, by means of canal or slack-water, along the Sinnamahoning and Clarion Rivers, or railway through Jefferson and Armstrong Counties to connect the French Creek division of the Pennsylvania Canal.

"*Resolved*, That Jefferson County is large in territory and embraces a body of land with soil unsurpassed in Pennsylvania, covered with timber of the first order, with large bodies of stone-coal, salt-wells, and iron ore in abundance, and, in fact, everything calculated to advance the interest and further the improvement of our county.

"*Resolved*, That we highly approve of the measures of the canal commissioners for the improvement of this our important section of the county.

"*Resolved*, That in the opinion of this meeting the facilities which will be afforded by the contemplated connection of the eastern and western waters are too vitally important to be looked over. The trade passing east and west by way of this communication will surpass the most sanguine expectations of the people.

"*Resolved*, That if the present contemplated connection is carried into effect it will ere long form the most prominent part of our improvement.

"A motion was then made that the meeting adjourn, and the people invited to keep their seats to hear the following resolution, which was unanimously adopted by the meeting with loud cheers of applause, every one responding to the sentiment :

"*Resolved*, That we appreciate the talents, stability, character, and public worth of the Hon. Thomas Burnside, and that the citizens of this county and members of the bar sincerely regret his departure as president judge of this district ; that the highest testimonial of respect we are able to pay him is the assurance that he carries with him our best wishes for his future happiness, and we will ever cherish a grateful remembrance of our former acquaintance."

BURNSIDE'S RESPONSE.

"GENTLEMEN,—I have this day received the flattering resolution passed unanimously by the meeting over which you presided last evening at the court-house.

"I want words to express my thanks and my feelings for this mark of respect from the people and the bar of Jefferson County.

"It is grateful to my heart to have their confidence both in my public and private capacity.

"I bear testimony to the kindness of the people, their regard for the law, and their promptness on all occasions to maintain it. It is due to the bar to declare my entire approbation of their correct and gentlemanly deportment, and I part with them all with feelings of kindness and respect. I shall always remember them with the deepest sense of gratitude.

"Accept, gentlemen, my most grateful respects, and permit me to tender through you to the people of Jefferson County and the bar my unfeigned thanks for the kind and flattering sentiments conveyed in their resolution.

"THOMAS BURNSIDE.

"Directed to the officers of the meeting."
—*The Jeffersonian*, February 19, 1835.

PIONEER HISTORY OF JEFFERSON COUNTY, PENNA.

SHOOTING-STARS IN 1833—A SHOWER OF FIRE—NATURAL PHENOMENON.

"The heavens declare thy glory, O Lord."

On Wednesday, November 13, 1833, about 5 o'clock A.M., the heavens presented a spectacle in this wilderness as has seldom been seen in the world. To those who saw it in this county it struck terror to their hearts, and many ran away from home to their neighbors, declaring that the "day of judgment had arrived." The duration of the display was about an hour. One account says,—

"Yesterday morning, between the hours of five and six o'clock, the heavens presented a very unusual and brilliant display of shooting meteors, a more full account of which, I hope, will be furnished by those better versed in astography than the writer of this.

"At one period probably more than one hundred, of various sizes and brightness, appeared shooting forth from zenith to the horizon, illuminating not only the azure vault, already bright and clear with the vast number of stars with which it was studded, but actually lighting up our very chambers, as if to allure the slothful to a scene very rarely to be witnessed. They were attended with no noise, at least distinguishable to us, but were remarkable for their number, their startling velocity, and brightness with which they seemed to dart athwart the sky, and the brilliant track they left behind.

"The phenomenon continued until the approach of the sun, when the light of the meteors was lost in the near effulgence of his blaze.

"In a book recently published, called 'The Geography of the Heavens, with a Celestial Atlas,' by E. H. Barritt, A.M., pages 104–195½, an account is given of a scene similar to the above.

"'Mr. Andrew Ellicott, who was sent out as our commissioner to fix the boundary between the Spanish possessions in North America and the United States, witnessed a very extraordinary flight of shooting-stars, which filled the whole atmosphere from Cape Florida to the West India Islands. This grand phenomenon took place the 12th of November, 1799, and is thus described: "I was called up," says Mr. Ellicott, "about three o'clock in the morning to see the shooting-stars, as they are called. The whole heavens appeared as if illuminated with sky-rockets, which disappeared only by the light of the sun after daybreak. The meteors, which at any one instant of time appeared as numerous as the stars, flew in all possible directions, except *from* the earth, *towards* which they all inclined more or less, and some of them descended perpendicularly over the vessel we were in, so that I was in constant expectation of their falling upon us."'

"The notion that this phenomenon betokens high winds is of great antiquity. Virgil, in the first book of 'Georgica,' expresses the same idea:

PIONEER HISTORY OF JEFFERSON COUNTY, PENNA.

> "'And oft, before temptations winds arise,
> The *seeming* stars fall headlong from the skies,
> And shooting through the darkness, gild the night
> With sleeping glories and long tails of light.'"
> —*The Jeffersonian.*

THE PIONEER TEMPERANCE WORK IN JEFFERSON COUNTY—THE PIONEER TEMPERANCE WORKERS—ORGANIZATION OF THE JEFFERSON COUNTY TEMPERANCE SOCIETY, AN AUXILIARY TO THE PENNSYLVANIA STATE TEMPERANCE SOCIETY—WASHINGTONIANS.

In what year this society was formed and by whom is unknown. I find the following call in *The Jeffersonian*, Thursday, April 3, 1834:

"TEMPERANCE MEETING.

"A meeting of the Jefferson County Temperance Society will be held in the court-house on Monday evening, the 7th day of April next. An address will be delivered by Mr. John Wilson. The ladies and gentlemen are invited to attend.

"J. J. Y. THOMPSON,
"*Secretary.*"

A temperance society was formed in Brookville by a small number, principally young men, on the evening of the 23d of September, 1836. At this meeting there were only ten names signed to the pledge. The following officers were duly chosen,—viz.: President, Andrew C. Hall; Vice-Presidents, Samuel Craig, William A. Sloan; Recording Secretary, James M. Craig; Corresponding Secretary, James McCrackin; Treasurer, James Park; Managers, Thomas McGinty, Thomas M. Barr, John Shrenk.

The pledge was at first "only to abstain from ardent spirits;" but on the 2d of January, 1837, after several meetings held in the school-house, it was changed "to that of total abstinence." The secretaries, in a report to the society, on the evening of March 6, 1836, say since the organization of the society *seven meetings* have been held, at which the names of *forty-one* persons, at different times, have been added.

"The secretaries feel that they, in common with all other members of this society, owe a tribute to the ladies of Brookville and vicinity, no less than *nineteen* of whom have nobly come out and attached their names to the pledge." Rev. Hallock, Rev. Barris, Thomas Lucas, and other speakers addressed the monthly meetings.

This society was the only one organized body in the temperance work in the county until 1842, when the Washingtonians organized their societies. Colonel Hugh Brady, S. B. Bishop, Esq., and others led this movement.

CONTINUOUS WATER COMMUNICATION BETWEEN THE EASTERN AND WESTERN WATERS.

"To carry out successfully the gigantic project of uniting the great eastern with the great western waters was supposed to require an amount of capital and of credit beyond the control of any joint-stock company, and the pre eminent power and credit of the State herself was enlisted in the enterprise. Unfortunately, to do this required legislative votes, and these votes were not to be had without extending the ramifications of the system throughout all the counties whose patronage was necessary to carry the measure. In March, 1824, commissioners were appointed to explore a route for a canal from Harrisburg to Pittsburg by the way of the Juniata and Conemaugh, and by the way of the West Branch of the Susquehanna, Sinnemahoning, and the Allegheny, and also between the head-waters of the Schuylkill, by Mahanoy Creek, to the Susquehanna, with other projects. In 1825 canal commissioners were appointed to explore a number of routes in various directions through the State. In August, 1825, a convention of the friends of internal improvement, consisting of delegates from forty-six counties, met at Harrisburg, and passed resolutions in favor of 'opening an entire and complete communication from the Susquehanna to the Allegheny and Ohio, and from the Allegheny to Lake Erie, by the nearest and best practicable route.' The starting impulse being thus given, the great enterprise moved on, increasing in strength and magnitude as each successive Legislature convened ; and the citizens of every section were highly excited, not to say intoxicated, with local schemes of internal improvement. Contemporaneously with these enterprises, anthracite coal began to be successfully introduced for family use ; and, besides, the discovery of vast and rich deposits of this mineral, almost exclusively in Pennsylvania, the circumstance was an additional reason for the construction of improvements. Iron-mines and salt-wells were also opened, stimulated by the high tariff of 1828, and the rich bituminous coal-fields west of the Allegheny invited enterprise and speculation to that quarter. To describe the various public works that grew out of the powerful impulse given from 1826 to 1836 would require itself a small volume. Suffice it to say that in October, 1834, the Philadelphia and Columbia Railroad was opened for travelling. The main line of canal had been previously completed, and in the same month, on the completion of the Allegheny Portage Railroad, an emigrant's boat, from the North Branch of the Susquehanna, actually passed over the Allegheny Mountains, with all its family on board, and being launched into the canal at Johnstown, proceeded on its route to St. Louis !"—*Day's Recollections.*

"Yesterday the report of B. Aycrigg, Esq., the engineer employed by the State to examine and report on the practicability of a continuous water communication between the Susquehanna and Allegheny Rivers, was received, accompanied by his estimate of the expense. The House ordered two thousand copies to be printed.

"The canal will be 129 miles long, and is estimated to cost $3,767,377; add five per cent., $188,368; making a total of $3,955,745.

"Mr. Aycrigg remarks that the estimate is not of the probable, but of the greatest expense, and that he believes if the work be properly constructed a considerable surplus will be left.

"The tunnel, according to his estimate, will cost two hundred and fifty thousand dollars, and will take two years longer to make than the other parts of the canal. He therefore recommends an immediate appropriation to that part of the work, including the heavy embankments forming the reservoir.

"We think this is the most important State object that can occupy the attention of the Commonwealth. It will open an avenue by water to Philadelphia, not only for the commerce of the Ohio, but the commerce of the Great Lakes. It will do away with the necessity of a transshipment over the mountains, and it will crown our canals, so as in a short time to require double locks, and not only contribute to our commercial prosperity, but enrich the treasury of the Commonwealth. The Legislature, then, ought not a moment to delay its action. If any improvement is to be delayed, let it be some of the almost useless ones that have received the favor of the Committee on Internal Improvements, as will be seen by a reference to the appropriation bill now on the files of the House."—*Pennsylvania Intelligencer*, March 9, 1837.

"We are pleased to learn by our Harrisburg papers that Mr. Aycrigg —the engineer who was engaged last summer in exploring the country between the waters of the Susquehanna and Allegheny Rivers—made his report to the Legislature on Thursday morning last, the 15th. What will be most gratifying to the citizens of this section of country is the fact that the report is favorable to the Red Bank route. The *Pennsylvania Intelligencer* says, 'We have taken the trouble to read his report in manuscript, and are pleased with the valuable information it contains. He has found a route by the way of Anderson's Creek, which empties into the West Branch, and Red Bank, which empties into the Allegheny, where a water communication can be made. He recommends a reservoir on the summit. By constructing a mound 40 feet high, across the valley of Sandy Lick Creek, three eighths of a mile in length, a reservoir of 3 square miles can be made, which will contain 1,672,704,000 cubic feet of water, and that water can be supplied there during 240 days to pass 115,600 boats. The lockage is 693 feet,—by 83 locks westward to the Allegheny River at the mouth of Red Bank, and by 99 locks eastward to the mouth of the Sinnamahoning. The whole distance from the mouth of the Sinnamahoning to the mouth of Red Bank is 128¼ miles.'

PIONEER HISTORY OF JEFFERSON COUNTY, PENNA.

"It may be remembered that we during the course of the past season took occasion to remark that it was our opinion, and we thought well founded, too, that Mr. Aycrigg would report in favor of this route. Though we do not pretend to the spirit of prophecy, yet we felt certain that our prediction would, as it did, prove true. But a word with regard to the great advantages that will arise to this county. Perhaps no document ever issued from the press is of more vital importance to our citizens than the report in question. It involves the interests of the farmer and mechanic, and deeply interests the merchant and tradingman. Our unimproved lands must immediately rise in value; our timber will prove a source of wealth, and for years an almost inexhaustible quantity of it will be found; our bituminous coal, iron ore, and other minerals make the prospects of our county equally flattering, should this contemplated improvement be completed, with any other in Western Pennsylvania."— *The Jeffersonian*, December 22, 1836.

It is needless to say this great enterprise was never consummated.

PIONEER COUNTY BRIDGE ACROSS RED BANK.

"Petition for a bridge across Red Bank Creek at Brookville. Recorded on Road Docket, January 19, 1836.

"THOMAS HASTINGS, *Clerk*.

"TO THE JUDGES OF THE COURT OF COMMON PLEAS OF THE COUNTY OF JEFFERSON NOW HOLDING A COURT OF QUARTER SESSIONS OF THE PEACE IN AND FOR SAID COUNTY:

"The petition of the subscribers, inhabitants of the township of Rose in said county, respectfully represent that a bridge is much wanted over Red Bank Creek at the place where the public highway from the borough of Brookville to Indiana crosses the said creek in the township of Rose in said county, and that the erection of said bridge will require more expense than it is reasonable the said township should bear.

"Your petitioners therefore pray the Court to appoint proper persons to view the premises, and to take such order on the subject as is required and directed by the act of Assembly in such case made and provided. And they will ever pray, etc.

"John J. Y. Thompson, Charles C. Gaskill, John Beck, Wm. Corden, John Rhoads, James Shields, Wm. Thompson, Joseph Magiffin, Robt. Andrews, Wm. B. Kennedy, Robert Morrison, Jacob Milliron, Sheridan McCullough, John Love, William Steele, John Jones, John McAninch, James Clover, Henry Smith, John Brownlee, Jacob M. ——, Isaac Hallon, John Rine, Peter Groff, Philip Burns, Wm. Clark, Robert E. Kennedy, Lewis Sharer, John Wilson, Thos. Lucas, Thomas Witherow, Robert Witherow, Frederick Heterick, Joseph Hughes, Isaac Covert, Joseph Hall, Ramsey Potter, Wm. Kennedy, Thomas Hastings, John A.

PIONEER HISTORY OF JEFFERSON COUNTY, PENNA.

Matthews, D. M. Riddle, Paul Vandevort, John Smith, Miran Gibbs, Jacob Mason, Cyrus Blood, James M. Craig, George Darling, James Fullerton, James Henry, Wm. Rodgers, Christopher Barr, William Ferguson, Joseph Sharpe, John Christy."

This pioneer county covered bridge was a wooden one, made of pine timber. It was erected across Red Bank Creek in the borough of Brookville, a few feet west of where the present iron structure on Pickering Street now stands. There were no iron nails used in its construction, and only a few *hand-made* iron spikes. The timbers were mortised and tenoned, and put together with wooden pins. This was a single span bridge of one hundred and twenty feet in length, with no centre pier, and of the burr truss plan. It had two strings of circle arches, resting on the stone abutments. I find the following official records in the court dockets:

"At the February session of court, February 13, 1836, 'upon the petition to the honorable judges of said court of many inhabitants of Jefferson County, setting forth that they labor under great inconvenience for want of a bridge across Red Bank Creek, where the Hamilton road enters Pickering Street in the borough of Brookville, asking the Court to appoint viewers, whereupon the Court appointed the following-named persons to view the road and make a report to the Court,—viz.: John Dougherty, John Matson, Sr., James K. Huffman, Daniel Coder, Robert Morrison, and John Philliber.'" These viewers made their report to the Court May 10, 1836, "that the bridge was indisputably necessary."

At the September session, 1836, the Court approved this report and ordered the county to pay four hundred dollars to the construction of the bridge.

The following official advertisement for bids I copy from the *Brookville Jeffersonian* for 1836:

"NOTICE.

"The building of a bridge across Red Bank Creek, on Pickering Street, will be sold to the lowest bidder on Thursday, the 15th day of September next, at 1 o'clock P.M.

"A plan of said bridge will be shown at the commissioners' office, on Monday, 12. Sufficient security will be requested of the undertaker for the faithful performance.

"By order of the commissioners.

"JOHN WILSON, *Clerk.*

"COMMISSIONERS' OFFICE, BROOKVILLE, November 24, 1836."

The bridge was let by the commissioners December 15, 1836, to Messrs. Thomas Hall and Richard Arthurs, contractors. The contract called for the completion of the bridge by September, 1837. The accepted contract bid was seven hundred and ninety-five dollars. When finished the bridge was a good solid structure, but was a curious pile of wood and stones.

Many memories to the old citizen clustered around this bridge, but time has effaced the bridge and will efface the memories. On its planks generations have met, passed, and repassed, and from its stringers fishers dropped many a hook and line. Up to and later than 1843, Brookville had three natatoriums, or swimming-pools,—viz., one at the head of what is now Heidrick, Coleman & Co.'s dam on the North Fork, one at the "Deep Hole" near the Sand Spring, on the Sandy Lick, and one at or underneath the covered bridge on Red Bank. In those days, from the time we had May flowers until the chilling blasts of November arrived, one of the principal sports of the men and boys was swimming in these "pools." We boys, in summer months, all day long played on the bosom of these waters or on the border-land. The busy men, the doctor, the statesman, the lawyer, the parson, the merchant, the farmer, the mechanic, and the day laborer, all met here in the summer eve with boisterous shouts of joy and mirth to welcome up the moon. Of course, we had some skilful plungers and swimmers, who were as much at home in these waters as the wild ducks and geese of that day. An artist could swim on his back, on either side, under the water, float on his back, tread or walk in the water, and plunge or dive from almost any height. The beginner or boy, though, always commenced his apprenticeship in this graceful profession by swimming with his breast on a piece of plank, board, or old slab. But alas to the pioneer,—

> "Swimming sports, once deemed attractive,
> Haunts amidst the bloom of laurel flowers,
> Radiant charms that pleased my senses
> In my boyhood's sunny hours,
> Have departed like illusions,
> And will never more be ours."

POPULATION OF PENNSYLVANIA.

Counties.	Year 1840.
Adams	23,044
Allegheny	81,235
Armstrong	28,365
Beaver	29,368
Bedford	29,335
Berks	64,569
Bradford	32,769
Bucks	48,107
Butler	22,378
Cambria	11,256
Centre	20,492
Chester	57,515

PIONEER HISTORY OF JEFFERSON COUNTY, PENNA.

Counties.	Year 1840.
Clarion	9,500
Clearfield	7,834
Clinton	8,323
Columbia	24,267
Crawford	31,724
Cumberland	30,953
Dauphin	30,118
Delaware	19,791
Erie	3,412
Fayette	33,574
Franklin	37,793
Greene	19,147
Huntingdon	35,484
Indiana	20,782
Jefferson	7,253
Juniata	11,080
Lancaster	84,203
Lebanon	21,872
Lehigh	25,787
Luzerne	35,906
Lycoming	22,649
McKean	2,975
Mercer	32,873
Mifflin	13,092
Monroe	9,879
Montgomery	47,241
Northampton	40,996
Northumberland	20,027
Perry	17,096
Philadelphia	258,037
Pike	3,832
Potter	3,371
Schuylkill	29,053
Somerset	19,650
Susquehanna	21,195
Tioga	15,498
Union	22,787
Venango	17,900
Warren	9,278
Washington	41,279
Wayne	11,848
Westmoreland	42,699
Wyoming	8,100
York	47,010
	1,725,601

Jefferson County was not organized in 1830, and the census was not reported, only as a whole. Males in county, 1065; females, 940; total, 2005.

PIONEER HISTORY OF JEFFERSON COUNTY, PENNA.

PIONEER AND EARLY COUNTIES, DATE OF FORMATION, AND NUMBER OF ACRES IN EACH.

No.	Name.	Date of Formation.			Acres.
1	Philadelphia	March 10, 1682	One of Penn's original counties		80,840
2	Chester	" 10, 1682	" " " "		472,320
3	Bucks	" 10, 1682	" " " "		387,200
4	Lancaster	May 10, 1729	From a part of Chester		608,000
5	York	Aug. 19, 1749	" "	Lancaster	576,000
6	Cumberland	Jan. 27, 1750	" "	Lancaster	348,160
7	Berks	March 11, 1752	" "	Philadelphia, Chester, and Lancaster	588,800
8	Northampton	" 11, 1752	" "	Bucks	240,000
9	Bedford	" 9, 1771	" "	Cumberland	636,160
10	Northumberland	" 27, 1772	" "	Cumberland, Berks, Bedford, and Northampton	292,480
11	Westmoreland	Feb. 26, 1773	" "	Bedford, and in 1785 part of the Indian purchase of 1784 was added	672,000
12	Washington	March 28, 1781	" "	Westmoreland	573,440
13	Fayette	Sept. 26, 1783	" "	Westmoreland	527,360
14	Franklin	" 9, 1784	" "	Cumberland	480,000
15	Montgomery	" 10, 1784	" "	Philadelphia	303,080
16	Dauphin	March 4, 1785	" "	Lancaster	357,760
17	Luzerne	Sept. 25, 1782	" "	Northumberland	896,000
18	Huntingdon	" 20, 1787	" "	Bedford	537,600
19	Allegheny	" 24, 1788	" "	Westmoreland and Washington	482,560
20	Mifflin	" 19, 1789	" "	Cumberland and Northumberland	286,800
21	Delaware	" 26, 1789	" "	Chester	113,280
22	Somerset	April 17, 1795	" "	Bedford	682,240
23	Greene	Feb. 9, 1796	" "	Washington	389,120
24	Wayne	March 26, 1796	" "	Northampton	460,800
25	Lycoming	April 13, 1796	" "	Northumberland	691,200
26	Adams	Jan. 22, 1800	" "	York	337,920
27	Centre	Feb. 13, 1800	" "	Mifflin, Northumberland, Lycoming, and Huntingdon	688,000
28	Armstrong	March 12, 1800	" "	Allegheny, Westmoreland, and Lycoming	408,960
29	Beaver	" 12, 1800	" "	Allegheny and Washington	298,240
30	Butler	" 12, 1800	" "	Allegheny	502,400
31	Crawford	" 12, 1800	" "	Allegheny	629,760
32	Erie	" 12, 1800	" "	Allegheny	480,000
33	Mercer	" 12, 1800	" "	Allegheny	416,000
34	Venango	" 13, 1800	" "	Allegheny and Lycoming	330,240
35	Warren	" 12, 1800	" "	Allegheny and Lycoming	551,040
36	Indiana	" 30, 1803	" "	Westmoreland and Lycoming	492,800
37	McKean	" 20, 1804	" "	Lycoming	716,800

PIONEER HISTORY OF JEFFERSON COUNTY, PENNA.

PIONEER AND EARLY COUNTIES, DATE OF FORMATION, AND NUMBER OF ACRES IN EACH.—*Continued.*

No.	Name.	Date of Formation.				Acres.
38	Clearfield	March 26, 1804	From a part of	Lycoming and Northumberland		761,600
39	Jefferson	" 26, 1804	"	"	Lycoming	412,800
40	Potter	" 26, 1804	"	"	Lycoming	384,000
41	Cambria	" 26, 1804	"	"	Huntingdon, Somerset, and Bedford	428,800
42	Tioga	" 26, 1804	"	"	Lycoming	714,240
43	Bradford *	Feb. 21, 1810	"	"	Luzerne and Lycoming	751,300
44	Susquehanna	" 21, 1810	"	"	Luzerne	510,080
45	Schuylkill	March 1, 1811	"	"	Berks and Northampton	485,400
46	Lehigh	" 6, 1812	"	"	Northampton	232,960
47	Lebanon	Feb. 16, 1813	"	"	Dauphin and Lancaster	195,840
48	Columbia	March 22, 1813	"	"	Northumberland	275,840
49	Union	" 22, 1813	"	"	Northumberland	165,120
50	Pike	" 26, 1814	"	"	Wayne	384,000
51	Perry	" 22, 1820	"	"	Cumberland	344,960
52	Juniata	" 2, 1831	"	"	Mifflin	224,640
53	Monroe	April 1, 1836	"	"	Northampton and Pike	384,000
54	Clarion	March 11, 1839	"	"	Venango and Armstrong	384,000
55	Clinton	June 21, 1839	"	"	Lycoming and Centre	591,360
56	Wyoming	April 4, 1842	"	"	Northumberland and Luzerne	261,760
57	Carbon	March 13, 1843	"	"	Northampton and Monroe	256,000
58	Elk	April 18, 1843	"	"	Jefferson, Clearfield, and McKean	446,720

* Previous to March 24, 1812, this county was called Ontario.

CHAPTER XIX.

PIONEER SETTLEMENT OF WESTERN PENNSYLVANIA—PIONEER PENNSYLVANIA INDIAN TRADERS—THE PIONEER ROAD BY WAY OF THE SOUTH BRANCH OF THE POTOMAC AND THE VALLEY OF THE KISKIMINITAS—THE PIONEER ROAD FROM EAST TO WEST, FROM RAYSTOWN, NOW BEDFORD, TO FORT DUQUESNE, NOW PITTSBURG, A MILITARY NECESSITY—GENERAL JOHN FORBES OPENS IT IN THE SUMMER AND FALL OF 1758—COLONEL GEORGE WASHINGTON OPPOSED TO THE NEW ROAD AND IN FAVOR OF THE POTOMAC ROAD—DEATH OF GENERAL JOHN FORBES—PIONEER MAIL-COACHES, MAIL-ROUTES, AND POST-OFFICES.

"WESTERN PENNSYLVANIA was untrodden by the foot of the white man before the year 1700. As early as 1715 and 1720 occasionally a trader would venture west of the Allegheny Mountain, and of these the first was James Le Tort, who resided in 1700 east of the Susquehanna, but took up his residence west of it, Le Tort Spring, Carlisle, in 1720. Peter Cheaver, John Evans, Henry DeVoy, Owen Nicholson, Alexander Magenty, Patrick Burns, George Hutchison, all of Cumberland County; Barnaby Currin, John McGuire, a Mr. Frazier, the latter of whom had at an early day a trading-house at Venango, but afterwards at the Monongahela, at the mouth of Turtle Creek, were all traders among the Indians. But no attempt had been made by the whites at settlements in the region now occupied by the several counties west of the Alleghenies before 1748, when the Ohio Company was formed. This company sent out the undaunted Christopher Gist, in 1750, to explore the country and make report. He, it is said, explored the country 'from the South Branch of the Potomac northward to the heads of the Juniata River, crossed the mountains, and reached the Allegheny by the valley of Kiskiminitas. He crossed the Allegheny about four miles above the forks, where Pittsburg now stands, thence went down the Ohio to some point below Beaver River, and thence over to the Muskingum valley.' The first actual settlement made was within the present limits of Fayette County, in 1752, by Mr. Gist himself, on a tract of land, now well known there as Mount Braddock, west of the Youghiogheny River. Mr. Gist induced eleven families to settle around him on lands presumed to be within the Ohio Company's grant.

"The more southern part of Western Pennsylvania (Greene, Washington, Fayette, and part of Somerset), which was supposed to be within the boundaries of Virginia, was visited by adventurers from Maryland prior to 1754. Among these were Wendel Brown and his two sons and Frederick Waltzer, who lived four miles west of Uniontown. David Tygart had settled in the valley which still bears his name in Northwestern Virginia; several other families came here a few years afterwards. These were the only settlements attempted prior to Braddock's defeat, and those made immediately afterwards, or prior to 1760, were repeatedly molested, families murdered, cabins burnt, and, for a time, broken up, alternately abandoned and again occupied.

"The treaty of 1762 brought quiet and repose to some extent to the English colonies, and the first settlers on the frontiers returned to their abandoned farms, but they were soon again obliged to leave their homes and retire for safety to the more densely settled parts. Bouquet prosecuted his campaign with success against the Indians, and in November, 1764, compelled the turbulent and restless Kyashuta to sue for peace and bury the hatchet on the plains of Muskingum, and finally humbled the Delawares and Shawanese. Soon after the refugee settlers returned to their cabins and clearings, resumed their labors, extended their improvements, and cultivated their lands. From this time forth the prosperity of Pennsylvania increased rapidly, and the tide of immigration with consequent settlements rolled westward, though the pioneer settlers were afterwards greatly exposed.

"Previous to 1758, Westmoreland was a wilderness trodden by the wild beast, the savage, and, like other portions of Western Pennsylvania, by an occasional white trader or frontiersman. No settlements were attempted prior to this date, when Fort Duquesne, afterwards Fort Pitt, was abandoned by the French, became an English military post, and formed a nucleus for an English settlement, and two years afterwards (1760) a small town was built near Fort Pitt, which contained nearly two hundred souls, but on the breaking out of the Indian war, in 1763, the inhabitants retired into the fort, and their dwellings were suffered to fall into decay. In 1765, Pittsburg was laid out."—*History of Western Pennsylvania.*

This southern exploration was through what is now Somerset, Fayette, Westmoreland, and Allegheny Counties. In 1754, Lieutenant-Colonel George Washington, then twenty-one years old, penetrated this wilderness and improved this road. In 1755, General Braddock, accompanied by Washington, marched his army over this road. Hence the road has always been called Braddock's road.

The pioneer road from east to west was opened up in September, 1758, by General John Forbes. He commanded an army of about eight thousand men. General Forbes marched in the spring from Philadelphia with his troops to Raystown (now Bedford), but on account of the smallpox in his army he was detained at Carlisle, and failed to reach what is now Bedford until the middle of September. At a consultation of his officers at this point it was decided to cut out a new road over the mountains from Raystown to Loyalhanna, now in Westmoreland County, a distance of forty-five miles.

This new road passed through what is now Bedford, Somerset, and Westmoreland Counties. Colonel Bouquet, with twenty-five hundred men, cut out the road in September and October of that year.

Colonel Washington was at this consultation, and was opposed to the new road. Washington's arguments in favor of the southern route were as follows:

"CAMP AT FORT CUMBERLAND, August 2, 1758.

"SIR,—The matters of which we spoke relative to the roads have, since our parting, been the subject of my closest reflection, and so far am I from altering my opinion that the more time and attention I bestow the more I am confirmed in it, and the reasons for taking Braddock's road appear in a stronger point of view. To enumerate the whole of these reasons would be tedious, and to you, who are become so much master of the subject, unnecessary. I shall, therefore, briefly mention a few only, which I think so obvious in themselves, that they must effectually remove objections.

"Several years ago the Virginians and Pennsylvanians commenced a trade with the Indians settled on the Ohio, and, to obviate the many inconveniences of a bad road, they, after reiterated and ineffectual efforts to discover where a good one might be made, employed for the purpose several of the most intelligent Indians, who, in the course of many years' hunting, had acquired a perfect knowledge on these mountains. The Indians, having taken the greatest pains to gain the rewards offered for this discovery, declared that the path leading from Will's Creek was infinitely preferable to any that could be made at any other place. Time and experience so clearly demonstrated this truth that the Pennsylvania traders commonly carried out their goods by Will's Creek. Therefore the Ohio Company, in 1753, at a considerable expense, opened the road. In 1754 the troops whom I had the honor to command greatly repaired it, as far as Gist's plantation, and in 1755 it was widened and completed by General Braddock to within six miles of Fort Duquesne. A road that has so long been opened and so well and so often repaired must be much firmer and better than a new one, allowing the ground to be equally good.

"But supposing it were practicable to make a road from Raystown quite as good as General Braddock's, I ask, have we time to do it? Certainly not. To surmount the difficulties to be encountered in making it over such mountains, covered with woods and rocks, would require so much time as to blast our otherwise well-grounded hopes of striking the important stroke this season.

PIONEER HISTORY OF JEFFERSON COUNTY, PENNA.

"The favorable accounts that some give of the forage on the Raystown road, as being so much better than that on the other, are certainly exaggerated. It is well known that on both routes the rich valleys between the mountains abound with good forage, and that those which are stony and bushy are destitute of it. Colonel Byrd and the engineer who accompanied him confirm this fact. Surely the meadows on Braddock's road would greatly overbalance the advantage of having grass to the foot of the ridge, on the Raystown road; and all agree that a more barren road is nowhere to be found than that from Raystown to the inhabitants, which is likewise to be considered.

"Another principal objection made to General Braddock's road is in regard to the waters. But these seldom swell so much as to obstruct the passage. The Youghiogheny River, which is the most rapid and soonest filled, I have crossed with a body of troops after more than thirty days almost continued rain. In fine, any difficulties on this score are so trivial that they really are not worth mentioning. The Monongahela, the largest of all these rivers, may, if necessary, easily be avoided, as Mr. Frazier, the principal guide, informs me, by passing a defile, and even that, he says, may be shunned.

"Again, it is said there are many defiles on this road. I grant that there are some, but I know of none that may not be traversed, and I should be glad to be informed where a road can be had over these mountains not subject to the same inconvenience. The shortness of the distance between Raystown and Loyal Hanna is used as an argument against this road, which bears in it something unaccountable to me, for I must beg leave to ask whether it requires more time or is more difficult and expensive to go one hundred and forty-five miles on a good road already made to our hands than to cut one hundred miles anew, and a great part of the way over impassable mountains.

"That the old road is many miles nearer Winchester in Virginia and Fort Frederick in Maryland than the contemplated one is incontestable, and I will here show the distance from Carlisle by the two routes, fixing the different stages, some of which I have from information only, but others I believe to be exact.

FROM CARLISLE TO FORT DUQUESNE BY WAY OF RAYSTOWN.

		Miles.
From Carlisle to Shippensburg		21
"	Shippensburg to Fort Loudon	24
"	Fort Loudon to Fort Littleton	20
"	Littleton to Juniata Crossing	14
"	Juniata Crossing to Raystown	14
		93
"	Raystown to Fort Duquesne	100
		193

PIONEER HISTORY OF JEFFERSON COUNTY, PENNA.

FROM CARLISLE TO FORT DUQUESNE BY WAY OF FORT FREDERIC AND CUMBERLAND.

		Miles.
From Carlisle to Shippensburg		21
" Shippensburg to Chamber's		12
" Chamber's to Pacelin's		12
" Pacelin to Fort Frederic		12
" Fort Frederic to Fort Cumberland		40
		97
" Fort Cumberland to Fort Duquesne		115
		212

"From this computation there appears to be a difference of nineteen miles only. Were all the supplies necessarily to come from Carlisle, it is well known that the goodness of the old road is a sufficient compensation for the shortness of the other, as the wrecked and broken wagons there clearly demonstrate."—*The Olden Time*, vol. i.

For many years all government supplies for western forts, groceries, salt, and goods of every kind, were carried from the east on pack-horses over this Forbes road. One man would sometimes have under his control from fifty to one hundred pack-horses. A panel pack-saddle was on each horse, and the load for a horse was about two hundred pounds. Forts were established along the line of the road, and guards from the militia accompanied these horse-trains, guarding them by night in their "encampments" and protecting them by day through and over the mountains.

This Braddock road and Raystown road were nothing more than trails or military roads, and it was not until 1784 or 1785 that the State opened a road from the east to the west over Forbes's military trail.

General John Forbes died in Philadelphia, Pennsylvania, on the 15th of March, 1759.

One hundred years ago this pioneer road was crowded by carriers with their pack-horses going westward, laden with people, salt, iron, and merchandise.

"The pack-horses then travelled in divisions of twelve or fifteen, going single-file, each horse carrying about two hundred-weight; one man preceded and one brought up the rear of the file. Later on the carriers, to their bitter indignation, were supplanted by the Conestoga wagons, with their proud six-horse teams, with huge belled collars, the wagon stored with groceries, linens, calico, rum, molasses, and hams, four to five tons of load; by law none of these wagons had less than four inch tires on its wheels."

From 1784 to 1834 was the stage-coach era in this country. In the year 1802 the government started a line of coaches between Philadelphia and New York, carrying their own mail. This was continued for three years, clearing an average profit yearly of four thousand dollars In 1834 the postmaster-general and the government preferred railroad transportation where it could be had. The government required from the railroads a schedule time of thirteen miles an hour for the mails. I give as near as I can learn the pioneer individual stage-coach mail lines.

PIONEER MAIL-COACHES EAST AND WEST, AND TO CROSS THE ALLEGHENY MOUNTAINS.

"PHILADELPHIA AND PITTSBURGH MAIL STAGES.

"A line of stages being established and now in operation to and from each of the above places. This line will start from John Tomlinson's, Market-street, Philadelphia, every Friday morning, via Harrisburgh and Chambersburgh, to Pittsburgh, and perform the trip in 7 days. It will also start from THOMAS FERREE'S the Fountain Inn, Water-street, Pittsburgh, every Wednesday morning, same rout to Philadelphia, and perform the trip in 7 days ; Fare—Passengers 20 dollars and 20 lb. baggage free ; all extra baggage or packages, if of dimentions such as to be admitted for transportation by this line, to pay 12 dollars per 100 lb. the baggage or the packages to be at the owner's own proper risque unless especially receipted for by one of the proprietors, which cannot be done if the owner is a passenger in the stage, same trip. These stages are constructed to carry three passengers on a seat, and more never shall be admitted.

"This line will also leave John Tomlinson's as above every Tuesday morning for Chambersburgh, making the trip in 2½ days, and leave Mr. Hetrick's tavern in Chambersburgh, every Wednesday at noon, for Philadelphia, and make the trip in 2½ days ; fare 9 dollars and 50 cents, under the same regulations as above.

"The public will perceive by this establishment, that they have a direct conveyance from Philadelphia and Pittsburgh once a week, and from Philadelphia and Chambersburgh twice a week.

"The proprietors being determined that their conduct shall be such as to merit support in their line.

"JOHN TOMLINSON & CO.

" July 3rd, 1804."

"PHILADELPHIA AND PITTSBURGH MAIL STAGES.

" The Proprietors

"With pleasure now inform the public that they run their line of stages twice in the week to and from the above places.

"They leave John Tomlinson's Spread Eagle, Market-street, Philadelphia, every Tuesday and Friday morning, at 4 o'clock, and Thomas

Ferry's Fountain Inn, Water-street, Pittsburgh, every Wednesday and Saturday morning, perform the trip in seven days. Fare each passenger 20 dollars; 14 lbs. of baggage free; extra baggage to pay 12½ cents per lb. This line runs through Lancaster, Elizabeth Town, Middle Town, Harrisburgh, Carlisle, Shippensburgh, Chambersburgh, McConnell's-town, Bedford, Sommerset, Greensburgh, &c.

"As usual they continue to run their line of Stages in conjunction with Mr. Scott, from Philadelphia, to the City of Washington, *via* Lancaster, Columbia, York, Hanover, Petersburgh, Frederick Town, &c. three times a week, Summer establishment, and twice a week in winter. Also their daily Stages from Philadelphia and Lancaster continue, as heretofore. All baggage transported by any of the above lines of Stages is to be and remain at the risque of the owner. The Proprietors of the above lines respectfully thank the public for their past favours : Would be glad they would increase them ; and they will pledge themselves, neither expence in reason, or attention, shall not be wanting on their part to make their several lines respectable.

"JOHN TOMLINSON & Co.

"Nov. 9th, 1804."

PIONEER MAIL-ROUTES AND POST-OFFICES—EARLY MAIL-ROUTES AND POST-OFFICES—TRANSMISSION OF MONEY THROUGH MAILS AND OTHERWISE.

The pioneer post-office was established in this State under an act of Assembly, November 27, 1700,—viz. :

"AN ACT FOR ERECTING AND ESTABLISHING A POST OFFICE.

"*Whereas*, The King and the late Queen Mary, by their royal letters patent under the great seal of England, bearing date the seventeenth of February, which was in the year one thousand and six hundred and ninety-and-one, did grant to Thomas Neal, Esquire, his executors, administrators and assigns, full power and authority to erect, settle and establish within the King's colonies and plantations in America, one or more office or offices for receiving and dispatching of letters and packets by post, and to receive, send and deliver the same, under such rates and sums of money as shall be agreeable to the rates established by act of parliament in England, or as the planters and others should agree to give on the first settlement, to have, hold and enjoy the same for a term of twenty-one years, with and under such powers, limitations and conditions as in and by the said letters patent may more fully appear ;

"*And whereas*, The King's Postmaster-General of England, at the request, desire and nomination of the said Thomas Neale, hath deputed Andrew Hamilton, Esquire, for such time and under such conditions as in his deputation is for that purpose mentioned, to govern and manage the said General Post Office for and throughout all the King's plantations and colonies in the main land or continent of America and the islands adjacent thereto, and in and by the said deputation may more fully appear:

"*And whereas*, The said Andrew Hamilton hath, by and with the good liking and approbation of the Postmaster General of England, made application to the proprietary and governor of this province and territories and freemen thereof convened in general assembly, that they would ascertain and establish such rates and sums of money upon letters and packets going by post as may be an effectual encouragement for carrying on and maintaining a general post, and the proprietary and governor and freemen in general assembly met, considering that the maintaining of mutual and speedy correspondencies is very beneficial to the King and his subjects, and a great encouragement to the trade, and that the same is best carried on and managed by public post, as well as for the preventing of inconveniences which heretofore have happened for want thereof, as for a certain, safe and speedy dispatch, carrying and recarrying of all letters and packets of letters by post to and from all parts and places within the continent of America and several parts of Europe, and that the well ordering thereof is matter of general concernment and of great advantage, and being willing to encourage such a public benefit:

"(SECTION 1.) *Have therefore enacted, and be it enacted by the said Proprietary and Governor of this Province and Territories, by and with the advice and consent of the Freemen thereof in General Assembly met, and by the authority of the same*, That there be from henceforth one general letter office erected and established within the town of Philadelphia, from whence all letters and packets whatsoever may be with speed and expedition sent into any part of the neighboring colonies and plantations on the mainland and continent of America, or into any other of the King's kingdoms or dominions, or unto any kingdom or country beyond the seas; at which said office all returns and answers may likewise be received, etc., etc."

The pioneer mail-route through this wilderness was over the old State Road; it was established in 1805. It was carried on horseback from Bellefonte to Meadville. The route was over the State Road to what is now the Clarion line; from there over a new road to the Allegheny River or Parker's Ferry, now Parker's City; up the river to Franklin, and from there to Meadville. The pioneer contractor's name was James Randolph, from Meadville. The next contractor was Hamilton, from Bellefonte; then by Benjamin Haitshour and others, until the turnpike was completed; then the first stage contract was taken by Clark, of Perry County. He sent on his coaches by John O'Neal, and from that time until the present the mail has been carried through this county;

and in 1812 we got our news from a Meadville paper, edited by Thomas Atkinson, called the *Crawford Weekly Messenger*. The nearest post-office west was Franklin, and east was Curwinsville. All papers that came through the county were carried outside the mail and delivered by the mail-carrier. Our nearest post-office south was at Kittanning, Armstrong County, and when any one in the neighborhood would go there they would bring the news for all and distribute the same.

In 1815 the United States had three thousand post-offices. The postage for a single letter, composed of one piece of paper, under forty miles, eight cents; over forty and under ninety miles, ten cents; under one hundred and fifty miles, twelve and a half cents; under three hundred miles, seventeen cents; under five hundred miles, twenty cents; over five hundred miles, twenty-five cents. The law was remodelled in 1816 and continued until 1845, as follows,—viz.: Letters thirty miles, six and a quarter cents; over thirty and under eighty miles, ten cents; over eighty and under one hundred and fifty miles, twelve and a half cents; over one hundred and fifty and under four hundred miles, eighteen and three-quarter cents; over four hundred miles, twenty-five cents. If the letter weighed an ounce, four times these rates were charged. Newspaper rates, in the State or under one hundred miles, one cent; over one hundred miles or out of the State, one and one-half cents. Periodicals, from one and one-half to two, four, and six cents. A portion of the records of the postmaster-general's office at Washington were destroyed by fire in the year 1836; but it has been ascertained that an advertisement was issued May 20, 1814, for once-a-week service on route No. 51, Bellefonte to Franklin, Pennsylvania, from January 1, 1815, to December 31, 1817, Jefferson Court-House being mentioned as an intermediate point; that on May 26, 1817, an advertisement was issued for service between the same points from January 1, 1818, to December 31, 1819; and on May 26, 1819, service as above was again advertised from January 1, 1820, to December 31, 1823; the service during these years connecting at Franklin with another route to Meadville.

Owing to the incompleteness of the records of the office at Washington, for the reason above stated, the names of all the contractors prior to 1824 cannot be given; but under advertisement of June 10, 1823, for once-a-week service on route 158, Bellefonte to Meadville, from January 1, 1824, to December 31, 1827, contract was made with Messrs. Hayes and Bennett, of Franklin, Pennsylvania, at the rate of sixteen hundred dollars per annum.

From the best information at hand, it appears that a post-office was established at Port Barnett, Pennsylvania, January 4, 1826, the name changed to Brookville, September 10, 1830; that from the date of the establishment of the post-office to December 31, 1839, the office was supplied by star route from Bellefonte to Meadville, Pennsylvania, Messrs. Bennett and Hayes being the contractors to December 31, 1831, Messrs. J. and B. Bennett to December 31, 1835, and Mr. Benjamin Bennett to December 31, 1839.

From January 1, 1840, Brookville was supplied by route from Curwinsville to Meadville, Pennsylvania (the service having been divided on Curwinsville, the eastern route being from Lewistown *via* Bellefonte and other offices to Curwinsville), Mr. Jesse Rupp being the contractor to June 30, 1844, and Mr. John Wightman to June 30, 1848.

Prior to 1826, or the completion of the turnpike, there was no post-office in this wilderness. Not until the county had been organized for twenty-two and the pioneers had been here for twenty-five years was a post-office created. The second mail-route in this county commenced at Kittanning, Pennsylvania, and ended in Olean, New York. The route was one hundred and ten miles long. It was established in 1826. Roswell P. Alford, of Wellsville, Ohio, contractor and proprietor. The mail was to be carried through once a week, and this was done on horseback, and the pay for this service was four hundred dollars a year. The following-named post-offices were created in this county to be supplied by the carrier on this route:

Port Barnett, Pine Creek township, January 4, 1826; Joseph Barnett, postmaster.

Montmorenci, Ridgeway township, February 14, 1826; Reuben A. Aylesworth, postmaster.

Punxsutawney, Young township, February 14, 1826; Charles R. Barclay, postmaster.

Hellen, Ridgeway township, April, 1828; Philetus Clarke, postmaster.

Brockwayville, Pine Creek township, April 13, 1829, Alonzo Brockway, postmaster.

From the information at hand it appears that an advertisement was issued in the year of 1825 for proposals carrying the mails on star route No. 79, from Bellefonte, by Karthaus, Bennett's Creek, Rockaway, Gillett's, and Scull's, to Smithport, Pennsylvania, once in two weeks, from January 1, 1826, to December 31, 1827; and that in 1827 an advertisement was issued for service on route No. 219, from Bellefonte, by Karthaus, Fox, Bennett's Branch, Ridgeway, Gillett's, Scull's, Montmorenci, Sergeant, and Smithport, Pennsylvania, to Olean, New York, once a week, from January 1, 1828, to December 31, 1831.

There is no record showing the contractors during the above terms.

In the year 1831 an advertisement was issued for star route No. 1127, from Bellefonte, by Milesburg, Karthaus, Bennett's Branch, Fox, Kerseys, Ridgeway, Montmorenci, Clermontville, Smithport, Allegheny Bridge, Pennsylvania, and Mill Grove, New York, to Olean, New York, once a week, from January 1, 1832, to December 31, 1835, and contract

PIONEER HISTORY OF JEFFERSON COUNTY, PENNA.

was awarded to Mr. James L. Gillis, of Montmorenci, with pay at the rate of six hundred and seventy-four dollars per annum.

In 1835 an advertisement was issued for service on route No. 1206, from Bellefonte, by Milesburg, Karthaus, Bennett's Branch, Caledonia, Fox, Kersey, Ridgeway, Williamsville, Clermontville, Smithport, Farmers Valley, Allegheny Bridge, Pennsylvania, and Mill Grove, New York, to Olean, New York, once a week, from January 1, 1836, to December 31, 1839, and contract was awarded to Mr. Bernard Duffey (address not given) at six hundred and twenty-eight dollars per annum.

In 1839 an advertisement was issued for service on route No. 1593, from Bellefonte, by Milesburg, Karthaus, Caledonia, Fox, Kersey, Ridgeway, Williamsville, Clermontville, Smithport, Farmers Valley, Allegheny Bridge, Pennsylvania, and Mill Grove, New York, to Olean, New York, once a week between Bellefonte and Smithport, and twice a week the residue of route, from January 1, 1840, to June 30, 1844, and contract was awarded to Mr. Gideon Ions (address not given) at eight hundred and forty-five dollars per annum.

EARLY POSTMASTERS, WHEN APPOINTED.

Brookville.—Jared B. Evans, September 30, 1830; Cephas J. Dunham, March 30, 1833; William Rodgers, January 19, 1835; John Dougherty, August 18, 1840; Samuel H. Lucas, June 25, 1841.

Brockwayville.—Dr. Asaph M. Clarke, March 14, 1838.

Clarion, now Corsica.—John McAnulty, February 8, 1833; John J. Y. Thompson, November 29, 1843.

Cool Spring.—James Gray, April 17, 1838.

Heathville.—Elijah Heath, September 24, 1841.

Montmorenci.—Jesse Morgan, March 13, 1828; James L. Gillis, April 7, 1828.

Punxsutawney.—John W. Jenks, December 15, 1828; David Barclay, November 2, 1830; Charles R. Barclay, December 21, 1831; John Hunt, October 17, 1837; James McConaughey, February 11, 1839; John R. Rees, December 29, 1843.

Prospect Hill.—Tilton Reynolds, May 18, 1842.

Summerville.—David Losh, February 14, 1839; Geo. Richards, October 4, 1839; Samuel B. Taylor, October 20, 1840; James Gardner, October 4, 1841; Ira Baldwin, January 12, 1843.

Warsaw.—Thos. McCormick, August 15, 1836; David McCormick, January 17, 1838; Moses B. St. John, May 12, 1839.

Whitesville.—John Keim, December 14, 1835.

Like every other business in those days, the postmaster trusted his patrons, as the following advertisement exhibits,—viz. :

"All persons indebted to C. J. Dunham for postage on letters or newspapers are notified to call and pay off their bills to James M. Steedman, or they may look for John Smith, as no longer indulgence can or will be given.

"February 18, 1834."

Barter was taken in exchange for postage. In those days uncalled-for letters were advertised in the papers. The pioneer advertisement of letters was in the *Philadelphia Gazette*, March 26, 1783.

In the thirties distance governed the postage on letters up to four hundred miles and more. The price of such a letter was twenty-five cents. The postmaster, who was also a merchant, took produce for letters the same as for goods, and for postage on such a letter as named would receive two bushels of oats, two bushels of potatoes, four pounds of butter, or five dozen eggs. To pay the postage on thirty-two letters such as named the farmer would have to sell a good cow. "In early times it was death by the law to rob the United States mails."

In the pioneer days, or previous to about 1860, there was no bank in Jefferson County. There was no way to transmit funds except sending them with a direct messenger or by some neighbor who had business in the locality where you desired to send your money. An adroit way was to secure a ten-, fifty-, or one-hundred-dollar bill, cut it in two, send the first half in a letter, wait for a reply, and then enclose the other half in a letter also. The party receiving the halves could paste them together. The pioneer merchants when going to Philadelphia for goods put their silver Spanish dollars in belts in undershirts and on other parts of their person, wherever they thought it could be best concealed. In this way on horseback they made journeys. Every horseback rider (tourist) carried a pair of leather saddle-bags.

In the United States on the 1st of July, 1837, the post roads were about 118,264 miles in extent, and the annual transportation of the mails was at the rate of 27,578,620 miles,—viz.:

On horseback and in sulkies, 8,291,504; in stages, 17,408,820; in steamboats and railroad cars, 1,878,297.

The number of post-offices in the United States on the 1st of July, 1835, was 10,770; on the 1st of July, 1836, it was 11,091; and on the 1st of December, 1837, 11,100.

In the year 1837 the postmaster-general recommended revision of the present rates of postage of about twenty per cent., to take effect on the 1st of July next. To this end he suggested the following letter postage:

75 miles and under	5 cents.
150 miles and over 75 miles	10 "
300 miles and over 150 miles	15 "
600 miles and over 300 miles	20 "
Over 600 miles	25 "

PIONEER HISTORY OF JEFFERSON COUNTY, PENNA.

Postage stamps were invented by James Chalmers, an Englishman, and first used May 6, 1840, in London.

The first issue of the United States stamps took place in 1845, but the postmasters of several places had issued stamps for their own convenience a few years before this. These "Postmasters'," or provisional stamps, of course, were not good for postage after the government issue took place.

The first stamp sold of this issue was bought by the Hon. Henry Shaw. This issue consisted of but two denominations, the five- and ten-cent ones, and were unperforated, as were the stamps of the next series, issued in 1851–56.

The pioneer post-office was established in this State under an act of Assembly, November 27, 1700.

CHAPTER XX.

PIONEER ROADS IN PROVISIONAL JEFFERSON COUNTY FROM 1808 TO 1830.

ABSTRACT OF INDIANA RECORDS.*

PIONEER ROAD.

"The petition of a number of citizens of Jefferson County and parts adjacent was presented to Court and read, praying for the view of a road from Brady's mill,† on Little Mahoning Creek, to Sandy Lick Creek, in Jefferson County, where the State Road crosses the same. Whereupon the Court did appoint Samuel Lucas, John Jones, Moses Knapp, Samuel Scott, John Park, and John Wier to view and make report to next Court. September sessions, 1808, report filed."

There is no report of the viewers on record, nor is the report in the file with the old papers.

SEPTEMBER SESSIONS, A.D. 1809.

"The petition of a number of the inhabitants of Jefferson County was presented to Court and read, praying for a view of a road from a bridge at the end of Adam Vasbinder's lane to Samuel Scott's mills on Sandy Lick Creek. Whereupon the Court did appoint William Vasbinder, Moses Knapp, Ludwick Long, Samuel Scott, Adam Vasbinder, and John Taylor to view and make report to next Court. Order issued. Distance, 2½ miles and 53 perches."

---

* By J. N. Banks, Esq., Indiana, Pennsylvania.
† Indiana County.

PIONEER HISTORY OF JEFFERSON COUNTY, PENNA.

MARCH SESSIONS, 1811.

"The petition of the inhabitants of Jefferson County was presented to Court and read, setting forth that they labored under great inconveniences from the want of a public road from the settlement in Jefferson County to the settlement in Mahoning township, Indiana County, to begin near Moses Knapp's mill, on the State Road, to Big Mahoning Creek, near John Bell's. Whereupon the Court did appoint John Taylor, John Bell, Thomas Lucas, Moses Knapp, John Matson, and John Jones to view and make report to next Court. Order issued. Distance, 15 miles and 95 perches; 20 feet wide."

"The petition of a number of the inhabitants of the county of Indiana and county district of Jefferson was presented to Court and read, setting forth that they labor under great inconvenience from want of a public road from Puxsutawney, to intersect the road leading from Brady's mills to the mouth of Anderson's Creek, at or near Lucas's camp. Whereupon the Court appointed John W. Jenks, Zephaniah Weakland, John Bell, Esq., Samuel Bell, Esq., Peter Dilts, and Moses Crawford to view the ground over which the proposed road is petitioned for and to to make return next sessions. Approved April 12, 1820. Distance, 7½ miles and 34 perches."

"The petition of the inhabitants of Perry township, in Jefferson County, and also of Mahoning township, in Indiana County, was presented to Court and read, setting forth that they labor under great inconvenience from the want of a public road from the four-mile tree, upon a road leading from John Bell's, Esq., in Jefferson County, to David Lawson's, in Armstrong County; from thence to intersect the road leading from Jacob Knave's to James Ewing's mill, at or near the north end of the farm of Joshua Lewis. Whereupon the Court appointed James Ewing, William Dilts, James McComb, William Davis, Samuel Bell, Esq., and David Cochran to view the ground over which said road is contemplated to be made and make report to next Court. Distance, 7½ miles and 26 perches; 25 feet wide. Approved March 29, 1820."

"The petition of a number of the inhabitants of Pine Creek township, in Jefferson County, was presented to Court and read, setting forth that they labor under great inconveniences from the want of a public road from the county line of Armstrong County, to which place there is a road leading out near William King's; from thence to the town of Troy, which is about a mile. Whereupon it is considered by the Court and ordered that Salmon Fuller, John Welch, John Lucas, James Shields, James Clemons, and Peter Bartle do view the ground over which the proposed road is petitioned for and make report to next Court. Distance, 253 perches. Approved December 28, 1820."

"The petition of a number of the inhabitants of Pine Creek township was presented to Court and read, setting forth that they labor under great inconvenience for the want of a road or cart-way from the eighty-mile post near Alexander Power's on the State Road, to intersect the road leading to Indiana at or near Little Sandy Creek, and praying the Court to appoint viewers to view and lay out the same. Whereupon the Court appointed John Bell, John Matson, Archibald Hadden, John Bartle, Joseph McCullough, and Robert Anderson to view the ground over which the said road is contemplated to be made and make report to next Court. Distance, 9 miles and 63 perches. December 28, 1820, order of view approved."

"The petition of a number of the inhabitants of Perry township, in Jefferson County, was presented to Court and read, setting forth that they labor under great inconvenience from the want of a public road from Punxsutawney, to intersect the road leading from Indiana to Barnett's, at or near John Bell's, Esq. Whereupon the Court appointed John Bell, Esq., Archibald Hadden, Michael Lantz, Hugh McKee, Jacob Hoover, and William P. Brady to view the ground over which the proposed road is contemplated to be made and make report to next Court. Distance, 6 miles and 120 perches. Approved December 28, 1820."

"The petition of a number of the inhabitants of the counties of Indiana and Jefferson was presented to the Court and read, setting forth that they labor under great inconvenience for the want of a road from the settlement on the Indiana and Susquehanna road to Punxsutawney and Barclay's mill, conveniently at the northeast corner of Abraham Wilcock's lots, or near it, to intersect the road from Punxsutawney Leasure's camp, at or near where said road crosses Canoe Creek. Whereupon it is considered and ordered by the Court that Moses Crawford, John Park, Robert Hamilton, John Jamison, William Hendricks, and James Work do view the ground over which the proposed road is contemplated to be made, and if they or any four of these actual viewers agree that there is occasion for said road, they shall make report to next Court.

"June 25, 1822, report of viewers approved and ordered to be opened.

"No distance is given in the return of viewers."

SUMMARY OF THE PRINCIPAL ROADS AND COUNTY BRIDGES FROM 1830 TO 1840.

DECEMBER SESSIONS, 1830.

Petition No. 1.—Petition of the commissioners of Jefferson County for a bridge over Sandy Lick Creek where public highway to Indiana crosses said creek in the township of Pine Creek in said county, etc.

December 7, 1830, the Court appointed Joseph Barnett, William Robinson, David Butler, Samuel Jones, John Christy, and Joseph Potter to view the same and report according to law.

The contract for this bridge was made August 11, 1829. The commissioners were Thomas McKee and Thomas Lucas. The contractors, William Morrison and William Kelso. Witnesses to agreement, Andrew Barnett and John McGhee. Consideration, $320, to be paid as follows, —viz.: to give them now in hand the subscription of $75, and a draft on the supervisors of Pine Creek township for $50, and the remainder, $195, in county orders when completed.

The bridge was 16 feet wide, with stone abutments 75 feet apart, sufficiently strong to support roofing, and to be finished in 113 days.

Petition No. 3.—Road from Barclay & Jenks's mill to Brookville.

December 7, 1830. Viewers: James Winslow, Charles G. Gaskill, William Maxwell, Reuben Hickox, Alexander Jordan, and John Hess. Confirmed September session, 1831.

Petition No. 2.—Road from Jacob Hoover's mill to intersect the road leading from Barclay & Jenks's mill to the Jefferson road through Gibson's clearing.

Viewers: James Winslow, Obed Morris, Stephen Lewis, Reuben Hickox, John Hess, and Alfred Carey. Read and confirmed and ordered to be opened 35 feet wide, unless where digging and bridging is necessary. December 13, 1831.

Petition No. 3.—Road from Brookville to David Hamilton's on the Indiana county line.

February 8, 1831. Viewers: David Postlethwait, Archibald Haddon, William Newcomb, John Christy, John Shields, and John Barnett. September 7, 1831, read and confirmed.

Petition No. 4.—Road from William McKee's on the turnpike to James Linn's improvement on the Olean road.

February 8, 1831. Viewers: Christopher Barr, Jared B. Evans, Thomas Lucas, Esq., Thomas Robinson, Samuel Knapp, and William Vasbinder. Read and confirmed. December 13, 1832, ordered to be opened.

Report No. 5.—Of a road from Brookville to Matson's mill.

Viewers report in favor of same February 7, 1831: Thomas Robinson, R. R. Scott, Samuel Hughey, William Vasbinder, Joseph Clements. Confirmed by the Court and ordered to be opened 25 feet wide. May 10, 1831.

MAY SESSIONS, 1831.

Petition No. 1.—For a road from Moses Knapp's mill to intersect the Sandy road at or near W. Godfrey's.

Viewers: James Corbett, Esq., Isaac McElvane, Nathan Carrier, Samuel Kennedy, James Hall, and Daniel Elgin. Reported. December 13, 1831, approved and ordered to be opened.

PIONEER HISTORY OF JEFFERSON COUNTY, PENNA.

Petition No. 4.—For a road from the thirty-fourth mile-stone on the Susquehanna and Waterford turnpike road to or near the house of Joseph McCullough.

Viewers: Peter Sutton, Thomas Lucas, Esq., A. Barnett, John Lattimer, David Butler, and James Stewart. May 10, 1831. February 8, 1832, read and approved.

Petition No. 5.—For a road from Troy to intersect the Olean road at John McAnulty's.

Viewers: John Shields, Thomas Robinson, Thomas Lacy, Alonzo Baldwin, John Shoemaker, and Hiram Carrier. May 9, 1831. Read *ni si* February 8, 1832.

MAY SESSIONS, 1832.

Petition No. 1.—For a road from Squire McCullough's shop to David Butler's.

Viewers: Andrew Barnett, Joseph McCullough, Esq., David Butler, Jacob Vasbinder, Samuel Jones, and John Lattimer. December 12, 1832. Read and approved *ni si*.

Report No. 7.—Of a road from Shields's Lane to the road running along Red Bank Creek.

Viewers report in favor of road January 31, 1833: William B. Kennedy, Thomas Robinson, Isaac McElvane, Darius Carrier. Confirmed May 11, 1833.

MAY SESSIONS, 1833.

Petition No. 2.—For a road from Shoemaker's to intersect the road from Hance Robinson's to Troy.

Viewers: John Milliron, Samuel Milliron, Isaac McElvane, John J. Y. Thompson, Hulet Smith, and Darius Carrier. December 12, 1833, approved.

DECEMBER SESSIONS, 1833.

Petition No. 2.—For a road from Thomas Barr's on the Olean road to the Union School-House.

Viewers: J. J. Y. Thompson, J. W. Monks, John Barnett, John Shields, Samuel Jones, and Israel Gray. May 13, 1834, approved.

FEBRUARY SESSIONS, 1834.

Petition No. 1.—For a road from Port Barnett on the Indiana road to the Ceres road at or near Punxsutawney.

Viewers: John Long, John J. Y. Thompson, James M. Steedman, George Gray, David Henry, and Stephen Lewis. February 12, 1834. September 11, read *ni si*. January 12, 1847, ordered to be opened.

Petition No. 2.—For a road from a public road leading from Brookville to Kittanning at the county line to McKinstry's saw-mill near the mill of John Robinson.

PIONEER HISTORY OF JEFFERSON COUNTY, PENNA.

Viewers: John J. Y. Thompson, Euphrastus Carrier, Aaron Fuller, John Nolf, Sr., William Ferguson, and John Shoemaker. February 12, 1834. December 13, 1843, approved and ordered to be opened 50 feet wide.

MAY SESSIONS, 1834.

Petition No. 1.—For a road from Israel Gray's fulling-mill and carding-machine to a point at or near where the Olean road crosses Little Mill Creek.

Viewers: William B. Kennedy, Israel Gray, John Monks, Samuel McGill, Rev. William Kennedy, and William Steel. September 11, 1834. June 11, 1835, ordered to be opened 20 feet wide.

Petition No. 2.—For a road from the bridge over Mill Creek to the house of William McCullough in Pine Creek township.

Viewers: John J. Y. Thompson, Henry Keys, Frederick Heterick, William Cooper, James Kyle, and Michael Long. September 11, 1834. Opening order issued October 23, 1835, to be 20 feet wide.

Report No. 3.—Of a road from Ball's mill on Tionesta to the Hepler Camp road near the four-mile tree.

Viewers report in favor of road November 15, 1834: Cyrus Blood, David Reynolds, William Armstrong, Trumble Hunt, and John Hunt. Opening order issued October 16, 1835.

MAY SESSIONS, 1835.

Petition No. 1.—For a road from Robert P. Barr's on the turnpike to Andrew Vasbinder's improvement on the North Fork.

Viewers: Hugh Brady, William B. Kennedy, Andrew Barnett, Frederick Heterick, William Long, and Michael Long. December 16, 1836. Read and ordered to be opened 50 feet wide.

Petition No. 6.—For a bridge across Red Bank Creek where the Brookville and Hamilton road crosses.

Viewers: John Dougherty, John Matson, Sr., James K. Huffman, Daniel Coder, Robert Morrison, and John Philliber. February 13, 1836. Viewers report in favor, March 8, 1836.

Petition No. 7.—For a bridge on Big Mahoning.

Viewers: Thomas Kerr, James E. Cooper, Daniel Henneigh, Christian Reischel, John Drum, and James W. Bell. February 13, 1836. August 20, 1836, report in favor and county pay $180.

Report No. 10.—Of a road from John Hoover's mill to intersect the Ceres road at or near Daniel Graffius's, Jr.

Viewers report in favor of road February 4, 1836: James H. Bell, Nathaniel Tindall, John Hoover (miller), Samuel Bowers, James E. Cooper. May term approved.

Petition No. 2.—For a road from James Ross's to intersect the Brockway road at or near S. Tibbetts's.

PIONEER HISTORY OF JEFFERSON COUNTY, PENNA.

Viewers: Frederick Heterick, Paul Vandevort, William Cooper, James Smith, John McLaughlin, and Jared B. Evans.

Petition No. 3.—For a road from the tan-yard of John W. Jenks in Punxsutawney to the saw-mill of Wm. Campbell.

Viewers: Thomas Kerr, James E. Cooper, Andrew Bowers, James Winslow, John Ham, and John Hunt. Approved May 10, 1836.

Report No. 8.—Of a road from the west end of Morrison's Lane to the west end of John Kennedy's.

Viewers report in favor of road (no date) 1835: John J. Y. Thompson, Moses Knapp, Nathan Carrier, John Love, Sr., Wallace Bratton. May 10, 1836, read and confirmed.

SEPTEMBER SESSIONS, 1836.

Petition No. 2.—For a road from Vasbinder's improvement to Frederick Heterick's.

Viewers: William Kennedy, Jr., Frederick Heterick, Michael Long, James Moorhead, Hugh Brady, Esq., and Jesse Clark. May 10, 1836. December 17, 1836, read and confirmed.

Petition No. 3.—For a road from Mill Creek road near John Wilson's to Maize's Gap on the Clarion River.

Viewers: William Armstrong, Nathan Phipps, Thos. Callin, Henry M. Clark, Daniel Elgin, and George Catz. September 16, 1836. May 10, 1837, read and approved.

Petition No. 6.—For a road from Ball's mill on Tionesta Creek to intersect the Warren and Hepler Camp road near the four-mile tree.

Viewers: Cyrus Blood, William Armstrong, Trumble Hunt, Thomas Maize, John Hunt, and David Reynolds.

DECEMBER SESSIONS, 1836.

Petition No. 1.—For a road from Jacob Smith's to intersect the Ceres road at or near John Rhoads's.

Viewers: David Kerr, John Hoover (miller), John Rhoads, Sr., John Pifer, Sr., John Bouthart, and Nathaniel Tindall. December 16, 1836.

Petition No. 2.—For a road from the house of James Smith to intersect the Ceres road at or near the farm of Wm. Smith.

Viewers: Isaac Packer, John Fuller, Andrew Barnett, John Matson, Sr., Henry Vasbinder, John J. Y. Thompson. December 16, 1836. October 14, 1837, viewers report in favor of road. May 16, 1838, confirmed.

FEBRUARY SESSIONS, 1837.

Petition No. 1.—For a road from Armstrong & Reynolds's mill at the mouth of Maple Creek to Thomas Mechan's farm on the line of Jefferson and Venango.

Viewers: John H. Maize, Nathan Phipps, John Cook, James Aharrah,

PIONEER HISTORY OF JEFFERSON COUNTY, PENNA.

George Armstrong, and Joseph Reynolds. February 14, 1837. July 24, 1837, viewers report in favor of road. September 15, 1837, read and confirmed *ni si*.

Petition No. 2.—For a road from the public road at or near David Milliron's to intersect the Troy road at or near Benjamin Shaffer's.

Viewers: John Robinson, John Bell, Esq., James Corbett, Wm. Newcomb, David Postlethwait, and John Alcorn. February 17, 1837.

MAY SESSIONS, 1837.

Petition No. 1—For a road from Daniel Elgin's to the turnpike near the Widow Mills's.

Viewers: Thomas Hall, John Monks, John J. Y. Thompson, Thomas Arthurs, John Barnett, and Samuel Davidson. May 10, 1837. Confirmed September 15, 1837.

Petition No. 2.—For a road from the road from Whitesville to Punxsutawney, one-half mile east of Whitesville, to intersect the road from Hamilton's to Brookville near Henry Philliber's.

Viewers: John Bell, Esq., William Newcomb, Wm. Stunkard, John J. Y. Thompson, Wm. Johnston, and Daniel Postlethwait. May 10, 1837. September 15, 1837, confirmed *ni si*. Order issued December 23, 1837, for opening to John C. Ferguson, and to be paid by him.

Petition No. 3.—For a road from the Smethport and Milesburg turnpike where it crosses Clarion River to the mouth of Spring Creek.

Viewers: Henry Kerns, Caleb Dill, Lyman Wilmarth, George Pelton, John Liram, and Gould Richards. May 10, 1837. September 15, 1837, read and confirmed *ni si*.

Petition No. 5.—For a road from John Bowers's to James H. Bell's grist-mill.

Viewers: Andrew Bowers, Joseph W. Winslow, James Winslow, James E. Cooper, James Hunter, and John Grube. May 10, 1837. September 15, 1837, read and confirmed *ni si*. February 10, 1845, on the application of George R. Barrett, deputy attorney-general, the Court order and direct that the road be opened 40 feet wide.

SEPTEMBER SESSIONS, 1837.

Petition No. 2.—For a road from David Dennison's to the seventy-first mile-stone.

Viewers: James Ross, Joseph McAfee, Henry Keys, Henry McIntosh, James M. Brockway, and A. Sibley. Confirmed May 16, 1838.

Petition No. 10.—For a bridge on Mahoning Creek near Charles C. Gaskill's.

Viewers: David Henneigh, John Hutchison, John Drum, John Grube, Samuel Steffy, and Philip Bowers to view and report on same. September 1837. The county builds this bridge. John Hutchison, foreman. The Court approve the finding of the grand jury and direct the within-named bridge to be recorded as a county bridge. December 13, 1837.

DECEMBER SESSIONS, 1837.

Petition No. 2.—For a road from the forks of Jones's Run to intersect the Olean road about one mile east of Mr. Gorden's near the Black Swamp.

Viewers: Joseph Hughes, John Barnett, John Wilson, Samuel Hughes, William Mendenhall, and John J. Y. Thompson. December 13. December 18, 1840, confirmed. Order to open, April 24, 1841.

Petition No. 3.—For a road from Thomas Wilkins's to Ebenezer Carr's.

Viewers: Samuel Clark, Thomas Wilkins, John Long, John J. Y. Thompson, Samuel McQuiston, and Daniel Chistiter. December 12, 1837. Read and confirmed May 16, 1838.

Petition No. 6.—For a bridge across Red Bank Creek at or near Carrier's mill.

Viewers: David Henry, John Lattimer, James Matson, John Smith, John Wynkoop, and Job McCreight. December 12, 1837. Approved by the grand jury, and the county to assist in building the same. February 16, 1838.

FEBRUARY SESSIONS, 1838.

Report No. 3.—Of a road from Curry's lot to John Bell's in Perry.

Viewers report in favor of road February 9, 1838: John Hutchison, James W. Bell, Samuel K. Williams, Andrew Gibson, William Haddon, William Marshall. February 16, 1838, confirmed *ni si*. May 17, 1838, confirmed.

Petition No. 1.—For a bridge across Red Bank Creek at the place where the road from Aaron Fuller's to Hance Robinson's crosses.

Viewers: Thomas Hastings, John Lucas, Robert Andrews, Isaac McElvane, Jesse Smith, and John Barnett. Approved September 12, 1838, by Court.

MAY SESSIONS, 1838.

Petition No. 1.—For a road from Benjamin Shaffer's to David Milliron's.

Viewers: Aaron Fuller, Hance Robinson, Conrad Nolf, Isaac McElvane, Thomas Gourley, and James Winslow, Esq. Read and confirmed February 16, 1839.

Petition No. 2.—For a road from Dennison's to William McConnell's.

Viewers: Henry Keys, Andrew Smith, James Moorhead, Stephen Tibbetts, James Ross, and Isaac Temple. May 17, 1838. Confirmed December 14, 1838. Ordered to be opened 50 feet wide, December 15, 1843.

PIONEER HISTORY OF JEFFERSON COUNTY, PENNA.

DECEMBER SESSIONS, 1838.

Petition No. 4.—For a road from the twentieth mile-stone on the Susquehanna and Franklin turnpike to the Sandy Lick Creek at the Irish Town path.

Viewers: William Reynolds, Samuel Rea, Henry McIntosh, Andrew Smith, Woodward Reynolds, and David Rhea. December 14, 1838. May 15, 1839, read and confirmed.

MAY SESSIONS, 1839.

Petition No. 1.—For a road from Wakefield's in Pine Creek township to the district line near Andrew McCormick's, Snyder township.

Viewers: Isaac H. Metcalf, David McCormick, John Wilson, Ira Brownson, and Elihu Clark. Approved *ni si* December 10, 1839.

Petition No. 2.—For a road from Aaron Fuller's to the Brockville and Hamilton road near Mr. Holt's.

Views: Alonzo Baldwin, John Robinson, Esq., Salmon Fuller, Jr., Joel Spyker, John Welsh, and John Shoemaker. May 14, 1839. Read and confirmed *ni si* December 13, 1839, and ordered to be opened February 10, 1840.

Petition No. 3.—For a road from Hance Robinson's mill to the Armstrong County line near the land of Hulet Smith.

Viewers: Joel Spyker, Alonzo Baldwin, Frederick Heterick, Samuel Newcomb, Hulet Smith, and Nathan Carrier. May 14, 1839. Read and confirmed *ni si* September 10, 1839. Order to open October 7, 1840.

Petition No. 4.—For a road from Daniel Elgin's in Eldred township to the mouth of Spring Creek in Ridgeway township.

Viewers: James Crow, John McLaughlin, James Moorhead, Henry Vasbinder, Jr., Peter Vasbinder, and James Fullerton. May 14, 1839. Read and confirmed *ni si* December 11, 1839.

Petition No. 6.—For a road from the borough of Brookville to the Beech Bottom on Clarion River.

Viewers: James Moorhead, John McLaughlin, William Long, Henry Vasbinder, Jr., Almond Sartwell, and William Humphreys. May 14, 1839. Read and confirmed December 13, 1839.

Petition No. 8.—For a road from the upper end of the Clearfield and Armstrong turnpike east of Punxsutawney to intersect the old State Road at or near John McHenry's.

Viewers: James Winslow, Samuel Steffy, David Barnett, Daniel Henneigh, Robert Cunningham, and Christian Reischel. May 14, 1839. Read and confirmed December 13, 1839.

SEPTEMBER SESSIONS, 1839.

Petition No. 1.—For a road from the farm of Levi G. Clover to the Olean road at or near James Cochran's.

Viewers: William Kennedy, James Summerville, Henry M. R. Clark, William Hindman, John McCracken, and John Wilson, Esq. September 11, 1839. Read *ni si* 1839. Ordered to be opened May 22, 1840.

Petition No. 8.—For a road from the twelfth mile-stone on the turnpike to intersect the road half a mile east of John McGhee's.

Viewers: John McIntosh, John Atwell, William Cooper, John McGhee, Oliver McClelland, and James Moorhead. September 11, 1839. May 12, 1840, confirmed and ordered to be opened 50 feet wide.

Report No. 9.—Of a road from the southeast corner of the Graham lot on the Punxsutawney road to intersect the turnpike at the northeast corner of Andrew Barnett's land.

Viewers report in favor of road August 23, 1839: Samuel McQuiston, Joseph Kerr, Elijah Clark, John J. Y. Thompson, John W. Baum. Petitioned for May 15, 1839. December 13, 1839, read and confirmed.

Report No. 16.—Of a bridge across the Big Mahoning Creek at the Bell's mills.

Viewers report in favor of bridge November 30, 1837: John Drum, Philip Bowers, Daniel Henneigh, John Grube, Samuel Steffy, John Hutchison. Petitioned for September, 1837. County appropriated $250 to build said bridge. David McCormick, foreman. Court concur September 11, 1839.

DECEMBER SESSIONS, 1839.

Petition No. 1.—For a road from Richards's mill on the Brookville and Beech Bottom road to intersect the Brockway road at or near the farm of Almon Sartwell.

Viewers: John McLaughlin, James K. Huffman, William Humphreys, Peter Chamberlain, Henry Vasbinder, Jr., and Thomas Drum. December 10, 1839. May 12, 1840, confirmed.

Petition No. 3.—For a road from the Hogback road near Frederick Lantz's to intersect the Brookville and Indiana road at or near T. S. Mitchell's store.

Viewers: George Bloss, David Postlethwait, Michael Lantz, Archibald Haddon, James Means, and David Lewis. Approved by Court, December 16, 1841.

Petition No. 4.—For a road from T. S. Mitchell's on the Indiana and Brookville road to intersect the road that leads from Irvin Robinson's to the Indiana County line.

Viewers: George Bloss, David Postlethwait, Michael Lantz, Archibald Haddon, James Means, and David Lewis. December 13, 1839. Confirmed December 18, 1840.

Petition No. 5.—For a road from John Quiggles's to the Big Mahoning Creek where the line between James Solesby and William Campbell crosses said creek.

PIONEER HISTORY OF JEFFERSON COUNTY, PENNA.

Viewers: James H. Bell, David Kerr, Samuel Steffy, Samuel Bowers Charles Shipman, and William Cochran. Read and confirmed February term, 1841.

Petition No. 6.—For a road from the road that has been of late made from the twentieth mile-stone to Sandy Lick Creek to the Beechwoods road, one and a quarter miles from the twentieth mile-stone road.

Viewers: Woodward Reynolds, Ramsey Potter, Henry McIntosh, Samuel Sprague, and Thomas Reynolds. December 9, 1839. Confirmed May 12, 1840.

Petition No. 7.—For a road from the Waterford turnpike one-half mile east of the twenty-fifth mile-stone to David Losh's grist-mill.

Viewers: William Reynolds, Isaac McElvane, Jacob Horm, Ramsey Potter, Woodward Reynolds, and David Rhea. December 9, 1839. Confirmed May 12, 1840.

FEBRUARY SESSIONS, 1840.

Petition No. 1.—For a road from the Brockway road at or near S. Tibbetts's to the Beehwoods road at or near James Ross's Lane.

Viewers: David Dennison, Henry McIntosh, Henry Keys, Findley McCormick, William Cooper, and Isaac Temple. February 11, 1840. Confirmed May 12, 1840.

Petitioned for to Shaw's from Ross's Lane, September, 1836. Confirmed to these points May 10, 1837.

MAY SESSIONS, 1840.

Petition No. 3.—For a road from the Brockway road at or near Peter Richards's smith-shop to the Beechwoods road at or near the top of Mill Creek Hill.

Viewers: John McLaughlin, James Ross, William Shaw, Henry Vasbinder, Jr., Henry Keys, and Milton Johnston. May 13, 1840. February 10, 1841, read and confirmed to be opened fifty feet wide.

SEPTEMBER SESSIONS, 1840.

Petition No. 5.—For a road from the Clearfield County line near Robert Dixon's to Osborne's mill.

"Viewers: John McLaughlin, John McGhee, Henry McIntosh, Henry Keys, William Reynolds, and Andrew Hunter. September 11, 1840. Read and confirmed February 10, 1841.

Report No. 9.—Of a road from the road leading from Barnett's to Punxsutawney, about one mile south of Barnett's, to the old Indiana road, near the Five-Mile Run.

Viewers report in favor of road, May 12, 1840: John McLaughlin, George L. Matthews, William Taylor, Ebenezer L. Kerr, William Wiley. September 17, 1840, read *ni si*. February 10, 1841, read and confirmed.

SUSQUEHANNA AND WATERFORD TURNPIKE—THE OLD TOLL-GATES ALONG THE ROUTE—A FULL HISTORY OF THE OLD TURNPIKE, A PART OF WHICH IS NOW MAIN STREET IN REYNOLDSVILLE.

In 1792 the first stone turnpike in the United States was chartered. It was constructed in Pennsylvania in 1794 from Lancaster to Philadelphia. In this year also began the agitation in Pennsylvania for internal improvement. An agitation that resulted in a great era of State road, canal, and turnpike construction, encouraged and assisted by the State government. From 1792 until 1832 the Legislature granted two hundred and twenty charters for turnpike alone.

These pikes were not all made, but there was completed within that time, as a result of these grants, three thousand miles of passable roads. The pioneer turnpike through our wilderness was the Susquehanna and Waterford turnpike. On February 22, 1812, a law was enacted by the Pennsylvania Legislature enabling the governor to incorporate a company to build a turnpike from the Susquehanna River, near the mouth of Anderson Creek, in Clearfield County, through Jefferson County and what is now Brookville, and through the town of Franklin and Meadville, to Waterford, in Erie County. The governor was authorized to subscribe twelve thousand dollars in shares towards building the road. Joseph Barnett and Peter Jones, of Jefferson County, and two from each of the following counties, Erie, Crawford, Mercer, Clearfield, Venango, and Philadelphia, and two from the city of Philadelphia, were appointed commissioners to receive stock. Each of the counties just named was required to take a specified number of shares, and the shares were placed at twenty-five dollars each. Jefferson County was required to take fifty shares.

The war of 1812 so depressed business in this part of the State that all work was delayed on this thoroughfare for six years. The company commenced work in 1818, and the survey was completed in October of that year. In November, 1818, the sections were offered for sale, and in November, 1822, the road was completed.

The commissioners employed John Sloan, Esq., to make the survey and grade the road. They began the survey in the spring and finished it in the fall of 1818, a distance of one hundred and four miles. The State took one-third of the stock. James Harriet, of Meadville, Pennsylvania, took the contract to build the road, and he gave it out to sub-contractors. Some took five miles, some ten, and so on. Work began in 1821, and was completed in 1824. The bridge over the Clarion River was built in 1821, by Moore, from Northumberland County; it was built with a single arch.

In March, 1821, an act was passed by the Legislature appropriating two thousand five hundred dollars for improving the road. Appointments were made in each county through which the road passed of people whose duty it was to receive the money for each county and to pay it out. Charles C. Gaskill and Carpenter Winslow represented Jefferson County.

Andrew Ellicott never surveyed or brushed out this turnpike. He was one of the commissioners for the old State Road.

Our turnpike was one hundred and twenty-six miles long. The individual subscriptions to its construction were in total fifty thousand dollars, the State aid giving one hundred and forty thousand dollars. This was up to March, 1822. The finishing of our link in November, 1824, completed and opened one continuous turnpike road from Philadelphia to Erie. Our part of this thoroughfare was called a "clay turnpike," and in that day was boasted of by the early settlers as the most convenient and easy travelling road in the United States. That, in fact, anywhere along the route over the mountain the horses could be treated to the finest water, and that anywhere along the route, too, the traveller, as well as the driver, could regale himself "with the choicest Monongahela whiskey bitters," clear as amber, sweet as musk, and smooth as oil.

"Immediately after the completion of the turnpike mile-stones were set up. They were on the right-hand side of the road as one travelled east. The stones when first erected were white, neat, square, and well finished. On each stone was inscribed, ' To S. oo miles. To F. oo miles.' Of course figures appeared on the stones where ciphers have been placed above. S. stood for Susquehanna, which is east, and F. for Franklin, which is west."

Only the commonest goods were hauled into this country over the old State Road, and in the early days of the turnpike, Oliver Gregg, with his six horses, and Joseph Morrow, with his outfit of two teams, were regularly employed for many years in carrying freight from Philadelphia to this section. It took four weeks to reach here from Philadelphia, and the charge for freight was about six dollars per hundred pounds. A man by the name of Potter in latter years drove an outfit of five roan horses. Each team had a Conestoga wagon and carried from three to four tons of goods.

THE TOLL-GATE.

With the completion of the turnpike came the toll-gate. One was erected every five or ten miles.

Gangs of men were kept busy constantly repairing the pike, and they were individually paid at these gates. The road was then kept in good condition.

"An Act to enable the Governor of this Commonwealth to incorporate a Company for making an Artificial Road, by the Best and Nearest Route, from Waterford, in the County of Erie, through Meadville and Franklin to the River Susquehanna, at or near the Mouth of Anderson's Creek, in Clearfield County.

"SECTION 13. *And be it further enacted by the authority aforesaid*, That the said company, having perfected the said road, or such part thereof, from time to time as aforesaid, and the same being examined, approved, and licensed as aforesaid, it shall and may be lawful for them to appoint such and so many toll-gatherers as they shall think proper, to collect and receive of and from all and every person and persons using the said road the tolls and rates hereinafter mentioned; and to stop any person riding, leading, or driving any horse or mule, or driving any cattle, hogs, sheep, sulkey, chair, chaise, phaeton, cart, wagon, wain, sleigh, sled, or other carriage of burden or pleasure from passing through the said gates or turnpikes until they shall have respectfully paid the same,—that is to say, for every space of five miles in length of the said road the following sum of money, and so in proportion for any greater or less distance, or for any greater or less number of hogs, sheep, or cattle, to wit: For every score of sheep, four cents; for every score of hogs, six cents; for every score of cattle, twelve cents; for every horse or mule, laden or unladen, with his rider or leader, three cents; for every sulkey, chair, chaise, with one horse and two wheels, six cents; and with two horses, nine cents; for every chair, coach, phaeton, chaise, stage-wagon, coachee, or light wagon, with two horses and four wheels, twelve cents; for either of the carriages last mentioned, with four horses, twenty cents; for every other carriage of pleasure, under whatever name it may go, the like sum, according to the number of wheels and of horses drawing the same; for every sleigh or sled, two cents for each horse drawing the same; for every cart or wagon, or other carriage of burden, the wheels of which do not in breadth exceed four inches, four cents for each horse drawing the same; for every cart or wagon, the wheels of which shall exceed in breadth four inches, and shall not exceed seven inches, three cents for each horse drawing the same; and when any such carriages as aforesaid shall be drawn by oxen or mules, in the whole or in part, two oxen shall be estimated as equal to one horse; and every ass or mule as equal to one horse, in charging the aforesaid tolls."

COMPLETION OF THE TURNPIKE.

The first stage line was established over the Waterford and Susquehanna turnpike from Bellefonte to Erie by Robert Clark, of Clark's Ferry, Pennsylvania, in November, 1824. It was called a Concord line, and at first was a tri-weekly. The first stage-coach passed through where Brookville now is about the 6th of November, 1824. In 1824 the route was completed to Philadelphia, through Harrisburg, and was a daily line.

"The arrival of the stages in old times was a much more important event than that of the railroad trains to-day. Crowds invariably gathered at the public houses where the coaches stopped to obtain the latest news, and the passengers were of decided account for the time being. Money

was so scarce that few persons could afford to patronize the stages, and those who did were looked upon as fortunate beings. A short trip on the stage was as formidable an affair as one to Chicago or Washington is now by railroad. The stage-drivers were men of considerable consequence, especially in the villages through which they passed. They were intrusted with many delicate missives and valuable packages, and seldom betrayed the confidence reposed in them. They had great skill in handling their horses, and were the admiration and envy of the boys. Talk about the modern railroad conductor, he is nothing compared with the importance of the stage-coach driver of sixty and seventy years ago

"The traffic on the turnpike began, of course, at its completion in November, 1824. It increased gradually until it reached enormous proportions. A quarter of a century after the road had been built it arrived at the zenith of its glory."

Pedlers of all kinds, on foot and in covered wagons, travelled the pike. From Crawford County came the cheese and white-fish pedler. Several people, including the hotel-men, would each buy a whole cheese.

The pioneer inns or taverns in Jefferson County along this highway were about six in number. Five of the six were built of hewed logs,— viz.: one where Reynoldsville is; the Packer Inn, near Peter Baum's; one near Campbell Run (Ghost Hollow); the William Vasbinder Inn; James Winter's tavern at Roseville; and John McAnulty's inn, kept by Alexander Powers, where Corsica is now located. The Port Barnett Inn at this time was a "frame structure," as its picture represents.

The early settlers along the pike east of Port Barnett were John and Rebecca Fuller in 1822, the Potters in 1824-25, Andrew McCreight and wife in 1832, Tilton Reynolds and wife in 1834, Valentine Smith in 1835, Woodward Reynolds in 1837, Thomas Doling, and others. These were all in what is now Winslow township. West of Port Barnett the settlers along the pike were Moses Knapp, Joseph Kaylor, E. M. Graham, Alexander Powers, John Scott, Samuel D. Kennedy, Rev. William Kennedy, John Christy, and John Monks. Lee Tipton had a store in 1835 about where Corsica is. See chapter on my early "Recollections of Brookville, Pennsylvania."

As Morrow, Gregg, and Potter carried our produce to the Lewistown market, I reproduce a market-table herewith:

LEWISTOWN MARKET, 1837.

Wheat flour per barrel	$10.00
Rye " " "	5.00
Wheat grain per bushel	1.95
Rye " " "	1.00
Corn " " "	.70
Oats " " "	.40
Potatoes " "	.31
Ham	.12
Butter	.15
Beeswax	.20
Timothy-seed per bushel	2.50
Clover- " " "	7.00
Flax- " " "	1.25

PIONEER HISTORY OF JEFFERSON COUNTY, PENNA.

"AN ACT TO AUTHORIZE THE COMMISSIONERS OF JEFFERSON COUNTY TO ALTER A CERTAIN PART OF THE SUSQUEHANNA AND WATERFORD TURNPIKE ROAD.

"SECTION 1. *Be it enacted by the Senate and House of Representatives of the Commonwealth of Pennsylvania in General Assembly met, and it is hereby enacted by the authority of the same,* That the commissioners of Jefferson County be, and they are hereby authorized and empowered to lay out and make one mile and ten perches of turnpike road through the village of Brookville in said county, said road not to exceed five degrees from a horizontal line, and to be connected with the Susquehanna and Waterford turnpike road at both ends.

"SECTION 2. *And be it further enacted by the authority aforesaid,* That as soon as the said road is finished, so much of the said Susquehanna and Waterford turnpike road as lies between the points of intersection aforesaid may be vacated; and the commissioners of said county are hereby authorized to draw their warrant on the treasurer of Jefferson County for the amount necessarily expended by them in making said road.

"SECTION 3. *And be it further enacted by the authority aforesaid,* That from and after the 1st day of April next it shall be the duty of the supervisors of the public highway in each and every township in the county of Jefferson to lay out and expend at least two-thirds of the amount of all the road taxes assessed each year in each and every township aforesaid, in opening and repairing the public highways within said township and county, on or before the 1st day of October in each and every year.

"Approved—the fourth day of April, one thousand eight hundred and thirty one.

"GEORGE WOLF."

This law authorized a change in the pike in Brookville from Jefferson Street to Main Street. The Commonwealth awarded the contract for this work to Thomas and James Hall, who completed the change.

Stage-passengers' rights were guarded as herein by legal statutes.

ACT OF MARCH 6, 1820.

"AN ACT RELATIVE TO THE OWNERS AND DRIVERS OF PUBLIC STAGES AND OTHER CARRIAGES FOR THE CONVEYANCE OF PASSENGERS, AND FOR OTHER PURPOSES.

"SECTION 1. From and after the 1st day of July next, if the driver of any public stage, mail-coach, coachee, or carriage shall leave the same with the horses attached thereto, without some suitable person to take care of such horses, or securely fastening the same, such driver, and the owner or owners, or any of them, of such stage, mail-coach, coachee, or carriage shall for every such offence forfeit and pay any sum not less than ten nor more than fifty dollars, one moiety whereof shall go to the person giving information of the commission of such offence, and the other moiety to the stock of the county where such offence shall have been committed : *Provided*, That the party aggrieved shall have a right to appeal to the next court of common pleas of the county wherein the offence was committed.

"SECTION 2. If any wagoner, carter, drayman, or driver of any stage, mail coach, coachee, or carriage shall wilfully and vexatiously obstruct or delay any person or persons travelling on the public highways of this Commonwealth, he shall for every such offence forfeit and pay the sum of twenty dollars, one-half whereof shall go to the person giving information of the commission of such offence, and the other moiety to the stock of the county where the offence shall have been committed.

"SECTION 3. The said penalties may be recovered before any alderman or justice of the peace, in the same manner as sums not above one hundred dollars are now by law recovered; and in any suit or action brought to recover the same, the informer shall be a competent witness, leaving his credibility, as in other cases, to be judged of by the proper authority determining the same. And no such suit or action shall be abated, nor a nonsuit therein ordered, on account of the names of all the owners of any such stage, mail-coach, coachee, or carriage not being embraced as defendants, but it shall be lawful to bring and sustain any such suit or action against any one or more of the said owners : *Provided*, That no such suit or action shall be brought against any person for the penalty incurred by a violation of the provisions of this act after the expiration of thirty days from the commission of the offence." *

CHAPTER XXI.

PIONEER COURT—PIONEER JUDGES—PRESIDENT AND ASSOCIATES—PIONEER BAR AND EARLY LAWYERS—MINUTES OF PIONEER SESSIONS OF COURT —DECEMBER SESSION, 1830, AND FEBRUARY SESSION, 1831—LIST OF RETAILERS OF FOREIGN MERCHANDISE IN THE COUNTY, FEBRUARY SESSIONS, 1831—EARLY CONSTABLES.

THE first legislation creating a judiciary in this State was called the provincial act of March 22, 1722. This court was styled "The Court of Quarter Sessions of the Peace and Gaol Delivery." The Orphans' Court was established in 1713. The constitution of 1776 provided for the continuance of these courts. By the constitution adopted in 1790

---

* For turnpike, see my " Recollections of Brookville."

the judicial power of the State was vested in a Supreme Court, in a Court of Oyer and Terminer and General Jail Delivery, Common Pleas, Quarter Sessions, Orphans' Court, and Register Court for each county, and for justices of the peace for boroughs and townships. The early judges were appointed by the governor.

In 1806, for the more convenient establishment of the Supreme Court, the State was made into two districts,—viz., the Eastern and Western. Jefferson County was in the Western.

By an act of the Legislature passed April 2, 1830, Jefferson County was attached to the Eighteenth Judicial District. Thomas Burnside was appointed president judge, and John W. Jenks and Elijah Heath asso-

Hon. Thomas Burnside, pioneer judge, 1830-35.

ciate judges. They were the pioneer judges of this county. The salary of an associate judge was one hundred and fifty dollars per year.

Both the president judge of a district and the associate judges for a county were appointed in this State until 1850, when the State constitution was changed to make them elective. The term of the president judge ran ten years, but the term of the associates was for five years.

In 1835, Burnside resigned and Nathaniel B. Eldred was appointed district judge. In a short time he resigned, when Alex. McCalmont was appointed and served ten years. Neither Burnside, Eldred, nor McCalmont lived in Jefferson County. The president judge's salary was sixteen hundred dollars a year and mileage.

The early associates, all of whom resided in the county, and whose service extended only until 1844, were,—viz.: William Jack, Andrew Barnett, James Winslow, and James L. Gillis.

PIONEER HISTORY OF JEFFERSON COUNTY, PENNA.

The early local or home lawyers were Hugh Brady, Cephas J. Dunham, Benjamin Bartholomew, Caleb A. Alexander, L. B. Dunham, Richard Arthurs, Elijah Heath, D. B. Jenks, Thomas Lucas, D. S. Deering, S. B. Bishop, and Jesse G. Clark. Many very eminent lawyers from adjoining counties attended our courts regularly at this period. They usually came on horseback, and brought their papers, etc., in large leather saddle-bags. Most of these foreign lawyers were very polite gentlemen, and very particular not to refuse a "drink."

The pioneer law student in the county was Lewis B. Dunham. He was admitted to the bar of the county at the September term, 1835. It may be a matter of pride to recall the fact that Benjamin Bartholomew had a son born while living in Brookville, who became distinguished as one of the great orators of the State, the Hon. Linn Bartholomew.

PIONEER SESSION—DECEMBER SESSION, 1830—HELD IN THE UPPER ROOMS OF THE OLD JAIL.

" Minutes of a Court of General Quarter Sessions of the Peace, held at Brookville, for the county of Jefferson, on Monday, the sixth day of December, 1830:

"Present, the Honorable Thomas Burnside, President, and John W. Jenks and Elijah Heath, Esquires, Judges of said Court. High Sheriff of Jefferson County, Thomas McKee. Constables, Alfred Cory, Constable of Young township, and Hulet Smith, Constable of Rose township, sworn.

"The Court order and direct that a Grand Jury of twenty-four and a Traverse Jury of thirty-six be summoned returnable to next term."

The following-named gentlemen were admitted to practise law in the several courts of Jefferson County, and were all sworn and affirmed,—to wit: Thomas Blair, Thomas White, George W. Smith, Josiah W. Smith, John Johnston, William Banks, and Hugh Brady, Esq. December 7, Robert E. Brown, Esq., admitted and sworn as an attorney of the several courts of Jefferson County.

James M. Brockway appointed constable of Ridgeway township and sworn in open court; Samuel Jones appointed constable of Pine Creek township and sworn in open court; William Hopkins appointed constable of Perry township for the present year and sworn in open court.

The following constables appeared and made their returns,—to wit: Alfred Cory, constable of Young township, and Hulet Smith, constable of Rose township.

FEBRUARY SESSIONS, 1831.

Grand jurors for February sessions, 1831. Thomas McKee, Esq., high sheriff of Jefferson County, returns his *præcipe* to him directed and the

PIONEER HISTORY OF JEFFERSON COUNTY, PENNA.

following named persons for grand jury at February sessions, 1831,—to wit:

No.	Name.	Township.
1	Andrew Barnett	Pine Creek.
2	Jacob Shaffer	Ridgeway.
3	Aaron Fuller	Rose.
4	Samuel Jordan	Perry
5	Joseph Sharp	Rose.
6	John Welsh	Rose.
7	Andrew Bowers	Young.
8	William Summerville	Rose.
9	John Christy.	
10	Archibald Hadden.	
11	Christ. Heterick.	
12	John H. Wise	Rose.
13	John Millen	Perry.
14	Henry Walborn	Ridgeway.
15	Darius Carrier	Rose.
16	John McGiffen	Rose.
17	Jacob Shillery	Young.
18	Clark Eggleston	Ridgeway.
19	Joseph Bell	Perry.
20	John Hughes	Rose.
21	Jacob Hoover	Young.
22	Robert K. Scott	Rose.
23	William Love, Sr.	Rose.
24	Thompson Barr	Rose.

CONSTABLES' RETURNS FOR FEBRUARY SESSIONS, 1831.

The following constables appeared and made their returns at February sessions, 1831,—to wit: Samuel Jones, Pine Creek township; Alfred Cory, Young township; William Hopkins, Perry township; Hulet Smith, Rose township; James Brockway, Ridgeway township.

List of retailers of foreign merchandise in the township of Rose, returned at February sessions, 1831,—to wit: William Douglass, Jared B. Evans, William Rodgers, Joseph Chambers, John Robinson, John McAnulty, Sr., Andrew Vasbinder, John Eason, William Clark.

"A list of retailers of foreign merchandise in the county of Jefferson, classified according to the act of Assembly in that case provided,—viz.: John W. Jenks, 8th class, Young township; William Douglass, 8th class, Rose township; Jared B. Evans, 8th class, Rose township; John Smith & Co., 8th class, Rose township; William Rodgers, 8th class, Rose township; Joseph Chambers, 8th class, Rose township; John Robinson, 8th class, Rose township.

"We, the undersigned Judges and Commissioners of Jefferson County, do certify the foregoing to be a correct list as returned by the several Constables, given under our hands the 9th day of February, 1831.

"JOHN W. JENKS,
ELIJAH HEATH,
Judges.
THOS. LUCAS,
ROBERT ANDREWS,
Commissioners of County."

PIONEER ADMISSIONS TO THE BAR FROM 1830 TO 1843

The names of the members of the Jefferson County bar as they have been recorded on the annals of the court in the order in which they were

Court-house and jail, 1896.

admitted. Some of these attorneys were not residents of this county, but were admitted to this bar, and practised regularly in our courts.

PIONEER HISTORY OF JEFFERSON COUNTY, PENNA.

ADMITTED AT DECEMBER TERM, 1830.

"Thomas Blair, of Kittanning ; Thomas White, of Indiana ; George W. Smith, of Butler, for ten or fifteen years was afterwards president judge of this district ; Joseph W. Smith, of Clearfield ; John Johnston, of Clearfield ; William Banks, of Indiana, practised in this court for many years ; Hugh Brady ; Robert E. Brown, of Kittanning."

FEBRUARY TERM, 1831.

"Joseph Martin ; William Watson, of Kittanning, Pennsylvania ; Joseph Buffington, of Bellefonte, practised at this bar for many years ; was appointed president judge of this district, and afterwards served as member of Congress from this district."

SEPTEMBER TERM, 1831.

"Cephas J. Dunham, of Brookville ; Ephraim Carpenter, of Indiana, came here for many years ; Lewis W. Smith, of Clearfield, came here occasionally ; Benjamin Bartholomew, resided in Brookville a number of years, and represented the district in the Legislature in 1846. He removed from Brookville to Warren, and then to Schuylkill County, where he was afterwards district attorney. Hon. Linn Bartholomew, his son, was born in Brookville."

DECEMBER TERM, 1833.

"Michael Gallagher, of Kittanning ; James McManus, of Bellefonte."

FEBRUARY TERM, 1834.

"William F. Johnston, of Kittanning, practised regularly at this bar for many years ; was afterwards governor of Pennsylvania."

MAY TERM, 1834.

"C. A. Alexander ; James Burnside, of Bellefonte."

FEBRUARY TERM, 1835.

"Michael Dan McGeehan, of Ebensburg ; General William R. Smith, from the eastern part of the State, was only here once ; removed to Dubuque, Iowa."

MAY TERM, 1835.

"Hiram Bayne, of McKean County, practised at this bar regularly for a number of years. He was engaged in the sale of lands, and was a member of the State constitutional convention of 1837."

SEPTEMBER TERM, 1835.

"Lewis B. Dunham, of Brookville, was the pioneer man admitted on examination to the Jefferson County bar, and the pioneer law student in the county. He practised here for a number of years, and then removed to the West,—Maquoketa, Iowa. Mr. Dunham did not practise his profession after he left Brookville. He represented Iowa in the State senate. Stewart Steele, of Blairsville."

DECEMBER TERM, 1835.

" Alexander McCalmont, of Franklin, practised for many years at this bar, and was president judge of the district. James Ross Snowden, of Franklin, a prominent attorney and politician, came here occasionally. Elijah Heath, of Brookville; David Barclay Jenks, of Brookville."

SEPTEMBER TERM.

" Richard Arthurs, of Brookville."

SPRING TERM, 1838.

" Jesse G. Clark."

SEPTEMBER TERM, 1839.

" John W. Howe, of Franklin, came here regularly for many years. He was a prominent attorney, and was elected member of Congress from his district. Thomas Struthers, of Warren, also came here regularly for many years."

DECEMBER TERM, 1839.

" William M. Stewart, of Indiana."

DECEMBER TERM, 1840.

" Thomas Lucas, of Brookville."

SEPTEMBER TERM, 1842.

" J. W. McCabe, of Kittanning, came here a few times."

FEBRUARY TERM, 1843.

" Carlton B. Curtis, of Warren, came here frequently; elected to the Legislature and Congress twice from the districts of which Jefferson County formed a part. Andrew Mosgrove, of Kittanning, came here occasionally."

MAY TERM, 1843.

" David S. Deering, of Brookville, read law, was admitted, and practised at this bar for several years. He now resides in Iowa."

PIONEER LEGAL CARD AND NOTICE IN "THE JEFFERSONIAN."

CEPHAS J. DUNHAM,
Attorney at Law.

OFFICE:
PICKERING STREET,
BROOKVILLE, PA.

April, 1834.

"TO THE PUBLIC.

"This is to inform the public that I employed C. A. Alexander, Esq., attorney-at-law, to conduct a suit for me, for which he agreed to take two dollars, and took my note for the same, to be paid when I collected the money, in two or three weeks, the time not exactly remembered; he kept the note and sued me on an account of three dollars for the same services, but only got judgment for two. If he has such an ambition for money the other lawyers will get my business.

"ANDREW VASTBINDER.

"BROOKVILLE, August 1, 1834."

PIONEER LAWS AND PIONEER HIGHWAYS.

Stewart H. Whitehill, Esq., of Brookville, Pennsylvania, has kindly prepared for me this summary of the pioneer laws specially enacted for Jefferson County, Pennsylvania, and for Brookville, Pennsylvania; also a summary of the pioneer laws pertaining to the townships and public highways of said county, as follows:

COUNTY.

March 26, 1804.—Jefferson County erected and boundaries named; but by the same act annexed to Westmoreland County for judicial purposes.

February 3, 1806.—Authority of commissioners of Westmoreland County and other county officers of said county extended over and within the county district of Jefferson.

February 24, 1806.—Jefferson County placed in the Western District for the Supreme Court, and the State divided into ten judicial districts, the counties of Somerset, Cambria, Indiana, Armstrong, and Westmoreland comprising the tenth.

March 10, 1806.—Jefferson County annexed to the county of Indiana, and the authority of the county commissioners and other county officers of said Indiana County to extend over and within the county of

Jefferson. It remained thus annexed to Indiana County for all purposes until 1824, and for judicial purposes until 1830.

March 31, 1806.—Jefferson County made into a separate election district, elections therein to be held at the house of "Joseph Barnett, on Sandy Lick, in said county."

March 21, 1808.—Jefferson County placed in a Senatorial District, composed of the counties of Armstrong, Indiana, and Jefferson, the return judges thereof to "meet at the house occupied by Widow Elder, in Blacklick township, Indiana County."

By the same act Jefferson County placed in a State Representative District, composed of the counties of Armstrong, Jefferson, and Indiana, the return judges of which were to meet at the house of Absalom Woodward in Armstrong County.

March 20, 1812.—Jefferson County placed in the Eleventh Congressional District, composed of the counties of Westmoreland, Armstrong, Jefferson, and Indiana.

March 14, 1814.—Authority granted for the subdivision of Jefferson County into six districts, for the election of justices of the peace.

March 8, 1815.—Jefferson County placed in the Sixteenth Senatorial District, composed of the counties of Westmoreland, Indiana, and Jefferson, the return judges thereof to meet at the house of John Kelly, in the town of Newport, in Blacklick township, Indiana County.

By the same act Jefferson County was placed in a State Representative District, along with Armstrong and Indiana Counties, the three counties being entitled to two members, and the return judges were to meet at the house of Absalom Woodward, in Indiana County.

1825.—The Milesburg and Smethport Turnpike Road Company, authorized "for the purpose of making a turnpike road from Milesburg in Centre County, past Karthaus in Clearfield County, and Smethport in McKean County, to the New York line," and Jonathan Colgrove, Paul E. Scull, John King, and Joseph Otto, of McKean County; Peter A. Karthaus, of Clearfield County; James L. Gillis, of Jefferson County; John Mitchell and Roland Curtin, of Centre County; George Vaux and Simon Gratz, of the city of Philadelphia, appointed commissioners to solicit subscriptions for said road, which passed through Ridgeway, then in the county of Jefferson. Notice of the time and place when and where books to be opened to receive subscriptions of stock to be published in the Bellefonte *Patriot* and the Lycoming *Gazette*, and one paper published in the city of Philadelphia. Upon subscription of twenty or more persons, representing six hundred or more shares of twenty dollars each, the governor to incorporate the company, which was to have power to erect and maintain toll-gates upon and across said turnpike, as will be seen by the following section of the act:

"SECTION 13.—*And be it further enacted by the authority aforesaid,*

PIONEER HISTORY OF JEFFERSON COUNTY, PENNA.

That whenever and as often as the said company shall have finished five miles or more of said road the president thereof may give notice to the governor, who shall thereupon forthwith appoint three skilful, judicious, and disinterested persons to view and examine the same and report on oath or affirmation to him whether the road is so far executed in a competent and workmanlike manner, according to the true meaning and intent of this act ; and if their report shall be in the affirmative, then the governor shall, by license under his hand and seal of the State, permit and suffer said company to erect and fix such and so many gates or turnpikes upon and across the said road as will be necessary and sufficient to collect from all persons travelling the same, otherwise than on foot, the same tolls which are hereinafter authorized and granted : *Provided*, That all persons attending funerals, military parades, or trainings or divine worship on the Sabbath-day shall at all times be exempt from the payment of any toll on said road."

1828.—"A SUPPLEMENT TO THE ACT ENTITLED 'AN ACT AUTHORIZING THE GOVERNOR TO INCORPORATE THE MILESBURG AND SMETHPORT TURNPIKE ROAD COMPANY.'

"SECTION 1. *Be it enacted by the Senate and House of Representatives of the Commonwealth of Pennsylvania in General Assembly met, and it is hereby enacted by the authority of the same*, That the governor be and is hereby authorized and required to subscribe twenty thousand dollars, in shares of twenty dollars each, to the stock of the Milesburg and Smethport Turnpike Road Company ; and as soon as any five miles of the road shall be completed, it shall be the duty of the governor to draw his warrant on the State treasurer for a sum in proportion to the whole distance, and a like sum for every five miles, until the whole sum shall be drawn : *Provided*, That previous to any payment from the treasury satisfactory evidence shall be furnished to the governor that sums equal at least in amount to the sums drawn from the treasury shall have been paid by individual stockholders and expended agreeably to the provisions of the twelfth section of the act incorporating the said turnpike road company, passed the eleventh day of April, one thousand eight hundred and twenty-five : *And Provided further*, That there shall not be more than five thousand dollars of the aforesaid sum of twenty thousand dollars drawn from the said treasury in any one year.

"Approved—the second day of February, A.D. one thousand eight hundred and twenty-eight.

"J. ANDW. SHULZE."

1831.—"A FURTHER SUPPLEMENT TO THE SAID ACT INCORPORATING SAID TURNPIKE ROAD COMPANY, BEING THE SECOND SECTION OF THE ACT OF THE 4TH DAY OF APRIL, A.D. 1831, AS FOLLOWS:

"SECTION 2. *And be it further enacted by the authority aforesaid,* That the proceedings which are authorized by the thirteenth section of the act entitled 'A Further Supplement to the Act entitled An Act authorizing the Governor to incorporate the Milesburg and Smethport Turnpike Road Company,' passed eleventh day of April, one thousand eight hundred and twenty-five, and a supplement to the said act, passed the second day of February, one thousand eight hundred and twenty-eight, in cases when the said company shall have finished five miles or more of said road, be and the same are hereby authorized and extended to portions less than five miles of said road, which are and shall hereafter be finished as aforesaid."

1836.—A further supplement authorizing the State to subscribe five thousand dollars additional stock in said turnpike.

March 24, 1817.—The county having been divided into two election districts,—Pine Creek and Perry,—the latter declared a separate election district by act of Assembly,—elections therein to be held at the house of John Bell, of said township.

April 22, 1822.—Jefferson County placed in the Seventeenth Congressional District, composed of the counties of Westmoreland, Indiana, and Jefferson.

December 23, 1822.—Sales of unseated lands in Jefferson County for taxes authorized.

January 21, 1824.—Election of county commissioners and county auditors first authorized; and when elected, to "hold their office and transact the public business at such places as shall be determined upon by a majority of the commissioners first elected until the seat of justice is ascertained."

1826.—County commissioners of the provisional county of Jefferson to draw their warrants on the county treasurer for expenses of laying out roads, criminal prosecutions, and all other costs and expenses incidental to said county; and the authority of the county commissioners of Indiana County over Jefferson County to cease.

1826.—One-half of all road taxes received by the treasurers of Jefferson and McKean Counties from unseated lands to be applied for seven years to the improvement of the "leading roads" in said counties; and C. C. Gaskill and James Gillis, of Jefferson County, and Jonathan Colgrove and Paul E. Scull, of McKean County, appointed commissioners to expend said fund in the "making, clearing, and opening" of said "leading roads."

1828.—The above act repealed as to Jefferson County.

PIONEER HISTORY OF JEFFERSON COUNTY, PENNA.

April 10, 1826.—Young township having been erected, now made a separate election district,—elections therein to be held at the house of Elijah Heath, in Punxsutawney.

April 16, 1827.—Ridgeway township, of Jefferson County, having been formed, the same is now made into a separate election district,—elections to be held at the house of James Gallagher in said township.

April 14, 1828.—Rose township having been erected, the same is now declared a separate election district,—elections therein to be held at the house of John Lucas, in said township.

March 3, 1829.—An act to encourage the destruction of foxes and wild-cats, awarding a bounty of thirty-seven and a half cents on the scalp of every fox produced, and one dollar on the scalp of every wild-cat.

April 8, 1829.—John Mitchell, of Centre County; Alexander McCalmont, of Venango County; and Robert Orr, of Armstrong County, appointed to meet at the house of Andrew Barnett, of Jefferson County, and from thence to view, select, and "determine the most eligible and proper situation for the seat of justice for the said county of Jefferson."

April 2, 1830.—"AN ACT TO ORGANIZE THE PROVISIONAL COUNTY OF JEFFERSON FOR JUDICIAL PURPOSES.

"SECTION 1. *Be it enacted by the Senate and House of Representatives of the Commonwealth of Pennsylvania in General Assembly met, and it is hereby enacted by the authority of the same,* That from and after the first day of October next the inhabitants of the county of Jefferson shall enjoy all and singular the jurisdictions, powers, rights, liberties, and privileges whatsoever within the same which the inhabitants of other counties of this State do, may, or ought to enjoy by the laws and constitution of this Commonwealth.

"SECTION 2. *And be it further enacted by the authority aforesaid,* That the county of Jefferson shall be attached to and form a part of the Fourth Judicial District, until otherwise ordered by law, and that the judges of the Supreme Court, and the president of the Fourth Judicial District, and the associate judges to be appointed in the said county of Jefferson, shall have like powers, jurisdictions, and authorities within the same, as are or may be warranted to and exercised by the judges in the other counties of this Commonwealth, and the said county of Jefferson is hereby annexed to the Western District of the Supreme Court of this Commonwealth.

"SECTION 3. *And be it further enacted by the authority aforesaid,* That the citizens and inhabitants of the said county of Jefferson, who are or shall be qualified to vote agreeably to the Constitution and laws of this Commonwealth, shall at the first general election, to be held on the second Tuesday in October next at their respective election districts, choose two fit persons for sheriffs, two for coroners, and all other officers necessary to be elected for the said county of Jefferson in the same manner and under the same rules, regulations, and penalties as by the laws of this Commonwealth similar officers are chosen in other counties, and said officers when chosen as aforesaid and duly qualified to enter on the duties of their respective offices shall have and enjoy all and singular the powers, authorities, privileges, and emoluments in or any way arising out of their respective offices, in and for the county aforesaid, as fully as such officers are entitled to in any other county within this Commonwealth; and it shall and is hereby declared lawful for all the public officers of the said county of Jefferson, from and after the first day of October next, to do, perform, and exercise all the duties of their respective offices in as full and ample manner as if the several courts should be opened on that day by the president and judges of the same, and any process that may issue returnable to the first term in said county shall bear test as of the first day of October next.

"SECTION 4. *And be it further enacted by the authority aforesaid,* That the Courts of Common Pleas and General Quarter Sessions of the Peace, and Orphans' Court for the county of Jefferson shall, from and after the first day of October next, commence and be holden on the first Monday after the courts in Clearfield County.

"SECTION 5. *And be it further enacted by the authority aforesaid,* That all suits which shall be pending and undetermined in the Court of Common Pleas of Indiana County on the first day of October next, when the defendant or defendants in such suit or suits shall at that time be resident in Jefferson County, shall be transferred to the Court of Common Pleas of Jefferson County, and shall be considered as pending in said court, and shall be proceeded on in like manner as if the same had been originally commenced in said court, except that the fees thereon, due to the officers in Indiana County, shall be paid to them when recovered by the prothonotary or sheriff of Jefferson County, and the prothonotary of Indiana County shall procure a docket and copy therein all the docket entries respecting the said suits to be transferred as aforesaid, and shall on or before the fourth Monday in November next have the said docket, together with the records, declarations, and other papers respecting said suits, ready to be delivered to the prothonotary of Jefferson County, the expense of said docket and copying to be paid by the prothonotary of Jefferson County, and reimbursed by the said county of Jefferson on warrants to be drawn by the commissioners of Jefferson County on the treasury thereof.

"SECTION 6. *And be it further enacted by the authority aforesaid,* That it shall and may be lawful for the commissioners of Jefferson County, and they are hereby required, as soon as they may deem it expedient, to erect or cause to be erected on such part of the public square in the town of Brookville as they may deem best suited thereto a court-house, and offices for the safe-keeping of the papers and records of the said county, and until such court-house is erected the courts of justice shall be opened and held in such house in said county as the judges and commissioners may obtain for that purpose.

"SECTION 7. *And be it further enacted by the authority aforesaid*, That the sheriff, coroner, and other public officers of Indiana County shall continue to exercise the duties of their respective offices within the county of Jefferson until similar officers are appointed and elected agreeably to law within and for the said county of Jefferson.

"SECTION 8. *And be it further enacted by the authority aforesaid*, That the sheriffs and coroners of the said county of Jefferson before they enter on the duties of their offices shall give security in like sums as similar officers do in the county of Indiana and in the same manner, and under the restrictions as similar officers are compelled to do in the several counties of this Commonwealth.

"SECTION 9. *And be it further enacted by the authority aforesaid*, That the seat of justice for the county of Jefferson shall be, and the same is established and confirmed at the mouth of the North Fork of Sandy Lick Creek, in the county of Jefferson, and it shall be the duty of the commissioners of said county to demand and receive from John Pickering, Esq., a sufficient deed or deeds in fee-simple, in trust to them and their successors in office for the use of said county, for all the lands or lots which the said John Pickering, Esq., has agreed to give for the purpose of aiding in the erection of public buildings, agreeably to the act of the General Assembly of the eighth day of April, A.D. one thousand eight hundred and twenty-nine, entitled 'An Act authorizing the Appointment of Commissioners to fix a proper Site for the Seat of Justice in Jefferson County, and also for one Public Square in the said Town of Brookville for the purpose of erecting Public Buildings thereon,' and the said commissioners shall procure the said deed or deeds when recorded in the office for the recording of deeds in the county of Indiana, to be recorded in the proper books directed to be kept for the county of Jefferson, and the said commissioners and their successors in office, or a majority of them, shall and are hereby authorized to sell and dispose of the said lands or lots aforesaid, and to make and execute deeds to the purchasers, and the moneys arising from such sales shall be by them applied to the erection of public buildings for the use of the said county of Jefferson.

"SECTION 10. *And be it further enacted by the authority aforesaid*, That the said commissioners shall, as soon as may be, proceed to lay out the said town of Brookville, and file a draught and return of the survey of the said town, together with the proceedings under and by virtue of this act, in the office for the recording of deeds in and for the county of Jefferson, and an exemplification of the same shall be evidence in all matters of controversy touching the same.

"Approved—the second day of April, A.D. one thousand eight hundred and thirty.
"GEO. WOLF."

1831.—An act relieving the prothonotary, register, and recorder of Jefferson County from payment of State tax on his fees and commissions, and refunding all such taxes already paid by him.

1831.—Commissioners of Jefferson County authorized to alter the location of, and to lay out and make one mile and ten perches of, the Susquehanna and Waterford turnpike, where it passes through the village of Brookville.

1831.—Township supervisors of Jefferson County authorized and required to expend at least two-thirds of the annual road tax in the repair and improvement of the public roads of their respective townships, on or before the 1st day of October in each and every year.

February 7, 1832.—Boundary line between Jefferson and Venango Counties fixed, Richard Irvin, Esq., having run and marked the same "to the entire satisfaction of both counties."

1833.—Jefferson County placed in the Eighteenth Judicial District by section 8 of the act of 1833, which reads as follows:

"*And be it further enacted by the authority aforesaid*, That from and after the first day of September, Anno Domini one thousand eight hundred and thirty-five, the said county of Potter, and the counties of McKean, Warren, and Jefferson, shall be formed into a separate judicial district, to be called the Eighteenth District, and a person of integrity, learned in the law, shall be appointed and commissioned by the governor to be president and judge of the Courts of Common Pleas within the said district, which president shall receive the like salary, and have and execute all and singular the powers, jurisdictions, and authority of president judge of the Court of Common Pleas, Court of Oyer and Terminer and General Jail Delivery, Orphans' Court, and justice of the Court of Quarter Sessions of the Peace, agreeably to the constitution and laws of this Commonwealth. The courts in Potter County shall be held on the first Mondays of February, May, September, and December of each year; the courts in McKean County on the first Monday after those in Potter County; the courts in Warren County on the first Monday after the courts in McKean County; and the courts in Jefferson County on the first Monday after the courts in Warren County, the courts in each county to continue one week if necessary."

1834.—Recognizances and bonds of the sheriff of Jefferson County fixed at $7000.

1835.—Courts of Jefferson County authorized to be held on the second Mondays of February, May, September, and December.

1835.—Wheat, rye, and corn flour, designed for exportation as a product of Jefferson County, to be stamped.

PIONEER HISTORY OF JEFFERSON COUNTY, PENNA.

1839.—An act authorizing one person to hold and exercise the several offices of prothonotary, clerk of the courts, register, and recorder in the county of Jefferson. This act remained in force until 1893.

1840.—Commission appointed to run and mark the division line between the counties of Jefferson, Warren, McKean, and Clearfield, consisting of Jonathan Coalgrove, of the county of McKean, Elijah Heath, of the county of Jefferson, and John S. Brockway, of the county of Clearfield.

1840.—An act to encourage the destruction of wolves and panthers, giving a bounty of twenty-five dollars on wolves and sixteen dollars on panthers. Repealed in 1841.

1841.—An act requiring township elections in the county of Jefferson to be held on the second Tuesday of February, annually.

1842.—Township elections to be held on the fourth Monday of February, annually.

1842.—County commissioners of Jefferson County authorized to issue orders to supervisors on county treasurer for road taxes collected on unseated lands, and prescribing the form thereof.

1842.—Jefferson County commissioners authorized to issue orders on county treasurer for school taxes collected on unseated lands in favor of the school treasurers of the respective townships, and the form thereof prescribed.

1843.—Act granting premiums on destruction of wild-cats and foxes repealed as to Jefferson County.

1843.—Mechanics' lien law extended to Jefferson County.

1843.—Elk County erected out of parts of Jefferson, Clearfield, and McKean Counties. Timothy Ives, Jr., of Potter County; James W. Guthrie, of Clarion County; and Zachariah H. Eddy, of Warren County, appointed commissioners to "ascertain and plainly mark the boundary lines of said county of Elk."

By same act, Jefferson County to receive and provide for all Elk County prisoners for three years, or until Elk County erects a jail.

1843.—Jefferson County placed in the Twenty-third Congressional District, composed of the counties of Erie, Warren, McKean, Clarion, Potter, and Jefferson.

1843.—Jefferson County placed in the Twenty-eighth Senatorial District, composed of the counties of Warren, Jefferson, Clarion, McKean, and Potter. Same act places Jefferson, Clarion, and Venango Counties together in one legislative district, and authorizes the three counties to elect two members.

1844.—Supplement to the act erecting Elk County, regarding the bringing of suits, liens, revival of judgments, and the issuing of execution writs, etc.

1845.—All expenses for laying out and opening roads in Jefferson County to be paid out of the road funds of the several townships through which the same may pass. All expenses for the election of township officers in said county to be paid out of township rates and levies. Supervisors in the county of Jefferson required to give bond in double the amount of the sum assessed for road purposes; and township auditors, within ten days after settlement with supervisors, to file a copy of said settlement with the clerk of the quarter sessions.

1845.—An act authorizing but three road and bridge viewers in Jefferson County, and requiring all to view.

1846.—Certain deeds made and improperly executed by Jefferson County commissioners legalized.

BROOKVILLE BOROUGH.

1830.—County commissioners authorized to lay out the town, and limits thereof defined by courses and distances.

1834.—Borough incorporated. Election of borough officers authorized, and Thomas Hastings and Jared B. Evans, Esqs., to publish notice "and see to the opening of the election."

1835.—Manner and time of electing constable for Brookville prescribed.

1837.—Six school directors to be elected in the borough on the first Monday of January annually.

1837.—Brookville to have and own the school taxes assessed against its own citizens by Rose township.

1838.—Brookville Academy established "for the education of youth in the English and other languages, and in the useful arts, sciences, and literature, under the care and directions of six trustees and their successors in office." The six trustees first appointed were C. A. Alexander, Thomas Hastings, John J. Y. Thompson, Levi G. Clover, John Pearce, and Richard Arthurs. By same act the State appropriated $2000 to said Brookville Academy.

1838.—Brookville Female Seminary authorized and established, and Andrew Barnett, Thomas Hastings, Levi G. Clover, William Jack, Elijah Heath, C. A. Alexander, John Bell, Charles K. Barclay, and John W. Jenks appointed trustees.

1841.—County commissioners authorized to subscribe $500 to the Brookville Academy. Three trustees thereafter to be elected annually "by the qualified voters of the county."

1842.—After payment of the $500 to the Brookville Academy, to be subscribed and paid by the county, trustees of the said academy to be elected by the voters of the whole county.

1842.—Brookville borough to elect two constables and one assessor annually.

1843.—Voters of Jefferson County not to vote for trustees until the

PIONEER HISTORY OF JEFFERSON COUNTY, PENNA.

county commissioners have subscribed and paid the aforesaid $500 heretofore authorized to be subscribed.

1845.—Borough officers to be elected on the first Monday of March annually.

1845.—Market, Water, Jefferson, and Church Streets, of the borough of Brookville, authorized.

TOWNSHIPS OF JEFFERSON COUNTY.

1804.—Pine Creek was the original township, coextensive with the county as erected in 1804.

PERRY.

1817.—Perry township made a separate election district, and elections therein to be held in the house of John Bell in said township.

1826.—Elections in Perry township to be held at the house of Jacob Heterick in said township.

1830.—Auditors of Young and Perry townships authorized to audit and settle the accounts of John Van Horn as supervisor of Perry township previous to its division into the said townships of Perry and Young, and to apportion the balance found due him between the said townships.

1835.—Elections in Perry township to be held at the house of William Stunkard in said township.

1842.—Perry township divided into two school districts,—Perry and Whitesville.

YOUNG.

1826.—Young township to hold its elections at the house of Elijah Heath, in the town of Punxsutawney.

RIDGEWAY.

1827.—Ridgeway township made a separate election district, and elections to be held at the house of James Gallagher.

ROSE.

1828.—Rose township made a separate election district, and elections to be held at the house of John Lucas in said township.

1834.—Rose township elections to be held at court house, Brookville, Pennsylvania.

1836.—Rose township divided for election purposes, the western end thereof to hold its elections at the house of Darius Carrier.

1838.—Rose township again divided for election purposes by a different line from that established by the act of 1836; but both parts of the township were required to vote at Brookville. This was very unsatisfactory, and so in 1840 this act of 1838 was repealed by a revival of the act of 1836, permitting again the western end of the township to vote at the house of Darius Carrier, the site of which is now, in 1897, within the limits of the borough of Summerville.

1838.—Boundaries of Rose township determined and fixed, extending to the Armstrong County line.

1842.—Rose township elections to be held at the court-house in the borough of Brookville.

BARNETT.

1832.—Barnett township elections to be held at the house of John Wyncoop in said township.

1835.—Barnett township elections to be held at the house of Alexander Murray in said township.

YOUNG.

1838.—Young township divided for election purposes by an east and west line, and all electors north of that line to hold their elections "at the Paradise School-House, near Jacob Smith's, in said district."

ELDRED.

1836.—Eldred township declared a separate election district, and elections to be held at the house of James Linn in said township.

SNYDER.

1835.—Snyder township declared a separate election district, and elections to be held "at the house of John McLaughlin on the Brockway road in said township."

1838.—Elections in Snyder township to be held on the third Tuesday of February, instead of the first Friday of March.

1842.—Elections in Snyder township to be held at the house of James M. Brockway in said township.

WASHINGTON.

1838.—Washington township declared a separate election district, and elections therein to be held at the house of John McIntosh in said township.

JENKS.

1838.—Jenks township in Jefferson County declared a separate election district, and elections therein to be held at the house of Cyrus Blood in said township.

PORTER.

1840.—Porter township declared a separate election district, and elections therein to be held at the house of Henry Freese in said township.

CLOVER.

1842.—Clover township elections to be held at the house of Darius Carrier, in the village of Troy in said township.

PIONEER HISTORY OF JEFFERSON COUNTY, PENNA.

GASKILL.

1842.—Elections in Gaskill township to be held at the house of Henry Miller in said township.

1844.—Elections in said township to be held at "Miller's District School-House."

WARSAW.

1842.—Warsaw township declared a separate election district, and elections therein to be held at the house of William Weeks in said township.

TIONESTA.

1838.—Tionesta township, in Jefferson County, declared a separate election district, and elections therein to be held at the house of John Noeff in said township.

1844.—One-fourth of the road taxes levied and collected in Tionesta township, in the county of Jefferson, to be applied annually for six years to repairs and improvement of the Warren and Ridgeway turnpike.

HIGHWAYS OF JEFFERSON COUNTY AS MADE BY ACT OF ASSEMBLY.

1798.—Red Bank Creek declared a public highway from its mouth to the "second great fork," which is the North Fork.

1817.—One thousand dollars appropriated by the State "for the purpose of improving the navigation of Red Bank Creek from the mouth thereof as far up as it is declared navigable."

1820.—Sandy Lick Creek declared a public highway up to Henry Nulf's saw-mill in the county of Jefferson.

1798.—Toby's Creek, now Clarion River, declared a public highway from its mouth up to the second great fork thereof.

1817.—Two hundred dollars appropriated by the State "for the purpose of improving the navigation of Toby's Creek."

1808.—Big Mahoning declared a public highway from its mouth up to the mouth of Canoe Creek, and permission given and regulated to erect dams in said creek.

1817.—Appropriation by the State of $800 "for the purpose of removing obstructions in Big Mahoning Creek, and improving the navigation of the same between the mouth of Little Mahoning and the confluence of said creek with the river Allegheny."

1835.—Big Mahoning Creek declared a public highway from the mouth of Canoe Creek to the forks of Stump Creek in Jefferson County.

1845.—Incorporation of the Mahoning Navigation Company authorized, and J. W. Jenks, William Campbell, and James Torrence appointed commissioners to procure books, solicit subscriptions, and organize the company.

PIONEER HISTORY OF JEFFERSON COUNTY, PENNA.

1812.—Incorporation of the Susquehanna and Waterford Turnpike Company authorized. Governor of Pennsylvania to subscribe $125,000 in the stock of said road.

1814.—Supplement to said act extending the time for subscriptions to the stock of said company three years from the 22d of February, 1815.

1818.—Supplement extending the time five years from March 20, 1818.

1821.—Governor of Pennsylvania, on behalf of the State, authorized to subscribe $15,000, in addition to the amount before subscribed, to the Susquehanna and Waterford Turnpike Company. By a report made in the Pennsylvania House of Representatives, March 23, 1822, it appears that the contemplated length of this road was one hundred and twenty-six miles, one hundred and seventeen of which were completed at that date. About twenty six miles of this turnpike were laid out within the limits of the county of Jefferson.

1838.—Susquehanna and Waterford Turnpike Road Company authorized to open their road one hundred feet wide through marshy places, "so as to let the light and air upon the same."

OLEAN ROAD.

1819.—This State road was authorized by the following act of Assembly :

"AN ACT AUTHORIZING THE GOVERNOR TO APPOINT COMMISSIONERS FOR THE PURPOSE OF LAYING OUT A STATE ROAD FROM THE TOWN OF KITTANNING TO THE STATE LINE, IN DIRAECTION TO THE VILLAGE OF HAMILTON, IN THE TOWNSHIP OF OLEAN, IN THE STATE OF NEW YORK, AND ALSO FROM MILESBURG IN CENTRE COUNTY TO CLARION RIVER IN JEFFERSON COUNTY.

"SECTION 1. *Be it enacted by the Senate and House of Representatives of the Commonwealth of Pennsylvania in General Assembly met, and it is hereby enacted by the authority of the same,* That the governor be, and is hereby authorized and required to appoint three commissioners, one of whom shall be a practical surveyor, to view, mark, and lay out a State road from the town of Kittanning, in the county of Armstrong ; thence on the nearest and best route to the State line, on a direction to the village of Hamilton, on the Allegheny River, in the township of Olean, in the State of New York ; and the commissioners so appointed shall proceed to perform the duties required of them by this act on or before the first Monday in June next, and shall make out and deposit a copy of the draft of said road in the office of the clerk of the Court of Quarter Sessions in each county through which said road shall pass, and the said clerks shall enter the same in their respective offices, which shall be a record of said road ; and from thenceforth the said road shall be, to all intents and purposes, a public highway, and shall be opened and kept in repair in the same manner as roads laid out by order of the Court of Quarter Sessions of the county through which said road passes."

Section 2 provides for the oath of the commissioners, their pay, and the settlement of their accounts.

Sections 3 and 4 pertain only to the other State road mentioned in the title of the act.

"Approved—the twenty-third day of March, one thousand eight hundred and nineteen."

1821. – Appropriation of $8000 to the Olean road by the nineteenth section of "An Act for the Improvement of the State," which reads as follows:

"SECTION 19. *And be it further enacted by the authority aforesaid,* That the sum of eight thousand dollars be, and the same is hereby appropriated for the opening and improving a State road, recently laid out from the town of Kittanning in Armstrong County to the State line, on a direction to the village of Hamilton, in the State of New York, which passes through Armstrong, Jefferson, and McKean Counties, to be expended in the said counties through which said road passes in proportion to the distance it passes through the same respectively. And the governor is hereby authorized to draw his warrant on the State treasurer in favor of the following named persons —that is, for that part of the said road which lies in Armstrong County in favor of David Lawson and James Cochran, Armstrong County; and for that part of said road which lies in Jefferson County in favor of John Sloan, Jr., of Armstrong County, John Matson, and John Lucas, of Jefferson County; and for that part of said road that lies in McKean County in favor of Brewster Freeman and Joseph Otto, of McKean County, who are hereby appointed commissioners to receive and expend the said sum in opening and improving the said road within the limits of the counties to which they are appointed to superintend, etc.

"Approved—March 26, 1821."

1819.—State road from Kittanning to the mouth of Anderson's Creek, in Clearfield County, authorized by

"AN ACT TO AUTHORIZE THE GOVERNOR TO APPOINT COMMISSIONERS TO LAY OUT A STATE ROAD FROM THE TOWN OF KITTANNING IN A DIRECTION TO THE MOUTH OF ANDERSON'S CREEK.

"SECTION 1. *Be it enacted by the Senate and House of Representatives of the Commonwealth of Pennsylvania in General Assembly met, and it is hereby enacted by the authority of the same,* That the governor is, and he is hereby authorized to appoint three commissioners, one of which shall be a practical surveyor, to view, mark, and lay out a State road from the town of Kittanning, thence by the nighest and best route on a direction towards the mouth of Anderson's Creek, in Clearfield County, to intersect a road from Bellefonte to Erie. And the commissioners so appointed shall proceed to perform the duties of their appointment at such time as the governor shall direct. And they shall make out and deposit a draft of said road in the office of the clerk of the Court of Quarter Sessions in each county through which said road shall pass, and the said clerks shall enter the same in their respective offices, which shall be a record of said road, and from thenceforth the said road shall be to all intents and purposes a public highway, and shall be opened and kept in repair in the same manner as roads laid by order of the Courts of Quarter Sessions of the counties through which said road passes.

"Approved—January 27, 1819."

1821.—Appropriation of $2500 to the State road from Kittanning to Anderson's Creek, Clearfield County, by "An Act for the Improvement of the State."

"SECTION 18. *And be it further enacted by the authority aforesaid*, That the sum of two thousand five hundred dollars be, and the same is hereby appropriated for the purpose of opening and improving a State road recently laid out from the mouth of Anderson's Creek, in Clearfield County, to the town of Kittanning, in Armstrong County, which passes through the counties of Clearfield, Jefferson, Indiana, and Armstrong, to be expended in the same counties through which said road passes in proportion to the distance it passes through the same, and the governor is hereby authorized to draw his warrant on the State treasurer in favor of the following-named persons,—that is, for that part of said road which lies in Armstrong County in favor of James Hannagan and Joseph Marshall, of Armstrong County; for that part of said road which lies in Indiana County in favor of James McComb and William Travis, of Indiana County; for that part of said road lying in Jefferson County in favor of Charles C. Gaskill and Carpenter Winslow, of Jefferson County; and for that part lying in Clearfield County in favor of David Ferguson and Moses Boggs, of said county, who are hereby appointed commissioners to receive and expend the said sum in opening and improving the said road within the limits of the counties to which they are appointed to superintend, and the said commissioners shall each be entitled to receive as a full compensation one dollar and fifty cents per day for every day they shall be necessarily employed in performing their respective duties.

"Approved—March 26, 1821."

1824.—State road from Warren to Brookville authorized.

1825.—"State road from Indiana through Punxsutawney, in the county of Jefferson, and Smethport, in the county of McKean, to the

PIONEER HISTORY OF JEFFERSON COUNTY, PENNA.

town of Ceres, in said county of McKean," authorized, and Meek Kelly, of Indiana County, John Sloan, Jr., of Armstrong County, and Charles C. Gaskill, of Jefferson County, appointed commissioners to view, lay out, and mark the same.

1826.—Warren and Jefferson County Turnpike Road Company authorized "for the purpose of making a turnpike road from the town of Warren, in Warren County, to the Susquehanna and Waterford Turnpike, at or near the bridge over the north fork of Sandy Lick Creek, in Jefferson County," and Joseph Hackney, John Andrews, and Archibald Tanner, of Warren County; Thomas Lucas, Charles C. Gaskill, and John Matson, of Jefferson County, appointed commissioners to solicit subscriptions and organize the company.

1826.—An act to improve the leading roads in McKean and Jefferson Counties.

1826.—Clearfield and Jefferson Turnpike authorized, and Charles C. Gaskill, Dr. John W. Jenks, Andrew Barnett, and Thomas Lucas, of the county of Jefferson; and Greenwood Bell, John Irvin, David Ferguson, and Alexander B. Read, of Clearfield County, appointed commissioners to procure books and solicit subscriptions for said road, and generally to assist in the organization of the company, to be known as "The President, Managers, and Company of the Clearfield and Jefferson Turnpike Road."

1826.—Sandy Lick or Red Bank Creek declared a public highway from the eastern boundary of Jefferson County to its mouth, for the passage of descending boats, rafts, etc.; and permission granted, and regulations prescribed, for the erection of dams in said creek.

1828.—Little Toby's Creek, in the counties of Clearfield and Jefferson, from the mouth of John Shaffer's mill-run, on the main branch of Toby's Creek, and from the forks of Brandy Camp (or Kersey Creek) to the Clarion River, declared a public highway for the passage of rafts, boats, and other craft, and permission given to erect and regulate dams on said creek.

1833.—North Fork Creek, in Jefferson County, from its mouth to Ridgeway, declared a public highway.

1834.—State road from Kittanning to Brookville authorized, and John Sloan, Jr., Alexander Duncan, and James Corbett appointed commissioners to view and lay out the same.

1835.—Commissioners appointed to lay out State road from Kittanning to Brookville: William Jack, John Cribbs, Jr., and Robert Richards.

1838.—Luthersburg and Punxsutawney Road Company authorized, "for the purpose of making a turnpike from the town of Punxsutawney, in the county of Jefferson, to the town of Luthersburg, in Clearfield County," and Lebbeus Luther, John Jordan, Benjamin Bonsall, David Irvin, Jacob Flick, Benjamin Carson, David Hoover, David Henny, and

Jeremiah Miles, of the county of Clearfield ; William Campbell, Charles R. Barclay, Charles C. Gaskill, James Winslow, James W. Bell, and John Hoover (miller), of the county of Jefferson, appointed commissioners to solicit subscriptions for stock, and generally to assist in the organization of the company to be known as "The Luthersburg and Punxsutawney Road Company."

1838.—The governor of Pennsylvania authorized and required to subscribe $4000 to the Luthersburg and Punxsutawney Turnpike Company "if incorporated the present session."

1830.—State road from Warren to Ridgeway's settlement, in Jefferson County, authorized, and Robert Falconer, John Andrews, and Lansing Witmore, of Warren County, and Reuben A. Aylsworth, and Enos Gillis, of Jefferson County, appointed commissioners to lay out the same.

1831.—Company organized and incorporated to build said road, called the Warren and Ridgeway Turnpike Road Company. "The said commissioners are hereby authorized to employ one surveyor, whose compensation shall not exceed one dollar and fifty cents per day, and two chain-bearers and one axe-man, at per diem allowance, not exceeding one dollar per day, and one packer and pack-horse, if necessary, for which a reasonable allowance shall be made. Further, that the compensation of the said commissioners shall be one dollar and fifty cents each for every day they may be necessarily employed by virtue of this act."

1836.—In consideration of privileges granted by the State to the State bank, it was authorized and required to pay $5000 to this Warren and Ridgeway Turnpike Road Company.

1838.—Governor of Pennsylvania authorized to subscribe $2000 stock in said Warren and Ridgeway Turnpike Road Company.

1842.—Having completed forty miles of the Warren and Ridgeway turnpike road, said company was authorized to demand, receive, and collect tolls thereon.

1844.—The managers and stockholders of the Warren and Ridgeway Turnpike Road Company having abandoned the same, it was enacted that one-half of the road taxes levied in the township of Sheffield, and one-fourth of the road tax levied in the township of Kinzua, in the county of Warren ; one-fourth of the road tax levied in the township of Tionesta, in the county of Jefferson ; one-fourth of the road tax levied in the township of Ridgeway, and one-eighth of the road tax levied in the township of Jones, in the county of Elk, should, for a period of six years, be paid and expended by Richard Dunham and Erastus Barnes, of the county of Warren, and Joseph S. Hyde, of the county of Elk, commissioners, to the best advantage, in repairing, mending, and improving said turnpike road through the counties of Warren, Jefferson, and Elk.

1831.—Armstrong and Clearfield turnpike road authorized to commence at Kittanning, pass through Punxsutawney, and to end at the

PIONEER HISTORY OF JEFFERSON COUNTY, PENNA.

mouth of Anderson's Creek, in Clearfield County. Thomas Blair, Jacob Pontius, and Joseph Marshall, of Armstrong County; Charles C. Gaskill, and John W. Jenks, of Jefferson County; John Ewing and Henry Kinter, of Indiana County; David Ferguson and John Irvin, of Clearfield County; and William A. Thomas and Hardman Phillips, of Centre County, were appointed commissioners by said act to solicit subscriptions, give notice of organization of company, etc.

1838.—Governor of Pennsylvania authorized and required to subscribe $5600 to said Armstrong and Clearfield Turnpike Road Company.

1844.—Time for the completion of the said Armstrong and Clearfield turnpike road extended for the term of ten years from April 16, 1844.

1834.—State road from the mouth of Little Bald Eagle Creek, in Huntingdon County, through Clearfield County, to Punxsutawney, in Jefferson County, authorized, and James Winslow, of Jefferson County; Elisha Fenton, of Clearfield County; and Benjamin Johnson, of Huntingdon County, appointed commissioners to lay out the same.

1835.—Supplement extending time for making out drafts of location of said State road from Little Bald Eagle Creek to Punxsutawney.

1834.—State road authorized from the settlement on the head-waters of Millstone Creek, in Jefferson County, to the State Road leading from the Clarion River bridge, on the Susquehanna and Waterford turnpike, in the county of Venango, at or near the farm of Peter Walley, Jr., and James Gillis and William Armstrong, of Jefferson County; and David Reyner, of Venango County, appointed commissioners to lay out the same.

1835.—State road from Shippenville to Ridgeway, in Jefferson County, authorized, and Daniel Rhyner and James Hasson, of Venango County; and William Armstrong, of Jefferson County, appointed commissioners to view, lay out, and mark the same.

1838.—State road from Brookville to Tionesta authorized, and James Huling and Richard Irvin, of Venango County, and Philip G. Clover, of Jefferson County, "appointed commissioners to view, lay out, locate, and mark the same by the nearest and best route."

1840.—Incorporation of the Armstrong, Jefferson, and Clearfield Turnpike Company authorized, to begin "at the northern termination of the Freeport and Kittanning turnpike road, on the top of the Mahoning hills, and continue by the most practical route, *via* the borough of Brookville, in Jefferson County, and the Brandy Camp, to the Milesburg and Smethport turnpike road, at or near Ridgeway, in Jefferson County. By same act James Kerr, Hance Robinson, Jacob Miller, of the county of Armstrong; and Hiram Wilson, William Jack, John Dougherty, and Jacob Shaffer, of the county of Jefferson; and Isaac Horton, Daniel Oyster, Uriah Rodgers, and Jonathan Nichols, of the county of Clearfield, were appointed commissioners to solicit subscriptions and organize the company.

PIONEER HISTORY OF JEFFERSON COUNTY, PENNA.

1840.—State road from Ebensburg to Punxsutawney authorized, to begin "at the town of Ebensburg, in Cambria County; thence by the nearest and best route to the Cherry Tree; thence by the nearest and best route to the town of Punxsutawney, Jefferson County;" and Stephen Lloyd and James Rhey, of Cambria County; James Bard, of Indiana County; David Ferguson, of Clearfield County; and James Winslow, of Jefferson County, appointed commissioners to view, lay out, and mark the same.

April 2, 1841.—Time for completing the survey and location of State road from Ebensburg to Punxsutawney extended one year from April 2, 1841, and Stephen Lloyd, John B. Douglass, of Cambria County; Richard Bard, of Clearfield County; William Thompson, of Indiana County; and James Winslow, of Jefferson County, appointed commissioners in place of those named in the act originally authorizing the road.

May 5, 1841.—Original act authorizing the State road from Ebensburg to Punxsutawney revived, "and William Thompson, of Indiana County; Richard Bard, of Clearfield County; and Stephen Lloyd, John B. Douglass, and James Rhey, of Cambria County, appointed commissioners to carry the provisions of the said act into execution."

1842.—Chutes of dams on the Red Bank and Sandy Lick Creek to be twenty feet long for every one foot high.

1841.—Jefferson County commissioners authorized to subscribe stock in the Mahoning Mouth Bridge Company "such number of shares as they may deem right and proper."

1842.—State road from Cherry Tree in Indiana County to Clarion authorized, and David Peelor, Heth F. Camp, and John Decker, of Indiana County; John Sloan, Jr., Peter Clover, Jr., of Clarion County; and Robert Woodward, of Armstrong County, appointed commissioners to view and lay out the said State road, which was to begin at "Cherry Tree in Indiana County, and to intersect the Susquehanna and Waterford Turnpike at or near the town of Clarion, in Clarion County, by the nearest and best route between the said points."

1843.—Time for executing and returning drafts of the survey of this State road from Cherry Tree to Clarion extended one year, and Henry Freese, of Jefferson County, added to the board of commissioners.

1843.—State road from Brookville to Ridgeway by way of the mouth of Little Toby authorized.

1843.—State road from Elderton to Punxsutawney authorized, and Thomas Armstrong, of Elderton; Peter Dilts, of Mahoning, Indiana County; and William Campbell, of Jefferson County, "appointed commissioners to view and lay out the road from Elderton, in Armstrong County, to Punxsutawney, in Jefferson County, by way of Plumville, in Indiana County, by the nearest and best route from point to point."

1844.—The county commissioners of the several counties through which the State road from Elderton by way of Plumville to Punxsutawney was laid out authorized and required to settle the accounts of the commissioners viewing and laying out said road.

1844.—State road from the borough of Warren, in Warren County, to the borough of Brookville, in Jefferson County, authorized, and Henry G. Sergeant and Orin L. Stanton, of Warren County; and Samuel Findley, of Jefferson County, appointed commissioners to view and lay out the same; drafts of the location of said State road to be made and deposited "in the office of the clerk of the court of the respective counties in which said road may be laid out."

1846.—Act relating to dams and obstructions in the Clarion River.

1846.—State road from Smicksburg, Indiana County, to the borough of Brookville, Jefferson County, authorized, and Hugh Brady, Levi G. Clover, of Jefferson County; and George Bernard, of Indiana County, appointed commissioners to view and lay out the same "on the nearest and best route, to a straight line, and in no place to exceed an elevation of five degrees."

Viewers required to make draft and file copy of same in both counties, and courts of the respective counties authorized to fill vacancies occurring in the board of commissioners.

CHAPTER XXII.

THE PIONEER PHYSICIAN IN THE COUNTY, DR. JOHN W. JENKS, OF PUNXSUTAWNEY—THE PIONEER PHYSICIAN ON THE LITTLE TOBY, DR. NICHOLS—OTHER EARLY PHYSICIANS, DR. EVANS, DR. PRIME, DR. DARLING, DR. BISHOP, DR. A. M. CLARKE, DR. JAMES DOWLING, DR. WILLIAM BENNETT—PIONEER MAJOR OPERATION IN SURGERY IN 1821—EARLY RIDES, FEES, ETC.

IN 1818, Dr. John W. Jenks came from Bucks County, Pennsylvania, and settled in what is now Punxsutawney, where he built a cabin, made improvements, and reared a family. He was quite a prominent man, and filled positions of profit and trust. He was one of the first associate judges, and father of Judge W. P. Jenks, Hon. G. A. Jenks and Mrs. Judge Gordon.

The pioneer physician and pioneer clergyman to settle in the Little Toby Valley was the Rev. Dr. Jonathan Nichols, who died in 1846, aged seventy-one. His wife, Hannah, died in Brookville in 1859, aged eighty-two years.

Rev. Dr. Jonathan Nichols migrated from Connecticut, and settled on Little Toby, Clearfield County, Pennsylvania, in the year 1818. He was a preacher and a doctor. He was the first minister to preach regularly in this county; also the pioneer physician in the northern part. The date of Dr. Nichols's first settlement in this wilderness was in 1812, on the Sinnamahoning. Dr. Nichols was a regularly educated physician, but, being of a very pious turn of mind, he studied and was ordained a Baptist minister. One who knew him well wrote of Dr. Nichols,—viz.: "He was a generous, kind-hearted gentleman, genial and urbane in his manners, with a helping hand ready to assist the needy, and had kind words to comfort the sorrowing. As a physician his visits were required over a large extent of the county. As a clergyman his meetings were well attended by the people."

PIONEER MAJOR SURGICAL OPERATION.

Moses Knapp moved to what is now called Baxter in the spring of 1821, and while cutting timber he got a foot and leg crushed so that his limb had to be amputated above the knee. Dr. Stewart, of Indiana, and Dr. William Rankin, of Licking, now Clarion County, performed the amputation in the summer of 1821. Knapp that year was constable, having been elected in the spring election.

Prior to 1825, Dr. R. K. Scott settled on what is now the Cowan farm, a little east of Roseville. The doctor was a pleasant, intelligent gentleman, and at one time was in the newspaper business. Where he removed to I do not know.

About the year 1831, Dr. Alvah Evans came to Brookville and opened an office for practice. He remained but a few months.

In the spring of 1832, Dr. G. C. M. Prime came to Brookville and commenced the practice of medicine. Dr. Prime was a man of skill. He amputated the arm of Henry (Hance) Vasbinder. Inflammation and gangrene in the arm, caused by a bite on his thumb while fighting, made this amputation necessary. Dr. Prime left Brookville in 1835.

In June, 1833, Dr. Geo. Darling (father of the late Paul Darling) came from Smithport, McKean County, Pennsylvania, and located in Brookville. In 1843, Dr. Darling left Brookville and located in Ohio. He was a well-bred, intelligent, educated physician.

In the summer of 1835, Rev. G. Bishop, M.D., located in Brookville, both preaching and practising medicine. He preached regularly to the Presbyterians of Beechwoods, Brookville, and where Corsica now stands.

In the spring of 1836, Dr. A. M. Clarke (who read and practised under Dr. Nichols) located in Brockwayville and commenced to practise for and by himself. Dr. Clarke was born in Granby, Connecticut, in 1808. His father was Philetus Clarke, who came into this wilderness in 1819. After a long and useful life Dr. Clarke died, May 2, 1884, leaving a family and his aged wife, *née* Rebecca M. Nichols. The following tribute was paid him at his death by a literary friend, Eugene Miller, Esq.,—viz.:

PIONEER HISTORY OF JEFFERSON COUNTY, PENNA.

"Deceased was intellectually a remarkable man. Denied the advantages of wealth and education, he became not only a learned and skilful physician, but a literary man of high order. Books were the mine in which he delved, and from their pages he brought forth jewels of information and thought most rare. He loved poetry with an ardor words cannot express, and was not only familiar with the leading poets of the past and present, but was himself the author of a number of fragments, which show him to have been possessed of a poetic fire that, in the hands of one less modest and unassuming than he ever proved himself to be, would have made him an enduring name. His qualities of heart were no less choice than were those of his head. He was generous to a fault, and as meek and gentle as a child. Nothing seemingly gave him more pleasure than to do good to his fellow-men, and many there are who have partaken bountifully of his store. In the sick-room his presence was always a sweet solace, and his delicate touch almost as soothing as a narcotic. In the social circle he was ever popular, the diversity of his knowledge and the easy flow of his language rendering him a delightful companion. As a man and citizen he was highly respected, as was proved by the spontaneity with which his neighbors gathered about his grave and dropped a tear to his precious memory. His death, like his life, was peaceful, and the name he leaves behind is as pure as the lily and as fragrant as the rose."

Dr. James Dowling came from Mercer County, Pennsylvania, in 1841, and located in what is now called Baxter. In 1843 he removed to Brookville. In 1844 he was elected a member of the Legislature. Dr. Dowling was a little man in stature, but a "big man in head and brain." He was greatly in advance of the many *theoretical*, narrow-minded, bigoted doctors of his time. He was popular in his manner and pleasing in his address. His practice was extensive and his reputation great. I remember his many kind acts to me, and I cherish his memory. He died December, 1860.

Dr. William M. Bennett was married to a Miss Orilla Ralston, of Angelica, Alleghany County, New York, about the year 1818 or 1819. He lived a short time where the city of Bradford now stands. He emigrated with his family to Jefferson County early in the year 1843, and settled on the Little Toby, in Snyder township, three miles below Brockwayville, where he built a saw-mill and engaged in the practice of his profession. Dr. Bennett was not a highly educated man, but he had a wonderful fund of common sense, and in his career of physician was popular, successful, and useful. In his treatment of diseases he was far in advance of what was then called science in medicine. He died October 11, 1875, and was buried at Temple's graveyard, Warsaw township, this county.

The pioneer and early doctor was a useful citizen, and his visits to the early settlers when afflicted was a great comfort. How we all long now to see the doctor when we are sick! These isolated people longed just the same for the coming of their doctor. The science of medicine then was very crude, and the art of it very imperfect, hence the early practitioner had but limited skill, yet while exercising whatever he professed for the relief of suffering, his privations and labor while travelling by night or day on horseback with his "old pill-bags" were hard and severe in the extreme. The extent of his circuit was usually from fifty to one hundred miles over poor roads and paths, swimming his horse through creeks and rivers as best he could. I have travelled a circuit of one hundred miles in my day. In those days every one had respect for the doctor, and every family along his circuit was delighted with an opportunity to extend *free* hospitality to the doctor and his horse.

In some of my long rides I have become so tired about midnight that I felt I could not go a step farther, when I would dismount from my horse, hitch him on the outside to a log of a log barn, slip the bridle around his neck, climb into the mow, throw the horse an armful of hay, and then fall asleep in the hay, only to awaken when the sun was an hour or two high. The pioneer doctor carried his pill-bags well stocked with calomel, Dover's powder, tartar emetic, blistering salve, a pair of old turnkeys for extracting teeth, and a spring and thumb lance for bleeding purposes, as everybody had to be bled, sick or well. Twenty-five cents was the fee for bleeding, and the amount of blood drawn from the arm was from half a pint to a quart. The custom of bleeding sick or well fell into disrepute about 1850. A town visit was from twenty-five to fifty cents, a visit in the country twenty-five cents a mile, an obstetric fee five dollars. The pioneer doctor always wore green leggings or corduroy overalls. I was no exception to this rule.

THE PIONEER MEDICAL SOCIETY OF JEFFERSON COUNTY, PENNSYLVANIA.

On July 3, 1857, a call was published in the Jefferson *Star* by Drs. A. P. Heichhold and J. G. Simons for the physicians of Jefferson County " to meet at the court-house in the borough of Brookville, on the 10th of July, 1857, at 10 o'clock A.M.," to organize a medical society.

The call was responded to, and below I give the minutes of the meeting as published in the *Star* of July 17, 1857:

" In compliance with a call to the members of the medical profession in Jefferson County, a meeting was held in Brookville and a county medical society was formed with the following members,—viz.: Drs. C. P. Cummins, Mark Rodgers, Charles Baker, A. J. Johnston, R. B. Brown, W. J. McKnight, D. A. Elliott, J. G. Simons, and A. P. Heichhold.

" The meeting was organized by calling Dr. M. Rodgers to the chair, and Dr. A. P. Heichhold was appointed secretary *pro tem*.

PIONEER HISTORY OF JEFFERSON COUNTY, PENNA.

"Dr. Simons was then called on to state the object of the meeting, which he did in a neat and appropriate manner.

"The following resolution was then offered: '*Resolved*, That in consequence of the indisposition of a portion of the members of the profession to the formation of a medical society, we deem it inexpedient to organize one at this time,' which was rejected, and a committee was then appointed to draft a constitution, and the society was organized permanently. The following officers for the ensuing year were then elected: President, Rev. Dr. C. P. Cummins; Vice-Presidents, Drs. A. J. Johnston, M. Rodgers; Secretary, D. A. Elliott; Treasurer, Dr. A. P. Heichhold; Censors, Dr. A. P. Heichhold, J. G. Simons, A. J. Johnston.

The society then adjourned to meet at the court-house, in Brookville, on Tuesday, the 28th day of July, at 7.30 P.M.

"C. P. CUMMINS,
"*President*.
"A. P. HEICHHOLD,
"*Secretary*."

In this same issue of July 17 the following official notice was published:

"A meeting of the Jefferson County Medical Society will be held in the court-house, in the borough of Brookville, on Tuesday evening, the 28th instant, at 7.30 o'clock P.M. An address will be delivered by the Rev. Dr. C. P. Cummins, the president of the society. The ladies and gentlemen of Brookville and vicinity are respectfully invited to attend.

"D. A. ELLIOTT,
"*Secretary*."

"Of this lecture the *Star* says, in an editorial of July 31, 1857,—

"COUNTY MEDICAL SOCIETY.—This body held a public meeting in the court-house on Tuesday evening last, which was addressed by Rev. C. P. Cummins, M.D. The remarks of the Rev. Dr. are highly extolled by those who had the pleasure of being present. The society met next morning at Dr. Heichhold's office for the transaction of business. We are glad to observe a great interest manifested in its proceedings by the physicians of the county."

The above address was published in full in the *Star*. The next meeting was publicly announced by the secretary "for September 14, at 7.30 o'clock. Dr. J. G. Simons will deliver an address, to hear which the ladies and gentlemen of Brookville and vicinity are invited to attend."

Of the members of the county medical society formed forty years ago in Brookville but two are now living,—viz., Dr. Charles Baker and the writer.

CHAPTER XXIII.

PIONEER TOWNSHIPS AND BOROUGHS AND PIONEER TAXABLES.

PINE CREEK.

CREATED in 1806 by an act of Assembly, and embraced all the county.

COMPLETE TAXABLE LIST IN PINE CREEK TOWNSHIP (THIS COUNTY) FOR THE YEAR 1807.

Joseph Barnett, farmer and distiller; John Dickson, weaver; Elijah M. Grimes, laborer; Lewis Heeb, farmer; Peter Jones, blacksmith; John Jones, farmer; Moses Knapp, farmer; Samuel Lucas, tailor; Thomas Lucas, farmer, and grist- and saw-mill; William Lucas, tailor; Ludwig Long, farmer and distiller; Alexander McCoy, farmer; Jacob Mason, laborer; Stephen Roll, cooper; Daniel Roadarmil, farmer; John Scott, Sr., farmer; Samuel Scott, miller, saw- and grist-mill; John Scott, Jr., farmer; Adam Vastbinder, farmer; Jacob Vastbinder (single man), farmer; John Vastbinder (single man), laborer; Fudge Van Camp (colored), farmer. Number of horses, 23; number of cows, 35.

PERRY.

Formed in 1818, and was taken from Pine Creek. Perry township as originally organized was bounded on the north by Pine Creek township, on the west by the Armstrong County line, on the south by the Indiana line, and on the east by the Clearfield County line.

PIONEERS IN PERRY TOWNSHIP AS PER ASSESSMENT IN 1818.

Names of Taxables.—Jesse Armstrong, John Bell, Esq., James W. Bell (single man), Joseph Bell (single man), John Bell (single man), Elijah Dykes, Benjamin Dykes, Archibald Hadden, Jacob Hoover, David Hamilton, Elizabeth McHenry, James Hamilton (single man), Adam Long, Michael Lantz, Henry Lott, Stephen Lewis, Isaac Lewis, Jacob Lane, James McClelland, David Milliron, Hugh McKee, James Hutchison, John Postlethwait, David Postlethwait (single man), Porter Reed, John Piper, James McKee, Thomas Page, Samuel States, James Stewart, John Stewart, James Wachob.

YOUNG.

Young township was organized in 1826, and was taken from Perry. It was bounded on the east by the Clearfield line, on the south by the Indiana line, on the west by Perry, and on the north by Pine Creek township.

PIONEER HISTORY OF JEFFERSON COUNTY, PENNA.

PIONEERS IN YOUNG TOWNSHIP AS PER ASSESSMENT IN 1826.

Names of Taxables.—Jesse Armstrong, John Archibald, David Burkhart, Andrew Bowers, Rev. David Barclay, house and lot in Punxsutawney, two-thirds of a grist-mill and two-thirds of a saw-mill; John Bowers, Philip Bowers, John Buck, Andrew Bowman, house and lot; Charles B. Barclay, house and lot; James Black, house and lot; Daniel Coffman, Charles Clawson, Matthias Clawson, Abraham Craft, James Caldwell, Benijah Corey, John Corey, house and lot; Isaac Carmalt, house and lot; Nichols Dunmire, Adam Dunmire, Daniel Graffius, Charles C. Gaskill, house and lot; Samuel Ganor, John Henderson, house and lot; Henry Hum, John Hum (single man), Jacob Hoover, one grist-mill; John Hoover, William Hemmingray, John Hess, house and lot in Long's Town; John Hutchison, Elijah Heath, house and lot; John W. Jenks, one third of a grist mill, one-third of a saw-mill, one bull; Adam Long, Joseph Long, house and lot; Adam Long, cooper; Francis Leach, George Leach, Isaac Lunger, Obed Morris, Joseph Potter, Frederick Rinehart, Christian Richel, Samuel Steffy, James Smith, Samuel States, Nathaniel Tindall, house and lot; James Williams, Benoni Williams, Ira White, James Winslow, Carpenter Winslow, Sr., Carpenter Winslow, Jr., Ebenezer Winslow, Charles Winslow, Reuben Winslow, Caleb Winslow (single man), Thomas Wheatcraft, William Webster, Abraham Weaver, house and lot; George Weaver (single man), Parlin White.

RIDGEWAY.

Organized in 1826, and was taken from Pine Creek. Ridgeway township was bounded on the east by McKean County line, on the north by the Warren County line, on the south by the Clearfield County line, and on the west by Pine Creek township.

PIONEERS IN RIDGEWAY TOWNSHIP AS PER ASSESSMENT IN 1827.
SEATED LIST.

Names of Taxables.—Aylesworth & Gillis Co., one grist- and sawmill; James Brockway, Collins Brooks (single man), Naphtalia Burns, Nehemiah Bryant, Sampson Crooker, Clark Eggleston, Henry Francis (single man), Enos Gillis, James Gallagher, Joseph P. King, George March (single man), William Maxwell (single man), Harvey B. Moorhouse (single man), James McDougal, Lorenzo Preaket (single man), Jacob Shaffer, John Stratton, William Taylor, Jacob Taylor (single man), Alanson Vial, Henry Walborn.

ROSE.

Organized in 1827, and was taken from Pine Creek. Rose township was bounded with Pine Creek on the east, Young and Perry on the south.

PIONEER HISTORY OF JEFFERSON COUNTY, PENNA.

PIONEERS IN ROSE TOWNSHIP, AS PER ASSESSMENT IN 1827.

Names of Taxables.—Robert Andrews, Johns Avery & Caleb Howard, one saw-mill, trade; Christopher Barr, Joseph Barnett, one saw-mill; John Barnett, David Butler, one-half of a saw-mill; Nathaniel Butler, Alonzo Baldwin, Lorenzo Brooks (single man), Euphrastus Carrier (single man), Christian Conrad, John Coon, one half of a saw-mill; John Christy, James E. Corbett, William Cooper, James Crow (single man), Samuel Kennedy, Joseph Clements, W. B. Clements, George Crispen, James Divin, trade; Samuel Davidson, Robert Dixon, John Dixon, William Douglass (colored), George Eckler, Henry Feye, Sr., Henry Feye, Jr., Samuel Feye, William Guthrie, John Fuller, trade; Elijah M. Graham, William Graham, —— Himes, one-half of a saw-mill; Frederick Heterick, one saw-mill; James Hall (single man), John Horam, Moses Knapp, Samuel Knapp, one saw- and grist-mill; Robert Knox, John Kelso, John Kennedy, Joseph Keys, Matthew Keys (single man), Henry Keys (single man), William Long (single man), John Lucas, William Love, Sr., William Love, Jr. (single man), John Love (single man), Thomas Lucas, one-half of a saw-mill, land; John Lattimer, one-half of a saw-mill; John Long, Alex. Lyons, Henry Lot, one saw-mill; Peter Lot, Daniel Long, William Lattimer, Isaac Matson, John McGiffin (single man), William Morrison, Samuel Magill, Isaac McElvaine, Abraham Milliron, Jacob Mason, Benjamin Mason (single man, Joseph McCullough, John Matson, John McIntosh, John McGhee, trade; Timothy Nightingale, P. B. Ostrander, Alexander Osburn, James Parks, grist-mill; Alexander Powers, Isaac Packer, William Rodgers, Hance (Robinson, one-half of a saw-mill; David Roll, one saw-mill; Joshua Rhea, Thomas Robinson, Robert Smith, James Shields, trade; John Shields, Peter Slogerbuck, Samuel Stiles, Michael Shadle, Heulet Smith, Andrew Shippen, Charles Sutherland (colored), Robert K. Scott, Joseph Sharp, Walter Templeton, Joshua Vandevort, Jesse Vandevort, Jacob Vastbinder, Adam Vastbinder, William Vastbinder, Henry Vastbinder, Andrew Vastbinder, Hugh Williamson, John Welsh, house and lot in Troy; John Walters, Beach Wayland, Patience Wheeler, John Webster (single man), Peter Walters, Robert Weir, Daniel Yeomans, William McDonald, Nathan Carrier, William Mendenhall, Alexander Scott, Benjamin Sies, Joseph Hastings, Robert Tweedy, James Sharp, Nicholas Sharp, Joseph Butler, Jeremiah McCallester, Samuel Rhodes, John Hayes, John Scott (single man), Samuel Johns, Robert Maxwell.

BARNETT.

Organized in 1833, and was taken from Rose. Barnett originally contained Jenks and Tionesta townships and all that part of Jefferson County lying north of the Clarion River. In 1838 the two above-mentioned townships were organized out of it.

PIONEER HISTORY OF JEFFERSON COUNTY, PENNA.

PIONEERS IN BARNETT TOWNSHIP AS PER ASSESSMENT IN 1833.

Names of Taxables.—William Armstrong & Co., one saw-mill; Luther Barns & Co., Israel Ball, Warren Barns (single man), John Cook, one saw-mill; Job Carr, Nathan & Elijah Tipps, David Meads, Thaddeus Meads, Erastus Gibson, William Manross, one saw-mill; David Reynolds, John Wyncoop, two saw-mills; John Mays, James W. Mays, Smith heirs, one saw-mill; Alexander Murray, Thomas B. Mays, Thomas Fords, John A. Kramer, John Fitzgerald, Smith N. Myers, James Orwin, William Beer, William Thomas, George & Samuel Armstrong, Ebenezer Kingly, William Gordon, William Forsythe.

SNYDER.

Organized in 1835, and was taken from Ridgeway and Pine Creek. Snyder township was bounded on the east by Clearfield County line, on the north by Ridgeway township, on the south and west by Pine Creek township.

PIONEERS IN SNYDER TOWNSHIP AS PER ASSESSMENT IN 1836.

Names of Taxables.—Dillis Allen, Hugh Anderson, George Addison, James & Alonzo Brockway, one saw-mill; Elihu Clark, David Carr, Joel Clark, Sr., Joel Clark, Jr. (single man), David Dennison, John Dougherty (single man), Thomas Dougherty (single man), Miron Gibbs, Francis Goodar, Benjamin Hulet, Frederick Heterick, Joseph Houston (single man), William Houston (single man), Milton Johnston, Joseph McAfee (single man), Robert McCurdy (single man), Joseph McCurdy (single man), John McLaughlin, Thomas McCormick, Hamilton Moody, Thomas Moody, Andrew McCormick, James Moorhead (single man), James W. Moorhead (single man), John Moorhead, David Moorhead (single man), John Pearsall, Arad Pearsall, James Ross, David M. Riddle, Henry Shaffer (single man), Jacob Shaffer, Ami Sibbley, William Shaw, Stephen Tibbetts, Isaac Temple, Andrew Vastbinder, Paul Vandevort, Joseph Whitehill.

ELDRED.

Organized in 1836, and was taken from Rose and Barnett. Eldred township was bounded on the north by Barnett, on the east by Ridgeway township, on the south by Rose, and on the west by the Armstrong County line.

PIONEERS IN ELDRED TOWNSHIP AS PER ASSESSMENT IN 1837.

Names of Taxables.—Thomas Arthurs, George Armstrong, William Anderson, Henry Boyles, David Barr, Thomas Barr, Samuel Barr, Abraham Bickler, Smith Benedict, Richard Burns, William Booth, Jacob Beer, Thomas Callen, Jacob Craft, Moses H. Carly, Peter Coonsman, John D. Kahle, George Catz, Henry Clark, Job Carly, William Douglass (colored), Daniel Elgin, Alexander Fredericks, Elijah M. Graham, Joseph Graham, Elias Gearhart, Dolly George, Isaiah Guthrie, William Gordon, Israel Hughes, Thomas Hughes, Thomas Hall, William Hopper, Malachi Hopper (single man), William M. Hindman, William Hughes, Richard Hague, Richard Hague, Jr., William & John Hutchison, William B. Kennedy, Frederick Kahle, William Kennedy, David Aikens, James Cochran, David McKee, John W. Monks, Isaac Matson, Sr., mill seat; James McManigle, James McNeal, John McCracken, David Miller, Robert McFarland, Stewart Ross, Jacob Riddleburger, Christian Ruffner, George Royer, Andrew Steel, James Stewart, Jr., Paul Stewart, Alexander Scott, Hiram Sampson, John Summerville, William Summerville, James Summerville, David Silvis, Jacob Trautman, James L. Thompson, James Templeton, Michael Traper, George Wilson, Jr. (single man), Robert Wilson, John Wilson, Jr., William Wallace, John Wilson, Esq., George Walford, Abram Yokey, Christy Yokey.

TIONESTA.

Organized in 1838, and was taken from Barnett.

PIONEERS IN TIONESTA TOWNSHIP AS PER ASSESSMENT IN 1838.

Names of Taxables.—James Adams, George Bests, Samuel Cupins, Erastus Gibson, Ebenezer Kingsley, Perry Kingsley, Ephraim Kingsley (single man), Edward Kingsley, Count Kingsley, John Lukins (single man), George Leadlie, one saw-mill with two saws; David W. Mead, sawyer; John Nolf.

JENKS.

Organized in 1838, and was taken from Barnett.

PIONEERS IN JENKS TOWNSHIP AS PER ASSESSMENT IN 1838.

Names of Taxables.—James Anderson, Cyrus Blood, Benjamin L. Baley, Aaron Brockway, Sr., Aaron Brockway, Jr., Amos Fitch, Isaac Fitch, John Hunt, Phelps Hunt, Jessie Jackson, Josiah Leary, John Lewis, Robert McLatchlie, Oran Newton, Samuel Reyner, Andrew J. Reyner.

WASHINGTON.

Organized in 1839, and was taken from Pine Creek and Snyder. Washington township was bounded on the east by Clearfield County line, on the north by Snyder township, and on the south and west by Pine Creek township.

PIONEERS IN WASHINGTON TOWNSHIP AS PER ASSESSMENT IN 1838.

Names of Taxables.—Dillis Allen, one saw-mill; Frederick Alexander, Hugh Alexander, John Atwell, James Alexander and father, James Bond, Samuel Beman, Samuel Crawford, John Clendennen, John Crawford, William Cooper, John P. Clark, Aaron Clark, Robert Douthard, one grist-mill; Thomas Dougherty, James Dougherty, James Downs,

PIONEER HISTORY OF JEFFERSON COUNTY, PENNA.

Robert Dickson, Michael Elliott, William Feely, John Fuller, Alexander B. Fowler, George Feely, George Hughes, Andrew Hunter, George Horam, Jacob & William Horam, John Horam, Sr., John Horam, Jr., Matthew Keys, Henry Keys, Joseph Keys, James Kyle, Samuel Kyle, Samuel Miles, John McGhee, Oliver McClelland, Andrew Moore, Robert Morrison, William McConnell, James McConnell, Joseph McConnell (single man), John McClelland, William McCullough, William McDonald, Robert McIntosh, occupation; Henry McIntosh, John McIntosh, William McIntosh, Jr., William McIntosh, Sr., Rebecca McIntosh, George Ogden, Joseph Potter, tavern; Ramsey Potter, Jacob Peters, Tilton Reynolds, William Reynolds, Thomas Reynolds (single man), David Reynolds, Joshua Rhea, Samuel Rhea, James Rany, James Smith, Andrew Smith, Matthew Smith, B. Sprague, Ephraim Stephen, Peter Sharp, John Sprague, Thomas Tedlie, Henry Vastbinder, James Waite, John Wilson, Oliver Welsh, Daniel Yeomans, Henry Yeomans.

PORTER.

Organized in 1840, and was taken from Perry. Porter township was bounded on the west by Armstrong County line, on the south by Indiana County line, on the north by Rose township.

PIONEERS IN PORTER TOWNSHIP AS PER ASSESSMENT IN 1841.

Names of Taxables.—John Alcorn, William Alcorn, Samuel Albert, Thomas Adams, Alexander Adams, George Barickhouse, Lawrence Bair, Ludwick Byerly, Gideon Bush, Powel Baughman, Robert Brice, Armstrong Bartley, Rev. Elisha Coleman, $30 on interest; John Coleman, William Callen, Benjamin Campbell, Henry Cherry, David Callen, Peter Callen, Andrew Callen, John Cherry (single man), Elisha Campbell, Frederick Coonrod, James Chambers, John Chambers, Harrison Coon, Jacob Dinger, Benjamin Dimick, Michael Tumas, Henry Dornhime, John Thomas, Edward Enty (colored), John Flisher, Jr., John Flisher, Henry Flisher, William Ferguson, Sr., William Ferguson, Jr., John Ferguson, Ebenezer Ferguson, Henry Faringer, William Foster, David Fairman, Francis Fairman, Henry Freece, Thomas Gaghagen, James Gaghagen, Gearhart & Spangler, Henry Glontz, Daniel Gaghagen, Peter Graver, Daniel Geist, one saw-mill; Solomon Geist, Samuel Geist, Jesse Geist, John Geist, Sr., John Geist, Jr., Pollie Gilbreth (widow), William Gillespie, occupation; Daniel Hinderlighter, Michael Hinderlighter, Daniel Hass, William Himes, James Hamilton, Elias Hulwick, David Hamilton, Michael Heterick, Peter Heterick, Samuel Hice, Michael Holloback, E. E. Hannager, Joseph Hannah, Adam Hane, Harry Heckendorn, John Hice, office; Isaac Hamilton, Jacob Huffman, Daniel Huffman, Andrew Hazlet (single man), John James, Robert Kennedy, John Conklin, Joseph Kinnear, George Knarr, Michael

PIONEER HISTORY OF JEFFERSON COUNTY, PENNA.

Lantz, John Lantz, Frederick Lantz, George Letich, Samuel Lerch David Langard, John Miller, John Mohney, John Motter, Henry Milliron (single man), William McAninch, Jr., William McAninch, Sr., Hugh McGuier, occupation; John McAninch, John McClelland, John Mower, Jr., John Mower, Sr., William Montier, William McNutt, Robert McNutt, Martin Miller, Peter Minich, George Milliron, David Milliron, Philip Milliron, William Milliron, Peter Milliron, Daniel Motter, Samuel Motter, Jacob Motter, George McGregor, M. McGregor, John Martz, Gillmore Montgomery, Daniel McGregor, Matthew McDavid, John Miller, Andrew McDaniel, Jacob Minich, David McDaniel, John McMillen, Thomas McMillen, Henry Minich, occupation; Samuel Mickle, Coonrod Nulf, N. J. Nesbit, occupation; Thomas Nice, William Niel, John Potts, George Potts, John Postlethwait, David Postlethwait, Elias Powel, Moses Powel, Peter Procius, Daniel Procius, Henry Peter, James Robinson, David Richard, George Reitz, John Robinson, Esq., one saw-mill; William Robinson, Irwin Robinson, Samuel Richard, Carl Randolf, Philip Reed, Joshua B. Farr, George Rinehart, Henry Ross, occupation; George Reitz (single man), John Silvas, occupation; Michael Shaffer, Simon Stahlman, Henry Spare, Sr., Isaac Shaffer, Frederick Steer, Jacob Snyder (single man), Abraham Shipe, Henry Shipe, one tan-yard; Philip Smith, Andrew Shaffer, Abraham Shaffer, Benjamin Shaffer, Valentine Shaffer, money on interest; Francis Shrawber, office; John Shrawber, Martin Shannon, occupation; Peter Spangler, Absalom Smith, John Shadle, John Steel, Jacob Startzel, John Shofner, Henry Spare, John Startzel, Coonrod Snyder, Walter Snyder, Daniel Snyder, Moses Shoffstall, Stephen Travis, Broce Taylor, Edward Chamberlin, Henry Truckmiller, Henry Chamberlain, George Chamberlain, George Travis, James Travis, Samuel Trayor, John Wilson, occupation; Edward Uptagraff, George Wise, Amos Weaver, Moses Weaver, James Watts, James Wilson, Esq., office; Benjamin Weary, Abraham Walker, Robert Wilson, Jacob Wise, George Young, Jr., George Young, Sr., Lawrence Yeager.

CLOVER.

Organized in 1841, and was taken from Rose. Clover township was bounded on the east and north by Rose, on the west by the Clarion County line, and on the south by Perry.

PIONEERS IN CLOVER TOWNSHIP AS PER ASSESSMENT IN 1843.

Names of Taxables.—Daniel Baldwin, Wallace Bratton, John H. Bish, Hudson Bridge, Samuel Bratton, Michael Brocius, John Brocius, Peter Brocius, Jacob Brocius, George Burns, Alonzo & Fred. Baldwin, one saw-mill, one yoke of oxen, one cow, and two horses; Adam Brocius, John Baughman, John Bruner, occupation as sawyer; John Campbell, Hiram Carrier, one saw-mill; Nathan Carrier, one fourth of a saw-mill;

PIONEER HISTORY OF JEFFERSON COUNTY, PENNA.

Darius Carrier, Lorenzo Campbell, Sanford Campbell, George and Nathan Carrier, George Cain (single man), Michael Crawford, George Carrier, one-fourth of a saw-mill; Darius Carrier, one-half of a saw-mill; Euphrastus Carrier, Darius & Hiram Carrier, one grist-mill; Isaac Covert, George Campbell, Matthew Dickey, Dr. James Dowling, James S. Dean, Andrew Doyle (single man), James Defords, George Eckler, William Edmond, Thomas Edmond, one saw-mill; David Edmond, John Fuller (single man), John H. Flemming, Solomon Fuller, Jr., Christopher Fogle, one tan-yard; David Farriweather, C. Jacox, house and lot; Ira Fuller, one saw-mill; William Fitzsimmons, transferred to Baldwin, James Ferguson, Abraham Funk, Hiram Fuller, Thomas Guthrie, Aaron Fuller, one saw-mill; George Gray, occupation; William Guthrie, James Guthrie (single man), Carder Gilmore, James B. Guthrie, James Guthrie, Sr., Alexander Guthrie, Jacob Grame, James Gardner, Elijah Heath, one grist-mill and one saw-mill; Jacob Heckman, James Hildebrand, Peter Himes, Joseph Hall, Sr., Joel & Porter Haskill, one saw-mill; Gideon Haskill, Simon Hays, one house and lot; Abram Hidelman, occupation as miller; John Johnston, William Jack, Samuel Johns, Hazard Jaycock, Charles Jaycock, Matson J. Knapp, Samuel Knapp, Moses Knapp, Jr., one grist-mill and one saw-mill; Joseph Knapp, one yoke of oxen and three cows; John Knapp, John Kelso, Jr., one dog; George Keck, James Kelso, William Kelly, William Lucas (single man), James S. Lucas, occupation; Peter Lucas, John Lucas, Jr., Daniel Leech, John Lucas, Sr., Samuel Lucas, Sr., John Lucas (of Samuel), Samuel Lucas, Jr., tradesman; John T. Love, John Love (Yankee), William Lucas (single man), Lucas & Knapp, guardians of Buttle's estate; James Long, trade; Rev. John McCauley, Samuel Magill, William Magill, Hugh McGiffin (Yankee), Daniel Milliron, Samuel Milliron, John McGiffin, Robert Morrison, David Moore, Isaac Motter, Andrew McElwaine, estate; Eli McDowel (single man), Abraham Milliron, Hugh McGiffin, Solomon Milliron, tradesman; Elijah McAninch, estate; George McAninch, William McAninch (of Samuel), Henry Milliron, Jonathan Milliron, William Miller, one house and lot; Samuel Newcomb, one saw-mill; Coonrad & Frank Nolf, William B. Newcomb, Joseph Osborne, William Rhoney, Levi Reed, William Rodgers, James Ross, one saw-mill; Hance Robinson, one grist-mill and saw-mill; Joseph Ross, William Robinson (single man), Richards Richard, George Richard, one house and lot; John Reitz, Isaac Reitz (single man), David Smith, William Simpson, Alexander Smith, Hulet Smith, John Shields, Sr., James Shields, Peter Swab, tradesman; Robert Shields, one yoke oxen and cow; Daniel and James Shields, one cow and yoke of oxen; James Shields, Jr., George Simpson, Benjamin Sowers, Abraham Stine, one house and lot; Henry Scott, Henry Sowers, John B. Shields, James Sowers, Jr., David Shields, James Sowers, Sr., Gideon Trumbull,

Joseph M. Thompson, Samuel B. Taylor, one lot and store; Jesse Vandevort, occupation; Paul Vandevort, one house and lot; David Vandevort, Stephen Webster, five lots; Beech Wayland, Patience Wheeler, John R. Welsh, Jackson Welsh (single man), Monroe Webster, Ezekiel White.

BROOKVILLE BOROUGH.

The pioneer borough, and taken from Rose, bounded on the east by Pine Creek.

BROOKVILLE BOROUGH AS PER ASSESSMENT IN 1844.

Names of Taxables.—Richard Arthurs (single man), house and lot, profession; Caleb Alexander, one patent-lever watch, $35; Charles Anderson (colored), one outlot and house; James Acheson (single man), Isaac Allen, two lots improved, one-half lot and house, and blacksmithshop; John Arthurs, James H. Ames, occupation; John Alexander, Rev. Garey Bishop, profession; Cyrus Butler, house and lot; Samuel B. Bishop, house and stable, profession, one gold watch, $50; Thompson Barr (single man). office; Robert P. Barr, house and lot, one grist-mill, mill lot and house, saw-mill; Hugh Brady, one lot improved, profession; Thomas Barr, house and lot, outlot, lot improved; John Brownlee, house and lot, printing-office; Samuel M. Bell, David Bittenbenner (single man), Wakefield Corbett (minor), one patent-lever watch; Barclay & Hastings, printing-office; Jesse G. Clark, house and lot, brick, tavern stand, lot improved, outlots improved, profession, one gold watch, $50; James Corbett, one lot, office, justice of peace; Levi G. Clover, house and lot, lots, outlots, office judgeship; Solomon Chambers, house and lot; Joseph Clements, house and lot, lots improved; Samuel Craig, house and lot, lot improved; James Craig, house and lot; Andrew Craig (single man), Corbett & Barr, house and lot, inlot and smith-shop; James C. Coleman, William F. Clark (single man), inlot, one lever watch, $35; George Darr, Joseph Deering (single man), Hugh Dowling (single man), George Darling, house and lot; Lewis B. Dunham, house and lot, outlot, profession, one pleasure carriage, $30; Daniel Dunkleburg (single man), David Deering (single man), profession, one lever watch, $35; John Dougherty, house and lots (tavern), house and lots (brick), house and lots, inlot improved, inlots, one gold watch, $45; James Dowling, profession; Jared B. Evans, four lots and houses and stables, eight lots; Samuel Espy, house and lot; Charles Evans, house and lot, brick, main street; Evan Evans, John Gallagher, lot improved, office justice of peace, outlot; Enoch Hall, house and lot; William Fleming (single man), John Hutchison, house, lot, and shop; Joseph Henderson, house and one and two-thirds lots; John Hastings, occupation, one lever watch, $35; Jamison Hendricks, occupation; James Hall estate, house and lot, outlot; Joseph Hughes, house and lot;

PIONEER HISTORY OF JEFFERSON COUNTY, PENNA.

George Irwin, David B. Jenks, house and two lots, profession ; William Jack, house and one-half lot, house and lot, inlots, inlots improved, outlots; William P. Jenks, Sr., Samuel H. Lucas, house and lot, one gold watch, $40; Thomas Lucas, house and lot, inlot improved, profession ; John Matson, Jr., house and lot; Uriah Matson, house and lot, James C. Matson, Joseph McAfee, inlot improved, outlots improved ; Benjamin McCreight, house and lot, brick, partly finished, house and lot, four lots ; Geo. McLaughlin (single man), house and lots, lot improved ; William McCandless (single man), Robert Matson (single man), John McCrea, office prothonotary ; George Porter, house and two lots ; John Richards, occupation, one gold watch, $75 ; John Ramsey, house and lot; William Rogers, occupation ; Alexander Scott, Jr. (single man), Philip Schrader, house and two lots ; John Smith, house and one-half lot, tavern, outlot; Daniel Smith, house and lot; Gabriel Vastbinder, inlot improved ; George Wilson (single man), William Wilkins (single man), one pleasure carriage ; Thomas Wilkins, James C. Wilson (single man), watch, value of $25 ; Wilkins & Irwin, one and one-half lots and house, tan-yard and house ; Michael Woods, Adam Goodman, T. B. McClellan, house and lot, lot improved ; Ephraim Washburn, occupation ; Alexander Scott, Sr., lot improved ; George Scott (single man), Wm. A. Sloan, house and lot, lot improved ; Samuel Truby, house and lot, lot improved ; John Templeton, house and lot ; James Humphrey (single man).

GASKILL.

Organized in 1842, and was taken from Young. Gaskill township was bounded on the east by the Clearfield County line, on the south by the Indiana County line, and on the west and north by Young township.

PIONEERS IN GASKILL TOWNSHIP AS PER ASSESSMENT IN 1842.

Names of Taxables.—Levi Anthony, unimproved land judgments, $38 ; Henry Bowman, Philip Bowers, Andrew Bowers, John Bowers, Eli Bowers, Henry & Samuel Beam, Calvin Brooks, William Brooks, Peter Buchite, George Culp, John Cary, Daniel Coffman, John Coffman, Oliver Cathers, Joseph Cofflett, Abraham Cofflett, Jacob Cofflett (single man), Josiah Covert, John Douthett estate, Francis Doros, John Deamer, James Dickey, Alexander Dickey, Thomas Davis, Josiah Davis, George Gregg, David Henry, John Hoover, Joseph Hoover, Sally Hess, Rufus Jorley, Frederick Kuhuley, Thomas Kerr, one promissory note, $20 ; George Keller, occupation ; Joseph Keller, Abraham Keller, Alexander Lyons, Henry Lot, Francis Leech, George Leech, occupation ; Abraham Ludwick, George Ludwick, Elizabeth Ludwick, John Long, Andrew McCreight, Sharp McCreight, James McCreight (single man), Henry Miller, mason ; John Miller, George Miller, Henry Miller, farmer ; William McElheny, George Pifer (single man), John Pifer, Jonas Pifer, Henry & John

PIONEER HISTORY OF JEFFERSON COUNTY, PENNA.

D. Philipi, Samuel Pershing, Adam Quigley, John Rider, George Rhodes, Jacob Smith, Sr., Jacob Smith, Jr., Jonathan Stouse, James Solesley, Samuel Smith, Adam States, Henry Sprague, Ashel Sprague, Milton Sprague, carpenter; Thomas Thompson, Adam Wise, Jacob Weaver; Joseph Wilson, Richard Wainwright, George Wainwright, William Williams, James Williams, Adam Yohey, Henry Yohey, Samuel Yohey (single man), Samuel Zufall, one saw-mill.

WARSAW.

Organized in 1842, and was taken from Pine Creek. Warsaw was bounded by Snyder and Washington on the east, by Ridgeway on the north, Eldred on the west, and Pine Creek on the south.

PIONEERS IN WARSAW TOWNSHIP AS PER ASSESSMENT IN 1843.

Names of Taxables.—William Anderson, John Alexander, Gilbert Burrows, Ira Bronson, John Bell, John W. Baum, Joseph Buell, Nathaniel Butler, Philo Bowdish, David Butler, Bartholomew Cavinore, ——— Chapman, one cow and trade; Peter Chamberlin, Elihu Clark, David Carlton, Sarah Dixon, John Dill, Thomas Dixon, Jared A. Evans, Thomas Ewing, John Fleming, George Frederick, Aaron Fuller, Milton Gibbs, William Gray, Francis Goodar, Miron Gibbs, William Humphrey, Matthew Humphrey, Philip Heterick, Samuel Howe, Joel Howe, Elijah Heath, James K. Huffman, George Hunter, John Heterick, Joseph E. Hannah, Joseph Hoey, Davis Ingraham, Eli I. Irvin, William Jack, Milton Johnson, Henry Keys, William Long, Michael Long, Sarah Ann Lithgow, Josiah Loomis, Sarah McCormick, Thomas McCormick, David McCormick, Jr., one silver watch; James & John Moorhead, David Moorhead, Joseph McConnell, Matthew Metcalf, one silver watch; William and James McElvain, Asa Morey, Jacob Moore, Mundale Metcalf, Ozias P. Mather, Robert Montgomery, Andrew McCormick, Samuel P. McCormick, Findley McCormick, one silver watch; David McCormick, Sr., Thomas McWilliams, Elnathan Marsh, Charles Munger, Nathan Perrin, John M. Phelps, Arad Pearsall, trade, John Pearsall, Solomon Riggs, George Russell, William R. Richards, two saw-mills, one silver watch; Peter Richards, Sr., Peter Richards, Jr., Abraham Rufsnyder, William Russell, John N. Riggs, Davis E. Riggs, James L. L. Riggs, Daniel Snyder, Eli Snyder, Abraham Snyder, Nathan Snyder, Samuel Shul, one saw-mill and house; Moses B. St. John, Gideon Trumbull, Isaac Temple, Jacob Vastbinder, Sr., Joshua Vandevort, Sr., Jacob Vastbinder, Jr. (single man), John Vastbinder, Andrew Vastbinder, Abram Vandevort, Levi Vandevort, Joshua Vandevort, Jr., Peter Vastbinder, James A. Wilkins, John J. Wilson, Isaac Walker, John Wakefield, John Walker, Solomon Wales, William Weeks, John R. Wilkins, Galbraith Wilson, Jeremiah Wilson, one tannery; Hiram Wilson.

PIONEER HISTORY OF JEFFERSON COUNTY, PENNA.

CHAPTER XXIV.

PIONEER NEWSPAPER IN THE WEST—PIONEER NEWSPAPER IN THE COUNTY
—TERMS—EARLY MARKET—OTHER PAPERS.

PREVIOUS to 1793 there were no postal or post-office facilities. Letters and papers had to be sent with friends, neighbors, or by special carriers. The first newspaper started in the western part of the State was the *Pittsburg Gazette.* It was published by John Scull, and issued in 1786. It was distributed to patrons by special carriers. The pioneer newspaper for Jefferson County was published in Indiana, Pennsylvania. It was established in 1826. It was a four-column paper, printed on paper eleven inches wide and seventeen inches long. I have No. 13 of vol. i., and reprint here from it,—viz. :

THE AMERICAN,
AND
INDIANA & JEFFERSON REPUBLICAN.

"He is a freeman whom the truth makes free and all are slaves besides."—COWPER.

ALEXANDER T. MOORHEAD, PROPRIETOR, AND EDITED BY JAMES MOORHEAD.

NEW SERIES—VOL. I.   MONDAY, MAY 22, 1826.   NO. 13.

PRINTED BY
WM. MOORHEAD,
in the frame house next door to Mr. Jos. Thompson, Chair Maker and Painter,
North of the Court House,
Water Street, Indiana, Pa.

Terms of Publication.

THE AMERICAN, AND INDIANA AND JEFFERSON REPUBLICAN will be published every Monday, at two dollars per annum, exclusive of postage; and two dollars and fifty cents, including postage, payable half yearly in advance.
No subscription taken for a shorter period than six months, and no withdrawal whilst in arrears.
A failure to notify an intention to discontinue at the end of six months is considered a new engagement.
Advertisements will be inserted at the rate of ONE DOLLAR per square for the three first insertions, and TWENTY-FIVE cents for every continuance; those of greater length in proportion.
All orders directed to the Editor must be post paid or they cannot receive attention.
GRAIN, RAGS, BEES-WAX, OR TALLOW, will be taken in payment of subscription, if paid within the current year.

Inside and local column :

THE AMERICAN.

INDIANA:

MONDAY, MAY 22, 1826.

The price of lumber by retail as advertised by the Diamond Mills, March 6th, 1826.
Bill of Price of Pine BOARDS, and SCANTLING at the MILLS.

Inch boards price per 100 feet	$0.80
¾ inch do do	0.75
½ inch do do	0.70
2 inch plank (selected)	0.50
1½ inch (do)	1.25
3 inch (do)	2.00
2 inch common plank for barn or stable floors	1.20
Scantling for Joists, &c. &c. 2½ inches by 10, running measure per 100 feet.	1.30
3 inches by 8, per 100 feet	1.37½
3 inches by 7, do	1.25
3 inches by 5, (selected)	1.25
3 inches by 4, (do)	1.12½
5 inches by 5, (do)	1.50
Scantling for Rafters in proportion.	
Lath for palings &c. per 100 feet	0.26
Selected boards of the best timber for Sash, or other particular uses	1.00

Purchasers are invited to give us a call.

ROBERT MITCHELL,
JAMES HAMILTON,
A. T. MOORHEAD.

A common advertisement of those days as found in the above paper :

"Six Cents Reward.

" RAN away from the residence of his father, in Green Township, Indiana County,
SIMON CONNER,
without any just cause; I therefore forbid any person from harboring said boy, or the law will be rigidly enforced against them. He had on when he absconded a drab coat and pantaloons, and other clothing; one fur and one wool hat. The above reward and all reasonable expenses paid if brought home.
JOHN CONNERS."
May 22, 1826.

The following market report is taken from the *Blairsville Record and Conemaugh Reporter*, dated February 18, 1830, published by L. McFarland :

" Butter, per pound, 11 cents ; bacon, per pound, 6 and 7 ; bags, 37 and 62 ; beans, per bushel, 87 and $1.00 ; boards, pine, per 100 feet, $1.50

PIONEER HISTORY OF JEFFERSON COUNTY, PENNA.

and $1.60; coal, per bushel, 2 and 3; candles, per pound, 10 and 10½; cheese, per pound, 7 and 8; eggs, per dozen, 12½; flour, per barrel, $5 and $5.50; feathers, per pound, 30; wheat, per bushel, 70 and 80; rye, per bushel, 40 and 50; corn, per bushel, 40 and 50; oats, per bushel, 31 and 37; sole leather, per pound, 23 and 26; lard, per pound, 5; pork, fresh, per pound, 3 and 3½; potatoes, per bushel, 25; salt, per barrel, $2.50; wool, per pound, 13 and 33; whiskey, per gallon, 27 and 30.

"PITTSBURGH, PENN'A, March 4th, 1834.

"PRICES CURRENT.

Wheat per bushel	65 and 70 cents.
Rye " "	50 and 56 "
Corn " "	45 and 59 "
Oats " "	31 and 33 "
Wheat flour per barrel	$3.
Buckwheat flour per hundredweight	$2.50 and $3.
Flaxseed per bushel	90 cents to $1.
Dried apples per bushel	40 and 50 cents.
" peaches	$1.
Feathers per pound	33 and 40 cents.
Rags " "	5 and 5½ "
Wool " "	30 cents.
Spanish hides per pound	16 and 19 cents.
Green " " "	5 cents.
Beeswax per pound	16 and 18 cents.
Havana coffee per pound	14 and 14½ cents.
Rio " " "	15½ and 17 "
Java " " "	16 and 18 cents.
Whiskey per gallon	23 and 25 "

—Copied from the *Olive Branch*, Freeport, Pennsylvania, April 26, 1834, vol. i., No. 30.

In the year 1832, John J. Y. Thompson established in Brookville, Jefferson County, Pennsylvania, and issued the first number of the pioneer paper within the confines of the county. This paper was printed on coarse paper, thirteen inches wide and twenty inches long. The terms of subscription were the same as printed for the *American*. In politics it was Democratic. In 1833, Thomas Reid purchased a half interest in the establishment. The paper then was published as a neutral or independent, and still called *Gazette*. Thompson and Reid not agreeing, Reid retired, and Thompson and James P. Blair continued the publication.

In 1833, Thompson disposed of his interest to Dr. R. K. Scott, and the firm became Blair & Scott. They changed the name to *Jeffersonian*, and in politics it was Democratic. On February 27, 1834, Blair & Scott sold out to George R. Barrett, who published it as the *Jeffersonian* for one year. It was printed and published each week on Thursday, and on the same terms as the *Indiana American*. The pioneer printing office under all these parties, except Thompson, was in a one story-and-a-half frame building, unpainted, on the corner of Main and Pickering Streets, opposite the old, and now the new, court-house. Matson's brick block is now located on the ground. For years this little office, as well as the village, which was named Brookville by Joseph Barnett, the patriarch of the county, was surrounded by a boundless forest, the tall and lofty pines

J. J. Y. Thompson, pioneer publisher of paper.

in the immediate vicinity towering up towards the clouds, obscuring the sun's rays until noontide, while nightly revels of hungry wolves awakened the pioneer in his cabin. Next Jesse G. Clark and Blair bought and ran the paper for six months, at which time James H. Laverty and James McCrackin bought and published the paper until 1836. At this time Laverty retired, and McCrackin changed the name to the *Brookville Republican*, and continued the publication until January 1, 1839, when he removed with his paper from the county.

Copy of George R. Barrett's indenture, the man who published the *Brookville Jeffersonian* in 1834:

PIONEER HISTORY OF JEFFERSON COUNTY, PENNA.

"Article of agreement made and concluded this first day of September, eighteen hundred and thirty-one, between John Bigler, of the borough of Bellefonte, Centre County, on the one part, and Daniel Barrett, of Clearfield County, on the other part.

"The said John Bigler, printer, doth agree to teach George Barrett, son of the said Daniel, the art and mystery of printing; and during the period that the said George shall so live with him the said Bigler is to

Hon. George R. Barrett, editor of paper.

board and clothe said George, and during his time give him one-quarter of day schooling, one-quarter night schooling, and when free give the said George a good suit of clothes, to be new at that time.

"And the said Daniel doth hereby covenant and agree that the said George shall remain with the said Bigler for the term of three years and six months from the date of these presents, and comport himself in such manner as is the duty of an apprentice to a master.

"JOHN BIGLER,
DANIEL BARRETT.

"Witness present—FRANKLIN B. SMITH."

PIONEER HISTORY OF JEFFERSON COUNTY, PENNA.

In June, 1838, Thomas Hastings and son started and published in Brookville a new paper called the *Backwoodsman*. In 1841, Colonel William Jack bought this paper and had it published by George F. Humes. This was not a success, and Humes, in a valedictory to his patrons, told them to go to h—ll and he would go to Texas. In 1843 the paper was owned and published by David Barclay and Barton T. Hastings. In a short time Barclay retired and Hastings continued the publication. Those papers were all printed on the old Ramage or Franklin press, and every publisher made his own "roller" out of glue and molasses, in the proportion of a pound of glue to a pint of molasses. In Brookville the "youngest devil" in the office carried to the residence of each subscriber his or her paper. The boy who delivered these papers was called the "carrier." Each New Year's day this carrier would have an address in poetry, written by some local bard, recounting the events of the year just closed. This New Year's address he offered for sale to his patrons.

"ADDRESS TO HIS PATRONS BY THE CARRIER OF THE BROOKVILLE DEMOCRAT-REPUBLICAN, JANUARY 1, 1837.

"Here I come, the 'little herald' of our town,
So early in the morning, to prance the streets around,
Bringing to you news from near and far,
Of murder, marriage, death, and war;
Through the bleak winter's snow-storm,
Through rain, hail, and weather of every form,
I my weekly courses round to your house run,
As regularly as the bright and unvarying sun;
And since I my first visit here have made,
Changes many and strange, it is said,
Have fallen to the poor creature man:
To some, many thousands is a clan.

"But since I have thus taken upon me
To be merry and busy as a honey-bee,
You will please bear with me awhile,—
I will tell you of wars strange and vile,
Which, within twelve months, have taken place,
On Texas's fair soil, by the Mexican race,
Who, like bloody monsters and fiend,
Butcher'd man, woman, and child.
Brave Crockett, like a hero has a fallen,
Far in Texas, while the Mexican malling.
His fame, may it be handed down,
Like the never-fading laurels of a crown.
May a lasting tribute be fully paid
To him that low in the Alamo was laid;
But, the commander, Santa Anna, soon in snare,
Was taken by Houston and his men of war;

PIONEER HISTORY OF JEFFERSON COUNTY, PENNA.

In chains and fetters he long lay,
Now turned at liberty, they say.
To Washington in haste he comes,
There in its lofty and pure domes,
To acknowledge TEXAS to be at liberty;
And that she shall no longer fear he,
In the presence of Jackson, noble and brave,
To declare her free as the sea-rolling wave.

"Another President has been made,
MARTIN VAN BUREN, it is truly said,
Will take this high nation's reins,
Will, on the fourth, if the Lord deigns,
Of March next President be,
Over this great nation of Liberty;
While Johnston, of Kentucky great,
Yet has to stand before the Senate.

"Now to you, fair lasses, a word.
I will speak to you of neither famine nor sword,
But of plenty and happiness, full and free,
Around well-furnished tables of tea.
Leap year has taken its flight,
And the bachelors are glad of the sight;
Beaus you will soon have in full store,
Since you have courted them no more;
But I would advise and warn you,
To beware lest they despise and scorn you,
That you pass not sweet twenty-five,
In single blessedness to live.
You will please take this friendly warning,
And I will bid you a good-morning.

"Old maids, like to have forgotten you I had;
Your condition is surprisingly bad;
Next to an old bachelor's dreadful state
I deplore your wonderfully hard fate.
But cheer up, ye lovely old dames,
Husbands you shall have in picture-frames.

"But of all IMPS I am the completest,
Of all patrons you are the neatest,
All so very kind, loving, and civil
To your young friend, the printer's devil;
Then take it not as impudent of me,
Little, poor, and despised you see,
To wish you a happy New Year;
And you need not feel anxiety or fear,

> About produce that may fall or rise,
> If you just hand over to me TWENTY-FIVE.
> To do this you may not be willing,
> Then extend unto me but one shilling.
>   "CARRIER.
>
> "*Republican Office*, BROOKVILLE, January 1, 1837."

CHAPTER XXV.

MILITIA AND TOWNSHIPS.

PIONEER MILITIA REGIMENT.

OUR pioneer militia regiment was the One Hundred and Forty-fifth, Second Brigade, Fifteenth Division, Pennsylvania Militia.

The first reference I can find of a militia company was in what is now Washington township. I am unable to give any further information of the militia at that date.

"ATTENTION.

"The enrolled militia, comprising the Seventh Company, First Battalion, One Hundred and Forty-fifth Regiment, Second Brigade, Fifteenth Division, Pennsylvania Militia, are ordered to meet, properly equipped for drilling, at the home of Joseph Keys, in Pine Creek township, on the first Monday of May next, at the hour of ten o'clock of said day.

"JOHN WILSON, *Captain*."

April 10, 1834.

The lieutenants of this company were Henry Keys and Oliver McClelland.

Our battalion seems to have been comprised of five companies, formed part of the One Hundred and Forty-fifth Regiment, and belonged to the Fifteenth Division. The regiment was composed of two battalions, one in Jefferson, and the division was composed of the counties of Allegheny, Armstrong, Indiana, and Jefferson. William F. Johnston, of Kittanning, afterwards governor of the State, was the colonel; Alexander McKnight (my father), of Brookville, was lieutenant-colonel; and William Rodgers, of Brookville, was major.

These regimental officers were commissioned August 3, 1835, for seven years, or during good behavior.

The companies were numbered, "first," "second," etc., instead of being designated by letters, as at present

PIONEER HISTORY OF JEFFERSON COUNTY, PENNA.

OFFICIAL FIRST COMPANY.

Pioneer Militia Company of Eldred and Barnett Townships.—List of the voters or enrolled men of the First Company of the militia of Jefferson County, Pennsylvania, March 21, 1836:

Thomas Arthurs, Jacob Craft, Henry M. R. Clark, Daniel Elgin, John West, Joseph B. Graham, Nathan Phipps.

At an election held at the house of Thomas Arthurs, on the 21st of March, 1836, John West was elected captain, Nathan Phipps was elected first lieutenant, and Joseph B. Graham second lieutenant.

Pioneer Militia Officers of the Third Company, for the Township of Perry.—At an election held on the 21st of March, 1836, at the house of John Sprankle, the following officers were elected:

For captain, Clark Kithcart had seven votes.
For first lieutenant, William Ferguson had seven votes.
For second lieutenant, John N. Shaffer had seven votes.

Pioneer Militia Officers of the Fourth Company of Militia, for the Township of Young.—At an election held at the house of A. Weaver, on March 21, 1836, the following officers were elected:

For captain, William Clawson had twelve votes.
For first lieutenant, John Drum had eleven votes.
For second lieutenant, James Torrence had ten votes.

Pioneer Militia Company, Sixth Company, for the Township of Rose.—At an election held March 21, 1836, at the house of Alonzo Baldwin, in the township of Rose, for company officers for the Sixth Company of the Jefferson County Militia, Second Brigade, and Fifteenth Division:

For captain, Isaac McIlvaine had thirteen votes.
For captain, Christopher Barr had one vote.
For first lieutenant, Enoch Hall had seven votes.
For first lieutenant, John Heterick had seven votes.
For second lieutenant, John Lucas, Jr., had nine votes.
For second lieutenant, William Godfrey had five votes.

J. J. Y. THOMPSON, *Clerk.*

Voters on enrollment:

Christopher Barr, Andrew McIlvaine, William Godfrey, John Williams, George McAninch, John Heterick, Isaac McIlvaine, Hiram Carrier, Andrew McIlvaine, Jr., Philip Burns, William McAninch, David Moore, John J. Y. Thompson, Alonzo Baldwin.

Pioneer Militia Company of Brookville.—At an election held March 21, 1836, at the house of Thomas Hastings, inn-keeper in Brookville, for the purpose of electing officers for the Seventh Company of the Jefferson County Battalion, Pennsylvania Militia, the following members polled their ballots:

Job McCreight, Robert Barr, Henry Dull, William McGarey, William

PIONEER HISTORY OF JEFFERSON COUNTY, PENNA.

Barr, Thomas Craddick, Jr., Andrew C. Vastbinder, Jared B. Evans, Thomas Hastings, John Gallagher, John Brownlee, Samuel Craig, Cephas J. Dunham, John Beck, Thomas Barr, Daniel Coder, Isaac Hallen, Joseph Sharp, Charles A. Wells, Joseph Clements, Jesse G. Clark, Benjamin McCreight, Hugh Brady, Samuel Truby, William Rodgers, Arad Pearsall, Alexander C. Hamilton, William Kelso, James Craig, Andrew C. Hall, Richard Arthurs, James Lucas, Caleb A. Alexander, James McCracken, John Barnett, James Templeton, Henry Smith.

William Kelso was elected captain, Daniel Coder first lieutenant, and Henry Smith second lieutenant.

The following notice, dated November 17, 1836, was published in the *Brookville Republican* by the brigade inspector, as required by law:

"An appeal for the First Battalion, One Hundred and Forty-fifth Regiment, will be held at the house of J. Pierce, in the borough of Brookville, on Monday, the 12th day of December next. The field officers of said battalion are requested to attend for the purpose of hearing excuses and exonerating constables, etc. Persons interested are requested to attend. All persons having claims for military services are requested to present them at the above time and place.
"S. S. JAMISON, *Brigade-Inspector*,
"*Second Bat., Fifteenth Div., P. M.*"

The pioneer musters and reviews were held either at Port Barnett, the McCullough farm, or Samuel Jones's farm; also on what is now Jackson Heber's farm, and on what is now our fair grounds. All marching was done to the tune of "Yankee Doodle." The militia carried all kinds of weapons, including "corn-stalks," and hence were called the "corn-stalk militia."

The militia drills ceased in this State about 1847 or 1848.

Marching was in single file. In drill it was "by sections of two, march." Instead of "file right" or "file left," it was "right" or "left wheel." Instead of "front" it was "left face." The Brookville militia and Jefferson Blues company drilled on the flat now covered with water by Heidrick, Matson & Co.'s dam.

VOLUNTEERS — THE PIONEER MILITARY COMPANY — JEFFERSON BLUES—CONSTITUTION OF THAT ORGANIZATION—MILITARY FOURTH OF JULY CELEBRATION.

As near as I can learn, the pioneer military volunteer company in the county was the Jefferson Blues. This body of men was organized at Brookville some time in 1836, and was a "Volunteer Rifle Association."

PIONEER HISTORY OF JEFFERSON COUNTY, PENNA.

The pioneer officers were, captain, John Wilson; lieutenants, William Kelso and Henry Vastbinder; orderly Sergeant, Samuel Chitister. Band: Samuel Lucas, fifer; Oliver George, snare drummer; Evans R. Brady, bass drummer.

From the *Brookville Democrat-Republican* of 1837 I quote the following account of the pioneer military celebration of the Fourth of July, 1776:

"JEFFERSON BLUES—ANNIVERSARY CELEBRATION.

"The sixty-first anniversary of American Independence was celebrated in this place on the memorable Fourth by the Jefferson Blues, commanded by Captain John Wilson, together with the citizens of Jefferson County, in a spirit worthy of the occasion. The company formed in procession, and after parading in the streets and through the borough for a time, adjourned to the public house of William Clark, Esq., where they partook of a sumptuous repast, served up in his best style.

"Dinner over, the procession marched to the grove southeast of Brookville, where an oration was spoken by Richard Arthurs, Esq., after which the following toasts were drunk:

"By Captain John Wilson. The young republic of Texas: may she soon be united into the confederacy of our happy Union, and with her sound the trumpet of liberty.

"By Lieutenant Vastbinder. The heroes of the army and navy of the last war: may their memories be cherished while the earth bears a plant or the sea rolls a wave.

"By Sergeant Samuel Chitister. The Jefferson Blues: may they have the pleasure of being commanded hereafter by a commander of their own who is capable of performing the duties assigned him.

"By Samuel Miller. The Jefferson Blues: it is now about one year since their organization; it it is hoped that hereafter they will agree better, and become a respectable volunteer company.

"By William Clark. The North Fork Company: may they last as long as laurel grows green or I keep a tavern in Brookville.

"By S. Miller. Carlton B. Curtis, Esq., our late representative in the Legislature. The talent and ability with which he represented us last winter insures him our suffrage for another term.

"Sent by Levi L. Tate. Universal education, the railroad to internal improvement: may it go ahead and prosper.

"By Samuel Lucas. The Jefferson Blues: may they never be compelled to slavery while the soil yields fruit or the ocean rolls a wave.

"By George O. George. May we stand firm in the field of battle, undaunted and unshaken by the toils and dangers of a military life.

"By Joseph Chitister. Free and independent Blues: may love and unity prevail among us.

PIONEER HISTORY OF JEFFERSON COUNTY, PENNA.

" By D. Chitister. Our Constitution: may we all fearlessly support it while we are able to beat a drum or shoulder our arms.

" By John W. Carr. The farmers of Jefferson County who sold their grain out of the county last winter: may they have the pleasure of living on potatoes for three months.

" By David Vandyke. The Reform Convention: consists of many men, many minds, and I believe of birds of various kinds, a great singing and humming, and at least not much doing.

"By Thomas Dixon. The people of Jefferson County: may virtue, liberty, independence, ever be their polar star.

" By George Matthews. The volunteers of Pennsylvania: may they have but one object, that the good of their country.

" By William W. Stewart. Daniel Webster, a Democrat and Anti-Mason, and the best statesman in the United States: may he be chosen President in eighteen hundred and forty.

" By Thomas Dixon. Nicholas Biddle, Daniel Webster, Henry Clay, and others will find they have ' barked up the wrong sapling' in their efforts to underrate the virtue of Old Hickory in his dealings towards the United States Bank.

" By John T. Crow. The Jefferson Blues: may her members increase in number and in knowledge of military tactics, and may our next choice of a captain result in the selection of one who understands the first principles of military duties.

" By U. Matson. Short shoes and long corns to be the enemies of liberty.

" By J. S. McCullough. May the Jefferson Blues be as gallant as the heroes of seventy-six under the gallant Washington.

" BY THE COMPANY.

" The Independence of the United States made the Fourth of July sixty-one years ago. Let us remember our leader Washington while we volunteer.

" The captain of our company: thanks to you for your good performance this day.

" May the Jefferson Blues be united unanimously, so that they may understand their duty to defend their country.

" May our company become more united together, and encourage one another to do their duty here and hereafter.

" The hero of Tippecanoe: may his name be handed down to posterity in letters of gold.

" (NOTE-QUERY.—Whether were the toasts drunk, or the persons by whom they were given? We hope not the latter.—EDITORS *Republican.*)"

The martial bands at every celebration and muster kept constantly beating the tune of all tunes that delighted the pioneer,—viz.:

"Yankee Doodle is the tune,
Yankee doodle dandy;
How we made the redcoats run
At Yankee doodle dandy!"

This tune was sometimes alternated with "The Girl I Left Behind Me."

AGREEMENT TO FORM COMPANY.

"The subscribers, whose names are hereunto affixed, agree to form themselves into a Volunteer Rifle Association, the name of which shall be the 'Jefferson Blues,' and have adopted the following constitution for our government:

"JEFFERSON BLUES' CONSTITUTION.

("Published by request.)

"ARTICLE 1. *Uniform.*—Citizen's blue coat, white pantaloons, white vest, red belt, black hat, with red scarf trimmed with white tape or cord, black cockades, white plumes with red tops, and black leather stocks or handkerchiefs.

"ARTICLE 2. *Time of Parade.*—The company shall parade upon the three days appointed by law, fixing upon the tenth of September for the third, and as many times thereafter as a majority of the company shall parade. Notice of the time and place of each parade shall be publicly given by the orderly sergeant at least ten days previous to the time of the parade.

"ARTICLE 3. *Fines.*—The fines shall be as follows: On law days, for each commissioned officer two dollars, for non-commissioned officer one dollar and fifty cents, and privates one dollar, and on days appointed by the company one-half of said fine.

"ARTICLE 4. The non-commissioned officers shall be elected and act during good behavior. The commissioned officers having the power to remove the non commissioned officers and hold another election, the officer so removed, if aggrieved, may appeal to the company.

"ARTICLE 5. The orderly sergeant shall act as clerk of the company, and the orderly sergeant shall collect all fines, etc.

"ARTICLE 6. The commissioned officers shall constitute a standing executive committee to manage all the concerns of the company, and court of appeals.

"ARTICLE 7. Signing the constitution and fulfilling the promises shall constitute a membership previous to the organization, after which, in addition to the above, every applicant shall be admitted by the concurrence of two-thirds of the company.

PIONEER HISTORY OF JEFFERSON COUNTY, PENNA.

"ARTICLE 8. The constitution shall not be altered or amended except with the consent of two-thirds of the company.

"Adopted this 4th day of July, 1836.

"JOHN WILSON,
HENRY VASTBINDER,
THOMAS DIXON,
WILLIAM DIXON,
JOHN DIXON,
JAMES DIXON,
DANIEL LONG,
WILLIAM LONG,
MICHAEL LONG,
JOHN KNAPP,
JOSHUA KNAPP,
SAMUEL KNAPP,
PAUL VANDEVORT,
DAVID VANDEVORT,
JOSHUA VANDEVORT,
J. B. GRAHAM,

WILLIAM KELSO,
SAMUEL CHITISTER,
DAVID CHITISTER,
DANIEL CHITISTER,
JOSEPH CHITISTER,
JAMES MURPHY,
DAVID MASON,
WILLIAM MASON,
JACOB MASON,
BENJAMIN MASON,
JAMES S. MCCULLOUGH,
WILLIAM MCCULLOUGH,
MOSES KNAPP, JR.,
DAVID MOORE,
JOHN HETERICK."

"ATTENTION, JEFFERSON BLUES!

"Notice is hereby given that an Appeal will be held at the house of William Clark on Monday, the sixth day of November next, when those concerned can have an opportunity of attending. Appeal to open at 10 o'clock.

"By order of the captain.

"SAMUEL CHITISTER, O. S.

"BROOKVILLE, October 19, 1837."

These Blues had an existence of seven years.

"MILITIA APPEAL.

"An appeal for the First Battalion, One Hundred and Forty-fifth Regiment, will be held at the house of J. Pierce, in the borough of Brookville, on Monday, the 12th day of December next. The field officers of said battalion are requested to attend for the purpose of hearing excuses and exonerating constables, etc. Persons interested are requested to attend.

"All persons having claims for military services are requested to present them at the above time and place.

"S. S. JAMISON, *Brigade Inspector*,
"*Second Bat., Fifteenth Div., P. M.*

"November 17, 1836."

—*Brookville Democrat-Republican.*

"THE AMERICAN BOY.

"A POEM OF 1836.

"'Father, look up and see that flag,
    How gracefully it flies;
Those pretty stripes, that seem to be
    A rainbow in the skies.'

"'It is your country's flag, my son,
    And proudly drinks the light,
O'er ocean's wave—in foreign climes,
    A symbol of our might.'

"'Father, what fearful voice is that,
    Like thundering of the clouds?
Why do the people wave their hats,
    And rush along in crowds?'

"'It is the noise of cannonry,
    The glad shout of the free;
This is a day to memory dear,—
    'Tis freedom's jubilee.'

"'I wish that I was now a man,
    I'd fire my cannon too,
And cheer as loudly as the rest;
    But, father, why don't you?'

"'I'm getting old and weak, but still
    My heart is big with joy;
I've witnessed many a day like this;
    Shout you aloud, my boy.'

"'Hurrah for Freedom's Jubilee!
    God bless our native land!
And may I live to hold the sword
    Of Freedom in my hand.'

"'Well done, my boy. Grow up and love
    The land that gave you birth;
A home where freedom loves to dwell
    Is Paradise on earth.'
                                "J. G. H."
—*Baltimore Chronicle.*

PINE CREEK—THE MOTHER TOWNSHIP.

Pine Creek in the Delaware language is "Cucoeu-harrue,"—*i.e.*, a pine creek, a stream flowing through pine woods.

This township was established by an act of Assembly in 1806, being the first and only township in the county, and named in honor of Pine Creek township, Lycoming County, from which the county and this town-

PIONEER HISTORY OF JEFFERSON COUNTY, PENNA.

ship were taken. This township was the mother of all the others, and its historic reminiscences are all commemorated in the general history of the county.

The resident taxables in 1807 were 23; in 1814, 35; in 1821, including Perry township, 161; in 1828, 60; in 1835, 103; in 1842, 98. The population by census in 1810 was 161; in 1820, 561; this also included Perry township; in 1830, not obtained; in 1840, 628.

Though the county was organized provisionally in 1804, there seems to have been no records kept nor any elections held untill 1807.

The pioneer election district in the county and in Pine Creek township, Jefferson County, was created by an act creating certain election districts, and making alterations in other districts already enacted. Approved 31st March, A.D. 1806, which read as follows,—viz., Jefferson County made a separate district :

"SECTION 9. *And be it further enacted by the authority aforesaid,* That the county of Jefferson shall be a separate election district, and the electors thereof shall hold their general elections at the house now occupied by Joseph Barnett, on Sandy Lick Creek, in said county."

The pioneer election returns are as follows :

" 1807—Jefferson County. At an election held at the house of Samuel Scott, in said county, on Friday, the 20th of March, A.D. 1807, the following persons were duly elected :

"Supervisors, John Scott had eighteen votes, Peter Jones had eighteen votes. Signed, Samuel Scott, Thomas Lucas, judges."

" 1808—At an election held at the house of Samuel Scott, in said county, on the 18th day of March, A.D. 1808, the following persons were duly elected as returned below :

"Supervisors, John Jones, Alexander McCoy, were duly elected; auditors, Samuel Lucas, Samuel Scott, Moses Knapp, and Adam Vastbinder were duly elected. Signed, Samuel Scott, John Dixon, judges."

These returns are as copied from the records of Indiana County, where the returns had to be made, this county then being under the legal jurisdiction of Indiana.

In June, about the year 1818, a terrible hail-storm swept through this region and extended its ravages several miles, killing and destroying the largest pine-trees, leaving them standing as dead. The width of this storm was about half a mile.

On the 6th of June, 1806, there was a total eclipse of the sun. Fowls went to roost and bees hastened to their hives. The pioneers and Indians were greatly alarmed.

Between the hours of three and seven o'clock in the morning of December 16, 1811, two distinct shocks of earthquake startled the pioneers of Jefferson County. The violence was such as to shake their log cabins.

PIONEER HISTORY OF JEFFERSON COUNTY, PENNA.

The pioneer explorers of the land were Andrew Barnett and Samuel Scott, in 1796.

The pioneer settler was Joseph Hutchison and wife in 1798. The patriarch was Joseph Barnett, who settled here in the fall of 1800. The pioneer birth was Rebecca Barnett, in 1802.

Andrew Barnett, Jr.

The pioneer marriage was Sarah Barnett to Elisha M. Graham, March 30, 1807.

The pioneer minister of the gospel to visit and preach was a Rev. Mr. Greer, a friend of Joseph Barnett. He came on a visit in 1801. He remained two weeks, and preached several times. He returned on a visit in 1802, and again preached.

The pioneer death was that of Andrew Barnett, in the fall of 1797.

PIONEER HISTORY OF JEFFERSON COUNTY, PENNA.

He was buried on the bank of Mill Creek, by Samuel Scott and two friendly Indians, and to this day no man knoweth the exact place of his burial.

The second family to follow the Barnetts into this wilderness was Peter Jones, from Centre County, Pennsylvania. He came in 1801. In the winter of 1801, Stephen Roll, August Shultz, and a negro named Fudge Van Camp started on foot near Easton for the Barnett settlement. When they struck "Meade's trail," at the mouth of Anderson's Creek, there yet remained for them to travel thirty-three miles of unbroken wilderness. They were foolish enough to start on this part of their journey without anything to eat on the way. After they started it snowed all day in this wilderness until the snow was two feet deep. Van Camp was a large and powerful man. He undertook to break the road for the other two, but hunger and cold overcame him when within a mile of Barnett's, and this last mile he had to make on his hands and knees.

He reached Barnett's at midnight, half frozen, and so exhausted as to be scarcely able to tell of the condition of his two companions. A rescue party of four or five men was at once started. Roll was met a few rods from the house, making his way on his hands and knees. Shultz was found some two miles farther, almost frozen. He lost several toes from his feet, and eventually died from this exposure. Roll and Van Camp lived to be old men. In 1802, John, William, and Jacob Vastbinder settled on what is now the Ridgeway road, near Kirkman Post-Office. In the year 1803, Ludwig Long, a hunter, settled on the Ridgeway road, two miles from Brookville. He was father of our great hunters, Mike, John, Dan, and William Long. He started the first distillery. At an early day he moved to Ohio, leaving his sons here. Jacob Mason and Master John Dixon came in 1802. In 1805 or 1806, John Matson settled where Robert now lives.

The second or third mill built in the county was at the head of what is now Heidrick, Matson & Co.'s mill pond. It was erected by Moses Knapp in 1800. In the thirties the Matsons and McCulloughs erected mills on the North Fork and Mill Creek. These were only mills in name, being the old up-and-down mills, or commonly called thundergust mills. The mill at Bellport was erected in 1830 by Benjamin Bailey. It was carried away in a flood, and then John J. Y. Thompson rebuilt it in 1838.

The pioneer graveyard in the county was located on the property now of William C. Evans, near the junction of the Ridgeway road with the pike. I found this graveyard in my boyhood, and thought they were Indian graves. My mother told me its history. The graves are now lost and the grounds desecrated. The second graveyard in the township was laid out in 1842, on Nathaniel Butler's farm, and is still called Butler's graveyard.

PIONEER HISTORY OF JEFFERSON COUNTY, PENNA.

In 1816, Cyrus, Nathaniel, and David Butler, and John Lattimer settled on farms near the Barnetts.

Pioneer efforts to secure a county road at September term, 1807, of Indiana Court:

William C. Brady, Thomas Lucas, Samuel Scott, James McHenry, Captain Hugh Brady, and James Johnston were appointed to lay out a road from Joseph Barnett's, on Sandy Lick Creek, Jefferson County, to Brady's mill, on the Little Mahoning, Indiana County.

The pioneer road was the Indiana and Port Barnett, for the creation of which the petition of a number of citizens of Jefferson County and parts of Indiana County was presented to the Indiana County Court at the September term, 1808. The points of the road were from Brady's mill, on Little Mahoning Creek, Indiana County, to Sandy Lick Creek, in Jefferson County (Port Barnett), where the State (Milesburg and Waterford) road crosses the same. The Court appointed as viewers Samuel Lucas, John Jones, Moses Knapp, and Samuel Scott, of Jefferson County, and John Park and John Wier, of Indiana County, to view and make a report at the next term. This road was probably built in 1810.

The pioneer justice of the peace was Thomas Lucas, appointed January 16, 1809.

The early settlers to erect cabins on the Indiana road in Pine Creek township were Joseph Carr in 1817, Manuel Reitz, George Gray, and Samuel McQuiston in 1827, John Matthews in 1830, Elijah Clark in 1833, Andrew Hunter and William Wyley in 1834, and Isaac Swineford in 1835. The pioneer school-house in this settlement was built in 1830; the pioneer graveyard was on the McCann farm in 1830.

"FINES FOR MISDEMEANORS.—In the early days of the county's history the penalties prescribed by the laws of the Commonwealth for any offence against any of the statutes was rigorously enforced, seemingly without regard to the social standing of the offender. Sabbath-breaking, swearing, and intoxication seem to have been the sins most vigorously punished by the arm of the law. In an old docket, opened on the 15th day of January, 1810, by Thomas Lucas, the first justice of the peace of Pine Creek township, are the following entries:

(Copy.)

"'(L. S.) JEFFERSON COUNTY, ss:

"'Be it remembered that on the seventh day of May, in the year of our Lord one thousand eight hundred and ten, Gabriel Puntus, of sd county, is convicted before me, Thomas Lucas, Esq., one of the Justices of the Peace in and for sd county, going to and from mill unnecessarily upon the sixth of May instant, being the Lord's day, commonly Coled Sunday, at the county aforesaid, contrary to the Act of Assembly in

Such cases made and provided, and I do adjudj him to forfeit for the same the sum of four dollars.

"'Given under my hand the day and year aforesaid.

"'THOMAS LUCAS.'

(Copy.)

"'COMMONWEALTH vs. JOHN DIXON.

"'(L. S.) JEFFERSON COUNTY, ss.:

"'Be it remembered that on the 13th day of January, in the year of our Lord one thousand eight hundred and twelve, John Dixkson, of Pine Creek township, in the county of Jefferson, is convicted before me, Thomas Lucas, one of the Justices of the Peace, in and for sd county, of being intoxicated with the drink of spirituous liquors, and for cursing one profane curse, in these words: "God dam," that it is to say this Day at Pine Creek township, aforesaid, contrary to the Act of General Assembly in such cases made and provided, and I do aguge him to forfeit for the same the sum of sixty-seven cents for each offence.

"'Given under my hand and seal the day and year afore s'd.

"'THOMAS LUCAS.

"'Justice's Cost 35 cents; Constable's Cost 31 cents.'

"Lewis Long is also convicted in 1815 for 'having hunted and carried the carcis of one deer on the 23d day of July instant, being the Lord's day, commonly Coled Sunday, up Pine Creek township aforesaid,' and sentenced to pay four dollars penalty.

"The first entry in this old docket is an action for debt. 'Thomas McCartney vs. Freedom Stiles, to recover on a promisory note, dated June 20th, 1805, for $4.25.'

"The next entry is an action of surety of the peace:

(Copy.)

"'COMMONWEALTH vs. HENRY VASTBINDER.

"'Surety of the peace and good behavour on oath of Fudge Van Camp, January 25th, 1810.

"'Warrant issued January 25th, 1810.

"'Fudge Van Camp, principal, tent. in $100, to appear, &c. Samuel Lucas, (bail,) tent. in $100, to prosicute, &c. referred to Samuel Scott, John Scott, Elijah M. Graham, Peter Jones, and John Matson.

"'Justice's Costs.—information 15 cents, Warrant 15 cents, 2 recognizances 40 cents, notice to refferees 15 cents, One Sum. 3 names 19 cents, One Sum. 1 name 10 cents, Swearing 3 witnesses 56 cents, Five referees 35 cents, Entering rule of renewment 10 cents, Constable's Cost $1.96, referees $2.50, Witnesses $1.50.

"'We, the refferees within named having heard the parties, the proofs and allegation to wit: We find from the evidence that the run is to be

PIONEER HISTORY OF JEFFERSON COUNTY, PENNA.

the line between Fudge Van Camp and Henry Vastbinder, from the line of the tract of land to the corner of —— by the camp, and thence along the old fence to the corner, thence by a direct line the same across the ridge to the run, and each party to enjoy these clearings till after harvest, next, Fudge Van Camp to enjoy the benefit of his sugar camp till the line is run, and John Jones and Moses Knap is for to run the line between the parties, and eavery one of the partis is to move there fence on their own ground, sd Van Camp is to leave sixteen feet and a half in the clear between the stakes of the fences for a lane or outlet between the partis, and each party is to give sureity for there good behavior unto each other, there goods and chattles, for the term of one year and one day from entering of sureity, to be entered ameditly if it can be had; if not to be had at the present time, bail is to be entered on Tuesday, the sixth day of February, A.D. 1810. The plaintiff to pay fifty cents costs, and the defendant the remainder of the costs of Sute.

" ' Witness our hands and seals this second day of february, A.D. 1810.

" ' SAMUEL SCOTT, (L. S.)
JOHN SCOTT, (L. S.)
ELIJAH M. GRAHAM, (L. S.)
PETER JONES, (L. S.)
JOHN MATSON, (L. S.)

" ' Before me THOMAS LUCAS.'

"The fines for Sabbath-breaking, profane swearing, and intoxication seem to have been rigidly enforced all through the term of office of Mr. Lucas, as we find numerous entries, in some instances the fines amounting to twelve dollars for one person. Numerous other offences are entered, the most curious being the indictments of the 'Commonwealth *vs.* Francis Godyear and Mollie Taylor for Poligamy,' September 12, 1835.

"In the same old docket is the account of Thomas Lucas's fees on probates on fox, wolf, and wild-cats, from February 14, 1832, to June 11, 1838. Among the hunters are the names of William and Michael Long, Adam, Philip, Henry, and William Vastbinder, John, Samuel and James Lucas, John and Thomas Callen, Jacob Shaffer, James Linn, Ralph Hill, John Wyncoop, William Dougherty, Frederick Heterick, Nelson T. McQuiston, William Horan, and William Douglass. The list embraces thirty wild-cats, forty-eight wolves, seventy-six foxes, and one panther (shot by Thomas Callen). The justice's fee on each probate was twelve and a half cents.

"On the whole, however, the early settlers of the county seem to have been a law-abiding people, for, with the exception of a few actions for 'assault and battery,' there were no serious breaches of the peace in the first quarter of a century that this old docket legally chronicles."—*Kate Scott's History of Jefferson County.*

PIONEER HISTORY OF JEFFERSON COUNTY, PENNA.

The following were the early settlers up to 1818 :

Jacob Mason, Richard Van Camp, Samuel States, John Hice, Henry Lott, Joseph Clements, Charles Sutherland (colored), Robert Dickson, Enos Van Camp (colored), Frederick Frants, George Evans, Robert Knox, William Hayns, Israel Stiles, Hulet Smith, John Templeton, and Joseph Greenawalt, and perhaps a few others.

Fudge Van Camp was the pioneer colored settler.

The pioneer school in the county was started here, a description of which will be found under the chapter on education.

"The first election in the county was held at Port Barnett, and up to 1818 it was the only polling and election precinct in and for the county. At the last election (when the township was the whole county), in 1817, Friday, March 14, the names of the contestants for office and the votes were as follows,—viz. : Constable, Elijah M. Graham, 22 votes; John Dixon, 13 votes. Supervisors, Joseph Barnett, 25 votes; Thomas Lucas, 28 votes. Overseer of the Poor, Henry Keys, 9 votes; John Matson, 6 votes. Fence Appraisers, Moses Knapp, 7 votes; William Vastbinder, 7 votes. Town Clerk, Elijah M. Graham, 22 votes.

"Signed and attested by the judges, Walter Templeton and Adam Vastbinder."—*Kate Scott's History of Jefferson County*.

From 1831 to 1842, Andrew Barnett kept a licensed tavern at Port Barnett. Jacob Kroh kept the tavern from 1842 until 1843. Isaac Packer kept the log tavern near Peter Baum's from 1834 until 1842. In 1834 there were but two buildings between Port Barnett and Reynoldsville,—Packer's tavern and Hance Vastbinder's house near where Emerickville now is. The pioneer store was opened by the Barnetts and Samuel Scott, who, in 1826, sold it out to Jared B. Evans, and he, in the fall of 1830, removed it to Jefferson Street, Brookville, Pennsylvania.

PORT BARNETT.

Port Barnett, where the pioneer settlers of Jefferson County founded a home for themselves, was the property of Joseph Barnett and Samuel Scott. The county records describe the ownership of this property as follows :

"The Port Barnett property containing two hundred and fifty-six acres and one hundred perches. One part conveyed to Samuel Scott by Jeremiah Parker, by deed dated 16th day of ——, 1818, recorded in Indiana County, in Deed Book No. 2, page 727, and by sundry conveyances to Andrew Barnett. Other moiety conveyed to Joseph Barnett by Jeremiah Parker, by deed dated 26th of June, 1821, recorded in Indiana County, in Deed Book No. 4, page 482, and by will of Joseph Barnett devised to Andrew Barnett."

In 1818 there were but three saw-mills in the county, and nineteen miles of county road. "The only road then in this region was one

PIONEER HISTORY OF JEFFERSON COUNTY, PENNA.

from Port Barnett, which crossed the Sandy near where Fuller's dam is now built, and from thence to Indiana. There were fourteen men employed in cutting it out, under the direction of Judge Shippen, of Meadville.

"The party had a wagon to haul their provisions, and was composed of Mr. Kennedy and two men named Halloway and Williamson. No respect was had for the future comfort of the traveller, or the poor horses that had to toil over the road, no digging was done, and it was up one hill and down another. The second road was from Port Barnett to Troy, and was made in the same manner as the other. These roads were made so as to pass the homes of as many settlers as possible. The unseated taxes were sufficient to pay all expenses. The nearest grist-mill was run by a man named Parks, and was the Knapp mill. This mill was in what is now Brookville. The bolting was done by hand, and William Kennedy says he often took his turn at this work when waiting for his grist."

Timber tracts could be bought for twenty-five and fifty cents per acre. In 1820 there were twenty-five saw-mills in the county, and one hundred and fifty miles of county road. The early paths of the settlers ran over the steepest part of the hills, and these paths were usually enlarged into roads. These paths and roads were run over the hills by sighting from peak to peak with a compass to keep from being lost in the wild woods.

THE PIONEER SQUARE TIMBER RAFT.

Ludwig Long and sons about 1834 ran the first square timber raft. It took them six days to reach the mouth. Up to the year 1830 our people were unable to run much timber to market in any other way than in boards. A Yankee by the name of Samuel Seeley moved into this county about the year 1830 or 1832 and located at Port Barnett. This man Seeley either invented or introduced into this wilderness the idea of rafting timber sticks together with white oak bows and ash pins.

About the year 1834, Long's timber raft was taken out near Port Barnett, hauled to the creek, and rafted in. It was three platforms long. The timber sticks were of uniform length, which left no stiffness in the structure. The oar-blades and stem, as was the custom then, were hewed out of a good-sized pine-tree in one body. The cables were hickory, and the halyards wild grape-vine. The pilot stood on the front end of the raft, and steered from there. The timber was marketed at Pittsburg.

"Although more or less of the lumber has from the origin of the business until now been annually exported, the trade in square timber and spars was not until 1842 considered remunerative. Prior to that it was carried on from necessity. It was important to clear the land that bread might be raised and population supported, and, whilst the growing trees were considered of little or no value, our citizens were satisfied if the pittance they then received for their timber would pay them for the labor of cutting and exporting.

"During all the early years of the settlement, varied with occasional pleasure and excitements, the great work of increasing the tillable ground went slowly on. The implements and tools were few and of the most primitive kinds, but the soil that had long held in reserve the accumulated richness of centuries produced splendid harvests, and the husbandman was well rewarded for his labor. The soil was warmer then than now, and the seasons earlier. The wheat was occasionally pastured in the spring to keep it from growing up so early and so fast as to become lodged. The harvest came early, and the yield was often from twenty to thirty bushels per acre. Corn grew fast, and roasting ears were to be had by the 1st of August in most seasons."

PERRY TOWNSHIP.

This was the second organized township, being taken, in 1818, from Pine Creek. The division line separating at that time these two townships was called the "Mason and Dixon line of Jefferson County." This township was named in honor of Commodore Perry, the hero of the navy on the Lakes, in the war of 1812; and its boundary then was, on the north by Pine Creek township, east by Clearfield County, south by Indiana County, and west by Armstrong County. There are two pioneer villages in the township,—viz., Perrysville and Whitesville; and the former has a post-office called Hamilton, and the latter's post-office is Valier; also the taxables were as follows: in 1828, 85; 1835, 209; 1842, 251. The population by census of 1840 was 1076.

The pioneer settler in what is now Perry township was John Bell. He erected his cabin there in 1809. His nearest neighbor was nine miles distant, in Indiana County, and the Barnetts were the nearest on the north side. Bell came from Indiana Town. He died on the 19th of May, 1855, in his eighty-sixth year. He was an intelligent, industrious farmer, a justice of the peace, appointed in 1818 by Governor Findley, and held this office for twenty-five years by appointment or election. Once, while on his way home from Port Barnett, he observed an Indian taking aim at him with his rifle from behind a tree. Mr. Bell said in his lifetime, "That Indian was never seen afterwards." Mr. John Bell was a great hunter, during his life in Jefferson County he killed two panthers, ninety-three wolves, three hundred and six bears, and over six hundred deer.

The next settler in Perry was Archibald Hadden. He came from Westmoreland County, Pennsylvania, in 1810, and settled near Mr. John Bell. In 1812, Hugh McKee, a soldier of this war, settled near Perrysville. John Postlethwait came in 1818, Reuben Hickox in 1822.

Reuben Hickox's hunting exploits alone would make a book. He, in three days, caught six bears, and in the early part of the season, in less than three months, secured over fifty of the "bruin" family. He trapped and hunted principally for bears and wolves. Wild cats were numerous, and often got into his traps, but he cared naught for them,

Perry township.

as their fur was valueless, only bringing in the market ten cents apiece. As for the deer, they formed the major portion of his bill of fare. Turkeys, wild ducks, etc., were numerous, and whenever he had a desire for fowl, his trusty rifle would soon secure an amount far in excess of the wants of his family.

Other early settlers in Perry were William Johnston, Benjamin McBride, William Stewart, Isaac Lewis, Samuel Newcomb, and Thomas S. Mitchell.

One of the most useful and prominent citizens of Perry township was Thomas Sharp Mitchell, who migrated in 1828, at the age of fifteen years, to the wilderness of Perry township, Jefferson County, Pennsylvania. He came in the employ of Alva Payne, from Armstrong County, Pennsylvania, who in the year 1828 opened the pioneer store in what is now Perrysville. Young Mitchell was Payne's clerk. In addition to being salesman in the store, Thomas peddled with a wagon among the pioneers, trading goods for deer pelts, furs, etc. In this vocation he sometimes extended his trips into the adjoining counties. He peddled and clerked in this way for about two years, when Payne left the country for parts unknown. From 1831 to 1837, Mitchell peddled for himself. In 1837 he and his brother James opened a general merchandise store in Perrysville, and continued in active operation as a firm until 1842, when James moved to Indiana County, Pennsylvania, leaving Thomas still engaged in merchandising, lumbering on the Mahoning, and droving. Our enter-

Early barn.

prising merchants were drovers of horses and cattle, and Thomas S. Mitchell was a successful one. For several years he "drove" several droves each season, a single drove sometimes containing as many as four hundred head of cattle. Thomas S. Mitchell's mother was Agnes Sarah Sharp, daughter of Captain Sharp, one of the pioneers on the Kiskiminitas, and of some fame as an Indian fighter. He died of wounds received in an engagement with redskins outside of Fort Pitt. But the hero captain landed his wife and children in Fort Pitt, where he died in fourteen days from his wounds.

Thomas S. Mitchell married Miss Sarah Blose, of Perry township, in 1831. She was a daughter of George Blose, who emigrated from West-

PIONEER HISTORY OF JEFFERSON COUNTY, PENNA.

moreland County, Pennsylvania, to Perry township, Jefferson County, in the twenties. George Blose owned the land where Perrysville is now located.

Thomas S. Mitchell was a large man of exceedingly fine presence, able, intelligent, genial, social, and popular. He served a term as sheriff. I knew him well, and remember him with great kindness and respect. He died in August, 1883. His wife died in 1875.

The pioneer church was built in 1835, at Perry; the pioneer schoolhouse in 1820, in what is now Perrysville. The pioneer saw-mill was built by Elijah Heath, above the Round Bottom. The pioneer hotel in Perrysville was kept by Irvin Robinson, and the pioneer store was opened by Alva Payne. The pioneer graveyard was located where Perry church was built, and Robert Stunkard was the pioneer burial.

At the pioneer election held at Bell's, on Friday, March 20, 1818, the following were contestants for the township offices,—viz.: "Constables, David Hamilton, 5 votes; Jacob Hoover, 3 votes. Supervisors, John Bell, 5 votes; Hugh McKee, 5 votes. Auditors, Archibald Hadden, 5 votes; Jesse Armstrong, 5 votes; James McClennen, 5 votes; Michael Lance, 5 votes. Fence Appraisers, Joseph Crossman, 5 votes; Adam Long, 5 votes. Overseers, Henry Lott, 5 votes; Elijah Dykes, 5 votes. Signed, Archibald Hadden, Hugh McKee, judges.

"At the next election the voters had increased to eight, and at the last election before Young township was formed the number of voters appears to have been seventy-seven. At this election in 1825 'schoolmen' appear to have been voted for, John W. Jenks, Charles C. Gaskill, and John Bell being elected. This is the only record of any such office in the election returns of the county from 1807 to 1830. These elections were held at the house of John Bell, and in the first ten years he was eight times elected to office, being supervisor, auditor, overseer of the poor, and schoolman."

Act of the Legislature, No. 174, establishing the polling-place:

"SECTION 29. The electors of the township of Perry, in the county of Jefferson, shall hereafter hold their general elections at the house of William Stunkard, in said township. Approved—April 15, 1835."

Among the pioneer and early settlers along Little Sandy Creek, in Perry township, were Andrew Shaffer, David Milliron, and Mr. Vanlear.

Daniel Geist erected his cabin there in 1834, and founded Geistown, now called Worthville. He built a grist-mill in 1840. Henry Frease located also near where the town of Ringgold now stands, and erected a grist-mill about 1840. John Philliber, Ludwick Byerly, Henry Nulf, Conrad Nulf, Solomon Gearhart, George Reitz, and Michael Heterick all erected cabins on farms in the early thirties. Thomas Holt, a veteran of the war of 1812, settled there in 1837. Samuel Lerch, a carpenter and cabinet-maker, erected his cabin near Ringgold in 1836. Farther

PIONEER HISTORY OF JEFFERSON COUNTY, PENNA.

up the stream from Geistown, near where the Indiana and Brookville road now crosses, William Hadden settled in 1831, and, being a great hunter, killed annually turkeys, bears, and deer. George and William Newcomb erected cabins in 1825, John Jones in 1826, Peter Depp in 1828, Alexander and William McKinstrey in 1833, Joseph Manners in 1835. James Gray, in 1836, opened a small store near McKinstrey's. James Gray was postmaster for Cool Spring. In 1833, Frederick Sprankle erected a gristmill near the junction of Big Run and Kellar's Run. Adam Dobson located his cabin in 1833, John and William Coulter in 1841, and Samuel Burket in 1842.

YOUNG TOWNSHIP.

Young, the third township, was organized in 1826, and was taken from Perry township. The township was then of very large proportions, but is now rather attenuated. It was named after Judge Young, then president judge of the Westmoreland judicial circuit.

The taxables in the township were, in 1828, 73; in 1829, 70; in 1831, 70; in 1835, 146; in 1842, 271. The population by the census in 1840 was 1321.

Abraham Weaver was the pioneer settler in Young township. In 1818, Dr. John W. Jenks, Rev. David Barclay, and Nathaniel Tindle came to what is now Young township, prospecting for a future home, and they were so well pleased that in the spring of 1819 they returned with their families and settled where Punxsutawney now stands. Phineas W. Jenks was the first white child born. Rev. Barclay and Dr. Jenks donated and laid out the ground for the present cemetery.

Isaac P. Carmalt, John B. Henderson, and John Hess came in 1821, Joseph Long came in 1824, James St. Clair came in 1831, William and Robert Campbell and John Dunn came in 1832, Obed Morris came in 1824, Daniel Graffius came in 1823.

Among the early lumbermen were Jesse Armstrong and William Neel.

The pioneer church erected was a hewed log building,—Presbyterian. The first school-house was built of round logs in 1822, on or near T. Pantall's farm. Rev. Barclay laid out Punxsutawney for "a white man's town" in 1821. In 1832 it contained fifteen dwellings, two taverns, and a store. Adam Long was the pioneer hunter.

The pioneer tavern was kept by Elijah Heath, and his first license to sell liquor was in 1824. This tavern was built by Elijah Heath in 1824.

The pioneer military company was organized in the thirties. William Long was captain in 1840. The company was attached to the Third Battalion, Second Brigade, Fifteenth Division, Pennsylvania Militia.

The pioneer election held for the township of Young after it was separated from Perry, as the returns appear in the office of the prothonotary at Indiana, are as follows:

"Young township return for 1826: Constable, Joseph Long had 32 votes, John Hum 11 votes. Signed Philip Bowers, judge, etc."

At an election held at the house of Elijah Heath, in Punxsutawney, Young township, on the 16th of March, 1827, the following persons contested for the township offices: Constable, Joseph Long, 22 votes; Obed Morris, 13 votes. Supervisors, Nathaniel Tindle, 29 votes; Benoni Williams, 32 votes. Auditors, Andrew H. Bowman, 30 votes; Josiah Caldwell, 27 votes; Matthias Clawson, 24 votes; Philip Bowers, 18 votes. Poor Overseers, Frederick Rinehart, 15 votes; Christian Rishel, 20 votes. Fence Appraisers, Adam Long (cooper), 20 votes; John Hum, 9 votes. Signed, Frederick Rinehart, Joseph Long, Josiah Caldwell, judges; Matthias Clawson, A. H. Bowman, clerks.

"TURNPIKE NOTICE.

"The stockholders of the Armstrong and Clearfield Turnpike Road Company are hereby notified that an election will be held at the house of James Caldwell, in Punxsutawney, on Wednesday, the 17th day of September next, to elect officers of said company for the ensuing year. By order of the President.

"WILLIAM CAMPBELL, *Secretary*.

"PUNXSUTAWNEY, August 17, 1834."

"One of the first settlers of the southern portion of the county, and, if tradition serves us right, one of the earliest lumbermen of the Mahoning, was Jesse Armstrong, who built his cabin in a bend of the creek, now called Armstrong's Bend, a short distance below where the mill of J. U. Gillespie now stands. He, with William Neel, devised the plan of constructing a raft, and early in the spring of 1818 the two men, with Sally, Armstrong's wife, and, tradition says, assisted by two Indians, who had been in the neighborhood, perhaps visiting the graves of their people, started on their raft to explore the lower waters of the Mahoning, a peaceful enough stream in summer, but when swollen by the spring rains and melting snows a veritable rushing, foaming river. The raft, which was not one of the deftly put together square timber or board rafts of the present day, but constructed of round logs roughly withed together, was swept down the mad current. The oars were poor, and the oarsmen and pilot unskilled and ignorant of the stream; and at length the frail craft struck on the rocks, and the crew barely escaped with their lives to the shore. Indeed, poor Sally Armstrong would have found a watery grave had not Billy Neel caught her long red hair and pulled her out of the seething flood. It is said that the eddy where this catastrophe occurred was ever after known as 'Sally's Eddy.' Just before this mishap occurred, Sally had prepared some food from the stores which they had with them; but Owenoco, one of the Indians, said, 'No, no, we no eat now; maybe never eat.' At the same time he was trying with great strength and skill to keep the tossing craft from dashing against the great rocks that loomed up on every side. Suddenly they were drawn into the fearful eddy, and, the oar of Owenoco breaking off suddenly, he lost control of the craft. Extricating themselves with difficulty from their perilous predicament, the white men and Indians finally got their broken raft safely moored to shore and tied fast to a tree. Then, by the aid of a flint and torch, the Indians called down a sacred fire, which they ascribed as a gift from their Manitou, and soon the little band of lumbermen and the poor drenched lumber-woman were gathered around the welcome fire. All their provisions, with the exception of some bread and salt Sally had placed in a box, which was saved, went down into the watery flood, with some crocks of honey, the product of wild bees, which Sally was taking to Pittsburg to purchase finery with. The bows and arrows of the Indians soon, however, procured them food, and in the cheerful light and warmth of the fire they soon regained their spirits, and after a night's rest were ready early the next morning to again undertake the perilous journey, and without any more serious mishaps gained their journey's end, being safely landed at Pittsburg, where their dusky companions bade them farewell forever and wended their way to Canada, there to join the remainder of their tribe.

"Armstrong and his wife exchanged their logs for such provisions and wearing apparel as they could carry, and returned on foot to Punxsutawney. It was after night when they came in sight of their cabin, where Adam Long and his wife dwelt with them. The loud barking of the dog announced their coming, and Adam said to his wife, 'I bet a deer-skin it bees Jess and Sall comin'; and soon the weary travellers were seated around their own fireside, enjoying the rest they so much needed; and while they partook of the repast of bear's meat, etc., that Mrs. Long hastily provided for them, they told the story of their perilous journey and its successful ending, and Adam Long in turn narrated the story of his fight with the bear whose skin was then drying on the wall of the cabin, and which he had killed near their very door. 'Oh, lor', but I am tired!' said Mrs. Armstrong. 'I would not do that again for all the plagued raft and honey. I feel so crippled up I can scarcely walk.' 'Yes,' said Adam, 'but you give the honey to the fish an' to te allegators.' 'Yes, I lost my seven crocks of honey, and if it hadn't been for Billy Neel I would have went with the honey. I'll always respect him for that. Jesse never tried to put out his hand to catch me,' said the irate dame. 'Why, Sally,' said Armstrong, 'you know that when you jumped in I was trying to save myself on the other side of the raft.' 'But what te tivel you do mit Neel?' said Adam. 'Did de Injun kill him, or did you sell him mit your raft?' 'Oh,' said Jesse, 'Neel went with us to Pittsburg, where we left him. We got on Leslie Ramsey's boat. I helped to push the boat up to Kittanning, and Sally and me come afoot from there along the Indian path. We come it in two days.'

"Then Adam Long told the story of the bear's death. His dog had started the bear on the hill above the creek, and they had followed it from crag to crag until at last, just on the bank of the creek, it turned and gave them battle, and caught the dog in its embrace, when the hunter dealt the huge beast a powerful blow with his hatchet. The furious animal relaxed its hold on the dog and sprang at Adam with extended jaws, and seemed to realize that the conflict was for life or death. The hunter's gun was useless. He had no time to aim at the bear, but, springing aside, he drew his long, keen hunting-knife and returned to the charge. The huge black beast was standing erect, and received the thrust of the knife in his neck, and as Long was about to give him another blow with his knife he struck him with his powerful paw and stretched him on the ground, while the knife flew from his hand into the creek; and had not the dog at this juncture come to the rescue, poor Adam would never have lived to tell of this exploit; but seeing his master at the mercy of their common enemy, he sprang upon the bear, and there ensued a fierce struggle; but the bear was badly wounded, and the dog at last threw him almost into the creek, when the bear gave up the contest, and, springing into the water, made for the other shore, the brave dog still holding on to his flank. Adam Long had by this time recovered his faculties, and, reloading his gun, fired at the bear, the ball taking effect in his shoulder. He then plunged into the creek and encountered him upon the other shore with his hatchet, and soon despatched him. He believed that the huge beast would have weighed at least four hundred pounds. Adam always loved to narrate this story."—*History of Jefferson County*.

Among the early settlers of Young township, east of Punxsutawney, on the Mahoning stream, were Jesse Armstrong and John Grube in 1833, Daniel Smeyers in 1839, Abraham Rudolph in 1833, Jacob Bowersock, and Daniel Graffius. John Hess built a saw-mill in 1828. James H. Bell settled on this stream in 1831, built a grist-mill in 1833, and opened a store in 1840. James McCracken erected his cabin near Bell in 1839, building saw-mills and farming. Mr. McCracken was an active, popular man. John Pifer erected his cabin in what is now known as Paradise in 1829.

The pioneer church in the Pifer settlement was built in 1840. Other early settlers to erect cabins on farms north of the Mahoning in 1830 were John Smith, John Deemer, William Best, Samuel McGhee, and others.

PIONEER HISTORY OF JEFFERSON COUNTY, PENNA.

Joseph and Daniel North erected cabins in the early thirties. The pioneer saw-mill was built on Big Run by William Best in 1830.

This illustration is of South Side pioneers who, by invitation of D. S. Altman, Esq., and wife, partook of a dinner at their home in Punxsu-

tawney, Pennsylvania, on the 8th day of February, A D. 1877. This picture was taken with the pioneers seated and standing in the snow. The first name is in the standing row, and the second name in the row of seated pioneers.

PIONEER HISTORY OF JEFFERSON COUNTY, PENNA.

Name.	Date of Birth.	Where Born.	Located in Jefferson Co., Pa.
Rev. Jacob F. Wall	June 29, 1805	Allegheny County, Pa.	1854
David Willard	June 11, 1801	Westmoreland County, Pa.	1837
Thomas McKee	Oct. 24, 1801	Centre County, Pa.	1839
Isaac P. Carmalt	Sept. 9, 1794	Philadelphia, Pa.	1819
Robert Law	Nov. 10, 1802	Huntingdon County, Pa.	1836
James Winslow	Apr. 14, 1798	Maine	1818
James H. Bell	Oct. 18, 1800	New York City	1826
Reuben Hickox	Nov. 11, 1794	New Haven, Conn.	1820
J. K. Coxen, Esq.	July 12, 1802	Mercer County, Pa.	1844
John Drum, Esq.	July 12, 1806	Westmoreland County, Pa.	1831
Dr. George Kurtz	Nov. 11, 1792	Germany	1836
Isaac Rodgers	June 18, 1806	Huntingdon County, Pa.	
Ellis Evans	Feb. 13, 1788	Schuylkill County, Pa.	1837
Joseph W. Winslow	Dec. 10, 1804	Maine	1818
Abraham Ruth.			
Obed Morris	Dec. 8, 1792	Bucks County, Pa.	1824

These old pioneers met after this event annually for a few years at the home of Mr. and Mrs. Altman, to partake of a dinner and relate incidents of pioneer hardships; but sickness, extreme old age, and death soon stopped their pleasant reunions.

"A PIONEER POSTAL ROUTE.

"More than sixty-seven years ago the first Tuesday of April, 1830, a bright, beautiful morning, I started forth from my log cabin home with a United States mail-bag, on my black pacing horse Billy, with Bob Thompson, then about my own age (twelve years), on his dwarf mule Bully, to penetrate the wilderness through a low grade of the Allegheny Mountains, between the Allegheny River at Kittanning and the west branch of the Susquehanna River at Curwensville, sixty-five miles and return each week, Robert going along to show me the way.

"I have climbed the Rockies with a burro since that period in search of gold and silver, but I have never met either so primitive a people or a rougher route of sixty-five miles than that wilderness route. The post-offices were Glade Run, Smicksburg, Ewing's Mill, Punxsutawney, and Curwensville. The first of these was eighteen miles from Kittanning, near where is now the little town of Dayton.

"In about three months the route was changed up the Cowanshannock, and the Rural Valley post-office established about two miles above Patterson's mill. The changed route intersected the old one at Glade Run post-office. The next place east of Glade Run was the residence of George McComb, where I rested for dinner and fed my horse. A stretch of over two miles brought me to Smicksburg, as now spelled, but the original founder spelled his name Schmick. Mr. Carr, the blacksmith, was postmaster. For more than four miles there was not a single house on the road, though a cabin was to be seen in the distance, until I reached Ewing's Mill, another post-office. My place of lodging for the first night was with James McComb, four miles from Punxsutawney, and never did a boy find a more pleasant home.

"The second day I rode ten miles for breakfast, passing Punxsutawney, where Dr. Jenks was postmaster. The town was a mere hamlet, principally a lumbering camp, surrounded with the finest of white pine, which was rafted in hewed logs down Mahoning Creek to the Allegheny River, and thence to Pittsburg. It is a rapid, rocky, crooked stream, and the logs were hewed square to make their transit over safe, both by reducing their size and securing a smooth, even surface. Six miles farther on was a farm, a few acres, the home of Andrew Bowers, where I ate breakfast, then entered a wilderness of sixteen miles. Those sixteen miles of wilderness were then a most dismal district of country, heavily timbered with pine, spruce, hemlock, and chestnut, with much undergrowth of laurel. In this dreary waste I saw every animal native to the clime, except the panther, of which more hereafter.

"After emerging from this wilderness, in which the sun was never visible, there was a settlement of Quakers, known as the Grampian Hills, near the centre of which was a fine farm, the home of a colored man, Samuel Cochran, where I took dinner, and then passed on to Curwensville, the end of my route. I returned to Cochran's for the second night's rest. The object of this return was to be ready to enter the wilderness and give good time to get through it before the shades of evening had fallen. Once I realized the wisdom of this plan when high water delayed me, so that I was compelled to stop at Bowers's place for the night and ride through the wilderness twice in a day, entering at the dawn of morning and reaching the place of departure amid darkness.

"Was I lonely? If the shriek of the panther, the growl of the bear, the howling of the wolf, the hooting of the owl is society, I was far from lonely. When I realized my situation I drove the spurs into my horse and rushed him with all his speed. My heart-beats seemed to drown the racket of his hoofs upon the stony road. The return was but a repetition of the outgoing journey. I never made such a trip again.

"My predecessor was John Gillespie, of whose history since I know nothing, but there was a story that in his ambition to create a favorable impression of the importance of his charge he frequently horrified a good Presbyterian preacher, who was the Glade Run postmaster, by stuffing the mail-bag with crab-apples, and made indignant the good Mrs. McComb, where he had lodged the night previously, by laying the mischief to the McComb children. A plethoric mail-bag always opened the eyes of the rural postmaster, and it was fun to John to witness the indignation of the good Mr. Jenks and hear the screaming of laughter of the villagers, just arrived to get the latest news, when a peck of crab-apples, but no letter, rolled out on the floor at Punxsutawney.

"Those were the days of William T. Barry as postmaster general. I used to collect government's moiety in each of the little post-offices in driblets of five to ten dollars, with the plain signature of 'Wm. T. Barry, P. M. G.,' attached to the orders, and looked at the great man's name with admiration, until I really think I could distinguish his handwriting now.

"On more than two-thirds of the little farms no wagon-tracks were to be seen, all the work being done with sleds. Nevertheless, there were occasional freighters through the wilderness, generally loaded with salt. The only stores in that sixty miles were one at Glade Run and one at Punxsutawney. The people made all their own clothes. Nearly every family that had a daughter as old as fourteen years had a weaver. The blooming miss who learned that art was an artist indeed. It was a treat for the boys who had no sister weaver to carry the yarn to the neighbor girl and help her adjust the web for the work. Their clothes were made from the backs of the sheep and the flax in the field. The girls wore linsey-woolsey and the boys linen and tow shirts, and indeed full suits of the same for common work. The fine clothes for the girls were barred flannel of their own spinning, and the boys satinet,—then generally called cassinet,—flax, and wool. The preachers and the teachers were reverenced and respected, but woe unto them if they even seemed to put on airs on account of their 'store clothes.'

"Many were the expedients for social gatherings; but to these brave, industrious pioneers it was essential to unite business with pleasure, and I rarely heard of a party which was not utilized for the advancement of improvements on the farm. The singing-school was the only exception. In the log-rolling, the wood-chopping, the flax-skutching, the sheep-shearing, all the neighbors would go the rounds helping each other, in the spirit of the song,—

"'Let the wide world wag as it will,
We'll be gay and happy still.'

"'Skutching' was the term used for the primitive mode of separating the woody part of the flax from the fibre used in weaving cloth, and a skutching was a jolly party, in which the boys took the heavier part, and passed the 'hank' to the girls for the lighter, more delicate work of polishing.

"Thus the logs were rolled in the clearings, the flax and wool prepared for the loom, and the firewood made ready for the winter. But the most primitive, most amusing, and the merriest gathering of all was the kicking frolic.

PIONEER HISTORY OF JEFFERSON COUNTY, PENNA.

"It is doubtful whether any of the readers of this book have ever seen a kicking frolic. Let me try to describe it. As I have said, the people made all their own clothes in those days. After the web was woven, the next process was fulling, whereby the cloth was properly shrunken for use. Generally it was taken to fulling-mills, but in some parts they were so far away and so expensive that the wits of the pioneers were compelled to invent a substitute. One night, at my journey's end for the day, near Punxsutawney, I was invited to go with the McComb boys to Henderson's kicking. The girls of the whole neighborhood had spent the afternoon at quilting, for the quilting was an accompaniment of nearly all the other frolics, and at dark the boys assembled for the kicking. The good old Mrs. Henderson had prepared a boiler full of soapsuds. The web of cloth was placed on the kitchen floor,—a floor generally made from puncheons,—that is, logs split and smoothed with the axe and adze. Around the web was placed a circle of chairs, with a plough-line or a clothes-line circling the chairs, to hold the circle together for work. Thus equipped the boys took off shoes and stockings, rolled up their pants to their knees, placed themselves on the chairs in the circle, and then the kicking began. The old lady poured on the soapsuds as hot as the boys' feet could stand, and they sent the web whirling and the suds splashing to the ceiling of the kitchen, and thus the web was fulled to the proper thickness and dimensions. Despite the good Mrs. Henderson's protestations that 'the hard work would kill the boys,' I stripped and went in, and never did a boy so sweat in his life. The work was done. The barred flannel was ready for the girls' dresses, the blankets for the beds, and the satin for the boys' clothes. A merrier time boys and girls never enjoyed, nor did a party ever have a better supper than Mrs. Henderson prepared. There was no dance, but the kissing plays of the time lent zest to the occasions, and

"'In the wee sma' hours ayont the twal'

all returned to happy homes.

"The threshing machinery was unknown to the farmers anywhere, and the flail did the work of threshing. Even the fanning-mill was uncommon, as I remember of but three on all that route. There was a mode of winnowing grain by three men, one shaking the wheat in the chaff through a ridder or sieve, and two waving a tightly drawn sheet, producing wind to separate the chaff from the grain.

"In places I have seen hand mills for grinding corn and wheat. They had an upper and nether millstone, the upper stone being turned by a 'handle' standing nearly perpendicularly above the centre of the stone.

"In the wilderness was every animal native to the clime,—the deer, the wild turkey, the fox, the raccoon, the wolf, the porcupine, the bear, and the panther. There I have seen scores of such animals. Frequently I have met bears in pairs, but I never saw a panther, though I frequently heard their familiar screams. It was a shy animal, but considered the most dangerous of all wild animals. On one occasion, when near the middle of that wilderness of sixteen miles, I was startled by the fearful screams of a panther, which, from the sound, seemed fast approaching me. Hurriedly breaking a limb from a spruce-tree, I lashed my horse into all his speed; still the screams became more distinct and frightful. I had perhaps run my horse a quarter of a mile, when a bear rushed through the thick underbrush across the road, not more than two rods ahead of me, the screaming of the panther sounding as if he was not a rod behind in the brush. The bear never stopped to look at me, and I plied my stick to the horse's back, shoulder, and flank with all my power, running him until the sounds gradually died away, and the exhausted horse gave out and I was compelled to slacken my speed. My first stopping-place was at the house of Mr. Andrew Bowers, at the edge of the wilderness. I told him my story, and he replied, 'John, that was a "painter," and that "painter" was after that bear, and if he had come up to that bear when you were near it, he would have jumped onto you quicker than the bear. Now, John,' he continued, 'don't run, nor don't advance on it. If you do either, the "painter" will attack you. But just stop and look the "painter" in the eye, and by and by he will quietly walk off.'

"I have twice seen in the wilderness that rarest of animals, the black fox, whose fur rivals the seal and the sable in ladies' apparel.

"Did I ever see ghosts? Of course I did. What could a poor post-boy know of cause and effect in the wilderness which has since developed some of the most wonderful gas-wells of the age? In that wild country the ignis-fatuus was frequently seen. Once I saw a floating light in the darkness, and in my fright was trotting my horse at his best speed, when he stumbled on a rock, throwing me clear over his head, the mail-bag following. I grabbed the bags and was on my horse's back before he could get off his knees. The 'ghost' in the mean time had vanished. Once, when about half-way between Smicksburg and Punxsutawney, a light as brilliant, it seemed to me, as Paul saw on his way to Damascus, shot up under my horse. I grabbed my hat, as my hair seemed to stand on end. I was so alarmed that I told my story to the postmaster at Ewing's Mill, and he relieved my mind greatly by explaining the phenomenon. He said, 'Was there snow on the ground?' 'Yes.' And then he went on to relieve my fears in the most kindly way, telling me that all the stories about ghosts, spooks, and hobgoblins could be explained on natural principles. He said that at times natural gas exuded from between the rocks, and that the snow confined it, and that my horse's shoe had struck fire from the flinty rock, and the gas exploded. I believed him, and my ghost story was exploded, too, but I would have killed a horse before I would have ventured over that spot in night-time again.

"The boys of that period had as much fun in their composition as those of the present age. One Halloween we sauntered 'on fun intent' near where Dayton now stands. We lodged a yearling calf in a haymow, changed the hind wheels of the only two wagons in the neighborhood to the forward axles, and *vice versa*, robbed a loom and strung the maiden's web from tree to tree across the road, and changed the natural order of things generally. I remember especially that in our mischief we accidentally broke a window in the house of a good old couple. We repaid damages by a boy slipping up and depositing fifty cents on the sill of the broken window. The old people were so universally esteemed that malicious mischief would have been investigated; but whether the motive for recompense was remorse for a bad act or esteem for their two beautiful daughters with raven locks and black eyes, this boy will only confess for himself. The McComb boys reported that one of the girls called on the way to the store the next day for glass and expressed the gratitude of the family for the kind consideration of the boys in making restitution.

"I distinctly remember how we all put in our utmost strength to place a log endwise against the door of Dr. Sims's house, so as to press it inward with such force that an urgent call before morning compelled the doctor to crawl out of the window."—*Punxsutawney News.*

RIDGWAY TOWNSHIP.

THE PIONEER SETTLER AND OTHER EARLY SETTLERS—PIONEER ROAD UP HOGBACK HILL—PIONEER GRIST-MILL FOR THE WILDERNESS—PIONEER PHYSICIAN AND MINISTERS—PIONEER BLACKSMITH—THE PIONEER ELECTION—JAMES L. GILLIS, ETC.

Ridgway, the fourth township, was organized in 1826, being taken from Pine Creek, and named after a Mr. Jacob Ridgway, residing in Philadelphia, a large landholder in the township. It was then bounded on the north and east by McKean County, and south and west by Pine Creek township. The taxables in 1826 were 20; in 1835, 40; in 1842, 75. The population by census in 1830 was 50; and in 1840, 195. In 1843 this township was separated from Jefferson County by the organization of a new county called Elk, and has now within its bounds the seat of justice for that county, and which is also named Ridgway.

The pioneer settler of Ridgway township was "a pioneer hunter named General Wade and family, with a friend named Slade, who came to the head-waters of the Little Toby in 1798, and settled temporarily. In 1803 the party returned east, but the same year came hither and built

Skidding logs in the woods.

a log house at the mouth of the Little Toby on the east bank. In 1806, while Wade and Slade were hunting near what is now Blue Rock, they saw an Indian girl watching them. Approaching her, Wade enticed her to follow him to his home, and there introduced her to Mrs. Wade. In 1809 this Indian girl married Slade, Chief Tamisqua performing the ceremony. Slade removed with his wife to where Portland now is and established a trading house there."—*Elk County History*.

Of the early settlers Dr. A. M. Clarke wrote as follows:

"About the time of the 'late war' with England, in 1812, some venturesome men pushed their way up the Susquehanna River and up the Sinnemahoning Creek to the mouth of Trout Run on Bennett's Branch, at which place Leonard Morey located and built a saw-mill. Dwight Caldwell, John Mix, and Eben Stephens came at the same time. These were the first settlers on Bennett's Branch. About the same time a large tract of country, containing some one hundred and forty thousand acres, which had been surveyed on warrants issued in the name of James Wilson, had come into the possession of Fox, Norris & Co., Quakers, of Philadelphia, who sent William Kersey as agent to construct a road into their lands and build a mill. The road started from a point on an old State road leading to Waterford, Pennsylvania, about eight miles west of the Susquehanna River, passed through the woods over Boon's Mountain, crossed Little Toby's Creek, without a bridge, where Hellen Mills now stand, followed up the creek seven miles to the point of Hogback Hill, up which it went, though steep and difficult, continued over the high and undulating grounds to the spot which had been selected for a mill site on a stream which was afterwards called Elk Creek, where the mill was built, about two miles from the present Centreville. Jacob Wilson was the miller who for many years attended this mill. Often the old man had to go a mile and a half from his own house to the mill to grind a small grist of a bushel, brought on horseback; but his patience was quite equal to the emergency, and he did it without complaining.

"A few settlers came into the county about the time the Kersey Mill was built; of these I may mention Elijah Meredith, James Green, Josiah Taylor, J. R. Hancock, David Reesman, John Kyler, and John Shafer, with their families; these constituted the Kersey settlement."

This settlement was in Clearfield County, but was along the line of Jefferson, and its history is a part of ours.

"In 1822, Alonzo and James W. Brockway settled on the Henry Pfeffer tract, Lottery Warrant No. 34; they had to cut their way down the creek five miles from Philetus Clark's. This was the first settlement in what afterwards became Snyder township, and where Brockwayville now stands. Rev. Jonathan Nichols settled on the Brandy Camp. He was the first clergyman who settled in this section, and spent his life in serving the people. He was the first physician, and his visits were re-

PIONEER HISTORY OF JEFFERSON COUNTY, PENNA.

quired over a large extent of country. As a clergyman, his ministrations were generally well accepted, and his meetings as well attended as could be in a country so sparsely settled; people frequently went six or eight miles to meeting. In the winter their carriages were sleds drawn by oxen; in the summer, men, women, and children could walk nine or ten miles and home again the same day."

The old State road spoken of here by Dr. Clarke was the Milesburg and Le Bœuf road that passed through Port Barnett.

One of the pioneers of Ridgway township was James L. Gillis. In June, 1820, he left his home in Ontario County, New York, to look over the land, and in December, 1820, he moved his family into the wilderness. They came in sleds, and it required two days; they had to camp out overnight. Gillis was an agent for Ridgway, and was furnished ample means for all expenses. He cleared five hundred acres of land, erected a large frame house, and built a grist-mill and a carding-machine. Reuben A. Aylesworth and Enos Gillis came with his family.

James L. Gillis was a man of State celebrity. He was absent nearly all the time, lobbying at Harrisburg, Pennsylvania, or at Washington. He was a very interesting man to talk with.

In 1826, William Morgan, of Batavia, New York, was abducted from his home at night and never heard of afterwards. Morgan had been a Mason, and published the alleged secrets of the Masonic order. The Masons were charged with abducting and murdering him. Mystery surrounds his disappearance to this day. Intense excitement prevailed all over the nation.

Mr. Gillis was a Mason, and was arrested at Montmorenci and carried to New York State, and there tried for the abduction and murder of Morgan. In the trial he was cleared.

Mr. Gillis was a cavalry soldier in the war of 1812, and took part in several severe engagements. He was taken prisoner by the British and suffered severely. He was a model man physically, and by nature endowed with much intelligence. This, added to his extensive travels and political experience, gave him a prominence in the State and nation that few men possessed. Gillis was the Patriarch in Ridgway township. He migrated in 1821 to what he named Montmorenci, Pine Creek township, then in Jefferson County. He brought his children and brother-in-law with him. He cleared four hundred acres of land in one chopping, and built a grist-mill and a carding-mill in those woods.

For five years he was monarch of all he surveyed, and without any post-office nearer than fifty miles of him. He came to Port Barnett, near Brookville, to vote, was liable to and for militia service, and for all legal business had to go to Indiana, Pennsylvania, a distance of ninety miles. While at Montmorenci in 1826 he was instrumental in securing a mail-route from Kittanning to Olean, New York. This gave him mail service once in two weeks. He was a great horseman and horseback rider.

Gillis was related to Jacob Ridgway, one of the richest men in the State, and he was agent for all his lands in Jefferson County. Gillis was slow and methodical in his habits; was fond of games,—viz., chess, backgammon, checkers, and euchre. He carried a snuff-box that held about a pint of the choicest snuff, in which was buried a Tonka bean, that imparted to the snuff a delightful aroma. He walked with a gold-headed cane, and in winter he wore a panther-skin overcoat. Physically he was a large man, and was sociable and agreeable. In 1830 he moved to where Ridgway now is. He was elected to several offices, including Congress. He moved to Mount Pleasant, Iowa, where he died in 1881, aged eighty-nine years.

> "Sleep, soldier, though many regret thee
> Who pass by thy cold bier to-day;
> Soon, soon shall the kindest forget thee,
> And thy name from the earth pass away.
> The man thou didst love as a brother
> A friend in thy place will have gained,
> And thy dog shall keep watch for another,
> And thy steed by another be reined."

The second saw-mill was erected by Enos Gillis in 1823, at the western end of what is now Ridgway, and is standing as it did seventy years ago, only it is transformed into part of an axe-factory.

James Gallagher and family arrived in 1825, over the same trail Gillis came. Enos Gillis and James Gallagher were the pioneers in what is now called Ridgway borough, by having erected there three or four log cabins and a saw-mill in 1824. About 1838, J. S. Hyde, father of Hon. W. H. Hyde, reached Ridgway clothed in overalls, and all his possessions tied up in a handkerchief. He entered the store of Gillis & Clover and wanted to buy an axe on credit; on being refused he told the storekeeper to keep his axe; that he would see the day when he could buy the whole store.

Caleb Dill was the "post-boy" in 1828.

The pioneer tannery was started in 1830. Enos Gillis, owner; James Gallagher, tanner.

"WANTED IMMEDIATELY.

"Two apprentices to the TANNING BUSINESS. Two boys, about 17 or 18 years of age, who can come well recommended, will find a good place. All pains will be taken to acquaint them with the business.

"JAMES GALLAGHER.

"RIDGWAY TOWNSHIP, March 13, 1834."
—*The Jeffersonian.*

PIONEER HISTORY OF JEFFERSON COUNTY, PENNA.

The pioneer road was the State road from Kittanning to Olean. There was great excitement and enthusiasm by the land-owners and settlers over this State road. But it all came to naught, for the road has never been used to any extent. It is still known as the Olean road where it is not grown up and abandoned.

The Ceres road was laid out in 1825 and finished in 1828. The Milesburg and Smethport Turnpike Company was incorporated in 1825, and the road was finished about 1830. (See Laws.)

In 1840 the waters of what is now called the Clarion were as clear as crystal, pure as life, and gurgled into the river from the mountain springs. No tannery or other refuse was to be found in it. In 1749 the French named the stream Gall River. It was declared a public highway as Toby's Creek by an act of the Legislature, March 21, 1798, up to the second great fork.

In early times this river was known as Stump Creek, and sometimes as Toby's Creek, and it is said that it got these two names after two Indian hunters, who were in the habit (in the winter) of going up this river in canoes, to hunt and trap. They would return each spring with their furs and meat to their villages down the Allegheny and Ohio Rivers.

It was called Toby's Creek as early as 1758. Unable myself to find any authority for a change to Clarion, I wrote to the Secretary of Internal Affairs, and received the following,—viz. :

"June 8, 1897.

"HON. W. J. MCKNIGHT, Brookville, Pa.

"DEAR SIR,—In answer to your letter of recent date, we beg to say that we are unable to find any act of Assembly changing the name of Toby's Creek to Clarion River. In an act to authorize the erection of a dam, passed in 1822, this stream is designated as 'Toby's Creek, otherwise called Clarion River.'

"Very truly yours,
"JAMES W. LATTA,
"*Secretary.*"

The early mills in and around Ridgway were the Elk Creek Mill, owned by J. S. Hyde, the Mill Creek Mill, owned by Yale & Healey, and the Dickinson Mill. This mill was erected by Hughes & Dickinson, and painted red. The boarding-house was also red.

In the year 1833 there were seven families in what is now Ridgway, —viz., Reuben Aylesworth and Caleb Dill west of the river, and Enos Gillis, James W. Gallagher, H. Karns, Thomas Barber, and Joab Dobbins on the east side.

About 1840, common hands on the river received one dollar per day and board. Pilots, two and three dollars per day and board. The "head" sawyer on the Red Mill received twenty-five dollars per month and board; the assistant, eighteen dollars per month and board; and common hands, fifteen dollars a month and board.

The usual religious exercises on Sunday at the Red Mill, in 1842, were wrestling, fishing, pitching quoits, shooting at mark, running foot-races, and "jumping by the double rule of three."

The Beech Bottom Mill belonged to the Portland Lumber Company. The diet at these old mills was bread, potatoes, beans, flitch, and molasses; brown sugar, old tasted butter, coffee and tea without cream, and for dessert dried apple-sauce or pie. Labor was cheap. Pine boards of the finest quality sold in Louisville, Kentucky, at seven and nine dollars per thousand. If the operator cleared twenty-five or fifty cents on a thousand feet he was thankful.

All goods and groceries were dear, they had to be hauled from Olean, New York, or Waterson's Ferry on the Allegheny River. Money was scarce, the people social and kind. Whiskey and New England rum was three cents a drink.

PIONEER TEAMSTERS—MELANCHOLY ACCIDENT.

"On Thursday, the 4th of July, a man by the name of John Schram, from Ridgway settlement, in Jefferson County, a wagoner, while at Freeport waiting the arrival of some store goods from Pittsburg, came to a sudden and untimely end by his wagon oversetting upon him, while driving rather faster than prudence would justify, along the towpath. An inquest was held by Robert Criswell, Esq. Verdict that he came to his death by the upsetting of his wagon in the Pennsylvania Canal. The unfortunate stranger was interred in decency and respect."—*Armstrong Democrat*, July 4, 1837.

Other early teamsters from Ridgway to Freeport, Kittanning, and Waterson's Ferry were Conrad Moyer, Coryell Wilcox, Barney McCune, and Charles B. Gillis. The pioneer and early teamsters from St. Mary's to those points were John Walker, Charles Fisher, and Joseph Wilhelm. The merchandise carried from Pittsburg to this region was by canal to Freeport, by keel-boat and steamboat to Kittanning and Waterson's Ferry. The teamsters loaded their wagons with wheat flour, etc., in barrels bound with hickory hoops, bacon and salt and whiskey in barrels bound with *iron* hoops. But, strange to say, there was always a soft stave in these whiskey-barrels through which a "rye straw" could be made to reach the whiskey for the teamster and his friends while *en route* home.

"From 1825 to 1845 the plan of Fourier—that of communities with a union of labor and capital and working under fixed rules—was actively put into operation in this section of Pennsylvania. On the main road from Ridgway to Smethport are the remains of the town of Teutonia, once a large community; but jealousies grew up, and the members dispersed among the people at large, and became industrious and useful citizens.

"The sudden advent and exit of this community had its prototype within half a mile of Teutonia. The mouldering wood and growth of trees of half a century mark the spot where was laid out the town of Instanter. Its plot is duly recorded in McKean County. Mr. Cooper, a large landholder, was the instigator, if not the forerunner of the settlement. As the streets were marked out, the buildings went up like magic; but Madam Rumor spread a report that the land-title was unsound, and on investigation such was found to be the fact. Work suddenly ceased and the settlers left."

Part of the Cooper lands were situated in what was then Jefferson County, and the flaming hand-bill which was gotten up to advertise these lands gave the following explicit directions for getting to them:

"*Title.*—Three hundred thousand acres of land for sale and settlement. In the counties of McKean and Jefferson, in the State of Pennsylvania, joining the New York line and the Genesee lands, extending for forty miles, and situate about two hundred and fifty miles northwest from Philadelphia, etc.

"Settlers and others wishing to go into the aforesaid lands from the northern part of Jersey, New York, and New England States, take the Newburg and Cohecton Turnpike, or such roads as will be most direct to the Painted Post; then cross the York and Pennsylvania line, taking the Tioga road to Dr. Willar's or Widow Barry's; thence to and on the east and west road, passing Wellsborough and Coudersport to Smethport; thence ten miles to Instanter (proposed county town of McKean). For settlers and others south of Easton, fall into the Lehigh and Berwick or Sunbury pike, from thence to Williamsport, passing by Jersey Shore to the aforesaid east and west road. For such as go on foot or horseback, they can take the Ellicott road from Jersey Shore, passing through Dunstown, and up the Susquehanna and Sinnemahoning to Cox's settlement and Instanter.

"BENJAMIN B. COOPER.

"COOPER'S POINT, April 25, 1812."
—*History of Pennsylvania.*

In 1835 a man by the name of Frank Goodar lived in Ridgway township, on the Beechwoods road, near what is now Brockwayville, Snyder township. He was married, but concluded that he ought to have two wives, so with the consent of wife No. 1 he married Mollie No. 2, Squire McCullough, of Pine Creek township, performing the ceremony in the summer of that year. For this offence against morals Isaac Temple prosecuted Goodar before Thomas Lucas, Esq., for bigamy; but at the

PIONEER HISTORY OF JEFFERSON COUNTY, PENNA.

hearing of September 12, 1835, he failed to prove a marriage with wife No. 1, and of course Goodar was discharged. All three lived together for seven years in a log cabin, on what was afterwards the Frost farm, and now the William Kearney place, where Frank and Mollie deserted Beckie, wife No. 1.

Ralph Hill settled at Portland Mills about 1832. He came from Massachusetts. He lived the life of a hermit. Portland becoming too much in civilization, he moved up Spring Creek, and lived in Forest County, the companion of wild animals, "where his right there was none to dispute." He died at a ripe old age.

The pioneer railroad was the Sunbury and Erie. "The Sunbury and Erie, now the Philadelphia and Erie, a portion of that magnificent system, the Pennsylvania Railroad, was chartered April 3, 1837, but it was not until 1852 that construction was commenced, and the road was not completed until 1864."

In the speculative times of 1836 non-residents of then Jefferson County bought largely of the wild lands in and around Ridgway township, which, of course, when railroad and other bubbles burst, was left on their hands. This land had been advertised to contain valuable iron ore and bituminous coal, and much of it could have been bought as late as 1841 at fifty and twenty-five cents an acre.

To build a railroad through a dense wilderness of worthless hemlock, ferocious beasts, gnats, and wintergreen berries required a large purse and great courage. Of course, there was no subject talked about in the cabin homes of that locality so dear to the hearts of the pioneers as this railroad.

There was not a cabin on the line of this proposed road from Shippen to Ridgway, and but one at Johnsonburg from Ridgway to the waters of Tionesta.

The pioneer justice of the peace was Reuben A. Aylesworth, appointed February 18, 1832.

In 1839, James Watterson, of Armstrong County, Pennsylvania, settled at the mouth of Spring Creek, and he and Job Paine built a sawmill. In 1833, Ralph Hill and a man named Ransom were living in a shanty at Beech Bottom.

"The pioneer school was held in Gallagher's log cabin (near the present Ridgway Central Graded School), in 1826, under the control of Hannah Gilbert, and attended by the children of the three families residing there. Subsequently Ann Berry and Betsey Hyatt taught in an old red school-house, which was situated at the present site of Dillon's meat market. In 1834 a house for common school purposes was erected above the old Dickinson homestead, on the west side of the race and north side of Main Street, by Messrs. Crow, Gallagher, Thayer, Dickinson, Cobb, and Cady, and Betsey (Elizabeth M.) Hyatt installed teacher.

PIONEER HISTORY OF JEFFERSON COUNTY, PENNA.

She was succeeded by Mr. Barnutz in 1835. A second building was erected in 1838, near where the B. R. & P. depot now stands.

In the winter of 1832, L. Wilmarth, Arthur Hughes, and George Dickinson erected the red saw-mill. Ridgway was laid out for a town in 1833.

"In 1834 the first bridge was put across the Clarion River. This was a toll-bridge. It was built of twelve by sixteen inch stringers resting on cribbing. Before this time teams forded the river, and in high water boats were used. The country was covered by a thick growth of hemlock-trees. Game, such as elks, deer, bears, panthers, and wild-cats were found in great abundance, fish abounded in the streams," and rattlesnakes and other reptiles were numerous and dangerous.

Up to 1835, Ridgway township included all that portion of Snyder township that is now Brockwayville borough, and even west of Sugar Hill, as well as a good portion of what is now Washington township. Ridgway in 1836 was a small village. At the west end of the town was George Dickinson's boarding-house, then Henry Gross's home, then Dickinson's saw-mill and barn, Caleb Dill's home, justice office, and blacksmith-shop, Stephen Weis's home and John Cobb's house, Hon. James L. Gillis's home and store, George Dickinson's home and store, and on the east side of the Clarion was the Exchange Hotel, owned by David Thayer, then Edward Derby's old red house, then the Lone Star Hotel, owned by P. T. Brooks.

When P. T. Brooks, who was quite a wag, very polite and demonstrative, was keeping this hotel in the wilderness, two finely dressed and appearing gentlemen rode up one day in front of and stopped at his hotel for dinner. Of course, this was an opportunity for Mr. Brooks to be demonstrative and polite. After seeing that the horses were properly cared for, Brooks approached the gentlemen in this way: "What kind of meat would you gentleman prefer for dinner?" "Why, Mr. Landlord, we would prefer venison." "I am sorry that we are just out of venison." "Oh, well," said the strangers, "a little good beef or mutton will do." "Well, well," replied Mr. Brooks, "I am sorry to say we are just out of beef and mutton." At this the strangers were a little nonplussed, but finally said, "We will be satisfied with fish." "Well, well," replied Mr. Brooks, rubbing his hands, "I am sorry to say that we are just out of fish, but we have some very excellent pickled pork."

Uncle Eben Stevens, an old hunter who came to the Sinnemahoning region about 1812, told me there was an Indian graveyard at the mouth of Mill Creek, that he used to go up there and hunt with the Indians, and in the spring they would paint their canoes red with that "iron paint" on the Clarion.

And down the Toby Creek—

PIONEER HISTORY OF JEFFERSON COUNTY, PENNA.

" Where the rocks were gray and the shores were steep,
Where the waters below looked dark and deep,
Where the shades of the forest were heavy and deep the whole day through,"

Stevens and the Indians in these red canoes would carry their game, skins, and furs to the Pittsburg market.

The pioneer effort to erect what is now the county of Elk was on Tuesday, February 28, 1837, when an act to erect the county of Ridgway was reported in the State Senate.

The present town or borough of St. Mary's was established in 1842. Father Alexander had the colony in charge then. Early in the summer of 1842 a number of Germans in the cities of Baltimore and Philadelphia associated themselves in a society to form a German settlement on the community plan, and appointed John Albert, Nicholas Reimel, and Michael Deileth to select the place for settlement. This committee selected Jefferson County, Pennsylvania, and the site where the borough of St. Mary's and the adjoining settlement now is. For this colony they purchased thirty-five thousand acres of land from Mr. Kingsbury. In October of this year the first instalment of settlers—one from Philadelphia and one from Baltimore—reached John Green's, in Kersey. From Kersey these men, in two instalments, opened a path to where St. Mary's now is, and immediately set to work to erect their log cabins on St. Mary's Street. In December, 1842, they moved their families to these cabins, and the county of Elk was organized in 1843.

The pioneer election for township officers was held in Ridgway township, at the house of James Gallagher, on the 16th of March, 1837. The following persons contested,—viz.: Constable, Nehemiah Bryant, 8 votes; Alanson Viall, 7 votes. Supervisors, James Gallagher and Alonzo Brockway, no opposition. Poor Overseers, Naphtala G. Barrun and William Maxwell, no opposition. Fence Appraisers, Nehemiah Bryant and William Taylor, no opposition. Town Clerk, James Gallagher. Officers of Election : Inspector, John Stratton ; Judges, Nehemiah Bryant, James Brockway, and Alonzo Brockway; Clerk, James Gallagher.

ROSE TOWNSHIP.

Rose, the fifth township, was organized in 1827, and was also taken from Pine Creek township. It was named for Dr. Rose, then a prominent landholder in its territory. He founded the village of Roseville, and labored hard to make it the county seat, but failed in this aspiration. Roseville was celebrated for the early horse-racing. The other village in the township is Bellview (post-office, Stanton), about five miles south of Brookville. The taxables in 1828, 123; in 1835, 252 (this included the taxables in the borough of Brookville). The town and township held their elections together for a number of years, and the taxables were as-

PIONEER HISTORY OF JEFFERSON COUNTY, PENNA.

sessed together up to 1845. The population of Rose township, including Brookville, in 1840, was 1421. The pioneer settlers in Rose township were John Matson and Mary, his wife. He built his cabin on the land now owned by his son, Robert L., in 1805. The next settler was Joseph Clements, the next Andrew Vastbinder. John Lucas came from Crooked Creek, Indiana County, in 1816, and settled at Puckety. John Kennedy came in the spring of 1822. Walter Templeton, grandfather of Thomas L. Templeton, the efficient cashier of the Brookville National Bank, was living in the township then. He was the mechanic of that time. He could do any and all kinds of repairing. In 1826, Samuel D. Kennedy settled on the pike near Corsica. There was a log house then in what is now Corsica, and a man by the name of Powers kept a tavern in it. Luther Geer settled in the township in 1833. Peter Thrush in 1837.

Square timber.

Peter Himes in 1838. The Enoch and Joseph E. Hall family came in 1833. Joel Spyker came in 1835. The Witherows came in 1833. William Thompson came in 1834.

James Corbett built the pioneer saw-mill on Red Bank, near Coders. The pioneer church building was the Bethel log, in 1824 (Presbyterian).

The pioneer brick-yard was started by Colonel William Jack and General Wise. It was situated on the head of what is now Heidrick, Matson & Co.'s mill-pond, on the east side of the North Fork, and was operated about 1830.

PIONEER HISTORY OF JEFFERSON COUNTY, PENNA.

The pioneer improvement in what is now Rose township was made by John Matson. He built the first pioneer grist-mill in the township, on the North Fork, above Verstine & Kline's saw-mill, in 1830. In 1829 he built the saw-mill now known as Verstine & Kline's mill.

The pioneer election polling-place was at the house of John Lucas. In 1836 it was changed as follows: By an act of the Legislature passed the 16th day of June, 1836, it was enacted "that all that part of Rose township, in the county of Jefferson, lying west of a line commencing at the home of Robert Morrison, on the line of Perry township; thence north along an old line to the Eldred township line, be, and the same is hereby, erected into a separate election district, and shall hereafter hold their general elections at the house now occupied by Darius Carrier within said bounds."

Among the pioneer industries was tar-burning. Kilns were formed and split fagots of pitch-pine knots were arranged in circles and burned. The tar was collected by a ditch and forced into a chute, and from there barrelled. John Matson, Sr., marketed on rafts as high as forty barrels in one season. Freedom Stiles was the king "tar-burner." Pioneer prices at Pittsburg for tar was ten dollars a barrel.

The pioneer licensed tavern was kept by John Matson on the old State Road in 1812.

The early tavern-keepers, or those to whom license to sell whiskey was granted, were William Vastbinder, William Christy, John Shoemaker, David Orcutt, Anthony Rowe, James Green, Isaac Mills, and Joshua McKinley. The two latter kept at Roseville. Joseph Henderson at Dowlingville in 1841.

The early brick-kilns were started in 1832, one by Robert P. Barr and the other by Joseph Kaylor.

The pioneer birth in the township was Jane, daughter of John and Mary Matson.

At the pioneer local election for 1828 the number of votes cast was 65, and at the general election in the fall, 66.

At an election held at the home of John Lucas, March 20, 1829, the following persons contested,—viz.: Supervisors, Moses Knapp, 39 votes; James Shields, 30 votes. Poor Overseers, John Lucas, 10 votes; John Avery, 10 votes. Auditor, John Hughes, 50 votes; Alonzo Baldwin, 42 votes; R. K. Scott, 36 votes; William Morrison, 32 votes. Constable, William Love, Jr., 51 votes. Fence-Viewers, John Kelso, 16 votes; Elijah M. Graham, 14 votes. Town Clerk, John Christy, 3 votes; James Corbett, 3 votes. Attest: Alonzo Baldwin, John Lucas, judges.

Election district according to the act of April 16, 1838:

"SECTION 52. That the citizens of Rose township, Jefferson County, within the following boundaries,—viz.: Beginning at the mouth of a run putting into the north side of Red Bank Creek, a short distance west of

PIONEER HISTORY OF JEFFERSON COUNTY, PENNA.

the mill of Dr. Dowling; thence up said creek till it strikes the Rose district line; thence west to county line between Armstrong and Jefferson Counties, and from a place or point the nearest opposite the mouth of the aforesaid run, by a line running due south till the same shall strike the northern line of Perry township, shall hold their elections in the borough of Brookville, at the place now appointed by law for holding the borough election."

A POLITICAL CANDIDATE.

" Prior to March, 1832, our neighboring county of Jefferson was without any newspaper, and the announcements of candidates for county offices were then made through the weekly papers of this county, and it might be incidentally added that then, as ever since over that way, there was no scarcity of candidates.

" The announcements were generally inserted prominently in large type, occupying from three to five times as much space as would be allowed in these days.

" One of these announcements, which was shown us a few days ago by one of our subscribers, appeared regularly in the *Indiana Free Press* for three months prior to the October election in 1831. It is a curiosity. Here it is in its original form and style :

" ' TO THE FREE AND INDEPENDENT ELECTORS OF JEFFERSON COUNTY.

" ' Solicited it's I have been,
To stand a poll by many,
For office of *Commissioner*
Before, have not agreed to any;
My name at length I will let go,
Through medium of the press.
By word of mouth and by hand-bills,
Which way they think it best;
It's free and independent times,
October you will see,
The second Tuesday, if I'm right,
The polls will ended be;
And now I'll say what I have said
Before, on such occasions,
That if elected to an office,
I'll do my best endeavors
To fill the office I'm put in
With punctuality,
And with the utmost of my skill,
Though best it may not be;
If I'm elected to that trust,
My best wishes shall be fervent,
Whilst here I stand a candidate,
Your most obedient servant.

PIONEER HISTORY OF JEFFERSON COUNTY, PENNA.

JOHN CHRISTIE is my name in full,
America is my nation,
Rose township is my dwelling place,
A Farmer is my station.

"'July 31, 1831.'"
—*Indiana Messenger.*

I copy the following advertisement from the *Brookville Democratic Republican* of the year 1837 :

" CAMP-MEETING.

"There will be a camp-meeting held by the Methodist Episcopal Church below Troy, to commence on Friday, the 1st day of September, 1837.

"DARIUS CARRIER."

HORSE-RACING.

Horse-racing was practised as early as when Troy was besieged by the Greeks. In the plain before the city the besiegers celebrated holidays by sports and horse-races, and Homer says the walls of Troy were covered with sporting Trojans watching the result.

The trotting horse is an institution of the present century. Before 1800 running was the only method of racing.

Horse-racing as practised in the pioneer days of our county was a great sport. People came here from all the northwest.

THE ROSEVILLE PIONEER RACE-GROUND.

"*Jefferson County Races.*—On Tuesday, the 14th of November, instant, will be run over the race-course on the Lewistown and Erie Turnpike, near the public house of Mrs. Mills, four miles west of Brookville, a *match race* of 600 yards between the celebrated racers *Robin* and *Zib*. The public and all others friendly are hereby invited to attend. By order of

"THE PROPRIETORS.

"November 2, 1837."

"Robin" was a Brookville horse, and won this race. He was a sorrel, and belonged to John Pierce and Major William Rodgers. These men purchased him from Ephraim Bushly for five hundred dollars, and they sold him to Benjamin Bennett, Sr., of Bellefonte, where he was taken and matched for a race. He had never been beaten in a race, but before this match took place in Centre County he was poisoned and ruined.

"Zib" was a dark bay horse, and was owned by a Mr. Chambers, of Crawford County, Pennsylvania. The "stake" in the above race was three hundred dollars. Great crowds attended these races. People came from Indiana, Armstrong, Crawford, Clearfield, and Centre. The stake was usually three hundred dollars, and the excitement and side-betting was lively.

The act of the Legislature No. 110, regulating election districts, approved July 11, 1842, established the polling-place for Rose township as follows:

"SECTION 11. That the qualified voters of Rose township, Jefferson County, shall hereafter hold their general election at the court-house of Brookville, in said county."

The pioneer to clear land in what might be called South Rose was Joseph Millen. Robert Morrison was the second.

The pioneer school-house was on the farm of William Carr. The one at Bellview was built in 1842.

The pioneer church was on the land of William Ohl in 1837.

The *Brookville Republican*, under date of June 13, 1837, contains the following:

"DISTRESSING ACCIDENT.

"On Saturday, the 24th day of May last, a few men were collected in building a church in this vicinity. While in the act of pushing up a log it accidentally slipped off the skates and fell upon Mr. Robert Morrison and crushed him, so that he survived but a few hours."

This church was on the farm now owned by Simon Reitz, of Beaver township.

"Between the years of 1830 and 1840 a number of German families came into the lower part of the county and settled near Red Bank Creek.

"The impulse given to the lumber trade by the speculations in the State of Maine was not without its influence in the remote sections of the Union. The keen sagacity of the Yankee discovered that there were vast bodies of pine lands lying around the sources of the Allegheny River, not appreciated at their full value by the few pioneers who lived among them. The Yankees had learned to estimate the value of pine land by the tree and by the log; the Pennsylvanians still estimated it by the acre. Somewhere between 1830 and 1837 individuals and companies from New England and New York purchased considerable bodies of land on the head-waters of Red Bank and Clarion Rivers from the Holland Land Company and other large land-holders. They proceeded to erect saw-mills and to drive the lumber trade after the most approved method. The little leaven thus introduced caused quite a fermentation among the lumbermen and land-holders of the county. More land changed owners, new water privileges were improved, capital was introduced from abroad, and during the spring floods every creek and river resounded with the preparation of rafts and the lively shouts of the lumbermen as they shot their rafts over the swift chutes of the mill-dams. The population of the county was trebled in ten years."

Matson dam.

In 1840-43 large bodies of original tracts were still held by rich proprietors at a distance. The price of land then was fifty cents, one dollar, and three dollars per acre.

BARNETT TOWNSHIP.

This township was so called for Joseph Barnett, the patriarch; it was the sixth organization, and was separated from Rose township in 1833. That part lying north of the Clarion River was taken away from it by the organization of Forest County. The taxables in 1835 were 70; 1842, 67. The census gave it for population, in 1840, 259.

In 1827, William, George, and Samuel Armstrong came to that section. In 1829, David and Joseph Reynolds, John Cook, John H. Maize, and Alex. Murray located. David Reynolds cleared the first land and ran the first lumber in 1829. Other early settlers were Alex. Forsythe, Robert Wallace, Richard Burns, and Orrin Butterfield. The pioneer birth was Evaline Armstrong, daughter of William.

The pioneer marriage was Thomas Maize, who married Martha Hall in 1836. The pioneer death was James Maize, who died in 1831. The first grave was at Troutman's Run. The pioneer school-house was built

PIONEER HISTORY OF JEFFERSON COUNTY, PENNA.

at the mouth of this run. The pioneer grist-mill was built on the Toby, now Clarion River, by William Armstrong, who also opened a store, in 1830. The pioneer hotel-keeper was Alex. Murray. The pioneer blacksmith was Andrew Clough. The pioneer saw-mill was built by Wm. Reynolds, at Maple Creek, in 1829.

The pioneer election for township officers was in 1833, and the following officers were elected: Constable, John Maize; Supervisors, David Mead, William Armstrong; Auditors, John Wynkoop, Edwin Forsythe, Wm. Manross; Poor Overseer, Enos Myers, John Maize.

From an act regulating election districts in the State:

"SECTION 29. *And be it further enacted by the authority aforesaid,* That the electors of Barnett township, in the county of Jefferson, shall hereafter hold their general elections at the house now occupied by John Wynkoop, in said township.

"Approved—the third day of May, A.D. one thousand eight hundred and thirty-two.

"SECTION 64. The electors of the township of Barnett, in the county of Jefferson, shall hereafter hold their elections at the house of Alexander Murray, in said township.

"Approved—the fifteenth day of April, one thousand eight hundred and thirty-five."

In 1833, Job Carr had a saw-mill about a mile above Millstone, on the river.

In Big Toby Creek (now Clarion River) and in the Little Toby Creek pike were occasionally shot and gigged weighing from thirty to fifty pounds. The Mahoning, Sandy Lick, North Fork, and Red Bank also were full of choice pike, catfish, bass, sunfish, suckers, and chubs. It was a common thing to shoot pike; the others were caught by hook and line, in seines, and gigged after night. The lesser streams, like the mill creeks, in addition to many of the others just mentioned, were alive with speckled trout, and every run in the county then contained these speckled beauties.

"In 1835, James Aharrah migrated with his family from Indiana, Pennsylvania, to Wynkoop Run, and erected a cabin eighteen by twenty feet with a few small windows in it. One night when James was absent a panther paid them a visit. Sitting up on his haunches, he peered into the small cabin. In desperation Mrs. Aharrah seized an axe which was standing near by and took her place at the side of the window, ready to receive the visitor should he decide to enter, while her son, armed with the old-time poking-stick, came to her assistance and took post at the opposite side of the window. Henry and his sister Jane (Jack Knopsnyder's mother), who were both quite young, took refuge under the bed and waited for the panther's departure.

"Mr. Panther soon tired of this, and bade them an affectionate farewell, which shook the earth with its vibrations."

The provisions were brought by canoes up the Clarion River from the place where Parker now stands. Two canoes were engaged in delivering groceries, etc. Ephraim and John Shawl were the two men who had control of one, and David Ridder and a man by the name of Sampson manned the other.

CRIME.

From 1778 to 1855, inclusive, three hundred and twenty-eight persons were hanged in Pennsylvania. Of these, five suffered the penalty of death for high treason, eight for robbery, fourteen for burglary, three for assault, one for arson, four for counterfeiting, and seven for unknown offences. On April 22, 1794, the death penalty was abolished except for murder in the first degree. Before 1834 hangings took place in public, and since then in jail yards or corridors.

The pioneer murder in Jefferson County was committed on May 1, 1844. Daniel Long, one of the mighty hunters of Pine Creek township, and Samuel Knopsnyder, were murdered in Barnett township, now Heath, near Raught's Mills. There was a dispute between Long and James Green about a piece of land. The land was a vacant strip. James Green and his son Edwin took possession of Long's shanty on this land while Long was absent. On Long's return to the shanty in company with Knopsnyder, Long was shot by young Green as he attempted to enter the shanty, with Long's own gun. Knopsnyder was so terribly cut with an axe in the hands of the Greens that he died in a few days. The Greens, father and son, were arrested, tried, and convicted of murder in the second degree, and each sentenced to four years in the penitentiary.

James Green, the father, served a year and was pardoned. Edwin served his time and returned to Jefferson County a few days only, as he was in terror of the Longs. He therefore returned to Pittsburg, and settled down somewhere and lived and died highly respected.

"In 1784, the year in which Pittsburg was surveyed into building lots, the privilege of mining coal in the 'great seam' opposite that town was sold by the Penns at the rate of thirty pounds for each mining lot, extending back to the centre of the hill. This event may be regarded as forming the beginning of the coal trade of Pittsburg. The supply of the towns and cities on the Ohio and Mississippi Rivers with Pittsburg coal became an established business at an early day in the present century or in 1800. Pittsburg coal was known long before the town became noted as an iron centre.

"Down to 1845 all the coal shipped westward from Pittsburg was floated down the Ohio in flat-bottomed boats in the spring and fall freshets, each boat holding about fifteen thousand bushels of coal. The

PIONEER HISTORY OF JEFFERSON COUNTY, PENNA.

boats were usually lashed in pairs, and were sold and broken up when their destination was reached. In 1845 steam tow-boats were introduced, which took coal-barges down the river and brought them back empty."

PIONEER FLAT-BOATS—PIONEER TIPPLES, ETC.

The pioneer boats in what is now Jefferson County were built at Port Barnett for the transportation of Centre County pig-metal. In 1830

Making a boat, Clarion River.

they were built on the North Fork for the same purpose. In after-years, when tipples were used, boats were built and tipples erected at the following points,—viz.: at Findley's, on Sandy Lick, by Nieman and D. S. Chitister; at Brookville, by John Smith; at Troy, by Peter Lobaugh; at Heathville, by A. B. Paine and Arthur O'Donnell; at the mouth of Little Sandy, by William Bennett; at Robinson's Bend, by Hance Robinson. This industry along Red Bank was maintained by the charcoal furnaces of Clarion and Armstrong Counties. The boats were sold at the Olean bridge at Broken Rock, and sold again at Pittsburg for coal-barges. Some of the boats were sold for the transportation of salt to the South from Freeport. The industry on Red Bank ceased in the fifties.

Anthony and Jacob Esbaugh built scaffolds and boats for the dealers on Red Bank. The pioneer boat was sixteen feet wide and forty feet long. These boats were always built from the best lumber that could be made from the choicest timber that grew in our forests. Each gunwale was hewed out of the straightest pine-tree that was to be found,—viz.: twenty-eight inches high at the "rake," fourteen inches at the stern, ten inches thick, and forty feet long, two gunwales to a boat. The ties were hewed six inches thick, with a six-inch face, mortised, dove-tailed, and keyed into the gunwale six feet apart. The six "streamers" for a boat were sawed three by twelve inches, sixteen feet long, and "pinned" to the ties with one pin in the middle of each streamer. These pins were made of white oak one and a half inches square and ten inches long. The plank for the "bottoms" were first-class white pine one and a half inches thick, and pinned to the streamers and gunwales with white oak pins, calked with flax or tow. All pioneer boats were built on the ground and turned by about ten men—and a gallon of whiskey—over

Rafting-in on the Clarion, at Armstrong's.

and on a bed made of brush to keep the planks in the bottom from springing. All boats were "sided up" with white oak studding two and a half by five inches and six feet (high) long. Each studding was mortised into a gunwale two feet apart. Inside the boat a siding eighteen inches high was pinned on. These boats were sold in Pittsburg, to be used as coal-barges for the transportation of coal to the Lower Mississippi. The boats were manned and run by two or three men, the pilot always at the stern. The oar, stem and blade, was made the same as for ordinary rafts. The pioneer boats were tied and landed with halyards made of twisted hickory saplings. The size of these boats in 1843 was eighteen feet wide and eighty feet long, built on tipples similar to the present method. The boats are now made from one hundred and twenty to one hundred and fifty feet long and from twenty to twenty-four feet wide, and from spliced gunwales.

Sixty years ago boats were built on the Big Toby at Maple Creek, Clarington, Millstone, Wynkoop, Spring Creek, Irvine, and Ridgway. The pioneer boat was probably built at Maple Creek by William Reynolds.

Turning a boat.

The pioneer boats were gems of the art as compared with those made to-day. Now the gunwales are spliced up of pieces to make the required length, and the boats are made of hemlock. The industry, however, is carried on more extensively on the Clarion now than ever and for the same market.

From this time forth, as has been the case for several years of the past, the boat bottom will be of hemlock, patched of many pieces, spiked together instead of built with long oak pins, and they will have to be handled with care to serve the purpose. Of such a kind of boat bottoms there is small danger of scarcity.

SNYDER TOWNSHIP.

THE BEGINNING OF ITS EXISTENCE AS AN ORGANIZED COMMUNITY—DR. A. M. CLARKE'S REMINISCENCES—JOEL CLARKE'S SETTLEMENT WITH HIS SONS—PIONEER LUMBERING ON LITTLE TOBY—PIONEER POST-ROUTE, 1828—POST-OFFICE AND POSTMASTER—PIONEER ELECTION—PIONEER HUNTER, ETC.

Snyder, the seventh township, was organized out of Pine Creek and Ridgway townships in 1835. It is situated and lies on the western and southwestern water-shed of the Elk Mountains, which consist of spurs of the Allegheny range. One of the most prominent of these high grounds is called Boone's Mountain, or frequently, in the common usage of the neighborhood, "The Mountain." The rock formation of this eminence is sandstone and conglomerates, giving rise to many springs of pure cold water. These are the sources of Little Toby and Sandy Lick Creeks.

The township was called for Governor Simon Snyder. The taxables in 1835 were 41; in 1842, 72. The population by census of 1840 was 291. In 1843 part of this township was detached and added to Elk

County. Owing to so many changes in the lines I am unable to tell the pioneer settlers.

Ami Sibley was one of the early hunters and trappers in this section, having arrived in 1818. The tales of his adventures in hunting would make an interesting volume. He died in 1861. His wife was Rachel Whitehill, to whom he was married in 1827, when they located in what is now Snyder.

PIONEER HISTORY OF JEFFERSON COUNTY, PENNA.

In 1819, Joel Clarke, with his wife and sons, Elisha and Joel, Jr., came to and settled on Little Toby from Russell, St. Lawrence County, New York. Later, the same year, Philetus, the third son of Joel Clarke, came also from Russell, New York, and settled on Little Toby. The late Dr. Clarke describes their coming as follows,—viz.:

"I was about eleven years old when my father, Philetus Clarke, came from St. Lawrence County, New York, into the Little Toby wilderness. The journey was long and tedious. We moved with oxen in wagons, which were covered with canvas, and which gave us shelter from sunshine and storm. I was the oldest child, and there were three of us. Sometimes I had to drive, while my father would support the wagon to keep it from upsetting. The Susquehanna and Waterford turnpike was being made, and we came along an old road near it to 'Neeper's Tavern,' about four miles from where Luthersburg now is. This was the old State Road from Bald Eagle's Nest, Mifflin County, to Le Bœuf, Allegheny County, at this time the Milesburg and Waterford road. I remember the motto that was over the sign-board at Neeper's:

"'It is God's will
This woods must yield,
And the wildwood turn
To a fruitful field.'

"From that place the road was very rough over the hills and mountains. We could not get through in one day, and had to stop one night at a place where the road-makers had built a shanty, but it had burned down and the place was called 'Burnt Shanty.' Our wagon gave us shelter, and a good spring was pleasant indeed. The next day we passed over Boone's Mountain, came to the crossing of Little Toby, near where the Oyster House was built many years afterwards. We pursued our journey onward to Kersey settlement. My father thought best to examine the lands for which he had exchanged his New York property before going any farther, and was utterly disappointed and disgusted with them. He made explorations in various directions in search of a mill site, and finally concluded to settle at what is now Brockport, where he built a saw-mill, the first ever built on Little Toby. He put a small grist-mill with 'bolts' in the saw-mill, which answered the requirements of the few settlers for a while, and afterwards built a good grist-mill, which did good service for the people." His first home was a cabin, twelve by fourteen, of round logs.

Old settlers, frequently carrying a peck or a half-bushel of corn on their backs, came to this mill and waited for their grist to be ground. Ofttimes a bushel or two of grain, too heavy to carry, was suspended across the yoke of an ox team.

In 1823, Jacob Shafer located about a mile and a half above Brock-

PIONEER HISTORY OF JEFFERSON COUNTY, PENNA.

wayville, on the Henry Sivert tract. He was a fine old German gentleman of the olden time. He was always a good Democrat, and voted for Jackson for many years. He died in 1851. Henry Walborn, brother-in law of Mr. Shafer, came at the same time, and located near Mr. Shafer on the stream which took his name,—Walborn Run. He sold his place to Joel Clarke, Jr., and went off, and his name, but for the run, would have been forgotten.

In 1828 the lumbermen of Little Toby commenced to open up the creek for a public highway. This was attended with much labor, and required two years' time. In 1830 the lumber from these mills was started to market,—viz., Brockway's, Philetus Clarke's, and Horton's, these being the only mills at that time on the creek. Dr. A. M. Clarke says, "I went with the first lumber that was sent from Little Toby to Pittsburg. It was a great company raft, awkwardly put in and poorly managed from beginning to end. After a great deal of trouble and much staving, the rafts were all collected and coupled together in one unwieldy raft at Miller's Eddy, on the Allegheny River. On account of the exceeding rough appearance of this raft it was called the 'Porcupine.' Want of experience and lack of skill nearly wrecked the whole business, for in their anxiety to get to market, and encouraged by their pilot, the unwieldy craft—I think it was three abreast and thirty-two platforms long—was started on very high water. They soon discovered their mistake, but were unable to land, and went rushing forward, and miles of foaming water were traversed before the frightened crew effected a landing. I was sent to take care of my father's share in the adventure. We went down in May, 1830, and came back in July. Our best sales were made for five and ten dollars per thousand feet for common and clear stuff."

In 1828 a post-route was established, and the mail ordered to be carried once a week on horseback from Kittanning to Smethport, McKean County. The route lay through this section of country, and in April of that year Hellen Post-Office was established, and Philetus Clarke was appointed postmaster; this was the first post-office in this neighborhood. Letter postages were six and a quarter, twelve and a half, eighteen and three quarters, and twenty-five cents, according to the distance over which they were conveyed. In 1829 a post-office was established at Brockwayville, and Alonzo Brockway appointed postmaster; this gave name to the place, which it has retained.

The first burial was an infant child of Alonzo and Huldah Brockway. The scathed stump of a pine-tree, which grew over the grave, until recently it was struck by lightning, marks the place, though the appearance of a grave has been entirely obliterated, and the unconscious passer-by, as he walks over the spot, has no thought that a human form lies mouldering under his heel. The second burial was also a child, one of the family of Mr. Jacob Shafer. They buried it in a corner of a field, on a somewhat elevated spot, between two ravines, by the roadside, near where Marvin Allen now resides. Others were afterwards buried there, until it came to be called "Shafer's Burying-Ground." In that "little city of the dead" rest the remains of Joel Clarke and Chloe, his wife, Baily Hughes, A. J. Ingalls, Joel Clarke and Mary, his wife, Philetus Clarke and Ada, his daughter, Annie Sibley, Mrs. Monahan, Mrs. Stephens, Samuel Beman and wife, Jacob Shafer and Mary, his wife, Hiram, Willis, and Jane, children of Joel and Mary Clarke, Jacob Myers, Comfort D. Felt, and others. It has lately been much neglected, and is rapidly going to decay. Some of the dead have been removed to Wildwood Cemetery.

"In 1821, John S. Brockway purchased at treasurer's sale, at Indiana, the 'Henry Peffer' tract on Little Toby, and the next year Alonzo and James M. Brockway moved over from Bennett's Branch and commenced improvements on the land. They had to cut their way five miles down the creek from Philetus Clarke's. They planted fruit-trees of various kinds as soon as the land was cleared, and peach- and plum-trees were soon in bearing. They also made large quantities of maple-sugar, raised all their own supplies, and, with game in abundance, lived luxuriously for those days. This was the first settlement in what is now Snyder township." Other early settlers were Baily Hughes, A. J. Ingalls, James Pendleton, Dr. William Bennett, A. R. Frost, Samuel Beman, Stephen Tibbetts, Jacob Myers, Alonzo Ferman, Bennett Prindle, Charles Matthews, Joseph W. Green, McMinns, and others.

The pioneer saw-mill was built in 1828 by the Brockway brothers. Dr. William Bennett built one of the first saw-mills in the township. In 1836, Hoyt and Wilson built a mill where Ferman's is now. In 1841, James Pendleton built a saw-mill, grist-mill, and carding-mill on Rattlesnake. Early school-teachers were Miss Clarissa Brockway, A. M. Clarke, John Kyler, and Mary Warner.

The first township election was held in 1835 at what is now Matthew Bovard's, and the following officers were elected,—viz.: Constable, Myron Gibbs; Supervisors, John McLaughlin, Ami Sibley; Auditors, Milton Johnston, Thomas McCormick, Joseph McCurdy; Town Clerk, Thomas McCormick; Overseers of the Poor, Myron Gibbs, Joseph McAfee; Assessor, Milton Johnston; Inspector, Myron Gibbs; Fence Appraiser, James Ross.

In 1836, Dr. A. M. Clarke moved into the township and laid out the town of Brockwayville. It is pretty hard to locate these old settlers. They are found in different townships, owing to the fact that new townships were being formed, county lines changed, and townships or parts thereof stricken from one county and added to either Clearfield or Elk.

PIONEER HISTORY OF JEFFERSON COUNTY, PENNA.

"No. 174. AN ACT ESTABLISHING AND ALTERING CERTAIN ELECTION DISTRICTS, AND FOR OTHER PURPOSES.

"*Be it enacted by the Senate and House of Representatives of the Commonwealth of Pennsylvania in General Assembly met, and it is hereby enacted by the authority of the same.* . . .

"SECTION 28. The township of Snyder, in the county of Jefferson, shall hereafter be a separate election district, and the electors thereof shall hold their general elections at the house of John McLaughlin, on the Brockway road, in said township. Approved April 15, 1835."

The act of the Legislature, No. 110, regulating election districts, approved July 11, 1842, established the polling-place for Snyder as follows:

"SECTION 27. That the qualified voters of the township of Snyder, in the county of Jefferson, shall hereafter hold their general and township elections at the house of James M. Brockway, in said township."

The pioneer justice of the peace was Stephen Tibbetts, appointed February 14, 1835.

Dr. A. M. Clarke relates the following incident: "When I was about twelve or thirteen years of age I was sent, in the winter season, with a yoke of oxen and a sled to procure a load of corn from any source from which it could be obtained, and found myself belated in the woods; but at last came to a little clearing, where there was an old man by the name of Stevens and his wife living in a poor log cabin. I was made welcome to the warmth of their fire, which was very pleasant, as I was cold, tired, and perhaps hungry. I had brought forage with me, and the team was soon cared for, and the old lady busied herself for some time in preparing a supper for me. She first fried some salt pork, then greased a griddle with some of the fat procured from the meat and baked some corn-cakes, then made what she called 'a good cup of rye coffee,' sweetened with pumpkin molasses. I was not hungry enough to much enjoy this repast. In the morning, on inquiry of my host, I learned that six miles farther down the stream (Bennett's Branch) I could likely get the corn at a Mr. Johnston's. I must not return without it, so onward we went in the morning, bought the corn and returned home."

ELDRED TOWNSHIP.

Eldred, the eighth township, was organized in 1836, and was taken from Rose and Barnett townships, and named for Hon. Nathaniel B. Eldred, then president judge of this judicial district. Taxables in 1835, 37; in 1842, 123. The census was, in 1840, 395.

The pioneer settler in Eldred was Isaac Matson, in 1828. In 1829, Walter Templeton, James Linn, and Robert McCreight. In 1830, Elijah M. Graham and John McLaughlin. In 1831, David English and Jacob

PIONEER HISTORY OF JEFFERSON COUNTY, PENNA.

Craft. In 1832, Paul Stewart, James Templeton, and James Trimble. In 1833, Stewart Ross, John Wilson, and Thomas Hall. In 1834, William and George Catz and James Summerville. In 1836, Frederick Kahle. In 1842, Professor S. W. Smith. Mr. Smith was a highly educated man, and served the county as teacher, professor in the academy, and county superintendent of schools.

The pioneer school-house was built at Hall's in 1839.

The first election for township officers was in 1836. The following persons were elected,—viz.: Constable, Elijah M. Graham ; Supervisors, Thomas Barr and Thomas Anthony; School Directors, George Catz, Henry Boil, Thomas Hughes, Thomas Hall, Jacob Craft, and John Maize ; Poor Overseers, Thomas Callen and Michael Long ; Town Clerk, Jacob Craft. The pioneer polling-place was at the home of James Linn, now the farm of Timothy Caldwell.

Joseph Matson, Esq., lived in Eldred township, and in the early days he built an outside high brick chimney. He employed a pioneer stonemason by the name of Jacob Penrose to do the job. Penrose was a very rough mason, but had a high opinion of his own skill, and was quite confiding and bombastic in his way. After he finished the chimney, and before removing the scaffold, he came down to the ground to blow off a little steam about his work. Placing his arms around Matson's neck, he exclaimed, pointing to the chimney, "There, Matson, is a chimney that will last you your lifetime, and your children and your children's children." "Look out!" said Matson. "God, she's a coming!" True enough, the chimney fell, a complete wreck.

JENKS TOWNSHIP—A LOST TOWNSHIP.

Jenks, the ninth township, organized in 1838, was taken from Barnett township. This and Tionesta township might be called twins, as both were separated at the same time from the same township. Taxables in 1842, 16; in 1849, 32. The population in 1840 was 40. The township was named in honor of Hon. John W. Jenks, then one of the associate judges of Jefferson County. It is now in the bounds of Forest County.

Cyrus Blood was the pioneer of Jenks and Tionesta townships. He brought his family into this wilderness in 1833. For years his farm was called the "Blood settlement." When he settled there, the region was full of panthers, bears, wolves, wild cats, and deer. Mr. Blood was a powerful man, of great energy and courage. He was well educated and a surveyor.

Cyrus Blood was born at New Lebanon, New Hampshire, March 3, 1795. He was educated in Boston. When twenty-two he migrated to Chambersburg, Pennsylvania, where he was the principal of the academy. He was afterwards principal of the Hagerstown Academy, Maryland.

He accepted and served as a professor in the Dickinson College, at Carlisle, Pennsylvania.

Ambitious to found a county, Cyrus Blood made several visits into this wilderness, and finding that the northern portion of Jefferson County was then an almost unbroken wilderness, he finally purchased a tract of land on which Marienville is now located, and decided to make his settlement there.

It was understood when Mr. Blood purchased in Jefferson County from the land company that a road would be opened into it for him. In 1833, when Mr. Blood arrived where Corsica now is, on the Olean road, he found to his annoyance that no road had been made. Leaving his family behind him, he started from what was then Armstrong's Mill, now Clarington, with an ox team, sled, and men to cut their way step by step through the wilderness twelve miles to his future home. Every night the men camped on and around the ox-sled. When the party reached Blood's purchase, a patch of ground was cleared and a log cabin reared. In October, 1833, Mr. Blood and his five children took possession of this forest home. For many years Mr. Blood carried his and the neighbors' mail from Brookville. Panthers were so plenty that they have been seen in the garden by the children, playing like dogs. For years they had to go with their grist to mill to Kittanning, Leatherwood, or Brookville.

Trumbull Hunt was the second pioneer.

The pioneer election was held in Jenks township in 1838. The following persons were elected to fill township offices: Constable, Cyrus Blood; Supervisors, Cyrus Blood, John Hunt; School Directors, Cyrus Blood, John Hunt, Aaron Brockway, Sr., Aaron Brockway, Jr., Josiah Lacey, and John Lewees; Auditors, John Hunt, Aaron Brockway, Sr., and Aaron Brockway, Jr.; Poor Overseers, Cyrus Blood, Aaron Brockway, Sr.; Town Clerk, John Hunt; Fence Viewer, Aaron Brockway, Jr.; Inspector, John Hunt.

The last and only beavers in this State made their homes here in the early thirties, in the great flag swamp or beaver meadows on Salmon Creek. These meadows covered about six hundred acres. Furs were occasionally then brought to Brookville from these meadows by trappers.

Pioneer election district according to the act of April 16, 1838:

"SECTION 48. That the township of Jenks, in the county of Jefferson, is hereby declared a separate district, the election to be held at the house now occupied by Cyrus Blood in said township."

The pioneer hunter was John Aylesworth. He came to Barnett township, Jefferson County, or what in 1838 became Jenks township, Jefferson County, and is now Jenks township, Forest County, in 1834. He was a Connecticut Yankee, but came to this wilderness from Ashtabula, Ohio. He was the most noted and famous hunter in this section of Jefferson

County. Other early professional hunters were Philip Clover and Ami Sibley.

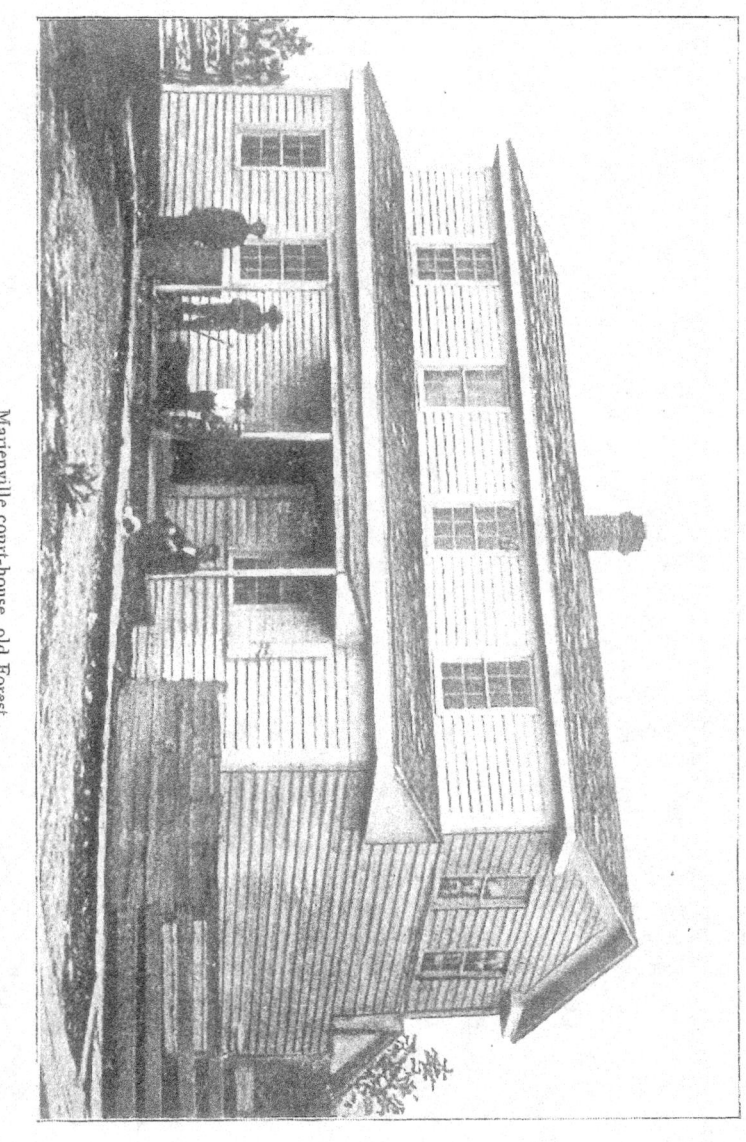

Marienville court-house, old Forest.

The pioneer path or trail was opened by Cyrus Blood from Clarington to Blood's settlement. This was in the year 1833. The pioneer

PIONEER HISTORY OF JEFFERSON COUNTY, PENNA.

road was this "path" widened and improved by Blood several years later.

The pioneer tavern was the home of Cyrus Blood. Mr. Blood built the pioneer saw-mill in 1834 and the pioneer grist-mill in 1840. These mills were erected by him on Salmon Creek.

The pioneer school-master was John D. Hunt. He taught in the winter of 1833-34 in Mr. Blood's home.

The pioneer preacher was Dr. Otis Smith. The pioneer sermon to white people was preached in Mr. Blood's house.

Brookville was the post-office for this settlement from 1833 to 1843.

The pioneer court house of Forest County was built in Marienville, of hewed logs, and afterwards weather-boarded and painted white. The work was done by Bennett Dobbs. (See illustration.)

What is now Marienville was called for many years "the Blood settlement."

TIONESTA TOWNSHIP—A LOST TOWNSHIP.

This, the tenth township organization, was taken from Barnett, in 1838, and named after a river in its boundary. Taxables in 1842, 9; population in 1840, 27. This township is now Howe, a member of Forest County.

Pioneer election district according to the act of April 16, 1838:

"SECTION 49. That the township of Tionesta, in the county of Jefferson, is hereby declared a separate election district, and the election shall be held at the house of John Noef, in said township."

WASHINGTON TOWNSHIP.

ANDREW HUNTER'S BIRTHDAY ANNIVERSARY AN HISTORICAL EVENT.

Washington, the eleventh township, was organized in 1839, and was taken from Snyder and Pine Creek. The township was named for the "Father of our Country." Taxables in 1842, 112. Population by census 1840, 367.

The township embraced Prospect Hill, Prescottville, Reynoldsville, and West Reynoldsville, until Winslow township was formed, hence the early settlers on the old State Road and on the turnpike were originally in Washington.

The pioneer settlers in what is now Washington township were Henry Keys, John McGhee, Thomas Moore, Alexander Osborne, and John McIntosh. These pioneers located in 1824. In 1826, Andrew Smith, William Cooper, and John Wilson settled. In 1829, James Smith, Esq., settled also. Other early settlers were as follows: John Millen, James Ross, David Dennison, William Shaw, Robert Morrison, Robert Smith, George Senior, William Smith, Thomas Tedlie, John Magee, William McConnell, Alvin H. Head, T. B. McLain, William B. McCullough,

PIONEER HISTORY OF JEFFERSON COUNTY, PENNA.

Alexander Keys, Robert Patton, Daniel Groves, James Groves, John Groves, James Welsh, Frederick R. Brown, James Bond, and John McClelland.

Joseph McCurdy came to Beechwoods from Indiana County in the year 1835. He was accompanied by his mother, two brothers, Robert and James, and three sisters, Martha, Margaret, who married John Millen, and Betsy, who married Andrew Hunter. They settled where James McCurdy now lives. As a man, he was very quiet and unassuming, without show or pretence. He was faithful as a Christian, firm and decided as an elder in maintaining discipline in the church, and mild in enforcing the same ; a firm believer in the doctrines of the Presbyterian Church as being the truth taught by the word of God. These truths he unflinchingly maintained and defended through life. He did much for the church, and after his death his mantle fell upon his brother James.

In 1830, John and Andrew Hunter settled on farms. Andrew lived to be over one hundred years old, and as the celebration of his centennial birthday was the first and only event of the kind in this county, I reprint my report of that interesting occasion, made at the time for the *Brookville Jeffersonian Democrat,*—viz. :

"A GREAT BIRTHDAY.

"CELEBRATION OF ANDREW HUNTER'S ONE HUNDRED YEARS OF LIFE.

"Jefferson County's Centenarian.

" Born in Ireland, October 1, 1790, living in Jefferson County, Pennsylvania, October 1, 1890. Has one sister living aged ninety-seven, and a brother ninety-five. Located on his farm in Washington township in 1830. He is bright, intelligent, and pleasant to converse with. Handsome, short in stature, rosy-cheeked, with a fine head of iron-gray hair. A widower for many years, and will probably not remarry. Always an early riser and a hard worker. Has never been sick, never used tobacco, but drinks tea and coffee, and believes that a little ' gude whuskey,' unless taken to excess, ' will not hurt ony man at all, at all.' Occasionally goes to a wedding, but attends church regularly. A strict Presbyterian. Leads the family devotions night and morning. Is lively, loves jokes, laughs heartily, and enjoys life. Is opposed to all modern innovations in the church, such as organs, improved psalmody, etc.

" A friend remarked to him, ' I suppose, Mr. Hunter, they are getting some new-fangled ideas in the church up here ?' ' Aye, feth, that's jest what they're doin'. They are singin' human composition in the church now. I fought it with all my might, but they overpowered me, and I did not go back for three months. I thought I never would go back ; but then I said for all the wee time I had to stay, I might just as weel go back. Our preacher came over to make us a visit, and I just took the opportunity to give him a piece of my mind, and after I was through he had not one word in reply to make, for he had not a particle of foundation to stand upon.'

Andrew Hunter, one hundred years old.

"The gathering at Mr. Hunter's home yesterday was an immense affair, worthy of the occasion,—the celebration of the one hundredth anniversary of his birth. Relatives, friends, and neighbors were present. The old, the middle-aged, and the infant were there.

PIONEER HISTORY OF JEFFERSON COUNTY, PENNA.

"The company numbered fully a thousand, coming from various parts of the county, and some from outside. At noon refreshments were served for all present, a special table being prepared for the old patriarch, with Judge Jenks, Rev. Filson, Dr. McKnight, James McCurdy, and other friends near him. The old gentleman laughed, joked, and ate a hearty meal. He hears ordinary talk and has nearly all his lower teeth.

"At one P.M. Rev. Filson preached an old-fashioned sermon, Rev. Hill explaining the psalm. The clerks in charge of the singing were A. McCullough and Elder William Smith, one lining the psalm and the other leading the music. Mr. Hunter joined in the singing.

"Addresses were made by Hon. W. P. Jenks and Dr. W. J. McKnight; an original poem, by Willie Wray, was read by Rev. Hill. Mr. Hunter's neighbors presented him with a gold-headed cane on which to lean in the second century of his life. A photograph of the company was taken by E. Clark Hall, of Brookville. This was the greatest event ever witnessed in this section of Jefferson County.

"The following old people were present: James Welsh, William McConnell, W. P. Jenks, W. McCurdy and wife, of Indiana, Dr. McCurdy, of Freeport, John Cooper, S. Patton, D. B. McConnell, J. Shaw, R. Osborne, I. Morrison, J. Sterrett and wife, N. Riggs, J. Snoddy, Dr. Niver and wife, J. Clover, W. Smith, R. Smith, J. R. Millen, W. Patton, J. McCurdy, M. Smith, T. Moore, J. Crawford, J. Dixon, R. Sterrett, James Cooper, H. Maginnis, D. Motherell, Mrs. Wray, Mrs. J. B. Henderson, Mrs. McClure, Mrs. Cooper, Mrs. McCurdy, Mrs. Harker, Mrs. Daily, Mrs. Patterson, Mrs. J. Hunter, Mrs. M. Smith, Miss A. McCurdy, Mrs. McIntosh, Mrs. Stewart, Mrs. Maxwell, Mrs J. J. Stewart, N. B. Lane and wife.

"Following is the address delivered by Dr. W. J. McKnight:

"'LADIES AND GENTLEMEN,—Ordinary birthday celebrations are pleasant to neighbors and friends, but the pleasure to celebrate the birthday of a friend and neighbor who has reached the age of one hundred years is seldom realized or enjoyed by any community. We are here to day to celebrate a centennial birthday. Our neighbor, Andrew Hunter, was born in county Tyrone, Ireland, October 1, 1790. It is now October 1, 1890. He emigrated to America in 1825, and located where he now resides in 1830, having lived here sixty years. He is what we Americans call a Scotch-Irishman. As Americans we are proud of this blood. In our struggle for independence they were loyal. A Tory was unheard of among them. Pennsylvania and the nation owe very much of their greatness to this race. Natural-born leaders and orators, they have given us statesmen, teachers, professors, ministers, physicians, judges, Congressmen, and generals, even to our Sheridan and Grant. They have furnished the nation with seven Presidents and our State with seven governors. Brave, intelligent, warm hearted, and true, their influence must and always will be potent.

"'But, ladies and gentlemen, others have spoken of Mr. Hunter and his virtues as a man and a citizen. I endorse all that has been said. To say more of him personally would be unseemly. Therefore let us

"'Lift the twilight curtains of the past
And, turning from familiar sight and sound,
Sadly and full of reverence, let us cast
A glance upon tradition's shadowy ground.'

"'When Andrew Hunter first saw the light of day George Washington was President, our territory small, only thirteen States, and our population but three million. He has lived to see our nation grow to forty-four States, our people increase to sixty-five million, and our country to rise from poverty to the wealth of fifty-six billion dollars. He has lived to see our territory become as large as Russia in Europe, Norway, Sweden, Denmark, Holland, Belgium, Germany, Austria-Hungary, Switzerland, Italy, Spain, Portugal, France, Great Britain, and Ireland, fronting on two great oceans, and populated, too, with a people only twenty per cent. of whom are unable to read and write.

"'In the year Andrew Hunter was born letter postage was twelve and a half cents every one hundred miles; to-day two cents will send a letter three thousand miles. Then we had but seventy-five post-offices; now we have sixty thousand one hundred and forty. In those days the mails were carried on horseback or in stage-coaches. Communications of news, business, or affection were slow and uncertain, but to-day, with rapid railroad transportation,

"'Letters are but affection's touches,
Lightnings from friendship's lamp.'

"'In 1790 railroads were unknown. To-day there is in the United States one hundred and seventy thousand miles of railroad. Over these roads there were carried last year five hundred million people and six hundred million tons of freight. Employed upon them are one million men, thirty thousand locomotives, twenty-one thousand passenger-cars, seven thousand baggage cars, and one million freight cars. The total capital invested is eight billion dollars. The disbursements for labor and repairs are yearly six hundred and fifty million dollars. As a Pennsylvanian I am proud to say our own Pennsylvania road is the greatest, the best, and most perfect in management and construction of any road in the world. We have smoking-cars, with bath room, barber-shop, writing-desks, and library. We have dining cars in which are served refreshments that a Delmonico cannot surpass. We have parlor-cars

PIONEER HISTORY OF JEFFERSON COUNTY, PENNA.

with bay-windows and luxurious furniture, and we have cars with beds for sleeping soft as the "eider down."

"'In the year Andrew Hunter was born training-day was a great event. All men were required by law to participate in a day of general military drill. No uniforms were worn, save the homespun dress of each soldier. Each company was armed with sticks, pikes, muskets, or guns, and were preceded in their marches by a fife or drum. An odd and comic sight it must have been. Royal amusements in 1790 were shooting-matches, rollings, huskings, scutchings, flax-breakings, apple-parings, and quiltings. Dancing was not entirely overlooked. Books were few and but little schooling to be had. Woman's extravagances in dress was then and is now a juicy topic for grumblers.

"'In 1790 no steamboat had ever navigated the water, nothing but old sail-crafts being used. A trip across the ocean required from four weeks to three months. Father Hunter was six weeks on the ocean. Now we skip across in six and seven days. Then it took weeks and months to hear the news from Europe or Asia; now we hear daily from the whole world. We have only to speak across the ocean, when our brother in Europe or Asia greets us and replies.

"'In the year Andrew Hunter was born Pennsylvania contained a population of four hundred and thirty-four thousand three hundred and seventy-three; now we have five million people. In 1790 the curse of slavery rested on Pennsylvania, for in that year three thousand seven hundred and thirty-seven human beings were considered "property" within her borders and held as slaves. Sixty-four of these slaves were still in our State in 1840.

"'In 1790, Jefferson County was unknown. No white man lived within her borders. Nature reigned supreme. The shade of the forest was heavy the whole day through. Now our county contains a population of forty-three thousand. We have schools, churches, telegraphs, telephones, and court all the time.

"'The great coal deposits that underlie forty-two of our counties was known to exist at that early date, but its use was not understood. Some hard coal was mined and shipped to Philadelphia for a market, but not knowing what to do with it, it was finally used to repair the roads. Our people are alive now to its use, as the following exhibit will show: In 1888 there was mined in Pennsylvania of hard coal forty-one million six hundred and thirty-eight thousand four hundred and eighty-four tons, giving employment to one hundred and sixteen thousand and forty-two people. In 1888 there was mined in Pennsylvania thirty-three million seven hundred and seventy-two thousand two hundred and eighty-five tons of bituminous coal, giving employment to sixty thousand nine hundred and forty-six people. Total output of hard and soft coal in 1888, seventy-five million four hundred and ten thousand seven hundred and sixty-nine tons. Total number of people employed in mining, one hundred and seventy-six thousand nine hundred and eighty-nine.

"'In the year 1790 men were imprisoned for debt and kept in prison until the last farthing was paid. The jails of that day were but little better than dungeons. There was no woman's Christian temperance union, no woman's relief corps, no society for the prevention of cruelty to animals or children.

"'In 1790 domestic comforts were few. No stove had been invented. Large, deep fireplaces with cranes, andirons, and bake-ovens were the only modes of heating and cooking. Friction-matches were unknown. If the fire of the house went out, you had to rekindle with a flint or borrow of your neighbor. I have borrowed fire. House furniture was then meagre and rough. There were no window-blinds or carpets. Rich people whitewashed their ceilings and rooms, and covered their parlor-floors with white sand. Hence the old couplet:

"'Oh, dear mother, my toes are sore
A dancing over your sanded floor.'

"'Pine-knots, tallow-dipped candles burned in iron or brass candlesticks, and whale oil burned in iron lamps were the means for light in stores, dwellings, etc. Food was scarce, coarse, and of the most common kind, with no canned goods or evaporated fruits. In addition to cooking in the open fireplace, women had to spin, knit, dye, and weave all domestic cloths, there being no mills run by machinery to make woollen or cotton goods. Mrs. Winslow's soothing syrup and baby-carriages were unknown. The bride of 1790 took her wedding-trip on foot or on horseback behind the bridegroom on a "pillion."

"'Men wore no beards, whiskers, or moustaches, their faces being as clean shaven and as smooth as a girl's. A beard was looked upon as an abomination, and fitted only for Hessians, heathen, or Turks. In 1790 not a single cigar had ever been smoked in the United States. I wish I could say that of to-day. There were no aniline dyes, no electric lights, no anæsthetics and painless surgery, no gun-cotton, no nitro glycerin, no dynamite, giant powder, audiphones, pneumatic tubes, or type-writers. No cotton-gin, no planting-machine, no mower or reaper, no hay-rake, no hay-fork, no corn-sheller, no rotary printing-press, no sewing-machine, no knitting-machine, no envelopes for letters, no india-rubber goods, coats, shoes, or cloaks, no grain elevator except man, no artificial ice, no steel pens, no telegraph or telephone, no street-cars, no steam-mills, no daguerreotypes or photographs, no steam-ploughs, no steam-thresher, only the old hand-flail, no wind-mill, and no millionaire in the whole country. General Washington was the richest man, and he was only worth eight hundred thousand dollars.

"'In 1790 slavery prevailed in all Christendom. It was everywhere

PIONEER HISTORY OF JEFFERSON COUNTY, PENNA.

in manner and in fact. Men, women, and children were bought and sold like cattle. Now there is no slavery in all Christendom. No more human auction-blocks, no more masters, no more driver's lash. Bless God!

"'Our fathers established the first Christian, non-sectarian government in the world, and declared as the chief corner-stone of that government Christ's teaching, that all men are "born free and equal;" love your neighbor as yourself. Since this thought has been carried into effect by our non-sectarian government, it has done more to elevate and civilize mankind in the last one hundred years than had ever been accomplished in all time before. Under the humane and inspiring influence of this grand idea put into practice the wheels of progress, science, religion, and civilization have made gigantic strides, and our nation especially, from ocean to ocean, from arctic ice to tropic sun, is filled with smiling, happy homes, rich fields, blooming gardens, and bright firesides, made such by Christian charity carried into national and State constitutional enactment.'"

The pioneer voting-place was at the cabin of James Wait.

The pioneer birth in the township was that of William McGhee in 1825. The pioneer marriage, Henry Keys and Catherine Wilson in 1826. The pioneer death, Mary, wife of John Hunter, in 1830. The pioneer graveyard, on Cooper's Hill in 1831. Pioneer merchant, Thomas B. McLain, near Beechtree. Other early merchants, W. B. McCullough, Alvin Head. Pioneer church, Presbyterian, organized December 3, 1832, with fourteen members. The pioneer cabin was constructed by three men only,—viz.: Thomas Moore, Henry Keys, and John McIntosh.

The pioneer township election was held in 1839, and the following persons were elected,—viz.: Constable, John McGhee; Supervisors, John McIntosh and Tilton Reynolds; Auditors, Andrew Smith, Oliver McClelland, William Reynolds, and Joshua Rhea; School Directors, Oliver McClelland, Andrew Smith, James McConnell, William Reynolds, John Fuller, and John Horm; Fence Appraisers, James Smith and Oliver Welch; Poor Overseers, Henry Keys and Tilton Reynolds; Town Clerk, John Wilson.

In 1831, John Wilson erected an up-and-down saw-mill near Rockdale.

Archie Campbell, James Wait, Samuel, James, and Robert Kyle were early settlers, too. Archie Campbell and James Kyle were brothers-in-law. They were odd, eccentric, and stingy, but each prided himself on being very generous. The Kyles and Campbell had the reputation of being wealthy. Early in the forties the women in that part of Washington township took a notion to fix up Prospect Graveyard, and in order to reach the Kyles and Campbell a subscription paper was put in the hands of Jimmie Kyle. Jimmie was an old bachelor. The first thing he did after getting the paper was to call on Archie Campbell, when the following conversation, in a dignified manner, took place:

" Gud-morning, Muster Cummell."

" Gud morning, Muster Kyle."

" Are yez all well this morning, Muster Cummell?"

" Yes, Muster Kyle, there's only me and Mary, and we're all well."

" Muster Cummell, I've got a subscription paper here to fix the graveyard beyand, and wud you be after putting something down?"

" Egad, no, Muster Kyle, not a cint for that ould cow-pasture. As long as I luv I won't be burried there. Egad, I won't."

" Wull, Muster Cummell, we duffer in opinion on that, for if I luv and kape me health, I wull."

Pioneer school-master, William Reynolds, in 1832. Other early instructors: Alexander Cochran, 1833; William Kennedy, 1834; Betsy McCurdy and Thomas Reynolds, 1835; Oliver and Nancy Jane McClelland, 1836; Fanny McConnell and Rev. Dexter Morris, 1838; Peggy McIntosh and Finley McCormick, 1839; Joseph Sterrett and Nancy Jane McClelland, 1840. The master taught three-month terms in the winter, the women two in the summer.

This township was settled by Scotch-Irish, mostly from the counties Antrim and Tyrone, Ireland. They were as a unit agricultural. One noted hunter was reared there,—viz.: George Smith. Before the advent of the settlers the Indians made maple-sugar here. Trees are still standing that were notched for this purpose by the savage tomahawk. The early Irish settlers took up this business and made tons and tons and barrels and barrels of maple molasses and sugar every spring. As a result no sugar trust or Claus Spreckels had any terrors for them.

Money was scarce, and the pioneers and early settlers of this township paid their debts usually " with sugar in the spring and oats after harvest." I lived in my boyhood four years with Joseph McCurdy, in this township. I desire to say here that he was an honest man and a true Christian gentleman.

The pioneer history of this section of the county has been graphically portrayed by Rev. Boyd McCullough, who settled with his parents in the Beechwoods in 1832, in his "Sketches of Local History" and the "Shamrock," published by him, from which the following incidents are taken:

" In 1833 there was a beautiful fall. Keys's folks sowed wheat in November. The next spring was favorable, and it was a bountiful crop. This was a great loss to the settlement, for the people were encouraged to sow as much as they could get in any time through October, and the rust generally ruined it, until they learned wit by dear experience.

" The winter of 1831 was a very cold one, and in the severest part of it the house of John Hunter was burned down. The neighbors soon gathered together and put up a log house for him, but he lost nearly everything he owned by the fire.

"It was in the spring of 1832 that we moved into the woods. There were seventeen families in the woods at that time. We stopped at Andrew Smith's. I was seven years old. The next morning I ran in with the news that there was an ass with very slim legs and a small nose in the yard. I was told it was a deer. They had petted several young deer at different times.

"That fall the first school was started in the place. (Waites) The log school-house had one regular window with six lights. The other window was made by removing a log and placing panes of glass in the cavity joining each other. A writing-desk was made by driving pins in the logs below this window, and laying rough boards upon it. The fireplace was made by building a stone wall against the logs as high as the loft; from this a kind of a flue was made of pine sticks and clay. Sometimes the smoke found its way up the chimney and sometimes it wandered through the house. William Reynolds taught this first school for ten dollars a month, half in cash and half in grain after harvest. People who do not know half as much would turn up their noses at treble that pay now.

"The kindly spring came gently on, and we then commenced to make sugar. Right pleasant it is to see the luscious juice drop, drop, dropping from trees all over the hill, while roaring fire makes the syrup go foaming and dancing in the kettle till it is time to take it out and put fresh sap in. It is hard work, but then you can see the progress you are making, and you get your pay immediately.

"There was no school in summer, but we attended Sabbath-school in the school-house. This school was organized by Rev. Mr. Riggs in 1831, but it existed before that. Robert McIntosh and Betty Keys had started it when there were but few families in the place. It went from house to house before there was any school house.

"James and Andrew Smith, father and son, Thomas Ledlie, and Alexander Cochran might be mentioned as men whose deep thought gave an intellectual tone to discussions. Robert McIntosh, Sr., was the first superintendent. He was not a man of extended information, but his devoted spirit and warm cordial impulse gave a great interest to his devotional exercises, and made him universally respected. Well do I remember the last time I saw him in the Sabbath-school. He closed by singing the sixth psalm, long meter, in the old version,—' Lord, in thy wrath, rebuke me not.' That was the fall of 1833, and he died in the fall of 1834.

"Betty Keys was also the life of the school, as long as her health enabled her to attend. She was said to be very self-willed and opinionative, and on one occasion the young women, returning from Sabbath-school, were walking ahead, and the men in a company behind, all except Oliver McClelland, who was walking with the girls. She invited him to fall back in the company of men, and so maintain the decorum due the day. That she loved to rule might be true, but certain it is that if she ruled it was by the gentle power of love. We children, no matter what class we belonged to, were accustomed to look up to her as to one superior to the rest, and as one who could scarcely do anything wrong. We carried our dinners with us, as there was Sabbath-school in the morning and prayer-meeting in the afternoon.

"When we came to the Beechwoods the soil was rich and the vegetation luxurious, but the subsoil was poor. Thousands of years ago great currents of water must have swept westward, carrying the soil into Ohio, Indiana, and Illinois, leaving the heavy deposits of iron and rock. When the climate became drier and the streams shrank to their present size, a growth of forest followed. The decaying leaves of two or three thousand years formed this rich mould. Scarcely was the snow of winter gone when the wild leeks peeped up like corn. At first they had not much of their rampant taste, and cattle nipped them off greedily. Before they got strong, the curley weed showed itself, vellera and broad leaf followed. All these had thick juicy roots, which lived over winter. By the middle of June the wild peavine gave pasturage. Besides these, which the cattle ate, there were many flowers that they did not eat, the mandrake, the sweet-william, the phlox, the honeysuckle, and the violet.

"Bees found homes in the hollow trees as conveniently as food in the flowers. The blossoms of the trees also gave them their choice honey. The crops were often good. In 1835 we planted a bushel and a half of potatoes in one patch of new ground, covering them with leaves, and scratching enough clay over them to keep the leaves down. It was a wet season, which was the most suitable for such planting, and we dug thirty-six bushels of potatoes. The same year the Keyses had four hundred bushels to the acre. Another year James Smith had as good a yield.

"One year, perhaps in 1836, William Smith, Sr., had soft corn, owing to the season, and the next year he thought he would plant more. His wife planted a patch by the house and took every care of it. The crop yielded at the rate of a hundred bushels of shelled corn to the acre. In those days people hardly ever sowed timothy seed at all. A little seed in the wheat got into the ground, and taking hold in fence corners and around stumps, was ready to spread when a field was thrown out. Two tons of hay to the acre was thought nothing remarkable, yet all this was the product of rich mould on the surface. People did not know how poor the subsoil was or they would have kept up the condition of their land.

"Rev. Joseph McGarrah assisted Rev. Mr. Riggs to hold the first communion in the Beechwoods. A son of Mr. McGarrah told me, in a chat about the old times, that in 1815 he went to a store with a bag of wheat. He went on horseback twelve miles, and got seventy-five cents a bushel for his wheat, and paid fifty cents a pound for coffee and twenty-five cents a piece for tin cups to eat mush and milk out of. It was night when he got back, and he brought two pounds of coffee and two tin cups for his bag of wheat.

"It was not so bad in 1836 as in 1815, but still we had the difficulty of cheap produce and dear store goods. It was five pounds of coffee, four yards of coarse muslin, or six yards of poor calico for a dollar, when a dollar represented two days' hard work. And then cash could not be had for work, and many articles the merchants would not sell without money.

"If the young people want to know how we got along in those days, I will tell them we got along exactly as we do now. When tired we grunted, when hurt we grinned, when pleased we laughed, exactly as we do now. The young men winked at the girls, and the girls smiled back as often and pleasantly as you do now. But to be more definite, the men shore the sheep, the women scoured the wool, and the girls made a frolic to pick it. It was sent to the carding-machine, and then spun by hand. The yarn was carried to the weaver. The cloth was soused in soapsuds and thrown on the kitchen floor, where the boys kicked it until it was fulled up; then, colored with butternut, it was made up into men's clothing. The women were a little more tasty, and wore barred flannel colored with indigo, madder, etc. If people did not look quite as well in homespun as in broadcloth, they felt as happy.

"In 1841, Billy Richards set up a fulling-mill on North Fork. This was a great relief, as before we had to carry our cloth to Frederick Holopeter's, somewhere in Clearfield County. Remember, this home-made cloth cost more, counting the labor, than fine cloth does now, but it was the best we had, and we felt proud of it.

"I think it was in 1830 that Rev. Gary Bishop came from Phillipsburg to marry James Waite and Mattie McIntosh. The temperance reform had not started then. Mr. Bishop carried a jug of whiskey in one end of his saddle-bags and a stone in the other to cheer the wedding-guests. It was the whiskey, not the stone, that cheered the guests. They had no fighting. He baptized Susan McIntosh, now Mrs. Stevenson, at the wedding. The reader will perceive that they were in the habit of killing two birds with one stone in those economical days."

The pioneer temperance society was the Washingtonians, organized in 1842, by Hugh Brady, S. B. Bishop, and Samuel Lucas, of Brookville, Pennsylvania. Fifty members were enrolled.

In 1831, Rev. Riggs made a missionary tour through the settlement. He made a pastoral visit to each family, and preached on two Sundays. The only capitalist in the "Woods" was Matthew Keys,—he had a five-dollar bill. Each settler agreed to give Keys twenty-five cents apiece as soon as he could get it if he would give Mr. Riggs the bill. This Keys did, and then the settlement was without a cent.

Archie Campbell married Mary Ann Kyle. Archie and his wife lived in the vicinity of what is now Reynoldsville, and one winter day they concluded to visit the Kyles. They hitched up their horse in a little jumper, and reached their destination, some four miles over the Ceres road, and remained overnight with their relations. During the night there was a heavy snow-fall. On starting home in the morning the Kyles presented Mary Ann with a small crock of apple-butter. The crock was stored between Mrs. Campbell's feet when she took her seat in the jumper. The road-track was covered with fresh snow, and Archie could not, of course, discern it. After driving some distance he struck a trot, the jumper went over a stump, and threw Archie and Mary Ann violently into the snow. Archie scrambled up and cried, "Mary Ann, my dear, are you hurted?" "My thigh is broken, my thigh is broken, Archie!" Archie rushed to her aid, and running his hand up her limb to ascertain her injury, he exclaimed, "It's wurse than that, it's wurse than that, Mary Ann; your bowels are busted, your bowels are busted!" And it was only apple-butter.

PORTER TOWNSHIP.

Porter, the twelfth township, organized in 1840, was taken from Perry township, and named for David R. Porter, then the governor of Pennsylvania. This township has a post-office called Porter, situated about twenty miles south of Brookville. Taxables in 1842, 192; population by census in 1840, 977.

"It is difficult to point out the distinguishing characteristics of the several townships, and we will not attempt to specify the advantages or the opposites of this division. It is similar to Perry and Ringgold, and its early settlers were cast in the same rugged mould. Agriculture ranks first in this section, and the farms generally are in excellent condition."
—*Atlas*.

Pioneer settlers: in 1803, James McClelland; in 1804, Benjamin Ions; in 1806, David Hamilton; in 1815, Elijah Ekis, Michael Lantz, and William Smith. The first person born in the township was Robert Hamilton. The pioneer graveyard was in 1843. The pioneer church society organized was by the Methodists in 1838. The pioneer church was built in 1843. The pioneer camp meeting was held in this township in 1836.

The pioneer election for township officers was in 1840, and the following officers were chosen,—viz.: Justice of the Peace, John Robinson; Constable, John Hice; Supervisors, Conrad Nolf, Geo. Miller; Auditors, John McAninch, John Robinson, William McAninch, William Ferguson;

PIONEER HISTORY OF JEFFERSON COUNTY, PENNA.

Judge of Election, William Foster; Inspectors, Robert E. Kennedy, Daniel McGregor.

CLOVER TOWNSHIP.

This was the thirteenth township, being organized in 1841. It was taken from Rose township, and called for Levi G. Clover, then prothonotary of the county. Troy (post-office Summerville) is the place where the people get their mails, and is now an important shipping-point and trade centre. Taxables in 1842, 145.

The pioneer settler in what is now Clover township was Samuel Baldwin, in 1812. Early settlers, Solomon Fuller, John Welch, before 1816; Darius Carrier, 1816; in 1818, Thomas and John Lucas; in 1819, Robert Andrews and Walter Templeton; in 1820, Frederick Heterick, Henry Lot, Alonzo Baldwin, and the Carrier brothers; and in 1821, Moses Knapp.

The pioneer church was organized in 1828, by the Associate Reformed Seceders. In 1831 the pioneer church building was erected by this association on the farm of Robert Andrews, and the Rev. Joseph Scroggs was pastor. The pioneer school-house was built on the John Lucas farm in 1825. The pioneer school-master was Robert Knox. Rev. William Kennedy preached here occasionally at that time. In 1827, Joseph McGiffin taught a six-months' term of school, at fifty cents a month per scholar, in the Lucas school-house.

In 1840, Dr. James Dowling organized a militia company called the "Independent Greens,"—a rifle company. The uniform of these soldiers consisted of green baize cloth trimmed with red fringe. The coat was made in the form of a shirt. The uniform of the band or drum corps was a bright red, and the members were the "Lucas Band." Muster and reviews at that time were occasionally held on the farm of Robert Andrews.

The pioneer physician in what is now Clover township was Dr. R. K. Scott, in 1826; Dr. James Dowling, in 1837.

The people of that day seemed to be as anxious for "salt territory" as we are now for "oil territory." Thomas and John Lucas settled on the flat called Puckerty. They bored for salt, found some salt water, but never made a success of their well. In 1840 Major Johnston sank a well with pole power, eight hundred and fifty feet deep, and struck what was then called a three barrel well. This was below Troy. James Anderson purchased these works from Johnston, and made salt at the "saltworks below Troy" for twenty-five years. Before these works were started our people had to go to Saltsburg, Indiana County, Pennsylvania, for salt, and bring the salt on horseback on pack-saddles. Salt sold then for five and six dollars a barrel.

Pioneer saw-mills: 1814, on Hiram's Run, Mr. Scott; 1820, Thos.

PIONEER HISTORY OF JEFFERSON COUNTY, PENNA.

Lucas, at Puckerty; 1822, Moses Knapp, at Baxter; 1825, Moses Knapp, at Knapp's Bend. In 1838, Moses Knapp built a grist-mill alongside of this mill at the Bend. In 1836, Darius Carrier built a grist-mill in what is now called Troy.

The pioneer election in Clover township was in 1842, and but one officer was elected,—viz. : Wm. Magill, fence viewer.

In 1843 the following-named persons were elected to fill the township offices,—viz. : Inspectors, Samuel Milliron, Euphrastus Carrier; Judge of Election, Solomon Fuller; Supervisors, James Sowers, Hazard Jacox; School Directors, Hiram Carrier, Matthew Dickey, John Shields, Henry Scott, Samuel Lucas, and Christopher Fogle; Constable, Charles Jacox; Assessor, Euphrastus Carrier; Auditors, D. Fairweather, P. I. Lucas; Poor Overseer, Elijah Heath, Robert Andrews; Town Clerk, A. Baldwin.

The act of the Legislature No. 110, regulating election districts, approved July 11, 1842, established the polling-place for Clover township as follows :

"SECTION 12. That the qualified voters of Clover township, Jefferson County, shall hereafter hold their general election at the house of Darius Carrier, in the village of Troy, in said township."

GASKILL TOWNSHIP.

Gaskill was the fourteenth township, organized in 1842, taken from Young township, and named after Hon. Charles C. Gaskill, then agent of the Holland Land Company, of Jefferson and adjoining counties. Taxables in 1842, 78.

" 'This is a good township,' an observing farmer from Eastern Pennsylvania remarked, and well he said, for the landscape is dotted with real farm-homes, and the products of the soil are of many kinds, and of a quantity and quality that would suit the fastidious taste of an Orange County (New York) agriculturist. This is the home of Joseph Winslow, the pioneer. The primitive tilling of the past has been followed by the advanced (theoretical as well as practical) culture of the present, and they who could not raise wheat in the early part of the century are known only by tradition. The times have changed, and with them the moon-consulting and sign-believing wiseacres of fifty years ago. We can only say, *Tempus fugit.*"—*Atlas.*

The pioneer settler was Carpenter Winslow, in 1818. He came from Maine. Other early settlers were Francis Leech, Daniel Coffman, Reuben Clemson, John and Philip Bowers, and John Van Horn, in 1820. The pioneer grist- and saw-mill in the township was built by William Neel in 1843.

"When these families settled in the neighborhood game was very plenty, and it is said that they were frequently obliged to go out at night and drive whole droves of deer out of their grain-fields. Like all the other early pioneers, these people had to encounter hardships, privations, and dangers, which called forth all their powers of endurance, and they were for many years obliged to practise the closest economy; but hope, faith, and endurance overcame all difficulties, and they lived to see beautiful farms as the result of those years of toil."

The pioneer lumberman was Philip Bowers, in 1836.

The pioneer graveyard was at Bowers's, in 1840.

The pioneer election was held in the township in 1841, and the following township officers were elected: Constable, Joseph Winslow; Supervisors, John Pifer, Henry Miller, John Kauffman; Auditors, Henry Phillips, Philip Bowers, Thomas Thompson; School Directors, Henry Miller, Jonathan Strouse, David Harney, Philip Bowers; Judge of Election, John D. Phillips; Poor Overseers, Thomas Thompson; Town Clerk, Henry Miller; Fence-Viewers, Andrew McCreight and John Pifer.

The act of the Legislature No. 110, regulating election districts, approved July 11, 1842, established the polling-place for Gaskill township as follows:

"SECTION 9. That the qualified voters of Gaskill township, Jefferson County, shall hereafter hold their general and township elections at the house of Henry Miller, in said township."

FENCE-VIEWERS.

It will be noticed that in each of these pioneer elections that one or more persons were annually elected as fence-viewers. This office was abolished by act of Legislature in 1842, and in order that the readers of this volume may understand the duties of this office I here reproduce the act creating this office:

"AN ACT FOR REGULATING AND MAINTAINING LINE-FENCES, AND FOR OTHER PURPOSES.

"SECTION 1. *Be it enacted, etc.*, That in addition to the duties now imposed upon the township auditors, they shall hereafter perform the duties hereinafter prescribed as fence-viewers. That in addition to the oath now prescribed to be taken by the auditors, they shall annually be sworn or affirmed to discharge their duties as such viewers faithfully and impartially.

"SECTION 2. In case of the death, removal, or resignation . . . so elected, the judges of the court of the proper county shall appoint a suitable person. . . .

"SECTION 3. When any two persons shall improve lands adjacent to each other . . . so that any part of the first person's fence becomes the partition fence between them, in both these cases the charge of such division fence, so far enclosed on both sides, shall be equally borne and maintained by both parties.

PIONEER HISTORY OF JEFFERSON COUNTY, PENNA.

"SECTION 4. On notice given the said viewers shall within five days thereafter view and examine any line fence as aforesaid, and shall make a certificate in writing, setting forth whether, in their opinion, the fence if one has been already built is sufficient, and if not, what proportion of the expense of building a new or repairing the old fence should be borne by each party, and in each case they shall set forth the sum which in their judgment each party ought to pay to the other in case he shall repair or build his proportion of the fence, a copy of which certificate shall be delivered to each of the parties; and the said viewers shall receive the sum of one dollar for every day necessarily spent by them in the discharge of their duties, which they shall be entitled to receive from the delinquent party, or in equal sums from each as they shall decide to be just.

"SECTION 5. If the party who shall be delinquent in making or repairing of any fence shall not, within ten days after a copy of the certificate of the viewers shall have been delivered to him, proceed to repair or build the said fence, and complete the same in a reasonable time, it shall be lawful for the parties aggrieved to repair or build the said fence; and he may bring suit before any justice of the peace or alderman against the delinquent party, and recover, as in other actions, for work, labor, service done, and materials found, and either party may appeal from the decision of the justice or aldermen as in other cases.

"SECTION 7. If any viewer shall neglect or refuse to perform any duty herein enjoined upon him, he shall pay for each such neglect or refusal the sum of three dollars, to be recovered by the party aggrieved as debts of a like amount are recoverable.

"Approved—the eleventh day of March, one thousand eight hundred and forty-two.

WARSAW TOWNSHIP.

PIONEER HISTORY OF THE LARGEST TOWNSHIP IN JEFFERSON COUNTY.

Warsaw, the fifteenth township, organized in 1842, was taken from Pine Creek and Snyder townships, and named by the people after a city of Poland, and lately the metropolis of that country, in the palatinate of Masovia. Taxables in 1842, 77.

Before the white man came to settle in this county a part of Warsaw was "a barren" and thickly settled with Indians, and what is now called Seneca Hill, on the M. Hoffman farm, is where they met for their orgies. They had a graveyard on the Temple place, and S. W. Temple has found a number of curious Indian relics from time to time since he lived there.

The pioneer settlers in what is now Warsaw township were John, Jacob, and Peter Vastbinder. They settled on farms in 1802.

"John Dixon settled in what is now Warsaw about the year 1803, on the farm now owned by C. H. Shobert. The venerable John Dixon, of

Polk township, a son of the above pioneer, relates some of the incidents of those early days. He remembers when coffee was seventy-five cents and tea four dollars a pound, and salt ten dollars a barrel. His father on one occasion walked to Indiana, where he bought a bushel of salt, for which he paid four dollars. He carried it home on his back, and then found that he had been cheated in the measurement, as it lacked considerably of a bushel. The family subsisted chiefly on wild game, deer, bears, and wild turkeys being abundant. Their corn was ground on hand-mills, or else taken to Blacklick, in Indiana County, until Joseph Barnett erected his little mill at Port Barnett.''

Mr. Dixon was the pioneer school-teacher in Jefferson County, and was an exemplary citizen. He died in 1834, aged about seventy-six years. Mrs. Dixon, *née* Sarah Ann Armstrong, died in 1860, aged about ninety-two years. In 1825, Joshua Vandevort located at the place where Mayville, otherwise Bootjack, now stands, the pioneer settler in what is now Bootjack. In 1834, Thomas McCormick, Myron Gibbs, and Milton Johnson, Esq., settled on farms about two miles from Vandevort's. In 1835, Elihu Clark, Isaac Temple, and Andrew McCormick moved into that neighborhood, which afterwards became Warsaw. Mrs. Chloe Johnson died, and was the first interment in the burying-ground near Isaac Temple's residence.

The pioneer settlement near Richardsville was made by James Moorhead, who built a house on the farm now owned by the heirs of Jackson Moorhead in 1835, but he did not move his family there until the spring of 1836. John Wakefield built a house and moved his family on the farm now owned by Joseph McCracken in 1836, but returned to Indiana to spend the following winter. William Humphrey built a house on the farm now owned by his son, Samuel M. Humphrey, in the fall of 1836, and moved his family there in April, 1837. Michael Long built a cabin on the farm now owned by Matthew Humphrey in 1836, and occupied it for a short time. Isaac Walker built a house the same year on the farm now owned by Thomas Brownlee, to which he moved his family the next spring. Matthew Humphrey commenced operations on the farm on which he still resides in 1837. He is the only one of the original settlers of West Warsaw remaining. He says when he came to the township there were no roads, only a trail leading through the woods to ''Bootjack.'' (Hazen.)

William Russell, father of ''Indian'' George Russell, the hunter, settled in what is now Warsaw in 1834, and built a saw-mill on the North Fork. This was the pioneer saw-mill.

In 1837, William R. Richards located on the north fork of Red Bank Creek, six miles from Brookville, built a saw-mill, woollen-factory, and grist-mill, and called the place Richardsville. He had cleared a farm in Snyder township the year before, which he left in care of Alex. Hutch-

PIONEER HISTORY OF JEFFERSON COUNTY, PENNA.

inson. Daniel Gaup and Thomas McCormick settled on farms this year also. In 1837, David McCormick, Moses B. St. John, John Wilson, and William Perrin settled on farms. In 1838, John Bell, Peter Ricord, and Nelson Riggs also located there.

The pioneer graveyard was in the pine grove at Vastbinder's, the second at Temple's. Warsaw is now the largest township in the county. The country is very hilly and much broken, though few of the hills rise more than four hundred feet above the level of the larger streams. Some bituminous coal of good quality is found in the hills, lying in veins of three feet above the water-level; it is therefore very accessible for mining. Fire-clay has a place among these coal-measures, and ought to be utilized. Various kinds of iron-ores are abundant, and white and blue sandstones suitable for building purposes may readily be found in many places. Limestone in very large deposits is found in many localities. The soil is moderately fertile, and will amply reward the careful cultivator for his well-directed efforts. For some reason, a large extent of the township was called by the early settlers "The Barrens." The hills, as well as the vales between them, were formerly covered by a dense and heavy growth of timber-trees of various kinds. Pine and hemlock predominated. Chestnut and oak grew in some localities. Birch, sugar-maple, ash, and hickory occupied a wide range. Birch- and cherry-trees were numerous, and linwood-, cucumber-, and poplar-trees grew on many of the hill-sides. Butternut and sycamore, black ash and elms, grew on the low grounds.

The pioneer grist-mill was built on Mill Creek by E. Holben. The pioneer hotel-keeper was Isaac Temple. The pioneer merchant was Solomon Wyant, in Dogtown, or at what is now John Fox's hotel.

The act of the Legislature No. 110, regulating election districts, approved July 11, 1842, established the polling-place for Warsaw township as follows:

"SECTION 26. That the township of Warsaw, in the county of Jefferson, be and the same is hereby erected into a separate election district, and that the general as well as the township elections shall be held at the house of William Weeks in said township."

In the forties, Peter Ricord, Sr., and his son Peter erected on their farm in what was then called "Jericho," and now Warsaw Post-Office, a frame grist-mill structure thirty by thirty feet. This mill had one run of stones, and the motive power was one yoke of oxen. I cannot describe it. The capacity was about thirty bushels of corn or grain a day. Ephraim Bushly was the millwright; Peter Ricord, Jr., the miller. The scheme not proving a financial success, the running gear was removed in a few years, and the building utilized as a barn by the Ricords, and afterwards by John A. Fox.

The pioneer election held in Warsaw township for local offices was

PIONEER HISTORY OF JEFFERSON COUNTY, PENNA.

in 1843, and the following-named persons were elected,—viz.: Judge of Election, John Moorhead; Inspectors, Thomas McCormick, Peter Chamberlin; Supervisors, William Weeks, James K. Huffman; School Directors, O. P. Mather, Ira Bronson, G. D. Frederick, Arad Pearsall, James A. Wilkins, Peter Chamberlin; Constable, David C. Riggs; Assessors, Andrew McCormick, Jacob Moore, Eli B. Irvin; Auditors, John Pearsall, Thomas McCormick, Finley McCormick; Poor Overseers, Jacob Vastbinder, William Richards; Town Clerk, Ira Bronson.

PARADISE TOWNSHIP—A DEAD TOWNSHIP.

It appears on the records of the county that prior to or about the year 1839 a township was organized and known from 1839 until 1842 as Paradise township. From the names embraced in the officers elected in this township the territory must have taken all of what is now Gaskill, Bell, Henderson, McCalmont, and part of Winslow. The township disappears from the records of the county as mysteriously as it appears.

Pioneer election in Paradise township in the year 1839: Assessor, David Barnett; Judge of Election, John Pifer; Inspectors of Election, Peter Deemer, John Rhoads.

Second election, 1840, Paradise township: Judge of Election, John Rhoads; Inspectors of Election, John Deemer, Henry Philipi.

Third election, 1842: Constable, James Dickey; Supervisors, John Pifer, Henry Miller; Auditors, Henry Philipi, Thomas Thompson, Philip Bowers; Town Clerk, Henry Miller; School Directors, Henry Miller, Thomas Kerr; Overseers of the Poor, Andrew McCreight, Andrew Bowers; Assessor, David Harvey; Judge of Election, John Pifer; Inspectors of Election, George Pifer, George Smith.

PIONEER CENSUS, 1840.

The following is the population of Jefferson County by the several censuses taken since 1810: in 1810, 161; in 1820, 561; in 1830, 2025; and in 1840, 7253, as follows:

Brookville	276
Washington	367
Ridgway	195
Tionesta	27
Jenks	20
Porter	977
Young	1321
Rose	1421
Snyder	291
Eldred	395
Barnett	259
Pine Creek	628
Perry	1076
Total	7253

	Horses.	Cattle.	Sheep.	Swine.	Wheat.	Oats.	Rye	Buck-wheat.	Corn.	Pot
. . . .	29	66	27	87	97	150	40	50	50	
. . . .	314	1315	2001	1444	10,805	17,035	5,813	4,011	5,548	13
. . . .	66	405	391	520	2,223	7 3,0	701	367	1,586	5
. . . .	36	248	190	254	1,757	3,930	349	531	1,142	3
. . . .	29	87	30	48	290	1,440	. . .	157	505	3
. . . .	91	332	403	651	1,777	4,180	2,046	775	660	2
. . . .	4	9	. . .	. . .	. . .	400	. . .	30	150	.
. . . .	23	85	68	248	547	1,065	560	521	365	2,
. . . .	4	25	. . .	12	40	500	. . .	. . .	170	
. . . .	79	485	456	621	3,488	7,300	2,393	1,042	1,732	8
. . . .	213	815	1234	1506	7,285	9,501	4,416	2,004	2,843	7
. . . .	299	1003	1582	1876	9,070	15,982	4,936	3,221	4,463	8,
. . . .	240	898	960	1631	6,219	8,184	3,213	1,695	4,155	8,
. . . .	1427	5773	7342	8898	43,598	77,077	24,467	14,404	23,369	64,

PIONEER HISTORY OF JEFFERSON COUNTY, PENNA.

Since 1840, Ridgway and part of Snyder townships were taken to Elk County. Clover township was taken from Rose; Union from Rose and Eldred; Heath from Barnett; Warsaw from Pine Creek, Washington, and Snyder; Gaskill from Young; Winslow from Gaskill, Washington, and Pine Creek. Punxsutawney is erected into a borough. Its census is separate from Young township. Porter is divided.

The accompanying tables show the number of horses, cattle, etc., amount of grain raised, value of home-made woollens and linens and lumber produced, and the number of grist- and saw-mills in the several townships of Jefferson County at this period.

	Value of Home-made Woollens and Linens.	Value of Lumber produced.	Grist-Mills.	Saw-Mills.
Brookville		$3,450	1	1
Rose	$2283	15,732	5	17
Washington	497	410	1	1
Snyder		1,550	1	3
Ridgway		4,720	..	7
Eldred	450	1,155	..	..
Tionesta		500	..	1
Barnett	104	6,310	..	9
Jenks		85	..	1
Pine Creek	653	4,140	1	8
Porter	1281	3,700	..	2
Perry	1771	826	2	4
Young	1334	8,025	3	14
Total	$8363	$50,603	14	68

In 1839 there were six tanneries, that tanned five hundred and twenty sides of sole leather and eight hundred and five of upper leather. In these six tanneries seven hands were employed.

In the produce of lumber three hundred and fifty-three hands were employed.

In 1840, Rose township took the lead in population, and in everything else except swine and sugar.

Perry took the lead in swine.

Washington was the sweetest, and Snyder next, for they made the most sugar; but we have only to remember the name, for both townships were called after good and great men.

The total value of skins and furs, $1029; number of stores in county, 19,—viz., Brookville, 8; Rose, 2; Snyder, 1; Ridgway, 1; Porter, 1; Perry, 2; Young, 4.

Bituminous coal used: Brookville, 2000 bushels, Charles Anderson, miner; Rose township, number of bushels used, 500. The second miner, and in Rose, was Isaac Hallam; two miners in the county and 2500 bushels of coal used.

PIONEER HISTORY OF JEFFERSON COUNTY, PENNA.

BROOKVILLE BOROUGH.

This borough, the seat of justice of Jefferson County, commenced its first building in June of 1830. After the lots were sold, it being then in Rose township, its citizens voted with the township until 1848, when it

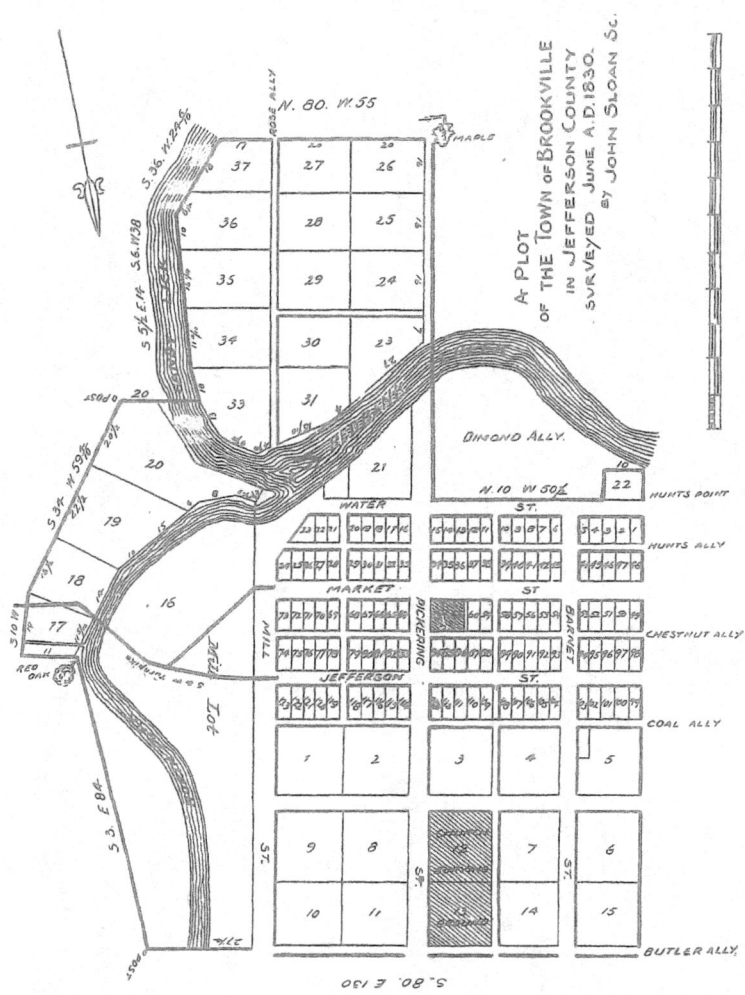

was set apart as a distinct polling place by act of the Legislature No. 285, regulating election districts, and for other purposes, approved the 7th day of April, A D. 1848.

Brookville was named for, or on account of, the springs or brooks on its hill-sides,—springs which here to all in these continuous woods did

PIONEER HISTORY OF JEFFERSON COUNTY, PENNA.

freely flow unbought. Brook, with the French "ville," or Latin "villa," a country-seat, in common English, a town; these put together formed the name. The population by the census of 1840 was 276.

Brookville was incorporated as a borough on April 9, 1834 (see pamphlet laws of that year, page 209). The pioneer election for the new borough, for borough officials, was in the spring of 1835. Joseph Sharpe was elected constable, and Alexander McKnight, my father, was elected school director.

"AN ACT (OF APRIL, 1834) TO ERECT BROOKVILLE, ARMAGH, SHREWS-
BURY, AND GREENFIELD INTO BOROUGHS, AND TO ALTER THE ACT
INCORPORATING THE BOROUGH OF MEADVILLE.

"SECTION 1. *Be it enacted, etc.*, That the town of Brookville, in the county of Jefferson, shall be, and the same is hereby erected into, a borough, which shall be called 'the borough of Brookville, in the county of Jefferson,' bounded and limited as follows,—viz.: Beginning at the southwest corner of lot number twenty-two in said town, near or adjoining Hunt's Point; thence due north along the marked line of said town to a post on the north side of Butler's Alley; thence along the north side of said alley to its extremity; thence by a continued east line to the northeast corner of the mill lot; thence south three degrees, east eighty-four perches, to a red oak; thence south eighteen perches to a post; thence south ten degrees, west seventeen perches, to a white pine; thence south twenty-four degrees, west fifty-nine perches, to a post; thence west twenty perches to the west side of Sandy Lick Creek at high-water mark; thence up said creek, following the several courses thereof, to a point east of and opposite the mouth of the south end of Rose Alley, being the extremity of the outlots; thence east to a maple opposite the south end of Pickering Street; thence north to the northeast corner of Water and Pickering Streets; thence along the south side of Water Street to the northeast corner of lot number twenty-two aforesaid; thence around the lines of said lot to the place of beginning.

"SECTION 2. It shall and may be lawful for all persons entitled to vote for members of the Legislature, who have resided in said borough twelve months immediately previous to such election, to meet at the court-house in said borough (or at such other place as may hereafter be appointed) on the second Monday in May in every year, and then and there elect by ballot, between the hours of twelve and six o'clock of the same day, one reputable citizen residing in said borough, who shall be styled the burgess of said borough, and five reputable citizens residing in said borough, who shall be a town council, and shall also elect one reputable citizen as town constable; but previous to such election the inhabitants shall elect two reputable citizens as judges, one inspector, and two clerks of said election, which shall be regulated and conducted according to the general election laws of this Commonwealth, so far as relates to receiving and counting votes, and who shall be subject to the same penalties for malpractices as by the said laws are imposed. And the said judges, inspector, and clerks respectively, before they enter upon the duties of their respective offices, shall take an oath or affirmation before any justice of the peace of said county to perform the same with fidelity; and after the said election shall be closed shall declare the persons having the greatest number of votes to be duly elected; and in case any two or more candidates shall have an equal number of votes, the preference shall be determined by lot, to be drawn by the judges and inspector; whereupon duplicate returns thereof shall be signed by the said judges, one of which shall be transmitted to each of the persons elected, and the other filed among the records of the corporation. And in case of death, resignation, removal, or refusal to accept, or neglect or refusal to act after acceptance, of any of the said officers, the burgess, or in case of his death, absence, or inability to act, or when he neglects or refuses to act, the first named of the town council shall issue his precept, directed to the high constable, or when there is no high constable, or when he refuses or neglects to act, then any of the members of the town council shall advertise and hold an election in manner aforesaid to supply such vacancy, giving at least ten days' notice thereof by advertisements set up at four of the most public places in the said borough.

"SECTION 3. From and after the passage of this act the burgess and town council, duly elected as aforesaid, and their successors, shall be one body politic and corporate, in law, by the name and style of 'The Burgess and Town Council of the Borough of Brookville, in the County of Jefferson,' and shall have perpetual succession; and the said burgess and town council aforesaid, and their successors, shall be capable in law to receive, hold, and possess goods and chattels, lands and tenements, rents, liberties, jurisdictions, franchises, and hereditaments, to them and their successors, in fee-simple, or otherwise, not exceeding the yearly value of five thousand dollars, and also to give, grant, sell, let, and assign the same lands, tenements, hereditaments, and rents; and by the name and style aforesaid they shall be capable in law to sue and be sued, plead and be impleaded, in any of the courts of law in this Commonwealth or elsewhere, in all manner of actions whatsoever, and to have and use one common seal, and the same from time to time at their will to change and alter."

The first complete set of borough officers was elected under this law and the act of the 23d of February, 1835, hereafter referred to. This first election was in the spring of 1837, and those elected were as follows: Burgess, Thomas Lucas; Council, John Dougherty, James Corbett, John Pierce, Samuel Craig, Wm. A. Sloan; Constable, John McLaughlin.

PIONEER HISTORY OF JEFFERSON COUNTY, PENNA.

This man McLaughlin was a great hunter, and could neither read nor write; he moved to Brockwayville, and from there went West.

By an act of Assembly passed April 2, 1830, it was provided that from and after the 1st day of October, thereafter, the inhabitants of Jefferson County should "enjoy all and singular the jurisdiction, powers, rights, liberties, and privileges whatsoever within the same which the inhabitants of other counties of this State do, may, or ought to enjoy, by the law and Constitution of this Commonwealth."

Our first president judge, Thomas Burnside, was born in the county of Tyrone, Ireland, July 28, 1782, and resided in Bellefonte, Centre County. His father, William Burnside, with his family, emigrated to Philadelphia, Pennsylvania, in 1792. In 1800, Thomas commenced to read law with Hon. Robert Porter, and on the 13th day of February, 1804, he was admitted to the Philadelphia bar. In the month of March of that year Thomas moved to, and settled in, Bellefonte, Centre County, Pennsylvania. In 1811 he was elected to the State Senate. In 1815 he was sent to Congress. In 1816 he was appointed a president judge. In 1823 he was again elected a State Senator and was made Speaker. In 1826 he was again appointed a president judge. In 1854 he was commissioned a judge for the Supreme Court of Pennsylvania.

In stature, Judge Burnside was of medium height, dark complexioned, and very homely. He was a learned lawyer, an able jurist, and a kind, blunt, honest, open-hearted gentleman.

Many of the details of the history of Brookville are given in fragments throughout this general history. The place was laid out in 1830 as the county seat, and in June of that year the lots were sold, the price ranging from thirty to three hundred dollars. In 1831 a traveller speaks of it as a "shanty town," and doubts that the population might amount to fifty. In 1840 the inhabitants numbered two hundred and seventy-six, and there were sixty dwellings and stores. From an early history, in speaking of Jefferson County, and especially of Brookville, we quote the following: "The scenery around this town would be fine were it not that all the hills, except on the north side, are still clothed by the original forest of pines, being held by distant proprietors, who neither sell nor improve. Its situation is on the Waterford and Susquehanna Turnpike, forty-four miles east of Franklin, and immediately at the head of Red Bank Creek, which is here formed by the confluence of two branches. The great State road, called the Olean road, between Kittanning and Olean, passes through the county about seven miles west of Brookville. North of the turnpike, however, the road has been suffered to be closed by obstructions, and is not now used." Another writer says "that Meade's trail from Port Barnett crossed the creek five times." Still another says, "This hole can never become a place of any importance, the county seat must be removed to Punxsutawney or Port Barnett."

PIONEER HISTORY OF JEFFERSON COUNTY, PENNA.

"A few straggling Indians occasionally called at the village, reminding one of former scenes." "Times are slow," says another; "our lumber at the creek will not bring more than three or four dollars." They had hard times in the past, and times that made the county seat what it is,— a commercial centre, a centre of religion and morals, a place for culture in literature and music, which for its age will compare with learned Boston. The population to-day is about three thousand.

PIONEERS AND PIONEER EVENTS IN BROOKVILLE.

"The deeds of our fathers in times that are gone,
Their virtues, their prowess, the toils they endured."

The pioneer settler to locate where Brookville is was Moses Knapp. The pioneer to locate in the county seat was John Eason, father of Rev. David Eason. He bought the lot on the corner of Main Street and Spring Alley, and erected the pioneer house in the county seat,—viz., in August, 1830, and opened it for a tavern. Mr. Eason died in 1835. In 1831, William Robinson lived in a little log house on the corner of Mill and Water Streets. This log house and log stable had been built by Moses Knapp in 1806. The next person to locate was perhaps Thomas Hall. Benjamin McCreight was an early settler. Mr. McCreight was a tailor and carried on the business. He was an honorable and useful man, and held many responsible positions during his life here. John Dougherty attended the sale of lots, bought several, and in 1831 moved to Brookville. Thomas M. Barr came here in 1830. He was a stone-mason and bricklayer, and assisted to build up the town by taking contracts. The pioneer blacksmith was Jacob Riddleberger, in 1832-33. Wm. Clark, Sr., came to Brookville in 1830, and erected a tavern on the northwest corner of Pickering and Jefferson Streets. In the fall of 1830, Jared B. Evans moved his store from Port Barnett to Brookville, and was appointed the pioneer postmaster for Brookville post-office. Brookville, by post-road, was one hundred and sixty-five miles northwest of Harrisburg, Pennsylvania, and two hundred and thirty-eight miles northwest of Washington, D. C. Mr. Evans's was the pioneer store. The second store was opened three days later by Major William Rodgers. Thomas Hastings located in 1831, and built the Jefferson Tavern. Robert P. Barr came in 1830. He was a useful and public-spirited man. He built the saw-mill and flouring-mill on the North Fork. Joseph Sharpe was the first shoemaker and the first constable. He lived on the lot now occupied by the National Bank of Brookville.

William Jack came to Brookville in 1831, and was sent to Congress from this district. Richard Arthurs, Esq., located here in 1831 or thereabouts. Cyrus Butler in 1830-31. James Corbett in 1830. Alexander McKnight located in Brookville in 1832. He taught the first term of school in the first school building, was the first school director elected for the new borough, held the office of justice of the peace, lieutenant-colonel in the militia, had served a year as private in the regular army of the United States, and was county treasurer when he died, in 1837, aged twenty-seven years.

Samuel Craig located in Brookville in 1832, Hugh Brady, Esq., in 1832, and John Ramsey, the pioneer wagon-maker, in 1834. Hugh Brady and family came from Indiana, Pennsylvania, in a Conestoga wagon drawn by four horses,—the lead horses having bells on. That was the wagon of that period. (See illustration.) There was no bridge across the North Fork. They came *via* Port Barnett. John Showalter located here in 1843. He lived in Snyder's Row, was a gunsmith, and had a confectionery. James R. Fullerton located in Brookville in 1833. The pioneer gunsmith was Isaac Mills. He located where Thomas L. Templeton now resides. The pioneer doctor was Alvah Evans; he came in September, 1831. He was a young, handsome, portly man. He remained four or five months and left. Where he came from or where he went to nobody knows. The second doctor was C. G. M. Prime. He came in the spring of 1832. Dr. Prime amputated the arm of Henry (Hance) Vastbinder. During his residence here he married a Miss Wagley. He was a hard drinker. He left here April 3, 1835, for Mississippi, where he was shot and killed at a card-table. He became a lawyer while here, delivered political speeches and Fourth of July orations.

The pioneer merchant to sell drugs and medicines in Brookville was Major William Rogers, in 1831. He sold Dover's powder, Hooper's pills, mercurial ointment, wine, brandy, whiskey, quinine, etc.

The pioneer fire-engine was bought June 29, 1839. Cost, two hundred and fifty dollars. It was a hand-engine. This same year it was resolved by the council that "the timber standing or lying on the streets and alleys be sold for the use of said borough." The first volunteer fire company in the United States was at Philadelphia, 1736.

The pioneer saddle and harness manufactory in Brookville was opened by John Brownlee, on May 8, 1834, in the rear of his lot facing Mill Street, and opposite D. E. Breneman's residence.

—— McDonald started the pioneer cabinet and furniture factory in 1831–32.

The pioneer foundry was started by a man named Coleman, in 1841. It was located where the Fetzer building now is.

The pioneer grist-mill was built by Moses Knapp.

The pioneer saw-mill was built by Moses Knapp.

The pioneer borough election was in 1835.

John J. Y. Thompson settled in Brookville in 1831, Andrew Craig in 1838, Robert Darrah in 1837, Arad Pearsall in 1833, Samuel C. Espy in

PIONEER HISTORY OF JEFFERSON COUNTY, PENNA.

1842, Hon. Philip Taylor in 1841, John Gallagher in the early thirties, William Farley in 1843. Isaac Allen was an early settler.

The pioneer silversmith and watch- and clock-maker was Andrew Straub, in 1833-34. Watches were then assessed as property.

The pioneer graveyard was on lands now owned by W. C. Evans, on Litch's Hill. The second one is now called the "old graveyard."

The pioneer dentists were Dr. A. M. Hills and T. M. Van Valzah. These were travelling dentists, and came here periodically. The first dentist to locate was William J. Chandler.

In 1832, Peter Sutton built and kept a tavern on the corner of Taylor Street, across the North Fork, now Litchtown. In 1832 or 1833 there was a frame tavern adjoining the Franklin Tavern. It was kept for a number of years by a man named Craig, Mrs. Wagley, and others.

The pioneer tannery was built in 1831 by David Henry, on the lot now occupied by the United Presbyterian church. As late as 1843 a great gully crossed Main Street, carrying the water from this institution over and through the lot now occupied by that model institution of the town, the National Bank of Brookville.

Miss Julia Clark opened the pioneer millinery and mantua-making business in Brookville. Prices: bonnets, leghorn, $5; silk, $2.50; gimp, $1.50; straw, $1. In her advertisement she says, "She can be seen at her residence, four doors east of E. Heath's store, on Main Street. Persons, so wishing, can be supplied by her with ladies' leghorn hats, flats and crown, from No. 32 to 42; ladies' Tuscan and French gimp; Italian braid hats; Leghorn braid, Tuscan and Italian edge, Misses' gimp hats, Tuscan; French gimp by the piece. She hopes, by giving her undivided attention to the above business, to merit a share of public patronage. Brookville, July 13th, 1834."

The pioneer tinner was Samuel Truby. He came from Indiana, Pennsylvania, arriving here on January 1, 1834. The last thirteen miles of the journey was through a dense forest, without house or clearing. They stopped at John Eason's tavern, and as soon as possible he commenced to cut down the trees on and clear his lot, corner of Jefferson and Pickering Streets, preparatory to building a house, a contract for the building of which was taken by the late R. Arthurs, he agreeing to furnish all the material and finish it as specified by April 1 for the sum of forty dollars, which was paid in silver quarters. The house was sixteen feet square and one and a half stories high.

Hon. Thomas Hastings came in May, 1831. "Nearly all of what is now the principal part of the town—Main Street and Jefferson Street—was then a forest. Only three houses had yet been built,—the Red Lion Hotel, where Gregg's barber-shop now is, the hotel now occupied by P. J. Allgeier, and another hotel, which stood where J. M. White's dwelling now stands. Besides these houses just built, a little log house stood down by the North Fork Creek. Such was Brookville in May, 1831, sixty-seven years ago. There was not a street opened, and the turnpike ran in a straight line from Allgeier's hotel to Dr. Hunt's residence."

There is one person (John Butler) still living in Brookville who has seen a slave that was owned in Brookville whipped with a blacksnake whip on Pickering Street, between Joseph Darr's residence and where the Methodist Episcopal church now stands.

In 1835, Brookville contained about one hundred and thirty-five people. The village had six merchants,—viz., Evans & Clover, William Rodgers, James Corbett, Jared B. Evans, Jack & Wise, and Steadman & Watson. Each storekeeper had a large dry pine block, called "upping block," in front of his store-room, to assist men and women to mount or alight from their horses. The stores were lighted with candles and warmed with wood-fires. Wood-fires in stoves and chimneys were very dangerous, on account of the accumulation of wood-soot in the chimney; for when this soot gathered in quantity it always ignited, burned out, and endangered the shingle roof. Towns and cities then had men and boys called professional "chimney-sweeps." These "sweeps" entered the chimney from the fireplace, climbing up and out at the top by the aid of hooks, announcing their exit in a song and looking as black as an African negro. In 1835 some of the legal privileges of the town were: "That no citizen of the town shall be permitted to keep on Main Street, at one time, more than ten cords of wood, not more than enough brick to build a chimney, or before his door more lumber than will build a spring-house; not more than two wagons and a half-sled; a few barrels of salt, five thousand shingles, or twenty head of horned cattle." Of course, there was no legal restriction as to the number of "chickens in the garden" or geese and hogs on the street. On dark nights the people then carried lanterns made of tin, holes being punched in them, and the light produced by a candle. The lantern had a side door to open, to light, blow out, and replace the candle.

"MAIL ARRIVALS AND DEPARTURES.

"The Mail arrives from Philadelphia by way of Harrisburg, Lewistown, and Bellefonte every Monday evening, Wednesday evening, and Friday evening in a four Horse Coach.

"From Erie, by way of Meadville, Franklin, &c., every Monday, Wednesday, and Friday evenings, and returns the same day, in a four Horse Stage.

"From Washington City, by way of Chambersburgh, Indiana, &c., every Friday and returns same day—carried on a Horse.

"From Pittsburg by way of Kittanning every Friday, and returns on Tuesday—carried on a Horse.

"Arrive at this place every Tuesday, from Smethport, McKean county by way of Gillis Post-office, and returns on Friday—carried on a Horse."—*Republican*, Brookville, January, 1835.

EARLY SCHOOLS — PIONEER ACT AUTHORIZING BROOKVILLE TO ELECT SCHOOL DIRECTORS—PIONEER ELECTION OF DIRECTORS AND PIONEER MASTERS.

The act of the Legislature No. 109, approved April 4, 1837, authorized the election of school directors. Section 7 and 8 read as follows:

"SECTION 7. *Be it enacted by the Senate and House of Representatives of the Commonwealth of Pennsylvania, in General Assembly met, and it is hereby enacted by authority of the same*, That the citizens of the borough of Brookville, in the county of Jefferson, be and are hereby authorized to meet at the usual place of holding borough elections, on the first Monday of January, in the year one thousand eight hundred and thirty-seven, and afterwards annually, at the time of holding their borough elections, and elect six school directors, in the manner provided for the election of school directors by law.

"SECTION 8. And that all moneys now in the treasury of Rose township school district, assessed on the citizens of the borough aforesaid, shall be paid to the use and for the support of schools in said borough, that now are, or that may be hereafter, organized under the provisions of the act aforesaid.

"Approved—the fourth day of April, A.D. one thousand eight hundred and thirty-seven."

The following notice of pioneer election for directors appeared in the *Brookville Republican*, Thursday, September 7, 1837:

"Saturday next, at three o'clock in the afternoon, is the time agreed upon by the citizens of Brookville for holding an election to elect six school directors for this borough. It is important that every friend of education, and we hope we have no citizen who would oppose it, should be in attendance and give his vote for delegates, in order to give weight to the proceedings. We repeat that we hope there will be a unanimous attendance of the citizens at said election."

On September 9, 1837, the people elected the following school directors: Levi G. Clover, Samuel Craig, David Henry, C. A. Alexander, William A. Sloan, James Corbett.

The pioneer school-house in the town was built in 1832. It was a small one-storied brick building, Major William Rodgers says, about twenty feet square. It stood near the northwest corner of the present location of the county jail. The building was erected under the provisions of the law of 1809, and was paid for by voluntary subscriptions. Alexander McKnight taught the pioneer term of school in it in 1832-33. Anticipating the want of a stove for the contemplated building, Major William Rodgers, then one of the business men of the new town, wrote the following "subscription-paper" and collected the money on it. The money was invested in what was then called a "ten-plate stove," so called because it was formed of ten pieces or "plates of metal." The fuel used in it was wood.

"We, the undersigned subscribers, do severally promise to pay the sums set to our names, on demand, to the trustees of the Brookville school, to be applied to the purchase of a stove for the use of the school-house in Brookville. Witness our hands, the 18th day of February, 1832:

"SUBSCRIBERS' NAMES.

William Clark	$0.50
Joseph Clements	.50
Elijah Heath	1.00
Isaac Mills	.50
Thomas Robinson	.50
Thomas Barr	.25
Joseph McCullough	.50
James Hall	.25

PIONEER HISTORY OF JEFFERSON COUNTY, PENNA.

James Corbett	.50
Aaron Fuller	.25
David Henry	.25
Thomas Hall	.50
Joseph Sharp	.25
Andrew Vastbinder	.25
Fr. Heterick	.50
Thomas Lucas	.50
Thomas Hastings	.50
C. J. Dunham	.50
William Kelso	.25
William Rodgers	.25
W. McCullough	.25
—— Sloan	.25
Total	$9.00"

As happens nowadays, a few of these subscriptions were not paid.

In the memories of some of our oldest citizens now cluster recollections of this little old brick school-house and the ten-plate stove thus purchased to warm it. About that little school-house were formed many ties which bound men and women together as friends in long succeeding years. Around that little temple of learning I have seen

> "The hoop, the bow and arrow,
> The soaring of the kite and swing,
> The humming of the 'over-ball,'
> And the marbles in the ring;
> The sleds, the rope, and sliding-boards,
> The races down the yard,
> And the war of snow-ball armies,
> The victors and the scarred."

In this little brick house the Methodists for years held their weekly prayer-meetings. The principal members were Judge Heath, Arad Pearsall, John Dixon, John Heath, David and Cyrus Butler, David Henry and wife, and Mary, Jane, and Sarah Gaston.

The pioneer Sunday-school teacher in Brookville was Cyrus Butler. Professor Blose and Miss Kate Scott both err in saying that Cyrus Butler taught the first or pioneer school in the old jail in Brookville in 1830. The old jail was not built until 1831, and Cyrus Butler never taught any school or class in this county but in the Sunday-school.

School-masters who taught in Brookville subscription schools under the law of 1809:

1832–33.—Alexander McKnight, pioneer.

1834.—Miss Charlotte Clark, Charles E. Tucker.

1835.—John Wilson.

1836.—Hannibal Craighead.

Masters who taught under the common school law of 1834:

1837.—Cyrus Crouch, pioneer, had sixty scholars in a house where the United Presbyterian church now stands.

1838.—Rev. Dexter Morris, a Baptist preacher.

1839.—John Smith.

Pioneer academy.

1840.—S. M. Bell, Mrs. M. T. H. Roundy.

1841.—D. S. Deering.

All or nearly all of the above masters taught in the little brick schoolhouse that was built on the back of the lot where the jail now stands.

1842.—R. J. Nicholson, Miss Elizabeth Brady, first to teach in the academy building.

1843.—R. J. Nicholson, Miss Nancy Lucas.

PIONEER SCHOOL DIRECTORS.

The following is a list of the pioneer and early school directors for the borough of Brookville, Pennsylvania, from 1834 to 1805:

Rose Township.

1834.—Colonel Alexander McKnight, James Green, Robert Andrews, Irwin Robinson, Darius Carrier.

1835.—Darius Carrier, Colonel Alexander McKnight.

PIONEER HISTORY OF JEFFERSON COUNTY, PENNA.

Brookville Borough.

1837.—General L. S. Clover, C. A. Alexander, David Henry, Samuel Craig, William A. Sloan, James Corbett.
1839.—Cyrus Butler, John Dougherty, Robert P. Barr.
1840.—John M. McCoy, Robert P. Barr.
1841.—John Smith, Esq., Samuel B. Bishop.
1842.—D. B. Jenks, Esq., J. G. Clark, Esq., Hugh Brady, Esq.
1843.—George Irwin, John Dougherty.
1844.—Samuel B. Bishop, C. A. Alexander, Thomas Wilkins, L. B. Dunham.
1845.—Dr. James Dowling, David S. Deering, Thomas M. Barr, Hon. J. B. Evans.

Fifty years ago spelling contests in schools were common, regularly every Saturday afternoon, and sometimes a neighborhood had rival school contests at night. It was one of the backwoods amusements, and a useful one, too. It was conducted in this wise: Two of the best spellers were chosen captains, these would alternately select other spellers, and form their followers on opposite sides, sitting or standing. The schoolmaster would give out the words from a book agreed upon, or sometimes at his option. When a scholar missed a word he vacated his place; this plan was pursued until but one scholar remained of either side. Then his side was declared victorious and the best speller was a hero. A spelling craze passed over the United States in 1875, and Brookville caught the fever and had a contest,—viz.:

"SPELLING-BEE" IN BROOKVILLE.

The following account of a spelling-bee in Brookville is taken from an issue of the *Jeffersonian* published in the fall of 1875. Its perusal will doubtless call up in the minds of many the incidents of the evening. It will be remembered how "Schuylkill" seated E. Heath Clark, and "inter-nos" settled Dr. Sweeney:

"The first spelling-match in Brookville came off on Thursday evening last. The original intention was to hold it in the room of the musical society, but it was found there would not be room there for the crowd, when the court-room was secured. The attendance was large, and the interest taken in it by both contestants and spectators was marked. The captains were William Dickey and David Eason, Esqs. Each side numbered twenty, and among the spellers were found lawyers, doctors, schoolteachers, etc. The difficult task of pronouncing was assigned to Hon. George A. Jenks, who probably discharged his duty as satisfactorily to all parties as any one could have done. After the arrangements necessary had been made, the spelling commenced, and was continued for one hour, when it was found that Captain Eason's side had missed thirty-one words, while Captain Dickey's side had missed thirty-two words. On Eason's side there were seven who had not missed a word, and on Dickey's side four. Between these eleven commenced the contest for the prize,—Macaulay's 'History of England,' in five volumes. In a short time but one speller was up on Eason's side, and he our old friend, Dr. McKnight, while Rev. A. B. Fields and Mrs. T. L. Templeton on Dickey's side were arrayed against him. The word 'soirée,' however, was too much for the doctor, and he retired as gracefully as a French dancing-master. The contest now was between Mrs. Templeton and Mr. Fields, both of Dickey's side; but 'apropos' soon left Rev. Fields master of the field and the possessor of the prize. We were surprised to hear so few words missed, and, taken altogether, the spelling was much above the average."

NOTE.—I should have been declared the victor in this match. After it became a *personal* contest, Mr. Fields went down on the word "guaranty," and after we had spelled several rounds he was permitted to take his place again. Great sympathy existed in this community for Rev. Fields on account of his domestic troubles. The management of the class acted outrageously in their determination to favor the reverend. I spelled the word "soirée" in this way: "s-o-i-r-e," and before pronouncing the word corrected the spelling in the last syllable by saying "double-ee," but still I was ruled out, because they wished the reverend to have the prize. I made no objection.

MINUTES OF THE PIONEER SESSION OF BROOKVILLE TOWN COUNCIL.

"On the 19th day of July, 1834, the following officers having been duly elected, chosen, and sworn to serve the borough of Brookville, in Jefferson County, for the current year,—viz.: Thomas Lucas, Esq., Burgess; William Jack, James Corbett, John Eason, Robert Larrimer, Thomas Hastings, Town Council; Cyrus G. M. Prime, Constable, met in session, when the following proceedings were had and done,—viz.:

"On motion, William Jack was duly chosen president of the board. Hugh Brady was appointed clerk. Benjamin McCreight was appointed treasurer, with directions that he give bond to the borough with one or more sureties in the sum of three hundred dollars, and that his compensation be two and a half per cent. on all moneys received and paid over by him. Joseph Sharpe was appointed street commissioner, with a compensation of one dollar per diem, and that the compensation of the clerk be ten dollars per annum.

"That James Corbett and Hugh Brady be appointed a committee to procure a seal for the said borough on the most reasonable terms, and that the device of said seal be 'The Seal of the Borough of Brookville.'

"That David Henry be appointed assessor; that the rate per cent. be one-third per cent. of the dollar for this year; that William Jack and James Corbett be appointed to assist the assessor in making a valuation; and that the assessor be directed at the time of making his assessment to show his duplicate to the person assessed the amount of his or their assessment. On motion, council adjourned."

"ORDINANCE NO. 1.

"AN ORDINANCE TO REPAIR MAIN STREET IN THE BOROUGH OF BROOKVILLE.

" *Be it ordained by the Town Council of the Borough of Brookville, in the County of Jefferson, and it is hereby ordained by the authority of the same,* That all the moneys about to be raised by the present assessment in said borough (except what may be needed for the payment of officers, procuring seal, books, and stationery for the use of the corporation) shall be paid over to the street commissioner, by orders drawn by the president of the council upon the treasurer, which said orders shall be countersigned by the clerk, for the purpose of repairing and amending Main Street from the east side of Mill Street to the western boundary of said borough; and that the said street commissioner is hereby authorized to proceed immediately, upon the receipt of any such moneys, to making the repairs as aforesaid, under the direction of the town council.

"Ordained in council the 2d day of August, 1834.

"Attest: HUGH BRADY,
"*Secretary.*"

In 1835 the burgess was Thomas Lucas. Council, William Jack, James Corbett, Jared B. Evans, Samuel Craig, Alexander McKnight.

An act of July 11, A.D. 1842, "Regulating Election Districts and for other Purposes":

"SECTION 14. That the qualified voters of the borough of Brookville, in the county of Jefferson, shall annually hereafter, at the time and place of electing a high constable, town council, and other borough officers, elect two reputable citizens of said borough as constables, and return the names of the persons so elected to the next Court of Quarter Sessions of said county, agreeably to the provisions and regulations of the act of Assembly passed the third day of February, A.D. one thousand eight hundred and thirty-five, and shall also on the same day and place aforesaid elect one reputable citizen of said borough as an assessor of all taxable property in said borough, and that all county rates, and levies, and other taxes shall be levied according to the valuation of said assessor, and that so much of the act passed the fifteenth day of April, A.D. one thousand eight hundred and thirty-four, entitled 'An Act relating to County Rates and Levies, and Township Rates and Levies,' as compels the assessors of said township with the commissioners to ascertain the real value of all property (made taxable by law) within the limits of said borough be and the same is hereby repealed."

Under this act of 1842 the pioneer and separate assessment of Brookville as a borough was made in 1844.

BROOKVILLLE'S HISTORIC SPRING—INDIANS AND THEIR WHITE CAPTIVES— JIM HUNT'S CAVE—THE OLD-TIME EMIGRANT.

As early as 1755 there is authentic record that the Delaware Indians carried white captives over a trail through what is now Punxsutawney and Brookville to the Allegheny River and Lake Erie region. These Indians stopped overnight occasionally where Sandy Lick and the North Fork unite, eating their corn-meal and drinking from the spring. It was here that the fugitive Indian, Jim Hunt, had a hiding-place in an artificial cave. Jim was a fugitive from his tribe for murder, and when apprised by the whoops of his friends always hid in this cave. The water was too cool for Jim's stomach, hence he spent most of his time about Barnett's, where he could get "fire-water." The old State Road lay on the left of the pike coming from Port Barnett, and came down what is now Litch Hill, close by and near to this spring; and for eighteen years the old-time emigrant, with his flint-lock gun, his dog, wagon, and family, always stopped at the foot of the hill, in a sly little nook of laurel blossoms, to quench his thirst with old rye and pearly, pure potations of water from this bubbling white-sand spring.

In my early days Sunday-school picnics and occasionally a Fourth of July was celebrated here. To the people of Brookville it was a great resort during the hot days of summer. As a rule, everybody went over on Sabbath with a tin cup to refresh themselves. I clip the following from the pen of Bion H. Butler:

"It is at the foot of the hill just below Heidrick, Matson & Co.'s mill, and it has poured refreshing drinks down many times more throats than did ever Clover's or Tommy Wesley's still, which stood on the pike not far away.

"The sand spring is a great pool in the white rock, where water enough gushes out to run a prohibition campaign and give every man a drink as often as he wants one. When I first knew the spring it was doing business single-handed and alone, although the distillery close by and the brewery across the creek were rivals for public favor, to say nothing of Heber's tavern on the corner. But the spring is there yet, while the distillery is gone; and the path that leads down to the spring has borne the footprint, often, too, of nearly every man, woman, or child who has travelled this forest or lived in Brookville in the last one hundred years."

PIONEER HISTORY OF JEFFERSON COUNTY, PENNA.

BROOKVILLE'S EARLY PUGILISTS.

I clip the following from the pen of Bion H. Butler: "Harry Clover was a strong man, and as supple as he was strong. He could lift with his teeth a chair on which was a man weighing two hundred and twenty-five pounds. He could take up a barrel of whiskey easy and drink from the bung-hole.

"Clover was a blacksmith. He weighed two hundred pounds, but he was as agile as any man you ever saw. One day, when he had gone with some lumber to Pittsburg in rafting season, he went into a store to buy a hat. The price did not suit him, so in the course of the banter he told the merchant to hang it on a hook that was screwed in the ceiling and let him kick at it. If he kicked it down it was to be his. If not, he would pay double for it. The first kick Clover brought the hat down, kicking a hole in the ceiling which was a sight for raftsmen for years.

"Harry had no scientific pugilistic training, and never sought a row. On the contrary, he was cowardly, and often would not fight when bullies set on him. But when his anger was aroused his great strength and his activity made him a terrible enemy. When he worked in the old blacksmith-shop by the bridge I have seen him shoe unruly horses, and he just held them by main force. His reputation had extended all along the creek; and in the spring, when we went to Pittsburg with lumber, the first question asked was as to whether Harry Clover had come down.

"More or less rivalry always existed between the raftmen and the furnace-men along the river. One time the Red Bank furnace hands concluded they would clean out the raftmen, and a fellow by the name of Tom Fagan, who had heard of Clover, came down from Catfish Furnace to do him up. Clover never wanted to quarrel when sober, and he hid behind a door when Fagan came to look for him. After much persuasion he was brought forth. When he stepped up before Fagan he closed an eye with each fist before Fagan could get a successful blow on Clover anywhere."

CHAPTER XXVI.

MY FIRST RECOLLECTIONS OF BROOKVILLE.

I WAS born in Brookville when wolves howled almost nightly on what is now known as our "Fair Ground;" when the pine in its lofty pride leaned gloomily over every hill-side; when the shades of the forest were heavy the whole day through; when the woods around our shanty town was the home of many wild animals, such as panthers, bears, wild-cats, foxes, deer, wolves, catamounts, coons, ground-hogs, porcupines, partridges, elks, rabbits, turkeys, and pheasants; when the clear sparkling waters of the North Fork, Sandy Lick, and Red Bank Creeks contained choice pike, many bass, sunfish, horned chubs, trout, and other fish; when the wild "bee trees" were quite numerous and full of luscious sweets for the woodsman's axe. As you will see, choice meals for hunters and Nimrods could easily be obtained from the abundance of this game.

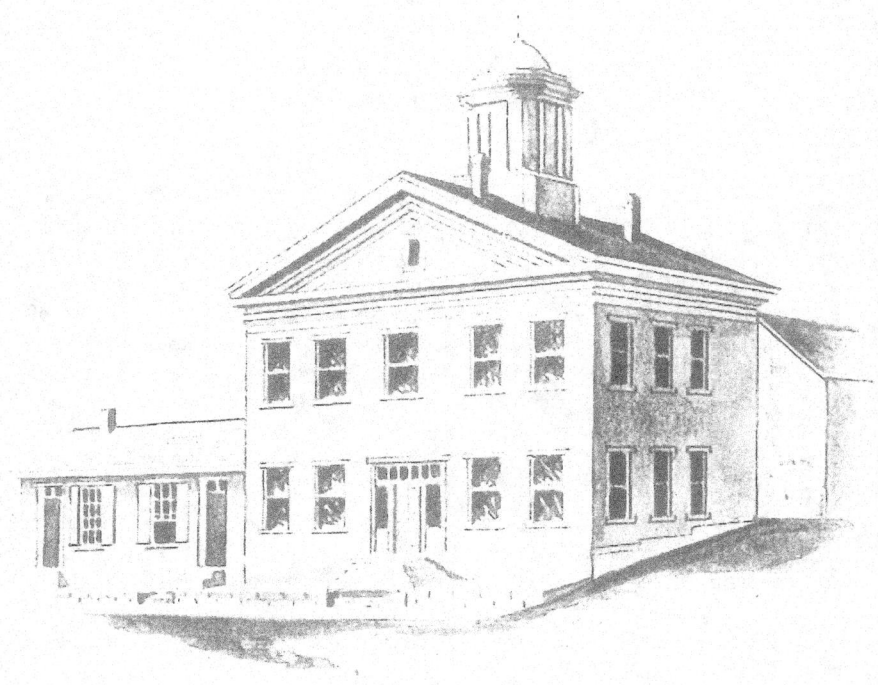

Pioneer court-house and jail, 1831,—
"Where gross misconduct met the lash,
And there see the rock-built prison's dreadful face."

The conditions and circumstances of the county made every man a hunter, and each and every one had his gun, bullet-moulds, shot-pouch, and powder-horn for any and every emergency. It was frequently found necessary before going to church on Sunday to shoot a wild turkey or a deer to "keep them off the grass." The "mighty hunters," though, were "Mike," "Dan," John, and "Bill" Long. Dan was murdered on the Clarion River, near Raught's mill. John was the father of Hon. James E. Long. In winter these hunters wore a white garment, called a "hunting-shirt," buckskin breeches, and moccasin shoes. In their shirt belts each carried a flint-knocker, spunk, hunting-knives, and a tomahawk.

PIONEER HISTORY OF JEFFERSON COUNTY, PENNA.

Animals were ruthlessly killed for their skins. Deer were thus slaughtered, only the "saddles" or hind quarters being saved for food. If a history of these Longs could be truthfully written,—a full narration of their adventures, perils, coolness, and daring while on the trail of bears, wolves, and panthers,—it would, perhaps, make a book equally as interesting as the "Life of Daniel Boone and Simon Girty."

In the way of a preface to these imperfect reminiscences of Brookville and our dear fathers I simply ask of you this:

> "Let not ambition mock their useful toil,
> These homely joys and destinies obscure,
> Nor grandeur hear with a disdainful smile
> These short and simple annals of the poor."

My first clear and distinct recollections of our town and the people in it are in the years 1840 to 1843. The ground where the *Democrat* is now printed was then covered with pines. Then Brookville was a town of forty or fifty "shanties" and eight or ten business places, including the "old brick court-house" and the "old stone jail." The number of people in the town was three hundred and twenty-two. These "shanties" were principally on Main Street, and extended from where the Baptist church now is in the east to where Judge Clark now lives in the west. There were a few scattered shanties on Jefferson Street. A great deep gully crossed Main Street about where the Brookville National Bank now stands.

A common sign in those days was, "Cakes & Beer For Sale Here,"—a bottle of foaming beer in a glass in the corner. The first of these signs which I remember was one on John Brownlee's house, on the northeast corner of Main and Mill Streets, and one on John Showalter's house (the late gunsmith), now the property of John S. Moore. The cakes were made of New Orleans molasses, and were delicious, more so than any you can make or buy now. They were sold for a cent apiece. The beer was home-made, and called "small beer," and sold for three cents a glass. It was made of hops, ginger, spruce, sassafras-roots, wheat bran, molasses, yeast, and water. About every family made their own beer. Mrs. Showalter and other old ladies living in the town now, I venture to say, have made "barrels" of it.

The hotels in the town then were four in number. First, the "Red Lion," located then where Frank P. Rankin now has his hardware store. This hotel was kept by John Smith, the step-father of David Eason. The second was the "Jefferson House," then kept by Thomas Hastings, now occupied and kept by Phil. J. Allgeier. In this hotel the "light fantastic toe" was tripped to the airs of "Money Musk," "Virginia Reel," "French Four," and "Pine Creek Lady." The orchestra for these occasions was George Hayes, a colored fiddler of the town, who could play the violin behind his back as well as before his face, with his left or right hand, and asleep or awake. I could name quite a number of ladies in the town now whom I used to see enjoying themselves in this way. The third was the "Franklin House," built by John Gelvin, and then kept by John Pierce. The Central Hotel, owned by S. B. Arthurs, has been erected on the ground occupied by the Franklin. The fourth was on the corner of Main and Barnett Streets, erected by John Dougherty. It swung the sign,—

"Peace and Poverty, by John Dougherty."

In 1840 it was occupied and kept by John Gallagher. Each of these hotels had license, and sold whiskey at three cents a drink, mostly on credit. You could have your whiskey straight, or have brown sugar or "tansy bitters" in it. The bars had to be opened regularly on Sunday for "morning bitters." Single meals were given for twenty-five cents, a "check" or cold meal for a "'leven-penny bit," and a bed for ten cents. You could stop overnight, have supper, bed, morning bitters, and breakfast, all for fifty cents.

The Susquehanna and Waterford turnpike was completed in 1822–23. It was a good road, and was kept in fair repair. In 1840 it passed from under State control, and the magnitude of the travel over it was great. The stage line was started in 1825. Morrow started his team in 1835, and cattle and other droving commenced in 1835. All this I am told; but I know the stage was a big factor in 1840. Morrow was on time, and droving was immense. I have seen passing through Brookville on their way east from four to six droves of cattle in a day. The droves were generally divided into three sections. At the head of the first would be a man leading a big ox, his extra clothing strapped on the ox's head, and the man would be crying out ever and anon, "K-o, b-o-s-s;" "Come, boss." I have seen two and three droves of sheep pass in a day, with occasionally a drove of hogs sandwiched between them. Horse droves were numerous, too. I have seen a few droves of colts, and a few droves of turkeys. I could not give an estimate of the number of these droves I have seen passing our home in a day. The business of droving began in June of each year, and ended in November. There was no other way to take this merchandise east than to drive it.

But you must not think everybody was going east. A big lot of people were going west, including their cousins and their aunts. This turnpike was the shortest line west. We lived where T. L. Templeton now lives, and every few days all through the summer months I would see, nearly opposite the Baptist church, in the middle of the street, two men and a dog, and one of the men usually carrying a gun. They were the advance-guard for an "emigrant train." In a few minutes from one to six wagons would come in sight and stop,—all stopping here for a

PIONEER HISTORY OF JEFFERSON COUNTY, PENNA.

short rest. "Where are you going?" was the usual inquiry. "Going West; going to Ohio." The wagons were heavy, wide-tracked, covered with hoops and a white canvas, and had a stiff tongue and iron pole-chains. The horses wore heavy harness with iron trace-chains. An occasional emigrant would locate in our county, but the great majority generally struggled on for the far West,—Ohio.

The usual mode of travel for the people was on foot or on horseback; but the most interesting mode was the daily stage, which "brought" and "took" the mail and carried the passengers who were going east or west. This was the "limited mail," and the "day and night express" of these days,—a through train, only stopping thirty minutes for meals. Of course this "limited mail," this "day and night express," over this "short route," eclipsed and overshadowed every other line and mode of travel. It was "grand, startling, and stupendous." There were no through tickets sold, to be

"Punched, punched with care,
Punched in the presence of the passengaire."

The fare was six cents a mile in advance, and to be paid in "bimetallism." When the officials made their usual tour of inspection over this "road," they had extended to them the genuine hospitality of everybody, including that of the landlords, and free whiskey. President Roberts, of the great Pennsylvania line, is a small potato to-day in contrast with the chief manager of our line in that day, for our line was then the vanguard of every improvement a passenger might desire or a traveller wish for.

The coaches were made in Concord, New Hampshire, and were called "rockaway coaches." Each coach had heavy leather belt-springs, and was a handsome vehicle, painted red, with gold stripes and letters, and was drawn by four horses. The coach was made to carry nine passengers, but I have often seen it with a dozen inside, two on the seat with the driver, and some on top. Trunks were carried on the top and in the "boot." Every driver carried a horn, and always took a "horn." When nearing a "relay" or a post-office, the valleys and hills were made to echo and re-echo to the "er-r-a h, er-r-a-h, tat, tat, t-a-h, tat t-a-h" of the driver's horn, which was to attract the attention of the landlord or postmaster by night or by day. Sometimes the coaches were the most ordinary hacks, and the horses could be "seen through," whether sick or well, without the aid of any X-rays.

The roads in spring, summer, and fall were a succession of mud-holes, with an occasional corduroy. Don't mention bad roads now. The male passengers usually walked up the hills.

I take from an old paper the experience of one who rode in these stages:

PIONEER HISTORY OF JEFFERSON COUNTY, PENNA.

> " Jolted, thumped, distracted,
> Rocked, and quite forlorn.
> Oh! wise one, what duties
> Now are laid on corn?
> Mad, disgusted, angry,
> In a swearing rage,
> 'Tis the very d—l
> Riding in this stage."

The prominent stage-drivers in 1840 were Gabriel Vastbinder, Bill Adams, Joe Stratton, and others. Each driver carried a whip made as follows: a hickory stock, and a buckskin lash ten or twelve feet long, with a silk cracker on the end. These whips were handled with marvellous dexterity by drivers, and were made to crack over the horses' heads like pistols. The great pride of a driver then was to turn a "coach-and-four" with the horses on a "complete run." Bill Adams was good at this. A laughable incident occurred in one of these turns on Main Street. The driver was showing off in his usual style, and in making the turn with the horses on a complete run the coach struck a stone, which upset it. The weight of all the passengers coming against the coach-door burst it open, and the passengers, one and all, were thrown out and literally dumped into the hotel bar-room. This was a perfection in stage driving not easily attained.

In 1840 the Brookville merchant kept his own books,—or, as he would have said, his own accounts,—wrote all his letters with a quill, and when they were written let the ink dry or sprinkled it with sand. There were then no envelopes, no postage stamps, no letter-boxes in the streets, no collection of the mail. The letter written, the paper was carefully folded, sealed with wax or a wafer, addressed, and carried to the post-office, where postage was prepaid at rates which would now seem extortionate.

In 1840, Brookville merchants purchased their goods in Philadelphia. These purchases were made in the spring and fall. It took about two and a half days continuous travelling in the "limited mail" day and night stage-coach to reach Lewistown, Pennsylvania, and required about one day and a half travelling over the canal and railroad to reach Philadelphia from that point. From Brookville to Philadelphia it required some four or five days' constant travelling. Our merchants carried their money on these trips as well as they could, mostly secreted in some way about their persons. After purchasing their goods in Philadelphia, they were ordered to be shipped to Brookville as "heavy freight," over the great corporation freight line of "Joe Morrow." Joe was a "bloated corporationist," a transportation monopolist of that day. He was a whole "trust" in himself. He owned and managed the whole line, and had no opposition, on this end at least. His line consisted of two Conestoga wagons, the bed on each at least four feet high and sixteen feet long. Each wagon was painted blue, and each was covered with a white canvas, this covering supported by hoops. The wagon was always loaded and unloaded from the rear end. The tires on the wheels were six inches wide. Each wagon would carry over three tons of freight, and was drawn over good roads by six magnificent horses, and over bad roads by

Bennett's stage and Morrow's team.

eight of such horses. This was the "fast" and heavy freight line from Philadelphia to Brookville until the canal was built to Lewistown, Pennsylvania, when Morrow changed his head-quarters from Philadelphia to Lewistown, and continued to run his semi-annual "freight train" from Lewistown to Brookville. Morrow's advent into town was always a great

PIONEER HISTORY OF JEFFERSON COUNTY, PENNA.

event. He always stopped his "train" in front of the Red Lion Hotel, then kept by John Smith. The horses were never stabled, but stood day and night in the street, three on each side of the stiff tongue of the wagon, and were fed in a box he carried with him, called his "feed-trough." The harness was broad and heavy, and nearly covered the horses; and they were "hitched up" to the wagon with iron "pole" and "trace-chains." The Brotherhood of Locomotive Engineers, the Switchmen's Union, the "American Railway Union," and all the Sovereigns and Debses put together, had no terrors for Joe, for he had but one employee, a "brakeman," for his second wagon. Joe was the employed and the employer. Like a "transportation king," like a "robber baron," he sat astride a wagon saddle on the hind near horse, driving the others with a single line and a blacksnake whip, to the words, "Gee," "Jep," and "Haw." Morrow always remained in Brookville four or five days, to buy our products and load his train for the home trip. He bought and loaded clover, timothy, and flaxseed, feathers, old rags, tar, beeswax, wheat, rye, chestnuts, furs, and dried elderberries. The western terminus of his line was Shippenville, Clarion County, Pennsylvania, and on his return from there he bought up these products.

Morrow's last trip to Brookville with his train was about the year 1850. He was an Irishman, slim, wiry, industrious, and of business habits. He was killed by the kick of a horse, at Cross's tavern, Centre County, Pennsylvania,—kicked on the 11th day of September, 1855, and died on the 12th. I remember that he usually wore a spotted fawn-skin vest, made from the skin with the hair on. The merchants in Brookville of that day who are still living, and for whom Morrow hauled goods, as far as I can recollect, are Uriah Matson, Harry Matson, Judge Henderson, Samuel Truby, Wm. Rodgers, and W. W. Corbett, who now reside in or near the town, Captain John Hastings, of Punxsutawney, W. F. Clark, of Maquoketa, Iowa, and S. M. Moore, of Minneapolis, Minnesota.

The town was laid out in 1830. My father moved here in 1832. He taught the first term of the school in the town, in the winter of 1832. He was lieutenant-colonel in the militia, a justice of the peace, and was county treasurer when he died, in 1837, at the early age of twenty-seven years, leaving my mother in this wilderness, a widow with three small children to support and rear. In 1840 my mother taught a summer term of school in what was then and is now called the Butler school-house. This school house is on the Ridgway road, in Pine Creek township, three miles from town. I was small, and had to go and come to and from this school with mother. We came home every Saturday to remain over Sunday, and to attend Presbyterian church, service being then held in the old brick court-house. The Presbyterians then called their church "Bethel." In 1842 it was changed to Brookville. We had no choir in the church then, but had a "clerk," who would stand in front of the pulpit, read out two lines, and then sing them, then read two more and sing them, and so on until the hymn or psalm was sung, the congregation joining in as best they could. Of these clerks, the only ones I can now recollect were Thomas Lucas, Samuel McQuiston, and John S. Lucas. I have no recollection of David's psalms being used other than is found in Watts's version, in combination with the hymns. I recollect two of the favorite hymns at that time with this church. The first verse of each hymn was as follows :

"When I can read my title clear
To mansions in the skies,
I'll bid farewell to every fear,
And wipe my weeping eyes."

The first verse of the second hymn was :

"There is a land of pure delight,
Where saints immortal reign ;
Infinite day excludes the night,
And pleasures banish pain."

One by one, these early pioneer Christians have left for this "land of pure delight!" to occupy these "mansions in the skies." I hope and pray that each one is now—

"In seas of heavenly rest."

After returning home from the Butler school-house one Saturday, I remember I asked my mother for a "piece." She went to the cupboard, and when she got there the cupboard was not bare, for, lo ! and behold, a great big snake was therein, coiled and ready for fight. My mother, in horror, ran to the door and called Mr. Lewis Dunham, a lawyer, who lived in the house now occupied by R. M. Matson, Esq. Mr. Dunham came on a run, and tried to catch or kill the snake with our "tongs," but it made good its escape through a big hole in the corner of the cupboard. Reptiles, such as black-, rattle-, house-, and other snakes were very plenty then in and around Brookville, and dangerous, too. These snakes fed and lived on birds, mice, etc., and were very fond of milk, which they drink after the manner of a horse.

In a former chapter I called Brookville a town of shanties. And so it was ; but there was one exception, there was one solid building, a dwelling occupied by a man named Bliss, on Water Street, on or near the lot at present owned and occupied by Billy Barr. It was built of logs. The other shanties were solid enough, for they were built in a different manner from shanties now, being put together with "frame timbers," mortised and tenoned, and fastened with oak pins, as iron and nails were scarce, people being poor and having little or no money. Every building had to have a "raising," and the neighbors had to be invited to help "raise." Cyrus Butler, a bluff, gruff Yankee, was the captain at all raisings. He would stand off by himself, crying out at the proper time, "All together, men, he-o he! he-o-he!"

My mother.
"Who ran to help me when I fell,
And would some pretty story tell,
And kiss the place to make it well?
My mother!"

No dwelling in the town was then complete without having in the back-yard an "out-oven," an "ash-hopper," a "dye-kettle," and a rough box fastened to the second story of the necessary, in which to raise early cabbage-plants. At the rear of each kitchen was a hop-vine with its pole, and each family raised its own catnip, peppermint, sage, and tansy.

"The hand of the reaper
Takes the leaves that are hoary,
But the voice of the weeper
Wails manhood in glory."

PIONEER HISTORY OF JEFFERSON COUNTY, PENNA.

In 1840 there was a law requiring the enrollment of all able-bodied men between twenty-one and forty-five years of age in the militia. These were formed into companies and battalions, and organized into brigades, each brigade to meet once a year in "encampment," for a period of three days, two days for "muster and drill" and one day for "review." The encampments were held in May or June, and for some reason or other these soldiers were called the "cornstalk militia," because some of the soldiers carried cornstalks for guns. No uniforms were worn in most cases. The soldier wore his homespun or store-clothes, and each one reported with his own pike, wooden gun, rifle, or musket, and, under the inspiring influence of his accoutrements, discipline, and drill,—

"Each bosom felt the high alarms,
And all their burning pulses beat to arms."

For non-attendance by a soldier at these encampments a fine of fifty cents was imposed for every day's absence. This fine had to be paid in cash, and was quite a severe penalty in those days of no money, county orders, and store barter.

The first encampment I remember was held on what is now called Granger (Jack) Heber's farm. Brigadier General Mercer was the commander then. He rode a sorrel horse, with a silver mane and tail, and a curled moustache. His bridle was ornamented with fine leather straps, balls, and tassels, and the blue saddle-cloth was covered with stars and spangles, giving the horse the appearance of a "fiery dragon." The general would occasionally dismount, to make some inspection on foot, when the army was drawn up in line, and then a great race, and frequently a fight, would occur among the small boys for the possession of the horse. The reward for holding him at this time was a "fippenny-bit." The camp grounds were alive with whiskey-sellers, ginger-bread and small beer dealers. Whiskey was to be had from barrels or jugs, in large or small quantities. When the army was in line it was dealt out to the soldiers from a bucket with a dipper. Anybody could sell whiskey and anybody could drink it. It was worth from twelve to twenty cents a gallon. The more brawls and fist-fights, the livelier, better, and greater was considered the muster. The bad blood between neighbors was always settled here. Each party always resolved to meet the other on review-day to fight it out, and after the fight to meet, drink together, and make up their difference. Pugilism was practised in that day, not on scientific principles, but by main strength. The terror of all public gatherings was a man called "Devil John Thompson." He lived in Indiana County, and came here always on reviews. Each military company had a fifer or drummer, seldom a complete band. I have seen the late Judge Taylor blowing his fife, the only musician of and for one of these companies. This occurred on Main Street, in front of our house;

PIONEER HISTORY OF JEFFERSON COUNTY, PENNA.

and when I look back on this soldier scene, it seems to me these soldiers, from their appearance, must have been composed of the rag-tag and bob-tail of creation. An odd and comic sight it really was. To be an officer or captain in one of these companies was considered a great honor, and something which the recipient was in duty bound to thank God for in his morning and evening prayers. I cannot do this subject justice. Such was the Pennsylvania militia as I saw it, and all that remains for me to say is, "Great the State and great her sons."

In 1840 we had two big men in the town,—Judge William Jack, who was sent to Congress, and who built and lived in the house on Pickering Street now owned and occupied by Joseph Darr, Esq., and General Levi G. Clover, who lived on Main Street, in a house that was burned down, which stood on the lot now owned by Mrs. Clarissa Clements, and is the place of business of Misses McLain and Fetzer. Clover was a big man physically, a big man in the militia, a big man in politics, and a big man in business. Like most big men in those days, he owned and ran a whiskey-still. This distillery was located on or near the property of Fred. Starr, in what is now Litchtown. I used to loaf occasionally in this distillery, and I have seen some of our old citizens take a pint tin cup and dip it full of whiskey from out of Clover's copper kettles, and then drink this whole pint of whiskey down apparently at one gulp. I might pause to say right here, that in drinking whiskey, racing, square pulling, swearing, and fighting the old settler was "right in it." The wrestling- and fighting-ground then for the men and boys was the ground now occupied by the Jenks machine-shop, and the highway to and from these grounds was down the alley between Ed. Snyder's blacksmith-shop and C. A. Carrier's store. I have had business on that ground with some boys myself.

In the woods in and around Brookville in 1840 there were many sweet-singing birds and beautiful wild-flowers. I remember the laurel. We used to adorn our mantels and parlor fireplaces with these every spring. I remember the honeysuckle, the wild rose, the crab-apple tree, the thorn, and others. The aroma from many of these flowers was delightful. House-plants were unknown. The garden flowers of that day were the pink ("a flower most rare"), the lilac, the hollyhock, the sunflower, and the rose. Each garden had a little bed of "sweet-williams" and "johnny-jump ups." The garden rose was a beautiful, sweet flower then, and it is a beautiful, sweet flower to-day, and it ever will be sweet and beautiful. My mother used to sing to me this hymn of Isaac Watts's as a lullaby:

"How fair is the rose, what a beautiful flower!
In summer so fragrant and gay;
But its leaves are beginning to fade in an hour;
And they wither and die in a day.

PIONEER HISTORY OF JEFFERSON COUNTY, PENNA.

"Yet the rose has one powerful virtue to boast
 Above all the flowers of the field:
When its leaves are all dead and its fine colors lost,
 Still how sweet a perfume it will yield.

"So frail are the youth and the beauty of men,
 Though they look gay and bloom like the rose,
Yet all our fond care to preserve them is vain,
 Time kills them as fast as he goes.

"Then I'll not be proud of my youth or my beauty,
 Since both will soon wither and fade,
But gain a good name by performing my duty;
 This will scent like the rose when I'm dead."

In 1840 there was no church building in the town. Our Presbyterian preacher in the town was the Rev. David Polk, a cousin to President Polk. The token was then given out on Saturday to all those who were adjudged worthy to sit at the Lord's table. These tokens were taken up on the following Sunday while seated at the table. Friday was "fast" or preparation day. We were not allowed to eat anything, or very little, until the sun went down. I can only remember that I used to get hungry and long for night to come. Rev. Polk preached half of his time in Corsica, the other half in Brookville. His salary was four hundred dollars per year,—two hundred dollars from Brookville and two hundred dollars from Corsica. He lived on the pike in the hollow beyond and west of Roseville. He preached in the courthouse until the Presbyterians completed the first church building in the town, in 1843. It stood where the church now stands, and was then outside of the borough limits. The building was erected through the efforts of a lawyer then residing in Brookville, named C. A. Alexander. The ruling elders of the church then were Thomas Lucas, John Matson, Sr., Elijah Clark, John Lattimer, Joseph McCullough, and John Wilson.

Other preachers came to town occasionally in 1840, and held their services in the court-house. One jolly, aged Welshman was called Father Thomas. He was a Baptist, a dear old man, and a great singer. I always went to his church to hear him sing. I can sing some of his songs yet. I will repeat a stanza from one of his favorites:

"Oh, then I shall be ever free,
 Happy in eternity,
 Eternity, eternity,
 Happy in eternity."

Dear old soul, he is in eternity, and I have no doubt is happy singing his favorite song there.

PIONEER HISTORY OF JEFFERSON COUNTY, PENNA.

A Methodist preacher named Elijah Coleman came here occasionally. Methodist head-quarters were at David Henry's and at Cyrus Butler's. The first Methodist prayer-meeting held in town was at Cyrus Butler's. It was held in the little yellow house occupied for years by Mrs. Rachel Dixon, and torn down by C. C. Benscoter, Esq., in 1887, in order to erect his present dwelling. In 1840 men and women were not permitted to sit on the same seat in church, or on the same side of the house.

The physicians in the town in 1840 were Dr. George Darling, father of the late Paul Darling, and Dr. Gara Bishop, father of Mrs. Edmund English. Dr. Bishop was also a Presbyterian preacher.

In 1840, Jefferson County contained a population of seven thousand two hundred and fifty-three people, and embraced nearly all of Forest and Elk Counties. Ridgway was then in the northeast corner of our county, and Punxsutawney was a village of about fifteen or twenty dwellings.

The politics of the county was divided into Whig and Democrat. The leading Whigs in Brookville, as I recollect them, were Thomas Lucas, Esq., James Corbett, father of Colonel Corbett, Benjamin Mc-Creight, father of Mrs. Dr. Hunt, Thomas M. Barr, and Samuel H. Lucas. The leading Democrats were Hon. William Jack, General L. G. Clover, Judge Joseph Henderson, John Smith, Daniel Smith, Jesse G. Clark, father of Judge Clark, D. B. Jenks, John Dougherty, Richard Arthurs, and Thomas Hastings. Politics ran so high that year that each party had its own Fourth of July celebration. The Whigs celebrated at Port Barnett. Nicholas McQuiston, the miller who died at Langville a few years ago, had one of his legs broken at this celebration by the explosion of a log which he had filled with powder. The Democrats celebrated in Brookville, in front of the Franklin Hotel, now the Central. I was big enough to have a full run and clear view of this table and celebration. The table was covered with small roasted pigs, roasted turkeys, venison, pies, gingerbread, "pound-cake," etc. I was not allowed to participate in the feast, although my father in his lifetime had been a Democrat. Boys and girls were then taught modesty, patience, and manners by parents. Children were taught and compelled to respect age and to defer to the wishes of father and mother. Now the father and mother must defer to the wishes of children. There was more home and less public training of children, and, as a result, children had more modesty and patience and less impudence. In 1840 children slept in "trundle-beds," and were required by their mothers to repeat every night before going to sleep this little prayer:

"Now I lay me down to sleep,
I pray the Lord my soul to keep;
If I should die before I wake,
I pray the Lord my soul to take."

PIONEER HISTORY OF JEFFERSON COUNTY, PENNA.

This home training was a constant building up of individual character, and I believe a much more effectual way for good than the present public way of building character collectively.

In 1840 our Congressman was Judge Jack, of Brookville, and our member of the Legislature was Hon. James L. Gillis, of Ridgway township. The county officers were: Prothonotary, General Levi G. Clover; Sheriff, John Smith; Treasurer, Jesse G. Clark; Commissioners, Daniel Coder, Irwin Robinson, and Benjamin McCreight. The county was Democratic by one hundred and twenty-five majority.

The postmaster in Brookville was John Dougherty, and Joseph Henderson was deputy United States marshal for Jefferson County. He took the census of 1840 for our county.

Of the above-named politicians and officials, Judge Henderson is the only one now living (1895). Every day yet the judge can be found at his place of business, pleasant, cheerful, and intelligent,—a fine old gentleman. In his many political contests I always admired, defended, and supported him. One thing I begin to notice, "he is not as young as he used to be."

"Oh, tell me the tales I delighted to hear,
    Long, long ago, long, long ago;
Oh, sing me the old songs so full of cheer,
    Long, long ago, long, long ago."

In 1840 we boys amused ourselves in the winter months by catching rabbits in box-traps,—the woods were full of them,—skating on Geer's pond, a small lake then located where Allgeier's brewery now stands (this lake was destroyed by the building of Mabon's mill-race), skating on Barr's (now Litch's) dam, and coasting down the town or graveyard hill. In the summer and fall months the amusements were alley-ball behind the court-house, town-ball, over-ball, sock-ball, fishing in the streams and in Geer's pond, riding floats of slabs on the creek, swimming in the "deep hole," and gathering blackberries, crab-apples, wild plums, and black and yellow haws. But the amusement of all amusements, the one that was enjoyed every day in the year by the boys, was the cutting of firewood. The wood for heating and cooking was generally hauled in "drags" to the front door of each house on Main Street, and there cut on the "pile" by the boys of each house. The gathering of hazel-nuts, butternuts, hickory-nuts, and chestnuts was an agreeable and profitable recreation. My boy associates of those days—where are they? I can only recall the following, who are now living in Brookville: David Eason, W. C. Evans, Dr. C. M. Matson, Thomas E. Espy, Thomas P. McCrea, Daniel Burns, Clover Smith, W. C. Smith, and W. R. Ramsey. I understand John Craig, Frederick and Lewis Dunham, Elijah and Lorenzo Lowell, and Alexander Barr live in the State of Iowa, Richard Espy in Kentucky, and John L. and Anson Warren in Wisconsin.

In 1840 every housewife in Brookville cooked over a fireplace, in which a crane was fastened so as to swing in, out, off, on, and over the fire. Every fireplace had a wooden poker, a pair of tongs to handle burning wood, and a shovel to remove the ashes. The fuel used was wood,—pine, maple, oak, birch, and hickory. To every fire there had to be a "back log," and the smaller or front pieces were supported on "andirons" or common stones. Matches were not in use, hence fires were covered at night so as to preserve some live coals for the morning fire. Rich people had a little pair of bellows to blow these live coals into a blaze, but poor people had to do the best they could with their

Kitchen and fireplace in 1840.

mouths. After having nearly smoked my eyes out trying to blow coals into life, I have had to give it up and go to a neighbor to borrow a shovel of fire. Some old settlers used "spunk," a flint, and a barlow knife to start a fire in an emergency like this. Spunk—punk or touchwood—was obtained from the inside of a hollow white maple-tree. When matches were first brought around great fear was entertained that they might burn everybody out of house and home. My mother secured a tin box with a safe lid in which to keep hers. For some reason they were called locofoco matches.

The crane in the fireplace had a set of rods with hooks on each end, and they were graduated in length so as to hang the kettle at the proper height from the fire. In addition to the kettles we had the long-handled frying-pan, the handle of which had to be supported by some one's hand, or else on a box or a chair. Then there was the three-legged, short-handled spider. It could support itself. And I must not forget the griddle for buckwheat cakes. It had to be suspended by a rod on the crane. Then there was the old bake-kettle, or oven, with legs and a closely-fitted cover. In this was baked the "pone" for the family. I can say truthfully that pone was not used more than thirty days in the month.

This was a hard way to cook. Women would nearly break their backs lifting these heavy kettles on and off, burn their faces, smoke their eyes, singe their hair, blister their hands, and "scorch" their clothes.

Our spoons were pewter and iron; knives and forks were iron with bone handles. The chinaware was about as it is now.

The every-day bonnet of women then was the "sun-bonnet" for summer, and a quilted "hood" for winter. The dress bonnet was made of paper or leghorn, and was in shape something like our coal-scuttles.

In 1840 nearly every wife in Brookville milked a cow and churned butter. The cows were milked at the front door on Main Street. These cows were ornery, ill-looking, ill-fed, straw-stealing, and blue-milk giving creatures. The water with which to wash clothes and do the scrubbing was caught in barrels or tubs from the house-roof. Scrubbing the floors of a house had to be attended to regularly once a week. This scrubbing had to be done with powdered sand and a home made "split broom." Every wife had to make her own soap, bake her own bread, sew and dye all the clothes for the family, spin the wool for and knit the mittens and socks, make the coverlets, quilt the quilts, see that the children's shoes for Sunday were greased with tallow every Saturday night, nurse the sick, give "sheep saffron" for the measles, and do all the cooking. About every family had a cow, dog, cat, pig, geese, and chickens. The town gave these domestic animals the right to "life, liberty, and the pursuit of happiness." Of course, under these sanitary conditions, the town was alive with fleas, and every house was full of bedbugs. Bats were numerous, and the "public opinion" then was that the bats brought the bedbugs. This may be given as an illustration of the correctness of public opinion. However, we were contented and happy, and used to sing,—

"Home, home, sweet, sweet home,
Be it ever so humble, there's no place like home."

In 1840 there were doubtless many fine horses in Jefferson County, yet it seemed to me nearly every horse had stringhalt, ring-bone, spavin, high-step, or poll-evil. Horses with poll-evil were numerous then, but the disease has apparently disappeared. It was an abscess on the horse's head, behind the ears, and was doubtless caused by cruelty to the animal. If a horse did not please his master in his work it was a common thing for his master to knock him down with a handspike, a rail, or the butt end of a blacksnake whip. Poor food and these blows undoubtedly caused this horrible disease. Sick horses were treated in a barbarous manner. When sick they were not allowed to lie down ; hence they were whipped, run, and held upon their feet. I have seen horses held up with handspikes, rails, etc. The usual remedies were bleeding and drenching with filthy compounds. "Bots" was the almost unfailing disease.

The cattle were home stock, big-horned, heavy-bellied, and long-legged. They could jump over almost anything, and could outrun the "devil and his imps." They were poorly fed, received little care, and had little or no stabling. In the spring it was common for cows to be on the "lift." The common trouble with cattle was "hollow horn," "wolf in the tail," and loss of "cud." These were little else than the results of starvation. I have witnessed consultations over a sick cow, when one man would declare positively she had hollow horn, and another declare just as positively it was wolf in the tail. After a spirited dispute they would compromise by agreeing to bore her horn and split her tail. If they had called it hollow belly and wolf in the stomach they would have been nearer the truth. A better remedy would have been a bucket of warm slop, a good stable, and plenty of hay. The remedy for "hollow horn" was to bore a gimlet hole in the horn near the head and then saturate a cloth with spirits of turpentine and wrap it around the horn. The cure for wolf in the tail was to split the tail near the end with a knife, and fill the cut with salt and pepper. The cure for "lifts" was to call the neighbors, lift the cow to her feet and prop her up so she could not lie down again. The cures for loss of "cud" were numerous and filthy. A "sure cure," and common, too, was to roll human excrement in dough and force it down the animal's throat. The same remedy was used for "founder." If the critter recovered, the remedy was the right one ; if it died, the reason was the remedy had been used too late. Of course, these conditions were all imaginary. They were only diseases resulting from exposure and want of nourishing food. A wild onion called "ramp," and a shrub called "tripwood," grew in the woods and were early in their appearance each spring. These, of which the cattle ate freely, were often their only dependence for food.

The hog of that time was a racer, and could outrun the average horse. His snort when startled was something terrible. He was of the "razor-back" variety, long-bodied, long-legged, and long-snouted. By means of his snout he could plough through everything. Of course he was starved in the winter, like all the other animals, and his condition resulting from his starvation was considered a disease and called "black teeth." The remedy for this disease was to knock out the teeth with a hammer and a spike.

Ignorance was the cause of this cruelty to animals. To the readers of this volume the things mentioned are astonishing. But I have only hinted at the barbarities then inflicted on these domestic animals, which had no rights which man was bound to respect. Not until 1866 was any effort made in this country to protect dumb animals from the cruelty of man. In that year Henry Berg organized the American society in New York, and to-day the movement is felt throughout a great portion of the world. In 1890 there were five hundred and forty-seven societies in existence for the prevention of cruelty to animals, two hundred and twenty-three of them in the United States. The work of humane organizations is not a matter of mere sentiment. "The economic necessity for the existence of societies having for their object the better care and protection of animals becomes manifest when it is considered that our industries, our commerce, and the supply of our necessities and comforts depend upon the animal world. In the United States alone it is estimated that there are 14,000,000 horses, valued at $979,000,000. There are also 2,330,000 mules, 16,000,000 milk cows, 36,800,000 oxen and other cattle, 44,000,000 sheep, and 50,000,000 swine. The total domestic animals in 1890 were estimated at 165,000,000, valued at over $2,400,000,000." To-day every good citizen gives these humane societies or their agents his support, and almost every one is against the man or men who in any way abuse dumb beasts.

Along about 1840 the winters were very severe and long, much more so than now. Regularly every fall, commencing in November,—

> "Soft as the eider down,
> Light as the spider gown,
> Came the beautiful snow, till
> Over the meadow lots,
> Over our garden plots,
> Over the ponds and the lakes,
> Lay only beautiful flakes.
> Then with this snowing,
> Puffing and blowing,
> Old Boreas came bellowing by,
> Till over the by-ways,
> And over the highways,
> The snow-drifts were ever so high."

The snow was several feet deep every winter. It came early and remained till late.

I have made frequent reference in these chapters to the old court-house. As I find there is some confusion in regard to its size, and as I find our county history contains this error: "The court-house, a one-story brick building, was finished in 1832," I deem it of sufficient importance to correct these errors, and to state that the court-house was a two-story building, with a one-story wing on the west extending along Main Street.

This wing was divided into two rooms, the first for the prothonotary's office and the other for the commissioners' office. The main building was two-storied, with an attic and belfry. The second story was divided into four good-sized rooms, called jury-rooms. The southwest room was used by the Methodists for a long time for their Thursday evening prayer-meeting. Alexander Fullerton was their janitor. The Union Sunday-school was held here for years also. The northwest room was used as an armory by the Brookville Rifles,—a volunteer company. The other two were used as jury-rooms. I have played in every room of the old building, and know every foot of it. The building cost three thousand dollars. The contractors were John Lucas and Robert P. Barr. It was torn down in 1866 to make room for the present fine structure. Our alley-ball games were all played for years behind the old court-house.

Our first jail was a stone structure, built of common stone, in 1831. It was two stories high, was situated on the northeast corner of the public lot, near Joseph Darr's residence, and fronting on Pickering Street. Daniel Elgin was the contractor. The building was divided into eight rooms, two down-stairs and two up-stairs for the jail proper, and two down-stairs and two up-stairs for the sheriff's residence and office. The sheriff occupied the north part. The early church services in this building were held in the jail part, up stairs. This old jail has a history, not the most pleasant to contemplate or write about. It was used to imprison runaway slaves, and to lodge them overnight, by slave captors. Imprisoning men for no other crime than desiring to enjoy life, liberty, and the pursuit of happiness ! There was a branch of the underground railroad for the escape of slaves running through Brookville at that time. As many as twenty-five of those unfortunate creatures have passed through Brookville in one day. Judge Heath, then living in our town,—a great Methodist and an abolitionist,—had to pay a fine of two thousand dollars for aiding two slaves to escape from this old stone jail ; a big sum of money to pay for performing a Christian, humane act. Was it not ? In this stone jail men were imprisoned for debt, and kept in it until the last penny was paid. I have seen some of the best men of that day in our county imprisoned in this old jail for debt or bail money. I have seen Thomas Hall, than whom I knew no better man, no better Christian, an elder in the Presbyterian church, incarcerated in the old stone jail for bail money. He had bailed a relative for the sum of fifty dollars, and his relative let him suffer. Honest, big-hearted, generous, Christian Thomas Hall ! Thank God that the day for such inhumanities as those stated above are gone forever. This old jail was rented after the new one was erected, and used as a butcher-shop until it was torn down to make room for the present court-house.

In these days of fine carriages and Brookville wagons it might be well to describe the wagon of 1840. It was called the Pennsylvania wagon, was wide-tracked, and had wooden axles with iron skeins on the spindles. The tongue was stiff, and reached about three feet ahead of the horses. The horses were hitched to these wagons by iron trace- and long tongue-chains. In rough roads I used to think every time the tongue would strike a horse on the leg it would break it. Old team horses understood this and would spread out to avoid these leg-blows. The wheels were kept in place by means of an iron strap and linch-pin. Every wagon carried its own tar on the coupling-pole under the hind axle. The carriage of that day was called a dearborn wagon. I am unable to describe these, although I used to see them. The making of tar was one of the industries then. It retailed at twenty and twenty-five cents a gallon, and brought from three to four dollars a barrel at Pittsburg. These old wagons would screech fearfully if they were not kept properly lubricated with this tar.

Big political conventions were held in those days, and a great custom was to have a young lady dressed in white to represent each of the different States, and have all these ladies in one wagon, which would be drawn by four or six horses.

In the hotels of that day the "bar" was constructed for the safety of the bartender. It was a solid structure with a counter in front, from which a sliding door on iron rods could be shoved up and locked, or shut down and locked; hence the hotel man could "bar" himself in and the drunken men out. This was for safety in dispensing whiskey, and is the origin of the word "bar" in connection with hotels. In 1840 all our hotel bars were so made.

Lumbering in 1840 was one of our principal industries. We had no eastern outlet, and everything had to be rafted to Pittsburg. The sawmills were nearly all "up and down" mills. The "thunder-gust" mills were those on small streams. All were driven by flutter-wheels and water. It required usually but one man to run one of these mills. He could do all the work and saw from one to two thousand feet of boards in twelve hours. Pine boards sold in the Pittsburg market then at three and four dollars per thousand; clear pine at ten dollars per thousand. Of course these sales were on credit. The boards were rafted in the creek in "seven-platform" pieces, by means of grubs. The oars were hung on what were called thole-pins. The front of each raft had a bumper and splash board as a protection in going over dams. The creeks then were full of short bends, rocks, and drift. Cables were unknown here, and a halyard made from hickory withes or water-beech was used as a cable to tie up with. "Grousers" were used to assist in tying up. A pilot then received four dollars to the mouth of the creek; forehands, two dollars and expenses. The logging in the woods was all done with oxen. The camp and mill boarding consisted of bread, flitch, beans, potatoes, Orleans molasses, sometimes a little butter, and coffee or

PIONEER HISTORY OF JEFFERSON COUNTY, PENNA.

tea without cream. Woodsmen were paid sixteen dollars a month and boarded, and generally paid in store-orders or trade.

We usually had three floods on which to run this lumber,—spring, June, and fall. At these times rafts were plenty and people were scarce, and, as time and tide wait for no man, whenever a flood came everybody had to turn out and assist to run the rafts. The boy had to leave his school, the minister his pulpit, the doctor abandon his patients, the lawyer his briefs, the merchant his yard-stick, the farmer his crops or seeding. And there was one great compensation in this,—nearly everybody got to see Pittsburg.

"Running down the creek and gigging back" was the business language of everybody. "How many trips have you made?" etc. It took about twelve hours to run a raft from the neighborhood of Brookville to the mouth, or the Allegheny River, and ordinarily it required hard walking to reach home the next day. Some ambitious, industrious pilots would "run down in the daytime and walk back the same night." James T. Carroll has made four of these trips in succession, Joseph Shobert five, and William Green four or five. Of course, these pilots remained down the last night. This extraordinary labor was accomplished without ever going to bed. Although some may be incredulous, these are facts, as the parties interested are still alive (1895). Pilots sometimes ran all night. Joseph Shobert has started from Brookville at five o'clock P.M. and reached the mouth at five o'clock in the morning. Other pilots have done this also.

Pine square timber was taken out and marketed in Pittsburg. No other timber was marketable, and then only the best part of the pine could be hewed and rafted. Often but one stick would be used from a tree. In Pittsburg this timber brought from four to eight cents a foot, running measure.

The square timber business was then *the* business. Every lumberman followed it, and every farmer ran one timber raft at least. The "taking out of square timber" had to be done in the fall, before snow came. The trees were felled, "cut in sticks," "scored in," and hewn smooth and square. Each "lumber tract" had its log cabin and barn. The "sticks" were hauled to the creek on a "bob" sled in the snow by oxen or horses, and banked until time to "raft in" and get ready for the "spring flood." It was the timber trade that made the pioneer prosperous and intelligent.

The lumbermen could contract with hewers for the cutting, scoring, and hewing of pine timber, complete, ready to be hauled, for from three-quarters to one and a quarter cents per foot. All timber was generally well faced on one side, and was rafted with lash-poles of iron-wood or white oak, and securely fastened in position by means of white-oak bows and ash pins. Bows and pins were an article of merchandise then. Bows sold at seventy-five cents a hundred, and ash pins brought fifty cents a hundred. Grubs for board rafts sold at two dollars and fifty cents a hundred. Oar stems were then made from small sapling dead pines,

Rafting on the North Fork.

shaved down. Pine timber or wild lands could then be bought at from one dollar to two dollars per acre.

Along the lower end of our creeks and on the Allegheny River there lived a class of people who caught and appropriated all the loose logs, shingles, boards, and timber they could find floating down the streams.

These men were called by the early lumbermen Algerines, or pirates. The name Algerine originated thus: In the war of 1812 "the dey of Algiers took the opportunity of capturing an American vessel and con-

Rafting on the North Fork.

demning her crew to slavery. Then a powerful squadron, under Porter and Perry, early in 1815, appeared in the Mediterranean, captured the largest frigate in the Algerine navy, and with other naval successes so terrified the dey that he immediately consented to a treaty of amicable relations, surrendered all his prisoners, made certain pecuniary indemnities, and renounced all future claim to any American tribute or payments."

As there has been considerable agitation over my paragraph on poll-evil in horses, I reprint here a slip that has been sent me:

"AN OLD TIME CURE FOR POLL-EVIL.

"ED. SPIRIT,—I am moved by your quotation from Dr. McKnight's article in the *Brookville Democrat* on the old-time nonsense in relation to poll-evil in horses to say that the doctor's explanation of the cause of that severe affliction on the poor brute's head is in part correct; but it was mainly owing to the low door-ways and the low mow-timbers just above the horse's head as he stood in the stall of the old-time log stables. The horse often struck his head on the lintel of the low door-way as he passed in and out; and as he stood in the stall, when roughly treated by his master, in throwing up his head it came in violent contact with the timbers, and continued bruising resulted ultimately in the fearful, painful abscesses referred to. There were those in that day who had reputations for skill in the cure of poll-evil, and their method was this: The afflicted animal must be brought to the doctor before the break of day. An axe was newly ground. The doctor must not speak a word to any person on any subject after the horse was given into his hand until the feat was performed. Before sunrise the doctor took the axe and the horse and proceeded out of sight of any human habitation, going towards the east. When such a spot was reached he turned towards the animal, bent down its head firmly and gently, drew the sharpened blade of the axe first lengthwise, then crosswise of the abscess sufficiently to cause the blood to flow, muttering meanwhile some mystic words; then, just below where the head of the horse was, he struck the bloody axe in the ground, left it there, turned immediately around, walked rapidly away, leading the animal, and not at all looking back until he had delivered it into the hand of the owner, who was waiting at a distance to receive it, and who took it home at once. The next morning at sunrise the axe was removed, and in due time the cure was effected.

"AN OLD-TIMER.

"SMICKSBURG, PA., September 7, 1894."

The first known person to live within the confines of the present borough was Jim Hunt, an Indian of the Muncy tribe. He was here as early as 1797, and was in banishment for killing a warrior of his own tribe. By an Indian law he was not allowed to live in his tribe until the place of the warrior he had slain was filled by the capture of another male from white people or from other Indians. In 1808, Jim's friends stole a white boy in Westmoreland County, Pennsylvania, and had him accepted into the tribe in place of the warrior Jim had killed. Jim Hunt's residence or cave was near the deep hole, or near the sand spring, on Sandy Lick, and was discovered in 1843 by Mr. Thomas Graham. After 1812 Jim Hunt never returned. He was a great bear-hunter, having killed seventy-eight in one winter. He loved "fire-water," and all his earnings went for this beverage; yet he never dared to get so drunk he could not run to his cave when he heard a peculiar Indian whoop on Mill Creek hills. His Indian enemies pursued him, and his Indian friends looked after him and warned him to flee to his hiding-place by a peculiar whoop. Little Snow, a Seneca chief, lived at the sand spring in 1800, and it was then called "Wolf Spring."

The first white person to settle in what is now Brookville was Moses Knapp. He built a log house about 1801 at the mouth of North Fork Creek, on ground now owned by Thomas L. Templeton, near Christ's brewery. The first white child born within the limits of what is now Brookville was Joshua Knapp, on Mr. Templeton's lot, at the mouth of the North Fork, in the month of March, 1810. He is still living (1895) in Pine Creek township, about two miles from the town. About 1806 or 1807, Knapp built a log grist-mill where the waters of the North Fork then entered the Red Bank. It was a rude mill, and had but one run of *rock*-stones. In 1818 he sold this mill to Thomas Barnett. James Parks, Barnett's brother-in-law, came to run this mill about 1824 (Barnett having died), and lived here until about 1830. Parks came from Westmoreland County, Pennsylvania, and brought with him and held in legal slavery here a negro man named "Sam," who was the *first* colored person to live in what is now called Brookville.

Joseph B. Graham, Esq., of Eldred township, informs me that he carried a grist on horseback to this mill of one half-bushel of shelled corn for this Sam to grind. Mr. Graham says his father put the corn in one end of the bag and a big stone in the other end to balance the corn. That was the custom, but the 'squire says they did not know any better. Joshua Knapp, Uriah Matson, and John Dixon all took grists of corn and buckwheat to this mill for "Sam," the miller, to grind.

"Happy the miller who lives by the mill,
For by the turning of his hand he can do what he will."

But this was not so with "Sam." At his master's nod he could grind his own "peck of meal," for his body, his work, his life, and his will belonged to Parks. Many settlers in early days carried corn to the grist-mill on their own shoulders, or on the neck-yoke of a pair of oxen. I have seen both of these methods used by persons living ten and fifteen miles from a mill.

The census of 1830 gives Jefferson County a population of 2003 whites, 21 free colored persons, and 1 colored slave. This slave, we suppose, was "Sam."

Brookville was laid out as the county seat in 1830, but it was not incorporated as a borough until April 9, 1834. (See pamphlet laws of 1834, page 209.) The first house was erected in August, 1830. The first election held in the new borough for officials was in the spring of 1835. Joseph Sharpe was elected constable. Darius Carrier and Alexander McKnight were elected school directors. The first complete set of borough officers were elected in 1835, and were as follows:

Burgess, Thomas Lucas; Council, John Dougherty, James Corbett, John Pierce, Samuel Craig, Wm. A. Sloan; Constable, John McLaughlin (this man McLaughlin was a great hunter, and could neither read nor write; he moved to Brockwayville, and from there went West); School Directors, Levi G. Clover, Samuel Craig, David Henry, C. A. Alexander, Wm. A. Sloan, James Corbett.

In 1840 the borough officers were:

Burgess, William Jack; Council, Elijah Heath, John Gallagher, Cyrus Butler, Levi G. Clover, John Dougherty, William Rodgers; Constable, John Dougherty.

Of these early fathers the only one now living (1895) is Major William Rodgers. He resides about a mile from town, on the Corsica road.

In 1840 the "itch" was in Brookville, and popular all the year round. As bath-tubs were unknown and family bathing rare, this itch was the seven-year kind. Head-lice among the people and in the schools were also common. Had I been familiar with Burns in my boyhood, many a time, while seeing a louse crawl on and over a boy or girl in our schools, I could have exclaimed,—

> "O, Jenny, dinna toss your head
> An' set your beauties a' abraed;
> Ye little ken what cussed speed
> The beast's a makin'."

The only cure for lice was to "rid" out the hair every few days with a big, coarse comb, crack the nits between the thumb-nails, and then saturate the hair with "red precipity," using a fine-tooth comb. The itch was cured by the use of an ointment made of brimstone and lard. During school-terms many children wore little sacks of powdered brimstone about their necks. This was supposed to be a preventive.

In 1840 the only music-books we had were "The Beauties of Harmony" and "The Missouri Harmony." Each of these contained the old "buckwheat" notes of me, fa, sol, la. Every one could not afford one of these books. Music-teachers travelled through the county and taught classes. A class was twenty-six scholars, a term thirteen nights, and the tuition-fee fifty cents for each scholar. Teachers used "tuning-forks," and some played a violin in connection with the class-singing. The teacher opened the singing by exhorting the class to "sound your pitches,—sol, fa, la."

PIONEER HISTORY OF JEFFERSON COUNTY, PENNA.

In 1840, Billy Boo, an eccentric, intelligent hermit, lived in a hut on the farm in Rose township now occupied by William Hughey. Although he lived in this hut, he spent most of his wakeful hours in Brookville. He was a man of good habits, and all that he would tell, or any one could learn of him or his nativity, was that he came from England. He was about five feet five or six inches high, heavy set, and stoop-shouldered. He usually dressed in white flannel clothes. Sometimes his clothing, from being darned so much, looked as if it had been quilted. He lived upon the charity of the people, and by picking up a few pennies for some light gardening jobs. He died as a charge on Brookville borough in 1863.

Indian relics were found frequently on our hills and in our valleys in 1840. They consisted of stone tomahawks, darts, arrows, and flints.

Prior to and during 1840 a form of legalized slavery was practised in this State and county in regard to minor children. Poor or destitute children were "bound out" or indentured by the poor overseers to masters or mistresses, boys until they were twenty-one years of age and girls until they were eighteen. Parents exercised this privilege also. All apprentices were then bound to mechanics to learn trades. The period of this indenture was three years. The law was severe on the children, and in favor of the master or mistress. Under these conditions cruelties were practised, and children and apprentices tried to escape them. Of course, there were bad children who ran away from kind masters and mistresses. The master or mistress usually advertised these runaways. I have seen many of these in our papers. I reprint one of these advertisements, taken from the *Gazette and Columbian*, published by J. Croll & Co., at Kittanning, Armstrong County, Pennsylvania, on August 8, 1832:

"$5 REWARD.

"Run away from the subscriber, living in the borough of Kittanning, on the 22d inst., an indentured apprentice to the Tailoring business, named Henry P. Huffman, between 18 or 19 years of age, stout made and black hair, had on when he went away a light cotton roundabout, and pantaloons of the same, and a new fur hat. Whoever apprehends the said runaway and delivers him to the subscriber in Kittanning shall receive the above reward.

"JOHN WILLIAMS.

"KITTANNING, July 25, 1832."

In the forties the election for State officers was held on the second Tuesday of October of each year, and in the absence of telegraphs, railroads, etc., it took about four weeks to hear any definite result from an election, and then the result was published with a tail to it,—"Pike, Potter, McKean, and Jefferson to hear from." It is amusing to recall

PIONEER HISTORY OF JEFFERSON COUNTY, PENNA.

the reason usually given for a defeat at these elections by the unsuccessful party. It was this: "The day was fine and clear, a good day for threshing buckwheat; therefore our voters failed to turn out." The editor of the defeated party always published this poetic stanza for the consolation of his friends:

> "Truth crushed to earth will rise again,
> The eternal years of God are hers,
> While error, wounded, writhes in pain,
> And dies amidst her worshippers."

In a Presidential contest we never knew the result with any certainty until the 4th of March, or inauguration-day.

In 1840, according to the census, the United States contained a population of 17,062,666 people, of which, 2,487,113 were slaves. The employments of the people were thus divided: Agriculture, 3,717,756; commerce, 117,575; manufactures and trades, 791,545; navigating the ocean, 56,025; navigating rivers, canals, etc., 33,067; mining, 15,203; learned professions, 65,236.

The Union then consisted of 26 States, and we had 223 Congressmen. The ratio of population for a Congressman was 70,680. In this computation five slaves would count as three white men, although the slaves were not allowed to vote. Our Territories were populated thus: District of Columbia, 43,712; Florida, 54,477; Wisconsin, 30,945; Iowa, 43,112. The chief cities and towns were thus populated:

New York	312,710
Philadelphia	228,691
Baltimore	102,313
New Orleans	102,193
Boston	93,393
Cincinnati	46,338
Brooklyn	35,234
Albany	33,721
Charleston	29,261
Washington	23,364
Providence	23,171
Louisville	21,210
Pittsburg	21,115
Lowell	20,796
Rochester	20,191
Richmond	20,133
Buffalo	18,210
Newark	17,293
St. Louis	16,469
Portland	15,218
Salem	16,083
Brookville	276

PIONEER HISTORY OF JEFFERSON COUNTY, PENNA.

Household or family goods were produced in 1840 to the amount of $29,230,380.

Total amount of capital employed in manufactures, $267,726,579.

The whole expenses of the Revolutionary War were estimated, in specie, at $135,193,703.

In 1840 it was the custom for newspapers to publish in one of their issues, after the adjournment of the Legislature, a complete list by title of all the enactments of that session.

In the forties fruit was scarce and inferior in these woods, and as "boys were boys then" all kinds of means, both fair and foul, were resorted to by the boys to get a fill of apples. Johnny Lucas, Johnny Jones, Yankee Smith, and Mrs. Fuller used to bring apples and peaches into the village and retail them out on the street. I have seen this trick played frequently on these venders by two boys,—viz.: a boy would go up to the wagon, holding his cap with both hands and ask for a sixpence worth of apples or peaches. The vender would then count the apples and drop them in the cap. The boy would then let go of the cap with one hand as if to pay, when boy No. 2 would snatch the cap and apples out of his hand and run for dear life down the street and into the first alley. The owner of the cap, in apparent anger, would immediately take after this thief, forget to pay, and in the alley help eat the apples.

In 1840 "shingle weavers" brought their shingles to Brookville to barter. A shingle weaver was a man who did not steal timber. He only went into the pine-woods and there cut the clearest and best tree he could find, and hauled it home to his shanty in blocks, and there split and shaved the blocks into shingles. He bartered his shingles in this way: he would first have his gallon or two-gallon jug filled with whiskey, then take several pounds of Baltimore plug-tobacco, and then have the balance coming to him apportioned in New Orleans molasses, flitch, and flour. Many a barter of this kind have I billed when acting as clerk.

Timothy Pickering & Co., Leroy & Linklain, Welhelm Willink, Jeremiah Parker, Holland Land Company, Robert Morris, Robert Gilmore, William Bingham, John Nicholson, Dr. William Cathcart, Dr. James Hutchinson, and a few others owned about all the land in Jefferson County. This goes a great length to disprove the demagogy you hear so much nowadays about the few owning and gobbling up all the land. How many people own a piece of Jefferson County to-day?

In 1840 the only newspaper published in Jefferson County was the *Backwoodsman*, published in Brookville by Thomas Hastings & Son. Captain John Hastings, who is still living in Punxsutawney, was the son. The terms of this paper were one dollar and seventy-five cents in advance,

PIONEER HISTORY OF JEFFERSON COUNTY, PENNA.

two dollars if paid within the year, and two dollars and fifty cents if not paid within the year. Hastings & Son sold the paper to William Jack. Jack rented the paper to a practical printer by the name of George F. Humes, who continued the publication until after the October election in 1843, when he announced in an editorial that his patrons might go to h—ll and he would go to Texas. Barton T. Hastings then bought and assumed control of the paper, and published it until 1846 as the *Brookville Jeffersonian*. Mr. Hastings is still living in Brookville.

I reprint here a large portion of the proceedings of an old-time celebration of the Fourth of July in 1843 in Brookville. We copy from the *Backwoodsman*, dated August 1, 1843, then edited by George F. Humes. The editorial article in the *Backwoodsman* is copied entire. The oration of D. S. Deering, all the regular toasts, and part of the volunteer toasts are omitted because of their length. Editor Humes's article was headed

"FOURTH OF JULY CELEBRATION.

"The citizens of Brookville and vicinity celebrated the sixty-seventh anniversary of American independence in a spirited and becoming manner. The glorious day was ushered in by the firing of cannon and ringing of bells. At an early hour the 'Independent Greens,' commanded by Captain Hugh Brady, formed into parade order, making a fine appearance, and marched through the principal streets, cheering and enlivening the large body of spectators, whose attention appeared to be solely drawn to their skilful rehearsals of military tactics; and, after spending some time in a course of drilling, joined the large assembly, without distinction of party or feeling, under the organization and direction of John McCrea, Esq., president of the day, and Samuel B. Bishop and Colonel Thomas Wilkins, marshals; when they proceeded to the court-house, where the Declaration of Independence was read in a clear and impressive tone by L. B. Dunham, Esq., after which David S. Deering, Esq., delivered an address very appropriate to the occasion, touching with point and pathos upon the inducements which impelled our fathers to raise the flag of war against the mother-country. The company then formed into line, and proceeded to the hotel of Mr. George McLaughlin, at the head of Main Street, where they sat down to a well-served, delicious, and plentiful repast, the ladies forming a smiling and interesting 'platoon' on one side of the table, which added much to the hilarity of the celebration. After the cloth was removed, and the president and committees had taken their seats, a number of toasts applicable to the times, and as varied in sentiment as the ages of the multitude, were offered and read, accompanied by repeated cheering and a variety of airs from the brass band, thus passing the day in that union and harmony so characteristic of Americans. It was indeed a 'Union celebration.'

PIONEER HISTORY OF JEFFERSON COUNTY, PENNA.

"VOLUNTEER TOASTS.

"By John McCrea. Our Brookville celebration: a union of parties, a union of feeling, the union established by our Revolutionary fathers of '76. May union continue to mark our course until time shall be no more.

"By W. W. Corbett. Liberty, regulated by law, and law by the virtues of American legislators.

"By William B. Wilkins. Henry Clay: a man of tried principles, of admitted competency, and unsullied integrity, may he be the choice of the people for the next Presidency in 1844.

"By Evans R. Brady. The Democrats of the Erie district: a *form*, *locked up* in the *chase* of disorganization; well *squabbled* at one side by the awkward formation of the district. If not *locked tight* by the *sidesticks* of regular nominations, *well driven* by the *quoins* of unity, and *knocked in* by the *sheep's foot* of pure principles, it will be *battered* by the *points* of whiggery, bit by the *frisket* of self-interest; and when the *foreman* comes to *lift it* on the second Tuesday of October, will stand a fair chance to be *knocked* into *pi*

"By Michael Woods. Richard M. Johnston, of Kentucky: a statesman who has been long and thoroughly tried and never found wanting. His nomination for the next Presidency will still the angry waves of political strife, and the great questions which now agitate the nation will be settled upon democratic principles.

"By Hugh Brady. The citizens of Jefferson County: they have learned their political rights by experience; let them practise the lesson with prudence.

"By B. T. Hastings. The Hon. James Buchanan: the Jefferson of Pennsylvania and choice for the Presidency in 1844. H s able and manly course in the United States Senate on all intricate and important subjects entitles him to the entire confidence and support of the whole Democracy.

"By Andrew Craig. Henry Clay: a worthy and honest statesman, who has the good of his country at heart, and is well qualified to fill the Presidential chair.

"By A. Hutcheson. American independence: a virtuous old maid, sixty-eight years old to-day. God bless her.

"By David S. Deering. The Declaration of Independence: a rich legacy, bequeathed us by our ancestors. May it be transmitted from one generation to another until time shall be no more.

"By the company. The orator of the day, David S. Deering: may his course through life be as promising as his commencement.

"By D. S. Deering. The mechanics of Brookville: their structures are enduring monuments of skill, industry, and perseverance.

"By George F. Humes. The American Union: a well-adjusted

form of twenty-six pages, fairly *locked up* in the *chase* of precision by the *quoins* of *good workmen.* May their *proof-sheets* be *well pointed* and their regular *impressions* a perfect *specimen* for the world to look upon.

"By John Hastings. James Buchanan: the able defender of the rights of the people and the *high wages* candidate for the Presidency in 1844. His elevation to that post is now without a doubt."

In 1840 the mails were carried on horseback or in stage-coaches. Communications of news, business, or affection were slow and uncertain. There were no envelopes for letters. Each letter had to be folded so as to leave the outside blank and one side smooth, and the address was written on this smooth side. Letters were sealed with red wafers, and the postage was six and a quarter cents for every hundred miles, or fraction thereof, over which it was carried in the mails. The postage on a letter to Philadelphia was eighteen and three-quarter cents, or three "fippenny bits." You could mail your letter without prepaying the postage (a great advantage to economical people), or you could prepay it at your option. Postage-stamps were unknown. When you paid the postage the postmaster stamped on the letter "Paid." When the postage was to be paid by the person addressed, the postmaster marked on it the amount due, thus: "Due, $6\frac{1}{4}$ cents."

In 1840 nearly half of our American people could neither read nor write, and less than half of them had the opportunity or inclination to do so. Newspapers were small affairs, and the owners of them were poor and their business unprofitable.

The candles used in our houses were either "dips" or "moulds." The "dips" were made by twisting and doubling a number of cotton wicks upon a round, smooth stick at a distance from each other of about the desired thickness of the candle. Then they were dipped into a kettle of melted tallow, when the ends of the sticks were hung on the backs of chairs to cool. The dipping and cooling process was thus repeated till the "dips" attained the proper thickness. This work was done after the fall butchering. "Moulds" were made in tin or pewter tubes, two, four, six, eight, ten, or twelve in a frame, joined together, the upper part of the frame forming a trough, into which the moulds opened, and from which they received the melted tallow. To make the candles, as many wicks as there were tubes were doubled over a small round stick placed across the top of the frame, and these wicks were passed down through the tubes and fastened at the lower end. Melted tallow was poured into the trough at the top till all the tubes were filled. The moulds were usually allowed to stand overnight before the candles were "drawn." The possession of a set of candle-moulds by a family was an evidence of some wealth. These candles were burned in "candlesticks," made of tin, iron, or brass, and each one had a broad, flat base, turned up around the rim to catch the grease. Sometimes, when the candle was exposed

PIONEER HISTORY OF JEFFERSON COUNTY, PENNA.

to a current of air, it would "gutter" all away. A pair of "snuffers," made of iron or brass, was a necessary article in every house and had to be used frequently to cut away the charred or burned wick. Candles sold in the stores at twelve to fifteen cents per pound. One candle was the number usually employed to read or write by, and two were generally deemed sufficient to light a store,—one to carry around to do the selling by, and the other to stand on the desk to do the charging by.

Watches were rare, and clocks were not numerous in 1840. The watches I remember seeing in those days were "English levers" and "cylinder escapements," with some old "bull's-eyes." The clocks in use were of the eight-day sort, with works of wood, run by weights instead of springs. Along in the forties clocks with brass works, called the "brass clock," came into use. A large majority of people were without "time pieces." Evening church services were announced thus: "There will be preaching in this house on —— evening, God willing, and no preventing providence, at early candle-lighting."

In 1840 the judge of our court was Alexander McCalmont, of Franklin, Venango County. Our associate judges from 1841 to 1843 were James Winslow and James L. Gillis. Our local or home lawyers were Hugh Brady, Cephas J. Dunham, Benjamin Bartholomew, Caleb A. Alexander, L. B. Dunham, Richard Arthurs, Elijah Heath, D. B. Jenks, Thomas Lucas, D. S. Deering, S. B. Bishop, and Jesse G. Clark. Many eminent lawyers from adjoining counties attended our courts regularly at this period. They usually came on horseback, and brought their papers, etc., in large leather saddle-bags. Most of these foreign lawyers were very polite gentlemen, and very particular not to refuse a "drink."

Moses Knapp, Sr., was our pioneer court crier. Elijah Graham was our second court crier, but I think Cyrus Butler served in this capacity in 1840.

In 1840 there was no barber-shop in the town. The tailors then cut hair, etc., for the people as an accommodation. My mother used to send me for that purpose to McCreight's tailor-shop. The first barber to locate in Brookville was a colored man named Nathan Smith. He barbered and ran a confectionery and oyster saloon. He lived here for a number of years, but finally turned preacher and moved away. Some high old times occurred in his back room which I had better not mention here. He operated on the Major Rodgers lot, now the Eddleblute property.

Then "Hollow Eve," as it was called, was celebrated regularly on the night of October 31 of every year. The amount of malicious mischief and destruction done on that evening in Brookville, and patiently suffered and overlooked, is really indescribable. The Presidential contest in 1840, between Harrison, Whig, and Van Buren, Democrat, was perhaps the most intense and bitter ever known in this nation.

PIONEER HISTORY OF JEFFERSON COUNTY, PENNA.

The first exclusively drug-store in Brookville was opened and managed by D. S. Deering, Esq., in 1848. It was located in a building where McKnight & Brothers' building now stands, on the spot where McKnight & Son carry on their drug business. The first exclusively grocery-store in Brookville was opened and owned by W. W. Corbett, and was located in the east room of the American Hotel. The first exclusively hardware-store in the town was opened and owned by John S. King, now of Clearfield, Pennsylvania. Brookville owes much to the sagacity of Mr. King for our beautiful cemetery.

In the forties the boring of pitch-pine into pump-logs was quite a business in Brookville. One of the first persons to work at this was Charles P. Merriman, who moved here from the East. By the way, Merriman was the greatest snare-drummer I ever heard. He also manufactured and repaired drums while here. He had a drum-beat peculiarly his own, and with it he could drown out a whole band. He introduced his beat by teaching drumming-schools. It is the beat of the Bowdishes, the Bartletts, and the Schnells. It consists of single and double drags. I never heard this beat in the army or in any other locality than here, and only from persons who had directly or indirectly learned it from Merriman. Any old citizen can verify the marvellous and wonderful power and skill of Merriman with a drum. No pupil of his here ever approached him in skill. The nearest to him was the late Captain John Dowling, of the One Hundred and Fifth Regiment, Pennsylvania Volunteers. It was the custom then for the different bands in the surrounding townships to attend the Fourth of July celebrations in Brookville. The Monger band, father and sons, from Warsaw township, used to come. They had a peculiar open beat that old Mr. Monger called the 1812 beat. The Belleview band came also. It was the Campbell band, father and sons. Andrew C. and James (1895), after going through the war, are still able on our public occasions to enliven us with martial strains. The Lucas band, from Dowlingville, also visited us in the forties. Brookville had a famous fifer in the person of Harvey Clover. He always carried an extra fife in his pocket, because he was apt to burst one. When he "blowed" the fife you would have thought the devil was in it sure.

In 1847 the town had water-works, the enterprise of Judge Jared B. Evans. The Spring that furnished the water was what is now known as the American Spring. The conduit-pipes were bored yellow-pine logs, and the plant was quite expensive, but owing to some trouble about the tannery, which stood on the spot where the American barn now stands, the water-plant was destroyed. Judge Evans was a useful citizen. He died some three years ago.

In 1840 the church collection was either taken up in a hat with a handkerchief in it or in a little bag attached to a pole.

H. Clay Campbell, Esq., has kindly furnished me the legal rights of married women in Pennsylvania from 1840 until the present date. The common law was adopted by Pennsylvania, and has governed all rights except those which may have been modified from time to time by statute. Blackstone's Commentaries, Book I., page 442, says, "By marriage, the husband and wife are one person in law; that is, the very being or legal existence of the woman is suspended during the marriage, or at least is incorporated and consolidated into that of her husband, under whose wing, protection, and cover she performs everything."

You see the rights surrendered by a woman marrying under the common law were two: First, the right to make a contract; secondly, the right to property and her own earnings. To compensate for this she acquired *one right*,—the right to be chastised. For as the husband was to answer for her misbehavior, the law thought it reasonable to intrust him with the power of restraining her, by domestic chastisement, with the same moderation that a man is allowed to correct his apprentice or his children.

In 1840 married women had no right to the property bequeathed to them by their parents, unless it was put into the hands of a trustee, and by marriage the husband became the immediate and absolute owner of the personal property of the wife which she had in possession at the time of marriage, and this property could never again revert to the wife or her representatives. She could acquire no personal property during marriage by industry, and if she obtained any by gift or otherwise, it became immediately by and through the law the property of her husband. This condition prevailed until the passage of an act, dated 11th of April, 1848, which in some slight degree modified this injustice of the common law. By that act it was provided that all property which belonged to her before marriage, as well as all that might accrue to her afterwards, should remain her property. Then came another modification by the act of 1855, which provided, among other things, that "whenever a husband, from drunkenness, profligacy, or other cause, shall neglect or refuse to provide for his wife, she shall have the rights and privileges secured to a *femme-sole* trader under the act of 1713." Modifications have been made from year to year, granting additional privileges to a wife to manage her own property, among which may be noted the act of 1871, enabling her to sell and transfer shares of the stock of a railroad company. By the act of May, 1874, she may draw checks upon a bank. During all these years of enlightenment the master has still held the wife in the toils of bondage, and it was with great grudging that he acknowledged that a married woman had the right to claim anything. The right to the earnings of the wife received its first modification when the act of April, 1872, was passed, which granted to the wife, if she went into court, and the court granted her petition, the right to claim her earnings. But legally the wife remained the most abject of slaves until the passage of the "married woman's personal property act" of 1887, giving and granting to her the right to contract and acquire property; and it was not until 1893 that she was granted the same rights as an unmarried woman, excepting as to her right to convey her real estate, make a mortgage, or become bail.

The higher education of women in the seminary and college is of American origin, and in 1840 there was an occasional young ladies' seminary here and there throughout the country. These isolated institutions were organized and carried on by scattered individuals who had great persistency and courage. Being of American origin its greatest progress has been here, and at present there are more than two hundred institutions for the superior education of women in the United States, and fully one-half of these bear the name of college. The women who graduate to-day from colleges and high schools outnumber the men, and as a result of this mental discipline and training women are now found throughout the world in every profession, in all trades, and in every vocation.

> "Preferring sense from chin that's bare
> To nonsense 'throned in whiskered hair."

Women are now admitted to the bar in nine different States of the Union, and by an act of Congress she may now practise before the United States Supreme Court.

In 1840 women had but one vocation for a livelihood,—viz., marriage and housekeeping. Then female suffrage was unknown. To-day (1895) women vote on an equality with men in two States, Colorado and Wyoming, and they can vote in a limited form in twenty other States and Territories.

In 1840 women had no religious rights. She did not dare to speak, teach, or pray in public, and if she desired any knowledge in this direction, she was admonished to ask her husband at home. The only exception I know to this rule was in the Methodist Church, which from its organization has recognized the right of women to teach, speak in class-meetings, and to pray in the public prayer-meeting.

In 1840 women had no industrial rights. I give below a little abstract from the census of 1880, fourteen years ago, which will show what some of our women were working at then and are working at now.

FEMALE WORKERS.

Artists, 2016; authors, 320; assayists, chemists, and architects, 2136; barbers, 2902; dress-makers, 281,928; doctors, 2433; journalists, 238; lawyers, 75; musicians, 13,181; preachers, 165; printers, 3456; tailors, 52,098; teachers, 194,375; nurses, 12,294; stock raisers, 216; farmers, 56,809; in government employ as clerks, 2171; managing commercial and industrial interests, 14,465. And now in 1894 we have 6000 post-

PIONEER HISTORY OF JEFFERSON COUNTY, PENNA.

mistresses, 10,500 women have secured patents for inventions, and 300,000 women are in gainful occupations. I confess that this statement looks to the intelligent mind as though "the hand that rocks the cradle" will soon not only move but own the world.

The earliest schools established by the settlers of Pennsylvania were the home school, the church school, and the public subscription school, the most simple and primitive in style. The subscription or public school remained in force until the law of 1809 was enacted, which was intended for a State system, and which provided a means of education for the poor, but retained the subscription character of pay for the rich. This 1809 system remained in force until 1834. The method of hiring "masters" for a subscription school was as follows: A meeting was called by public notice in a district. At this gathering the people chose, in their own way, three of their number to act as a school committee. This committee hired the master and exercised a superintendence over the school. The master was paid by the patrons of the school in proportion to the number of days each had sent a child to school. A rate-bill was made out by the master and given to the committee, who collected the tuition-money and paid it to the master. The terms of these schools were irregular, but usually were for three months.

The studies pursued were spelling, reading, writing, and arithmetic. The daily programme was two or four reading lessons, two spelling lessons,—one at noon and one at evening,—the rest of the time being devoted to writing and doing "sums" in arithmetic. It was considered at that time (and even as late as my early schooling) that it was useless and foolish for a girl to learn more at school than to spell, read, and write. Of course there was no uniformity in text-books. The child took to the school whatever book he had, hence there was, and could be, no classification. Black-boards were unknown. When any information was wanted about a "sum," the scholar either called the master or took his book and went to him.

The first school-master in Jefferson County was John Dixon. His first term was for three months, and was in the year 1803 or 1804. The first school-house was built on the Ridgway road, two miles from Brookville, on the farm now owned by D. B. McConnell. I give Professor Blose's description of this school-house:

"The house was built of rough logs, and had neither window-sash nor pane. The light was admitted through chinks in the wall, over which greased paper was pasted. The floor was made with puncheons, and the seats from broad pieces split from logs, with pins in the under side, for legs. Boards laid on pins fastened in the wall furnished the pupils with writing-desks. A log fireplace, the entire length of one end, supplied warmth when the weather was cold."

The era of these log school-houses in Jefferson County is gone,—gone forever. We have now (1895) school property to the value of $269,300. We have 196 modern school-houses, with 262 school-rooms, 295 schools, and the Bible is read in 251 of these. There is no more *master's* call in the school-room, but we have 131 female and 149 male *teachers*,—a total of 280 teachers in the county. The average yearly term is six and a half months. The average salary for male teachers is $39 50, and for female teachers, $33. Total wages received by teachers each year, $64,913.20. Number of female scholars, 5839; number of male scholars, 6073. The amount of tax levied for school purposes is $56,688.23. Received by county from State appropriation, $42,759.72.

The act of 1809 made it the duty of assessors to receive the names of all children between the ages of five and twelve years whose parents were unable to pay for their schooling, and these poor children were to be educated by the county. This law was very unpopular, and the schools did not prosper. The rich were opposed to this law because they paid all the tax-bills, and the poor were opposed to it because it created a "caste" and designated them as paupers. However, it remained in force for about twenty-five years, and during this period the fight over it at elections caused many strifes, feuds, and bloody noses. This was the *first* step taken by the State to evolve our present free-school system. The money to pay for the education of these "pauper" children was drawn from the county in this way: "The assessor of each borough or township returned the names of such indigent children to the county commissioners, and then an order was drawn by the commissioners on the county treasurer for the tuition-money."

One of the most desirable qualifications in the early school-master was courage, and willingness and ability to control and flog boys. Physical force was the governing power, and the master must possess it. Nevertheless, many of the early masters were men of intelligence, refinement, and scholarship. As a rule, the Scotch-Irish master was of this class. Goldsmith describes the old master well:

> "He was kindly, and if severe in aught,
> The love he bore to learning was in fault.
> The village all declared how much he knew,
> 'Twas certain he could write and cipher, too.
> In arguing the parson owned his skill,
> For e'en though vanquished he would argue still."

The government of the early masters was of the most rigorous kind. Perfect quiet had to be maintained in the school-room, no buzzing, and the punishment for supposed or real disobedience, inflicted on scholars before, up to, and even in my time, was cruel and brutal. One punishment was to tie scholars up by the thumbs, suspending them in this way over the door. "Spare the rod and spoil the child" was the master's slogan. Whippings were frequent, severe, and sometimes brutal. Thorn, birch, and other rods were kept in large number by the master. Other and milder modes of punishment were in vogue, such as the dunce-block, sitting with the girls, pulling the ears, and using the ferule on the hands and sometimes on the part of the body on which the scholar sat.

> "What is man,
> If his chief good and market for his time
> Be but to sleep and feed? A beast, no more."

In 1840 the country master boarded round with the scholars, and he was always given the best bed in the house, and was usually fed on doughnuts and pumpkin-pie at every meal. He called the school to order by rapping on his desk with his ferule.

During the twenty-five years of the existence of the pauper schools the agitation for a better system was continually kept up by isolated individuals. This was done in various ways,—at elections, in toasts to a "free-school system" at Fourth of July celebrations, and in conventions of directors. The first governor who took a decided stand in favor of the common schools was John A. Schultze. He advocated it in his message in 1828. Governor Wolf, in 1833, found that out of four hundred thousand school children of the legal age, twenty thousand attended school, and that three hundred and eighty thousand were yearly uninstructed. Therefore, in his message to the Legislature, he strongly recommended the passage of a law to remedy this state of affairs. William Audenreid, a senator from Schuylkill County, introduced a bill during the session of the Legislature of 1833, which became what is known as the school law of 1834,—the establishment of the common-school system. Our second State superintendent of public instruction was appointed under this law. His name was Thomas H. Burrowes. The first State aid for schools in Jefferson County was in 1835, and through Mr. Burrowes. The amount received was one hundred and four dollars and ninety-four cents.

"Barring the master out" of the school-room on Christmas and New Year's was a custom in vogue in 1840. The barring was always done by four or five determined boys. The contest between the master and these scholars was sometimes severe and protracted, the master being determined to get into the school-room and these boys determined to keep him out. The object on the part of the scholars in this barring out was to compel the master to treat the school. If the master obtained possession of the school-room, by force or strategy, he generally gave the boys a sound flogging, but if the boys "held the fort," it resulted in negotiations for peace, and in the master eventually signing an agreement in writing to treat the school to apples, nuts, or candy. It took great nerve on the part of the boys to take this stand against a master. I know this, as I have been active in some of these contests.

PIONEER HISTORY OF JEFFERSON COUNTY, PENNA.

In 1840 a woman could teach an A, B, C, or "a-b ab," school in summer, but the man that desired to teach a summer school was a lazy, worthless, good-for-nothing fellow. Cyrus Crouch taught the first term in Brookville under the common school law of 1834.

In the forties the school-books in use were the New England Primer, Webster's Spelling-Book, Cobb's Spelling-Book, the English Reader, the New England Reader, the Testament and Bible, the Malte Braun Geography, Olney's Geography, Pike's Arithmetic, the Federal Calculator, the Western Calculator, Murray's Grammar, Kirkham's Grammar, and Walker's Dictionary. A scholar who had gone through the single rule of three in the Western Calculator was considered educated. Our present copy-books were unknown. A copy-book was then made of six sheets of foolscap-paper stitched together. The copies were set by the master after school hours, at which time he usually made and mended the school pens for the next day. Our pens were made of goose-quills, and it was the duty of the master to teach each scholar how to make or mend a goose-quill pen. One of the chief delights of a mischievous boy in those days was to keep a master busy mending his pens.

The first school-house in Brookville that I recollect of was a little brick on the alley on the northeast side of the American Hotel lot. Mrs. Pearl Roundy was the first teacher that I went to. She taught in this house. She was much beloved by the whole town. I afterwards went to Hamlin and others in this same house.

When the first appropriation of seventy-five thousand dollars was made by our State for the common schools, a debt of twenty-three million dollars rested on the Commonwealth. A great many good, conservative men opposed this appropriation, and "predicted bankruptcy from this *new* form of extravagance." But the great debt has been all paid, the expenses of the war for the Union have been met, and now (1895) the annual appropriation for our schools has been raised to five and a half million dollars. This amount due the schools for the year ending June 5, 1893, was all paid on November 1, 1893, and our State treasurer had deposits still left, lying idle, in forty-six of our banks, amounting to six and a half million dollars, which should have been appropriated for school purposes and not kept lying idle. This additional appropriation would have greatly relieved the people from oppressive taxation during these hard times.

The act of May 18, 1893, completed the evolution in our school system from the early home, the church, the subscription, the 1809 pauper, the 1834 common, into the now people's or *free* school system.

This free school is our nation's hope. Our great manufacturing interests attract immigrants to our land in large numbers, and to thoroughly educate their children and form in them the true American mind, and to prevent these children from drifting into the criminal classes, will task to

PIONEER HISTORY OF JEFFERSON COUNTY, PENNA.

the utmost all the energies, privileges, and blessed conditions of our present free schools. In our free schools of Pennsylvania the conditions are now equal. The child of the millionaire, the mechanic, the widow, and the day laborer all stand on the same plane. We have now, for the first time in the history of our State, in addition to the free schoolhouses, free desks, free fuel, free black-boards, free maps, free teachers, free books, free paper, free pens, free ink, free slates, free pencils, free sponges, and, in short, *free schools*.

In 1840 our houses and hotels were never locked at night. This was from carelessness, or perhaps thought to be unnecessary. But every store-window was provided with heavy outside shutters, which were carefully closed, barred, or locked every night in shutting up.

Then every merchant in Brookville was forced, as a matter of protection, to subscribe for and receive a weekly bank-note detecter. These periodicals were issued to subscribers for two dollars and fifty cents a year. This journal gave a weekly report of all broken banks, the discount on all good bank-notes, as well as points for the detection of counterfeit notes and coin. The coin department in the journal had woodcut pictures of all the foreign and native silver and gold coins, and also gave the value of each.

Money was scarce then, and merchants were compelled to sell their goods on credit, and principally for barter. The commodities that were exchanged for in Brookville stores were boards, shingles, square timber, wheat, rye, buckwheat, flaxseed, clover-seed, timothy-seed, wool, rags, beeswax, feathers, hickory-nuts, chestnuts, hides, deer-pelts, elderberries, furs, road orders, school and county orders, eggs, butter, tow cloth, linen cloth, axe-handles, rafting bows and pins, rafting grubs, maple-sugar in the spring, and oats after harvest.

In those days everybody came to court, either on business or to see and be seen. Tuesday was the big day. The people came on horseback or on foot. We had no book-store in town, and a man named Ingram, from Meadville, came regularly every court and opened up his stock in the bar-room of a hotel. An Irishman by the name of Hugh Miller came in the same way, and opened his jewelry and spectacles in the hotel bar-room. This was the time for insurance agents to visit our town. Robert Thorn was the first insurance agent who came here, at least to my knowledge.

In 1840 every store in town kept pure Monongahela whiskey in a bucket, either on or behind the counter, with a tin cup in or over the bucket for customers to drink free of charge, early and often. Every store sold whiskey by the gallon. Our merchants kept chip logwood by the barrel, and kegs of madder, alum, cobalt, copperas, indigo, etc., for women to use in coloring their homespun goods. Butternuts were used by the women to dye brown, peach-leaves or smartweed for yellow, and cobalt for purple. Men's and women's clothing consisted principally of homespun, and homespun underwear. Men and boys wore warmusses, roundabouts, and pants made of flannels, buckskin, Kentucky jean, blue drilling, tow, linen, satinet, bed-ticking, and corduroy, with coon-skin, seal-skin, and cloth caps, and in summer oat-straw or chip hats. The dress suit was a blue broadcloth swallow-tail coat with brass buttons, and a stove-pipe hat. "Galluses" were made of listing, bed-ticking, or knit of woollen yarn. Women wore barred flannel, linsey-woolsey, tow, and linen dresses. Six or eight yards of "Dolly Varden" calico made a superb Sunday dress. Calico sold then for fifty cents a yard. Every home had a spinning-wheel, some families had two,—a big one and a little one. Spinning-parties were in vogue, the women taking their wheels to a neighbor's house, remaining for supper, and after supper going home with their wheels on their arms. Wool-carding was then done by hand and at home. Every neighborhood had several weavers, and they wove for customers at so much per yard.

About 1840, Brookville had a hatter,—John Wynkoop. He made what was called wool hats. Those that were high-crowned or stove-pipe were wreath-bound with some kind of fur, perhaps rabbit-fur. These hatters were common in those days. The sign was a stove-pipe hat and a smoothing-iron. There was a standing contest between the tailors, hatters, and printers in drinking whiskey (doctors barred).

Then, too, coopers were common in every town. These coopers made tubs, buckets, and barrels, all of which were bound with hickory hoops. Ours was a Mr. Hewitt. His shop was on the alley, rear of the Commercial Hotel lot. These are now two lost industries.

In 1840 there was but one dental college in the world,—the Baltimore College of Dental Surgery, established in Baltimore, Maryland, in 1839, —the first dental college ever started. Up to and in that day dentistry was not a science, for it was practised as an addenda by the blacksmith, barber, watch-maker, and others. In the practice no anatomical or surgical skill was required. It was something that required muscular strength and manual dexterity in handling the "turnkey." With such a clumsy, rude condition of dentistry, is it any wonder that Tom Moore wrote these lines?

> "What pity, blooming girl, that lips so ready for a lover,
> Should not beneath their ruby casket cover one tooth of pearl,
> But like a rose beneath a churchyard stone,
> Be doomed to blush o'er many a mouldering bone."

All the great discoveries and improvements in the science and art of dentistry as it is to-day are American. Dentistry stands an American institution, not only beautified, but almost perfected upon a firm pedestal, a most noble science. Through the invention, by Charles W. Peale, of Philadelphia, of porcelain teeth, our molars shall henceforth be white as milk. If Moore lived to-day, under the condition of American dentistry, he might well exclaim, in the language of Akenside,—

> "What do I kiss? A woman's mouth,
> Sweeter than the spiced winds from the south."

In 1796, when Andrew Barnett trod on the ground where Brookville now stands, slavery existed throughout all Christendom. Millions of men, women, and children were held in the legal condition of horses and cattle. Worse than this, the African slave-trade—a traffic so odious and so loudly reproved and condemned by the laws of religion and of nature—was carried on as a legal right by slave-dealers in and from every Christian nation. The horror with which this statement of facts must strike you is only proof that the love of gold and the power of evil in the world is most formidable. The African slave-trade was declared illegal and unlawful by England in 1806–7, by the United States in 1808, by Denmark, Portugal, and Chili in 1811, by Sweden in 1813, by Holland in 1814–15, by France in 1815, and by Spain in 1822.

When Andrew Barnett first trod the ground where Brookville now stands the curse of slavery rested on Pennsylvania, for in that year three thousand seven hundred and thirty-seven human beings were considered "property" within her borders and held as slaves.

> "Chains him and tasks him, and exacts his sweat
> With stripes, that Mercy with a bleeding heart
> Weeps when she sees it inflicted on a beast."

In 1840 slavery still existed in Pennsylvania, the total number being 75, distributed, according to the census of that year, as follows: Adams County, 2; Berks, 2; Cumberland, 25; Lancaster, 2; Philadelphia, 2; York, 1; Greene, 1; Juniata, 1; Luzerne, 1; Mifflin, 31; Union, 3; Washington, 2; Westmoreland, 1; Fayette, 1.

It will be seen there was no slave held or owned in Jefferson County. There is not to-day a slave in all Christendom, after a struggle of nearly two thousand years.

> "Little by little the world grows strong,
> Fighting the battle of Right and Wrong.
> Little by little the Wrong gives way;
> Little by little the Right has sway;
> Little by little the seeds we sow
> Into a beautiful yield will grow."

In 1840, according to the census, there were fifty-seven colored people and no slaves in Jefferson County. The most prominent of these colored people who lived in and around Brookville were Charles Sutherland, called Black Charley; Charles Anderson, called Yellow Charley; John

PIONEER HISTORY OF JEFFERSON COUNTY, PENNA.

Sweeney, called Black John; and George Hays, the fiddler. Charles Sutherland came to Jefferson County and settled near Brookville in 1812. He came from Virginia, and was said to have held General Washington's horse at the laying of the corner-stone of the national capitol at Washington. He was a very polite man, a hard drinker, reared a family, and died in 1852, at the advanced age of nearly one hundred years.

Charley always wore a stove-pipe hat with a colored cotton handkerchief in it. He loafed much in Clover's store. The late Daniel Smith was a young man then, and clerked in this store. Mr. Smith in his manhood built the property now owned and occupied by Harry Matson. Charley Sutherland, if he were living now, would make a good Congressman, because he was good on appropriations. One day there was no one in the store but Smith and Charley. There was a crock of eggs on the counter. Smith had to go to the cellar, and left the store in the charge of Charley. On returning he glanced in the direction of the eggs, and discovered that Charley must have pilfered about a dozen of them. Where were they? He surmised they must be in Charley's hat; so stepping in front of Sutherland, he brought his right fist heavily down on his hat, with the exclamation, "Why the h——ll don't you wear your hat on your head?" Much to the amusement of Smith and the discomfort of Sutherland, the blow broke all the eggs, and the white and yellow contents ran down over Charley's face and clothes, making a striking contrast with his sooty black face.

The lives of many good men and women have been misunderstood and clouded by the thoughtless, unkind words and deeds of their neighbors. Good men and women have struggled hard and long, only to go down, down, poisoned and persecuted all their days by the venomous and vicious slanders of their neighbors; while, strange to say, men and women who are guilty of all the vices are frequently apologized for, respected, and are great favorites with these same neighbors.

Charles Anderson, or, as he was called, "Yellow Charley," came to Brookville in May, 1831. From his first entry into the town until his death he was a public and familiar character, a kind of family visitor. He was the pioneer coal merchant. He was the first man to mine, transport, and sell coal in this city. He mined his coal on what is now the John Matson property, opposite Samuel Truby's, on the Sigel road, and also on the Clements farm. He dug this coal from the spring ravine where our school building receives its supply of water. The vein of this mine was about two feet thick. Anderson stripped the earth from the top of the vein, dug the coal fine, and transported it in a little, old, rickety one-horse wagon, offering, selling, and retailing the coal at each family door in quantities of a peck, half-bushel, and bushel. The price per bushel was twelve and a half cents, or an eleven-penny bit, and a fippenny bit for a half-bushel. I had a free pass on this coal line, and rode on it a great deal.

PIONEER HISTORY OF JEFFERSON COUNTY, PENNA.

To me it was a line of "speed, safety, and comfort." Anderson was a "Soft Coal King," a baron, a robber, a close corporationist, a capitalist, and a monopolist. He managed his works generally so as to avoid strikes, etc. Yet he had to assume the *rôle* of a Pinkerton or a coal policeman at one time, for "there was some litigation over the ownership of this coal-bank, and Charley took his old flint-lock musket one day and swore he would just as soon die in the coal-bank as any other place. He held the fort, too."

Charley was a greatly abused man. Every theft and nearly all outlawry was blamed on him. Public sentiment and public clamor were against him. He tried at times to be good, attend church, etc., but it availed *him* nothing, for he would be so coldly received as to force him back into his former condition. As the town grew and other parties became engaged in mining coal, Charley changed his business to that of water-carrier, and hauled in his one-horse wagon washing- and cooking-water in barrels for the women of the town. He continued in this business until his death, which occurred in 1874. In early days he lived on the lot now owned by Dr. T. C. Lawson. He died in his own home, near the new cemetery.

It is unfortunate enough in these days to have been painted black by our Creator, but in 1840 it was a terrible calamity. A negro then had no rights; he was nothing but a "d—d nigger;" anybody and everybody had a right to abuse, beat, stone, and maltreat him. This right, too, was pretty generally exercised. I have seen a white bully deliberately step up in front of a negro, in a public street, and with the exclamation, "Take that, you d—d nigger!" knock him down, and this, too, without any cause, word, or look from the negro. This was done only to exhibit what the ruffian could do. Had the negro, even after this outrage, said a word in his own defence, the cry would have been raised, "Kill the d—d nigger!" I have seen negro men stoned into Red Bank Creek, for no crime, by a band of young ruffians. I have seen a house in Brookville borough, occupied by negro women and children, stoned until every window was broken and the door mashed in, and all this for no crime save that they were black. It used to make my blood boil, but I was too little to even open my mouth. A sorry civilization this, was it not?

The accompanying cut represents Brookville as I first recollect it,— from 1840 to 1843,—a town of shanties, and containing a population of two hundred and forty people. It is made from a pencil sketch drawn on the ground in 1840. It is not perfect, like a photograph would make it now. To understand this view of Main Street, imagine yourself in the middle of the pike then, street now, opposite the Union or McKinley Hotel, and looking eastward. The first thing that strikes your attention is a team of horses hauling a stick of timber over a newly laid hewed log bridge. This bridge was laid over the deep gully that can be now seen in

G. B. Carrier's lot. Looking to the left side of the street, the first building, the gable end of which you see, was the Presbyterian church, then outside of the west line of the borough. The next, or little house, was Jimmie Lucas's blacksmith shop. The large house with the paling fence was the residence and office of John Gallagher, Esq., and is now the Judge Clark property. The next house was east of Barnett Street, and the Peace and

Brookville, 1843.

Poverty Hotel. East of this hotel you see the residence and tailor-shop of Benjamin McCreight. Then you see a large two-story house, which stood where the Commercial Hotel now stands. This building was erected by John Clements, and was known as the Clements property. Then there was nothing until you see the court-house, with its belfry, standing out, two stories high, bold and alone. East of this and across Pickering Street, where Harry Matson now resides, was a large frame building, occupied by James Craig as a store-room for cabinet work. Rev. Gara Bishop resided here for a long time. Next to this, where Guyther & Henderson's store now stands, were several brick business buildings belonging to Charles Evans. Next came Major William Rodgers's store, on what is now the Edelblute property. Then came Jesse G. Clark's home; then the Jefferson House (Phil. Allgeier's house); and the present building is the original, but somewhat altered. Then across the alley, where Gregg's barber-shop now is, was the Elkhorn, or Red Lion Hotel, kept by John Smith, who was sheriff of the county in 1840. The next house was on the Mrs. Clements property, and was the home and blacksmith-shop of Isaac Allen. Then came the Matson row, just as it is now down to the Brownlee house, northeast corner of Main and Mill Streets.

Now please come back and look down the right-hand side. The first building, the rear end of which only can be seen behind the tree, was the first foundry built in town. It stood near or on the ground where Fetzer's brick building now stands, and was built and owned by a man named Coleman. It was afterwards the Evans foundry. When built it was outside the borough. The second house, with the gable next the street, was the home of James Corbett, Esq., father of Colonel Corbett, and it stood where the gas-office now is. The next and large building, with the gable-end next the street, was called the James Hall Building, and stood on the ground now occupied by the Bishop Buildings. This building was used for day-school and singing-school purposes. I went to day-school here to Miss Jane Clark then, now Mrs. E. H. Darrah. It was also used by a man named Wynkoop, who made beaver hats. The next building was a house erected by a Mr. Sharpe, and was located on the lot west of where the National Bank of Brookville now stands. The building having the window in the gable-end facing you was the Jack Building, and stood on the ground now occupied by McKnight & Son in their drug business. East of this, on the ground now occupied by R. M. Matson's brick, stood a little frame building, occupied by John Heath, Jr. It cannot be seen. East and across Pickering Street you see the Franklin House and its sign. Here now stands the Central Hotel of S. B. Arthurs. East of the Franklin House, but not distinctly shown on the picture, were the houses of Craig, Waigley, Thomas M. Barr, Levi G. Clover, Mrs. Mary McKnight, Snyder's row, and Billy McCullough's house and shop, situate on the corner of Main and Mill Streets, or where the Baptist church now stands.

The buildings on each side of Pickering Street, east of the courthouse, you will see, are not very plain or distinct on the picture.

PIONEER HISTORY OF JEFFERSON COUNTY, PENNA.

CHAPTER XXVII.

CORNPLANTER—OUR CHIEF—CHIEF OF THE SENECAS, ONE OF THE SIX NATIONS—BRIEF HISTORY—SOME SPEECHES—LIFE AND DEATH—MOSES KNAPP—SAW-MILLS—JOHN JONES.

In the year 1784 the treaty to which Cornplanter was a party was made at Fort Stanwix, ceding the whole of Northwestern Pennsylvania to the Commonwealth, with the exception of a small individual reserve to Cornplanter. The frontier, however, was not at peace for some years after that, nor, indeed, until Wayne's treaty in 1795.

Notwithstanding his bitter hostility, while the war continued, he became the fast friend of the United States when once the hatchet was buried. His sagacious intellect comprehended at a glance the growing power of the United States, and the abandonment with which Great Britain had requited the fidelity of the Senecas. He therefore threw all his influence at the treaty of Fort Stanwix, now Rome, New York, and Fort Harmar in favor of peace. And notwithstanding the large concessions which he saw his people were necessitated to make, still, by his energy and prudence in the negotiation, he retained for them an ample and beautiful reservation. For the course which he took on those occasions the State of Pennsylvania granted him the fine reservation upon which he resided on the Allegheny. The Senecas, however, were never satisfied with his course in relation to these treaties, and Red Jacket, more artful and eloquent than his elder rival, but less frank and honest, seized upon this circumstance to promote his own popularity at the expense of Cornplanter.

Having buried the hatchet, Cornplanter sought to make his talents useful to his people by conciliating the good will of the whites and securing from further encroachment the little remnant of his national domain. On more than one occasion, when some reckless and bloodthirsty whites on the frontier had massacred unoffending Indians in cold blood, did Cornplanter interfere to restrain the vengeance of his people. During all the Indian wars from 1791 to 1794, which terminated with Wayne's treaty, Cornplanter pledged himself that the Senecas should remain friendly to the United States. He often gave notice to the garrison at Fort Franklin of intended attacks from hostile parties, and even hazarded his life on a mediatorial mission to the Western tribes.

The following is an extract from a speech of Cornplanter to representatives of the United States government appointed to meet him at Fort Franklin, 8th of March, 1796:

PIONEER HISTORY OF JEFFERSON COUNTY, PENNA.

"'I thank the Almighty for giving us luck to meet together at this time, and in this place as brethren, and hope my brothers will assist me in writing to Congress what I have now to say.

"'I thank the Almighty that I am speaking this good day. I have been through all Nations in America, and am sorry to see the folly of many of the people. What makes me sorry is they all tell lies, and I never found truth amongst them. All the western Nations of Indians, as well as white people, have told me lies. Even in Council I have been deceived, and been told things which I have told to my chiefs and young men, which I have found not to be so, which makes me tell lies by not being able to make good my word, but I hope they will all see their folly and repent. The Almighty has not made us to lie, but to tell the truth one to another, for when two people meet together, if they lie one to the other, them people cannot be at peace, and so it is with nations, and that is the cause of so much war.

"'General Washington, the father of us all, hear what I have now to say, and take pity on us poor people. The Almighty has blest you, and not us. He has given you education, which enables you to do many things that we cannot do. You can travel by sea as well as by land, and know what is doing in any other country, which we poor people know nothing about. Therefore you ought to pity us. When the Almighty first put us on this land he gave it to us to live on. And when the white people first came to it they were very poor, and we helped them all in our power; did not kill them, but received them as brothers. And now it appears to me as though they were agoing to leave us in distress.'"—*Pennsylvania Archives.*

"After peace was permanently established between the Indians and the United States, Cornplanter retired from public life and devoted his labors to his own people. He deplored the evils of intemperance, and exerted himself to suppress it. The benevolent efforts of missionaries among his tribe always received his encouragement, and at one time his own heart seemed to be softened by the words of truth, yet he preserved in his later years many of the peculiar notions of the Indian faith.

"In 1821-22 the commissioners of Warren County assumed the right to tax the private property of Cornplanter, and proceeded to enforce its collection. The old chief resisted it, conceiving it not only unlawful, but a personal indignity. The sheriff again appeared with a small posse of armed men. Cornplanter took the deputation to a room around which were ranged about a hundred rifles, and, with the sententious brevity of an Indian, intimated that for each rifle a warrior would appear at his call. The sheriff and his men speedily withdrew, determined, however, to call out the militia. Several prudent citizens, fearing a sanguinary collision, sent for the old chief in a friendly way to come to Warren and compromise the matter. He came, and after some persuasion, gave his note for the tax, amounting to forty-three dollars and seventy-nine cents. He addressed, however, a remonstrance to the governor of Pennsylvania, soliciting a return of his money and an exemption from such demands against lands which the State itself had presented to him. The Legislature annulled the tax, and sent two commissioners to explain the affair to him. He met them at the court-house in Warren, on which occasion he delivered the following speech, eminently characteristic of himself and his race :

"'Brothers, yesterday was appointed for us all to meet here. The talk which the governor sent us pleased us very much. I think that the Great Spirit is very much pleased that the white people have been induced so to assist the Indians as they have done, and that he is pleased also to see the great men of this State and of the United States so friendly to us. We are much pleased with what has been done.

"'The Great Spirit first made the world, and next the flying animals, and found all things good and prosperous. He is immortal and everlasting. After finishing the flying animals, he came down on earth and there stood. Then he made different kinds of trees and weeds of all sorts, and people of every kind. He made the spring and other seasons and the weather suitable for planting. These he did make. But stills to make whiskey to be given to the Indians he did not make. The Great Spirit bids me tell the white people not to give Indians this kind of liquor. When the Great Spirit had made the earth and its animals, he went into the great lakes, where he breathed as easily as anywhere else, and then made all the different kinds of fish. The Great Spirit looked back on all that he had made. The different kinds he had made to be separate and not to mix with or disturb each other. But the white people have broken his command by mixing their color with the Indians. The Indians have done better by not doing so. The Great Spirit wishes that all wars and fightings should cease.

"'He next told us that there were three things for our people to attend to. First, we ought to take care of our wives and children. Secondly, the white people ought to attend to their farms and cattle. Thirdly, the Great Spirit has given the bears and deers to the Indians. He is the cause of all things that exist, and it is very wicked to go against his will. The Great Spirit wishes me to inform the people that they should quit drinking intoxicating drink, as being the cause of disease and death. He told us not to sell any more of our lands, for he never sold lands to any one. Some of us now keep the seventh day, but I wish to quit it, for the Great Spirit made it for others, but not for the Indians, who ought every day to attend to their business. He has ordered me to quit drinking intoxicating drink, and not to lust after any woman but my own, and informs me that by doing so I should live the longer. He made known to me that it is very wicked to tell lies. Let no one suppose this I have said now is not true.

PIONEER HISTORY OF JEFFERSON COUNTY, PENNA.

"'I have now to thank the governor for what he has done. I have informed him what the Great Spirit has ordered me to cease from, and I wish the governor to inform others what I have communicated. This is all I have at present to say.'"—*Day's Recollections.*

The old chief appears after this again to have fallen into entire seclusion, taking no part even in the politics of his people. He died at his residence on the 7th of March, 1836, at the age of one hundred and four years. " Whether at the time of his death he expected to go to the fair hunting-grounds of his own people or to the heaven of the Christian is not known."

" Notwithstanding his profession of Christianity, Cornplanter was very superstitious. ' Not long since,' says Mr. Foote, of Chautauqua County, ' he said the Good Spirit had told him not to have anything to do with the white people, or even to preserve any mementos or relics that had been given to him from time to time by the pale-faces, whereupon, among other things, he burnt up his belt and broke his elegant sword.' "

In reference to the personal appearance of Cornplanter at the close of his life, a writer in the *Democratic Arch* (Venango County) says,—

" I once saw the aged and venerable chief, and had an interesting interview with him about a year and a half before his death. I thought of many things when seated near him, beneath the wide-spreading shade of an old sycamore, on the banks of the Allegheny,—many things to ask him, the scenes of the Revolution, the generals that fought its battles and conquered, the Indians, his tribe, the Six Nations, and himself. He was constitutionally sedate, was never observed to smile, much less to indulge in the luxury of a laugh. When I saw him he estimated his age to be over one hundred ; I think one hundred and three was about his reckoning of it. This would make him near one hundred and five years old at the time of his decease. His person was stooped, and his stature was far short of what it once had been, not being over five feet six inches at the time I speak of. Mr. John Struthers, of Ohio, told me, some years since, that he had seen him near fifty years ago, and at that period he was at his height,—viz., six feet one inch. Time and hardship had made dreadful impressions upon that ancient form. The chest was sunken and his shoulders were drawn forward, making the upper part of his body resemble a trough. His limbs had lost size and become crooked. His feet (for he had taken off his moccasins) were deformed and haggard by injury. I would say that most of the fingers on one hand were useless ; the sinews had been severed by the blow of a tomahawk or scalping-knife. How I longed to ask him what scene of blood and strife had thus stamped the enduring evidence of its existence upon his person ! But to have done so would, in all probability, have put an end to all further conversation on any subject. The information desired would certainly not have been received, and I had to forego my curiosity.

He had but one eye, and even the socket of the lost organ was hid by the overhanging brow resting upon the high cheek-bone. His remaining eye was of the brightest and blackest hue. Never have I seen one, in young or old, that equalled it in brilliancy. Perhaps it had borrowed lustre from the eternal darkness that rested on its neighboring orbit. His ears had been dressed in the Indian mode, all but the outside ring had been cut away. On the one ear this ring had been torn asunder near the top, and hung down his neck like a useless rag. He had a full head of hair, white as the driven snow, which covered a head of ample dimensions and admirable shape. His face was not swarthy, but this may be accounted for from the fact, also, that he was but half Indian. He told me he had been at Franklin more than eighty years before the period of our conversation, on his passage down the Ohio and Mississippi with the warriors of his tribe, in some expedition against the Creeks or Osages. He had long been a man of peace, and I believe his great characteristics were humanity and truth. It is said that Brandt and Cornplanter were never friends after the massacre of Cherry Valley. Some have alleged, because the Wyoming massacre was perpetrated by Senecas, that Cornplanter was there. Of the justice of this suspicion there are many reasons for doubt. It is certain that he was not the chief of the Senecas at that time. The name of the chief in that expedition was Ge-en-quah-toh, or He-goes-in-the-smoke. As he stood before me—the ancient chief in ruins—how forcibly was I struck with the truth of that beautiful figure of the old aboriginal chieftain, who, in describing himself, said he was ' like an aged hemlock, dead at the top, and whose branches alone were green' ! After more than one hundred years of most varied life,—of strife, of danger, of peace,—he at last slumbers in deep repose on the banks of his own beloved Allegheny.

"Cornplanter was born at Conewongus, on the Genesee River, in 1732, being a half-breed, the son of a white man named John O'Bail, a trader from the Mohawk Valley. In a letter written in later years to the governor of Pennsylvania he thus speaks of his early youth : ' When I was a child I played with the butterfly, the grasshopper, and the frogs ; and as I grew up I began to pay some attention and play with the Indian boys in the neighborhood, and they took notice of my skin being of a different color from theirs, and spoke about it. I inquired from my mother the cause, and she told me my father was a resident of Albany. I still ate my victuals out of a bark dish. I grew up to be a young man and married a wife, and I had no kettle or gun. I then knew where my father lived, and went to see him, and found he was a white man and spoke the English language. He gave me victuals while I was at his house, but when I started to return home he gave me no provisions to eat on the way. He gave me neither kettle nor gun.'

"Little further is known of his early life beyond the fact that he was

PIONEER HISTORY OF JEFFERSON COUNTY, PENNA.

allied with the French in the engagement against General Braddock in July, 1755. He was probably at that time at least twenty years old. During the Revolution he was a war chief of high rank, in the full vigor of manhood, active, sagacious, brave, and he most probably participated in the principal Indian engagements against the United States during the war. He is supposed to have been present at the cruelties of Wyoming and Cherry Valley, in which the Senecas took a prominent part. He was on the war-path with Brandt during General Sullivan's campaign in 1779, and in the following year, under Brandt and Sir John Johnson, he led the Senecas in sweeping through the Schoharie and the Mohawk Valleys. On this occasion he took his father a prisoner, but with such caution as to avoid an immediate recognition. After marching the old man some ten or twelve miles, he stepped before him, faced about, and addressed him in the following terms:

"'My name is John O'Bail, commonly called Cornplanter. I am your son. You are my father. You are now my prisoner, and subject to the custom of Indian warfare; but you shall not be harmed You need not fear. I am a warrior. Many are the scalps which I have taken. Many prisoners have I tortured to death. I am your son. I was anxious to see you and greet you in friendship. I went to your cabin and took you by force; but your life shall be spared. Indians love their friends and their kindred, and treat them with kindness. If you now chose to follow the fortunes of your yellow son and to live with our people, I will cherish your old age with plenty of venison, and you shall live easy. But if it is your choice to return to your fields and live with your white children, I will send a party of trusty young men to conduct you back in safety. I respect you, my father. You have been friendly to Indians, and they are your friends.' The elder O'Bail preferred his white children and green fields to his yellow offspring and the wild woods, and chose to return.

"Cornplanter was the greatest warrior the Senecas, the untamable people of the hills, ever had, and it was his wish that when he died his grave would remain unmarked, but the Legislature of Pennsylvania willed otherwise, and erected a monument to him with this beautiful inscription:

"'CYANTWAHIA, THE CORNPLANTER,
JOHN O'BAIL, ALIAS CORNPLANTER,
DIED
AT CORNPLANTER TOWN, FEB. 18, A. D. 1836,
AGED ABOUT 100 YEARS.'

"Upon the west side is the following inscription:

"'Chief of the Seneca tribe, and a principal chief of the Six Nations from the period of the Revolutionary War to the time of his death. Distinguished for talent, courage, eloquence, sobriety, and love for tribe and race, to whose welfare he devoted his time, his energy, and his means during a long and eventful life.'"

PIONEER HISTORY OF JEFFERSON COUNTY, PENNA.

In the above I have copied largely from Rupp's history, and from the "History of Warren County, Pennsylvania."

MOSES KNAPP.

In the spring of 1797, Joseph Barnett, of Linesville, Dauphin County, Pennsylvania, Samuel Scott and Moses Knapp, of Lycoming County, Pennsylvania, left the mouth of Pine Creek, on the west branch of the Susquehanna, in Lycoming County, and wended their way over Meade's Trail to the confluence of Mill Creek with Sandy Lick, now Port Barnett, for the purpose of starting a settlement. Port Barnett was then in Pine Creek township, Lycoming County. Upon their arrival they commenced the erection of a saw-mill. "Samuel Scott was a millwright by trade, and was assisted in his work by Moses Knapp, who was an adopted son, then about nineteen years of age. They first built a saw-mill on Mill Creek, about where the present mill of Mr. Humphrey now stands. This mill was the property of Mr. Scott. Young Knapp exhibited a good deal of mechanical ingenuity in this work, and the next year built a mill for himself on the North Fork, on a site about the head of Heidrick, Matson & Co.'s mill-pond. Leaving his mill in the fall to stand still during the winter, young Knapp went to Indiana to attend a term of school. While there he became acquainted with Miss Susan Matson, a daughter of Uriah Matson, of that place. The acquaintance thus made soon ripened into an engagement, and Moses Knapp and Susan Matson were united in matrimony, and thus in one short absence from the scene of his labors Moses had accomplished much, and when all this was accomplished she returned with him to Port Barnett. He then built a camp or residence at his saw-mill on the North Fork, and there they commenced keeping house, a beginning which resulted in the production of a family of eleven children. Here, in 1801, was born Polly, and afterwards Isabel and Samuel.

"He sold out his mill and 'betterments' at the head of Heidrick, Matson & Co.'s pond to Samuel and William Lucas, and then began house-keeping in a new place, at the mouth of the North Fork, now Brookville. After he had got his family in living shape here, he built another saw-mill on what was known as Knapp's Run. The name of this stream has since been changed to Five-Mile Run. This mill Knapp sold to Thomas Lucas, Esq. He then built a log grist-mill on the North Fork, near his residence, only a few rods from the Red Bank Creek. This mill had one run of rock-stones. The water was gathered by a wing-dam of brush and stones, that extended nearly up to where the road now crosses below Heidrick, Matson & Co.'s dam, and was thus brought into a chute, that passed it under a large under-shot water-wheel. A 'face-gear' wheel upon the water-wheel shaft 'meshed' into a 'trundle-head' upon the 'spindle' which carried the revolving-stone, comprised the propelling machinery. This mill was often taxed to its utmost capacity. People would come here to get their grain ground from distances of twenty and thirty miles, through the woods on horseback and on barefoot carrying the grain on their backs. A big day's grind was from six to ten bushels of grain."

While residing at this place, in what is now Brookville, John Knapp was born in 1807, and afterwards Amy, Joshua, Moses, Clarissa, and Joseph, the last in 1818.

During the time of Knapp's residence at the head of what is now Heidrick, Matson & Co.'s pond, and many years thereafter, "the cheapest and most expeditious method of obtaining such supplies as could not be produced on the ground was to go to Pittsburg for them. Rafts of sawed lumber were run to Pittsburg in the spring of the year. A canoe was taken along, and when the raft was sold most of the avails would be invested in whiskey, pork, sugar, dry goods, etc. These goods were then loaded into the canoe, and the same men that brought the raft through to market would "pole" or "push" the loaded canoe up the river and up the creek to Port Barnett. This was a "voyage" that all men of full strength were very desirous of making, and was the subject of conversation for the remaining part of the year.

These canoes were hewed out of a large pine-tree, large enough to receive a barrel of flour crosswise. A home-made rope of flax was attached to the front end of the canoe to be used in pulling the canoe up and over ripples. The men with these canoes had to camp in the woods wherever night overtook them, and their greatest terror and fear was rattlesnakes, for the creek bottoms were alive with them.

The pioneer keel-boat built on these western waters was at Pittsburg in 1811,—viz., the "New Orleans." The first river steamboat was built in 1817.

In 1821, Moses Knapp "articled" with the Holland Land Company for a quantity of land in what is now Clover township. The land was taken from warrants numbered 3082 and 3200, which included the land upon which Dowlingville is situated, and also that upon which the Baxter property and mills now are.

After building a cabin and moving his family into it, he commenced the building of a dam pretty much on the site of the present dam, and a saw-mill on the site of the present mill. He took a partner in the business and vigorously prosecuted the work. In cutting timber for the mill he in some way got his foot crushed so badly that it became necessary to have the leg amputated above the knee. The mill was completed, and the business of manufacturing lumber, etc., was carried on for a few years by Knapp & Ball.

He had two children born here,—Isaac M. and Eliza. He was elected constable while here in 1821, the year he was hurt.

PIONEER HISTORY OF JEFFERSON COUNTY, PENNA.

Moses Knapp was the pioneer pilot on Red Bank Creek. The pioneer board-raft contained about eight thousand feet of boards. Pilots received but two dollars per trip and found; common hands but one dollar per trip and found. The pioneer pilots steered the rafts then with the front oar. The pioneer oars and stems were then hewn out of a single dry pine-tree. Elijah M. Graham was the first to saw oar-blades separate from the stem.

SAW-MILLS.

The earliest form of a saw-mill was a "saw-pit." In it lumber was sawed in this way: by two men at the saw, one man standing above the

A pioneer saw-mill erected on Rattlesnake Creek, in Snyder township, in 1841, by James Pendleton.

pit, the other man in the pit, the two men sawing the log on trestles above. Saws are prehistoric. The ancients used "bronzed saws." Saw-mills were first run by "individual power," and water-power was first used in Germany about 1322. The primitive water saw-mill consisted of a wooden pitman attached to the shaft of the wheel. The log to be sawed was placed on rollers, sustained by a framework over the wheel, and was fed forward on the rollers by means of levers worked by hand. The pioneer saw-mill erected in the United States was near or on the dividing line of Maine and New Hampshire, in 1634.

The early up-and-down saw-mills were built of frame timbers mortised and tenoned and pinned together with oak pins. In size these mills were from twenty to thirty feet wide and from fifty to sixty feet in length, and were roofed with clapboards, slabs, or boards The running-gear was an undershot flutter-wheel, a gig-wheel to run the log-carriage back, and a bull-wheel with a rope or chain attached to haul the logs into the mill on and over the slide. The capacity of such a mill was about four thousand feet of boards in twenty-four hours The total cost of one of these up-and-down saw-mills when completed was about three hundred dollars, one hundred dollars for iron used and two hundred dollars for the work and material. Luther Geer, an old pioneer, built about twenty-eight of such mills. Moses Knapp died near Dowlingville, in 1853, and is buried in the graveyard of the Jefferson United Presbyterian Church. Mr. Knapp was a Seceder in belief, and was a leading member of that church,—to wit, the Jefferson.

JOHN JONES.

"The subject of this sketch was born in Northumberland County, Pennsylvania, the 10th of February, 1781, and in the year 1797 he came to what is now Port Barnett, about one and a half miles east of Brookville, Jefferson County, as an apprentice to the millwright trade with his uncle, Samuel Scott. After the erection of this mill (being assisted by the Indians) he engaged in the lumber business with his uncle, and became quite a woodsman, killing as many as one hundred deer in a season. The Indians being quite numerous at that time in the forest, he even camped and hunted in partnership with them. He was often heard to remark that he could beat them killing deer, but they could beat him on the bear. In the year 1811 he settled on his farm, east of Strattonville. He erected a cabin and commenced clearing, and in a short time he was drafted into the military service. After clearing off a portion of ground and sowing his wheat and fencing the same, he was, with several of his neighbors, ready for the call, and on the 25th of September they started for Pittsburg, Pennsylvania, and they remained there for a short time and elected their officers. A man by the name of Wallace was elected captain, and Robert Orr, major. They then marched through the State of Ohio to the Maumee River, and there they built Fort Meigs; remained there until spring, then returned to their home.

"Jones then commenced opening up more land, but still lumbering occasionally on Red Bank, and canoeing provisions and groceries from Pittsburg, there being no store of any account nearer. After they got to raising some grain, it had to be taken to Samuel Scott's at Port Barnett, fifteen miles distant. When the mill failed, some of the neighbors had to go to Mudlic, Indiana County. Some went to a horse mill on Bear Creek, below Parker City. There were also quite a number of hand mills in use in the country for grinding corn. The first store in what is

PIONEER HISTORY OF JEFFERSON COUNTY, PENNA.

now Clarion County was located where Reimersburg now stands, in 1812, and owned by James Pinks, and if you happened to run out of salt for your venison, you could get a bushel from him for five dollars, and all other things in proportion.

"In the year 1818 the mildew struck the wheat and it was totally destroyed, and starvation stared them in the face; but he knew where to go. So off he starts to the pine-woods, selects a place for himself and brothers, and at it they went, and gathered and split, and burned each of them a kiln of tar; and when they got the tar barrelled, they then had to haul it four miles to the Clarion River, made a canoe and run the tar to Pittsburg, and traded it for the necessaries of life. He also piloted the viewers and surveyors of the Brookville and Meadville turnpike, or, more properly, the Bellefonte and Erie turnpike, and many other roads, he being considered the best posted in regard to location."

CHAPTER XXVIII.

JOSEPH BARNETT—BIOGRAPHICAL SKETCH OF THE PATRIARCH OF JEFFERSON COUNTY.

JOSEPH BARNETT, the patriarch of Jefferson County, was the son of John and Sarah Barnett, and was born in Dauphin County, Pennsylvania, in 1754. His father was born in Ireland, and located in Pennsylvania in the early part of the eighteenth century, and was a farmer up to the time of his death in 1757. His mother died a few years later, and Joseph was "brought up" by his relatives. He was raised on a farm, and was thus peacefully employed when the Revolution commenced. As a son of a patriotic sire he could not resist taking part in the struggle, and so joined the army and served for some years. The exact duration of his service cannot now be ascertained, but this we learn: "he was a brave and efficient soldier, and never faltered in the path of duty." He also served in the State militia in the campaign against the Wyoming boys. After the war he settled in Northumberland County, where he owned a large tract of land, but was dispossessed of it by some informalities of the title. Here he was married to Elizabeth Scott, sister of Samuel Scott and daughter of John Scott, July 3, 1794.

I find Joseph Barnett assessed in Pine Creek township, Northumberland County, April 28, 1786. I find him in 1788 assessed in the same township and county with a saw-mill and as a single freeman. This was his saw-mill at the mouth of Pine Creek, and the mill on which he lost his eye. The property is now in Clinton County. After losing his mill and land Barnett returned in the nineties to Dauphin County, Pennsylvania, and engaged in contracting for and building bridges. In 1799 I find him again assessed in Pine Creek township, then Lycoming County, Pennsylvania, with two hundred and twenty-five acres of land. This was his Port Barnett property, where he migrated to with his family in 1800, and here he engaged in the erection of mills and in the lumbering business that eventually made Port Barnett, then in Lycoming County, the centre of business for a large extent of territory. In a short time a tub grist-mill was added to his saw-mill, and, with his "Port Barnett flint-stone binns," he made an eatable, if not a very desirable, quality of flour. The Indians (Cornplanters and Senecas) then in the country were good customers of our subject, and what few whites there were for thirty or forty miles around would make his cabin a stopping-place for several days at a time. His log cabin became a tavern, the only one in a seventy-five miles' journey, and was frequented by all the early settlers.

"His Indian guests did not eat in the house, but would in winter make a pot of mush over his fire and set it out in the snow to cool; then one fellow would take a dipper and eat his fill of the pudding, sometimes with milk, butter, or molasses; then another would take it and go through the same process until all were satisfied. The dogs would then help themselves from the same pot, and when they put their heads in the pot in the Indian's way he would give them a slap over the head with the dipper."

He kept a store, rafted lumber on Sandy Lick and Red Bank, and at the same time attended to his saw- and grist-mills. I find him assessed in Pine Creek township in 1800 as a farmer.

"The Senecas of Cornplanter's tribe were friendly and peaceable neighbors, and often extended their excursions into these waters, where they encamped, two or three in a squad, and hunted deers and bears, taking the hams and skins in the spring to Pittsburg. Their rafts were constructed of dry poles, upon which they piled up their meat and skins in the form of a haystack, took them to Pittsburg, and exchanged them for trinkets, blankets, calicoes, weapons, etc. They were friendly, sociable, and rather fond of making money. During the war of 1812 the settlers were apprehensive that an unfortunate turn of the war upon the lakes might bring an irruption of the savages upon the frontier through the Seneca nation.

"Old Captain Hunt, a Muncy Indian, had his camp for some years on Red Bank, near where is now the southwestern corner of Brookville. He got his living by hunting, and enjoyed the results in drinking whiskey, of which he was inordinately fond. One year he killed seventy-eight bears,—they were plenty then; the skins might be worth about three dollars each,—nearly all of which he expended for his favorite beverage.

"Samuel Scott resided here until 1810, when, having scraped together, by hunting and lumbering, about two thousand dollars, he went down to the Miami River and bought a section of fine land, which made him rich.

"It is related that Joseph Barnett at one time carried sixty pounds of flour on his back from Pittsburg. Their supplies of flour, salt, and other necessaries were frequently brought in canoes from that place. These were purchased with lumber, which he sawed and rafted to that city, and which in those days was sold for twenty-five dollars per thousand. The nearest settlement on Meade's trail eastward of Port Barnett was Paul Clover's, thirty-three miles distant, on the west branch of the Susquehanna, where Curwensville now stands; and westward Fort Venango was forty-five miles distant, which points were the only resting-places for the travellers who ventured through this unbroken wilderness. The Seneca Indians, of Cornplanter's tribe, heretofore mentioned, often extended their hunting excursions to these waters, and encamped to hunt deer and bears and make sugar. They are said to have made sugar by catching the sap in small troughs, and, after collecting in a large trough, hot stones were dipped into it to boil it down."—*Day's Collections.*

About the year 1802, Joseph Barnett consented to act as banker for the Indians around Port Barnett. The Indians were all "bimetallists," and had the "silver craze," for their money was all silver; and bringing their monometallism to Mr. Barnett, he received it from them and deposited it in their presence in his private vault,—viz., a small board trunk covered with hog-skin, tanned with the bristles on. On the lid were the letters "J. B.," made with brass tacks. The trunk was now full; the bank was a solid financial institution. In a short time, however, the red men concluded to withdraw their deposits, and they made a "run" in a body on the bank. Barnett handed over the trunk, and each Indian counted out his own pieces, and according to their combined count the bank was insolvent; there was a shortage, a deficiency of one fifty-cent piece. Mr. Barnett induced the Indians to recount their silver, but the fifty-cent piece was still missing. The Indians then declared Mr. Barnett must die; they surrounded the house and ordered him on the porch to be shot. He obeyed orders, but pleaded with them to count their pieces the third time, and if the fifty-cent piece was still missing, then they could shoot him. This the Indians considered fair, and they counted the silver pieces the third time, and one Indian found he had one more piece than his own; he had the missing fifty-cent piece. Then there was joy and rejoicing among the Indians. Banker Barnett was no longer a criminal; he was the hero and friend of the Indians.

PIONEER HISTORY OF JEFFERSON COUNTY, PENNA.

The following sketch of the first white settlement within the county was principally derived from Andrew Barnett, Jr., Esq., in 1840:

"Old Mr. Joseph Barnett was the patriarch of Jefferson County. He had done service on the West Branch under General Potter during the Revolution, and also under the State against the Wyoming boys. After the war he settled in Northumberland County, at the mouth of Pine Creek, and very probably might have been one of the Fairplay boys; at any rate, he lost his property by the operation of the common law, which superseded the jurisdiction of fair play. Again, in 1797, he penetrated the wilderness of the Upper Susquehanna by the Chinklacamoose path, and, passing the headlands between the Susquehanna and the Allegheny, arrived on the waters of Red Bank, then called Sandy Lick Creek. He had purchased lands here of Timothy Pickering & Co. He first erected a saw-mill at Port Barnett, where Andrew Barnett, Jr., now resides, at the mouth of Mill Creek, about two miles east of Brookville. His companions on this expedition were his brother, Andrew Barnett, and his brother-in-law, Samuel Scott. Nine Seneca Indians, of Cornplanter's tribe, assisted him to raise his mill. Leaving his brothers to look after the new structure, he returned to his family in Dauphin County, intending to bring them out. But Scott soon followed him with the melancholy news of the death of his brother Andrew, who was buried by the friendly Indians and Scott in the flat opposite the present tavern. This news discouraged him for a while; but in 1800 he removed his family out, accompanied again by Mr. Scott. They sawed lumber and rafted it down to Pittsburg, where it brought in those days twenty-five dollars per thousand. The usual adventures and privations of frontier life attended their residence. The nearest mill was on Black Lick Creek, in Indiana County. Mr. Barnett knew nothing of the wilderness south of him, and was obliged to give an Indian four dollars to pilot him to Westmoreland. The nearest house on the eastward was Paul Clover's (grandfather of General Clover), thirty-three miles distant on the Susquehanna, where Curwensville now stands; westward Fort Venango was distant forty-five miles. These points were the only resting-places for the travellers through that unbroken wilderness."

Their children were as follows: Sarah and Thomas, twins, born in Pine Creek township, Northumberland County, in 1790, now Clinton County. John was born in Linesville, Dauphin County, June 16, 1795. Andrew, born in Dauphin County, November 22, 1797, where Joseph Barnett was engaged in contracting for and building bridges in the nineties. He emigrated with his family from Dauphin County to Mill Creek, Port Barnett, Lycoming County, in 1800, now Jefferson County; and Rebecca was born at Port Barnett, Lycoming County, August 6, 1802. She was the first white female child born within the present limits of Jefferson County. J. Potter was born at Port Barnett, Lycoming County,

PIONEER HISTORY OF JEFFERSON COUNTY, PENNA.

May 23, 1800. Margaret Annie was born October 22, 1805, at Port Barnett, Pine Creek township, Jefferson County. Joseph Scott, the youngest child and the first white male child born in the county, was born April 12, 1812, at Port Barnett, Pine Creek township, Jefferson County; and Juliet was born April 12, 1808, at Port Barnett, Pine Creek township, Jefferson County.

The original Pine Creek township was erected in Northumberland County at the August term of court in 1785. In 1795, when Lycoming was organized, Pine Creek township became a part of that county. In 1804, when Jefferson County was organized and taken from Lycoming, Pine Creek township was divided, and that part taken from Lycoming was thrown into Jefferson and made into Pine Creek township, and was the whole of Jefferson County until the year 1818.

The census of 1800 shows that Lycoming had a population of 5414. The population of Pine Creek township, Lycoming County, in 1800, when Joseph Barnett migrated and located at Mill Creek, now Jefferson County, was: whites, 682; colored, 24; slaves, 5; total, 711.

The following advertisement is a relic of the institution of slavery in Pennsylvania at the time Joseph Barnett migrated to what is now Jefferson County:

"2 S. (SHILLINGS) REWARD.

"Ran away on the 2d inst. negro man John, about 22; also negro girl named Flora, about 18, slender made, speaks bad English and a little French. Has a scar on her upper lip and letters branded on her breast. Whoever secures the runaways in any place where their master can get them shall have the above reward and reasonable charges paid by

"JOHN PATTON.

"CENTRE FURNACE, MIFFLIN COUNTY, July 26, 1799."

—*History of Centre County.*

When Joseph Barnett settled on Mill Creek, Pine Creek township, Lycoming County was divided into two election districts,—the third and fourth,—viz.: "3. That part of Lycoming township west of Pine Run, and that part of Pine Creek east of Chatham's Run, and the township of Nippenose, to form the third district. Elections to be held at the house of Thomas Ramey, Pine Creek.

"4. All that part of Pine Creek township west of Chatham's Run to constitute the fourth district, and elections to be held at the house of Hugh Andrew, Dunnsburgh." Dunnsburgh, or Dunnstown, as it is now called, is in Clinton County, Pennsylvania. It was founded in 1768 by William Dunn, and is about one-half mile down the river from Lock

Haven, and on the opposite or east side of the river. This fourth district was the polling- or voting-place for the Port Barnett settlement.

Hon. Jacob Rush was then president judge. He was the president judge of the third judicial district, formed, in part, of Northumberland County, from which Lycoming County was taken, the act of April 13, 1795, providing that it shall be within his jurisdiction. He was born in Philadelphia in 1746, was a brother of the famous Benjamin Rush, of that city, and a graduate of Princeton College.

The first road we have any account of in Lycoming County was the "pack-horse" road into the valley of Loyalsock; it was cut across the mountain from Muncy to Hillsgrove, for the use of explorers and surveyors, and was called the "Wallis road," because it was made by Samuel Wallis. In 1793 another "pack-horse" road was cut. It left the Wallis road at the foot of the Alleghenies, then ran northward to the left of Hunter's Lake and on the forks of the Loyalsock, where Forksville is now situated. It was called the "Courson road." In 1792, Williamson cut his famous road through from Trout Run to the Block House and beyond to enable him to conduct a company of colonists to the Genesee country.

In stature, Mr. Barnett was five feet eight inches, and would weigh about one hundred and eight pounds. His presence was prepossessing, and with his smooth-shaved face, and a countenance open and frank, his appearance was such as to attract the attention of all.

In 1800 the only road was Meade's trail. Before the axe of the lumberman had visited these forests, the trees stood tall, lordly, and free from undergrowth, the great trunks standing straight in the air, with the ground cool and damp in the shade. You could ride a horse almost anywhere through the woods. In 1801, Barnett got out of salt. The nearest place to obtain it was in Westmoreland County, Pennsylvania. Barnett could not make the trip through the woods himself, and he bargained for three days with an Indian to guide him. The Indian wanted just as much more as Barnett felt able to give. At the end of three days the bargain was closed for what the Indian believed to be half-price,—viz., two dollars. The trip to Westmoreland was then made, and after Barnett secured his salt, the Indian coolly remarked, "Me no go back; me no go back." All then that was left for Barnett to do was to give him his original price of four dollars. Joseph Barnett was rather a homely man in face and features. He was Scotch-Irish. He was a practical business man, a strict Presbyterian, a true Christian of that time. He had his left eye gouged out in a rough-and-tumble fight on his saw-mill. He died as he had lived, a true-hearted man, on the 15th of April, 1838, and was buried in our old graveyard above Church Street. His wife passed away four months later, in her sixty-fifth year, and was buried there also.

BIOGRAPHY OF BILL LONG.

THE "KING HUNTER"—THE HUNTER OF HUNTERS IN THIS WILDERNESS—SOME OF THE ADVENTURES AND LIFE OF "BILL LONG" FROM HIS CHILDHOOD UNTIL HE WAS SEVENTY YEARS OLD.

William Long, a son of Louis (Ludwig) Long, was born near Reading, Berks County, Pennsylvania, in 1794. His father and mother were Germans. In the summer of 1803, Louis Long, with his family, moved

Bill Long.

into this wilderness and settled near Port Barnett (now the McConnell farm). Ludwig Long's family consisted of himself, wife, and eleven children,—nine sons and two daughters,—William, the subject of this sketch, being the second child. The Barnetts were the only neighbors

PIONEER HISTORY OF JEFFERSON COUNTY, PENNA.

of the Longs. Louis Long brought with him a small "still" and six flint-lock guns, the only kind in use at that time. It was not until about the year 1830 that the percussion-cap rifles were first used, but they were not in general use here for some years after that. As soon as Mr. Long raised some grain he commenced to operate his "still" and manufacture whiskey, this being the first manufactured west of the mountains and east of the Allegheny River.

This part of Pennsylvania was then the hunting-grounds of the Seneca Indians,—Cornplanter tribe. The still-house of Long soon became the resort for these Indians. Pittsburg was the nearest market for pelts, furs, etc., and the only place to secure flour and other necessaries, etc. From the mouth of Red Bank Creek these goods had to be poled up to Barnett's in canoes. By scooping the channel, wading, and polling, a round trip to the mouth could be made in from one to two weeks. Although the woods swarmed with Seneca Indians, as a rule, they never committed any depredations.

In the summer of 1804, when William was ten years old, he killed his first deer. One morning his father sent him into the woods for the cows. Nature was resplendent with verdure. William carried with him a flint-lock gun, and when a short distance from the house he found the cows and a deer feeding with them. This was William's opportunity. He shot and killed this deer, and, as a reward for merit, his father gave him a flint-lock gun as a present. This circumstance determined his course in life, for from that day until his death it was his delight to roam in the forest and pursue wild animals, and hunting was his only business. He was a "professional hunter," a "still hunter," or a man who hunted alone.

In this summer of 1804, William went with his mother to Ligonier, in Westmoreland County, to get some provisions. The only road was an Indian path, the distance sixty miles. They rode through the brush on a horse, and made this trip in about five days.

The Indians soon became civilized, as far as drinking whiskey and getting drunk was an evidence. They visited this still-house for debauchery and drunken carnivals. As a safeguard to himself and family, Louis Long had a strong box made to keep the guns and knives of these Indians in while these drunks were occurring. The Indians desired him to do this. Mr. Long never charged the Indians for this whiskey, although they always offered pelts and furs when they sobered up. In consideration of this generosity, the Indians, in broken English, always called Louis Long, "Good man; give Indian whiskey. Indian fight pale-face; Indians come one hundred miles to give 'good man' warning."

Ludwig Long kept his boys busy in the summer months clearing land, farming, etc. The boys had their own time in winter. Then William, with his gun and traps, traversed the forest, away from the

PIONEER HISTORY OF JEFFERSON COUNTY, PENNA.

ocean's tide, with no inlet or outlet but winding paths used by the deer when he wished to slake his thirst in the clear, sparkling water of the North Fork.

The boy hunter, to keep from being lost while on the trail, followed up one side of this creek and always came down on the opposite. When he grew older he ventured farther and farther into the wilderness, but always keeping the waters of the North Fork, Mill Creek, and Sandy Lick within range until he became thoroughly educated with the country and woods.

In his boyhood he frequently met and hunted in company with Indians. The Indians were friendly to him on account of his father's relations to them, and it was these Indians that gave young William his first lesson in the art of hunting. Young William learned the trick of calling wolves in this way. One day his father and he went out for a deer. William soon shot a large one, and while skinning this deer they heard a pack of wolves howl. William told his father to lie down and be ready to shoot, and he would try the Indian method of "howling" or calling wolves up to you. His father consented, and William howled and the wolves answered. William kept up the howls and the wolves answered, coming closer and closer, until his father became scared; but William wouldn't stop until the wolves got so close that he and his father had to fire on the pack, killing two, when the others took fright and ran away. The bounty for killing wolves then was eight dollars a piece. A short time after this William and his father went up Sandy to watch an elk lick, and at this point they killed an elk and started for home. On the way home they found where a pack of about twenty wolves had crossed their path, near where the town of Reynoldsville now is. Looking up the hill on the right side of Sandy they espied the whole pack, and, both father and son firing into the pack, they killed two of them. William then commenced to "howl," and one old wolf through curiosity came to the top of the hill, looking down at the hunters. For this bravery William shot him through the head. On their return home that day Joseph Barnett treated them both to whiskey and "tansy," for, said he, "the wolves this day have killed one of my cows." When Long was still a young man, one day he went up the North Fork to hunt. About sundown he shot a deer, and when he had it dressed there came up a heavy rain. Being forced to stay all night, he took the pelt and covered himself with it, and lay down under the bank to sleep. After midnight he awoke, and found himself covered with sticks and leaves. In a minute he knew this was the work of a panther hunting food for her cubs, and that she would soon return. He therefore prepared a pitch-pine fagot, lit it, and hid the burning fagot under the bank and awaited the coming of the panther. In a short time after this preparation was completed the animal returned with her cubs, and when she was within about thirty feet of him, Long thrust his torch up and out, and when it blazed up bright the panther gave out a yell and ran away.

John Long and William started out one morning on Sandy Lick to have a bear-hunt, taking with them nine dogs. William had been sent out the day before with two dogs, and had a skirmish with one on Sandy Lick, near where Fuller's Station now stands. The two brothers went to this point and found the track, and chased the bear across the creek at Rocky Bend, the bear making for a windfall; but the dogs stopped him before he reached the windfall and commenced the fight. They soon heard some of the dogs giving death-yells. They both hurried to the scene of conflict, and the first sight they beheld was three favorite dogs stretched out dead and the balance fighting. William ran in and placed the muzzle of his gun against bruin's breast and fired. The bear then backed up to the root of a large hemlock, sitting upright and grabbing for dogs. John and William then fired, and both balls entered bruin's head, not more than an inch apart. In this *mêlée* three dogs were killed and the other six badly wounded. When William was still a boy he went up the North Fork and killed five deer in one day. On his way home about dark he noticed a pole sticking in the hollow of a tree, and carelessly gave this pole a jerk, when he heard a noise in the hole. The moon being up, he saw a bear emerge from this tree some distance up. Young Long shot and killed it before it reached the earth. In that same fall, Bill Long killed in one day, on Mill Creek, nine deer, the largest number he ever killed in that space of time. At that time he kept nothing but the pelts, and carried them home on his back. Panthers often came around Louis Long's home at night, screaming and yelling. So one morning, after three had been prowling around the house all night, William induced his brother John to join him in a hunt for them. There was snow on the ground, and they took three dogs with them. The dogs soon found the "tracks." Keeping the dogs back, they soon found three deer killed by the brutes, and then they let the dogs go. The dogs soon caught these three panthers feasting on the fourth deer. The dogs treed two of the panthers. John shot one and Billy the other, the third escaped. The hunters then camped for the night, dining on deer- and panther-meat roasted, and each concluded the panther-meat was the sweetest and the best.

In the morning they pursued the third panther, treed it, and killed it. These were the first panthers the Long boys ever killed. This stimulated young William, so he took one of the Vastbinder boys and started out again, taking along two dogs. They soon found one, the dogs attacking it. Young Vastbinder fired, but missed. The panther sprang for Long, but the dogs caught him by the hams and that saved young Long. The panther broke loose from the dogs and ran up on a high root. Long then fired and broke the brute's back. The dogs then rushed in, but the panther whipped them off. Then Long, to save the dogs, ran in and tomahawked the creature. Long was about eighteen years of age now. At another time a panther sprang from a high tree for Long. Long fired and killed the panther before it reached him, but the

Shooting a panther.

weight of the animal striking Long on the shoulder, felled him to the earth.

In 1815 six brothers of Cornplanter's tribe of Indians erected wigwams in the Beaver Meadows, where Du Bois now stands. These brothers called themselves respectively "Big" John, "Little" John, "Black" John, "Saucy" John, "John" John, and "John" Sites. In 1823, Long coaxed these Indians to go with him to Luther's tavern to shoot at mark with Lebbeus Luther. Luther made on purpose several careless shots, when the Indians were greatly elated at their victory; but then, to their amazement and fear, all at once he pierced the centre every time. The Indians were then afraid, and casting superstitious glances at Luther, said, "We are not safe. Luver is a bad medicine-man. Let us go." This was great fun for Long. Long told me this story in 1862 in Hickory Kingdom.

In 1826, Ludwig Long moved to Ohio, and young Bill went with the family. He remained there about twenty months; but finding little game, concluded to return to the mountain-hills of Jefferson County, then the paradise of hunters. In 1828, William Long married Mrs. Nancy Bartlett, formerly Miss Nancy Mason, and commenced married life in a log cabin on the North Fork, three miles from where Brookville now is, and on what is now the Albert Horn farm, formerly the Gaup place. About this time, game being plenty, and the scalps, skins, and saddles being hard to carry in, Bill Long induced a colored man named Charles Sutherland to build a cabin near him on what is now known as the Jacob Hoffman farm. Long was to provide for Charlie's family.

Long sees one.

The cabin was built, and Sutherland served Long for about five years. Charles never carried a gun. I remember both these characters well in my childhood, and doctored Long and his wife in my early practice and as late as 1862. In 1830, taking Charlie, Long started up the North Fork for bear; it was on Sunday. After Long killed the first bear, he called Charlie to come and bring the dogs. When Charlie reached him he yelled out, "Good God, massa, hab you seed one?" They continued the hunt that day, and before dark had killed seven bears. Charlie had never seen any bears killed before, but after this day was crazy to be on a hunt, for, he said, if "dem little niggers of mine hab plenty of bear-grease and venison, they will fatten well enough." This fall Long killed sixty deer and twenty-five bears, all on the North Fork, and the bears were all killed near and around where Richardsville now is. This locality was a natural home for wild animals,—

> "With its woodland dale and dell,
> Rippling brooks and hill-side springs."

> "A life in the forest deep,
> Where the winds their revels keep;
> Like an eagle in groves of pine,
> Long hunted with his mate."

In 1832, the day after Long killed the seven bears, he took Charlie Sutherland, and travelled over the same ground that he had been over the day before. He heard nothing, however, during the day but the sigh of the breeze or the speech of the brook until near evening, when, within about a mile of home, he saw a large buck coming down the hill. He fired and wounded the buck, and then motioned Charlie to come up to him while he was loading. Charlie came with a large pine-log on his back. Long asked him what he was doing with that log. Sutherland replied, he wanted it for dry wood. Long told him to throw the wood away, and made him carry the buck home for food. Long then yoked his two dogs up and told Charlie to lead them, but soon discovering bear signs, told Charlie to let the dogs go. The dogs took the trail, and found two bears heading for the laurel on the head of the North Fork. Long knew the route they would take, and beat them to the laurel path. Soon Long heard them coming, the dogs fighting the bears every time the bears would cross a log, catching them from behind. The bears would then turn around and fight the dogs until they could get over the log. When the bears came within about thirty yards of Long, he shot one through the head and killed him. At this time Long only took the pelts, which he always carried home, the meat being of no account. This same year Long took Charlie with him to get some venison by watching a lick, and he took Charlie up a tree with him. In a short time a very large bear came into the lick. Long shot it while he and Charlie were up the tree. Much to Long's amusement, Charlie was so scared that he fell from the tree to the ground, landing on his back with his face up. He was, however, unhurt, and able to carry home to his cabin the pelt and bear oil. The next morning they saw a bear, and Long fired, hitting him in the lungs. This same fall, on the head of the North Fork, Long saw something black in the brush, which, on closer inspection, proved to be a large she bear. On looking up, he saw three good-sized cubs. Long climbed up, and brought the whole three of them down, one at a time. He then handed them to Charlie, who tied their legs. Long put them in his knapsack and carried them home. Bears have from one to four cubs annually, about the 1st of February.

Knapsacks were made out of bed-ticking or canvas, with shoulder-straps. One of these young bears Long sold to Adam George, a butcher in Brookville. Even at this late day Long only took the skins and what meat he wanted for his own use. This fall Long was not feeling well, and had to keep out of the wet. He therefore made Charlie carry him across the streams. He also made Charlie carry a wolf-skin for him to sit on at night, when he was watching a lick. At another time Charlie and Long went out on a hunt near the head of the North Fork. In lonely solitude the dog started a bear, and Long could not shoot it for fear of hitting the dog, so he ran up and made a stroke at the bear's head with a tomahawk, wounding it but slightly. The bear jumped for Long, and the dogs came to the rescue of their master by catching "the tip of the bear's tail end," and, with the valor and fidelity of a true knight, held

A common bear-pen.

it firmly, until Long, who had left his gun a short distance, ran for it. Charlie thought Long was running from the bear, and took to his heels as if the "Old Harry" was after him. Long tried to stop him, but Charlie only looked back, and at this moment his foot caught under a root, throwing him about thirty feet down a hill. Charlie landed on a rock hard enough to have burst a shingle-bolt. Long, seeing this, ran to the bear with his gun and shot him. He then hurried down the hill to see what had become of Charlie, calling to him. Charlie came out from under a bunch of laurel, saying, "God Almighty, Massa Long, I am falled from heben to hell! Are you still living? I tot that ar bar had done gon for you when I seed him come for you with his mouth open. Bless de good Lord you still live, or this nigger would never git out of dese woods!" That night Charlie and Long laid out in the woods. The wolves came up quite close and commenced to howl. Long saw there was a chance for a little fun, so he commenced to howl like a wolf. Charlie became nervous. "When lo! he hears on all sides, from innumerable tongues, a universal howl, and in his fright" said there must be five thousand wolves. Long said he thought there was, and told Charlie that, if the wolves came after them, he must climb a tree. In a few minutes Long made a jump into the woods, yelling "The wolves are coming," and Charlie bounded like a deer into the woods, too. The night was dark and dreary; but deep in the forest Charlie made out to find and climb a majestic oak. Long, therefore, had to look Charlie up, and when he got near to our colored brother, he heard him soliloquizing thus: "Charles, you have to stick tight, for if this holt breaks you are a gone nigger." Long then stepped up to the tree and told Charlie the danger was over; but coming down the tree was harder than going up, for Charlie fell to the earth like a thunder-bolt and doubled up like a jack-knife.

Charlie's domestic life was not all peace, as the following newspaper advertisement will explain:

"CAUTION.

"Whereas my wife Susey did on the 26th day of March last leave my bed and board, and took with her two of my sons and some property, having no other provocation than 'that I would not consent to my son marrying a white girl, and bring her home to live with us.' Therefore I hereby caution all persons against harboring or trusting her on my account, as I will pay no debts of her contracting.

"If she will come home I promise to do all in my power to make her comfortable, and give an equal share of all my property.

"CHARLES SOUTHERLAND.

"April 7, 1847."

When this wilderness commenced to settle up, Long visited Broken Straw Creek, in Warren County, on the head of the Allegheny River, to see a noted hunter by the name of Cotton, and to learn from him his method of hunting young wolves. He learned much from this man Cotton, and afterwards secured many young wolves by the instruction given him by Cotton. In the winter of 1835, Mike and Bill Long went to

PIONEER HISTORY OF JEFFERSON COUNTY, PENNA.

Boone's Mountain to hunt. This mountain was a barren region in those days, that always looked in winter-time like

"Rivers of ice and a sea of snow,
A wilderness frigid and white."

During the season Bill killed one hundred and five deer and Mike one hundred and four, and together they killed four bears. At this time there was some local demand in Brookville and other towns for venison, and in this year the Long's sent loads of venison to Harrisburg, making a trip to the capital in seven or eight days. In 1839, Long moved into Clearfield County, and his history in this county ceased.

Number of animals killed by Long in his life-time: bears, 400; deer (in 1835 one white one), 3500; panthers, 50; wolves, 2000; elks, 125; foxes, 400; wild-cats, 200; catamounts, 500; otters, 75.

Long used to catch fawns, mark their ears, turn them loose, and kill them when full-grown deer. Elks were easily domesticated, and sold as follows,—viz.: for a living male elk one year old, $50; two years old, $75; three years old, $100; and for a calf three months old, $25. In 1835, Long had five wolf-dens that he visited annually for pups, about the 1st of May each year.

In 1834, Bill Long, his brother Mike, and Ami Sibley started on a hunt for elk near where Portland now is. At the mouth of Bear Creek these three hunters came across a drove of about forty elks. Bill Long fired into the herd and broke the leg of one. This wounded elk began to squeal, and then the herd commenced to run in a circle around the injured one. Sibley's gun had the wiping-stick fastened in it, and he could not use it. Bill and Mike then loaded and fired into the drove as rapidly as they could, the elks continuing to make the circle, until each had fired about twenty-five shots, when the drove became frightened and ran away. On examination, the hunters found eight large elks killed. They then made a raft, ran the load down to where Raught's mill is now, and hauled the meat, pelts, and horns to Brookville.

In 1836, Bill Long took Henry Dull and started on a hunt for a young elk. On the third day Long saw a doe elk and calf. He shot the mother, and his dog caught the calf and held it without hurting it. Long removed the udder from the mother, carrying it with the "teats" uppermost, and giving the calf milk from it until they reached Ridgway, where a jug of milk was secured, and by means of an artificial "teat" the calf was nourished until Long reached his North Fork home. Dull led the little creature by a rope around its neck. Mrs. Long raised this elk with her cows, feeding it every milking-time, and when the calf grew to be some size he would drive the cows home every evening for his supper of milk. When this elk was full grown, Long and Dull led him to Buffalo, New York, *via* the pike westward to the Allegheny River, and up

PIONEER HISTORY OF JEFFERSON COUNTY, PENNA.

through Warren, and sold the animal for two hundred dollars,—one hundred dollars in cash and a note for the other hundred, that was never paid.

In the fall of 1836, Long took Henry Dull with him to hunt wolves. The second evening, Long found an old wolf with six half-grown pups. He shot two and the rest ran away. Long and Dull then climbed a hemlock, and Long began his wolf *howl.* On hearing the howl, two pups and the old wolf came back. Long then shot the mother, and afterwards got all the pups. Dull became so frightened that he fell head first, gun and all, through the brush, striking the ground with his head, producing unconsciousness and breaking his shoulder. "Thanks to the human heart, by which we live," for Long nursed Dull at his home on the North Fork for three months. Scalps then brought twelve dollars a piece. In that same year Fred. Heterick and Bill killed an elk at the mouth of Little Toby which weighed six hundred pounds. In 1824, Bill Long had a thrilling adventure with a huge panther in what is now Warsaw township. He, in a hand-to-hand encounter, killed the animal near where Bootjack now stands.

In the winter of 1834, William Dixon, Mike and Bill Long, with dogs, went out to "rope" or catch a live elk. They soon started a drove on the North Fork, and the dogs chased the drove over to the Little Toby, a short distance up from the mouth. The dogs separated one buck from the drove, and this elk, to protect himself from the dogs, took refuge on a ledge of rocks. Bill Long, while Mike and Dixon and the dogs attracted the attention of the elk from below, scrambled in some way to the top of the rocks and threw a rope over the elk's horns, and then cabled the elk to a small tree. This infuriated the elk, so that he jumped out over the rocks and fell on his side. Mike and Dixon now had the first rope. Bill Long then rushed on the fallen elk and threw another rope in a slip-noose knot around the elk's neck, and fastened this rope as a guy to a tree. Each rope was then fastened in an opposite direction to a tree, and after the buck was choked into submission, his feet were tied, and the elk was dragged by these three men on the creek ice to where Brockwayville now is. Here they secured a yoke of oxen and sled from Ami Sibley, a mighty hunter. A small tree was then cut, the main stem being left about five feet long and the two forks about three feet in length. Each prong of the tree was fastened to a horn of the buck, and the main stem permitted to hang down in front over the buck's nose, to which it was fastened with a rope. A rope was then tied around the neck and antlers, and the loose end tied around the hind bench of the sled; this drove the elk close up to the hind part of the sled. The ropes around the feet of the elk were then cut, and the buck lit on his feet. After the animal had made many desperate efforts and plunges, he quieted down, and no trouble was experienced until within a few miles

PIONEER HISTORY OF JEFFERSON COUNTY, PENNA.

of Brookville, when, meeting an acquaintance, Dixon became so much excited over the success in capturing a live elk, that he ran up and hit the elk on the back, exclaiming, "See, we have done it!" and this so scared the elk that he made a desperate jump, upsetting the sled into a ditch over a log. The oxen then took fright, and in the general *mêlée* the elk had a shoulder knocked out of place and the capture was a failure.

There grew in abundance in those days a tree called moose or leatherwood. The pioneers used the bark for ropes, which were very strong.

ELK AND VENISON JERK.

This was "venison flesh cut off in a sheet or web about half an inch thick and spread on the tops of pegs driven into the ground, whilst underneath a fire was kindled, fed with chips of sassafras and other odorous woods, that gradually dried it." The web would be removed and replaced until the jerk was thoroughly dried. The old hunter used to carry a little jerk always with him to eat with his bread. This jerk was a delicious morsel. Bill Long gave me many a "cut." I think I can taste it now. Mike and Bill Long would bring it to Brookville and retail it to the people at five cents a cut.

AN INCIDENT ON THE PIKE.

In the spring of 1820, when the pike was being constructed, there was an early settler by the name of George Eckler living near Fort Barnett. This man Eckler liked a spree, and the Irish that worked on the pike were not averse to "a wee drop at ony time." A jug or two of Long's "Mountain Dew" whiskey, fresh from the still, was secured, and a jolly "Donnebrook fair" time was had one night in the woods. Eckler came in for the worst of it, for his eyes were blackened and he was battered up generally. On sober reflection he concluded to swear out a warrant before Thomas Lucas, Esq., for the "Paddies of the pike." The warrant was placed in the hands of the constable, John Dixon, Sr. There were about twenty-five in this gang of Paddies, and Constable Dixon summoned a posse of eight to assist in the arrest. This posse consisted of the young Dixons, Longs, and McCulloughs, and when this solid column of foresters reached the Irish on the pike, one of the Paddies told the constable to "go home and attend to his own business." He then commanded the pike battalion to remove the handles from their picks and charge on the posse. This they did, to the complete rout of the natives, chasing them all in confusion like a herd of deer through and across Mill Creek. Young Bill Long was with this posse, and he ran home, too, but only to arm himself, not with a shillelah, but with his flint-lock, tomahawk, and knife. Thus armed and single-handed he renewed the conflict, keeping in the woods and above the Irish, and sending balls so close to their heads that the whiz could be heard, until he drove the whole pack, with their carts, etc., from above Port Barnett to where Brookville now stands.

As I remember Long, he was about five feet and four inches high, chubby, strongly built, active, athletic, and a great dancer,—danced what he called the "chippers" and the "crack,"—was cheerful, lively, and good-natured. He carried a heavy single-barrel, muzzle-loading rifle. His belief was that he could shoot better with a heavy rifle than with a light one. Although there were dozens of professional hunters in this wilderness, this man was the king. He had an enduring frame, a catlike step, a steady nerve, keen eyesight, and a ripe knowledge of all the laws governing "still hunts for deer and bear." To reach the great skill he attained in mature life required natural talents, perseverance, sagacity, and habits of thought, as well as complete self-possession, self-control, and quickness of execution.

In these woods Long had great opportunities for perfecting himself in all that pertained to proficiency in a great hunter. Of the other hunters that approached him, I only recall his brothers, the Knapps, the three Vastbinders, the Lucases, the Bells, the Nolfs, Sibley, Fred. Heterick, Indian Russell, and George Smith, who is still living.

The professional hunter was created by the law of 1705 under the dynasty of William Penn. The law reads as follows:

"AN ACT FOR THE KILLING OF WOLVES. FOR PREVENTING THE DE-
STRUCTION OF SHEEP AND CATTLE BY WOLVES.

"SECTION 1. *Be it enacted by John Evans, Esquire, by the Queen's royal approbation Lieutenant-Governor under William Penn, Esquire, absolute Proprietary and Governor-in-Chief of the Province of Pennsylvania and Territories, by and with the advice and consent of the freemen of the said Province in General Assembly met, and by the authority of the same,* That if any person within this province shall kill a dog-wolf, he shall have ten shillings, and if a bitch-wolf, fifteen shillings, to be paid out of the county stock. *Provided* such person brings the wolf's head to one of the justices of the peace of that county, who is to cause the ears and tongue of the said wolf to be cut off. And that the Indians, as well as others, shall be paid for killing wolves accordingly.

"SECTION 2. *And be it further enacted by the authority aforesaid,* That all and every person or persons who are willing to make it their business to kill wolves, and shall enter into recognizance before two or more justices of the peace of the respective counties where he or they dwell, with sufficient security in the sum of five pounds, that he or they shall and will make it his or their sole business, at least three days in every week, to catch wolves, shall have twenty-five shillings for every wolf, dog or bitch, that he or they shall so catch and kill within the time mentioned in the

PIONEER HISTORY OF JEFFERSON COUNTY, PENNA.

said recognizance, to be paid out of the county levies where the wolves are taken as aforesaid."

Repealed by the acts of 1782 and 1819.

Long's early dress was a coon-skin cap, moccasin shoes, a hunting-shirt, and generally buckskin breeches. The hunting-shirt was worn by all these early hunters, and sometimes in militia drill. It was a kind of frock, reached down to the thighs, had large sleeves, was open before, and lapped over a foot or so when belted. This shirt was made of linsey, coarse linen, or of dressed buckskin. The deer-skin shirt was cold and uncomfortable in wet and cold rains. The bosom of the shirt served as a receptacle for rye bread, wheat cakes, tow for cleaning the rifle, jerk, punk, flint and knocker to strike fire with, etc. Matches were first made in 1829, but were not used here for many years after that. The belt was tied behind; it usually held the mittens, bullet-bag, tomahawk, and scalping-knife in its long buckskin sheath. The moccasin in cold weather was sometimes stuffed with feathers, wool, and dry leaves. The heavy early rifles carried about forty-five bullets to a pound of lead. The hand-to-hand conflicts of this noted hunter with panthers, bears, catamounts, wolves, elks, and bucks, both on the land and in the streams, if written out in full, would make a large volume of itself. Elks and deer frequently took to the creeks, and a battle royal with knife and horns would have to be fought in the water. Long was several times mistaken while in a thicket for a wild animal, and careless hunters shot at him. Once his cheek was rubbed with a ball. Dozens of Indians and pale-faced men hunted in this wilderness as well as he, and the table giving an exhibit of the aggregate number of animals killed by Long during his life as a hunter only goes to show what a great zoological garden of wild animals this wilderness must have been. For some of the data in this article I am indebted to Mrs. Dr. Gibson, *née* Anna McCreight, of Reynoldsville, Pennsylvania.

William Long died in Hickory Kingdom, Clearfield County, Pennsylvania, in May, 1880, and was buried in the Conway Cemetery, leaving two sons,—Jack, a mighty hunter, and a younger son, William.

Peace to his ashes. In the haunts of this wilderness, scorched by the summer sun, pinched by the winds of winter wailing their voices like woe, separated for weeks at a time in his lonely cabins from the society of men and women, and then, too, awakened in the dark and dreary nights by the howl of the wolf, the panther's scream, and the owl's to-hoo! to-hoo! Long steadily, year in and year out, for sixty years pursued this wild, romantic life.

THE HABITS OF SOME OF THE GAME LONG HUNTED.

Our bears cub in February, have two cubs at a birth, and these cubs are about the size of a brown rat, without hair, and blind for nine days.

PIONEER HISTORY OF JEFFERSON COUNTY, PENNA.

They are suckled by the mother for about three months, when they reach the size of a cat; then the mother takes them out and teaches them to eat nuts, berries, bugs, little animals, green corn, vegetables, hogs, sheep, and sometimes cattle. A full-grown bear will weigh four hundred pounds. He is exceedingly strong. He can carry a heavy burden and walk on his hind legs for a long distance.

He frequently gnawed himself out of hunters' pens, is a bold, intelligent beast, and his meat was considered a delicacy by the hunters.

Bears lived in "homes," holes, or dens, and sometimes in a rocky place there would be a "community." They, like deer, follow their own paths.

Our panther was fully as strong as the bear, but was rather cowardly, and especially fearful of dogs. A single blow from one forefoot or a bite from a panther would kill a dog. As a preservation, the panther hunter always had a trained dog with him, for a single bark from a dog would often scare a panther up a tree. The panther, as a rule, sought and sprang upon his victim in the dark. He could throw a buck, hog, or cow without a struggle. A panther attained sometimes a length of ten feet from nose to end of tail. They lived in dens and had two cubs at a time.

Rowe, of Clearfield, says of the hunter Dan Turner, "Once, when going out to a 'bear wallow,' his attention was attracted by a panther acting in a strange manner. He soon saw a large bear approaching it. With hair erect and eyes glaring, the panther gnashed his teeth, and, waiting until bruin came up, sprang upon him. A mortal struggle ensued. Turner watched with much interest the fight, which lasted some ten minutes or more. At last the growls of the fierce combatants became faint, and the struggle ceased. The panther slowly disengaged himself from his dead enemy and took position upon the carcass. It was now Turner's time, and, raising his rifle, he shot the panther in the head. After examining it, he was of the opinion that it could have lived but a very few minutes longer. Nearly every bone in its body was broken, and its flesh was almost reduced to a pulp by the blows and hugs of the bear."

Our wolves always had their dens in the wildest, most hidden part of the wilderness. They always manage to get under the rocks or ground to shelter themselves and young from all storms. The male fed the female when the "pups" were small. He would travel a great distance in search of food, and if what he found was too heavy to carry home, he would gorge himself with it and go home and vomit it up for the family. The wolf and fox were very chary and hard to trap. But Long and other hunters knew their habits so well that they could always outwit them.

A wolf could carry a sheep for miles in this way : seize it by the throat and throw it over or on his back. Wolves hunted the deer in packs; they all hunted together until a deer was started. The pack would keep up the chase until they were tired; then one wolf would keep up the chase at full speed, while the balance of the pack watched, and when the deer turned a circle, fresh and rested wolves struck in and pursued; thus the deer was pursued alternately by fresh wolves and soon tired out, and would then fly to some stream; the wolves would follow, and while the deer would remain in the stream the wolves would separate, a part of the pack forming in line on each side of the stream, when the deer would become an easy prey to these ravenous creatures.

The most dangerous animal or reptile was the rattlesnake. We had these colors: the black, yellow, or spotted. Millions of them inhabited these woods, and some were four and five feet long. Snakes, as well as other wild animals, travel and seek their food in the night. To escape this danger, each pioneer kept a large herd of hogs, who would kill and eat snakes with impunity. Dogs, too, were faithful in this direction. But how did the woodsman and hunter escape? Well, he wore woollen stockings, moccasins with anklets, and buckskin breeches. A snake could not bite through these, and at night he usually laid his head on the body of his dog to protect his upper extremities.

It was seldom that the elk or deer had twins. The bear, panther, and wolf always had a litter. Wolves reared in the same pack lived friendly, but strange males always fought.

The deer, when frightened, circled round and round, but never left his haunt. The elk would start on a trot, and never stop under ten or fifteen miles. The bear was and is a wanderer,—here to-day and away to-morrow. The wolf and panther were fierce and shy.

APPENDIX.

SOME LOCAL HISTORY—A LINCOLN STORY—THE MEMORABLE CAMPAIGN OF 1864.

IN the spring of 1864 we had thirty thousand human, living skeletons in rebel prisons. The war had been carried on for three years. The following great and sanguinary battles had been fought,—viz.: Bull Run, Seven Pines, Fort Donelson, Fort Pillow, Shiloh, Seven Days' battle in Virginia, second battle of Bull Run, Antietam, Fredericksburg, Stone River, Chancellorsville, Gettysburg, Chickamauga, Cold Harbor, Spottsylvania, and the Wilderness. These battles, or most of them, had been the bloodiest that modern history records. In our sorrow and despair, the most bitter antagonisms existed at home between the war and antiwar people. A new President was to be elected that year, and in order to save the country and to punish rebellion, nearly all patriots—this included war Democrats—believed that the re election of Lincoln was absolutely necessary. Actuated by these impulses, Judge Joseph Henderson, of Brookville, was chosen our Congressional delegate to the national convention, which was to meet on the 7th of June, 1864, in Baltimore, Maryland. Judge Henderson, Major Andrews, and myself were warm friends. The judge was a great friend of Lincoln and Johnson. On the 5th of June I accompanied the judge to Baltimore. Our State delegation consisted of fifty-two men,—forty-eight district delegates and four at large,—viz., Simon Cameron, W. W. Ketcham, Morrow B. Lowry, and A. K. McClure. Simon Cameron was made chairman of the delegation. The following States were represented in that body: Maine, Vermont, New Hampshire, Massachusetts, Rhode Island, Connecticut, New York, New Jersey, Pennsylvania, Delaware, Maryland, Louisiana, Arkansas, Tennessee, Ohio, Indiana, Illinois, Michigan, Wisconsin, Iowa, Minnesota, California, Oregon, West Virginia, Kansas, Nebraska, Colorado, Nevada, and Missouri. There was a dispute as to the right of Tennessee to representation, but the convention voted them in. In this the judge voted aye, and on the first ballot Lincoln received every vote except Missouri, which cast a solid vote for General Grant. For Vice-President, Andrew Johnson, of Tennessee, was nominated on first ballot over Hamlin, of Maine, Dickinson, of New York, and Rosseau, of Kentucky. It was thought by the convention expedient to strengthen the ticket by nominating a man for this office who was known to be a war Democrat and from the South, and as this was a convention of freemen, wise leaders, and not of bosses, the people and wisdom ruled.

From Baltimore I went to Washington on business to see Stanton. I found him haughty and austere. I therefore sought and received an audience at the White House. I had heard Lincoln denounced verbally and in the newspapers as "Lincoln, the gorilla," "Lincoln, the ape," "Lincoln, the baboon," etc., and, true enough, I found him to be a very homely man, tall, gaunt, and long-limbed, but courteous, sympathetic, and easily approached. My business with him was this: In 1863 a thirteen-year-old boy from Jefferson County, whose father had been killed in battle, was recruited and sold for bounty into the Fourteenth United States Regulars at Pittsburg, Pennsylvania. After a few months' service, this boy, tired of military life, was told by his soldier companions that he could not be held in the service, and, instead of demanding his discharge in a proper way, unceremoniously left and deserted, for which he was afterwards arrested, court-martialled, and sentenced to be shot. As early as April 28, and after that, legal efforts were put forth, and military influence used by myself and others to save this boy, but without avail.

"ADJUTANT-GENERAL'S OFFICE,
"WASHINGTON, D.C., April 28, 1864.

"SIR,—I have the honor to acknowledge the receipt of your communication of the 9th ultimo, requesting the discharge of —— —— from the military service of the United States, of the Fourteenth United States Infantry, on the ground of minority, and to inform you in reply that he is now under arrest for trial by court-martial for desertion, and no action can be taken for his discharge, or that will prevent his punishment if found guilty.

"I am, sir, very respectfully,
"Your obedient servant,
"THOMAS M. VINCENT,
"*Assistant Adjutant-General.*

"W. J. MCKNIGHT, Brookville, Pa."

My business was to save this boy's life, and while everything else had been done by legal talent and military influence, I went to Lincoln with a sad heart. He was at that time perhaps the busiest man in the world. He listened patiently to my story, and then said, "Is all this true, Dr. McKnight, that you have told me? Will no one here listen to you?" I replied, "Yes, Mr. President, it is all true." He arose, reached for his hat, and remarked to me, "I'll be a friend to that fatherless boy." He put his arm in mine and took me to Stanton's office, and, after a few minutes' talk with the Secretary, he turned to me and said, "You can go home, doctor, and if that boy has not been shot, you can rest assured he will be discharged." In due time, after my return home, I received by mail the following :

"ADJUTANT-GENERAL'S OFFICE,
"WASHINGTON, D. C., July 13, 1864.

"SIR,—I have the honor to inform you that, by direction of the President, —— ——, alias John Scott, Fourteenth United States Infantry, was discharged the military service of the United States, by special orders No. 204, Par. 25, current series, from this office.

"I am, sir, very respectfully,
"Your obedient servant,
"SAMUEL BRECK,
"Assistant Adjutant-General.
"MR. W. J. MCKNIGHT, Brookville, Pa."

Washington at this time was the greatest panorama of war in modern times. It took me days to secure an audience with Mr. Lincoln. I was then, and am yet, perhaps too ultra and bitter a Republican, but after this humane act of President Lincoln I was as bitter a partisan as ever, and, in addition to that, a personal admirer of Lincoln from the crown of my head to the end of my toes. The call for our county convention that year was issued July 13, 1864, as follows,—viz. :

"DELEGATE ELECTION.

"The Republicans of Jefferson County will meet in their respective townships and boroughs on Tuesday, the 2d day of August, between the hours of two and six o'clock P.M., to elect two delegates of each township and borough, to meet at the court-house in the borough of Brookville, on Friday, the 5th day of August, at one o'clock, to nominate candidates to be supported for the different county offices.

"M. M. MEREDITH,
"Chairman County Committee."

The county then had twenty-three townships and four boroughs, giving us fifty-four delegates. The date fixed for the primaries was on the day set by the law of the State, passed in the spring of that year, for the special election for three amendments to our Constitution, one of which was to permit the soldiers in the field to vote. The date fixed for this call was a shrewd policy, as it materially assisted in bringing out a full Republican primary, and was a great aid in carrying that "soldier vote" issue in the county, which we did, as the full return gave fourteen hundred and ninety-seven for this amendment and twelve hundred and twenty against it, a majority of two hundred and seventy-seven. This

PIONEER HISTORY OF JEFFERSON COUNTY, PENNA.

issue was bitterly fought. After the national convention I had been appointed a member of the Union State Central Committee by Simon Cameron, who was then chairman of that committee, and this soldier campaign in the county was conducted by Captain Meredith. The county convention was held on August 5, as called, and the following ticket selected: For District Attorney, A. C. White; County Commissioners, I. C. Jordan, Eli B. Irvin; Auditor, Joseph P. North; Trustees of Academy, P. H. Shannon, M. M. Meredith, Calvin Rodgers.

G. W. Andrews was made county chairman. Our Representative district was Clarion and Jefferson, and on September 9, at Corsica, Hunter Orr, of Clarion County, was declared the nominee for the Legislature. On September 15, G. W. Schofield was declared in Ridgway our nominee for Congress. Dr. A. M. Clarke and S. W. Temple were our conferees there. This completed our ticket. There were no State officers to be elected. Nothing but district and county tickets in that October election. I do not recollect who was the Democratic chairman, but it is immaterial, for ex-Senator K. L. Blood dominated and controlled the Democratic party in this county then, and a bold, wiry, vigorous antagonist he was. Our Democratic Dutch friends used to make this reply: "I do not know how I votes. I votes for der Kennedy Blute anyhows." Schoolhouse meetings were held in all the townships. Local speakers were scarce. Most of them were in the army, and this labor then principally devolved upon Andrews and me. Dr. Heichhold was furloughed about October 20 to help us. In our meetings we all abused Blood, and he in return abused us. Major Andrews was a great worker, and usually took a number of papers and documents to read from. What little I said was off-hand. The major would always say in his speeches that "the common people of the Democrats were honest, but the leaders of that party were rascals, traitors, and rebels." He was a Maine Yankee. We elected him to the State Constitutional Convention in 1872, and after his service there he removed to Denver, where he lived and died.

For the August and October elections we had no funds except our own, and we were all poor alike. Our newspaper editor was John Scott, Esq. He was poor, too; paper was high and hard to get, and, as a consequence of this, our organ, the *Republican*, was only published occasionally, and often only half-sheets: hence our meetings had to be advertised verbally and by written and printed posters. I had one horse. I traded some books for a second-hand buggy, and bought another horse that I would now be ashamed to own, and in this buggy and behind this team the major and I drove the circuit in October and November, stopping for dinner and over night, Methodist preacher fashion, with the brethren. It was a rainy fall, and all through October and November there was mud,—mud rich and deep, mud here and there, mud on the hill and everywhere, mud on the ground and in the air, and to those who

PIONEER HISTORY OF JEFFERSON COUNTY, PENNA.

travelled politically it was a mud-splashing as well as a mud-slinging campaign. We had a mass-meeting on October 8 in Brookville and on that day we had a strong address published, reviewing the issues to the people, signed by I. G. Gordon, Philip Taylor, T. K. Litch, A. S. Rhines, R. G. Wright, and J. P. Wann. The speakers for the mass-meeting were Chairman Andrews, Colonel Childs, of Philadelphia, Congressman Myers, and A. L. Gordon. J. W. Pope, the great campaign singer, from Philadelphia, by his patriotic songs, impelled us all to greater earnestness. In the October struggle we lost our county and Representative ticket, but Schofield was re-elected to Congress. A Congressman then never thought of having one or two bosses in a county to dispense post-offices. The Democrats carried the State on the home vote; but, with the aid of the soldiers, we carried the State by a small majority. The anti-war Democrats greatly rejoiced at their victory on the home vote, and they confidently expected, as McClellan was a Pennsylvanian, that State pride would carry him through in November. The two elections were about one month apart. The soldier vote was denounced as the "bayonet vote" and "bayonet rule." Simon Cameron, our State chairman, was greatly disappointed at the loss of our State on the "home vote." After the October election Cameron sent me a draft for two hundred dollars in "rag-money," which I expended as judiciously as I knew how. We gained in the county sixty votes for the November election. I am sorry that I cannot give the manner of expenditure of this money. My accounts were all audited and the settlement-paper left with G. W. Andrews. McClellan had been the idol of the army and the people, and although he and Pendleton were nominated at Chicago on August 31, 1864, on a peace platform that the war had been a failure and a call to suspend hostilities, there never was a day that McClellan would not have been overwhelmingly elected in 1864, until in September, when Sherman captured Atlanta and Sheridan went whirling through the valley of Virginia. Everybody, Lincoln and all, knew this. These two victories gave the Union people great heart for hard work. After these victories, Fremont and Cochrane, who had been nominated at Cleveland, Ohio, on May 31, 1864, for President and Vice-President by radicals of the Republican party, withdrew, and both supported Lincoln. Our army before Richmond was idle, and, to effectually stop the "bayonet rule" charge, Meade furloughed five thousand soldiers for two weeks. Sheridan did the same, making ten thousand in all, and they were home and voted. This gave us the State on the home vote by about five, and with the "bayonet vote," by about twenty, thousand. In this election our county went as follows:

	Lincoln.	McClellan.
Home vote	1614	1756
Army vote	207	111
Total vote	1821	1867

PIONEER HISTORY OF JEFFERSON COUNTY, PENNA.

In the November election our county went Democratic; but we Republicans had a grand jubilee after the returns came in from the nation, as McClellan only carried three States,—viz., Kentucky, Delaware, and New Jersey. Brevity requires many things that I would delight to say about Lincoln and this campaign to be omitted. Republican success gave assurance to the world that "the war for the Union would still be prosecuted," and it was, and Pennsylvania performed her duty, both politically and on the battle-fields. Pennsylvania gave to the national government during the war three hundred and sixty-seven thousand four hundred and eighty-two soldiers, and during the same period organized and put in the field eighty-seven thousand men for State defence, making a grand total of four hundred and fifty-four thousand four hundred and eighty-two soldiers. Three times during the war Pennsylvania was invaded, and it remained for the Rebellion to receive its Waterloo at Gettysburg and from a Pennsylvania commander.

In conclusion, it was the soldiers' bayonets and the "bayonet voters" of "Lincoln's hirelings" that crushed rebellion and saved the Union.

"BROOKVILLE'S PIONEER RESURRECTION; OR, 'WHO SKINNED THE NIGGER?'—THE TRUTH TOLD FOR THE FIRST TIME, BY THE ONLY ONE NOW LIVING OF THE SEVEN WHO WERE ENGAGED IN IT—ORIGIN OF THE STATE ANATOMICAL LAW.*

"On Sunday morning, November 8, 1857, Brookville was thrown into a state of the greatest commotion and excitement, occasioned by the discovery by W. C. Smith (then a lad of fifteen) of the mutilated remains of a human being in an ice-house belonging to K. L. Blood, on the corner of Pickering Street and Coal Alley, or where Mrs. Banks now lives. When discovered by Smith, the door was broken open, having been forced during the night, and the body was found lying on the ice, with a board under the shoulders and head, the legs and arms spread apart, the intestines taken out, a lump of ice placed in the abdominal cavity, and the body literally skinned, the cuticle having been removed entirely from the crown of the head to the soles of the feet.

"Filled with terror, young Smith ran from the spot, telling his discovery to all he met. Men, women, and children rushed *en masse* to the ice-house. Thoughts of savage butchery, suicide, and horror took hold of the people. Women cried, and men turned pale with indignation. The news of Smith's discovery spread like wildfire, and the excitement and indignation became more and more intense as hundreds of men,

---

* By W. J. McKnight, M.D.

women, and children from the town and vicinity gathered around the lonely ice-house. It was at first supposed to be murder most foul; but, on a closer inspection of the 'remains' by Henry R. Fullerton, a little 'curly hair,' resembling 'negro wool,' was found lying loose near the body. This was a clue. Fullerton then declared it was the mutilated corpse of one Henry Southerland, who had died about ten days before and been buried in the old graveyard. Tools were at once procured by the excited mob, led by Henry R. Fullerton, Cyrus Butler, Sr., Richard Arthurs, Esq., and others, and a rush was made for Southerland's grave. Arriving there, and upon the removal of a few shovelfuls of dirt, a loose slipper was found, and farther on its mate. When the coffin was reached, the body was found to be gone, and only the clothes, torn off and lying inside, were to be seen. What was this desecration for? Cyrus Butler, Sr., a gruff old man, said, 'For money.' He boldly asserted that men nowadays would do anything for money. 'Yes,' he said, 'skin human excrement and eat the little end on't.' Soon, in the absence of any better theory, everybody seemed to accept his belief, and it was positively asserted from one to another that 'a negro hide would sell for five hundred dollars, to make razor-strops,' etc.

"During the entire day the mob were at sea. The officials permitted the body to remain exposed,—a revolting spectacle to men, women, and children. To all of this I was an interested spectator.

"At nightfall an inquest was summoned of twelve men by Justices John Smith and A. J. Brady, as appears from the following Quarter Sessions' record :

(Copy.)

" COMMONWEALTH'S SUMMONS TO JURORS.

"'November 8, 1857. Served personally on all the within-named jurors. Cost, $1.20.

"'C. BUTLER,
"' Constable.

"' The Commonwealth of Pennsylvania to C. Butler, constable of the township of Pine Creek, in the county of Jefferson : We command you immediately upon sight hereof, to summon twelve good and lawful men of Jefferson County aforesaid, whose names are hereto annexed, to be and appear before A. J. Brady and John Smith, two of the justices of the peace of the county of Jefferson, at the ice-house of K. L. Blood & Brother, in the borough of Brookville, at four o'clock P.M. of this day ; then and there to inquire of, do, and execute all things as in our behalf shall be lawfully given them in charge, touching the supposed body of Henry Southerland ; and be you then and there to certify what you shall have done in the premises; and, further, to do and execute what in our behalf shall be then and there enjoined you.

"'Given under our hands and seals, this 8th day of November, 1857.

"'A. J. BRADY, [L. S.]
JOHN SMITH, [L. S]

"'The Commonwealth of Pennsylvania, greeting, to E. R. Brady, John J. Y. Thompson, A. Craig, John Boucher, L. A. Dodd, Christopher Smathers, Henry Fullerton, G. W. Andrews, S. C. Arthurs, John Carroll, John Ramsey, D. Smith.

"SUBPŒNA FOR WITNESSES.

"'November 8, 1857. Served personally on the within names by reading. Cost, $1.75.

"'C. FULLERTON,
"'Constable.

"'The Commonwealth of Pennsylvania to K. L. Blood, Thomas Espy, J. P. George, Joseph Darr, Thomas Graham, John Hamilton, William J. McKnight, T. B. McLain, James Dowling, James Scott, J. S. Steck, George Smith, A. B. McLain, Charles Windsor, Robert St. Clair, J. P. Miller, West. Bowman, greeting: We command you and every of you, that you set aside all business and excuses whatsoever, you do in your proper persons appear before A. J. Brady and John Smith, two of the justices of the peace in and for said county of Jefferson, and an inquisition now sitting at the office of John Smith, Esq., in the borough of Brookville, in said county, to testify the truth and give such information and evidence as you and every of you shall know touching the manner in which the said body of Henry Southerland, or some person unknown, lying at the ice-house of K. L. Blood & Brother, in the borough of Brookville, dead, came by his death or came there, and touching all other matters in relation to which you shall be examined. And this you are in nowise to omit, under the penalty that may ensue.

"'Witness our hands and seals, at Brookville, the 8th day of November, A.D. 1857.

"'A. J. BRADY, [L. S.]
JOHN SMITH, [L. S.]

"CORONER'S INQUEST.

"'Proceedings of the coroner's inquest, held in the borough of Brookville, upon the body of a man found in the ice-house belonging to K. L. Blood, on the corner of Pickering Street and Spring [Coal] Alley, on the morning of Sunday, November 8, 1857.

"'In pursuance of the summons issued by Justices John Smith and A. J. Brady, the following persons were called and sworn,—to wit: E.

PIONEER HISTORY OF JEFFERSON COUNTY, PENNA.

R. Brady, J. J. Y. Thompson, Andrew Craig, John Boucher, Levi A. Dodd, Christopher Smathers, Henry R. Fullerton, G. W. Andrews, S. C. Arthurs, John E. Carroll, John Ramsey, Daniel Smith, who repaired to the ice-house and made an examination of the body there deposited, and found the remains of a male human being, with the breast sawed open, the bowels and entrails removed, the toe-and finger-nails cut off at the first joint, and the skin of the entire body removed.

" 'The grave in which Henry Southerland (colored), of Pine Creek township, had been buried having been opened in the presence of a number of the jurors and other persons, and it being found that the body of said deceased had been removed from the said grave, the following witnesses were called and sworn :

" ' David Banks, sworn : I helped open the grave in which the body of Henry Southerland (colored) had been buried ; found no body in the coffin ; found the burial clothes rolled up in a bundle and placed in the head of the coffin ; found one of the slippers in which deceased was buried in the clay about a foot above and before coming to the coffin ; the body had evidently been removed.

" ' F. C. Coryell, sworn : Was present at the opening of the grave to-day ; saw the coffin opened and no body there ; found the clothes thrown in carelessly in a heap ; one slipper with the clothes in the coffin and another in the clay some distance above the coffin ; these slippers had my cost mark on, and are the same as purchased from me by the friends of Henry Southerland for his funeral.

" ' A. R. Marlin, sworn : Henry Southerland was buried in the graveyard at Brookville on Wednesday or Thursday last ; helped to bury him ; the grave opened to-day is the one in which deceased was placed ; no body in the coffin when opened to-day.

" ' Richard Arthurs, sworn : I examined the body in the ice-house this day ; looked at the mouth and tongue ; they resembled those of a person who had died of a disease ; two double teeth out ; seemed as if they had recently been drawn ; found some hair about the back of the neck, which was black and curly ; think it was the hair of a negro, or whiskers ; think this is the body of Henry Southerland ; toes, fingers, and skin taken off.

" ' After making these enquiries and believing the body found in the ice-house to be that of Henry Southerland, which had been removed from the graveyard in the borough of Brookville, the jury caused the same to be taken up and deposited in the coffin, and placed in the grave from which the body of said Southerland had been removed, and the same filled up in their presence ; then returning to the office of John Smith, Esq., a justice of the peace, adjourned, to meet at nine o'clock to-morrow (Monday) morning.

" ' The jury render their verdict as follows : That the body found in

PIONEER HISTORY OF JEFFERSON COUNTY, PENNA.

the ice-house is, to the best of their knowledge and belief, the body of Henry Southerland, stolen from the grave in which the same had been deposited; and that the skin, bowels, and toe- and finger-nails had been removed by some person or persons to the jury unknown.

" ' E. R. BRADY, *Foreman*.
A. J. BRADY, [L. S.]
JOHN SMITH, [L. S.]
" ' E. R. BRADY, [L. S.]
JOHN J. Y. THOMPSON, [L. S.]
ANDREW CRAIG, [L. S.]
JOHN BOUCHER, [L. S.]
LEVI A. DODD, [L. S.]
H. R. FULLERTON, [L. S.]
C. SMATHERS, [L. S]
G. W. ANDREWS, [L. S.]
S. C. ARTHURS, [L. S.]
JOHN E. CARROLL, [L. S.]
JOHN RAMSEY, [L. S.]
D. SMITH, [L. S.]
" *Coroners Jury.*

"BILL OF COST ON INQUISITION.
" ' Fee of coroner, or justices $4.00
Viewing dead body 2.75
Summoning and qualifying inquest 1.37½
" witnesses, each 25 cents, 4 . . . . 1.00
Jurors, 12, each 2 days 24.00
Constable Fullerton 1.75
Constable Butler 1.20
Witnesses' costs:
David Banks, 1 day 62½
F. C. Coryell, 1 day 62½
A. R. Marlin, 1 day 62½
R. Arthurs, 1 day 62½
$38 57½

" ' JEFFERSON COUNTY, *ss.*:

" ' We hereby certify that the above is a true bill of the costs in this above case.

" ' Witness our hands and seals, this 15th day of December, A.D. 1857.
" ' A. J. BRADY, [L. S.]
JOHN SMITH, [L. S.]

" ' December 17, 1857. It is adjudged that there was probable cause for holding the inquest.
" ' By the Court,
" ' J. S. MCCALMONT.'

"This coroner's verdict was supposed to have been manipulated by the 'Masons.' It was the custom then to charge all unpopular verdicts on 'the Masons.'

"After the inquest jurors viewed the body and ice-house on Sunday evening, a rope was tied around Southerland's neck, he was dragged into Coal Alley, thrown into his coffin, and reburied in the old graveyard, where lie

"'Hearts once pregnant with celestial fire,
Hearts that the rod of empire might have swayed,
Or waked to ecstacy the living lyre.'

"Who were the ghouls? As usual, stupidity and prejucice came to the front, and picked out for vengeance two innocent and inoffensive colored men living in the suburbs of the town. 'The law ordained in reverence we must hold,' and so on Sunday evening Theresa Sweeney, a sister of Southerland's, was sent for, and she made information against Charles Anderson and John Lewis. Cyrus Butler, Jr., a constable then in Pine Creek township, arrested forthwith these two harmless colored men and thrust them into jail. On Monday morning, the 9th, Anderson and Lewis had a hearing before Justices Smith and Brady. George W. Zeigler, an able lawyer, represented the Commonwealth; but the poor negroes were without friends or a lawyer. However, as there was no evidence against them, they were discharged. The excitement was now so intense that several newly made graves were opened to see if friends had been disturbed. A few timid people placed night-guards in the cemetery.

"In commenting on this atrocity, the *Jeffersonian* said, 'Taking everything into consideration, it was one of the most inhuman and barbarous acts ever committed in a civilized community; and although the instigators and perpetrators may escape the punishment which their brutality demands, they cannot fail to receive the indignant frowns of an insulted community. They may evade a prosecution through the technicalities of the law, and they may laugh it off, and when we have no assurance but our bodies, or those of our friends, may be treated in the same manner, cold and hardened must be the wretch who does not feel the flame of indignation rise in his breast at the perpetration of such an offence.

* * * * * * * * *

"'Since the above was in type and the excitement somewhat allayed, it is now believed by every person that the body was placed in the ice-house for dissection, and it is supposed that those who had the matter in charge had the key to the door and left everything safe and secure on Saturday night, and that some thief, knowing that during the warm weather butter had been placed there for protection, broken open the door and entered the place for the purpose of stealing, and on striking a

PIONEER HISTORY OF JEFFERSON COUNTY, PENNA.

light or groping around in search of butter, he came across the "dead darky," and, in his haste to get away, forgot to shut the door, and we have no doubt that the fellow who broke open the door left in a hurry. This is, no doubt, the true state of the case.'

"All this confusion was a good thing for the guilty parties, as it gave time for the angry populace to cool off.

"Who was this Henry Southerland? He was a stout, perfect specimen of physical manhood. He was a son of Charles and Susan Southerland, *née* Van Camp. Charles Southerland came here in 1812,—a runaway slave. Miss Van Camp came to Port Barnett with her father, Fudge Van Camp, in 1801. Henry Southerland was born on the farm now owned by John Hoffman. He was a North Forker, and, like the other 'North Fork' boys, could drink, swear, wrestle, shoot, jump, 'pull square,' and raft. In the latter part of October, 1857, he took the fever and died in a few days, aged about thirty years. He lived then on what is called the Charles Horn farm. He was married and had one child. His widow and daughter now reside in the county, highly respectable people.

"Dr. J. C. Simons was then living in Brookville, practising medicine under his father in law, Dr. James Dowling. Simons was ambitious to become a surgeon. He believed, like all intelligent doctors then, that a knowledge of anatomy was the foundation of the healing art. Dissection of human bodies then in Pennsylvania was a crime. You could dissect mules and monkeys, but not men. It was legal in New York State, and was made so in 1789, and this law in New York was greatly improved in 1854. New York was the first State in the New World to legalize 'the use of the dead to the living.'

"The first human body dissected was in Alexandria, Egypt, the cradle of anatomy. England legalized dissection in 1820. The first subject dissected in Jefferson County was in Brookville, in the winter of 1854–55, by Dr. George Watt, Dr. McClay, Samuel C. Arthurs, and a student, G. W. Burkett, now a doctor in Tyrone City, Pennsylvania. This subject was stolen from a graveyard in Clarion County, Pennsylvania. He was an Irishman who froze to death. He drank too much water in his whiskey.

"Ambition is something like love,—laughs at law and takes fearful risks. The death of Southerland, Simons thought, was a good chance for a subject and a surgical school to advance himself and assist the rest of us. On the day of Southerland's death Dr. Simons visited separately each of the following doctors in the town, and appointed a meeting to be held on Saturday night, October 31, at ten o'clock, in K. L. Blood's drug-store, for the purpose of organizing and resurrecting the dead negro: Drs. J. G. Simons, John Dowling, Hugh Dowling, A. P. Heichhold, and W. J. McKnight. By request, I secured, on Friday, October

PIONEER HISTORY OF JEFFERSON COUNTY, PENNA.

30, permission from Dr. Clark to use for our school the empty house then owned by him, and where John Means now lives. Augustus Bell, an educated gentleman from Philadelphia, who lived and died here, and K. L. Blood, both medically inclined, were taken in as friends. Promptly at ten o'clock, Saturday night, October 31, 1857, all these parties met in council in the drug-store. Simons, the two Dowlings, and 'Little Bell' filled themselves full to the brim with Monongahela whiskey. Blood, Heichhold, and McKnight remained dry and took not a drop. At about eleven o'clock P.M. we all marched up Pickering Street, with a mattock, shovel, and rope. John Dowling and I were quite young men, and were stationed as watchers, or guards. The others were to resurrect. Simons and 'Little Bell' worked like 'bees,' and were as brave as lions as long as the whiskey stimulated them; but when that died out they kicked and balked badly. Mr. Blood then took hold like a hero. He dug, shovelled, broke open the coffin, and 'there, down there in the earth's cold breast,' placed the rope around the subject and assisted in the resurrection of Southerland. Remember this:

> "'It was a calm, still night,
> And the moon's pale light
> Shone soft o'er hill and dale,'

when we, seven ghouls, stood around the empty tomb of Henry Southerland. The grave was then hastily filled, and carefully too. The naked corpse was now placed on a 'bier.' John Dowling and I took one side side, K. L. Blood and Simons the other, and under the autumn's full moon we left the graveyard; down Barnett Street, crossed Coal Alley, across Jefferson Street, down to Cherry Alley, at the rear of Judge Clark's property now, and up Cherry Alley to the rear of the lot now owned by John Means, and down that lot to the kitchen part of the house, into which the body was carried and placed in a little bedroom west and south of the kitchen. This was done between the hours of one and two A.M., unobserved. Tired and weary, we all went home to rest, and expected to open the school on Monday night, the 2d, but for reasons I will give you farther on this was not done.

"On the evening of the 2d of November, 1857, my mother called me to one side and said, 'You have gotten yourself into trouble. You have been out nights. Don't say a word to me, just listen. You have been helping the other doctors to dig up Henry Southerland. Dr. Heichhold told Captain Wise all about it, Wise told his wife, she told Mrs. Samuel C. Arthurs, she told Mrs. Richard Arthurs, and Mrs. Richard Arthurs told me this afternoon. Now take care of yourself. As you are poor, you will have to suffer; the others are all rich and influential.'

"This was a nitro-glycerin explosion to me. I made no reply to my dear mother, but left for Blood's drug-store, and repeated to him what mother had told me. His left hand went up as if struck by a Niagara electric current. I said to him, ' I want Dr. Clark protected now; Southerland must be removed from his house.' Blood agreed with me. A caucus was then called for that night at the store, when it was decided to remove the body from the house down through the cellar and secrete it under those present front steps of John Means's house, and there it lay naked from Monday night until Wednesday night, when the cadaver was removed from there to Blood's ice-house, in a large coffee-sack, about nine P.M., as follows: McElhose had his printing-office in a little building east and on the same lot. It was on that vacant piece next to Corbett's house now. It was built for and used as a drug-store. There was a door under the west side that opened into the under part of the porch and the front steps. If McElhose or any of his imps had ever opened that door, ' a dreadful sight would have met their startled view.' I was a printer and had learned the art in part with McElhose, and I was detailed to go into his office and make all kinds of noises and detract the attention of the printers from any sounds under the porch. This I did by dancing, kicking over furniture, etc. I could hear the other parties at times; but McElhose thought I was drunk, or such a fool that he only watched and heard me. Everything worked favorably, and ' Black Hen' was successfully removed to a house whose inside walls were frigid and white. ' In the icy air of night' the school for dissection was opened on Wednesday and closed on Saturday morning. As our secret was known to so many, and realizing that we could not dissect in Brookville without being caught up, we only mutilated the cadaver for our personal safety.

"At this time Brookville was full of burglars, thieves, and housebreakers. On Friday night, the 6th, A. B. McLain was patrolling for robbers in Coal Alley, and under the ' ebon vault of heaven, studded with stars unutterably bright,' he espied what he thought to be three suspicious persons, and pounced down on them like a hawk on a chicken. The suspects proved to be Drs. Hugh Dowling, Heichhold, and ' Little Bell' (Augustus Bell). McLain was then taken a prisoner by the suspects, dumped into the ice-house, and for the first time in his life saw ' a man skinned.' The job was completed that night, and the cuticle, toes, fingers, and bowels were buried under a large rock in the ' Dark Hollow,' on Saturday forenoon, by Drs. Heichhold and John Dowling.

"For dissection the cadaver is divided into five parts: the head is given to one party, the right arm and side to another, the left arm and side to a third person, the right leg to a fourth, and the left leg to a fifth. In this way Dr. Simons and the four doctors skinned Henry Southerland. For us to dissect Southerland would have required about fifteen to twenty days.

"As dissection is a slow and intricate work, and to avoid discovery and arrest, efforts were made to remove as early as possible the subject

PIONEER HISTORY OF JEFFERSON COUNTY, PENNA.

from town. Dr. David Ralston, then practising medicine in Reynoldsville, was seen, and he agreed to come after the cadaver and take it home on Saturday night, the 7th. Dr. W. H. Reynolds, who resides now at Prescottville, this county, was then a young man, living on a farm near Rathmel, and Dr. Ralston secured his co-operation. On Saturday these two gentlemen came to Brookville with two mules in a wagon, and stopped at the American Hotel, J. J. Y. Thompson, proprietor. At a conference of all parties, it was arranged that Ralston and Reynolds should drive to the ice-house from the west end of Coal Alley about eleven o'clock P.M. They had a large store-box in the wagon to carry the corpse. The night was black dark. At ten P.M. J. Y. said, 'I'll be danged to Harry, what are so many doctors loafing here to-night for?' A little later, when Ralston ordered out the mules and wagon, Thompson was perfectly astonished, and exclaimed, 'I'll be dod danged to Harry and dangnation, if you men will leave my house at this late hour and this kind of a night for Reynoldsville.' But his objections were futile. We ghouls were detailed as follows: Blood and Bell as watchers, Heichhold and Hugh Dowling to open the ice-house door, and John Dowling and myself to hand the 'cadaver' out of the house to the men in the wagon. Explicit directions were given to avoid meeting there and forming a crowd.

"Dr. John Dowling and I were there at our appointed time, but the door was unopened, and so we left. Dr. Heichhold in some way lost the key at or near the ice-house, and had to go and find a hatchet to open the door. This he did, and the wagon came along, and, finding no one there, stopped a moment and left without the subject. On the North Fork bridge they pushed their box into the creek. I always felt that Dowling and myself were somewhat to blame; but we were young and had received orders not to loiter around, and if the door was not opened to leave.

"About eight or nine o'clock on Sunday morning I went up to Dowling's and told John we had better go up and 'view the land.' When we arrived on the tragic scene we found the door open and broken. We peeped in, and while doing so we observed William C. Smith on Pickering Street watching us. We walked briskly away up Coal Alley; but our actions and the 'broken door' excited his curiosity, and, hurrying over to the ice-house, he looked in, only to be horrified, and with arms extended towards heaven, pale as death, he ran home, exclaiming excitedly to those he met, that a man had been 'skinned alive in Blood's ice-house. He had seen the man, and also saw Dr. John Dowling and Tom Espy looking at the man in the ice-house. William C Smith has told his version of the discovery to me many times, and always puts 'Tom Espy' in my place.

"In the evening of Sunday, the 8th, loud mutterings against the doc-

PIONEER HISTORY OF JEFFERSON COUNTY, PENNA.

tors were heard, and we all hid. I hid in the loft above our old kitchen. At midnight, 'in the starlight,' I left for McCurdy's, in the Beechwoods. Monday morning, Blood had business in Pittsburg. David Barclay, a very able man and lawyer, was then our member of Congress, and he took charge of the prosecution. He and Blood had a political feud, and Barclay thought now was his time to annihilate Blood. Hearing of Barclay's activity, my brother, the late Colonel A. A. McKnight, then a young lawyer, made information against me before Esquire Smith, under the act of 1849, to protect graveyards. I returned on Tuesday night, and was arrested, taken before Smith, pleaded guilty, and was fined twenty-five dollars and costs, which I paid in full to the county commissioners, and I was the only one who had to pay a penalty. Under the above act the penalty was fine or imprisonment, or both. My conviction before Smith was to give me the benefit in court of that clause in the constitution which says, ' No person for the same offence shall be twice put in jeopardy of life or limb.' Barclay was a Republican, Blood was a Democrat. I was a Republican, without money or friends, therefore Barclay commenced his prosecution against Blood and me, leaving the others all out for witnesses. The criminal records of Justices Smith and Brady for some reason have been destroyed, therefore I cannot give them. Barclay kept up his prosecution until 1859, as the following legal records of the court show.

(Copy.)

"'No. 14 Feby. 1859. Q. S.

"'Commonwealth vs. Kennedy L. Blood and William J. McKnight.

"'Indictment for removing a dead body from burial-ground. Prosecutrix, Tracy Sweeney.

"'Witnesses, Charles Anderson, F. C. Coryell, L. A. Dodd, John McGiven, A. P. Heichhold, Richard Arthurs, John Dowling, John Carroll, William Smith, Thomas Espy, Myron Pearsall, Hugh Dowling, Aug. Beyle, William Reynolds, Henry Fullerton, Matthew Dowling, William Russell, Sinthy Southerland, Zibion Wilber, James Dowling, A. M. Clarke, George Andrews, A. B. McLain, William Lansendoffer, I. D. N. Ralston, Charles McLain, James McCracken, Charles Matson. In the Court of Quarter Sessions for the County of Jefferson, February Session, 1859.

"'The grand inquest of the Commonwealth of Pennsylvania, inquiring for the body of the county, upon their oaths and affirmations respectfully do present, that Kennedy L. Blood and William J. McKnight, late of the County of Jefferson, on the fifth day of November, in the year of our Lord one thousand eight hundred and fifty seven, with force and arms, at the County of Jefferson, the burial-ground of and in the borough of Brookville there situate, unlawfully did enter and the grave there in

PIONEER HISTORY OF JEFFERSON COUNTY, PENNA.

which the body of one Henry Southerland deceased had lately before then been interred ; and these two, with force and arms, unlawfully, wantonly, wilfully, and indecently, did dig open, and afterwards,—to wit, on the same day and year aforesaid,—with force and arms, at the county aforesaid, the body of him, the said Henry Southerland, out of the grave aforesaid, unlawfully and indecently, did take and carry away, against the peace and dignity of the Commonwealth of Pennsylvania.

"'And the grand inquest aforesaid, upon their oaths and affirmation, do further present, that Kennedy L. Blood and William J. McKnight, late of the County of Jefferson, on the fifth day of November, in the year of our Lord one thousand eight hundred and fifty-seven, with force and arms, at the County of Jefferson, the burial-ground of and in the borough of Brookville there situate, unlawfully and clandestinely, did enter, and the grave there in which the body of one Henry Southerland, deceased, had lately before then been interred ; and these two, with force and arms clandestinely, did dig open, and afterwards,—to wit, on the same day and year aforesaid, with force and arms, at the county aforesaid, the body of him, the said Henry Southerland, out of the grave aforesaid, clandestinely and indecently, did take, remove, and carry away, against the peace and dignity of the Commonwealth of Pennsylvania, and contrary to the form of the statute in such case made and provided.

"'A. L. GORDON,
"'District Attorney.

"'Commonwealth vs. K. L. Blood and William J. McKnight.
"'In the Court of Quarter Sessions of Jefferson County.
"'No. 14 Feby. Session, 1859. Q. S. D. No. 2, page 87.
"'Indictment for removing a dead body. Not a true bill. County to pay costs.

"'WILLIAM M. JOHNSTON,
"'Foreman.

"'Received of A. L. Gordon, my costs, Hugh Dowling, Charles Anderson, John E. Carroll, A. P. Heichhold, W. C. Smith, M. A. Dowling, A. B. McLain, H. R. Fullerton, M. M. Pearsall. Justice Brady, $4.52 ; attorney, $3.'

"This indictment was under the act of 1855, 'To protect burial-grounds,' the penalty of which was : If any person shall open any tomb or grave in any cemetery, graveyard, or any grounds set apart for burial purposes, either private or public, held by individuals for their own use, or in trust for others, or for any church or institution, whether incorporated or not, without the consent of the owners or trustees of such grounds, and clandestinely or unlawfully remove, or attempt to remove, any human body, or part thereof, therefrom, such person, upon conviction thereof, shall be sentenced to undergo an imprisonment in the county jail or penitentiary for a term of not less than one year, nor more than three years, and pay a fine of not less than one hundred dollars, at the discretion of the proper court.

"The witnesses before the grand jury were of two kinds,—those who knew and those who didn't know. Those who knew refused to testify, on the ground of incriminating themselves, and Judge McCalmont sustained them.

"The attorneys for the Commonwealth were A. L. Gordon, district attorney, and Hon. David Barclay. Our attorneys were Amor A. McKnight, Benjamin F. Lucas, and William P. Jenks.

"K. L. Blood and Dr. Heichhold, until the day of their death, were opposite political party leaders, and whenever either one addressed a political assembly some wag or opponent in ambush would always interrogate the speaker with ' Who skinned the nigger ?'

"Before concluding this article it might be well to say that the 'icehouse' was never used for any purpose after November 8, 1857.

"In 1883, when I was a State senator, I was invited to dine with Professor W. H. Pancoast, of Philadelphia. The city, State, and nation was agitated over the robbing of 'Lebanon Cemetery,' in that city. It was thought that these subjects were for dissection in Jefferson Medical College. Dr. Pancoast was then professor of anatomy in that school. While at dinner the question was raised as to what effect this scandal would have upon the college. During this talk I broached the idea that now would be an opportune time to secure legal dissection for Pennsylvania. The wisdom of my suggestion was doubted and controverted. I defended my position in this wise : The people of the city and State are excited, alarmed, and angered, and I would frame the 'act to prevent the traffic in human bodies and to prevent the desecration of graveyards.' This would appeal to the good sense of the people, as an effort, at least, in the right direction. Dr. Pancoast soon coincided with me, and from that moment took an active interest in the matter. He met with opposition at first from those who ought to have supported him ; but I assured the doctor if he would get the Anatomical Association of the city to draft a suitable law and send it to Senator Reyburn, of that city, I would support it from the country, and that we would push it through the Senate. Dr. Pancoast deserves great praise for his energy in overcoming the timidity and fears of the college deans and others in the city, and in finally inducing the 'Association' to frame the present act and send it to Senator Reyburn. This law in Pennsylvania legalizing dissection was passed finally on June 4, 1883. Its passage met serious and able opposition in both Houses. I firmly believe that had I not been connected with and prosecuted in this pioneer resurrection case in Brookville, I would not

PIONEER HISTORY OF JEFFERSON COUNTY, PENNA.

have been impelled to propose such a law or to champion it in the Senate. As introduced by Senator Reyburn, the title was, 'Senate bill 117, entitled An Act for the promotion of medical science, by the distribution and use of unclaimed human bodies for scientific purposes, through a board created for that purpose, and to prevent unauthorized uses and traffic in human bodies.'

"The act as passed and approved reads as follows,—viz.:

"'No. 106. AN ACT FOR THE PROMOTION OF MEDICAL SCIENCE BY THE DISTRIBUTION AND USE OF UNCLAIMED HUMAN BODIES FOR SCIENTIFIC PURPOSES THROUGH A BOARD CREATED FOR THAT PURPOSE, AND TO PREVENT UNAUTHORIZED USES AND TRAFFIC IN HUMAN BODIES.

"'SECTION 1. *Be it enacted, etc.*, That the professors of anatomy, the professors of surgery, the demonstrators of anatomy, and the demonstrators of surgery of the medical and dental schools and colleges of this Commonwealth, which are now or may hereafter become incorporated, together with one representative from each of the unincorporated schools of anatomy or practical surgery, within this Commonwealth, in which there are from time to time, at the time of the appointment of such representatives, shall be not less than five scholars, shall be and hereby are constituted a board for the distribution and delivery of dead human bodies, hereinafter described, to and among such persons as, under the provisions of this act, are entitled thereto. The professor of anatomy in the University of Pennsylvania, at Philadelphia, shall call a meeting of said board for organization at a time and place to be fixed by him within thirty days after the passage of this act. The said board shall have full power to establish rules and regulations for its government, and to appoint and remove proper officers, and shall keep full and complete minutes of its transactions; and records shall also be kept under its direction of all bodies received and distributed by said board, and of the persons to whom the same may be distributed, which minutes and records shall be open at all times to the inspection of each member of said board, and of any district attorney of any county within this Commonwealth.

"'SECTION 2. All public officers, agents, and servants, and all officers, agents, and servants of any and every county, city, township, borough, district, and other municipality, and of any and every almshouse, prison, morgue, hospital, or other public institution having charge or control over dead human bodies, required to be buried at the public expense, are hereby required to notify the said board of distribution, or such person or persons as may, from time to time, be designated by said board or its duly authorized officer or agent, whenever any such body or bodies come to his or their possession, charge, or control; and shall, without fee or reward, deliver such body or bodies, and permit and suffer the said board and its agents, and the physicians and surgeons from time to time designated by them, who may comply with the provisions of this act, to take and remove all such bodies to be used within this State for the advancement of medical science; but no such notice need be given nor shall any such body be delivered if any person claiming to be and satisfying the authorities in charge of said body that he or she is of kindred or is related by marriage to the deceased, shall claim the said body for burial, but it shall be surrendered for interment, nor shall the notice be given or body delivered if such deceased person was a traveller who died suddenly, in which case the said body shall be buried.

"'Section 3. The said board or their duly authorized agent may take and receive such bodies so delivered as aforesaid, and shall, upon receiving them, distribute and deliver them to and among the schools, colleges, physicians, and surgeons aforesaid, in manner following: Those bodies needed for lectures and demonstrations by the said schools and colleges incorporated and unincorporated shall first be supplied; the remaining bodies shall then be distributed proportionately and equitably, preference being given to said schools and colleges, the number assigned to each to be based upon the number of students in each dissecting or operative surgery class, which number shall be reported to the board at such times as it may direct. Instead of receiving and delivering said bodies themselves, or through their agents or servants, the board of distribution may, from time to time, either directly or by their authorized officer or agent, designate physicians and surgeons who shall receive them, and the number which each shall receive: *Provided always, however*, That schools and colleges incorporated and unincorporated, and physicians or surgeons of the county where the death of the person or such person described takes place, shall be preferred to all others: *And provided also*, That for this purpose such dead body shall be held subject to their order in the county where the death occurs for a period not less than twenty-four hours.

"'Section 4. The said board may employ a carrier or carriers for the conveyance of said bodies, which shall be well enclosed within a suitable encasement, and carefully deposited free from public observation. Said carrier shall obtain receipts by name, or if the person be unknown by a description of each body delivered by him, and shall deposit said receipt with the secretary of the said board.

"'Section 5. No school, college, physician, or surgeon shall be allowed or permitted to receive any such body or bodies until a bond shall have been given to the Commonwealth by such physician or surgeon, or by or in behalf of such school or college, to be approved by the prothonotary of the court of common pleas in and for the county in which such physician or surgeon shall reside, or in which such school or college may be situate, and to be filed in the office of said prothonotary, which bond shall be in the penal sum of one thousand dollars, conditioned that all such bodies which the said physician or surgeon, or the said school or college shall receive thereafter shall be used only for the promotion of medical science within this State; and whosoever shall sell or buy such body or bodies, or in any way traffic in the same, or shall transmit or convey or cause to procure to be transmitted or conveyed said body or bodies, to any place outside of this State, shall be deemed guilty of a misdemeanor, and shall, on conviction, be liable to a fine not exceeding two hundred dollars, or be imprisoned for a term not exceeding one year.

"'SECTION 6. Neither the Commonwealth nor any county or municipality, nor any officer, agent, or servant thereof, shall be at any expense by reason of the delivery or distribution of any such body; but all the expenses thereof and of said board of distribution shall be paid by those receiving the bodies, in such manner as may be specified by said board of distribution, or otherwise agreed upon.

"'SECTION 7. That any person having duties enjoined upon him by the provisions of this act who shall neglect, refuse, or omit to perform the same as hereby required, shall, on conviction thereof, be liable to fine of not less than one hundred nor more than five hundred dollars for each offence.

"'SECTION 8. That all acts or parts of acts inconsistent with this act be and the same are hereby repealed.

"'Approved—the 13th day of June, A.D. 1883.

"'ROBERT E. PATTISON.'

"In closing this narrative I quote a paragraph from my remarks in the Senate in support of the passage of the law and in reply to the speeches of other senators:

"'Where would the humanity exist then, especially that kind of which so much is said in regard to the dead? Humanity, I think, should first be shown to the living, and the Great Physician, whom senators quote on this floor as having had a regard for humanity, said, "Let the dead bury the dead." He took the same practical view that humanity should be practised for the living. We take a harsh view as medical men in regard to the dissection of dead bodies. We consider subjects just as clay. I know this is repugnant to the common idea of mankind, but it is the true idea. It is the idea that will enable a medical man to be of sound, practical good, professionally, in the world. For the crushed, relief in life is the great object, not relief after death. We have nothing to do with that. Beautiful poetry and nice homilies can be delivered here by senators about death, but it is the living that we want to be humane to and not the dead, and if it requires the dissection of ninety-nine dead persons to relieve one living sufferer, I would dissect the ninety-nine dead persons and relieve the one living person. Other

PIONEER HISTORY OF JEFFERSON COUNTY, PENNA.

senators here would have us do just the reverse of that. I repeat, Mr. President, this measure is in the interest of the laboring man; it is in the interest of the mechanic; it is in the interest of science; it is in the interest of the poor the world over; it is in the interest of the man who gets torn and lacerated in our mines and workshops, and who is too poor to travel to Philadelphia for his surgical aid. Enact this law, and the young man can go from Allegheny, from Jefferson, and from Armstrong Counties to Philadelphia, and he can legally take the human body, which is the A B C of all medical knowledge, and he can dissect it there, and learn by that means just where each artery is, and where each vein is, and where the different muscles lie and the different relations they sustain to one another, and then he is qualified to return to Allegheny or Jefferson Counties, locate at the cross-roads or in the village, and perform the operations that are so much needed there for the relief of suffering humanity and the suffering poor.

"'You all know that the surgeons of Philadelphia are famous, not only in Philadelphia, but throughout the world, and why? It is because they have studied the anatomy of the human body so thoroughly and so perfectly.

"'We must have anatomical dissections. No man learns anatomy in any other way in the world than through anatomical dissections. Pictures, models, and manikins won't do. He must not only dissect one body, but he must dissect a large number of bodies. He cannot dissect too many, neither can he dissect too often; therefore humanity requires that this dissection be legalized and go on.

"'Of course, we must have some regard for the sentiment of the living, and to respect that, we, in this bill, only ask that the unclaimed bodies of paupers be given to the medical colleges, not the bodies of those having friends. No body can be taken if any one objects.'

"We have now, in 1897, legalized dissection of the human body in twenty-four States, and, as a result, the skill of the physician in the future 'shall lift up his head, and in the sight of great men he shall stand in admiration.'"—*Jeffersonian Democrat*, January, 1897.

THE TEACHERS' INSTITUTE.

The following is an extract from the proceedings held in Brookville, Pennsylvania, November 23, 1896:

"The Jefferson County Teachers' Institute met in the court-house, Brookville, on Monday, at two P.M. After the enrollment of teachers and the selection of T. T. Millen as secretary, the following address of welcome to the teachers was delivered by Dr. W. J. McKnight, of Brookville:

PIONEER HISTORY OF JEFFERSON COUNTY, PENNA.

"'MR. CHAIRMAN AND TEACHERS,—This is an assemblage of teachers, called an "institute"—the institute of Jefferson County. What is its history? Let us lift the veil from the past and ascertain. The Rev. John C. Wagaman, of Punxsutawney, was our first county superintendent, elected in 1854, and paid a salary of three hundred dollars a year. He resigned in 1856, and Samuel McElhose, of Brookville, succeeded him by appointment. Our first county institute was held by McElhose, in the old Academy building, in Brookville, in October of 1856, continuing two weeks. The published call for it read as follows:

"'"TO TEACHERS.

"'"Believing that much good can be done to the cause of common school education by means of a county institute for the benefit of teachers, I hereby issue this call to teachers and those who wish to teach, requesting and urging each one of them to meet in Brookville on Monday, the 20th day of October, at which time will commence in the Academy the first session of the Jefferson County Teachers' Institute. It will last two weeks.

"'"Professor S. W. Smith will be present during the session. He is a graduate of the best of the New England schools, and has the advantage of several years' practice as a teacher. The course of instruction will extend to a general review of the branches required to be taught in our common schools. It will be our leading object to treat at large on the subjects of school government, classification of scholars, and the improved methods of teaching.

"'"Persons who attend the institute will be at no expense except for their own boarding. Several gentlemen have tendered their services and will deliver lectures on topics connected with education at the proper times in the session. We again solicit the attendance of those who desire to teach in this county, and also extend a cordial invitation to the friends of education in this and other counties to be present

"'"S. MCELHOSE,
"'" *County Superintendent.*

"'" BROOKVILLE, September 22, 1856."

"'This institute was opened with prayer by Professor Smith. The work consisted largely of daily class drills, conducted by Professor Smith and Superintendent McElhose. Professor Smith was an educated gentleman, and died in Brookville a few years ago, after serving two terms as county superintendent most acceptably.

"'The evening lectures before this first institute were free, delivered in the Presbyterian church by local talent. They were by Rev. Thomas Graham, on "The Duties of Teachers;" A. L. Gordon, Esq., on "Self-Knowledge," and I. G. Gordon, Esq., on "Discipline." All these evening entertainments were announced to be held at "candle-lighting." Day lectures were given before the institute by Superintendent McElhose, Professor Smith, on astronomy, and Dr. Cummins, on physiology. Numerous essays were read by the teachers present, on the beauties of nature, on education, on teaching, etc. Of the forty-two teachers who attended, I can recall but these: A. H. Brown, A. L. Gordon, J. C. Wilson, William Monks, T. Evans, John H. McKee, A. J. Monks, R. A. Travis, J. Kelso, Misses Maggie Polk, Jennie Craig, M. Kinnear, Abbie McCurdy, Martha Dennison, Emma Bishop, Mary McCormick, H. Thomas, Martha McCreight, and Messrs. C. M. Matson, David Dickey, and S. A. McAllister. The last three named are present with us to-day.

"'Extended discussion was had, and resolutions were passed, in regard to the construction of school-houses and concerning school furniture and school-books. The county then had one hundred and five school-houses and sixty-eight male and fifty female teachers.

"'Samuel McElhose served as superintendent a part of a term by appointment and two full terms by election, at a yearly salary of five hundred dollars. He was an educated and popular gentleman, a great worker, and the first in the county to agitate institutes. He held many of these,—sometimes three or four in a year,—some lasting three or four weeks. He was a good citizen and a patriot, and died a private soldier in the army in 1863.

"'Ninety-two years ago, in the winter of 1804, John Dixon, father of the venerable John Dixon, of Polk township, taught the first school in this county. It was a subscription school, and the term was three months. The "school-house" was two miles east of Brookville, on what is now the McConnell farm. It was twelve feet wide and sixteen feet long, was built of rough logs, and had no window-sash or glass. The light was admitted to the school-room through chinks in the walls, over which greased paper was plastered. The floor was of "puncheons," and the seats of broad pieces split from logs, with pins underneath for legs. The roof was covered with "clapboards" held down by poles. Boards laid on pins driven into auger-holes in the walls furnished writing-desks. A log fireplace, occupying an entire end of the room, supplied warmth when the weather was cold.

"'The second school was taught by John Johnson, in 1806, on the old "State road," near the present residence of William C. Evans, between Port Barnett and Brookville. The house was similar to the first one named, with the exception of a single window of six lights of eight-by-ten glass. This school cabin was heated by a ten-plate wood-stove, the invention of Franklin in 1800, and called by the people "The Little Devil." This was a subscription school also, and was known in those days as a "neighborhood," to distinguish it from the "family" school. The building was erected by those interested. The tools used

PIONEER HISTORY OF JEFFERSON COUNTY, PENNA.

in constructing it were a pole-axe and an auger. The master was hired by a committee of three, elected by the people at their own time and in their own way. This committee supervised the school. Children had to travel three or four miles, in some cases over trails and paths where the Indian lurked and the wild beast prowled.

"'Although Penn had declared in founding his colony that "wisdom and virtue must be carefully propagated by a virtuous education of the youth," and although the constitution of 1790 declared in favor of the establishment of schools throughout the State that the poor might be taught gratis, yet it was not until 1809 that the Legislature attempted to obey this mandate. Colleges and academies were, it is true, sparsely inaugurated, but they were not for the poor. Education was carried on by voluntary effort. The law of 1809 simply provided that it should be the duty of the county commissioners and assessors of the townships to ascertain from the parents the names of all the children between the ages of five and twelve years who reside in each township, and whose parents were unable to pay for their schooling. These children then had the privilege of attending the nearest subscription school, under the restrictions of the committee, and the county had to pay for each pauper scholar by the month, the same as the subscribers paid. This law was in existence for twenty-five years. It was despised by the poor and hated by the rich. The poor would not accept it because it declared them paupers. Its existence, however, kept up an agitation for a better system, which culminated, in 1834-36, in what is known as the common school law.

"'In 1833, Governor Wolf ascertained by careful inquiry that under this law of 1809, out of four hundred thousand children in the State between the ages of five and twelve years, only twenty thousand attended any school whatever.

"'The pioneer school-house in the southern part of the county was built of logs, in the fall of 1820, near John Bell's, a little more than a mile northeast of Perrysville. It was built after the fashion of the first school-house in the county,—lighted, warmed, and furnished in the same manner. John B. Henderson taught the first school in this pioneer house in the winter of 1820.

"'Our oldest school-master in the county is Joseph Magiffin, hale and hearty at the age of ninety. He taught near Dowlingville in 1827. The books used in the pioneer schools were generally the Bible, Columbian Reader, Murray's Grammar, Pike's Arithmetic, Catechism, United States Speller, and New England Primer. As a matter of care and economy these books were covered by the mothers with paper or cloth, generally calico or bed-ticking. The pioneer school-masters were nearly all Irishmen, and, as a rule, well-educated. In the winter they usually wore a red flannel warmus, and sometimes white flannel pants. They

PIONEER HISTORY OF JEFFERSON COUNTY, PENNA.

taught their scholars from the proverbs of the poets, from the maxims of the surrounding forests, and from the tenets of the blessed Bible, whose apocalypse is love. Is it any wonder, then, that the log cabin and log school house proved to be the birthplace and nursery of mental giants, of men who have blessed our country as rulers, statesmen, soldiers, scholars, orators, and patriots? What nation, old or new, has produced the equal of our Washington? What nation has equalled our Jefferson, with his declaration "that all men are created free and equal"? What nation has equalled our Lincoln, born and reared in a cabin, one of the people and for the people? With a heart alive to pity, like an angel of mercy, he was ever at home in his office of President to the most humble citizen. This I know by personal experience. What nation has produced the superior of Chief Justice Marshall? What orators have been more eloquent than Clay or Webster? What nation has produced a greater than our military chieftain, Grant, who commanded larger armies, fought more battles, and won more victories than any other general history records? Napoleon's career is pigmy-like when compared to Grant's successes. What nation has equalled our inventors? Fulton, born in Pennsylvania's woods, who harnessed steam to water-craft; Whitney, who invented the cotton-gin; Morse, who sought out the telegraph; McCormick, who made the reaper; Howe, who made the sewing-machine, and Edison, the intellectual wonder and marvel of the world,—born in Ohio and reared in the woods of Michigan? Such a mental genius as he is could only be the son of an American "school-marm."

"'I have not time to recapitulate the history of our country and its achievements. I can only say that what we are to-day we owe to the log cabin, the log school house, and the pioneer school-master.

"'We live in the age of steam and railroads, telegraphs, telephones, and of a free school system. "We live in an age on ages telling; to be living is sublime." Yet you are pioneers, pioneers of a new era, an era of moral courage, of the fatherhood of God and the brotherhood of man; an era of honesty, of temperance, of plenty, of virtue, of wisdom, and of peace. And you, teachers, are the leaders in this grand new era. As such we welcome you to Brookville. We welcome you most heartily as friends and neighbors. We welcome you as citizens of our county, whose hills and valleys are sacred to us. We welcome you as the children of noble, courageous, patient, toiling pioneer heroes and heroines, who subdued the savage and the wild beasts of the forest and reclaimed these lands. We welcome you as teachers under the free school system of the great State of Pennsylvania, made great by her forests, her fertile valleys, her mountains of coal, rivers of oil, and the enterprise of her sons and daughters, and whose free school system is the continued assurance of American liberty. We welcome you as teachers in an empire whose State insignia proclaims to the world Virtue, Liberty, and Inde-

PIONEER HISTORY OF JEFFERSON COUNTY, PENNA.

pendence. We welcome each one of you to Brookville for your individual worth, and we welcome you as an aggregation of intelligent force assembled in our midst for the public good. Finally, we welcome you as teachers convened to learn more thoroughly how to impart intelligence, teach virtue, wisdom, and patriotism under our flag, the emblem of all that is dear to man and woman in and for the best government on the face of the earth.'"

ORGANIZATION OF THE REPUBLICAN PARTY IN JEFFERSON COUNTY—THE PIONEERS AND FATHERS.

On February 22, 1856, a number of self-appointed delegates from all parts of the republic,—

> Men of principle,
> " Men who had opinions and a will,
> Tall men, sun-crowned, who lived above the fog,
> In public duty and in private thought,"—

met at Lafayette Hall, Pittsburg, Pennsylvania, and organized the National Republican party, the first national convention of which was held that year in Philadelphia, Pennsylvania. There was then in existence two other parties,—viz., the Democratic and the American National. This gave the country in the Presidential race of that year three candidates for the Presidency,—viz., Buchanan, Democrat, Fillmore, American, and Fremont, Republican. The Democrats were successful and Buchanan was elected. The Republicans were next strongest, and the Americans third in the race. In 1856 the Republicans in our county had more votes than the Americans, yet they had no organization. In 1857 the Republicans of Jefferson coalesced with the Americans and swallowed them by organizing a party in the county as the American Republican. The pioneer primaries for this organization to choose delegates were held on the last Saturday of June, at each election precinct, between the hours of two and six P.M. The county convention was held in the court-house at Brookville on the first Tuesday of July following. Each township or borough was to elect two delegates, except Heath and Polk, and they but one each.

There were then twenty townships and two boroughs in the county, and at the county convention, held July 7, 1857, the following delegates were present,—viz.:

Beaver.—G. Montgomery, R. Dinger.
Barnett.*—Not represented.
Bell.—John Grube, James Miller.
Brookville.—A. B. McLain, D. C. Gillespie.
Clover.—C. McCullough.
Eldred.—William Hall, J. B. Graham.

PIONEER HISTORY OF JEFFERSON COUNTY, PENNA.

Heath.—Not represented.
Knox.*—M. E. Steiner, William Davidson.
McCalmont.—J. P. North, S. McGhee.
Oliver.—J. P. McKee, W. P. Gastin.
Porter.—Jacob Howard.
Polk.*—Not represented.
Perry.*—C. R. B. Morris.
Pine Creek.*—Oliver Brady, J. P. Black.
Rose.*—E. P. Cochran, T. Witherow.
Ringgold.—R. T. Perry, J. A. Frees.
Snyder.*—Not represented.
Punxsutawney.*—J. R. Reese, W. A. Dunlap.
Union.*—John S. Barr, John Gibson.
Washington.*—John Crawford, Robert Morrison.
Warsaw.*—I. M. Temple, Emory Bartlett.
Winslow.*—G. Burrows, R. Ross.
Young.—S. B. Hughes, Thomas North.

The nominees of that convention were: Sheriff, Lawrence McQuown; Prothonotary, etc., Joseph Henderson; Treasurer, Samuel Craig; Commissioner, John North; Auditor, John Thompson. The townships marked thus * were carried for the Republicans in 1857, therefore the pioneer Republican townships in the county.

The election on the second Tuesday of October went Democratic, both State and county. Our county was carried by the Democrats by majorities ranging from six to one hundred.

The campaigns then were educational, and conducted by oratory in school-houses, etc. The pioneer "stumpers" in the county for the Republican party were I. G. Gordon, B. F. Lucas, A. A. McKnight, A. P. Heichhold, A. B. McLain, D. C. Gillespie, W. W. Wise, L. D. Rogers, Dr. W. J. McKnight, and J. K. Coxson. All evening meetings were announced to be held at "early candle-lighting." In stumping the speaker gave his own time and furnished his own transportation. If too poor to do this, some Republican would convey him in a hack, free of charge, or a number of workers would chip in and hire a team and go along. There was no campaign boodle to draw upon. We always had a begging committee; A. B. McLain was always on it, and the best beggar I ever knew. When we imported a "foreign speaker," McLain had to hustle to get money for the speaker's expenses, and he never failed. We had a county vigilance committee of one or two in each township. This committee was appointed at the county convention by the presiding officer, and was usually selected from the delegates present.

State delegates were selected as follows: An editorial notice was published in the *Star* that a meeting would be held at the court-house in

PIONEER HISTORY OF JEFFERSON COUNTY, PENNA.

Brookville on the evening of ——, at "early candle-light," to appoint a delegate to the State Convention. The crowd that gathered elected him *viva voce*.

EARLY HISTORY OF RIDGWAY — SOME SKETCHES ABOUT THE TOWN AND VICINITY FROM 1852 TO 1856.*

In the fall of 1852 I made my pioneer trip as a mail-boy on the "Star Route" from Brookville to Ridgway, Pennsylvania. In 1852 this was still a horseback service of once a week, and was to be performed weekly, as follows: Leave Brookville Tuesday at five o'clock A.M., and arrive at Ridgway same day at seven o'clock P.M. Leave Ridgway Wednesday at five o'clock A.M., and arrive same day at Brookville at seven o'clock P.M.

The proprietor of the route was John G. Wilson, then keeping the American Hotel in Brookville. To start the service on schedule time was easy enough, but to reach the destined point in the schedule time was almost impossible. The mail was usually from one to three hours late. Indeed, it could not be otherwise, for the route was through a wilderness, over horrid roads, and about seven miles longer than the direct road between the points.

It was too much work in too short a time for one horse to carry a heavy mail-bag and a boy. On my first trip I left Brookville at five A.M., James Corbett, the postmaster, placing the bag on the horse for me. I rode direct to Richardsville, where William R. Richards, the pioneer of that section, was postmaster. From Richardsville I went to Warsaw, where Moses B. St. John was postmaster. He lived on the Keyes farm, near the Warsaw graveyard. From St. John's I rode by way of what is now John Fox's to the Beechwoods McConnell farm, or Alvan post-office, Alex. McConnell, postmaster. From Alvan I went direct to what is now Brockwayville for dinner. Dr. A. M. Clarke was postmaster, and it was at his house I ate, to my disgust, salt-rising bread.

The doctor and his father lived in a large frame house near where the old grist-mill now stands. The old up-and-down saw-mill across the creek was then in operation. C. K. Huhn, I think, lived near it. The old frame school-house stood on a prominence near the junction of the Brookville and Beechwoods roads. Henry Dull, one of the pioneer stage-drivers in Jefferson County, lived in an old frame building near where D. D. Groves now resides, and John McLaughlin lived in an old log house down by the Rochester depot.

With these exceptions, all west of the creek in what is now Brockwayville was a wilderness. East of the creek the bottom land was

---

* This "Early History of Ridgway" was published in pamphlet form, and is republished here, revised and corrected.

cleared, and along the road on each side was a log fence. W. D. Murray and the Ingalls family lived near the Pennsylvania depot.

There was no other family or store or industry, to my recollection, in what is now the beautiful town of Brockwayville.

About five miles up the Little Toby, and in Elk County, Mrs. Sarah Oyster kept a licensed hotel, the only licensed tavern in that year outside of or between Brookville and Ridgway. Near this hotel Stephen Oyster lived and had erected a grist-mill and saw-mill. Oyster was postmaster, and the office was named Hellen Mills.

Stephen Oyster's house and mills were alongside or on the pioneer road to this region. The road was surveyed and opened about 1812, and over it the pioneers came to Brandy Camp, Kersey, and Little Toby. The history of the road is something like this: Fox, Norris & Co. owned about one hundred and forty thousand acres of land in this vicinity, and, being desirous to open these lands for settlement, employed and sent a surveyor by the name of Kersey to survey, open a road, and build a mill on their lands.

Kersey and his men started the road on the Susquehanna River near Luthersburg, on the old State road, crossed over Boone's Mountain, reached Little Toby at what is now Hellen, went up the creek seven miles over what is called "Hog-Back Hill" to a point on Elk Creek near where Centreville now is, and then located and built "Kersey Mill."

Kersey had an outfit and a number of men, and erected shanties wherever necessary while at his work. One of these he built on Brandy Camp. Among other necessaries, Kersey had some choice brandy with him. The men longed for some of this brandy, but Kersey kept it for himself. One day, in the absence of Kersey, the cabin burned down.

On Kersey's return he was chagrined, but the men told him that the Indians in the neighborhood had drunk his brandy and burned the shanty. This story had to be accepted, and hence the stream has ever since been called Brandy Camp. "The Travellers' Home Hotel" was on this stream. It was famous for dancing parties, blackberry pies, and sweet cake, but was closed this year and occupied as a private residence by a man named Brown.

Night came upon me at the farm of Joel Taylor, and through nine miles of wilderness and darkness I rode on a walk. There was a shanty at Bootjack occupied by a man named McQuone. From Taylor's to Ridgway was a long ride to me. It was a wearisome time.

I reached Ridgway, a small village then, about nine o'clock P.M. John Cobb was postmaster, and the office was in his store, near where Powell's store is now. My horse knew the route perfectly, and I left all details to her.

Two hotels existed in the village,—the Exchange, kept by David Thayer, near the river, and the Cobb House, kept by John Cobb, on

PIONEER HISTORY OF JEFFERSON COUNTY, PENNA.

the ground where Messenger's drug-store now is. Mr. P. T. Brooks was in charge that night. My horse stopped at the Cobb. For some reason the house was unusually full that night, and after supper I expressed to the landlord a doubt about a bed.

Mr. Brooks patted me on the back and said, "Never mind, my son, I'll take care of you, I'll take care of you." Bless his big heart, he did. Boy-like, my eyes and ears were open. I took in the town before leaving it. The only pavement was in front of the Gillis house. I knew of the judge's reputation as a Morgan killer, and I wanted to see where and how he lived. I had seen him in Brookville many a time before that.

There was a board fence around the public square. Charles Mead was sheriff, and lived in the jail. The village had a doctor, one Chambers. The school-teacher was W. C. Niver, afterwards Dr. Niver, of Brockwayville, Pennsylvania.

Of the village inhabitants then, I can recall these: Judge Gillis, E. C. Derby, M. L. Ross, Henry Souther, Caleb Dill, James Love, J. C. Chapin, Lebbeus Luther, a hunter and great marksman; Lafe Brigham, 'Squire Parsons, E. E. Crandall, Charles McVean, Judge Dickinson, J. S. Hyde, and Jerome Powell, editor of the *Advocate*.

I have an old issue of the *Advocate* of that date, from which I copy two advertisements, one of the coal industry of the county then, and the other on stage and transportation facilities:

"GREAT EXCITEMENT IN THE COAL REGIONS!

"*Removal of the Deposits from the Miners' Bank of Fox Township!*

"Providence having in days of yore deposited in the above bank a choice supply of coal for the use of mankind, to be drawn as need requires, the proprietor is now engaged in removing the funds from bank to his office adjoining, where he will always be ready to distribute liberally, at a trifling charge for his services, to those who call, whether Vulcans, people, or common folks.

"JESSIE KYLER.

"OFFICE OF THE MINERS' BANK OF FOX TOWNSHIP,
November 13, 1851."

"NEW ARRANGEMENT.

"*Through and Back by Daylight!*

"Having taken the contract for carrying the mail from Bellefonte to Smethport, the subscriber is happy to announce to the travelling public and the world in general that he is going to 'crack her threw' regularly, rain or shine, hot or cold, mud or dust, from this time forth, leaving Smethport every Monday morning, arriving at Ridgway same evening,

PIONEER HISTORY OF JEFFERSON COUNTY, PENNA.

passing along so as to reach Bellefonte on Wednesday night. On the return trip leaves Bellefonte on Thursday morning, arrives at Ridgway Friday night, and Smethport Saturday night.

" ☞ Good horses and coaches and *sober* drivers will always be kept on this route.

" ☞ Particular attention will be paid to baggage, which will be carried at my risk where freight is paid. Also, all kinds of errands promptly attended to along the line. Patronage is respectfully solicited.

"TOWNSEND FALL.

"CENTREVILLE, July 9, 1852."

I lived in Ridgway and worked on the *Advocate*, and afterwards in the *Reporter* office from August, 1854, to September, 1856. Ridgway was then but a village, containing three stores,—J. S. Hyde's, George Dickinson's, and Hall & Whitney's; two hotels, the Exchange and the Ridgway, née Fountain, née Oyster, née Cobb. One grist-mill and a little saw-mill on Elk Creek; one shoe shop, Parson & Crandall; one gunsmith, Horace Warner; one blacksmith, Caleb Dill; one tailor, M. L. Ross. Lawyers, Souther, Willis, Chapin, Mickel, and Pattison.

The town was too small and healthy for a physician to remain. There was a school-house near the residence of Caleb Dill, and the winter term of 1854-55 was taught by C. M. Matson, of Brookville, Pennsylvania; also a court-house and a stone jail. William N. Whitney was postmaster. The town and township contained about eighty-one voters.

The county officers were: President Judge, R. G. White, of Tioga County; Associate Judges, George Dickinson, of Ridgway, and W. P. Wilcox, of Jones township; Prothonotary, etc., Charles Horton; Treasurer, Jerome Powell; Sheriff, Alvan H. Head. The commissioners I do not remember.

The following lawyers, afterwards distinguished, then attended the courts: Brown, Curtis, and Johnson, of Warren; Barrett, Wallace, McCullough, and Larimer, of Clearfield; J. G. Gordon, W. P. Jenks, McCahon, and Lucas, of Jefferson; and Goodrich and Eldred, of McKean.

The merchants hauled their goods from Watterson's Ferry, on the Allegheny River, or Olean, New York. Minor Wilcox drove on the road with Charles B. Gillis, Ben. McClelland, and others. In 1855-56 there was one colored teamster in Ridgway,—viz., Charles Matthews. He had a wife, and drove for Sheriff Healy. Although the town water was as pure as the snow on the mountain, yet it did not agree with Charles's stomach. Like other teamsters, he had to take "something a little warmer and stronger."

There was no church edifice of any kind in the town, and but few church members. Sheriff Mead tried to run a Sunday-school, with a few scholars. The pioneer Sunday-school was organized by the Rev. R. L.

PIONEER HISTORY OF JEFFERSON COUNTY, PENNA.

Blackmarr, April 14, 1850. The circuit riders of the Methodist church that year were Revs. Shaffer and Colburn. They preached in the courthouse, and service was held once in two or four weeks, I cannot recall which. The elder's name was Poisdell. All of these gentlemen were appointed by the Baltimore Conference.

These ministers always travelled on horseback. The horse was usually "bobbed," and you could see that he had a most excellent skeleton. These itinerants all wore leggings, and carried on the saddle a large pair of saddle-bags, which contained a clean shirt, a Bible, and a hymn-book. The sermon was on a cylinder in the head of the preacher, and was ready to be graphophoned at any point or time.

Rev. John Wray was the first Presbyterian minister to regularly " cry aloud" to the people of Ridgway, "Repent, for the kingdom of Heaven is at hand. Come buy wine and milk without money and without price." During my two years' stay he preached regularly once in four or six weeks. He may have had a few female members in his church, but to my observation the people generally preferred the "world, the flesh, and the devil," whiskey and New England rum.

Rev. Wray was the pastor of the Beechwoods church in Jefferson County, and came to Ridgway as a missionary. His first advent was in 1850. He had been a missionary in India for seven years. He was a pleasant, earnest, good Irishman, and always stopped with Mr. Luther. He was small of stature, and rode astride his horse and saddle-bags as stiff and upright as though he were a keg of nails. He died at Brockwayville in August, 1883, aged eighty-nine years.

J. S Hyde was then a young, active business man. He came to Ridgway "as poor as a church mouse," and died, at a ripe old age, a millionaire. He was ambitious, an untiring worker, and an honorable citizen. In 1855 he twice solicited me to enter his service; I was flattered, but refused, and told him that "a doctor I would be." Mr. Hyde had great force and a habit of carrying his hands in front of him with the "thumbs up," especially if he was in earnest or excited. Whenever his thumbs were up in the presence of any one, there was sure to be something happen,—an explosion of Christian imagination.

Elk County then was one vast wilderness, and was so called on account of the great herds of elks that once roamed through those wilds. There were no elks killed during my residence, but Grandpap Luther told me that in 1852 a drove of twelve or fifteen was found by two hunters near the village, and seven of them were killed. Indians camped near Ridgway as late as 1850 to hunt for elks. Elks are gregarious. Where Portland now is was a great rendezvous for the elks. It was a great wintering-place for them. All other wild animals were numerous. Erasmus Morey told me that in March, 1853, he and Peter Smith killed in one week six full-grown panthers.

PIONEER HISTORY OF JEFFERSON COUNTY, PENNA.

The total bounty paid by the county in 1854 for killing wolves and panthers in 1853 was $225.50. There lived on the Smethport pike, between Ridgway and Montmorenci, two hunters with their families,— viz., Bill Easton and Nelse Gardner, the latter the father of James K. Gardner, who now resides in Ridgway.

These men were professionals. Chasing the wild deer was their daily life and delight. They both possessed in a high degree the agile, cat-like step, the keen eye, the cool nerve, and the woodcraft of the "still hunter."

I knew them well, but was not intimate enough to learn the story of their encounters and adventures. The buffaloes that once roamed in great numbers, the beavers that built their dams, and the stately elks that once traversed the forests of Elk are now extinct, and I believe the screaming panther and the prowling wolf can now, too, be so classed.

The pioneers to settle where Ridgway now is were James Gallagher and Enos Gillis. About 1824 they built two log houses and a saw-mill. Gallagher was the pioneer tanner, and built a tannery there in the early thirties. He died February 22, 1850, aged seventy years. James L. Gillis christened the village Ridgway. I came to Ridgway in 1854 by invitation of Jerome Powell, Esq., to work for him on the *Advocate*. I received eight dollars per month and boarding. I made my home with Lebbeus Luther. His wife was a most excellent cook, tidy, kind, and as neat in her housework as a pink.

About the first of August, 1854, I left Brockwayville for Ridgway. This was the stage era for Ridgway, and I took passage in Murray & Thayer's stage. My fare was one dollar.

The *Advocate* was a five column to the page paper, each column about eighteen inches long. The press was an old Franklin. We made our own rollers out of glue and molasses. The work on the paper was all done by Mr. Powell, Ben. Dill, and myself. The composing, press-work, and sanctum were all in one room. The paper was in its fifth volume. No. 1, vol. i., was issued March 9, 1850. Henry Souther was editor for about one year. Mr. Powell was the pioneer publisher and father of the craft in Elk County.

Some of the happiest days of my life I spent in this old court-house office. True, I was poor and ragged, but I had the confidence of my employer, I was free from cares, and there in that old office in winter's snows and summer's heat, "Happy hearts, happy hearts, with mine have laughed in glee, the charms of which time can never efface."

Mr. Powell was a polite, affable, genial employer, and Ben. Dill was a pleasant associate.

In August, 1854, the supervisors let a job to take the great stumps out of and straighten Main Street. The stumps were removed, and the spring water was brought to the public grounds. An eagle was shot that year near Ridgway that weighed twenty-four pounds.

PIONEER HISTORY OF JEFFERSON COUNTY, PENNA.

Elk County then had in the navy of the United States a passed midshipman,—viz., J. Henry Gillis,—who, by his bravery and long service, is now a commodore in Uncle Sam's "navee."

James L. Gillis, who lived in Ridgway, was a man of State celebrity. He was absent nearly all the time, lobbying at Harrisburg, Pennsylvania, or at Washington. He was a very interesting man to talk with. I used to go over to his house, when he was at home, to be entertained in an evening.

In 1854 the bridge across Big Toby Creek, now called the Clarion River, was destroyed. William Crawford had the contract for that year and built a new one.

In looking over old copies of the *Advocate* I used to read advertisements something like this:

"HUNTERS.—Several young fawns are wanted. for which a liberal price will be given. Enquire at this office."

In some of the old papers published before 1854, Caleb Dill, of Ridgway, advertised for elk, something like this: "For a living male elk one year old I will give $50; two years old, $75; three years old, $100; and for a calf three months old, $25." Elk were easily tamed.

In 1854 the principal part of Elk County was covered with white pine and hemlock. Pine-lands could be bought from three to five dollars an acre. Hemlock had no value only for farm lands. The bark even was not used for tanning. Pine was about the only timber manufactured. Tall, straight "pine in lofty pride leaned gloomily on every hill-side."

The streams were alive with pike, sunfish, bass, chubs, magnificent trout, and other fish. Every fall and spring hunters with dogs and fishermen from the adjoining counties and from across the line in New York State would flock to these hills, valleys, and streams for recreation or profit. The principal owners of all this wild land in 1854 lived in Philadelphia,—viz., Ridgway estate, Jones estate, Parker estate, and Fox and Norris estate.

I said in a former article that 1854 was the beginning of Ridgway's stage era. Prior to that time isolated attempts had been made in the establishment of lines, but all the efforts in that direction, with the exception of the Smethport or Townsend Fall's line were failures. I copy an editorial from the *Advocate* of June 10, 1854, giving a *résumé* of the stage in operation at that time:

"STAGING.—As an evidence of the rapid increase of the business of this county and of its general prosperity, it is not necessary to refer to every branch of business that is conducted here, but a reference to the single item of staging will make it clear to all that we are a rising nation.

PIONEER HISTORY OF JEFFERSON COUNTY, PENNA.

Two years ago there was no mode of communication through these interminable forests except that only true republican way, a 'footback,' and wading through the mud up to your knees, at least, into the bargain.

"About that time the pioneer stager of the county, Townsend Fall, coroner of Elk County and landlord in McKean County, commenced running a one-horse mud-boat from Bellefonte to Smethport. That was considered a great enterprise, and everybody predicted that Fall must get lost in the mud, and his hazardous undertaking would certainly be the ruination of that visionary man. These predictions would probably all have been verified had it not been for the fact that Mr. Fall is one of those live Yankees who is always ready to whittle out a wooden nutmeg while waiting for his horse to gain wind when stuck in the mud.

"He added another branch of trade to his staging which served to make up the losses that caused him, and assisted him in keeping body, soul, horse, and mud-boat together. He procured a quantity of steel-traps suitable for bears, wolves, and such animals, which he stationed along at intervals, and while waiting for his old horse to browse he could examine them and take care of their contents without losing any time. The furs, skins, and scalps he thus procured soon enabled him to purchase another horse and put by the side of the old veteran that had long served him so faithfully.

"From that day his prosperity and the prosperity of the stage interests of this region have been rapidly onward. He soon was enabled to get a wagon with a top to it. The first trip was a proud day for Elk County. Now Mr. Fall is running a tri-weekly line of splendid four-horse coaches between Smethport and Ridgway, for particulars of which see advertisement in this paper.

"There is also a weekly line running regularly between here and Bellefonte, and a semi-weekly line between here and Brookville, in connection, by Murray & Thayer, as will be seen by their advertisement in this paper. And with all these stage facilities, we receive no mails oftener than once a week. Where is Uncle Sam with his daily mails?"

In the stage advertisements of that year each proprietor advertised "sober drivers," otherwise the passenger would never have dreamed that the driver was in a sober condition. The proprietor occasionally drove over the route himself. I do not recall any of the drivers except Jim Clark, of the Brookville line.

One of the pioneers of Ridgway was David Thayer. He was an all-round business man, hotel-keeper, lumberman, and stage man. He was the father of a large family. Henry S. Thayer, living in Ridgway, is his son. He was the proprietor of the pioneer line of stages to Warren and Brockwayville, Pennsylvania.

PIONEER HISTORY OF JEFFERSON COUNTY, PENNA.

The following advertisements published at that time speak for themselves:

"ANOTHER STAGE LINE.

"David Thayer announces to the travelling public that he has taken the contract for carrying the mail between Ridgway and Brookville. He has put on a line of stages, and will run regularly between these two points named. Leaving Brookville every Tuesday morning, and leaving Ridgway every Wednesday morning.

"BROOKVILLE, January 4, 1854."

"SEMI-WEEKLY LINE TO BROOKVILLE.

"The undersigned have commenced running a line of stages between Brookville and Ridgway. Will leave Brookville Tuesday and Friday mornings, arrive at Ridgway same evenings. Will leave Ridgway Wednesday and Saturday mornings, and arrive at Brookville same evenings. This is a permanent arrangement, and may be relied upon. This line connects at Brookville with daily lines east, south, and west; and at Ridgway with semi-weekly and weekly lines north and northeast. Good coaches, fast horses, and sober drivers will always be kept on this line.

"MURRAY & THAYER.

"June 7, 1854."

David Thayer had opened a stage line in 1853 through the wilderness to Warren. It failed, but was revived, and a livery stable opened in connection with it in 1854, as you will see in this advertisement.

"STAGE LINE REVIVED.

"The undersigned, having taken the contract for carrying the mail between Ridgway and Warren, will commence running a stage on Saturday, July 8, and will continue to run it regularly hereafter, going out on Saturdays and back on Sundays as heretofore. This line may be depended on, as it will go through every time without fail. Good horses and coaches and sober drivers will always be kept on the route.

"JOSEPH GRANDPREY.
WM. CORLEY.

"RIDGWAY, June 30, 1854.

"N. B.—We will also keep on hand Horses and Carriages, so that persons travelling thro' here, and others, can at all times be carried to any point to which they may wish to go.

"G. & C."

This line failed also, and the old horseback method had to be resorted to. There were too many panthers, bears, wolves, etc., on the route and too few people.

PIONEER HISTORY OF JEFFERSON COUNTY, PENNA.
"THREE TIMES A WEEK."

"Fall has commenced running his stages three times a week between Ridgway and Smethport. He will leave Smethport every Monday, Wednesday, and Friday morning, and leave Ridgway every Tuesday, Thursday, and Saturday.
"June 10, 1854."

In 1854, Ridgway by stage was "forty miles from anywhere," forty miles from Brookville, forty miles from Warren, and forty miles from Smethport. The pioneer coaches were neither rockaways nor palaces. They were the most ordinary hacks, and the horses could be "seen through," whether sick or well, without the aid of any X-rays.

The roads in spring, summer, and fall were a succession of mud-holes, with an occasional corduroy. Don't mention bad roads now. The male passengers usually walked up the hills.

In the year 1855 a man by the name of Nicholas Collins, from the Centreville region, had a contract to repaint the court-house. The court-house was a frame, and was painted white. The board fence around the square was white, too. He boarded with Mr. Luther, and, with true Christian patience, he and William Lahey painted on the outside of the building one entire Sunday.

However, the stores were open, the shops, too, and some men were shooting at mark. Our State motto then was, "Virtue, Liberty, and Independence," and evidently the latter part of the motto was lived up to in Ridgway.

In 1855 the county consisted of eight townships,—viz., Benezette, Benzinger, Fox, Gibson, Jay, Jones, Ridgway, and Spring Creek, containing a voting population of seven hundred and sixty-five. Lumbering was the principal industry.

In 1784, the year in which Pittsburg was surveyed into building lots, the privilege of mining coal in the "great seam" opposite the town was sold by the Penns, at the rate of thirty pounds for each mining lot, extending back to the centre of the hill. This event may be regarded as forming the beginning of the coal-trade of Pittsburg. The supply of the towns and cities on the Ohio and Mississippi Rivers with Pittsburg coal became an established business at an early day in the present century or in 1800. Pittsburg coal was known long before the town became noted as an iron centre.

Down to 1845 all the coal shipped westward from Pittsburg was floated down the Ohio in flat-bottomed boats, in the spring and fall freshets, each boat holding about fifteen thousand bushels of coal. The boats were usually lashed in pairs, and were sold and broken up when their destination was reached. In 1845 steam-towboats were introduced, which took coal-barges down the river and brought them back empty.

PIONEER HISTORY OF JEFFERSON COUNTY, PENNA.

The mills in and around Ridgway were the Eagle Valley mill, conducted by Isaac Horton, Jr.; the Elk Creek mill, owned by J. S. Hyde; the Mill Creek mill, owned by Yale & Healey; and the Dickinson mill. In 1855 there were still some remnants of the old boat scaffold at the "Red Mill."

This mill was erected by Judge Dickinson, and painted red. The boarding-house was also red. The boat scaffold was erected in the spring of 1844. The work was done by "Brush" Baxter for John S. Barr and William McMahill. These men built eleven boats that summer, each twenty feet wide and a hundred feet long. Lumber was carried to market in them for one dollar per thousand, and fifteen thousand feet was a load. In Pittsburg, Barr and McMahill sold their boats for one hundred dollars each.

Common hands on the river received one dollar per day and board; pilots, two and three dollars per day and board. Lebbeus Luther kept the Red Mill boarding-house in 1843-44. Then the "head" sawyer on the Red Mill received twenty-five dollars per month and board; the assistant, eighteen dollars a month and board; and common hands, fifteen dollars a month and board.

Mr. John S. Barr, who is still living, informs me that the usual religious exercises on Sunday at the Red Mill in 1844 were wrestling, fishing, pitching quoits, shooting at mark, running foot-races, and "jumping by the double rule of three."

The Bear Creek mill was run by Alvan H. Head, and the Beech Bottom mill by Cobb & Ruloffson. The logging was conducted with cattle. Cobb & Ruloffson had that year an advertisement in the paper for hands to drive oxen. The diet at these old mills was bread, potatoes, beans, flitch, and molasses, brown sugar, old-tasted butter, coffee and tea without cream, and, for dessert, dried apple-sauce or pie. Labor was cheap. Pine boards of the finest quality sold in Louisville, Kentucky, at seven and nine dollars per thousand. If the operator cleared twenty-five or fifty cents on a thousand feet he was thankful.

What pilots and hands on the river received, I cannot recall. All goods and groceries were dear; they had to be hauled from Olean, New York, or Watterson Ferry, on the Allegheny River. Money was scarce, the people social and kind. Whiskey and New England rum were three cents a drink. The landlords, being generally hard up, were always a little short, but managed to get a fresh supply of whiskey for court week,—I suppose for the judges.

In 1855 the township officers were:

Assessor.—Horace Warner.
Assistant Assessors.—M. L. Ross, D. S. Luther.
School Directors.—H. A. Pattison and H. Souther for three years each, and Isaiah Cobb for two years.

PIONEER HISTORY OF JEFFERSON COUNTY, PENNA.

Supervisors.—P. T. Brooks and Harvey Henry.
Auditor.—H. A. Pattison.
Justice of the Peace.—Matthew L. Ross.
Judge of Election.—Caleb Dill.
Inspectors of Election.—H. A. Parsons, R. Maginnis.
Overseers of the Poor.—Horace J. Thayer, Charles McVean.
Town Clerk.—M. L. Ross.
Constable.—A. H. Head.

In this year the first Protestant church was commenced in the county. All I know about that is this: One day a large, fine-looking, well-dressed man came into the office and requested Mr. Powell to subscribe something for a church. Mr. Powell was poor, and demurred. The man persisted, but Mr. Powell further objected, whereupon the stranger became indignant, and vehemently declared, "It is a God damn shame there isn't a Protestant church in the county, and I'll be God damned if I stop till there is one!" At the end of this Christian exhortation Mr. Powell subscribed five dollars. The scene was so dramatic and ridiculous, I inquired who the stranger was, and Mr. Powell told me he was Alfred Pearsall, from Jay township. I understood afterwards Mr. Pearsall succeeded and erected his church, called Mount Zion Methodist Church.

FOURTH OF JULY IN RIDGWAY IN 1854.*

"As usual, the Fourth was a happy day in Ridgway, on Tuesday last. The old baby-waker proclaimed about eleven o'clock the night previously that the Fourth was coming, but it did not actually arrive till about twelve o'clock, when it caught some of us napping. The 'wind-fall' boys say the Fourth arrived there about eleven o'clock; but we don't believe it, for it generally gets here about as quick as anywhere else.

"When it had become light enough to see, and the smoke from the thousand battle-fields of the Revolution had cleared away, the patriotic old Fourth was seen, sweating and foaming with heat, smoking with the fires of '76, and roaring like a lion, seeking a Britisher whom he might devour. General Frank Dill had charge of the flying artillery, and Clark, the judge, and Hank controlled the small arms, such as firecrackers and torpedoes, making in all an effective force, which, under charge of Field Marshal Maginnis, might well spread panic and confusion among the enemies of the 'glorious Fourth.'

"Soon after daylight the people from the surrounding country began to flock in, and long before noon the streets were thronged with an intelligent and happy people. At eleven o'clock the citizens assembled at the court-house, where the exercises were as follows: Hon. James L. Gillis was chosen president of the day. The chaplain, Charles Mead,

---

* By Jerome Powell.

PIONEER HISTORY OF JEFFERSON COUNTY, PENNA.

Esq., offered up a fervent prayer to the throne of grace. The audience were for a few moments highly entertained by a few patriotic songs by the choir. The Declaration of Independence was then read by William B. Gillis. Albert Willis, Esq., was then introduced as the orator of the day, who entertained the audience with a highly instructive and interesting address, which was listened to with marked attention by all present.

"After the oration was concluded, Henry Souther, Esq., was called upon, who made a few remarks.

"H. A. Pattison, Esq., and others also were called upon, and entertained the audience with interesting, pointed, and appropriate speeches.

"After the performance at the court-house was closed, a procession was formed, under the direction of Major Maginnis, marshal of the day, and marched to the Bowery prepared by Joseph Grandprey, Esq., proprietor of the Exchange, where a dinner was served up that did honor to Mr. Grandprey and his excellent lady, and to which the company did ample justice. The table fairly groaned under the weight of good things that were spread before the hungry multitude.

"After the removal of the cloth, the following regular toasts, which had been previously prepared by the committee, were announced by the president of the day :

"REGULAR TOASTS.

"1. The day we celebrate : a day around which will cluster sacred memories, while liberty has a resting-place in a single human heart. (Three cheers and three guns.)

"2. George Washington. (Drunk standing and in silence.)

"3. The signers of the Declaration of Independence : men who had the heart to desire, the mind to conceive, and the nerve to execute. Their memory will ever be cherished.

"4. The heroes of '76 : they will soon all be in heaven.

"5. The Star-Spangled Banner : may it continue to wave until its ample folds encircle the world.

"6. The Constitution and the Union : the Gibraltar of strength and national glory.

"7. The President of the United States : President of the whole Union.

"8. The governor of Pennsylvania : a Pennsylvanian all over.

"9. The citizen soldiery : the right arm of our nation's defence.

"(Major Maginnis, being called upon, responded to this toast, in a few appropriate and timely remarks.)

"10. The ladies : ' God bless them.'

"11. The orator of the day : may he live to a good old age, and in the evening of his days may the fires of patriotism burn in h s bosom as brightly as now in the morning of his life.

"(Mr. Willis returned his thanks to the audience in a very neat and appropriate manner.)

"12. The reader of the Declaration: may he ever be guided by the immortal principles set forth in the Declaration he has read to us to-day.

"13. Mine host: we seldom meet with as good fare.

"The toasts were received with cheers and guns. The aged seemed to have their youth renewed by memories of the past, the young were fired with the spirit of '76. All seemed to enter into the spirit of the day and the occasion. Even the old gun, which has stood the test of 'five hundred Fourths of July,' felt as young as on the day it came from its maker's hands, and spoke in eloquent tones of the times that tried men's souls, until patriotism got so thick throughout this whole valley that it could hardly be cut with a two-edged sword.

"A number of volunteer toasts were then announced, only a part of which we can now remember. The following were among them:

"By William B. Gillis. The Elk *Advocate* and its editor. The Elk being called upon, responded in ' his usual happy style.'

"By a young lady. The gentlemen: may the ladies bless them. (Cheers and guns.)

"There was no response to this, but it is hoped they will all respond by giving the ladies a chance to—' bless them.'

"Judge Gillis was toasted by some one, and responded only as he can respond to a Fourth of July sentiment. Each returning ' Fourth' finds the judge 'at home' and on hand with any quantity of patriotic speeches. He is worth a whole regiment of ordinary men at a Fourth of July celebration.

"By H. A. Pattison. Thomas Jefferson: the author of liberal principles, as embodied in the Constitution and government of the United States. (Cheers and guns.)

"By a lady. The young gentlemen of Ridgway: may they be blessed with good wives and fat babies. (A 'fat baby' eloquently responded.)

"By J. Powell. The Fourth of July: may it be celebrated five hundred million years from now by a free and happy people.

"The president announced five hundred million cheers and a like number of guns for this toast.

"By a guest. The gunner: may rejoicings always attend his labors. (The gun responded in a very eloquent speech.)

"There were many other volunteer toasts offered, which were lost to our reporter, and we are consequently compelled to omit them.

"After the toasts were concluded, those who enjoy such recreations adjourned to the ball-room of the Exchange, where, we are told, they had a very happy time. It is suspected that they 'ran all night.'

"The day was pleasant, and the celebration, from beginning to end,

PIONEER HISTORY OF JEFFERSON COUNTY, PENNA.

passed off in an unexceptional manner. The celebration was a sober one, no intoxicating liquors being used.

"The fireworks, under the direction of Captain Souther, went off admirably."

In 1854, Dr. C. R. Earley lived at Kersey. The year he came to Elk I do not know. He was energetic, kind, and industrious. He had to keep himself busy, and for some time he and Jesse Kyler, rival pioneers, were the baron soft coal kings of the county. The following is Earley's card as it appeared in the *Advocate*:

IMPORTANT FROM THE MINES.

"Having recently commenced operations at the new 'placer' in the 'San Francisco' coal-mine, the subscriber wishes to inform the public that he is prepared to furnish those wishing it an article of coal far superior to any ever before offered in Elk County at his mines in Fox township. He would also say that he has a lime-kiln in full blast at the mines aforesaid, and will keep constantly on hand a superior article of lime. All of which will be sold on reasonable terms.

"C. R. EARLEY.

"SAN FRANCISCO, February 8, 1851."

The following is Kyler's announcement as it appeared in the *Advocate*. He was the pioneer dealer.

COAL.

"The subscriber, thankful for the very liberal patronage he has hitherto and is still receiving, takes this opportunity to inform his friends and the public generally that he still continues the mining and sale of coal at his old establishment, being the centre of the coal basin, and the identical bed recently opened in another place. He is unwilling to admit inferiority, nor is he bombastic enough to claim superiority, where neither one nor the other can possibly exist. In respect to the quality of coal, it is true, by removing the dirt from the top of the outcrop coal may be got in larger chunks and will seem to burn more free, because the air circulates through it better. But he that buys a bushel of coal by measure, mixed fine and coarse together, gets more for the same money in mining under. However, no section of the country has an advantage over another, and but little can be obtained without. He will therefore furnish coal as usual in quality and price, and abide the judgment of a discerning public.

"JESSE KYLER.

"Fox, February 10, 1851."

In 1854 there lived in Ridgway one Major Robert Maginnis. He was full of military enthusiasm, and through his exertion a military company was organized in August,—viz., the Elk County Guards. Captain, R. Maginnis ; first lieutenant, Harvey Henry ; second lieutenant, William N. Whitney ; ensign, J. F. Dill. I think its life was of short duration, if it ever mustered. Maginnis, failing in war, bought a few medical books from Dr. Farwell, and left town in the spring of 1855 to practise the healing or killing art somewhere in the West.

The result of the election on the second Tuesday in October, 1854, resulted in the choice of the following county officers: Prothonotary, Charles McVean ; Commissioner, Wm. A. Bly ; Auditor, W. N. Whitney.

In the winter of 1854-55,—

> " There was snow, snow everywhere,
> On the ground and in the air,
> On the streets and in the lane,
> On the roof and window-pane."

It snowed every day for thirty days,—

> " Until over the highways,
> And over the byways
> The snowdrifts were ever so high."

The supervisors had to shovel turnouts along the public roads so that teams could pass.

In December, Mr. Powell wrote an editorial on the weather, a part of which I reproduce:

" Yes, winter is here. The season for the hunter to don his white cap and shirt and, properly armed and equipped, hie to the woods away, intent on depriving the innocent denizens of the forest of ' life, liberty, and the pursuit of happiness.' Our hunters are now reaping their harvest. The ' tracking snow' never was better, and it is too early in the season for the rascally York State hunters to molest the deer or make them afraid. Crack ! crack ! goes the rifle, and at every flash down comes an antlered monarch, which is soon ' hung up,' and off goes the hunter in search of another. Fine sport to the hunter, but death to the deer. So goes the world,—the weaker must ever fall a victim to the rapacity of the stronger. In vulgar parlance, the ' big fish always eat the little ones.'

" In this country winter is the season. As we are seated in our sanctum, made comfortable and cheerful by the glowing heat of McCready's black diamonds, listening to the wind as it whistles through the old court hall and moans dismally for admission, and as the space between the brick fire-proofs is turned into an eddy of snow-flakes, the feathery rafts floating about in such beautiful confusion that it is impossible to tell whether the current runs up-stream or down, we are almost inclined to become poetical, but will endeavor to keep cool. We once read some poetry written by a love-sick swain, upon seeing a snow-flake fall upon the bosom of his lady-love. It seemed by his description that a snow-flake couldn't begin to compare with 'that whiter skin of hers than snow, and smooth as monumental alabaster,' yet it had the temerity to place its charms in competition with the lady's, with the most disastrous result, for the snow-flake had no sooner laid itself upon the more than snowy breast than it saw that its own charms were suffering by the comparison, when, ' grieved to see itself surpassed, melted into a tear.' Served the snow-flake right. It had no business there. Another chap, less poetical and more practical, perpetrated a similar one upon his ' gal' and snow-flakes. He said the snow kept falling upon her bosom and melting, ' until at last, at last, oh, dear, her shirt was wet as water!' "

One of the modes of Mike Long and other pioneer hunters on the Clarion River was to ride a horse with a cow-bell on through the woods over the deer-paths. The deer were used to cow-bells and would allow the horse to come in full view. While the deer was looking at the horse the hunter usually shot one or two. I don't know whether Daniel Davison, of Portland, ever practised this or not.

In November the following-named physician located in Ridgway, and published his card in the *Advocate*:

"DR. S. S. FARWELL,

" Having changed his residence from Second Fork to Ridgway, tenders his professional services to the citizens of the town and vicinity. Office in the Oyster House, where he can be found at all times, unless professionally absent.

"November 13, 1854."

The doctor was a good-looking little man; he stuttered and stammered and received no encouragement from the people. He had a good medical library. There were but few people sick, and nearly everybody employed either Dr. Earley, Dr. A. M. Clarke, or Dr. W. C. Niver. In January, 1855, Dr. Farwell brought into the office this poem. It was given to me to "set up." Here it is:

"SAY NOT MY HEART IS COLD.

"BY DR. S. S. FARWELL.

" Say not my heart is cold,
   Because of a silent tongue;
The lute of faultless mould
   In silence oft hath hung.
The fountain soonest spent
   Doth babble down the steep;
But the stream that ever went
   Is silent, strong, and deep.

"The charm of a secret life
　　Is given to choicest things;
　Of flowers, the fragrance rite
　　Is wafted on viewless wings.
　We see not the charmed air
　　Beating some witching sound;
　And ocean deep is where
　　The pearl of price is found.

"Where are the stars by day?
　　They burn, though all unseen,
　And love of purest ray
　　Is like the stars, I ween.
　Unmarked is the gentle light,
　　When the sunshine of joy appears;
　But even in sorrow's night
　　'Twill glitter upon thy tears."

A few weeks after notifying the people in this poetry that he had a warm heart the doctor left for parts to me unknown.

In 1854 or 1856, Elk County had no medical society, but they had an adopted fee-bill, which I here reproduce :

"TO ALL CONCERNED.

"We, the undersigned, physicians of the county of Elk, would respectfully announce the following as our lowest fee-bill,—to wit :

1. Call and medicine near residence, or medicine in office . . . $ .50
2. At night 1.00
3. Visit in country one mile 1.00
4. Each subsequent mile under 12 25
5. Visit of 12 miles 5.00
6. do.　　20 miles 10.00
7. do. at night, fifty per cent. to be added to the ordinary charge above.
8. All necessary medicine to be included in the above.
9. Consultation with additional mileage (as above) 5.00
10. Obstetrics, natural labor (with additional mileage) 5.00
11. Instrumental, or by turning 7.00
12. Cupping in office 1.00
13. Vaccination (including after attendance) 1.00
14. Reducing fractures and dislocation of the femur (with mileage as above) 10.00
15. All other fractures and dislocations 5.00
16. Amputation of inferior extremities 40.00
17. Amputation of superior extremities 30.00
18. Operation for strabismus 25.00
19. Strangulated hernia 30.00
20. Hydrocele 10.00
21. Single hairlip 20.00
22. Double do. 30.00

PIONEER HISTORY OF JEFFERSON COUNTY, PENNA.

23. Paracentesis abdominis $10.00
24. Excising enlarged tonsils 10.00
   All necessary after attendance, surgical and obstetrical cases,
   to be charged for at the usual rates.
25. Examination of persons for certificates to exempt from military duty 1.00

"C. R. EARLEY.
A. E. PULLING.
LEWIS IDDINGS.
G. BACHMANN.

"May, 1851."

Dr. Fuller, a root and herb doctor, lived in Jones township, and in 1855 came to Ridgway, boarded at the hotel, and practised medicine. His panacea for every ill was lobelia and capsicum. He was there, I think, when I left in 1856. He "called" for the cotillon parties, and was himself a fiddler. Jim Harm and Frank Dill composed the orchestra for all dancing parties. Dr. Fuller was a genial, pleasant old gentleman, and if his remedies were not compounded with the highest skill or prescribed accurately, his intentions were good.

Like a great many men of that time, he never permitted himself to get too dry. I have only kind words for him.

> "Let us speak of a man as we find him,
> And heed not what others may say,
> And if a man is to blame let us remind him
> That from faults there are none of us free.
> If the veil from the heart could be torn,
> And the mind could be read on the brow,
> There are many we've passed by in scorn
> We would load with high honors now."

In January, 1855, I carried the mail one trip on horseback to Warren from Ridgway. A man by the name of Lewis was the proprietor, and he boarded at Luther's. I performed this service free, as I was anxious to see Warren.

I had to start from Ridgway on Friday night at nine P.M., ride to Montmorenci, and stop all night. A family by the name of Burrows lived there. I stopped on Saturday in Highland for dinner with Townley's. There were living in that township then Wells, Ellithcrpe, Campbell, and Townley. I arrived in Warren Saturday after dark, and stayed over night at the Carter House. I returned on Sunday from Warren to Ridgway, and, the weather being intensely cold, "I paid too dear for my whistle."

In 1855–56, Ben. McClelland, then a young man, was driving team for Sheriff Healey. In the winter he was sent to Warren with two horses and a sled. On his way home he expected to stop over night at Highland. Before Ben. reached "Panther Hollow"—a few miles north of Townley's—it became quite dark.

PIONEER HISTORY OF JEFFERSON COUNTY, PENNA.

At the hollow Ben.'s horses snorted, frightened, and ran. In the dark Ben. quickly recognized the form of a panther after him. The horses had the beaten track, the panther the deep snow alongside, and afraid to attack the heels of the horses on account of the sled, the horses crazy and furious.

It was a neck-to-neck race for Highland. The panther never gave up the race until the cleared land was reached. Ben. was a hunter, but was unarmed and almost dead from fright. When Townley's farm was reached the horses were all in a lather of sweat and nearly exhausted. A posse of hunters started in the early morning, and found the big brute near the hollow and killed him.

This was Ben.'s ride, not Sheridan's. Had Ben. been on a horse he would never have seen Highland.

Lebbeus Luther, with whom I boarded, was a great old joker. He was president of the school board in 1854. I spent many an hour hearing his reminiscences. He migrated in 1820 to Clearfield County from Massachusetts and settled in what is now Luthersburg. Luthersburg took its name from him.

In what year he moved to Ridgway I cannot exactly recall. He was appointed postmaster in 1855, and lived where P. T. Brooks now resides. Lebbeus Luther, Sr., kept a hotel while in Luthersburg, and was an active proprietor. In addition to his jovial good qualities, he was a great marksman. Bill Long, the king hunter of Jefferson County, visited this hotel frequently for pure air and when he had a dryness in his throat. On these occasions he used to try his hand with Grandpap Luther shooting at target. Luther's coolness always counted.

D. S. Luther, a son, and Jim Harm, a grandson of 'Squire Luther, were hunters, killing wolves and a great many deer. Jim lived with his grandparents, and used to furnish us venison.

In 1854, William B. Gillis was elected county superintendent. He was the pioneer. Pennsylvania in school matters was behind New York and some of the Western States, and in that year adopted the county superintendent idea from these States. The foreign population of the State was bitterly opposed to this change, to this advance. The law of 1854 also required orthography, reading, writing, English grammer, geography, and arithmetic to be taught in every district. The State superintendent also recommended the adoption of uniformity in books.

The law of 1854 was a dreadful blow to the old log school-house, with its poor light, high boards around the walls for writing-desks, unqualified and incompetent teachers, short terms, and diversity of books. The appropriation from the State to the township in that year was forty-two dollars and eighty-four cents.

W. C. Niver taught the summer and winter terms of 1850, '51, '52, '53. Miss Statira Brown, now Chapin, a summer term in 1853. A Mr. Buckley, from New York State, a winter term in 1853-54. C. M. Matson, from Brookville, a winter term in 1854-55. S. J. Willis, from New York State, summer and winter term in 1855-56. I give below a roll of the scholars who attended the summer term of the Ridgway school, commencing May 6, 1850, W. C. Niver, teacher.

Males.—James Harm, Barrett Cobb, Roland Cobb, John Ross, George F. Dickinson, Benezette Dill, Robert Gillis, Ezra Dickinson, George W. Connor, Patrick Cline, Calvin Luther, Claudius Gillis, Joseph Fost, Franklin Dill, Bosanquet Gillis.

Females.—Esther J. Thayer, Augusta Gillis, Clarissa D. Thayer, Mary E. Thayer, Mary Weaver, Sarah Ann Thayer, Albina E. Thayer, Ellen C. Gillis, Lovina Harm, Angeline Wilcox, Clementine Harm, Phœbe M. Wilcox, Anna E. Connor, Sarah Weaver, Alzinah Weaver, Semiramis Brown, Louisa V. Brooks, Mary M. Meddock, Ann Eliza Goff, Ardissa Wilcox, Elizabeth Luce, Martha Dill, Amanda Mead, Elizabeth Winslow, Laura Cook, Emily Cook.

The winter term commenced October 14, 1850, under W. C. Niver, teacher, and had on the roll, in addition to the above enumerated scholars, the names of,—

Males.—George Ellithorpe, Henry Thayer, W. P. Luce, Edward Derby, Melville Gardiner, J. P. Pearce, J. W. Pearce.

Females.—Malonia Ely, Statira Brown, Christina Gray, Eliza A. Hyde, Caroline Pearsall, Rosamund Jackson, Margaret Mohen, Emily Clark, Elizabeth Wescott, Maria Cobb, Emeline King.

William B. Gillis resigned the superintendency in the winter of 1855. His salary was three hundred dollars. Dr. C. R. Earley, of Kersey, was appointed to the position. His salary was four hundred dollars a year. The doctor made an efficient superintendent. He held the pioneer county institute in the court-house in June, 1856. I reproduce the full proceedings of that institute, as taken from an issue of the *Reporter* of June 22, 1856:

"TEACHERS' INSTITUTE.

"*First Day.*"

"Monday, June 2, 1856, pursuant to previous call, the Elk County Teachers' Institute met at the Academy at three o'clock P.M., and organized by appointing the following persons as permanent officers during the session:. Dr. C. R. Earley, president; S. J. Willis and Miss Olive J. Brown, vice presidents; and H. A. Pattison, secretary.

"On motion, the chair appointed the following business committee: E. F. Taylor, S. S. Buckley, Miss Mary Warner, Mrs. E. S. Thurston, and H. A. Pattison, who are to report the business of each day every morning.

PIONEER HISTORY OF JEFFERSON COUNTY, PENNA.

"On motion, the following gentlemen were appointed a committee on resolutions: Albert Willis, H. Souther, H. A. Pattison, J. L. Brown, and E. F. Taylor, who are to report at the close of the session.

"On motion, it was resolved that the institute hold its sessions in the court-house.

"On motion, adjourned, to meet to-morrow morning, June 3, in the court-house.

"The second day was occupied with exercises in the several branches taught in the common schools, conducted by Dr. William C. Niver, of Jefferson County, Pennsylvania. D. F. Brown, Esq., of Brooklyn, New York, delivered a very interesting and instructive lecture on penmanship.

"Third day's proceedings same as above, with a lecture on alphabetical characters, by H. A. Pattison.

"The sessions of the institute were occupied in reviewing the branches taught in the common schools, each teacher giving his or her method of teaching. The evening sessions were devoted exclusively to penmanship, under D. F. Brown, Esq.

"*Second Week.*

"Monday, June 9. The usual exercises omitted, for discussion on the best method of school government.

"On Tuesday morning, F. A. Allen, county superintendent of McKean County, made his appearance in the institute. Mr. Allen, by request, took charge of the exercises, and gave instructions of the most interesting character in the several branches under review.

"The exercises in penmanship closed on Tuesday evening. On Wednesday the usual exercises were conducted by Mr. Allen and Dr. Niver.

"During the evening session Mr. Allen delivered a very interesting lecture on the subject of education generally.

"The exercises of Thursday were conducted by Mr. Allen and Samuel Earley, Esq.

"The evening session was devoted to instruction on mathematical geography, by Mr. Allen.

"Friday was devoted to the usual exercises, accompanied by remarks on the general character of institutes, by Mr. Allen. After some remarks by Dr. Earley, A. Willis, and H. A. Pattison, A. Willis, chairman of the Committee on Resolutions, made, on behalf of the committee, the following report:

"'WHEREAS, We regard a system of common school education as one of paramount importance, lying at the foundation of all truly free and enlightened governments, and especially the chief, if not the only, safeguard of our own, whose very existence depends upon the virtue and intelligence of its citizens; therefore,

PIONEER HISTORY OF JEFFERSON COUNTY, PENNA.

"'*Resolved*, That we regard the present law creating the county superintendent as giving a new impetus to the cause of education, and look upon its continuance as essential to the efficiency and well-being of the common school system.

"'*Resolved*, That we recognize in our worthy county superintendent, Dr. C. R. Earley, an efficient and zealous laborer in the educational field, and that we look with feelings of pride upon the changes that are now taking place in our county with regard to our common schools through his labors, and that we most cordially invite the co-operation of all friends of the people's college—the common schools—to aid him in the good work begun.

"'*Resolved*, That we, as members of the institute, hereby express our heartfelt thanks to Mr. Allen, the able county superintendent of McKean County, Dr. William C. Niver, and Samuel Earley, who, by their disinterested and most valuable services, have made the exercises of the institute interesting and instructive.

"'*Resolved*, That we as an institute will most heartily co-operate with organizations of a similar character throughout the State in advancing the interests of education by the common school system.

"'*Resolved*, That teaching should be considered a profession equal in importance with that of any other, and that the compensation ought to correspond with that importance.

"'*Resolved*, That the teacher while teaching ought not to study any other profession than that of teaching.

"'*Resolved*, That females ought to receive equal compensation with the males for equal services rendered.

"'*Resolved*, That we recommend to our State Legislature to grant a State appropriation, for the purpose of sustaining a County Teachers' Institute in each and every county in the Commonwealth.

"'*Resolved*, That we recommend to our County Superintendent the propriety of calling another institute as soon as he may think practicable.

"'*Resolved*, That a synopsis of the proceedings of this institute be published in the Elk *Reporter*, McKean *Citizen*, and the Pennsylvania *School Journal*.

"'On motion, the institute adjourned *sine die*.

"'C. R. EARLEY,
President.
H. A. PATTISON,
Secretary.

"'RIDGWAY, June 13, 1856.''

Colonel Corbett, who clerked for Gillis in 1845, informs me that the court-house was built in the summer of that year. The contractors were

General Levi G. Clover and Edward H. Derby. The supplies for the men were furnished through the store of James L. Gillis. S. M. Burson was the first lawyer to locate in Ridgway. In 1854 the court crier was M. L. Ross. On public occasions he wore a blue broadcloth swallow-tailed coat, with brass buttons in front. "This coat had pocket-holes behind for 30 years or more." The commissioners were E. C. Schultze, C. F. Luce, L. Luther.

John C. McAllister, Esq., of Brandy Camp, was clerk to the commissioners in 1855. He would walk over and back home, and take his meals while in Ridgway with Mr. Luther. The 'squire was a red-hot Democrat then. In looking over the records of Jefferson County I find that Enos Gillis, of Ridgway township, was assessed first in 1830 with one grist-mill and one tannery, and James Gallagher was assessed with an occupation tax of tanner. This tannery was on Elk Creek, nearly opposite Powell's store.

Gallagher tanned with both hemlock and oak bark, and made a difference in the price of his leather of six cents per pound between cash and trade. He ground bark in a mill made on a large scale, something like an old-fashioned coffee-mill.

I venture the assertion that W. H. Osterhout, with all his experience and ability, could not to-day run this pioneer tannery successfully. Sole leather sold per pound for about thirty cents. Gallagher kept the pioneer hotel. He never had license. His wife would not permit him to have liquor about the house. Whiskey or its odor always made Mr. Gallagher very sleepy.

Powell sold the *Advocate* to J. L. Brown, of Jones township, I think about September, 1855. Mr. Brown was a promising poor young man, but knew nothing about the "art preservative." He changed the name of the paper to *Reporter*, and continued the terms about as they had been. He and I ran the paper; he was the editor, of course. During the ten or eleven months that Mr. Brown published the *Reporter* he lived in a little frame house on the rear of a lot along an alley near the residence of W. C. Healey. The house was set on blocks. It was well ventilated, for it was neither painted, weather-boarded, lined, nor plastered. Mr. Brown had been newly married, and commenced house-keeping here. I boarded with him. Notwithstanding the little deficiencies mentioned, we enjoyed ourselves. It was home, and "be it ever so humble, there is no place like home."

Mr. Brown had two brothers, W. W. and I. B. Brown. W. W. lived in Ridgway that year awhile and clerked in a store. I. B. used to come down on a visit, and then the three Browns and myself would all be seated at a "sumptuous repast" within those "palace walls." Who owned the shanty I do not know. Strange to say, these three Browns and myself were all in public life at the same time. We met in Harris-

PIONEER HISTORY OF JEFFERSON COUNTY, PENNA.

burg in 1881, W. W. as a Congressman, J. L. as Elk's representative, I. B. as an Erie County representative, and myself as a State senator. The three Brown boys deserve great credit. They had a superior mother.

Mr. Brown, having tired of newspaper life, advertised the plant for sale, and a Methodist minister from Philadelphia, Pennsylvania, Rev. J. A. Boyle, came out into the wilderness and bought the *Reporter*. He had a wife, five boys,—Richard, Melville, Olin, Samuel, and Harlow, the latter born in December, 1856, in the Brown "palace" which I have just described,—and two daughters,—Harriet and Jennie. I boarded with him. He lived later near the Gillis house. Two of his boys worked on the paper with me. I remained in his employ until about the last of September, 1856.

Mr. Boyle was a man of intellectual power and an eloquent orator, but in rather feeble health. He changed his residence and occupation for the mountain air and rest. When the Rebellion broke out Mr. Boyle enlisted, was commissioned a captain, and was killed at Wauhatchie, Tennessee, October 29, 1863, having been promoted to major of the One Hundred and Eleventh Pennsylvania Volunteers. Elk County lost in him a good citizen, an able man, and the country a brave soldier. His wife was one of the dearest motherly women I ever met. After the major's death the family returned to Philadelphia.

In the issue of September 27, 1856, a week after I left Ridgway, Mr. Boyle paid me this compliment in the *Reporter*:

"MR. W. J. M'KNIGHT.

"This young gentleman, who has been at work in the *Reporter* office for some time past, has just left us. It is seldom we meet a young man who seems to us to have in view the great object of life, but when we do our heart rejoices and our hopes for humanity and the world are enlarged. Self-culture is our highest duty. To produce a harmony between the intellectual and moral of our nature, and have both striving for the highest development, is the true road to usefulness and respectability. Mr. McKnight has resolved to devote himself to a useful profession, and to do this he has determined to lay a foundation of thorough training. Self-reliant, with a good constitution and a well-developed intellect, he is about to commence a regular course of medical lectures. He has sufficient enthusiasm to impel him forward in the arduous toil required to master the science, and we trust he has too high an ambition to stop at any of the resting-places of Quackery, but will push forward until he reaches the highest pinnacle in the temple of Æsculapius.

"One of the grandest sights presented in this working world of ours is to see a young man, unaided by wealth, pushing his way through untoward circumstances to a useful position in society and an honorable post. Go forward, Mac, and may the blessing of a thousand hearts cheer you in your labors!"

THE TOWNSHIP OF RIDGWAY.

Ridgway township was originally formed as a part of Jefferson County in 1826, and remained there until 1843, when it was taken from that county by the following act of Assembly to create the county of Elk:

"AN ACT ERECTING PARTS OF JEFFERSON, CLEARFIELD, AND McKEAN COUNTIES INTO A SEPARATE COUNTY, TO BE CALLED ELK.

"SECTION 1. *Be it enacted by the Senate and House of Representatives of the Commonwealth of Pennsylvania in General Assembly met, and it is hereby enacted by the authority of the same,* That all those parts of the counties of Jefferson, Clearfield, and McKean lying between the following boundaries,—viz.: Beginning at the northeast corner of Jefferson County; thence due east about nine miles to the northeast corner of lot number two thousand three hundred and twenty-eight; thence due south to Clearfield County; thence east along said line to the east line of Gibson township; and thence south so far that a westwardly line to the mouth of Mead's Run shall pass within not less than fifteen miles of the town of Clearfield; and thence westwardly to Little Toby's Creek, along said line to the mouth of Mead's Run; thence in a northwesterly direction to where the west line of Ridgway township crosses the Clarion River; thence so far in the same direction to a point from whence a due north line will strike the southwest corner of McKean County; thence along said line to the southwest corner of McKean County; and thence east along the south line of McKean County to the place of beginning, be and the same is hereby erected into a separate county, to be henceforth called Elk.

"SECTION 2. That Timothy Ives, Jr., of Potter County, James W. Guthrie, of Clarion County, and Zachariah H. Eddy, of Warren County, are hereby appointed commissioners, who, or any two of whom, shall ascertain and plainly mark the boundary lines of said county of Elk; and it shall be the duty of the said commissioners to receive proposals, make purchase, or accept donation land in the eligible situations for a seat of justice in the said county of Elk, by grant, bargain, or otherwise, all such assurances for payment of money and grants of land that may be offered to them, or their survivors, in trust for the use and benefit of the said county of Elk; and to lay out, sell, and convey such part thereof, either in town lots or otherwise, as to them, or a majority of them, shall appear

PIONEER HISTORY OF JEFFERSON COUNTY, PENNA.

advantageous and proper, and to apply the proceeds thereof in aid of the county : *Provided*, That before the commissioners aforesaid shall proceed to perform the duties enjoined on them by this act, they shall take an oath or affirmation before some judge or justice of the peace, well and truly and with fidelity to perform said duties according to the true intent and meaning of this act : *Provided also*, That as soon as the county commissioners are elected and qualified, the duties enjoined on the said commissioners shall cease and determine, and shall be performed by the county commissioners so chosen and elected.

"SECTION 10. That it shall be lawful for the commissioners of the county of Elk, who shall be elected at the annual election in one thousand eight hundred and forty-three, to take assurances to them and their successors in office of such lot or lots, or piece of ground as shall have been approved of by the trustees appointed as aforesaid, or a majority of them, for the purpose of erecting thereon a court-house, jail, and offices for the safe-keeping of the records.

"SECTION 11. That the judges of the Supreme Court shall have like powers, jurisdictions, and authorities within the said county of Elk as by law they are vested with, and entitled to have and exercise in other counties of this State ; and said county is hereby annexed to the western district of the Supreme Court.

"SECTION 12. The county of Elk shall be annexed to and compose part of the eighteenth judicial district of this Commonwealth ; and the courts in the said county of Elk shall be held on the third Monday of February, May, September, and December in each and every year, and continue one week at each term, if necessary.

"Approved—the eighteenth day of April, one thousand eight hundred and forty-three."

POST-OFFICES AND POST-ROADS.

From 1854 to 1856 there was a continual agitation over railroads, frequent public meetings, addresses made, and resolutions passed. These three were the most favored : the Allegheny Valley, the Pittsburg and Rochester, and the Sunbury and Erie.

All State elections were then held on the second Tuesday of October each year. The city papers always published the result in full, with this note, "Potter, McKean, Elk, Forest, and Jefferson to hear from."

The bridge over the Clarion up to 1854 was a toll-bridge. The pioneer jewelry-store, etc., was started west of the bridge by Ed. Gillis, April 23, 1853. The pioneer dentist to visit Ridgway was Dr. A. Blake, of Albion, New York, in May, 1853.

The pioneer tin and hardware store was opened by George Gillis in June, 1853. The pioneer millinery-store was opened by Caroline Gillis in 1856.

PIONEER HISTORY OF JEFFERSON COUNTY, PENNA.

It was a custom in 1854 to send to the printer with the wedding-notice a piece of the bride's cake or a gold dollar.

Rattlesnakes were occasionally killed on the streets as late as 1854. A paper of June, 1853, said in an issue that "this is a great country for timber. A man over on the Sinnemahoning has got a tract of land containing two acres, on which there is timber enough to make twenty-five canoes, forty timber rafts, fifty spars, forty thousand rattlesnakes, and one hundred thousand porcupines."

H. S. Jaquish was the pioneer daguerrian artist, who visited the town in 1850.

The names of post-offices and the postmasters supplied on the route from Warren to Ridgway in the year 1855, and the name of the contractor for such service, were as follows:

Warren.—C. Masten and S. J. Goodrich.
Mead.—Jonathan Mott.
West Sheffield.—J. P. Blanchard.
Sheffield.—John Gilson.
New Highland.—Charles Stubbs.
Ridgway.—William N. Whitney.

The contractor was David Thayer, of Ridgway, and his compensation was at the rate of one hundred and ninety-seven dollars and fifty cents per annum.

THE COUNTY SEAT FIGHT.

"At a meeting of the citizens of Elk County, held at the court-house in Ridgway on the 20th day of January, 1849, for the purpose of taking into consideration the best means to prevent the removal of the county seat of said county from Ridgway to St. Mary's, as the question was about being agitated in the State Legislature, Hon. George Dickinson was called to the chair, Joseph S. Hyde and James Gallagher, Esqs., were chosen vice-presidents, and Henry Souther and Caleb S. Dill, Esqs., secretaries.

"On motion, a committee of six were appointed to draft and report resolutions to the meeting, who reported the following, which were unanimously adopted :

"'WHEREAS, We are apprised that secret movements are in progress to effect a removal of the county seat in Elk County, by privately circulating petitions in certain sections of the county, and simultaneous efforts by one or more individuals at Harrisburg (who are personally and peculiarly interested) to procure hasty and (of course) unfair legislation, to effect their object, that as citizens of Elk County, we regard such a course as an attempt to forestall and coerce legislation as impolitic, unfair, and mischievous. Impolitic, as the county is yet new, population sparse, and the county buildings already erected and finished, the location convenient, and fixed by commissioners appointed by a former Legislature. Unfair, as the grounds were conveyed and the buildings constructed principally by private donations, insuring but little expense comparatively to the county. Mischievous, inasmuch as changing the county seat, when judiciously and legally located with regard to present and future conveniences, would be establishing a precedent which in a few years may again agitate the citizens of the county whenever aspiring and interested land-holders, or the more subtle and private intriguing of the temporary sojourn may see fit again to disturb its location, its prospects, or permanency. With these views we do, as citizens of Elk County,

"'*Resolve*, That we will use our best endeavors to defeat any and every attempt to remove the seat of justice of Elk County from its present location ; and that our representatives in the Senate and Assembly are earnestly requested to interpose their influence in exposing its nature and injustice.

"'*Resolved*, That copies of the proceedings of this meeting be transmitted to the Hon. Timothy Ives, of the Senate, and A. I. Wilcox, Esq., of the Assembly, and the proceedings published in the *Union* at Harrisburg, and in the *Jefferson Democrat and Elk County Advertiser*, of Brookville.

"'Signed by the officers.

"'February 6, 1849.'

"At a very large and general meeting of the people of Elk County, held on the 11th of February, 1849, during court week, in the court-house at Ridgway, Hon. E. C. Winslow was called to the chair, and John Johnston and Edward McQuone were appointed secretaries.

"On motion of George Weis, Esq., a committee of seven was appointed by the chair to prepare resolutions in regard to the expediency of removing the county seat.

"The following gentlemen were appointed as the committee,—viz., Joseph F. Comely, C. F. Law, Bob Weed, Patrick Malone, Rasselas W. Brown, James McIntosh, and Alfred Pearsall, who reported the following preamble and resolutions :

"'WHEREAS, A few persons, mostly inhabitants of or visitors to Ridgway, met in the court-house on the 20th of January, and without notice to the citizens at large, passed resolutions in favor of retaining the county seat at Ridgway, in the name of the citizens of the county, but without their knowledge, presence, or authority, which resolutions have been published in the newspapers, and are circulated to deceive the Legislature ;

"'AND WHEREAS, The settled and permanent inhabitants of Elk County are almost unanimous in desiring the removal of the county seat, aware that it was located at Ridgway by unfair means and improper influence, and that its continuance there is burthensome, expensive, inconvenient, and unjust ;

PIONEER HISTORY OF JEFFERSON COUNTY, PENNA.

"'AND WHEREAS, The borough of St. Mary's offers a location proper and convenient in all respects for the county seat; therefore we, the people of Elk County, assembled during court from township, and embracing most of the citizens of the county, without distinction of party, do

"'*Resolve*, That we repudiate the proceedings of the meeting above referred to, and repel the insult offered us by persons whose only power lies in their presumption, pretending to speak in our names, but without our knowledge or authority, and in direct opposition to our views, wishes, and interests; and especially do we disown the acts of strangers and temporary sojourners who have participated in these proceedings.

"'*Resolved*, That we have carefully examined and thoroughly approve the bill for removing the county seat from Ridgway to St. Mary's, without expense to the county, because Ridgway is near the western limits of the county, distant many miles from the mass of the population, a place having no agricultural country to support it, without trade or manufactures, containing no internal means of increase, affording only the most insufficient accommodations for visitors, and in all respects improper, inconvenient, and expensive. While St. Mary's is a large and growing town, surrounded by a large and flourishing country, central both geographically, and, in reference to population, convenient, easy of access, having excellent hotels, stores, mechanics of all kinds, and is in all respects the only fit and proper place for the county seat.

"'*Resolved*, That we call on the representatives of the people in the Senate and House to respect the popular will and to use their best exertion to procure forthwith the removal of the county seat from its present improper location to the borough of St. Mary's.

"'*Resolved*, That these proceedings be laid before both branches of the Legislature by their respective speakers and published in the *Jeffersonian, McKean Yeoman, Democratic Union, Keystone,* and *Intelligencer* at Harrisburg.'

"The resolutions and the question of the removal of the county seat were debated at length by William A. Stokes, Esq., and Reuben Winslow, Esq., in favor of, and Hon. James L. Gillis, and Henry Souther, Esq., against the removal.

"The question being taken, the resolutions and preamble were adopted by a large majority.

"E. C. WINSLOW,
"*Chairman.*"

"A NIGHT IN THE NORTH.

"Mr. Brady: Having occasion to visit Ridgway, the county seat of Elk County, this week, I was so amused with some of the performances which were transacted during my stay that I cannot refrain from giving you a report for the columns of your paper. The scenes were rich, and if I should rub rather close on some individuals I hope they will excuse me. But to my story.

"It was court week, or rather the week appointed for court ; but, as there was no president judge, and only one associate in attendance, no business could be transacted. I observed that a general feeling of dissatisfaction prevailed, and many, indeed, were the imprecations heaped upon the president judge. But I shall leave those interested to settle this matter among themselves and pass on to something more interesting.

"About two or three o'clock on Monday afternoon I observed a number of sleds and sleighs coming into town, loaded with Germans ; my first impression was that an emigrant vessel had just landed, but on inquiry I was informed that it was 'Gulliver and the Lilliputians' coming to remove the county seat, and that they were going to have a meeting in the court-house that evening for the purpose.

"After supper, in company with several others, I went to the courthouse, anticipating some fun, as I had learned that several 'big guns' would be there ; and sure enough, there they were, ready primed, and only waiting the application of the torch to send forth their powerful discharges.

"As we entered we found that the meeting had already been organized, although it was quite early ; and after a few minutes' conversation among those gathered in the centre of the bar, a motion was made that a committee of six be appointed to draft a preamble and resolutions expressive of the sense of the meeting, etc.

"I observed the president reach out his hand and receive a small slip of paper, from which he read the names of the committee. He then handed the paper to one of the committee, who took a candle and proceeded towards the jury-room ; on arriving at the door which led into the hall he called over the names, but from the slow and reluctant response it was evident that the committee had been selected before the meeting had been opened.

"In the absence of the committee a motion was made that William A. Stokes, Esq., of St. Mary's, address the meeting. Mr. S. responded to the call, and then the 'bear-dance' commenced ; the ball was opened.

"Mr. Stokes commenced by referring to the preamble and resolutions of the meeting held at Ridgway on the 20th of January, ult., asserting that an unprovoked and wanton attack had been made by that meeting on an absent citizen ; he believed it was intended for him, and if so he hurled back the charges to those who made them as false.

"He appeared ready to defend himself, and called upon the six persons who framed those resolutions to meet him, as he was prepared to meet his accusers face to face. He hoped the opportunity would be afforded to any of the opposite party to reply to his remarks ; he desired them to do so, and he would claim the privilege of answering them.

"Mr. Souther: Mr. President, I was one of those who held that meeting, and I hurl back the charges of the gentleman who has just addressed you with as much fury as they were given. (Tremendous cheers.)

"Here such an excitement was created that it was impossible for him to proceed.

"Mr. Stokes hoped the audience would hear Mr. Souther; he had called upon him to speak, and he wanted to hear him. The Ridgway people had paid attention to him while speaking, and he thought those from St. Mary's would be as liberal.

"Mr. Souther: Mr. President, I am not going to be gagged. I have been called upon to speak, and I am going to do it. Just grounds were had for holding the meeting on the 20th. Letters received from Harrisburg informed them that a strong effort would be made at the present session to remove the county seat to St. Mary's, and urged the propriety of holding meetings and sending on remonstrances immediately.

"He thought this looked very much like forming legislation without giving the citizens of the county an opportunity to canvass the subject. He could prove by documents that Mr. Stokes had been at Harrisburg boring for the passage of the bill; while there he called upon Messrs. Wilcox, Hastings, McCalmont, and others, asking their support and influence in the measure.

"He (Mr. Stokes) had called upon Mr. Wilcox, and had told him he could vote as he pleased; the bill could be passed without him. Considerable excitement ensued, which prevented our hearing his further remarks.

"Mr. Stokes admitted that he had been at Harrisburg, and proceeded to read a bill which had been read in Senate on the 7th of February by Hon. Timothy Ives.

"The bill provided that the citizens of St. Mary's should procure a suitable lot of ground for the erection of public buildings; they should erect a good and sufficient court-house and public offices, under the supervision of a committee appointed for that purpose, and should also erect a suitable county prison, to be built by direction of the county commissioners, by donation, etc.; and after said buildings were completed and accepted the seat of justice of Elk County should cease to be at Ridgway, and the public records should be removed and safely deposited in the buildings erected for their reception.

"The same bill also provides that so soon as the county seat shall be removed from Ridgway the present public buildings shall be sold and the proceeds thereof placed in the county treasury; and that the commissioners of Elk County shall not pay out any moneys for the erection of the new buildings at St. Mary's.

"Mr. Stokes further said that the population of the county was nearly all east of St. Mary's, therefore justice to the citizens demanded a removal.

While the country in the neighborhood of Ridgway was one unbroken forest, that about St. Mary's was fertile and thickly settled.

"Four hundred farms were already opened and being improved. One man on the Driftwood Branch had to travel sixty-one miles to Ridgway when he came to court; but if the county seat were removed to St. Mary's no person would have to travel more than twenty miles. Ridgway, he humorously remarked, was twenty one years old,—just of age,—consequently full grown, as large as she ever would be; but St. Mary's, yet in her infancy, being only six years old, beat her two hundred to one. Petitions had been sent to all parts of the county relative to removal.

"Mr. Souther (interrupting) asked if any petitions were at Harrisburg previous to the reading of the bill in the Senate.

"Mr. Stokes said he could not tell, but presumed there were, as they were sent through the county on the 27th of January, and ample time had passed between that and the 7th of February to have them signed and forwarded. After various other remarks, which were not distinctly heard, he resumed his seat.

"Mr. Souther obtained the floor, and dwelt chiefly on the injustice of the proposed removal. The question, he said, should be submitted to the people; they ought to have an opportunity of deciding upon its merits by ballot. He entered into a detail of the manner in which the public buildings at Ridgway had been erected. They cost five thousand four hundred and thirty-two dollars and thirty-two cents.

"Of this sum, John J. Ridgway donated three thousand dollars, Dickinson and Wilmarth eight hundred dollars, and James L. Gillis two hundred dollars. John J. Ridgway advanced to the county one thousand dollars in payment of his taxes.

"Mr. Souther gave it as his opinion that if the public buildings were sold and the proceeds placed in the county treasury, the donors could bring an action for the recovery of the money, and any panel of jurors would decide that it should be refunded. The use of it by the county would be nothing less than a bold attempt to rob the givers of the amount subscribed. He referred to the project of annexing Shippen township, McKean County, to Elk, for the purpose of making St. Mary's a more central point, and unfolded a scheme which, if carried into effect, would ultimately create disturbance in parts then uninterested.

"The noise again commencing, his concluding remarks could not be heard, but, quiet being again in a manner restored, Mr. Stokes obtained the floor.

"He said that Mr. Souther gave it as his opinion that, suits being brought, the money donated for the present public could be recovered.

"Mr. Souther: I did, and I don't charge anything for it.

"Mr. Stokes: Well, there is one thing, and every lawyer present will bear me out in it, that a lawyer's opinion which he charges nothing for is not worth much. (Great cheering). But I will give my opinion, and if any one tenders a fee, I will take it. If suits are brought, they will not lay, and the donors cannot recover a cent. This is my opinion, and I will take a fee in order to make it good.

"Mr. Souther (interrupting, and handing him a copper coin) said, 'Mr. Stokes, here is a fee some gentleman requested me to give you.'

"The applause elicited by this sally was so loud and continued so long that the further remarks of Mr. Souther were lost. A tumult then arose. Some shouted for Souther and Gillis and others for Stokes. Mr. Gillis mounted a table and endeavored to make some remarks of a general character, when the committee appeared and asked leave to report.

"The preamble and resolutions were read by Mr. Reuben Winslow, but in so low a tone that a call was made to have them read by a louder voice. Mr. Barr then read them, when a motion for their adoption was made.

"Mr. Gillis then resumed his speech in opposition to the resolutions, but the noise was so great that I could not hear his remarks sufficiently correct to report them, but I heard him say that he had been told by a person from St. Mary's that they had the power in Elk County, and they were going to make use of it.

"Here one of the secretaries, dressed in a blue overcoat, rose and interrupted him and said, 'You mean me; I told you so.'

"Mr. Gillis replied that he mentioned no names, and did not personally implicate any one, but he had been told so, and could prove it.

"The same person interrupted him, saying, 'You meant me; I can tell by the wink of yer eye, Jim Gillis, who you referred to.'

"Mr. Gillis: If the coat fits, wear it. But it will not do for St. Mary's to come out so bold at this early day.

"Here a call was made for a vote on the resolutions, which was taken, but the confusion became so loud that the chairman was unable to decide upon the vote.

"Mr. Johnson, of Warren, rose to make a few remarks; said he felt a delicacy in participating in a matter which in no way concerned him. He thought the measures adopted by the removal party were only calculated to breed disturbance and prolong the consummation of their object. His sympathies were with the citizens of Ridgway, and believed it would be an injustice to remove the county seat from its present location. He recommended that the passage of the resolutions should not be insisted upon, and would move that they be laid upon the table.

"Several voices: He has no business to make a motion! He don't live in the county!

"Mr. Gillis: I live in the county. I have a right to speak, and I make the motion.

PIONEER HISTORY OF JEFFERSON COUNTY, PENNA.

"Mr. Stokes : I move as an amendment that Mr. Gillis's motion be laid on the table.

"Here a discussion ensued in relation to parliamentary usage (a thing very common in such places), in which some half a dozen voices participated at the same time.

"The chairman called for a division of the house on the passage of the resolutions, but no division could be made ; the house was too full. But it was amusing to see the few of the removal party who understood English running to and fro, gathering their flock together.

"The chairman then put the motion *viva voce*, when one of the leaders of the 'Lilliputian' band jumped upon the judge's desk and waved his hand, when one tremendous, unearthly, unmeaning 'yaw' burst forth, which caused the walls of the building to tremble for its fate ; which being partially subsided, without calling for the negative, the president declared the resolutions passed unanimously.

"We doubt very much whether the resolutions could have been passed fairly, as the largest portion of the meeting was opposed to the removal.

"Immediately after the announcement of the chairman several persons endeavored to obtain the floor, and each party called for its speaker ; but before it could be decided which should have it the candles were blown out, and all was darkness.

"A general rush was made for the doors and windows, and if the court-house was not removed, we are certain that considerable glass in the windows was destroyed.

"I am sorry that I could not procure a copy of the resolutions, etc., as they were no doubt drawn up for publication, but at the time when darkness prevailed, neither resolutions, president, secretaries, nor anything relating to them could be found. But I have no doubt the above report will be received by your readers as well without as with them. It was a 'bear fight' certain, and, like the old woman, I did not care which whipped, but I am of the opinion that the removal party met with a warmer reception than was anticipated, and when I left the next day the court house and jail were still in Ridgway. The meeting adjourned to meet in two weeks, whether in St. Marys or in Ridgway, I cannot say, but if I can get to it I will let you hear from me again.

"Yours truly,
"A RAMBLER.

"February 22, 1849."

ELK COUNTY MEETING.

"At a large meeting of the citizens of Benzinger township and the county of Elk generally held at the borough of St. Marys, on Monday evening, February 12, 1849, George Weis, Esq., was called to the chair, and Ignatius Garner and James P. Barr were appointed secretaries.

"William A. Stokes, Esq., in compliance with the unanimous call of the assemblage, addressed them in plain and practical speech on the subject of the county seat.

"Anthony Hanhauser, Esq., moved for the appointment of a committee of three to draft resolutions, whereupon the following were appointed : Dr. B. D. Holcomb, I. Garner, and A. Volmer, who, having retired, reported on their return the following preamble and resolutions :

"'WHEREAS, Petitions now before this meeting from the various townships of this county, prove by the names thereto, that a large majority of the permanent inhabitants and substantial farmers and freeholders of the county desire the removal of the county seat from Ridgway to St. Marys, and whereas the former location is inconvenient, expensive, and improper, and the latter location is central, easy of access, convenient, and suitable in all respects ; and whereas, we are able, willing, and ready to erect the public buildings without cost to the county, by individual and private subscription ; therefore,

"'*Resolved*, That we unite in application to the Legislature for the removal of the seat of justice of Elk county from Ridgway to St. Mary's, according to the provisions of the bill before the Senate.

"'*Resolved*, That the attempt of a part of the small population of Ridgway to anticipate expected action of those who are favorable to the removal of the county seat and to forestall public opinion on this has been ludicrously ineffective, except in so far as it has precipitated what otherwise might have been delayed, a movement of the people to an end always desired by them, the removal of the county seat from Ridgway, where it was located against their wishes, and by intrigue and arrangement, directed only to answer the selfish purposes and private ends of a few interested individuals.

"'*Resolved*, That the people of this county feel quite competent to the management of their own business, and consider it derogatory to their character that gentlemen from other States, and other persons, not residents of this county, should have largely participated in the efforts made to keep the county seat at Ridgway.

"'*Resolved*, That the will of the people should always be the supreme law, and that what the citizens of this county desire in regard to the removal of the county seat should be done without respect to the influence of wealth, or the representations of self-appointed leaders, who have for years, by the mere power of presumption, managed all the public affairs for their own private ends ; and we call on our senators and representatives in the General Assembly to hear and respect that popular voice which at the polls is decisive, and now emphatically demands that justice be done to the oppressed people of this county, by removing the courts and offices from the inconvenient, expensive, and improper location at Ridgway to the central and convenient point which the borough of St. Mary's presents, free of cost for that purpose.'

PIONEER HISTORY OF JEFFERSON COUNTY, PENNA.

"The preamble and resolutions were unanimously adopted.

"On motion of George F. Schaefer, a committee was appointed to attend to the petitions and other business connected with the removal of the county seat.

"The following gentlemen constituted the committee: J. Walker, Charles Fisher, G. Schaefer, G. Schœning, X. Brieberger, J. Fitzpatrick, J. Dill, A. Pearsall, E. C. Winslow, A. Fochtmann, M. Spuler, J. Schaus, J. Ganser, M. Schissle, A. Ostermann, M. Wellendorf, L. Stockmann, A. Andrews, L. Diez, Dr. Sap, M. Munich, P. Steavens, M. Frey, J. Seel, A. Hoffman, J. Meyer, John A. Durgind, David Hubbard, James C. Parkhurst, S. B. Gardner, C. Clinton, John Keller, William Rodroch, William Hicks, and William Myers.

"On motion of Mr. William A. Stokes, Esq.,

"'*Resolved*, That copies of these proceedings be sent to the Senate and House of Representatives, and be published in the *Jefferson Democrat, McKean Yeoman, Harrisburg Union,* and *Philadelphia Pennsylvanian.*'

"GEORGE WEIS,

"*Chairman.*"

PUBLIC MEETING IN KERSEY.

"At a large meeting, held at Kersey, on the 3d of March, 1849, Joseph T. Comely, Esq., was called to the chair, and C. Spely and P. Malone were appointed secretaries.

"A committee, consisting of John T. Comely, Matthew McEwen, and Charles Lewis, was appointed to prepare resolutions, who reported the following, which were considered and unanimously passed:

"'*Resolved*, That the county of Elk, being poor and thinly settled, it is particularly important that the public expenses should be as moderate as possible, and with this view the seat of justice should be central and convenient to the mass of the people, and not (as it is at Ridgway) on one side of the county and remote for the people generally, thereby subjecting the county for the public charges and the citizens for their private expenses, to great and unnecessary loss and inconvenience.

"'*Resolved*, That we are in favor of repairing the great injustice which was done by locating the county seat at Ridgway, and of removing it from that place at the earliest moment to St. Mary's.

"'*Resolved*, That we protest against a division of this county,—a movement made for the mere purpose of retarding the removal of the seat of justice. The county is already too small, and if reduced in size and the courts are held at Ridgway, the taxes will necessarily be increased to a most ruinous and oppressive extent.

"'*Resolved*, That we hereby instruct our Senator and Representative to use all honorable means to carry out these views by having the bill for that purpose passed without delay, according to the resolutions of the county meeting, which truly represented and fairly spoke the views, interests, and opinions of the large majority of the people of the county, who are in favor of the removal of the seat to St. Mary's.'

"The meeting was addressed by William A. Stokes, Esq., Joseph T. Comely, Patrick Malone, Edward McQuone, and Charles Lewis.

"On motion, '*Resolved*, That these proceedings be communicated to the Legislature, and be published in the *Philadelphia Spirit of the Times, Harrisburg Keystone and Intelligencer, McKean Yeoman*, and *Brookville Jefferson Democrat*.'

"J. T. COMELY,
"*Chairman*."

Meetings were held in Fox and other townships, of which there is no printed record.

During the progress through the State Legislature of the bill for the removal of the county seat of Elk County, an important amendment was proposed by the Hon. Timothy Ives, repaying to the donors the whole amount of money expended by them in erecting the present county buildings.

The bill being brought up on second reading in the Senate on Monday, the 26th of March, Mr. Ives offered an amendment so as to make the fifth section read as follows:

"The commissioners of Elk County are hereby required, so soon as the aforesaid seat of justice is removed, to sell the court-house and jail of Ridgway, and to pay the proceeds thereof to the several persons who have contributed towards the erection and completion of said buildings; the balance, if any, to be paid into the county treasury, for the use of said county," which was agreed to.

The bill, as amended, was then read a second time (yeas, fifteen; nays, ten), and afterwards a third time, and passed finally.

Colonel A. I. Wilcox, who is still living in his eightieth year, was opposed to the change, and the removal act failed in the House. This agitation in Elk County started an epidemic of "removal of county seats." A petition was introduced in the Senate of Pennsylvania asking the removal of the county seat from Warren to Youngsville. Agitators were desirous to remove the county seat from Smethport, McKean County, the county seat from Clearfield to Curwensville, and from Brookville to Punxsutawney. The cause of this agitation was land speculation and the "cursed love of gold."

LOCAL HISTORY.

PIONEERS OF RIDGWAY TOWNSHIP, ELK COUNTY, PENNSYLVANIA, AS PER ASSESSMENT IN 1843, IN JEFFERSON COUNTY SEATED LIST.

Names of Taxables.—William Armstrong, Watts Anderson, Thomas Graniff, Pierce T. Brooks, Ephraim Barnes, David Benninger, William S. Brownell, William Crow, James Cochran, John G. Clark, Jesse Cady,

PIONEER HISTORY OF JEFFERSON COUNTY, PENNA.

James Crow, John Cobb, Job Carr, William H. Clyde, Absalom Conrad, 'Squire Carr, William Daugherty, Henry Dull, Caleb Dill, George Dickinson, Eli Frederick, John Evans, Daniel Fuller, Ridgway O. Gillis, Caroline Gillis, James L. Gillis, Silas German, Rufus Galusha, Enos Gillis, William H. Gallegher, James Gallegher, Esq., Charles Gillis, Richard Gates, Miles German, Arthur Hughes, Peter Hardy, Joseph S. Hyde, Ralph Hill, Charles H. & L. Horton, Frederick Heterick, Chester Hayes, Harvey Hoyt, Hughes & Dickinson, James A. Johnston, Henry Karns, Frederick Kiefer, Benjamin Kiefer, John Knox, Reuben Lyles, Thomas Lynn, Ebenezer Lee, William McLatchey, Erasmus Morey, John McLatchey, Joseph Meffert, William Meade, Horace Olds, Riverus Prindle, Paine & Watterson, Chester Paine, George Phillips, Willoughby Redline, D. S. Ramsey, Amos Sweet, John Snyder, John Sharley, George L. Smith, Samuel Stoneback, Ephraim Shawl, James Shawl, David H. & L. Thayer, Cornelius Van Orsdale, Jamison Veasey, Van Schirk, Elisha Weaver, David Worden, Maria Wilcox, Boston Lumber Company.

THE FIRST PAPERS PUBLISHED.

As I have given you the history of the first paper published in the county,—viz., the *Elk Advocate*,—I will now give the name of the first paper published for the county,—viz., the *Jefferson Democrat and Jefferson and Elk County Advertiser*.

This paper was published every Wednesday morning, in Brookville, by Evans R. Brady and Clark Wilson; terms, one dollar and fifty cents a year. This paper was published to and ended with the issue of April 6, 1850. I find in vol. iv., No. 1, of the *Jeffersonian*, in the issue of January 5, 1848, the following:

"Having made arrangements with some of the officers of Elk County to furnish blanks, to do their advertising, etc., we have changed the name of our paper to suit this arrangement."

I see by the paper that David Thayer was sheriff, Charles Horton, prothonotary, and Henry Souther, treasurer.

The only item of interest that I can find in these papers is in relation to two or three Democratic meetings in Ridgway.

The total vote of the county in 1848 was four hundred and twenty-eight.

THE FIRST POLITICAL MEETING.

The first political gathering in Ridgway of which there is any published record was held in the court-house, February 28, 1848. It was a Democratic meeting. Hon. Isaac Horton was appointed president, Nathaniel Hyatt and John S. Brockway, vice-presidents, and Charles Horton and W. A. Simpson, secretaries.

The object of the meeting having been stated by S. M. Barson, Esq., on motion, a committee of eight—viz., Thomas Dent, Samuel Overturf,

PIONEER HISTORY OF JEFFERSON COUNTY, PENNA.

John Mead, H. Reburger, Joseph Taylor, Joseph S. Hyde, Isaac Keefer, and Thomas Irwin—was appointed to draft resolutions.

In their absence, B. Rush Petriken and D. B. Jenks addressed the meeting at length.

A. I. Wilcox was appointed delegate to the 4th of March convention as representative delegate.

The committee returned and reported the following preamble and resolutions, which were unanimously adopted :

"WHEREAS, The sovereign power of this government, vested in the people of these United States, is again to be called into action in the choice of agents through whom this power is to be exercised, it becomes the pleasure and duty of freemen by a public expression of their will, to announce to the world the principle by which they will be governed in the selection of their agents, therefore,

"*Resolved*, That we will sustain our present administration in all its measures, and that we will support no man for office who will not carry out the same in principle and in detail.

"*Resolved*, That those who denounce the present war and give aid and comfort to the enemy secure for themselves present shame and eternal infamy.

"*Resolved*, That the Hon. James Buchanan, by his dintinguished services and unwavering fidelity to the principles of the Democratic party, has secured our entire confidence, and that we will reward him for his services by using our influence to secure his nomination for the Presidency ; and that our representatives be, and they are hereby instructed, to give him their support at the 4th of March convention.

"*Resolved*, That our delegates to the 4th of March convention be instructed to support Timothy Ives for canal commissioner.

"On motion, *Resolved*, That a copy of the foregoing resolutions be transmitted to John S. McCalmont and A. I. Wilcox.

"On motion, *Resolved*, That the proceedings of this meeting be published in the *Democratic Union* at Harrisburg, and in all the Democratic papers in this senatorial district.

"On motion, *Resolved*, That the proceedings of this meeting be signed by the officers.

"ISAAC HORTON,
President.
CHARLES HORTON,
W. A. SIMPSON,
Secretaries.
NATHANIEL HYATT,
JOHN S. BROCKWAY,
Vice Presidents."

PIONEER HISTORY OF JEFFERSON COUNTY, PENNA.

The pioneer court held in the county was at Caledonia, twenty miles east of Ridgway, on the Milesburg and Smethport turnpike, in Jay township. The judges present were; Associates, James L. Gillis and Isaac Horton; Prothonotary, etc., W. J. B. Andrews; Commissioners, Reuben Winslow, Chauncey Brockway, and a Mr. Brooks. But little business was transacted. Attorneys present: George R. Barrett, Ben. R. Petriken, and Lewis B. Smith. The first court held in Ridgway was in the schoolhouse, February 19, 1844, Alexander McCalmont, president judge; Isaac Horton, associate judge; and Eusebius Kincaid, sheriff.

The pioneer court crier was Nathaniel Hyatt, from Kersey, and, like everybody else in those days, was fond of attending court, for the sake of visiting, seeing the judge, telling stories, and "smiling with his neighbors."

Mr. Hyatt was a large man, peculiar, and had a coarse voice. Judge McCalmont, of Venango, was on the bench, a very easy-going, mild-mannered man.

One day, while the court was in session, Mr. Hyatt, in a loud tone of voice, was busy telling stories to his neighbors in the court-room. The judge thought there was a little too much noise, and, to personally reprimand Mr. Hyatt, he commenced "a rapping, gently tapping, tapping" three times on the desk, and addressing Mr. Hyatt thus: "Crier, there is a little too much noise in court."

Promptly Mr. Hyatt responded by stamping his right foot violently on the floor, and, in his loud, coarse voice, exclaimed, "Let there be silence in court! What the h— are you about?"

EARLY RAILROADS.

The Sunbury and Erie Railroad, now the Philadelphia and Erie, was chartered April 3, 1837, but it was not until about 1852 that construction was commenced, and it was not completed until about the fall of 1864.

In the speculative times of 1836 non-residents of then Jefferson County bought largely of the wild lands in and around Ridgway township, which, of course, when railroad and other bubbles burst, was left on their hands. This land had been advertised to contain valuable iron ore and bituminous coal, and much of it could have been bought as late as 1851 at fifty cents an acre.

To build a railroad through a dense wilderness of worthless hemlock, ferocious beasts, gnats, and wintergreen berries, required a large purse and great courage. Of course, there was no subject talked about in the cabin homes of that locality so dear to the hearts of the pioneers as this railroad. Living, as they were, in the backwoods, they were perfectly excusable when the subject of railroads was broached, even if they did cut all kinds of fantastic tricks.

PIONEER HISTORY OF JEFFERSON COUNTY, PENNA.

The first railroad meeting held in Ridgway, Elk County, was in the fall of 1845. Gentlemen were present from Erie, Warren, McKean, Centre, Philadelphia, and other counties. The deliberations were held in the old school-house, and there the road was constructed in words, as it was all through the seasons for years afterwards.

In any event, I suppose those railroad barons enjoyed themselves in Ridgway, and were fed on elk-steak for breakfast, blackberry-pie for dinner, speckled trout and bear meat for supper, with nothing stronger to *drink than sassafras tea*. This generous diet, in sleep at least, would build railroads.

1852 was the railroad era. Engineers surveyed the route through Ridgway for the Allegheny Valley Railroad, the Venango Road, and the Sunbury and Erie Road. Numerous other railroads were talked about,— viz., the Clearfield and the Buffalo, Rochester and Pittsburg. In anticipation of the completion of all these railroads, I suppose, the county commissioners, in September of this year, erected a stone wall around the jail-yard two feet thick and fourteen feet above the ground, and to civilize the Whistletown section for these iron horses, my old friend, B. F. Ely, Esq., in this month, killed three bears in fifteen minutes.

EARLY HOME OF THE WILD PIGEON.

In 1845, Ridgway township was the nesting and roosting home of the wild pigeon. There was a roost at or near what is now Bootjack, one near Whistletown, and another near Montmorenci. These big roosts were occupied early in April each year. They were usually four to five miles long and from one to two miles wide. Every tree would be occupied, some with fifty nests. The croakings of the pigeons could be heard for miles.

The wild pigeon laid one or two eggs, and both birds did their share of incubating, the female from two P.M. until nine A.M., and the male then to two P.M. These roosts were great feeding-places for animals as well as for man. As late as 1851 the American Express Company carried in one day, over the New York and Erie Railroad, over seven tons of pigeons to the New York markets. A wild pigeon can fly from five hundred to one thousand miles in a day.

Like the buffalo and elk of this region, the wild pigeon has been doomed.

FULLNAME INDEX

----, Boaz 236 Corneliu 236
Cornelius 234 Jacob M 328 John
35 234 443 Mary 37 Michael
236 Nathaniel 236 Peter 236
Sister Esther 236
ACHESON, James 404
ADAIR, Blaney 302
ADAMS, Alexander 401 Bill 517
Edward 225 James 400 John
Quincy 318 Thomas 401
ADDISON, Alexander 302 George
399
ADLUM, John 51
AFTON, 169
AHARRAH, Henry 461 James 225-
226 315 352 461 Jane 461 Mrs
461
AIKENS, David 400
ALBERT, George Dallas 132 John
454 Samuel 401
ALCORN, Andrew 225 John 353
401 William 401
ALDEN, Roger 142-144 146
ALEXANDER, C 309 C A 198 215
250 305 313 369 371 380 505
508 524 538 Caleb 404 Caleb A
366 416 545 Father 454
Frederick 400 Hugh 400 James
400 John 404 406
ALFORD, Roswell P 343
ALLEGIER, 526
ALLEN, Benoni 261 Dillis 399-400
F A 642 Isaac 404 502 558
Marvin 469 Mr 643 Rev 262
ALLGEIER, 503 P J 502 Phil 558
Phil J 514
ALLSHOUSE, Henry 303
ALTMAN, D S 438 Mr 439 Mrs
439

AMES, James H 226 404
AMOS, 278-279 Butler B 277
ANDERSON, 557 Charles 404 495
555-556 603 608-609 Dr 209
Hugh 399 James 400 487 Robert
348 Samuel 210 Watts 658
William 406
ANDREW, Hugh 574
ANDREWS, A 657 Chairman 597 G
W 596-597 600-602 George 608
Jane 248 John 387-388 Maj 593
R 309 Robert 177 197-198 212
220 248 305 354 368 398 487-
488 507 Robt 328 W J B 661
William 177
ANNE, Queen 78
ANSERSON, William 399
ANTHONY, Levi 405 Thomas 471
ARCHIBALD, John 397
ARMSTRONG, 436 Col 34-35
Evaline 460 George 353 399 460
James 261 Jesse 124 178 223
396-397 433-435 437 Lieut 184
Mary 261 Sally 435-437 Samuel
399 460 Sarah Ann 491 Thomas
390 W P 215 William 211-212
219 311 351-352 389 399 460-
461 658
ARTHURS, Frank 168 John 404 R
502 602 Richard 198 306 318-
319 329 366 370 380 404 416-
417 500 525 545 599 601 605
608 S B 515 559 S C 600-602
Samuel C 604-605 Thomas 353
399 415
ATKINSON, Thomas 342
ATLEE, Col 43 66 Samuel F 60-61
65 71 74 Samuel J 39 Samuel
John 43 68 76

ATWELL, John 356 400
AUDENREID, Sen 209 222 William 207 551
AVERY, John 398 456
AYCRIGG, B 326 Mr 327-328
AYERS, John C 254
AYLESWORTH, 397 John 472 R A 322 Reuben 449 Reuben A 219 308 312 343 447 452
AYLSWORTH, Reuben A 388
BABCOCK, James 253
BACHMANN, G 639
BAILEY, Benjamin 424
BAILY, Richard 292
BAIN, John 255
BAIR, Ephraim 245 262 Jacob 262 Lawrence 401
BAKER, Charles 394-395 Mr 124
BALDWIN, A 309 488 Alonzo 195 350 355 398 402 415 456 487 Daniel 402 Fred 402 Ira 344 Samuel 487 Summers 177
BALEY, Benjamin L 400
BALL, 567 Israel 399
BALLIOTT, Stephen 76
BANKS, David 601-602 John 303 Mrs 598 William 275 302 304 366 369
BARBER, Thomas 449 Thomas W 224-225
BARCLAY, 349 404 C R 309 Charles 208 Charles B 397 Charles K 380 Charles R 219 223 244-245 309 314 343-344 388 David 123 208 244 344 397 412 434 608 610 Elizabeth 244 Mary 244 Rev 434 William D 303-304
BARD, James 390 Richard 390
BARDEN, Capt 291
BARICKHOUSE, George 401
BARNES, A C 254 Ephraim 658 Erastus 388
BARNETT, 101 132 301 424 571 576-577 A 215 350 And 309 Andrew 120-121 177 193 195 212 216 219-220 241 309-310 349-352 356 365 367 375 380 387 423 428 555 573 Andrew Jr 573 David 225 355 493

BARNETT (cont.)
  Elizabeth 570 J P 121 J Potter 573 John 177 195 223 305 349-350 353-354 398 416 570 573 Joseph 9 32 84 116-117 120-121 177 193 195 211 222-223 227 238 305 343 348 358 372 396 398 410 422-423 425 428 460 491 566 570 572-575 578 Joseph Scott 574 Juliet 574 Margaret Annie 574 Rebecca 423 573 Sarah 121 238 423 570 573 Sarah Ann 85 Thomas 177 537 573
BARNS, Luther 399 Warren 399
BARNUTZ, Mr 453
BARR, 219 526 Alexander 526 Billy 520 Christopher 248 309 313 329 349 398 415 David 399 Elizabeth 248 James 209 James P 655 John S 121 620 631 Mr 654 R P 260 Robert 197-198 415 Robert P 193 198 351 404 456 500 508 531 Robert Sr 241 Samuel 399 Sarah 248 Thomas 350 399 404 416 471 505 Thomas M 198 241 325 500 508 525 559 Thompson 310 367 404 William 416
BARRET, E D 243
BARRETT, 624 Daniel 411 G R 322 George 411 George R 318 321 353 409-410 661
BARRIS, Joseph S 255 Rev 325
BARRITT, E H 324
BARRUN, Naphtala G 454
BARRY, Widow 451 William T 441
BARTHOLOMEW, Benjamin 304 310 366 369 545 Linn 366 369
BARTLE, John 348 Peter 177 347
BARTLETT, 546 Emory 620 Israel 177 Nancy 581
BARTLEY, Armstrong 401
BASTIAN, 33
BAUGHMAN, John 402 Powel 401
BAUM, Frederick 116 John 260 John W 356 406 Peter 362
BAXTER, 567 Brush 631
BAYLOR, Anna Maria 279 Richard 278 Thomas G 279

BAYNE, Hiram 369
BEAM, Henry 405 Samuel 405
BEAR, R M 254
BEATTY, William 303
BECK, J 321 John 220 310-311 318 322 328 416
BEER, Jacob 399 William 399
BELL, 588 607 Ann 262 Archibald 122 Augustus 605-606 Greenwood 387 James 124 178 308 James H 262 322 351 353 357 437 439 James W 351 354 388 396 John 117 122 178 195 208 305 307 347-348 353-354 374 380-381 396 406 430 433 492 617 Joseph 178 367 396 S M 507 Samuel 347 Samuel M 404
BEMAN, Samuel 400 469
BENEDICT, Smith 399
BENN, J P 254 Thomas 254
BENNETT, B 343 Benjamin 343 Benjamin Sr 458 J 343 Mr 342-343 Oran 226 Orilla 393 William 463 469 William M 393
BENNINGER, David 658
BENSCOTER, C C 525
BENSCOTTER, 284
BERG, Henry 530
BERNARD, George 391
BERRY, Ann 452
BEST, Charles C 254 William 437-438
BESTS, George 400
BEYLE, Aug 608
BICKLER, Abraham 399
BIDDLE, Clement 302 James M 303 King 317 Nicholas 418
BIGLER, John 411
BINGHAM, 81 William 53 80 541
BIOREN, 139
BIRD, Col 169 Milton 245
BISH, John H 402
BISHOP, Dr 525 Emma 616 G 392 Gara 240-243 525 558 Garey 404 Gary 485 S B 325 366 485 545 Samuel B 404 508 542
BITTENBENNER, David 404
BLACK, J P 620 James 397 Mr 208
BLACKMARR, R L 625

BLACKSTONE, 547
BLACKWELL, Robert 53
BLAIR, 410 David 249 James P 409 Thomas 366 369 339
BLAKE, A 647
BLANCHARD, J P 648
BLISS, 520
BLOOD, 606-608 C 318 Cyrus 212 215 219-220 225 308 315 329 351-352 382 400 471-474 K L 284 596 598-600 604-605 610 Kennedy L 608-609 Virginia 266
BLOSE, Boaz D 265 G Ament 222 George 432-433 George Sr 218 Professor 506 549 Sarah 432
BLOSS, George 356
BLUTE, Kennedy 596
BLY, Wm A 636
BOALS, Francis 303
BOGGS, John 76 Moses 386
BOIL, Henry 471
BOILEAU, N B 170-171
BOND, James 400 475
BONER, Charles 250
BONNECAMP, Father 132
BONSALL, Benjamin 387
BOO, Billy 539
BOONE, Daniel 514
BOOTH, Ezra 253 William 399
BOSLEY, Harmen 177
BOUCHER, John 266 600-602
BOUQUET, 335 Col 336
BOUTHART, John 352
BOVARD, Matthew 469
BOWDISH, 546 Philo 406
BOWEN, J 177
BOWERS, Andrew 352-353 367 397 405 440 443 493 Eli 405 John 353 397 405 488 Philip 353 356 397 405 435 488-489 493 Samuel 351 357 William 224 305
BOWERSOCK, Jacob 437
BOWMAN, A H 435 Andrew 208 397 Andrew H 308 435 Henry 405 West 600
BOYD, John 76 William 210
BOYLE, J A 645
BOYLES, Henry 399
BRACK, Samuel 210

665

BRADBURN, Sophia 252
BRADDOCK, Gen 335-337 565
BRADFORD, W 76
BRADY, 31 A J 599-600 602 Capt
    30 E R 600-602 Elizabeth 507
    Evans R 417 543 659 Hugh 310
    325 351-352 366 369 391 404
    416 425 485 501 508-510 542-
    543 545 James Jr 178 Justice
    603 608-609 Mr 650 Oliver 620
    William C 425 William P 42 51
    83-84 348
BRANDT, 564-565
BRATTON, Margaret 248 Samuel
    402 Wallace 352 402
BRECK, Samuel 209 595
BRECKENREACH, David 36-37 40
BRECKENRIDGE, David 36
BRENEMAN, D E 501
BRICE, Robert 401
BRIDGE, Hudson 402
BRIEBERGER, X 657
BRIGHAM, Lafe 623
BROADHEAD, John 51 83-84
BROADLEY, Paul 184
BROCIUS, Adam 402 Jacob 402
    John 402 Michael 402 Peter 402
BROCKWAY, A 215 Aaron Jr 400
    472 Aaron Sr 400 472 Alonzo
    312 343 399 446 454 468-469
    Chauncey 661 Clarissa 469
    Huldah 468 J 309 James 367 397
    399 454 James M 224 353 366
    382 469-470 James W 446 John
    S 379 469 659-660
BRODHEAD, 31 Gen 30
BRONSON, Ira 406 493
BROOKS, Calvin 405 Collins 397
    Lorenzo 398 Louisa V 641 Mr
    661 P T 453 623 632 640 Pierce
    T 658 William 405
BROWN, 622 624 A H 616 Charles
    278-280 D F 642 Frederick R
    475 Harlow 645 Harriet 645 I B
    81 644-645 Isaac B 84 126 139-
    140 J L 642 644-645 Jacob 172
    Jennie 645 John 246 273
    Melville 645 Moses 297 Olin
    645 Olive J 641 Polly 248 R B
    394 Rasselas W 649 Rev 260

BROWN (cont.) Richard 645 Robert
    E 366 369 Samuel 251 645
    Semiramis 641 Statira 640-641
    W W 644-645 Wendel 335
BROWNELL, William S 658
BROWNING, Andrew 302
BROWNLEE, 559 John 226 328
    404 416 501 514 Thomas 491
BROWNSON, Ira 355
BRUNER, John 402
BRYAN, A M 245 George 270
    Samuel 302
BRYANT, Nehemiah 224 397 454
BUCHANAN, 619 James 543-544
    660 John 82
BUCHITE, Peter 405
BUCK, John 397
BUCKLEY, Mr 641 S S 641
BUELL, Joseph 406
BUFFINGTON, Joseph 369 Judge
    279
BUFFUM, Russell 309
BULLERS, John 260 Samuel 121
BUMP, Rev 254
BUND, 292
BUNDY, 265
BURKE, 279
BURKET, Samuel 434
BURKETT, G W 604 Jacob 266
BURKHART, David 397
BURNES, Philip 328
BURNS, Daniel 526 George 402
    Naphtalia 397 Patrick 334 Philip
    415 Richard 399 460
BURNSIDE, James 369 Thomas 310
    322-323 365-366 499 William
    499
BURROWES, Thomas H 200 214
    551 Thos H 221
BURROWS, 639 G 620 Gilbert 406
BURSON, S M 644 659
BUSH, Gideon 401
BUSHLY, Ephraim 458 492
BUTLER, Bion H 511-512
    Constable 602 Cyrus 254 404
    425 500 506 508 521 525 538
    545 Cyrus Jr 603 Cyrus Sr 599
    David 177 181 212 216 254 349-
    350 398 406 425 506 Edw 76
    John 503 John B 318 Joseph 398

BUTLER (cont.)
  Nathaniel 216 308-309 398 406
  424-425 Richard 60 65 68 70-71
  74 76 Wm 76
BUTT, Rev 254
BUTTERFIELD, Oran 308 Orrin
  460
BUTTLE, 403
BYERLY, Ludwick 401 433
BYRD, Col 337
CADY, Jesse 658 Mr 452
CAIN, George 403
CALDWELL, Alexander 87 Dwight
  446 James 310 397 435 Josiah
  435 Timothy 471
CALLEN, Andrew 401 David 401
  John 427 Peter 401 Thomas 399
  427 471 William 401
CALLENDER, Nathaniel 253
CALLIN, Thos 352
CAMERON, Simon 593 596-597
CAMP, Heth F 390
CAMPBELL, 639 Alex 76
  Alexander 70 74 Andrew C 546
  Archie 481-482 Arhcie 486
  Benjamin 219 401 Charles 302
  Elisha 401 Elizabeth 249 George
  403 H Clay 546 James 546 John
  402 Lorenzo 403 Mary Ann 486
  Paul 177 Robert 434 Sanford
  403 William 212 262 304 314
  356 383 388 390 434-435 Wm
  215 352
CANAN, John 51
CAR, Joseph 177
CAREY, Alfred 349 Hannah 261
  Lemuel 308 Lemuel Jr 262
  Lemuel Sr 261 Samuel 304
CARLEY, Job M 226
CARLTON, David 406
CARLY, Job 399 Moses H 399
CARMALT, 282 Hannah A 281
  Isaac 397 Isaac P 123 275 281
  434 439
CAROTHERS, John 244
CARPENTER, Ephraim 303 369
CARR, David 399 Ebenezer 354 Job
  399 461 659 John W 418 Joseph
  315 425 Mr 439 Squire 659
  William 459

CARRIER, 414 C A 523 D 219
  Darius 212 254 259 308 350 367
  381-382 403 456 458 487-488
  507 538 Euphrastus 177 351 398
  403 488 G B 558 George 403
  Hiram 350 402-403 415 488
  Nathan 254 349 352 355 398
  402-403
CARROLL, James T 533 John 600
  608 John E 601-602 609 William
  255
CARSON, Benjamin 387
CARTER, 639
CARY, John 405
CASTON, Zerah P 255
CATHCART, William 541
CATHERS, Oliver 405
CATLIN, 26
CATZ, George 352 399 471 William
  471
CAUFMAN, Mr 218
CAVINORE, Bartholomew 406
CHALMERS, James 346
CHAMBERLAIN, Edward 402
  George 402 Henry 402 Peter 356
CHAMBERLIN, Peter 406 493
CHAMBERS, 623 James 243-244
  401 John 401 Joseph 367 Martha
  249 Mr 458 Sarah 243 Solomon
  248 404
CHANDLER, William J 502
CHAPIN, 624 J C 623 Statira 640
CHAPMAN, ---- 406 Thomas 182
CHARLES, Ii 268 Ii King 78
CHEAVER, Peter 334
CHERRY, Henry 401 John 401
CHESLY, Mattie 266
CHILDS, Col 597
CHISTITER, Daniel 354
CHITISTER, D 418 D S 463 Daniel
  420 David 420 Joseph 225 417
  420 Samuel 417 420
CHRISTY, J 310 John 224 309 329
  349 362 367 398 456 William
  456
CHURCHILL, S 254
CLARK, 341 632 Aaron 400
  Charlotte 506 Dr 605-606 E
  Heath 508 Elihu 355 399 406
  491 Elijah 356 425 524 Emily

CLARK (cont.)
641 G R 76 Henry 399 Henry M
352 Henry M R 356 415 J G 309
508 James 268 Jane 559 Jesse
318 352 Jesse G 306 310 366
370 404 410 416 525-526 545
558 Jim 628 Joel Jr 399 Joel Sr
399 John 121 272 John G 658
John P 400 Judge 514 525 558
605 Julia 502 Philetus 446
Robert 360 Samuel 354 W F 519
William 211-212 224 250 302
310 321 367 417 420 505
William F 404 Wm 303 318 328
Wm Sr 500
CLARKE, A M 392 446 468-470
596 608 621 637 Ada 469 Asaph
M 308 344 Chloe 469 Dr 158
447 Elisha 467 George Rogers
71 74 Hiram 469 James 210 Jane
469 Joel 467 469 Joel Jr 467-468
Mary 469 Philetus 343 392 467-469 Rebecca M 392 Willis 469
CLAWSON, Charles 397 Matthias
397 435 William 224 313 415
CLAY, 317 618 Henry 303 318 418
543 Sen 319
CLEMENTS, 556 Clarissa 523 John
558 Joseph 177 195 349 398 404
416 428 455 505 Mrs 558 W B
398
CLEMONS, James 347
CLEMSON, Reuben 488
CLENDENNEN, John 400
CLINE, Patrick 641
CLINTON, C 657
CLOUGH, Andrew 461
CLOVER, 314 448 503 511 556
Gen 573 Harry 512 Harvey 546
J 477 James 322 328 L G 309
525 L S 508 Levi G 198 220 250
304 310 355 380 391 404 487
505 523 526 538 559 644 Paul
572-573 Peter 116 Peter Jr 390
Philip 473 Philip G 389 Philip Jr
118 Philip Sr 118
CLYDE, David 197 William H 659
COALGROVE, Jonathan 379
COBB, 265 552 623-624 631 Barrett
641 Isaiah 631 John 453 622 659

COBB (cont.)
Maria 641 Mr 452 Roland 641
COCHRAN, Alexander 209 482-483
David 347 E P 620 James 288
355 385 400 658 Joseph 224-225
Samuel 302 440 William 357
William M 224
COCHRANE, 597 Eliza 262
CODER, Daniel 250 266 306 309
313 329 351 416 526
COFFLETT, Abraham 405 Jacob
405 Joseph 405
COFFMAN, Daniel 397 405 488
John 226 405
COLBURN, Rev 625
COLEMAN, 330 501 559 Elijah 253
525 Elisha 401 J M 198 James C
404 John 401
COLGROVE, Jonathan 372 374
COLLINS, Nicholas 630
COLWELL, A 284
COMELY, Joseph F 649 Joseph T
657-658
CONKLIN, John 401
CONNELLY, Isaac 149
CONNER, Simon 408
CONNERS, John 408
CONNOR, Anna E 641 George W
641
CONRAD, Absalom 659 Christian
398 Henry W 213
COOK, Emily 641 John 352 399
460 Laura 641
COON, Harrison 401 John 398
Jonathan 309 William 275 284
COONROD, Frederick 401
COONSMAN, Peter 399
COOPER, Benjamin B 451 James
477 James E 245 351-353 John
477 Martha 242 Mr 209 451
Mrs 477 William 124 212 216
242 351-352 356-357 398 400
474 Wm 215
CORBETT, 404 606 Col 525 559
643 James 195 220 241 288 308-310 349 353 387 404 455-456
498 500 503 505-506 508-510
525 538 559 621 James E 398
Jas 309 John C 118 Philip 239
241-242 Robert 239 Samuel 177

CORBETT (cont.)
  Samuel T 181 Squire 288 W W
  181 519 543 546 Wakefield 404
  William 239 241
CORDEN, Wm 328
CORE, John 239
COREY, Benijah 397 John 397
CORLEY, Wm 629
CORY, Alfred 366-367
CORYELL, F C 601-602 608
COTTON, 584
COUCH, John 245
COULTER, James 303 John 434
  Richard 303-304 William 434
COURLEY, George 243
COVERT, Isaac 328 403 Josiah 405
COWAN, 392
COX, 451
COXE, John 183 Richard 183 Tench 143 Widow 183
COXEN, J K 439
COXSON, J K 254 620 John K 28 Mr 30
CRADDICK, Thomas Jr 416
CRAFT, 81 Abraham 397 Jacob 399 415 471
CRAIG, 502 559 A 600 Andrew 404 501 543 601-602 James 260 404 416 558 James M 250 325 329 Jane 260 Jennie 616 John 183 526 Samuel 241 304 309 325 404 416 498 501 505 508 510 538 620
CRAIGHEAD, 216 Hannibal 506
CRAMMOND, William 56
CRANDALL, 624 E E 623
CRAWFORD, J 477 John 400 620 Michael 403 Moses 347-348 Samuel 400 Thomas H 210 William 627
CRIBBS, John Jr 387
CRISPEN, George 398
CRISWELL, Robert 450
CRITTENDEN, Judge 281
CROLL, J 539
CROOKER, Sampson 397
CROOKS, 181
CROSSMAN, Asa Jr 178 Asa Sr 178 Joseph 178 433
CROUCH, Cyrus 216 507 552

CROW, James 355 398 659 John T 418 Mr 452 William 658
CULP, George 405
CUMMINS, C P 394-395 Dr 616
CUNNINGHAM, Judge 209 Robert 209 355 Thomas 209
CUPINS, Samuel 400
CURRIN, Barnaby 334
CURTIN, 181 Roland 372
CURTIS, 624 C B 304 Carleton B 313 Carlton B 370 417
CUTHBERTSON, John 245
DAGUERRE, 228
DAILY, Mrs 477
DALLAS, Mr 139
DANIEL, Shamokin 231
DARLING, Geo 392 George 217 219 329 404 525 Paul 217-218 392 525
DARR, 273 George 404 Joseph 198 503 523 531 600
DARRAH, E H 559 Jane 559 Robert 149 501
DAUGHERTY, William 659
DAVIDSON, Samuel 239 353 398 William 620
DAVIS, Josiah 405 Mary 262 Stewart 303 Thomas 405 William 262 308 347
DAVISON, Daniel 637 Samuel 209 241
DAY, Rev 254
DEAMER, John 405
DEAN, James 61 65 67 70 James S 403
DEBIENVILLE, Celeron 132
DECKER, John 390
DEEMER, John 437 493 Peter 493
DEERING, D S 366 507 542 545-546 David 404 David S 370 508 542-543 Joseph 404
DEFORDS, James 403
DEHAVEN, Absalom 226
DEILETH, Michael 454
DELGARN, Stephen 278-279
DENNISON, David 242 250-251 353 357 399 474 Martha 242 616
DENNY, Capt 138 Ebenezer 139
DENT, Thomas 659

DEPP, Peter 434
DERBY, E C 623 Edward 453 641
  Edward H 644
DEVOY, Henry 334
DEXTER, Thomas A 197
DICKENSON, 314
DICKEY, Alexander 405 Capt 509
  David 616 Elizabeth 248 James
  226 405 493 John 249 Matthew
  248 403 488 Mr 218 William
  508
DICKINSON, 449 593 653 659 Ezra
  641 George 225 453 624 648
  659 George F 641 John 76-77
  Judge 623 631 Mr 452 President
  43 45
DICKSON, John 117 396 Robert
  401 428
DIEHL, Patricia S 13
DIEZ, L 657
DIKE, Benjamin 178 Elisha 178
DILL, Ben 626 Benezette 641 Caleb
  224 353 448-449 453 623-624
  627 632 659 Caleb S 648 Frank
  632 639 Franklin 641 J 657 J F
  636 John 406 Martha 641
DILLON, 452
DILTS, Peter 347 390 William 347
DILWORTH, 205
DIMICK, Benjamin 401
DINGER, Jacob 401 R 619
DINWIDDIE, Gov 115
DIVEN, James 223 310
DIVIN, James 398
DIXKSON, John 426
DIXON, 85 J 477 James 420 John
  121 177 182 223 398 420 422
  424 426 428 490 506 537 549
  616 John Jr 254 John Sr 224 587
  Mr 491 Rachel 525 Robert 177
  357 398 Sarah 406 Sarah Ann
  491 Thomas 225 406 418 420
  William 420 586
DOBBINS, Jacob 224 Joab 449
DOBBS, Bennett 474
DOBSON, Adam 434
DODD, L A 600 608 Levi A 601-
  602
DODDRIDGE, Joseph 91
DOLING, Thomas 362

DORNHIME, Henry 401
DOROS, Francis 405
DOTTERER, Henry 292
DOUGHERTY, Bernard 76 James
  400 John 225 263-264 317 329
  344 351 389 399 404 498 500
  508 515 525-526 538 Kate 264
  Thomas 399-400 William 427
DOUGLASS, John B 390 Sarah 272
  William 239 241 272 302 367
  398-399 427
DOUTHARD, Robert 400
DOUTHETT, John 405
DOWLING, Dr 457 Hugh 404 604
  606-609 James 304 393 403-404
  487 508 600 604 608 John 546
  604-605 607-608 M A 609
  Matthew 608
DOWNS, F 181 James 400
DOYLE, Andrew 403
DRINKER, Henry 81
DRUM, John 224 245 309 351 353
  356 415 439 Thomas 356
DUBOIS, John 100
DUFFEY, Bernard 344
DUFFIELD, George 302
DULL, Henry 415 585-586 621 659
DUNCAN, Alexander 387
DUNGAN, Thomas 259
DUNHAM, 288 314 C J 317-318
  321 506 Cephas J 344 366 369
  416 545 Frederick 526 L B 316
  318-320 366 508 542 545 Lewis
  520 526 Lewis B 304 366 369
  404 Mr 370 Richard 388
DUNKLBURG, Daniel 404
DUNLAP, W A 620
DUNMIRE, Adam 397 Nichols 397
DUNN, Capt 172 John 434 Samuel
  171 William 574
DURGIND, John A 657
DYKES, Benjamin 396 Elijah 396
  433
EARHEART, John 310 318
EARLEY, C R 635 639 641 643 Dr
  637 Samuel 642-643
EARLY, John Z 177
EASON, 509 Catherine 266 David
  500 508 514 526 John 266 305
  367 500 502 509

EASTON, Bill 626
ECKLER, George 398 403 587
EDDY, Ira 253 Zachariah H 379 646
EDELBLUTE, 558
EDISON, 618
EDMOND, David 403 Thomas 403 William 403
EGGLESTON, Clark 224 367 397
EKIS, Elijah 486
ELDER, Widow 372
ELDRED, 624 Nathaniel B 310 365 470
ELGIN, Daniel 198 349 352-353 355 399 415 531
ELLICOTT, Andrew 57 59 127 138-140 302 324 359 Joseph 127 129 140
ELLIOT, Daniel 76
ELLIOTT, D A 394-395 James 302 Michael 226 401 W C 190
ELLIS, William 51
ELLITHORPE, 639 George 641
ELY, B F 662 Malonia 641
EMBURY, Mr 252
ENGLISH, David 470 Edmund 525
ENTY, Edward 401
ESBAUGH, Anthony 463 Jacob 463
ESPY, Richard 526 Samuel 404 Samuel C 260 501 Thomas 600 608 Thomas E 526 Tom 607
ETTEWEIN, John 234 237
ETTWEIN, 40 John 41
EVANS, 258 314 503 559 Alvah 392 501 Charles 404 558 Ellis 439 Evan 404 G 70 76 G G 298 George 428 Griffith 61 68 70-71 74-75 J B 309 508 Jared A 406 Jared B 312 314 344 349 352 367 380 404 416 428 500 503 510 546 John 334 588 659 Mrs 245 T 616 W C 85 502 526 William C 424 616
EWING, James 347 John 389 Thomas 406
FAGAN, Tom 512
FAIRMAN, David 401 Francis 401
FAIRWEATHER, D 488
FALCONER, Robert 388
FALL, 630 Townsend 624 627-628

FARINGER, Henry 401
FARLEY, 31 William 502
FARR, Joshua B 402
FARRIWEATHER, David 403
FARWELL, S S 637
FAULKNER, Justus 265
FEELY, George 401 William 401
FELT, Comfort D 469
FENTON, Elisha 389 James 172
FERGUSOM, Wm 309
FERGUSON, David 386-387 389-390 Ebenezer 401 James 248 403 John 401 John C 353 Mary A 249 William 243 308 329 351 415 486 William Jr 401 William Sr 401
FERMAN, Alonzo 469
FERREE, Thomas 339
FERRIER, Thomas 248-249
FERRY, Thomas 340
FETTERMAN, N B 209
FETZER, 559 Miss 523
FEYE, George 177 Henry 181-182 223 Henry Jr 177 398 Henry Sr 177 398 Samuel 398
FIELD, Elijah H 253 John 56
FIELDS, A B 509 Rev 237 509
FILLMORE, 619
FILSON, Rev 477 W H 242
FINDLAY, Gov 229 James 212
FINDLEY, Gov 430 Samuel 391
FIR, Henry 117
FISH, Nich's 197
FISHER, Charles 450 657 Jaboy M 197 Redwood 197
FITCH, Amos 400 Isaac 400
FITZGERALD, John 399
FITZPATRICK, J 657
FITZSIMMONS, John 219 William 403
FLECK, Rev 254
FLEMING, Jno 145 John 142-143 148 406 William 404
FLEMMING, John H 403 John M 239 241
FLICK, Jacob 387
FLISHER, Henry 401 John 401 John Jr 401
FOCHTMANN, A 657
FOGLE, C 219 Christopher 256 275

FOGLE (cont.)
  282-283 403 488 Jane 284
  Mother 256
FOOTE, Mr 563
FORBES, John 335 338
FORDS, Thomas 399
FORSTER, R H 42
FORSYTH, Sen 319
FORSYTHE, Alex 460 Edwin 212
  224 461 William 399
FOST, Joseph 641
FOSTER, A W 143 Alexander M
  279 Nathaniel 178 William 401
  487
FOUNTAIN, 624
FOURIER, 450
FOWLER, Alexander B 401
FOX, 446 622 627 George 143 John
  492 621 John A 492 Joseph 303
  Joseph M 304
FRAMPTON, John 243 Mary 243
  Mr 262
FRANCIS, Henry 397
FRANKLIN, Benjamin 52
FRANTS, Frederick 428
FRAZIER, Mr 334 337
FREAS, Henry 218
FREASE, Henry 310 433
FREDERICK, Eli 659 G D 493
  George 406
FREDERICKS, Alexander 399
FREECE, Henry 401
FREEMAN, Brewster 385
FREES, J A 620
FREESE, Henry 382 390
FREMONT, 597 619
FREY, M 657
FROST, 452 A R 469
FUDGE, Enos 273
FULLER, Aaron 177 351 354-355
  367 403 406 506 Daniel 659 Dr
  639 Hiram 403 Ira 403 John 124
  177 352 362 398 401 403 481
  Mrs 541 Rebecca 362 Salmon
  347 Salmon Jr 355 Solomon 177
  487-488 Solomon Jr 403
FULLERTON, Alexander 531 C
  600 H R 602 609 Henry 600 608
  Henry R 599 601 James 329 355
  James R 501

FULTON, 228 618 James 248
  Jonathan 251
FUNK, Abraham 403
GAGHAGEN, Daniel 401 James
  401 Thomas 401
GALBRAITH, Robert 42 82
GALLAGHER, 452 J 215 309
  James 212 308 375 381 397 448
  454 626 644 James W 449 John
  225 264 318 322 404 416 502
  515 538 558 Michael 369
GALLEGHER, James 659 William
  H 659
GALLGAHER, James 648
GALLGHER, James 310
GALUSHA, Rufus 659
GAMBLE, H D 279
GANOR, Samuel 397
GANSER, J 657
GAPEN, Stephen 54
GARDINER, Melville 641
GARDNER, James 344 403 James
  K 626 Nelse 626 S B 657
GARLAND, Sylvester 29
GARNER, I 656 Ignatius 655
GASKILL, C C 216 374 Charles C
  87-88 123 178 219 307 328 353
  359 386-389 397 433 488
  Charles G 349 Hannah A 281
GASTIN, W P 620
GASTON, Jane 506 Mary 506
  Robert 243 Sarah 506
GATES, Richard 659
GAUP, 581 Daniel 492
GEARHART, 401 Elias 400
  Solomon 433
GEER, 526 Luther 455 569
GEIGER, Lieut 39
GEIST, Daniel 401 433 Jesse 401
  John Jr 401 John Sr 401 Samuel
  401 Solomon 401
GELLATLY, Alexander 245
GELVIN, John 515
GEORGE, Adam 224 583 Dolly 400
  George O 417 J P 600 John 224
  King 317 Oliver 417
GERMAN, Miles 659 Silas 659
GEYER, Andrew 197
GIBB, Nancy 247
GIBBS, Milton 406 Miram 225

GIBBS (cont.)
   Miran 329 Miron 399 406
   Myron 469 491
GIBSON, Andrew 212 225 354
   Anna 589 Crawford 208 Erastus
   399-400 James 56 Joseph K 249
   Levi 132 Mrs Dr 589 Owen 37-
   40
GILBERT, Hannah 452
GILBRETH, Pollie 401
GILBSON, John 620
GILHAUSEN, Samuel 262 Sarah
   262
GILLESPIE, 282 D C 619-620 J U
   435 John 440 William 401
   William E 226
GILLIS, 397 448 623 643 645
   Augusta 641 Bosanquet 641
   Caroline 647 659 Charles 226
   659 Charles B 450 624 Claudius
   641 Ed 647 Ellen C 641 Enos
   314 388 397 447-449 626 644
   659 George 647 J Henry 627 J L
   212 James 374 389 James L 220
   304 310 312 344 365 372 447
   453 526 545 626-627 632 644
   650 653 659 661 Jas L 309 Jim
   654 Mr 654-655 Ridgway O 659
   Robert 641 William B 633-634
   640-641
GILMORE, Carder 403 Robert 53
   541
GILPIN, 87-88
GILSON, John 648
GIRTY, Simon 514
GIST, Christopher 334
GLONTZ, Henry 401
GODDARD, Dennis 253
GODFREY, W 349 William 415
GODYEAR, Francis 427
GOFF, Ann Eliza 641
GOLDSMITH, 550
GOODAR, Beckie 452 Francis 399
   406 Frank 451-452 Mollie 451-
   452
GOODER, Albert 168
GOODMAN, Adam 405
GOODRICH, 624 S J 648
GORDEN, Mr 354
GORDON, A L 597 609 615-616

GORDON (cont.)
   Capt 172 I G 597 615 620 J G
   624 James 302-303 Mrs Judge
   391 Nathaniel 276 Samuel 171
   William 399-400
GOURLEY, Eleanor 243 John 243-
   244 Thomas 243 315 354
GRAFFIUS, Daniel 397 434 437
   Daniel Jr 351
GRAHAM, E M 362 Elijah 117 177
   223 545 Elijah M 84-85 169 225
   398-399 426-428 456 470-471
   568 Elisha 84 Elisha M 423 J B
   85 420 619 John 84-85 254
   Joseph 400 Joseph B 169 415
   537 Sarah 121 238 423 Sarah
   Ann 85 Thomas 537 600 615
   William 398
GRAME, Jacob 403
GRANDPREY, Joseph 629 633
GRANIFF, Thomas 653
GRANT, 477 618 Gen 593 Thomas
   115
GRATZ, Simon 372
GRAVER, Peter 401
GRAY, Christina 641 George 350
   403 425 Israel 350-351 James
   309 344 434 William 406
GREEN, Edwin 462 James 212 446
   456 462 507 John 454 Joseph W
   469 William 533
GREENAWALT, Joseph 428
GREER, Rev Mr 423
GREGG, 181 256 362 502 558
   George 405 Oliver 359
GREY, John 184
GRIFFITH, Robert 53
GRIMES, Elijah M 396
GRINDER, Andrew 177
GRODON, A L 610
GROFF, Peter 328
GROSS, Henry 453
GROVE, Armenia 266
GROVES, D D 621 Daniel 475
   James 475 John 475
GRUBE, John 315 353 356 437 619
GUTHRIE, Alexander 403 Isaiah
   400 James 403 James B 403
   James Sr 403 James W 379 646
   Thomas 403 William 398 403

GUYTHER, 558
HACKNEY, Joseph 387
HADDEN, Archibald 178 208 348 367 396 430 433 Archie 123 William 434
HADDOCK, James 263
HADDON, Archibald 349 356 William 354
HAGUE, Richard 400 Richard Jr 400
HAITSHOUR, Benjamin 341
HALL, 624 Andrew C 325 416 E Clark 477 Enoch 309 404 415 455 James 198 349 363 398 404 505 559 Joseph 328 Joseph E 455 Joseph Sr 403 Martha 460 Miss 260 Thomas 215 329 353 363 400 471 500 506 531 William 619
HALLAM, Isaac 495
HALLEN, Isaac 416
HALLOCK, J A 254 Rev 325
HALLON, Isaac 328
HALLOWAY, 429
HAM, John 352
HAMILTON, 353 Alexander 296 Alexander C 416 Andrew 340-341 David 178 223 349 396 401 433 486 Isaac 401 James 82 84 178 275 396 401 408 John 600 Robert 348 486
HAMLIN, 593 O 304
HAMPTON, Richard 302
HANCOCK, J R 446
HANE, Adam 401
HANEY, Eliza 260
HANHAUSER, Anthony 656
HANK, 632
HANKS, Nancy 94
HANNAGAN, James 386
HANNAGER, E E 401
HANNAH, Joseph 401 Joseph E 406
HANNIBAL, 216
HARDY, Peter 659
HARKER, Mrs 477
HARL, David 243
HARM, Clementine 641 James 641 Jim 639 Lovina 641
HARMER, 55 Col 57 Jos 76

HARNEY, David 489
HARRIET, James 358
HARRISON, 545 Samuel S 303 William H 303
HARTSHORN, George 281
HARVEY, David 493
HASKILL, Gideon 403 Joel 403 Porter 403
HASS, Daniel 401
HASSON, James 389
HASTINGS, 404 542 B T 543 Barton T 412 542 John 404 519 541 544 Joseph 398 Mr 652 Thomas 198 304 306 310 322 328 354 380 412 415-416 500 502 506 509 514 525 541
HATTER, Alexander 177
HAWKINS, John 268
HAYES, Chester 659 George 514 John 398 Mr 342-343
HAYNS, William 428
HAYS, George 556 Samuel 303 Simon 403 Wm 149
HAZELHURST, Isaac 292
HAZLET, Andrew 401
HEAD, A H 632 Alvan H 624 631 Alvin 481 Alvin H 474
HEALEY, 449 631 Sheriff 639 W C 644
HEALY, Sheriff 624
HEARD, S 254 Stephen 254
HEATH, 265 281 288 314 E 316 502 Elijah 123 157 178 195-196 223 275 279 284 305 308-310 313 317 322 344 365-366 368 370 375 379-381 397 403 406 433-435 488 505 538 545 John 506 John Jr 559 Judge 208 279 506 531
HEBER, 511 Granger 522 Jack 522 Jackson 416
HECK, Barbara 252
HECKENDORN, Harry 401
HECKEWELDER, John 40 232
HECKMAN, Jacob 403
HEEB, Lewis 396
HEICHHOLD, 605-607 A P 394-395 604 608-609 620 Dr 596 610
HEIDRICK, 182 193 330 416 424

HEIDRICK (cont.)
  455 511 566-567
HEISY, Mr 218
HELLER, Jacob 142
HEMMINGRAY, William 397
HENDERSON, 558 J 309 J B 477
  John 397 John B 123 208 434
  617 Joseph 303 310 404 456
  525-526 593 620 Judge 519 Mrs
  442 Rev 246
HENDRICKS, Jameson 241 Jamison
  404 William 348
HENNEIGH, Daniel 351 355-356
  David 353
HENNIGHAUSEN, 296
HENNY, David 387
HENRY, David 284 304 313 350
  354 405 502 505-506 508-509
  525 538 Harvey 632 636 James
  329
HESS, John 123 305 309 349 397
  434 437 John Sr 308 Sally 405
HETERICK, Christ 367 Christopher
  212 F 309 Fr 506 Fred 586 588
  Frederick 305 328 351-352 355
  398-399 427 487 659 Jacob 381
  John 406 415 420 Michael 401
  433 Peter 401 Philip 406
HETRICK, Frederick 177 Mr 339
HEWITT, Mr 554
HICE, John 218 225-226 401 428
  486 Samuel 218 401
HICKOX, Reuben 92 349 430 439
HICKS, 149 William 657
HIDELMAN, Abram 403
HILDEBRAND, James 403
HILL, Aaron 63 65 67 70 74 Ralph
  427 452 659 Rev 477
HILLS, A M 502
HIMES, ---- 398 Christopher 177
  Hannah 266 Peter 403 455
  William 177 401
HINDERLIGHTER, Daniel 401
  Michael 401
HINDMAN, 181 219 James 241
  John 239 249-250 William 356
  William M 400 Wm M 215
HINTER, Henry 389
HISE, John 177
HITCHCOCK, H S 254

HOCH, Abraham 265
HODGDON, 81
HOEY, Joseph 406
HOFFMAN, A 657 Ferd 168 Jacob
  264 581 James K 182 224 John
  604 M 490
HOGE, John 54
HOLBEN, E 492
HOLCOMB, B D 656
HOLEMAN, Eli 140 148
HOLLOBACK, Michael 401
HOLMAN, Charles 149
HOLOPETER, Frederick 485
HOLT, Mr 355 Thomas 266 433
HOOVER, David 387 Jacob 123 178
  223 253 305 348-349 367 396-
  397 433 John 178 220 351-352
  388 397 405 Joseph 405
HOPKINS, William 213 366-367
HOPPER, Malachi 400 William 400
HORAM, George 401 Jacob 401
  John 398 John Jr 401 John Sr
  401 William 401
HORAN, William 427
HORM, Jacob 357 John 481
HORN, Albert 581 Charles 604
HORSEFIELD, Joseph 142
HORTON, Charles 624 659-660
  Charles H 659 Isaac 389 659-
  661 Isaac Jr 631 L 659
HOUSTON, Joseph 399 Samuel 304
  William 304-305 399
HOWARD, Caleb 398 Jacob 620
HOWE, 618 Joel 406 John W 370
  Samuel 309 406
HOWELL, Reading 131
HOYT, 265 469 Harvey 659
HUBBARD, David 657
HUFFMAN, Daniel 401 Henry P
  539 Jacob 401 James K 329 351
  356 406 493
HUGHES, 314 449 659 Arthur 453
  659 Baily 469 George 401 I D
  175 Isaac 226 Isaac D 238 Israel
  400 John 209 367 456 Joseph
  238 328 354 404 S B 620
  Samuel 354 Thomas 400 471
  William 400
HUGHEY, Samuel 349 William 539
HUHN, C K 621

HULET, Benjamin 399
HULING, James 389 Robert 225
HULWICK, Elias 401
HUM, Henry 397 John 397 435
HUMES, George F 412 542-543
HUMPHREY, James 405 Matthew 406 491 Mr 566 Samuel M 491 Thomas 260 William 260 406 491
HUMPHREYS, William 355-356
HUNT, Capt 92 122 571 Dr 503 Jane 262 Jim 511 536-537 John 212 245 262 344 351-352 400 472 John D 474 Mrs Dr 525 Phelps 400 Samuel 197 Trumble 212 351-352 Trumbull 472
HUNTER, Andrew 250 357 401 425 475 477-479 Betsy 475 Father 479 George 406 J 477 James 51 83-84 353 John 243 475 481-482 Mary 481 Mr 476-477
HUSON, L 292
HUTCHESON, A 543
HUTCHINSON, Alex 492 Alexander 250 Isabella 244 James 178 541 John 244-245
HUTCHISON, George 334 James 396 John 353-354 356 397 400 404 Joseph 121 151 423 William 400
HYATT, Betsey 452 Elizabeth M 452 Nathaniel 659-661
HYDE, Eliza A 641 J S 448-449 623-625 631 Joseph S 388 648 659-660 W H 448
IDDINGS, 281 Lewis 639
INDENTURED, Dutch Girl Maria 292
INDIAN, A Belt 75 A Large Belt 67 Anigwendahonji 68 70 Atyatonenghtha 68 70 Bald Eagle 126 Big Cat 74 76 Capt Bull 116 Chief Ge-en-quah-toh 564 Chief He-goes-in-the-smoke 564 Chief Little Snow 537 Chief Tamisqua 446 Conemah 31 Conewyando 116 Cornplanter 14 17 27 32 62 116 560-561 563-565 571-573 577 580 Council Door 74 76 Cyanthwahia 565

INDIAN (cont.)
Deungquat 73 76 Farmer's Brother 17 Five Strings 75 Four Strings 61 Gaghsawweda 67 Galasko 33-34 Guyasutha 14 27 Half King 73 75-76 Honeghariko 67 Hyngapushes 74 76 Kanonghgwenya 68 70 Kayenthogkke 67 Keatarondyon 68 70 Keeskanohen 74 76 Kyashuta 335 Noshaken 31 Obendarighton 68 70 Obendirighton 67 Odaghfeghte 67 Ojestalale 67 Onefaghweughte 67 Onequiandahonjo 67 Oneyanha 67 Ononghsawanghti 68 70 Oraghgwanentagon 68-69 Otoghfelonegh 67 Owenoco 436 Peechemelind 74 76 Pipe 74 76 Pisquetumen 230 Present 74 76 Pukeesheno 30 Red Jacket 17 29 560 Russell 588 Sagoyahalongo 67 Sheklemas 30 Shemenkenwhol 29 Six Strings 66 Sweat House 74 76 Tatabaughsey 74 76 Tatahonghteayon 68 70 Tauwarah 73 76 Tayagoneatageghti 68-69 Tecumseh 30 Tehonweeaghreyagi 68-69 Teweghnitogon 68 70 Teyagonendageghte 67 Thaghnaghtanhari 68 Thaghnagtanhari 69 Thaghneghtanhari 67 Tharondawagon 67-68 70 The Prophet 30 Thoneeyade 67 Three Strings 75 Twisting Vine 74 76 Volunteer 74 76 Wangomen 233 Whingohatong 74 76 Wialindeoghin 74 74 76 Wingenum 74
INGALLS, 622 A J 469 Isaac 309
INGERSOLL, Atty-gen 56
INGRAHAM, Davis 406
INGRAM, 553
INK, 55
IONS, Benjamin 486 Gideon 344

IRVEN, James 178
IRVIN, David 387 Eli B 493 596 Eli
  I 406 John 387 389 Judge 278
  Richard 378 389
IRVINE, James 76 William 59-60
  127 138-140
IRWIN, George 405 508 Thomas
  660
IVES, Timothy 649 652 658 660
  Timothy Jr 379 646
JACK, 503 559 D H 254 Judge 526
  William 182 303 310 321-322
  365 380 387 389 403 405-406
  412 455 500 509-510 523 525
  538 542 Wm 316-317
JACKSON, 468 Abner 254 Andrew
  303 317-318 320 Jessie 400
  Rosamund 641 William 210
JACOBS, Capt 183-184
JACOX, C 403 Charles 226 488
  Hazard 488
JAMES, George 175 George R 225-
  226 I 299 Ii 268 John 401 Joseph
  Y 304 King 300
JAMISON, John 246-247 303 348
  Nancy 247 Rev 247 S S 416 420
  William 251
JAQUISH, H S 648
JAYCOCK, Charles 403 Hazard 403
JEFFERSON, 618 Thomas 57 152
  185 296 317 634
JENKS, 349 523 D B 366 508 525
  545 660 David B 405 David
  Barclay 370 Dr 208 216 440 G
  A 391 George A 508 J W 215
  309 383 John W 123 178 195
  212 244-245 310 312 344 347
  352 365-368 380 387 389 391
  397 433-434 471 Judge 477
  Mary D 244 Mr 440 Phineas W
  434 W P 391 477 624 William P
  175 610 William P Sr 405
JOHNS, Samuel 266 398 403
JOHNSON, 593 624 Andrew 593
  Benjamin 389 Chloe 491 Francis
  68 74 James 302 John 254 565
  616 Mary 266 Milton 406 491
  Mr 654 Thomas 304 Wm 197
JOHNSTON, A J 394-395 F 77
  Francis 43 60-61 65 71 James

JOHNSTON (cont.)
  82-84 425 James A 659 John
  366 369 403 649 M 309 Maj 487
  Milton 308 357 399 469 Mr 470
  Richard M 543 William 431
  William F 369 414 William M
  609 Wm 353 Wm M 244
JONCAIRE, 30
JONES, 25 85 181 228 627 John
  122 177 328 346-347 396 422
  425 427 434 569 Johnny 541
  Peter 117 121 237-238 358 396
  422 424 426-427 Samuel 181
  212 215 238 349-350 366-367
  416
JORDAN, Alex 244 Alexander 244-
  245 349 Archibald S 170
  Benjamin 146 Flora 244 I C 596
  John 387 Mr 234 Samuel 367
JORLEY, Rufus 405
JUNGMAN, Brother 236
KAHLE, Frederick 400 471 Jack 92
  John 92 219 John D 226 399
KAILOR, Henry 177
KARNS, H 449 Henry 659
KARTHAUS, Peter A 372
KAUFFMAN, John 489
KAYLOR, Joseph 266 362 456
KEARNEY, William 452
KECK, George 403
KEEFER, Isaac 660
KEIM, John 344
KELLAR, A 254
KELLER, Abraham 405 George 405
  John 657 Joseph 405
KELLEY, Elbon S 303 James M
  303-304 Meek 303 305
KELLY, Eben Smith 27 Elizabeth
  243 John 372 Margaret 243
  Meek 387 Samuel 243 William
  403
KELSO, Isabella 248 J 616 James
  403 John 248 398 456 John Jr
  403 William 182 225 308 313
  349 416-417 420 506 Wm 215
  309
KENDALL, Richard 244
KENNEDY, Ann 248 John 248 352
  398 455 Mr 219 Robert 401
  Robert E 225 328 487 Samuel

KENNEDY (cont.)
  349 398 Samuel D 362 455
  William 182 239 241 305 351
  356 362 400 429 482 487
  William B 350-351 400 William
  Jr 352 William M 198 310 Wm
  328 Wm B 328
KENWORTHY, Hugh 209
KEPPELE, Heinrich 295
KERNS, Henry 353
KERR, David 352 357 Ebenezer L
  357 James 389 Joseph 250 356
  Thomas 351-352 405 493
KERSEY, 622 William 446
KETCHAM, W W 593
KEYES, 621
KEYS, 482 484 486 Alexander 475
  Betty 260 483 Catharine 260
  Catherine 481 Eliza 262 Henry
  124 260 262 315 351 353-354
  357 398 401 406 414 428 474
  481 Joseph 262 398 401 414
  Matthew 242 398 401 485 Mr
  209 Susan 242
KEYSER, Mr 107
KIEFER, Benjamin 659 Frederick
  659
KINCAID, Eusebius 661
KING, Emeline 641 John 372 John
  S 546 Joseph P 397 William 347
KINGLY, Ebenezer 399
KINGSBURY, Mr 454
KINGSLEY, Count 400 Ebenezer
  400 Edward 400 Ephraim 400
  Perry 400
KINNEAR, G D 256 Joseph 401 M
  616 Rev 254
KINTER, Henry 302
KIP, Leonard 197 Maria I 197
KIRKHAM, 552
KIRKLAND, Samuel 61 65 67 70
KIRKMAN, 121 Thomas 216
KITHCART, Clark 415
KLINE, 456
KNAP, Joshua 157 Moses 427
KNAPP, 121 429 588 Amy 567
  Annie 248 Clarissa 567 Eliza
  567 Isaac M 567 Isabel 566 John
  403 420 567 Joseph 403 567
  Joshua 420 537 567 Matson J

KNAPP (cont.)
  403 Moses 117 120-121 177 223
  248 346-347 349 352 362 392
  396 398 422 424-425 428 456
  487-488 500-501 537 566-569
  Moses Jr 403 420 Moses Sr 545
  Polly 566 Samuel 133 349 398
  403 420 566 Susan 566 Susanna
  248
KNARR, George 401
KNAVE, Jacob 347
KNOPSNYDER, Jack 461 Jane 461
  Samuel 462
KNOX, John 199 208 659 Robert
  177 209 398 428 487
KRAMER, John A 399
KRAUSE, Peter 116
KROH, Jacob 428
KUHN, Abraham 74 76
KUHULEY, Frederick 405
KURTZ, George 439
KYLE, James 351 401 481 Jimmie
  481 Mary Ann 486 Robert 481
  Samuel 226 401 481
KYLER, Jesse 635 Jessie 623 John
  446 469
LACEY, Josiah 472
LACY, Thomas 350
LAFAYETTE, Gen 316 318
LAHEY, William 630
LAMB, David 239 308
LAMBERTON, James 170 Maj 171
LANCE, Michael 433
LANE, Jacob 396 N B 477
LANGARD, David 402
LANSENDOFFER, William 608
LANTZ, Frederick 356 402 Jacob
  178 John 402 Michael 123 178
  348 396 402 486
LARIMER, 624
LARRIMER, Robert 198 509
LARRIMORE, Robert 318
LATT, Henry 177
LATTA, James W 137 142 449
LATTIMER, John 177 212 216 219
  305 309 350 354 425 524
  William 398
LATTIMRE, John 398
LAUGHLIN, James 119 Thomas
  227 303

LAVERTY, James H 410
LAW, C F 649 Robert 439
LAWRENCE, Joseph 214
LAWSON, David 304 347 385 T C 557 William 304
LEACH, Francis 397 George 397
LEADLIE, George 400
LEARY, Josiah 400
LEDLIE, Thomas 483
LEE, 87 Arthur 60 65 68 70-71 74 76 Ebenezer 659
LEECH, Daniel 403 Francis 405 488 George 405
LEET, Daniel 54 58 Jonathan 54
LEININGER, Barbara 32-34 36-38 237 Regina 33
LERCH, Samuel 402 433
LEROY, 541 Herman 53 James D 81 Marie 32-34 36-37 39
LESHER, Mr 293
LETICH, George 402
LETORT, James 334
LEWEES, John 472
LEWIS, 639 Ann 243 Charles 657-658 David 212 219 243 356 Elizabeth 243 Isaac 178 215 243 305 396 431 John 400 603 Joshua 302-304 347 Mr 262 Stephen 178 243 349-350 396
LINCKLEAN, Jan 53
LINCOLN, 593-594 597-598 618 President 229 595
LINKLAEN, Jan 86
LINKLAIN, 541
LINN, James 212 349 382 427 470-471
LIRAM, John 353
LITCH, T K 597
LITHGOW, Sarah Ann 406
LITLE, John 148
LLOYD, Stephen 390
LOBAUGH, Peter 463
LOCKE, J R 254
LOGAN, George 302
LONDON, Hiram 261 Isaac 261 Stephen 262
LONG, 85 90 96 102 514 580 582-584 586 588-589 Adam 124 178 396-397 433-437 Bill 91-92 94 100 513 579-580 584-587 640

LONG (cont.)
Dan 424 513 Daniel 398 420 462 Jack 589 Jackson 91 James 403 James E 513 John 89 218 254 350 354 398 405 424 513 579 Joseph 223 305 397 434-435 L 117 Lewis 177 426 Louis 576-577 Ludwick 121 346 Ludwig 396 424 429 576-577 580 Michael 351-352 406 420 427 471 491 Mike 89 92 424 513 584-587 637 Mrs 585 Nancy 581 William 89 225 351 355 398 406 420 424 427 434 576-579 581 589
LOOMIS, Josiah 406
LOSH, David 344 357
LOT, Henry 398 405 487 Peter 398
LOTT, Henry 396 428 433
LOVE, James 623 John 118 328 398 403 John Sr 352 John T 403 William 224 William Jr 398 456 William Sr 367 398 William T 249
LOWELL, Elijah 526 James Russell 104 Lorenzo 526
LOWREY, Alexd 76
LOWRY, Joseph 224 Morrow B 593 Mrs 281
LUCAS, 122 546 588 624 B F 620 Benjamin F 610 James 416 427 James S 403 Jane 248 Jimmie 558 John 177 195 197-198 211 218 305 309-310 347 354 375 381 385 398 403 427 455-456 487 531 John Jr 403 415 John S 520 John Sr 403 Johnny 541 Margaret 249 Nancy 507 P I 488 Peter 403 Samuel 239 241 315 346 396 417 422 425-427 485 488 566 Samuel H 344 405 525 Samuel Jr 403 Samuel Sr 403 Sarah 248 Thomas 157 177 196-198 307 310 322 325 347 349 349-350 366 370 387 396 398 405 422 425-428 451 487 498 506 509-510 520 524-525 538 545 566 587 Thos 309 328 368 488 William 302 396 403 566
LUCE, C F 644 Elizabeth 641 W P

LUCE (cont.)
641
LUDWICK, Abraham 405 Elizabeth 405 George 405
LUKINS, John 400
LUNGER, Isaac 397
LUTHER, 639 Calvin 641 D S 631 640 Jim Harm 640 L 644 Lebbeus 387 580 623 626 631 640 Lebbeus Sr 640 Martin 199 Mr 625 630
LYLES, Reuben 659
LYNN, Thomas 659
LYONS, Alex 398 Alexander 405
M'CLAY, William 68
M'KEAN, Thos 70
M'KEE, Judge 278
M'KNIGHT, Alx 278 W J 645
MABON, 526
MACAULAY, 509
MACK, Wilder P 255
MACLAY, Samuel 302 William 43
MAGEE, John 474
MAGENTY, Alexander 334
MAGIFEN, Joseph 209
MAGIFFIN, Joseph 313 328 617
MAGILL, Samuel 398 403 William 403 Wm 488
MAGINNIS, Field Marshal 632 H 477 Maj 633 R 632 636 Robert 635
MAIZE, James 460 John 224 461 471 John A 308 John H 352 460 Martha 460 T B 225 Thomas 352 460
MAJOR, Jane 262
MALONE, Lashley 116 P 657 Patrick 649 658
MANNERS, Jane 243 Joseph 243-244 434
MANROSS, William 399 Wm 461
MARCH, George 397
MARCHAND, David 303
MARKLE, Joseph 303
MARLIN, A R 601-602
MARSH, Elnathan 406
MARSHALL, Chief Justice 56 86 618 Joseph 130 386 389 Rebecca 243 William 212 243 354
MARTIN, Joseph 369 Thomas 115

MARTZ, John 402
MASON, Benjamin 398 420 David 420 Jacob 117 157 177 223 329 396 398 420 424 428 John 178 Nancy 581 William 420
MASTEN, C 648
MATHER, O P 493 Ozias P 406
MATLACK, Timothy 302
MATSON, 182 193 410 416 511 566-567 C M 526 616 624 641 Charles 608 Harry 519 556 558 Isaac 398 470 Isaac Sr 400 James 354 James C 405 Jane 456 John 117 177 222 309 347-348 385 387 398 424 426-428 455-456 556 John Jr 405 John Sr 122 195 329 351-352 456 524 Joseph 471 Mary 455-456 R M 520 559 Robert 405 424 Robert L 455 Susan 566 U 418 Uriah 133 181 306 405 519 537 566
MATTHEWS, Charles 469 624 Elijah 116 Geo S 218 George 225 418 George L 357 George S 225 John 425 John A 329
MAXWELL, Mrs 477 Robert 398 William 349 397 454 Wm H 197
MAYS, James W 399 John 399 Thomas B 399
MCAFEE, Joseph 315 353 399 405 469
MCALLISTER, John C 644 S A 616
MCANDRISH, William 224
MCANINCH, Elijah 403 George 403 415 John 226 328 402 486 Samuel 403 William 403 415 486 William Jr 402 William Sr 402
MCANULTY, 241 John 344 350 362 John Sr 367 John W 223
MCAULEY, John 248-250
MCBRIDE, Benjamin 124 431
MCCABE, J W 370
MCCAFFERTY, Philip 93
MCCAHAN, James 302
MCCAHEN, Alexander 251
MCCAHON, 624
MCCALLESTER, Jeremiah 398
MCCALMONT, Alex 365

MCCALMONT (cont.)
   Alexander 193 310 370 375 545
   661 J S 602 John S 660 Judge
   610 661 Mr 652
MCCANDLESS, William 405
MCCANN, 425
MCCARRELL, James 248-249
MCCARTNEY, John 178 Thomas
   426 Thos 302
MCCAULEY, John 403
MCCLAY, Dr 604 Mr 63 William
   60-61 65
MCCLEAN, Thomas B 82 Thomas
   Brown 82
MCCLELLAN, 597-598 T B 405
MCCLELLAND, Ben 624 639-640
   James 123 178 396 486 John 178
   250 305 401-402 475 Maj 170
   Mrs 260 Nancy Jane 482 Oliver
   356 401 414 481-482 484
   William 169-171
MCCLENNEN, James 433
MCCLINTOCK, Thomas 249
MCCLURE, A K 593 Mrs 477
MCCMORMICK, David 356
MCCOLLOUGH, James 224
MCCOLLUM, Samuel 245
MCCOMB, 442 444 George 439
   James 347 386 440 Mrs 440
MCCONAUGHEY, James 262 344
MCCONNELL, 576 616 Alex 621
   D B 477 549 Fanny 482 James
   260 262 401 481 Joseph 401 406
   Margaret 260 Mary Ann 260
   William 242 354 401 474 477
MCCOOL, John 54
MCCORMICK, 618 Andrew 250
   399 406 491 493 Andrw 355
   David 250 252 344 355 492
   David Jr 406 David Sr 406
   Findley 357 406 Finley 493
   Mary 616 Samuel P 406 Sarah
   406 Thomas 250 399 406 469
   491-493 Thos 344
MCCOY, Alexander 396 422 John
   M 508
MCCRACKEN, Elizabeth 262
   James 416 437 608 John 356 400
   Joseph 491
MCCRACKIN, James 325 410

MCCREA, John 310 405 542-543
   Thomas P 526
MCCREADY, 636
MCCREIGHT, 545 Andrew 362
   405 489 493 Anna 589 B 215
   309 Benjamin 250 315 405 416
   500 509 525-526 558 James 405
   Job 250 354 415 Martha 616
   Robert 470 Sharp 405
MCCULLOUGH, 416 424 587 624
   A 477 Billy 559 Boyd 482 C 619
   J 309 J S 418 James S 420 John
   121 237 Joseph 177 195 229 308
   348 350 398 505 524 Sheridan
   328 Squire 350 451 W 506 W B
   481 William 124 250 351 401
   420 William B 474
MCCUNE, Barney 450
MCCURDY, 608 A 477 Abbie 616
   Betsy 475 482 Dr 477 J 477
   James 178 180 475 477 Joseph
   178 180 243 399 469 475 482
   Margaret 475 Martha 475 Mrs
   477 Robert 399 475 W 477
MCDANIEL, Andrew 402 David
   402
MCDAVID, Matthew 402
MCDERMOTT, Elizabeth 262
MCDONALD, ---- 501 David 223
   John 178 Matthew 124 William
   124 250 398 401
MCDOUGAL, James 397
MCDOWEL, Eli 403
MCDOWELL, 183 John 76
MCELHANEY, Alexander 149
MCELHENY, William 405
MCELHOSE, 606 Samuel 615-616
MCELVAIN, James 405 William
   406
MCELVAINE, Isaac 398
MCELVANE, Isaac 349-350 354
   357
MCELWAINE, Andrew 403
MCEWEN, Matthew 657
MCFADDEN, James 118
MCFARLAND, L 408 Robert 209
   400
MCGARA, Clements 302-303
MCGAREY, Clement 248 Mary 248
   William 226 415

MCGARRAH, Joseph 484
MCGARRAUGH, Mr 239 Robert
  238 242
MCGEE, John 124
MCGEEHAN, Michael Dan 369
MCGHEE, John 225 349 356-357
  398 401 474 481 Mrs 92 Nancy
  260 S 620 Samuel 437 William
  481
MCGIFFEN, John 367
MCGIFFIN, Elizabeth 248 Hugh
  403 James 248 John 398 403
  Joseph 181-182 487 Rebecca 249
  Sarah 248
MCGILL, Hugh 249 Margaret 248
  Samuel 177 248 351
MCGINTY, Thomas 325
MCGIVEN, John 608
MCGREGOR, Daniel 402 487
  George 402 M 402
MCGUIER, Hugh 402
MCGUIRE, John 334
MCHATTEN, Alexander 149
  Samuel 149
MCHENRY, Elizabeth 178 396
  Isaac 223 244 James 425 John
  124 355 John Sr 245
MCILVAINE, Andrew 415 Andrew
  Jr 415 Isaac 415
MCINTOSH, Henry 353 355 357
  401 James 649 John 124 356 382
  398 401 474 481 Mattie 485 Mr
  209 Mrs 477 Peggy 482 Rebecca
  401 Robert 225 242 260 401 483
  Robert Sr 483 Susan 485
  William Jr 401 William Sr 401
MCKEAN, Gov 201 Joseph B 302
  Samuel 317 Thomas 70 144 146
  192 301
MCKEE, David 400 Elizabeth 243
  Hugh 123 178 208 348 396 430
  433 J P 620 James 178 396 John
  H 616 Thomas 196 224 245 305
  310 349 366 439 Thos 309
  William 254 349
MCKENNON, James 314
MCKINLEY, Hannah 266 Isaac 195
  Joshua 456
MCKINSTREY, Alexander 434
  William 434

MCKINSTRY, 350 A 309 Margaret
  243
MCKISSICK, John 302
MCKNIGHT, 546 559 605 A 309
  315 322 A A 608 620 Alexander
  209 212 308 313 321 414 497
  500 505-507 510 538 Amor A
  610 Dr 149 209 477 509 536
  James 302-303 Mary 216 559
  Treasurer 309 W J 81 126 137
  139 142 279 394 449 477 594-
  595 604 614 620 William J 600
  608-609
MCLAIN, A B 600 606 608-609
  619-620 Alexander 303 Charles
  608 James 302 Miss 523 T B
  474 600 Thomas B 481
MCLATCHEY, John 659 William
  659
MCLATCHLIE, Robert 400
MCLAUFHLIN, John 356
MCLAUGHLIN, 499 Geo 405
  George 542 John 225 352 355
  357 382 399 469-470 498 538
  621 Squire 168
MCLEAN, Daniel 249 John 320
MCMAHILL, William 631
MCMANIGLE, James 400
MCMANUS, James 369
MCMILLAN, Esther 262
MCMILLEN, Dr 243 John 402
  Thomas 402
MCMINNS, 469
MCMURRAY, Archd 218
MCNEAL, James 400
MCNEIL, Christ 225 William 308
MCNUTT, Robert 402 William 402
MCQUISTON, Nelson T 427
  Nicholas 226 525 Samuel 354
  356 425 520
MCQUONE, 622 Edward 649 658
MCQUOWN, Lawrence 620
MCVEAN, Charles 623 632 636
MCWILLIAMS, Thomas 406
MEAD, Amanda 641 Charles 623
  632 David 315 461 David W 400
  John 660 Sheriff 624
MEADE, 597 Darius 116 David
  115-116 George 53 John 115-
  116 William 659

MEADS, David 399 Thaddeus 399
MEANS, Edward 245 James 356
   John 605-606
MECHAN, Thomas 352
MECHLING, Philip 303-304
MEDDOCK, Mary M 641
MEFFERT, Joseph 659
MENDENHALL, William 354 398
MERCER, Brig Gen 522 Col 39
MEREDITH, Capt 596 Elijah 446
   M M 595-596
MERRIMAN, Charles 266 Charles
   P 546
MERSHON, Rev 254
MESSENGER, 623
METCALF, 279 Isaac H 355
   Matthew 406 Mundale 406
MEYER, J 657
MICKEL, 624
MICKLE, Samuel 402
MIFFLIN, Thomas 138-139 142-143
MILES, Col 145 Frederick 119
   Jeremiah 388 Jno 143 Richard
   144 Samuel 142-144 146 260
   262 401 Samuel Lieut 39
MILLEN, Chambers 249 Esther 248
   Hugh 248 J R 477 John 243 248
   367 474-475 Joseph 248 459
   Margaret 475 Polly 248 T T 614
MILLER, 107 David 400 Eugene
   392 Geo 486 George 405 Henry
   383 405 489 493 Hugh 553 J P
   600 Jacob 389 James 619 John
   123 402 405 John J 219 Martin
   402 Olive Thorne 103 Samuel
   417 William 403
MILLIRON, Abraham 177 398 403
   Daniel 403 David 123 178 353-
   354 396 402 433 George 402
   Henry 123 402-403 Jacob 328
   John 123 178 350 Jonathan 403
   Peter 402 Philip 177 402 Samuel
   350 403 488 Solomon 403
   William 177 402
MILLS, Isaac 456 501 505 John 242
   Mrs 458
MINICH, Henry 402 Jacob 402
   Peter 402
MINISH, James 282 James A 275
MITCHELL, Agnes Sarah 432 Dr

MITCHELL (cont.)
   275 James 432 John 193 372 375
   Judge 28 Robert 304 408 Sarah
   432 T S 356 Thomas S 431-433
   Thomas Sharp 431
MIX, John 446
MOHEN, Margaret 641
MOHNEY, John 402
MONAHAN, Mrs 469
MONGER, 546
MONKS, A J 616 Dallas 219 H W
   254 J W 350 John 351 353 362
   John W 209 215 400 William
   254 616
MONROE, Joshua 255
MONTGOMERY, G 619 Gillmore
   402 Robert 406 Samuel 70
MONTIER, William 402
MONTOUR, 73 John 71 74 76
MOODY, Hamilton 399 Thomas
   399
MOOR, Andrew 250
MOORE, 358 555 Andrew 401
   David 403 415 420 David L 226
   Jacob 406 493 James 218 John
   54 John Kelso 249 John S 514 S
   M 519 T 477 Thomas 474 481
   Tom 554
MOORHEAD, A T 408 Alexander
   407 David 399 406 Jackson 491
   James 275 352 354-356 399 406-
   407 491 James W 399 John 399
   406 493 Joseph 303
MOORHOUSE, Harvey B 397
MOREHEAD, Samuel 302
MOREY, Asa 406 Erasmus 625 659
   Leonard 446
MORGAN, 175 Jesse 344 John 245
   William 447
MORRIS, 81 C R B 245 620 Dexter
   482 507 J B Sr 244 Mary 244
   Obed 244 349 397 434-435 439
   Robert 53 80 83 86 296 541
MORRISON, I 477 Nancy 248
   Robert 242 328-329 351 401 403
   456 459 474 620 William 177
   248 310 349 398 456
MORROW, 362 515 518-519 Joe
   517 Joseph 359
MORSE, 618

MOSGROVE, Andrew 370
MOTHERELL, D 477
MOTT, Jonathan 648
MOTTER, Daniel 402 Isaac 403
   Jacob 402 John 402 Samuel 402
MOWER, John Jr 402 John Sr 402
MOYER, Conrad 450
MUHLENBERG, 303
MUNGER, Charles 406
MUNICH, M 657
MUNSON, John 239
MURPHY, James 420
MURRAY, 552 617 626 628-629
   Alex 460-461 Alexander 212
   382 399 W D 622
MYERS, Congressman 597 Enos
   461 Jacob 469 Smith N 399
   William 657
NAPOLEON, 618
NEAL, James C Sr 208 Thomas 340
NEALE, Thomas 340
NEEDLES, 283
NEEL, 437 Billy 435-436 William
   434-435 488
NEGRO, Girl Flora 574 Man John
   574 Man Sam 537
NESBIT, N J 402
NEWBOLD, Charles 152
NEWCOMB, George 224 434
   Samuel 225 309 355 403 431
   William 349 353 434 William B
   403 Wm 244 353
NEWCOME, John 178 Samuel 124
NEWENHOUSE, Adam 178
NEWTON, Oran 400
NICE, Thomas 402
NICHOLS, 260 Dr 392 Hannah 259
   391 Jonathan 259 389 391 446
   Rebecca M 392
NICHOLSON, 81 John 42 53 55 57
   80 83 541 Joseph 71 74 Owen
   334 R J 507 Samuel 54
NICKLIN, Philip 53
NIEL, William 402
NIEMAN, 463
NIGHTINGALE, Timothy 398
NIVER, Dr 477 E C 110 W C 623
   637 640-641 William C 642-643
NOEF, John 474
NOEFF, John 383

NOLF, 588 Conrad 354 486
   Coonrod 403 Frank 403 Henry
   123 John 400 John Jr 178 John
   Sr 178 351 Lawrence 123
NORRIS, 446 622 627
NORTH, Daniel 438 J P 620 John
   620 Joseph 438 Joseph P 596
   Thomas 620
NULF, Conrad 433 Coonrod 402
   Henry 433
NULJ, Henry 383
NUNER, John 266
O'BAIL, John 564-565
O'BALE, Capt 62-65
O'DONNELL, Arthur 463
O'HARA, James 58
O'NEAL, John 341
O'NEILL, John 263
OGDEN, George 401
OHL, Andrew 265 William 459
OLDEN, John 53
OLDS, Horace 659
OLNEY, 552
ORCUTT, David 456
ORR, Hunter 596 Robert 375 569
   Robert Jr 193 303-304 Samuel C
   132
ORWIN, James 399
OSBORN, Alexander 124
OSBORNE, Alexander 474 Joseph
   403 Mrs 262 R 477
OSBURN, Alexander 398 Joseph
   251
OSTERHOUT, W H 644
OSTERMANN, A 657
OSTRANDER, P B 398 Peter 224
   Peter B 178 181
OTTO, Joseph 372 385
OVERTURF, Samuel 659
OYSTER, 624 Daniel 389 Sarah 622
   Stephen 622
PACKER, Isaac 223 352 398 428
PAGE, Thomas 396
PAGNE, Thomas 178
PAINE, 659 A B 463 Chester 659
   Job 452
PALMER, M 226 Michael 226
PANCOAST, W H 610
PANTALL, T 434
PAPANHUNK, Anthony 232 John

PAPANHUNK (cont.)
  232
PARK, James 224 325 John 346 348
  425
PARKER, 627 Jeremiah 53 428 541
  William 278-279
PARKHURST, James C 657
PARKS, 429 James 272 398 537
PARSON, 624
PARSONS, H A 632 Squire 623
PATTERSON, Mrs 477 William
  210
PATTISON, 624 Alexander 303 H
  A 631-634 641-643 Robert E
  613
PATTON, John 180 574 Robert 475
  S 477 W 477
PAYNE, 432 Alva 431 433 Alvah
  224
PEALE, Charles W 554
PEARCE, J P 641 J W 641 John
  380
PEARSALL, 281 A 657 Alfred 649
  Arad 275 277-279 399 406 416
  493 501 506 Caroline 641 John
  399 406 493 M M 609 Myron
  608
PECK, R 254
PEELOR, David 390
PEFFER, Henry 469
PELTON, George 353 George W 89
PENDLETON, 597 James 469
PENN, 27 332 462 617 John 79
  Richard 79 Thomas 79 William
  29 78 81 185 281 588 William Jr
  78
PENROSE, Charles B 210 Jacob
  471
PERRIN, Nathan 406 William 492
PERRY, Commodore 430 James
  309 John 243 R T 620
PERSHING, Samuel 406
PETER, Henry 402
PETERS, Jacob 401
PETRIKEN, B Rush 660 Ben R 661
PFEFFER, Henry 446
PHELPS, John M 406
PHILIPI, Henry 406 493 John D
  406
PHILLIBER, Henry 225 353 J 309

PHILLIBER (cont.)
  John 212 215 220 329 351 433
PHILLIPS, George 659 Hardman
  389 Henry 489 James 143 John
  D 489 Mr 182
PHIPPS, Nathan 224 352 415
PICKERING, 81 Dr 32 Jno 197
  John 195-196 198 377 Octavius
  197 Timothy 82 541 573
PICKET, Francis 229
PIERCE, J 416 420 Jacob 178 John
  198 309 313 458 498 515 538
PIFER, George 405 493 John 178
  309 405 437 489 493 John Sr
  352 Jonas 405
PIKE, 552 617
PILES, James 229
PIM, 55
PINKS, James 570
PIPE, Capt 72-73
PIPER, John 396
PLIMPTON, Alured 256 B O 253
PLUMMER, Rev 303
POE, Thomas 172
POISDELL, 625
POLK, David 241-242 524 James K
  241 303 Maggie 616
POLLOCK, James 304
PONTIUS, Jacob 389
POPE, J W 597
PORTER, David R 303 486 George
  405 Robert 499
POST, 236 Agnes 231 Chrisian
  Frederic 230 Christian Frederic
  229 231 Frederick 36 Rachel
  231
POSTELTHWAIT, David 356
POSTLETHWAIT, D 309 Daniel
  353 David 124 178 349 353 396
  402 James R 225 John 124 178
  396 402 430 John Sr 123 208
  William 212 Wm 218
POTTER, 359 362 Gen 573 James
  51 82-84 118 Joseph 223 349
  397 401 Ramsey 328 357 401
POTTS, George 402 John 402
POWEL, Elias 402 Moses 402
POWELL, 622 644 ---- 304 J 634
  Jerome 623-624 626 Mr 626 632
  636

685

POWER, Alexander 348
POWERS, 455 Alexander 178 223 362 398 William 54
PREAKET, Lorenzo 397
PRESCOTT, Mr 218
PRESSLY, Joseph H 251
PRICHARD, D 254
PRIME, C G M 316-317 320-321 501 Cyrus G M 509 G C M 392
PRINDLE, Bennett 469 Riverus 659
PROCIUS, Daniel 402 Peter 402
PULLING, A B 639
PUNTUS, Gabriel 425
PURVIS, Robert 275
QUIGGLES, John 356
QUIGLEY, Adam 406
RAIKES, Robert 252
RALSTON, David 607 I D N 608 Orilla 393
RAMBLER, A 655
RAMEY, Thomas 574
RAMSEY, D S 659 John 405 501 600-602 Leslie 437 W R 526
RANDOLF, Carl 402
RANDOLPH, James 341 James F 115 Robert F 116
RANKIN, Frank P 514 Joseph 304 Rev 246 William 392
RANSOM, 452
RANY, James 401
RAUGHT, 585
REA, Samuel 355
READ, Alexander B 387 Almon H 210
REBURGER, H 660
REDLINE, Willoughby 659
REED, ---- 250 Chas M 303 John 178 243 303 John R 261 Levi 403 Margaret 261 Peter 178 Philip 402 Porter 396 Stephen 223
REES, John R 344
REESE, J R 620 Thomas 54
REESER, G F 254 George 254
REESMAN, David 446
REID, Thomas 409
REILLY, Capt 292
REIMEL, Nicholas 454
REISCHEL, Christian 351 355
REITZ, George 402 433 Isaac 403

REITZ (cont.) John 403 Manuel 425 Simon 459
RELF, 291
RENGAN, John 266
REYBURN, Sen 610-611
REYNER, Andrew J 400 David 389 Samuel 400
REYNOLDS, 88 David 351-352 399 401 460 John 226 Joseph 353 460 Thomas 216 218 357 401 482 Tilton 344 362 401 481 W 309 W H 607 William 308 355 357 401 465 481-483 608 Wm 461 Woodward 355 357 362
RHEA, David 355 357 Joshua 398 401 481 Samuel 401
RHEY, James 390
RHINES, A S 597
RHOADS, John 328 352 493 John Sr 352
RHODES, George 406 Samuel 398
RHONEY, William 403
RHYNER, Daniel 389
RICHARD, David 402 George 403 Richards 403 Samuel 402
RICHARDS, Billy 485 Geo 344 Gould 353 John 405 Peter 357 Peter Jr 406 Peter Sr 406 Robert 387 William 493 William R 406 491 621
RICHARDSON, Gould 307
RICHEL, Christian 397
RICKARD, Peter 226 Peter Jr 225
RICORD, Peter 492 Peter Jr 492 Peter Sr 492
RIDDER, David 462
RIDDLE, D M 329 David M 399 James 303
RIDDLEBEERGER, Jacob 500
RIDDLEBURGER, Jacob 400
RIDER, John 406
RIDGWAY, Jacob 444 448 John J 653 Smith 291
RIGDON, S 264
RIGGS, Cyrus 239 241-242 David 225 David C 226 493 Davis E 406 James L L 406 John N 406 Mary 243 Mr 486 N 477 Nelson 492 Rev 243 485 Rev Mr 483-484 Solomon 406

RILEY, Henry 181
RINE, John 328
RINEHART, Frederick 397 435
   George 402
RISHEL, Christian 435 Daniel 245
RITNER, Joseph 303
RITTENHOUSE, David 297
ROADARMIL, Daniel 396
ROBERTS, President 516
ROBINSON, H 309 Hance 350 354-
   355 389 398 403 463 Irvin 356
   433 Irwin 212 309 402 507 526
   James 314 402 John 255 308 350
   353 355 367 402 486 Robert 302
   Robt 303 Thomas 195 349-350
   398 505 William 225 349 402-
   403 500
ROBISON, Thomas 223-224
RODGERS, Calvin 596 Isaac 439 M
   395 Maj 545 Mark 394 Uriah
   389 William 182 226 306 310
   321 344 367 398 403 414 416
   458 500 503 505-506 538 558
   Wm 309 329 519
RODROCH, William 657
ROGERS, Job 250 L D 620 W 250
   William 405 501
ROLAND, Jonathan 293
ROLL, David 398 John Sr 117-118
   Mr 121 Stephen 273 396 424
ROSE, Dr 454
ROSENCRANTS, Nicholas 116
ROSS, A 215 Henry 402 James 184
   351 353-354 357 399 403 469
   474 John 641 Joseph 403 M L
   623-624 631-632 644 Mary 243
   Matthew L 225 632 R 620
   Stewart 400 471
ROSSEAU, 593
ROTH, 235 Brother 234 John 237
ROTHE, 40
ROUNDY, M T H 507 Pearl 552
ROWE, 590 Anthony 456 S B 146
ROYER, George 400
RUDOLPH, Abraham 437
RUFFNER, Christian 400
RUFSNYDER, Abraham 406
RULOFFSON, 631
RUPP, 566 Jesse 343
RUSH, Benjamin 575 Jacob 575

RUSSELL, George 406 491 William
   260 406 491 608
RUTH, Abraham 439
SAINTCLAIR, Gen 57 James 226
   434 Robert 600
SAINTCLARE, 55
SAINTJOHN, Moses B 344 406 492
   621
SALEM, Peter 269
SALLY, Silas 223
SAMPSON, 462 Hiram 400
SAP, Dr 657
SARTWELL, Almon 356 Almond
   355
SAUR, Christoph 295
SAVA, John 254
SCHAEFER, George F 657
SCHAUS, J 657
SCHIMMELPENNINCK, Ruter Jan
   53 87
SCHISSLE, M 657
SCHNELL, 546
SCHOENING, G 657
SCHOFIELD, 597 G W 596
SCHRADER, Philip 405
SCHRAM, John 450
SCHULTZE, E C 644 John A 551
SCHWENCK, Tobias 292
SCOFIELD, I 254 Isaac 254 Robert
   168
SCOTT, 9 121 132 Alexander 398
   400 Alexander Jr 405 Alexander
   Sr 405 Elizabeth 570 George
   405 Henry 403 488 James 600
   John 117 307 362 398 422 426-
   427 570 595-596 John Jr 396
   John Sr 396 Kate 32 87 427-428
   506 Miss 252 Mr 340 R K 392
   409 456 487 R R 349 Robert K
   313 367 398 Samuel 116 120
   122 346 396 422-428 566 569-
   570 572-573
SCROGGS, Joseph 248-249 487
SCULL, John 407 Paul E 372 374
SEEL, J 657
SEELEY, Samuel 429
SENIOR, George 474
SENSEMAN, Gottlob 233
SERGEANT, 55 Henry G 391
SEYE, Hendrick 88

SHADLE, John 402 Michael 398
SHAEFER, G 657
SHAFER, Jacob 467 469 John 446
  Mary 469 Mr 468
SHAFFER, Abraham 402 Andrew
  402 433 Benjamin 353-354 402
  Henry 225 399 Isaac 402 Jacob
  367 389 397 399 427 John 133
  387 John N 415 Michael 402
  Rev 625 Samuel 178 Valentine
  402
SHANNON, Martin 402 Martin H
  308 P H 596
SHARER, Lewis 328
SHARLEY, John 659
SHARP, Agnes Sarah 432 Capt 432
  Henry 178 James 398 Joseph
  224-225 310 367 398 416 506
  Nicholas 398 Peter 401 Thomas
  227 303
SHARPE, Joseph 329 497 500 509
  538 Mr 559
SHAW, Henry 346 J 477 William
  357 399 474 Wm 215
SHAWL, Ephraim 462 659 James
  659 John 462
SHEARER, Richard 83-84
SHERIDAN, 477 597 640
SHERMAN, 597
SHICK, Christ 181
SHIELDS, 181 Daniel 403 David
  403 Eleanor 244 Elizabeth 248
  James 178 195 248 328 347 398
  403 456 James Jr 403 John 219
  248 349-350 398 488 John B 403
  John Sr 403 Robert 403 William
  244
SHILLERY, Jacob 367
SHINEBAUGH, Rev 254
SHINGAS, 183
SHIPE, Abraham 402 Henry 402
SHIPMAN, Charles 357
SHIPPEN, Andrew 398 Edward 302
  Judge 29 278 429
SHOAF, Martin 308
SHOAP, John 219 239 242 Mr 240
SHOBERT, C H 490 Joseph 533
SHOEMAKER, John 350-351 355
SHOFF, Martin 212
SHOFFSTALL, Moses 402

SHOFNER, John 402
SHOWALTER, John 501 514 Mrs
  149
SHOWMAKER, John 456
SHRAWBER, Francis 402 John 402
SHRENK, John 325
SHUL, Samuel 406
SHULTZ, August 273 424 J Andw
  134
SHULZE, J Andw 193 373
SHUNK, Francis R 303
SIBBLEY, Ami 399
SIBLEY, 588 A 353 Ami 466 469
  473 585-586 Annie 469 Rachel
  466
SIES, Benjamin 398
SILVAS, John 402
SILVIS, David 400
SIMONS, 605 Dr 395 606 J C 604 J
  G 394-395 604
SIMPSON, George 403 W A 659-
  660 William 403
SIMS, Dr 444
SITES, Big John 580 Black John 580
  John 580 John John 580 Little
  John 580 Saucy John 580
SIVERT, Henry 468
SLADE, 444 446
SLAVE, Robinson 278 Sam 272 537
  William Jack 272
SLAYSMAN, George M 175
SLOAN, ---- 506 John 358 John Jr
  385 387 390 W A 241 William
  A 325 505 508 Wm A 309 405
  498 538
SLOGERBUCK, Peter 398
SMATHERS, C 602 Christopher
  600-601
SMEDLEY, 275
SMEYERS, Daniel 437
SMITH, 80 88 399 Absalom 402
  Alexander 248 403 Andrew 124
  242 308 354-355 401 474 481
  483 Annie 248 Clover 526 D
  600 602 Daniel 309 319 405 525
  556 601 David 403 Esquire 608
  Franklin B 411 George 100 482
  493 588 600 George L 659
  George W 366 369 Henry 225
  328 416 Herbert 224 Heulet 398

SMITH (cont.)
   Hulet 178 350 355 366-367 403
   428 Hulett 284 Jacob 178 352
   382 Jacob Jr 406 Jacob Sr 406
   James 242 302 352 397 401 474
   481 483-484 Jesse 216 219 273
   309-310 Jo 264-265 John 26 94
   224 303 310 313 316 318 329
   345 354 367 405 437 463 507-
   508 514 519 525-526 558 599-
   602 Joseph 264 Joseph W 369
   Josiah W 366 Justice 603 Lewis
   B 661 Lewis W 369 M 477
   Matthew 401 Mr 101 Nathan
   545 Otis 474 Peter 625 Philip
   402 Professor 616 R 477 Ralph
   197 Robert 398 474 S W 471
   615 Samuel 406 Sen 209 T S Sr
   218 Theophilus 219 Valentine
   362 W 477 W C 526 598 609
   William 118 178 224 242 474
   477 486 608 William C 607
   William R 322 369 William Sr
   484 Wm 352 Yankee 541
SNODDY, J 477
SNOWDEN, James Ross 370
SNYDER, 559 Abraham 406
   Christopher 115 Coonrod 402
   Daniel 402 406 Ed 523 Eli 406
   Gov 298-299 Jacob 402 John
   659 Nathan 406 Simon 149 170-
   171 204 302 466 Walter 402
SOLESBY, James 356
SOLESLEY, James 406
SOUTHER, 624 Capt 635 H 631
   642 Henry 623 626 633 648 650
   659 Mr 652-654
SOUTHERLAND, 603 606 Charles
   584 604 Henry 599-602 604-606
   609 Sinthy 608 Susan 604 Susey
   584
SOWERS, Benjamin 403 Henry 403
   James 488 James Jr 403 James
   Sr 403
SPANGLER, 401 Peter 402
SPARE, Henry 402 Henry Sr 402
SPEER, James 302
SPELY, C 657
SPIRIT, Ed 536
SPRAGUE, Ashel 406 B 401 Henry

SPRAGUE (cont.)
   406 John 401 Milton 406 Samuel
   357
SPRANKLE, Frederick 434 John
   244 415
SPRECKELS, Claus 482
SPULER, M 657
SPYKER, Joel 265 309 355 455
   Mary 266 Mr 219
STADNITSKI, Pieter 53
STAHLMAN, Simon 402
STAKE, Jacob 171-172
STANARD, Daniel 227
STANNARD, Daniel 303
STANTON, 594 Orin L 391
STARTZEL, Jacob 402 John 402
STATES, Adam 406 Samuel 396-
   397 428
STEADMAN, 503 James 275 279
STEARS, Frederick 218
STEAVENS, P 657
STECK, J S 600 Jacob 266
STEDMAN, J M 309 James M 322
   John 285
STEEDMAN, James M 308 322 344
   350
STEEL, Andrew 400 John 402
   William 254 351
STEELE, James 226 Stewart 370
   William 328
STEER, Frederick 402
STEFFY, Samuel 353 355-357 397
STEINER, M E 620
STEPHEN, Ephraim 401
STEPHENS, Eben 446 J 177 Mrs
   469
STERRETT, J 477 Joseph 482 R
   477
STEVENS, 454 470 Eben 453
   Thaddeus 209 213
STEVENSON, Susan 485
STEWART, Dr 392 J J 477 James
   124 178 208 350 396 James Jr
   400 James M 304 James P 313
   John 178 396 Mrs 477 Paul 400
   471 Prudence 262 William 124
   431 William M 370 William W
   418
STILES, Freedom 117 426 456
   Israel 428 Ruth 272 Samuel 398

STINE, Abraham 403 Michael 315
STOCKMANN, L 657
STOKELY, Benjamin 54 Thomas 54
STOKES, Mr 652-655 Samuel 178
    William A 650-651 655 657-658
STONEBACK, Samuel 659
STOUGHTON, Rev 262
STOUSE, Jonathan 406
STRATTON, Joe 517 John 308 397
    454
STRAUB, Andrew 502
STRAWBRIDGE, James 53
STRICKLAND, 257
STROUSE, Jonathan 489
STRUTHERS, John 563 Thomas
    370
STUBBS, Charles 648
STUNKARD, Robert 433 Ruth 243
    William 243 308 381 433 Wm
    353
STURTEVANT, Dr 32
STYLES, Freedom 223
SULLIVAN, Gen 565
SUMMERVILLE, James 356 400
    471 John 400 Rev 254 William
    367 400
SUTHERLAND, Charles 178 272
    398 428 555-556 581 Charlie
    582-584 Susan 272
SUTTON, Garvin 303 Garwin 227
    Peter 305 350 502 Thos 302
SWAB, Peter 403
SWARTZLANDER, F 259
SWEENEY, Dr 508 John 556
    Theresa 603 Tracy 608
SWEET, Amos 659
SWINEFORD, Isaac 425
SYNOD, Gen 265
T, Robinson 309
TACKETT, I H 253
TANEWOOD, Nicholas 116
TANNER, Archibald 387
TATE, Levi L 417
TAYLOR, Alexander 195 302 Broce
    402 E F 641-642 Jacob 397
    James 304 Joel 622 John 227
    302-304 346-347 Joseph 660
    Josiah 446 Judge 522 Lawson
    Lee 268 Mollie 427 Philip 502
    597 Samuel B 344 404 William

TAYLOR (cont.)
    357 397 454
TEDLIE, Thomas 401 474
TEMPLE, 15 I M 620 Isaac 250 252
    354 357 399 406 451 491-492 S
    W 490 596 Samuel 25
TEMPLETON, James 400 416 471
    John 405 428 T L 509 515
    Thomas L 455 501 537 Walter
    178 398 428 455 470 487
THATCHER, 298 Judge 297
THAYER, 626 628 Albina E 641
    Clarissa D 641 David 225-226
    453 622 628-629 648 659 David
    H 659 Esther J 641 Henry 641
    Henry S 628 Horace J 632 L 659
    Mary E 641 Mr 452 Sarah Ann
    641
THOMAS, Father 524 H 616 John
    401 Rev 262 Thomas E 260-262
    William 399 William A 389
THOMPSON, 410 Bob 439 Devil
    John 522 Elizabeth 248 J J Y
    309 316-317 321 325 415 601
    607 James 210 James L 400
    John 248 620 John J 284 John J
    Y 198 308 328 344 350-354 356
    380 409 415 424 501 600 602
    John Y 306 Jos 407 Joseph 175
    248 Joseph M 404 T M 144
    Thomas 406 489 493 Thomas
    Mckean 201 William 178 390
    455 Wm 328
THORN, Robert 553
THRUSH, Peter 265-266 455
THUMAS, Michael 401
THURSTON, E S 641
TIBBETS, Stephen 224
TIBBETTS, S 351 357 Stephen 308
    354 399 469-470
TIBBITS, Stephen 288
TIMBLIN, 216
TINDALL, Nathaniel 351-352 397
TINDLE, Nathaniel 123 434-435
TIPPS, Elijah 399 Nathan 399
TIPTON, Lee 362
TOD, John 249-250
TOMLINSON, John 339-340
TORANCE, William 262
TORRENCE, James 216 383 415

TOWNLEY, 639-640
TRAPER, Michael 400
TRAUTMAN, Jacob 400
TRAVIS, George 402 James 402 Mr
   218 R A 616 Stephen 402
   William 130 386
TRAYOR, Samuel 402
TRIMBLE, James 471 William 302
TROY, Michael 260
TRUBY, Samuel 405 416 502 519
   556
TRUCKMILLER, Henry 402
TRUMBULL, Gideon 403 406
TUCKER, Charles E 506
TURNER, Dan 590 John 184
TWEEDY, Robert 209 398
TYGART, David 335
TYRCONNELL, Earl 299
TYRONE, Earl 299
UPTAGRAFF, Edward 402
VANBUREN, 545 Martin 303 318
VANCAMP, 273 Enos 178 272 428
   Fudge 117 121 178 181 272 396
   424 426-428 604 Richard 178
   272 428 Ruth 272 Sarah 178 272
   Susan 272 604
VANDERCAMP, John J 87
VANDEVORT, Abram 406 David
   404 420 Jesse 398 404 Joshua
   398 420 491 Joshua Jr 406
   Joshua Sr 406 Levi 406 Paul 329
   352 399 404 420
VANDYKE, David 418
VANEEGHAN, Christian 53
VANEEGHEN, Pieter 87
VANHORN, Cornelius 115 John
   381 488
VANLEAR, Mr 433
VANORSDALE, Cornelius 659
VANSCHIRK, 659
VANSTAPHORST, Jan Gabriel 88
   Nicholas 53 87 Roelif Jr 88
VANVALZAH, T M 502
VASBINDER, 85 90 96 117 352 A
   250 Adam 121 346 Adam Sr 178
   Andrew 89 223 351 367 Andrew
   Jr 178 Hance 392 Henry 178
   352 392 Henry Jr 355-357 Jacob
   91 122 178 350 John 122 178
   Old William 100 Peter 91 93

VASBINDER (cont.)
   355 William 121-122 178 223
   346 349 362
VASTBINDER, 492 579 588 Adam
   396 398 422 427-428 Andrew
   371 398-399 406 455 506
   Andrew C 416 Gabriel 405 517
   Hance 428 501 Henry 401 417
   420 426-427 501 Jacob 396 398
   424 490 493 Jacob Jr 406 Jacob
   Sr 406 John 396 406 424 490
   Lieut 417 Peter 406 490 Philip
   427 William 398 424 427-428
   456
VASTVINDER, Henry 398
VAUGHAN, John 81
VAUX, George 372
VEASEY, Jamison 659
VERSTINE, 456
VIAL, Alanson 397
VIALL, Alanson 454
VINCENT, Thomas M 594
VIRGIL, 324
VOLLENHOVEN, Cornelius 88
   Hendrick 53 87
VOLMER, A 656
VONSHROEDER, Maria 266
WACHOB, James 178 223-224 396
   Sarah 243
WADE, 446 Gen 444 Mrs 446
WAGAMAN, John C 615
WAGLEY, Miss 501 Mrs 502
WAGNER, Anna Maria 292
WAIGLEY, 559
WAINWRIGHT, George 406
   Richard 406
WAIT, James 243 481
WAITE, James 401 485 Mattie 485
   Robert 141
WAKEFIELD, 175 John 406 491
WALBORN, Henry 367 397 468
WALBURN, Henry 224
WALES, Solomon 406
WALFORD, George 400
WALKER, 228 552 Abraham 402
   Isaac 406 491 J 657 John 406
   450
WALKUP, Joe 281
WALL, Jacob F 439
WALLACE, 569 624 A G 251

WALLACE (cont.)
  Robert 226 460 William 246 400
WALLEY, Peter Jr 389
WALLIS, Samuel 53 575
WALTERS, John 398 Peter 398
WALTZER, Frederick 335
WANN, J P 597
WARD, M A 27
WARNER, Horace 624 631 Mary
  469 641
WARREN, Anson 526 John L 526
WARWICK, Rev 246
WASHBURN, Ephraim 405
WASHINGTON, 297 418 618 Col
  336 Gen 17 480 556 561 George
  57 115 169 316 335 478 633
  President 296
WATSON, 503 Job 254 John 115
  William 369
WATT, 247 George 604
WATTERS, William 253
WATTERSON, 659 James 452
WATTS, 520 Isaac 523 James 402
WAYLAND, Beach 398 Beech 404
WAYNE, 55 560
WEAKLAND, Zephaniah 347
WEARY, Benjamin 402
WEAVER, A 415 Abraham 397 434
  Abram 123 Alzinah 641 Amos
  402 Elisha 659 George 397 Isaac
  302 Jacob 406 Mary 641 Moses
  402 Sarah 641
WEBB, Thomas 252
WEBSTER, 317 552 618 Daniel 418
  John 398 Monroe 404 Stephen
  404 William 397
WEED, Bob 649 N C 251
WEEKS, William 383 406 492-493
WEIR, Robert 398
WEIS, George 649 655 657 Stephen
  453
WEISER, Capt 39 Conrad 44
  Samuel 44
WELCH, John 347 487 Oliver 481
WELLENDORF, M 657
WELLS, 639 Charles A 416
WELSH, George 170 Jackson 404
  James 475 477 John 178 305 309
  355 367 398 John R 404 Mr 171
  Oliver 401

WESCOTT, Elizabeth 641
WESLEY, Charles 256 John 252
  256 Tommy 511
WEST, John 415
WESTLAKE, William 253
WESTON, James 148
WHEATCRAFT, Thomas 397
WHEELER, Patience 398 404
WHIPPLE, L 254
WHITE, A C 596 Charles R 245 De
  Witt C 226 Ezekiel 404 Ira 208
  397 J M 502 Jacob C 275 James
  27 John 244 Kesiah 244 Parlen
  219 Parlin 397 R G 624 Thomas
  366 369 William 232
WHITEHILL, Christwell 239
  Jopseh 399 Rachel 466 Robert
  302 Stewart H 371
WHITNEY, 618 624 William N 624
  636 648
WICKSTED, Polycarp 262
WIEGAND, John 210
WIER, John 346 425
WIGDEN, 30
WIGHTMAN, John 343
WIKOFF, Ann 197 J C 197
WILBER, Zibion 608
WILCOX, A I 649 658 660
  Angeline 641 Ardissa 641
  Coryell 450 Maria 659 Miner
  624 Mr 652 Phoebe M 641 W P
  624 William P 304
WILEY, William 357
WILHELM, Joseph 450
WILKINS, Gen 139 James 226
  James A 406 493 John R 406
  Thomas 354 405 508 542
  William 318 405 William B 543
WILLAR, Dr 451
WILLARD, David 439
WILLCOCK, Abraham 348
WILLIAMS, Benoni 397 435 Enion
  51 83-84 James 397 406 John
  415 539 John B 224 Mr 262
  Rachel 244 Samuel K 354
  Thomas 215 William 406
WILLIAMSON, 429 575 Hugh 178
  398 John G 308
WILLING, Charles 53 Thomas M
  53

WILLINK, Jan Jr 88 Welhelm 541
  Wilhelm 53 86-87 Wilhelm Jr 88
WILLIS, 624 Albert 633 642 Mr
  634 S J 641
WILMARTH, 653 L 212 215 453
  Lyman 219 308 315 353
WILSON, 469 Catherine 481 Clark
  659 David 118 Galbraith 225
  406 Geo 129 George 127 127
  140 405 George Jr 400 Hiram
  389 406 J C 616 Jacob 446
  James 53 402 446 James C 405
  Jeremiah 406 John 118 124 216
  224-225 239 303 308 310 315
  325 328-329 352 354-356 400-
  402 414 417 420 471 474 481
  492 506 524 John G 621 John J
  406 John Jr 400 Joseph 406 Lib
  281 M H 251 Robert 118 400
  402 Samuel 118 Samuel Sr 118
  Thomas 260 262 William 118
WINDSOR, Charles 600
WINKLEBLICK, 292
WINSLOW, Caleb 397 Carpenter
  359 386 488 Carpenter Jr 397
  Carpenter Sr 397 Charles 397 E
  C 649-650 657 Ebenezer 397
  Elizabeth 223 641 J 215 James
  123 216 309-310 349 352-355
  365 388-390 397 439 545 Jas
  309 John 308 Jos 212 Joseph
  226 488-489 Joseph W 353 439
  Mrs 245 480 Reuben 397 650
  654 661
WINTER, James 362
WIRT, William 303
WISE, 503 Adam 406 Capt 605 Gen
  455 George 402 Jacob 402 John
  H 367 W W 620
WISTER, Casper 295
WITHEROW, 455 Robert 328 T
  620 Thomas 328
WITMORE, Lansing 388

WOLCOTT, Gen 61 Oliver 60 65
  68 70
WOLF, Geo 303 378 George 131
  200 363 Gov 205 212 316 551
  617
WOLFGANG, Jacob 266
WOOD, George Jr 82 James 172
  Jethro 152
WOODS, George 184 Michael 405
  543
WOODWARD, Absalom 372
  Robert 390
WORDEN, David 659
WORK, James 348
WORTHINGTON, Wilmer 210
WRAY, John 625 Mrs 477 Willie
  477
WRIGHT, R G 597 Samuel 273
  William 274
WYANT, Solomon 492
WYETH, 175
WYLEY, William 425
WYNCOOP, John 382 399 427
WYNKOOP, 559 John 354 461 554
YALE, 449 631
YATES, John 278-279
YEAGER, Lawrence 402
YEATES, Judge 86
YEOMANS, Daniel 398 401 Henry
  401 Mary A 266
YOHEY, Adam 406 Henry 406
  Samuel 406
YOKEY, Abram 400 Christy 400
YOUNG, 123 Brigham 264 George
  265 George Jr 402 George Sr
  402 John 178 302 Judge 434 Rev
  266 Robert 303 William Sr 118
YOUNGS, 218
ZEIGLER, George W 603
ZEISBERGER, 234 David 40 232-
  233
ZUFALL, Samuel 406

www.ingramcontent.com/pod-product-compliance
Lightning Source LLC
Chambersburg PA
CBHW071214290426
44108CB00013B/1176